T0350276

Big Data Concepts, Theories, and Applications

Shui Yu • Song Guo

Editors

Big Data Concepts, Theories, and Applications

Editors
Shui Yu
School of Information Technology
Deakin University
Burwood, VIC, Australia

Song Guo
School of Computer Science
and Engineering
The University of Aizu
Aizu-Wakamatsu City, Fukushima, Japan

ISBN 978-3-319-27761-5   ISBN 978-3-319-27763-9   (eBook)
DOI 10.1007/978-3-319-27763-9

Library of Congress Control Number: 2015958772

Springer Cham Heidelberg New York Dordrecht London

Printed on acid-free paper

Springer International Publishing AG Switzerland is part of Springer Science+Business Media (www.
springer.com)

Preface

Big data is one of the hottest research topics in science and technology communities, and it possesses a great potential in every sector for our society, such as climate, economy, health, social science, and so on. Big data is currently treated as data sets with sizes beyond the ability of commonly used software tools to capture, curate, and manage. We have tasted the power of big data in various applications, such as finance, business, health, and so on. However, big data is still in her infancy stage, which is evidenced by its vague definition, limited application, unsolved security and privacy barriers for pervasive implementation, and so forth. It is certain that we will face many unprecedented problems and challenges along the way of this unfolding revolutionary chapter of human history.

Big data is driven by applications and aims to obtain knowledge or conclusions directly from big data sets. As an application-oriented field, it is inevitably needed to integrate domain knowledge into information systems, which is similar to traditional database systems, which possess a rigorous mathematical foundation, a set of design rules, and implementation mechanisms. We imagine that we may have similar counterparts in big data.

We have witnessed the significant development in big data from various communities, such as the mining and learning algorithms from the artificial intelligence community, networking facilities from networking community, and software platforms from software engineering community. However, big data applications introduce unprecedented challenges to us, and existing theories and techniques have to be extended and upgraded to serve the forthcoming real big data applications. With a high probability, we need to invent new tools for big data applications. With the increasing volume and complexity of big data, theoretical insights have to be employed to achieve the original goal of big data applications. As the foundation of theoretical exploration, constant refinements or adjustments of big data definitions and measurements are necessary and demanded. Ideally, theoretical calculation and inference will replace the current brute force strategy. We have seen the effort from different communities in this direction, such as big data modeling, big task scheduling, privacy framework, and so on. Once again, these theoretical attempts are still insufficient to most of the incoming big data applications.

Motivated by these problems and challenges, we proposed this book aiming to collect the latest research output in big data from various perspectives. We wish our effort will pave a solid starting ground for researchers and engineers who are going to start their exploration in this almost uncharted land of big data. As a result, the book emphasizes in three parts: concepts, theories, and applications. We received many submissions and finally accepted twelve chapters after a strict selection and revision processing. It is regretful that many good submissions have been excluded due to our theme and space limitation. From our limited statistics, we notice that there is a great interest in security and application aspects of big data, which reflects the current reality of the domain: big data applications are valuable and expected, and security and privacy issue has to be appropriately handled before the pervasive practice of big data in our society. On the other hand, the theoretical part of big data is not as high as we expected. We fully believe the theoretical effort in big data is essential and highly demanded in problem solving in the big data age, and it is worthwhile to invest our energy and passion in this direction without any reservation.

Finally, we thank all the authors and reviewers of this book for their great effort and cooperation. Many people helped us in this book project, we appreciate their guidance and support. In particular, we would like to take this opportunity to express our sincere appreciation and cherished memory to late Professor Ivan Stojmenovic, a great mentor and friend. At Springer, we would like to thank Susan Lagerstrom-Fife and Jennifer Malat for their professional support.

Melbourne, VIC, Australia   Shui Yu
Fukushima, Japan   Song Guo

Contents

Chapter 1
Big Continuous Data: Dealing with Velocity by Composing Event Streams

Genoveva Vargas-Solar, Javier A. Espinosa-Oviedo, and José
Luis Zechinelli-Martini

Abstract The rate at which we produce data is growing steadily, thus creating even larger streams of continuously evolving data. Online news, micro-blogs, search queries are just a few examples of these continuous streams of user activities. The value of these streams relies in their freshness and relatedness to on-going events. Modern applications consuming these streams need to extract behaviour patterns that can be obtained by aggregating and mining statically and dynamically huge event histories. An *event* is the notification that a happening of interest has occurred. Event streams must be combined or aggregated to produce more meaningful information. By combining and aggregating them either from multiple producers, or from a single one during a given period of time, a limited set of events describing meaningful situations may be notified to consumers. Event streams with their volume and continuous production cope mainly with two of the characteristics given to Big Data by the 5V's model: volume & velocity. Techniques such as complex pattern detection, event correlation, event aggregation, event mining and stream processing, have been used for composing events. Nevertheless, to the best of our knowledge, few approaches integrate different composition techniques (online and post-mortem) for dealing with Big Data velocity. This chapter gives an analytical overview of event stream processing and composition approaches: complex event languages, services and event querying systems on distributed logs. Our analysis underlines the challenges introduced by Big Data velocity and volume and use them as reference for identifying the scope and limitations of results stemming from different disciplines: networks, distributed systems, stream databases, event composition services, and data mining on traces.

G. Vargas-Solar (✉) • J.A. Espinosa-Oviedo
CNRS-LIG-LAFMIA, 681 rue de la Passerelle BP 72, Saint Martin d'Hères,
38402 Grenoble, France
e-mail: genoveva.vargas@imag.fr; javier.espinosa@imag.fr

J.L. Zechinelli-Martini
UDLAP-LAFMIA, Exhacienda Sta. Catarina Mártir s/n, San Andrés Cholula,
72810 Cholula, Mexico
e-mail: joseluis.zechinelli@udlap.mx

© Springer International Publishing Switzerland 2016   1
S. Yu, S. Guo (eds.), *Big Data Concepts, Theories, and Applications*,
DOI 10.1007/978-3-319-27763-9_1

1.1 Introduction

The rate at which we produce data is growing steadily, thus creating even larger streams of continuously evolving data. Online news, micro-blogs, search queries are just a few examples of these continuous streams of user activities. The value of these streams relies in their freshness and relatedness to on-going events.

Massive data streams that were once obscure and distinct are being aggregated and made easily accessible. Modern applications consuming these streams require to extract behaviour patterns that can be obtained by aggregating and mining statically and dynamically huge event histories. An *event* is the notification that a happening of interest has occurred. Event streams are continuous flows of events stemming from one or several producers. They must be combined or aggregated to produce more meaningful information. By combining and aggregating them either from multiple producers, or from a single one during a given period of time, a limited set of events describing meaningful situations may be notified to consumers.

Event streams with their volume and continuous production cope mainly with two of the characteristics given to Big Data by the 5V's model [1]: volume & velocity. Event-based systems have gained importance in many application domains, such as management and control systems, large-scale data dissemination, monitoring applications, autonomic computing, etc. Event composition has been tackled by several academic research and industrial systems. Techniques such as complex pattern detection, event correlation, event aggregation, event mining and stream processing, have been used for composing events. In some cases event composition is done on event histories (e.g. event mining) and in other cases it is done on-line as events are produced (e.g. event aggregation and stream processing). Nevertheless, to the best of our knowledge, few approaches integrate different composition techniques (online and post-mortem) for dealing with Big Data velocity and volume.

This chapter gives an analytical overview of event stream processing and composition approaches that can respond to the challenges introduced by Big Data volume and velocity. Examples of these approaches are complex event languages and event querying systems on distributed logs. Our analysis underlines the challenges introduced by Big Data velocity and volume and use them as reference for identifying the scope and limitations of results stemming from different disciplines: networks, distributed systems, stream databases, event composition services, and data mining on traces.

Accordingly, this chapter is organized as follows. Section 1.2 introduces the problem related to Big Data velocity by studying two main techniques: event histories and online event processing. It also describes target applications where data velocity is a key element. Section 1.3 gives an overview of existing event stream models. It discusses the main principles for modelling event streams. Section 1.4 gives an overview of event composition techniques. In particular, it compares existing approaches for exploiting streams either by composing them or by applying analytics techniques. Finally, Sect. 1.5 concludes the chapter and discusses Big Data velocity outlook.

1.2 Big Data Velocity Issues

This section introduces the challenges associated with Big Data velocity. In particular it describes stream processing challenges and results that are enabling ways of dealing with Big Data velocity. The section first gives the general lines of stream processing and existing prominent systems. Then it discusses event histories, which provide a complementary view for dealing with continuous data produced in a producers/consumers setting. The notion of event histories can be seen as Big Data produced at high rates and that must be analysed taking into consideration their temporal and spatial features. Finally, the section describes target applications families where Big Data velocity acquires particular importance.

1.2.1 Stream Processing and Velocity

Stream processing is a programming paradigm that processes continuous event (data) streams. They arise in telecommunications, health care, financial trading, and transportation, among other domains. Timely analysis of such streams can be profitable (in finance) and can even save lives (in health care). In the streaming model, events arrive at high speed, and algorithms must process them in one pass under very strict constraints of space and time. Furthermore, often the events volume is so high that it cannot be stored on disk or sent over slow network links before being processed. Instead, a streaming application can analyse continuous event streams immediately, reducing large-volume input streams to low-volume output streams for further storage, communication or action.

The challenge is to setup a processing infrastructure able to collect information and analyse incoming event streams continuously and in real-time. Several solutions can be used in that sense. For instance, stream database systems were a very popular research topic a few years ago. Their commercial counterparts (such as Streambase[1] or Truviso[2]) allow users to pose queries using declarative languages derived from SQL on continuous event streams. While extremely efficient, the functionalities of such systems are intrinsically limited by built in operators provided by the system. Another class of systems relevant to Big Data velocity are distributed stream processing frameworks. These frameworks typically propose a general-purpose, distributed, and scalable platform that allows programmers to develop arbitrary applications for processing continuous and unbounded event streams. IBM InfoSphere, StreamBase [2], Apache S4 [3], Storm [4], SAMOA [5] and Twitter Storm[3] are popular examples of such frameworks.

---

[1]http://www.streambase.com.

[2]http://www.dbms2.com/category/products-and-vendors/truviso/.

[3]https://storm.apache.org.

Streaming algorithms use probabilistic data structures and give fast, approximated answers. However, sequential online algorithms are limited by the memory and bandwidth of a single machine. Achieving results faster and scaling to larger event streams requires parallel and distributed computing.

The streaming paradigm is necessary to deal with the data velocity, and distributed and parallel computing to deal with the volume of data. Much recent work has attempted to address parallelism by coping data structures used for composing streams with physical architectures (e.g., clusters). This makes it easier to exploit the nested levels of hardware parallelism, which is important for handling massive data streams or performing sophisticated online analytics. Data models promoted by the NoSQL trend is addressing variety and also processing efficiency on clusters [6].

There are two approaches for dealing with streams consumption and analytics. The first one, event histories querying, supposes that there are histories or logs that are continuously fed with incoming events and that it is possible to perform dynamic and continuous (i.e., recurrent) querying and processing. The second one, complex event processing (CEP) [7], supposes that streams cannot be stored and that on-line processing and delivery are performed at given rates eventually combining them with stored data. The following sections describe these approaches.

1.2.2   Querying Event Histories

Events can be stored in event histories or logs. An event history is a finite set of events ordered by their occurrence time, and in which no two events have the same identifier. Because the number of produced events can reach thousands of events per second or higher [8], the size of an event history can be huge, increasing the difficulty of its analysis for composing events.

Distributed event processing approaches, deal with events with respect to subscriptions managed as continuous queries, where results can also be used for further event compositions. According to the type of event-processing strategy (i.e., aggregation, mining, pattern look up or discovery), event-processing results can be notified as streams or as discrete results. In both cases, event processing is done with respect to events stemming from distributed producers. Provided that approaches enable dynamic and post-mortem event processing, they use different and distributed event histories for detecting event patterns. For example, the overall load of a cluster system is given by memory and CPU consumption. So, in order to compute the load model of the cluster, the event histories representing memory and CPU consumption of each computer in the cluster have to be combined and integrated with on-line event streams. Thus, histories must be analysed and correlated with on-line event streams to obtain the load (memory and CPU consumption) of the cluster.

Furthermore, event processing must handle complex subscriptions that integrate stream processing and database lookup to retrieve additional information. In order to do such kind of event processing, a number of significant challenges must be addressed. Despite the increasingly sizes of event histories, event processing needs to be fast. Filtering, pattern matching, correlation and aggregation must all be performed with low latency. The challenge is to design and implement event services that implement event processing by querying distributed histories ensuring scalability and low latency.

Continuous query processing have attracted much interest in the database community, e.g., trigger and production rules processing, data monitoring [9], stream processing [10], and publish/subscribe systems [11–13]. In contrast to traditional query systems, where each query runs once against a snapshot of the database, continuous query systems support queries that continuously generate new results (or changes to results) as new data continue to arrive [14]. Important projects and systems address continuous query processing and data streams querying. For example, OpenCQ [11], NiagaraCQ [12], Alert [15], STREAM (STanford stream datA Management) [2], Mobi-Dic [16], PLACE (Pervasive Location-Aware Computing Environments) [17, 18] and PLASTIC—IST FP6 STREP.

Concerning query languages, most proposals define extensions to SQL with aggregation and temporal operators. Languages have been proposed for expressing the patterns that applications need to observe within streams: ESPER [19], FTL, and Streams Processing Language (SPL) [20]. For example, SPL is the programming language for IBM InfoSphere Streams [21], a platform for analysing Big Data in motion meaning continuous event streams at high data-transfer rates. InfoSphere Streams processes such events with both high throughput and short response times. SPL abstracts away the complexity of the distributed system, instead exposing a simple graph-of-operators view to the user. To facilitate writing well-structured and concise applications, SPL provides higher-order composite operators that modularize stream sub-graphs. Optimization has been addressed with respect to the characteristics of sensors [22]. Other approaches such as [23] focus on the optimization of operators. For example, to enable static checking while exposing optimization opportunities, SPL provides a strong type system and user-defined operator models.

1.2.3 Complex Event Processing

A special case of stream processing is Complex Event Processing (CEP) [7]. CEP refers to data items in input streams as raw events and to data items in output streams as composite (or derived) events. A CEP system uses patterns to inspect sequences of raw events and then generates a composite event for each match, for example, when a stock price first peaks and then dips below a threshold. Prominent CEP systems include NiagaraCQ [24], SASE (Stream-based and Shared Event processing) [18], Cayuga [17], IBM WebSphere* Operational Decision Management (WODM) [25], Progress Apama [14], and TIBCO Business Events [26].

The challenge of CEP [7] is that there are several event instances that can satisfy a composite event type. *Event consumption* has been used to decide which component events of an event stream are considered for the composition of a composite event, and how the event parameters of the composite event are computed from its components. The *event consumption modes* are classified in recent, chronicle, continuous and cumulative event contexts (an adaptation of the parameter contexts [27, 28]).

Consider the composite event type $E_3 = (E_1 ; E_2)$ where E_1 and E_2 represent event types and "$;$" denotes the operator sequence. The expression means that we are looking for patterns represented by E_3 where instances of E_1 are produced after instances of E_2. Consider the event history $H = \{\{e_{11}\}, \{e_{12}\}, \{e_{13}\}, \{e_{21}\}\}$. The event consumption mode determines which instances e_1-events to combine with e_{21} for the production of instances of the composite event of type E_3. An instance of the type E_1 will be the initiator of the composite event occurrence, while an instance of type E_2 will be its terminator.

Recent Only the newest instance of the event type E_1 is used as initiator for composing an event of type E_3. In the above example, the instance e_{11} of event type E_1 is the initiator of the composite event type $E_3 = (E_1 ; E_2)$. If a new instance of type E_1 is detected (e.g. e_{12}), the older instance in the history is overwritten by the newer instance. Then, the instance e_{21} of type E_2 is combined with the newest event occurrence available: (e_{13}, e_{21}).

An initiator will continue to initiate new composite event occurrences until a new initiator occurs. When the composite event has been detected, all components of that event (that cannot be future initiators) are deleted from the event history. Recent consumption mode is useful, e.g. in applications where events are happening at a fast rate and multiple occurrences of the same event only refine the previous value.

Chronicle For a composite event occurrence, the (initiator, terminator) pair is unique. The oldest initiator and the oldest terminator are coupled to form the composite event. In the example, the instance e_{21} is combined with the oldest event occurrence of type E_1 available: (e_{11}, e_{21}).

In this context, the initiator can take part in more than one event occurrence, but the terminator does not take part in more than one composite event occurrence. Once the composite event is produced, all constituents of the composite event are deleted from the event history. The chronicle consumption mode is useful in application where there is a connection between different types of events and their occurrences, and this connection needs to be maintained.

Continuous Each initiator event starts the production of that composite event. The terminator event occurrence may then trigger the production of one or more occurrences of the same composite event, i.e. the terminator terminates those composite events where all the components have been detected (except for the terminator). In the example, e_{21} is combined with all event of type E_1: (e_{11}, e_{21}), (e_{12}, e_{21}) and (e_{13}, e_{21}); and does not delete the consumed events.

The difference between continuous and recent consumption mode, and the chronicle consumption mode, is that in the latter one initiator is coupled with one terminator, whereas the continuous consumption mode one terminator is coupled with one or many initiators. In addition, it adds more overhead to the system and requires more storage capacity. This mode can be used in applications where event detection along a moving time window is needed.

Cumulative All occurrences of an event type are accumulated until the composite event is detected. In the example, e_{21} is combined with all event occurrences of type E_1 available (e_{11}, e_{12}, e_{13}, e_{21}).

When the terminator has been detected, i.e. the composite event is produced; all the event instances that constitute the composite event are deleted from the event history. Applications use this context when multiple occurrences of component events need to be grouped and used in a meaningful way when the event occurs.

1.2.4 Target Applications

Big Data is no longer just the domain of actuaries and scientists. New technologies have made it possible for a wide range of people—including humanities and social science academics, marketers, governmental organizations, educational institutions and motivated individuals—to produce, share, interact with and organize data. This section presents three challenges where Big Data velocity is particularly important and it is an enabling element for addressing application requirements: digital shadow analytics that relates velocity, volume, and value; smart cities, urban computing and industry 4.0 that relate velocity, volume and veracity [1].

1.2.4.1 Extracting Value Out of the Digital Shadow

The digital shadow of individuals is growing faster every year, and most of the time without knowing it. Our digital shadow is made up of information we may deem public but also data that we would prefer to remain private. Yet, it is within this growing mist of data where Big Data opportunities lie—to help drive more personalized services, manage connectivity more efficiently, or create new businesses based on valuable, yet-to-be-discovered, intersections of data among groups or masses of people.

Today, social-network research involves mining huge digital data sets of collective behaviour online. The convergence of these developments—mobile computing, cloud computing, Big Data and advanced data mining technologies—is compelling many organizations to transition from a "chasing compliance" mind set, to a risk management mind set. Big streams' value comes from the patterns that can be derived by making connections between pieces of data, about an individual, about individuals in relation to others, about groups of people, or simply about the structure of information itself.

Advertisers, for instance, would originally publicize their latest campaigns statically using pre-selected hash-tags on Twitter. Today, real-time data processing opens the door to continuous tracking of their campaign on the social networks, and to online adaptation of the content being published to better interact with the public (e.g., by augmenting or linking the original content to new content, or by reposting the material using new hash-tags). Online social networks, like Facebook or Twitter, are increasingly responsible for a significant portion of the digital content produced today. As a consequence, it becomes essential for publishers, stakeholders and observers to understand and analyse the data streams originating from those networks in real-time. However, current (de-facto standard) solutions for Big Data analytics are not designed to deal with evolving streams.

Open issues are related with the possibility of processing event streams (volume) in real-time (velocity) in order to have a continuous and accurate views of the evolution of the digital shadow (veracity). This implies to make event streams processing scale, and provide support for making decisions on which event histories should persist from those that are volatile, and those that should be filtered and correlated to have different perspectives of peoples (and crowds) digital shadow according to application requirements. Event stream types, processing operators, adapted algorithms and infrastructures need to be understood and revisited for addressing digital shadow related challenges.

1.2.4.2 Smart Cities and Urban Computing

The development of digital technologies in the different disciplines, in which cities operate, either directly or indirectly, is going to alter expectations among those in charge of the local administration. Every city is a complex ecosystem with a lot of subsystems to make it work such as work, food, cloths, residence, offices, entertainment, transport, water, energy etc. With the growth there is more chaos and most decisions are politicised, there are no common standards and data is overwhelming.

Smart cities are related to sensing the city's status and acting in new intelligent ways at different levels: people, government, cars, transport, communications, energy, buildings, neighbourhoods, resource storage, etc. A vision of the city of the "future", or even the city of the present, remains on the integration of science and technology through information systems. For example, unlike traditional maps, which are often static representations of distributed phenomena at a given moment in time, Big Data collection tools can be used for grasping the moving picture of citizens' expressions, as they are constantly changing and evolving with the city itself (identifying urban areas and colour them according to the time period of the day they are pulsing the most) [29].

Big Data streams can enable online analysis of users' perceptions related to specific geographic areas, and post-mortem analysis for understanding how specific user groups use public spaces. It can also discover meaningful relationships and connections between places, people and uses. Big event histories can be analysed for understanding how specific features of city spaces, services and events affect people's emotions. It can also detect post-event/fair reactions and comments by citizens and participants. These analytics processes can support the development of tools aimed at assisting institutions and large operators, involved in monitoring, designing and implementing strategies and policies oriented to improve the responsiveness of urban systems to the requests of citizens and customers.

1.2.4.3 Robotics and Industry 4.0

Big Data analytics and cloud architectures allow leveraging large amounts of structured, unstructured and fast-moving data. Putting this technology into robotics can lead to interesting dimensions to well-known problems like SLAM and lower-skilled jobs executions (assembly line, medical procedures and piloting vehicles). Rather than viewing robots and automated machines as isolated systems, Cloud Robotics and Automation is a new paradigm where robots and automation systems exchange data and perform computation via networks. Extending work linking robots to Internet, Cloud Robotics and Automation builds an emerging research in cloud computing, machine learning, Big Data, and industry initiatives in the Internet of Things, Industrial Internet and Industry 4.0.

For example, SLAM is a technique used by digital machines to construct a map of an unknown environment while keeping track of the machine's location in the physical environment. This requires a great deal of computational power to sense a sizable area and process the resulting data to both map and localize. Complete 3D SLAM solutions are highly computationally intensive as they use complex real-time particle filters, sub-mapping strategies or combination of metric topological representations. Robots using embedded systems cannot fully implement SLAM because of their limitation in computing power. Big Data can enable interactive data analysis with real-time answers that can empower intelligent robots to analyse enormous and unstructured datasets (Big Data analytics) to perform jobs. This of course requires the processing of huge amounts of event streams coming from robots that must be processed efficiently to support on-line dynamic decision-making.

1.3 Event Stream Models

A vast number of event management models and systems have been and continue to be proposed. Several standardization efforts are being made to specify how entities can export the structure and data transported by events. Existing models have been defined in an ad hoc way, notably linked to the application context (active DBMS event models), or in a very general way in middleware (Java event service, MOMs). Of course, customizing solutions prevents systems to be affected with the overhead of an event model way too sophisticated for their needs. However, they are not adapted when the systems evolve, cooperate and scale, leading to a lack of adaptability and flexibility.

This section introduces the background concepts related to event streams and related operators. It mainly explains how event types become streams and how this is represented in models that are then specialized in concrete event stream systems.

1.3.1 From Event Types to Streams

The literature proposes different definitions of an event. For example, in [30] an event is a happening of interest, which occurs instantaneously at a specific time [31] characterizes an event as the instantaneous effect of the termination of an invocation of an operation on an object. In this document we define an event in terms of a source named *producer* in which the event occurs, and a *consumer* for which the event is significant.

An event type characterizes a class of significant facts (events) and the context under which they occur. An event model gives concepts and general structures used to represent event types. According to the complexity of the event model, the event types are represented as sequences of strings [32], regular expressions— patterns—[33] or as expressions of an event algebra [27, 34, 35]. In certain models, the type itself contains implicitly the contents of the message. Other models represent an event type as a collection of *parameters* or *attributes*. For example, UpdateAccount(idAccount:string, amount:real) is an event type that represents the updates executed on an account with number idAccount and where the amount implied in the operation is represented by the attribute amount. Event types have at least two associated parameters: an *identifier* and a *timestamp*.

In addition, an event type can have other parameters describing the circumstances in which events occurred. This information describes the **event production environment** or **event context**. In some models, the event type is represented by a set of tuples of the form (*variable, domain*). Generally, these parameters represent for instance the agents, resources, and data associated with an event type, the results of the action (e.g., return value of a method), and any other information that characterizes a specific occurrence of that event type. For example, in active systems, the parameters of an event are used to evaluate the condition and to execute the action of an ECA rule.

Event types can be classified as *primitive event types* that describe elementary facts, and *composite event types* that describe complex situations by event combinations.

A **primitive event type** characterizes an atomic operation (i.e., it completely occurs or not). For example, the update operation of an attribute value within a structure, the creation of a process. In the context of databases, primitive event types represent data modification (e.g. the insertion, deletion or modification of tuples), transactions processing (e.g. begin, commit or abort transactions). In an object-oriented context, a method execution can be represented by a primitive event type.

Many event models classify the primitive event types according to the type of operations they represent (databases, transactional, applicative). These operations can be classified as follows:

- **Operations executed on data**: an operation executed on a structure, for example, a relational table, an object. In relational systems this operation can correspond to an insert/update/delete operation applied to one or more n-tuples. In object-based systems, it can be a read/write operation of an object attribute.
- **Operations concerning the execution state of a process**: events can represent specific points of an execution. In DBMS, events can represent execution points of a transaction (before or after the transaction delete/commit). In a workflow application, an event can represent the beginning (end) of a task. The production of exceptions within a process can be represented by events.
- **User operations**: an operation on a widget in an interactive interface, the connection of the user to the network, correspond to events produced by a user.
- **Operations produced within the execution context**: events can represent situations produced in the environment: (1) specific points in time (clock), for example, it is 19:00 or 4 h after the production of an event; (2) events concerning to the operating system, the network, etc.

A **composite event type** characterizes complex situations. A composite event type can be specified as a regular expression (often called a *pattern*) or as a set of primitive or other composite event types related by event algebra operators such as disjunction, conjunction, sequence). For example, consider the composite event type represented as the regular expression $(E_1 \mid E_2) * E_3$ where E_1, E_2, and E_3 are event types, "|" represents *alternation*,[4] and "$*$" represents the *Kleene closure*.[5] The composite event type $E_4 = E_1$ op $(E_2$ op $E_3)$ is specified by an event algebra where E_1, E_2, and E_3 are primitive or composite event types, and op can be any binary composition operator, e.g. disjunction, conjunction, sequence.

The *occurrence* or *instance* of an event type is called an event. Events occur in time and then they are associated to a point in time called *event occurrence time* or *occurrence instant*. The occurrence time of an event is represented by its timestamp. The timestamp is an approximation of the event occurrence time. The accuracy of timestamps depends on the event detection strategy and on the *timestamping* method.

The granularity used for representing time (day, hour, minute, second, etc.) is determined by the system. Most event models and systems assume that the *timeline* representation corresponds to the Gregorian calendar time, and that it is possible to transform this representation as an element of the discrete time domain having 0 (zero) as origin and ∞ as limit. Then, a point in time (event occurrence time) belongs to this domain and it is represented by a positive integer. The event (updateAccount(idAccount:0024680, amount:24500), t_i) is an

---

[4] $E_1 \mid E_2$ matches either events of type E_1 or E_2.

[5] $E*$ is the concatenation of zero or more events of type E.

occurrence of the event type `UpdateAccount(idAccount:string,`
`amount:real)` produced at time t_i, where the time may represent an instant,
a duration or an interval. A *duration* is a period of time with known length, e.g. 8 s.
An *interval* is specified by two instants as `[01/12/2006, 01/12/2007]`.

The notion of event type provides a static view of a happening of interest or a
behaviour pattern in time. Yet it is not sufficient to represent the dynamic aspect
of events flowing (i.e., being produced at a continuous rate). The notion of stream
provides means to represent event flows.

1.3.2 Event Streams

An event stream is represented by an append-only sequence of events having the
same type T. We note *Stream(T)* the stream of events of type T. Event streams can
be continuous, or potentially unbounded (i.e. events can be inserted in a stream at
any time). A finite part of an event stream of type T is noted *Stream$_f$(T)*. In order
to define how to deal with this "dynamic" structure used to consume a continuous
flow of event occurrences, several works have proposed operators to represent the
partition of the stream so that this partitions can be processed and consumed in
continuous processes [36].

The operator `window` is the most popular one. A `window` partitions an event
stream into finite event streams. The result is a stream of finite streams, which we
note `Stream(Streamf(E))`. The way each finite stream is constructed depends
on the window specification, which can be time-based or tuple-based.

1.3.2.1 Time Based Windows

Time based windows define windows using time intervals.

- *Fixed window*: `win:within(t`$_b$`, t`$_e$`, ES`$_i$`)`. Defines a fixed time
  interval `[tb, te]`. The output stream contains a single finite event
  stream $E_i S_{jf}$ such that an event e_i of type E_i belong to ES_{if} iff
  $t_b \leq e_i.\texttt{receptionTime} \leq t_e$.
- *Landmark window*: `win:since(t`$_b$`, ES`$_i$`)`. Defines a fixed lower bound time
  t_b. The output stream is a sequence of finite event streams $ES_{i,kf}$ $k = 1, \ldots n$
  such that each $ES_{i,kf}$ contains events e_i received since the time lower bound
  t_b. That is, $\forall k, e_i \in ES_{i,kf}$ iff $t_b \leq e_i.$ *receptionTime*.
- *Sliding window*: `win:sliding(t`$_w$`, t`$_s$`, ES`$_i$`)`. Defines a time duration t_w
  and a time span t_s. The output stream is a sequence of finite event streams
  $ES_{i,kf}$ $k = 1, \ldots n$ such that each $ES_{i,kf}$ contains events of type E_i produced
  during t_w time unit. The finite event streams in the sequence are produced each
  `ts` time unit. That is, if $ES_{i,kf}$ is produced at time t, then $ES_{i,k+1}$ will be
  produced at time $t + t_s$.

1.3.2.2   Tuple Based Windows

Tuple based windows define the number of events for each window.

- *Fixed size windows*: `win:batch(n`$_b$`, ESi)`. Specifies a fixed size n_b of each finite stream. The output stream is a sequence of finite event streams $ES_{i,kf}$ $k = 1, \ldots n$, each finite event stream $ES_{i,kf}$ containing n_b most recent events and are non-overlapping. If we consider windows of size 3, the event stream $ES_i, = \{e_{i,1}, \ e_{i,2}, \ e_{i,3}, \ e_{i,4}, \ e_{i,5}, \ e_{i,6}, \ \ldots\}$ will be partitioned in finite event streams $\{ES_{i,1f}, \ ES_{i,2f}, \ldots\}$ such that $ES_{i,1f} = \{e_{i,1}, e_{i,2}, \ e_{i,3}\}, ES_{i,2f} = \{e_{i,4}, \ e_{i,5}, \ e_{i,6}\}$, and so on.
- *Moving fixed size windows*: `win:mbatch (nb, m, ES`$_i$`)`. Defines a fixed size n_b of each finite stream, and a number of events m after which the window moves. The output stream is a sequence of finite event streams $ES_{i,kf}$ $k = 1, \ldots n$ such that each $ES_{i,kf}$ contains n_b most recent events of type E_i,. $ES_{i,k+1}$ is started after m events are received in $ES_{i,kf}$ (moving windows). As result, an event instance may be part of many finite event streams. This is the case if $m \leq nb$. For example, if we consider windows of size $nb = 3$ moving after each $m = 2$ events, the event stream $ES_i = \{e_{i,1}, \ e_{i,2}, \ e_{i,3}, \ e_{i,4}, \ e_{i,5}, \ e_{i,6}, \ e_{i,7}, \ \ldots\}$ will be partitioned into finite event streams $\{ES_{i,1f}, \ ES_{i,2f}, \ ES_{i,3f}, \ \ldots\}$ such that $ES_{i,1f} = \{e_{i,1}, \ e_{i,2}, \ e_{i,3}\}$, $ES_{i,2f} = \{e_{i,3}, \ e_{i,4}, \ e_{i,5}\}, ES_{i,3f} = \{e_{i,5}, \ e_{i,6}, \ e_{i,7}\}$, and so on.

The notions of type and event occurrence are useful for dealing with event streams processing phases. Event types are important when addressing the expression of interesting happenings that can be detected and observed within a dynamic environment. As discussed in this section, it is possible to associate to the notion of type, operators that can be applied for defining complex event types. An event definition language can be developed using such operators. The notion of event occurrence is useful to understand and model the association event—time, and then model a continuous flow under the notion of stream. Then it is possible to define strategies for composing streams (on-line) and for analysing streams. These strategies are discussed in the following section.

1.4   Complex Event Composition

Event composition is the process of producing composite events from detected (primitive and composite) event streams. Having a composite event implies that there exists a relation among its component events, such causal order and temporal relationships.

Several academic research and industrial systems have tackled the problem of event composition. Techniques such as complex pattern detection [34, 35, 37, 38], event correlation [39], event aggregation [8], event mining [40, 41] and stream processing [42–44], have been used for composing events. In some cases event composition is done on event histories (e.g. event mining) and in other cases it is done dynamically as events are produced (e.g. event aggregation and stream processing). Analysing an event history searching or discovering patterns produces events. Composite events can be specified based on an *event composition algebra* or *event patterns*.

This section introduces different strategies used for composing event streams. In general these strategies assume the existence of a history (total or partial) and thus adopt monotonic operators, in the case of algebras, or monotonic reasoning in the case of chronicles or codebooks and rules used as composition strategies. Rule based approaches assume that events streams patterns can be detected and they can trigger rules used to notify them.

1.4.1 Composition Algebras

An algebra defines a collection of elements and operators that can be applied on them. Thus, the event composition algebra defines *operators* for specifying composite event types based on primitive or composite event types related by event operators.

An event composition algebra expression is of the form E_1 op E_2. The construction of such an expression produces composite events. The types of these events depend on the operators. Operators determine the order in which the component events must occur for detecting the specified composite event. The occurrence time and parameters of a composite event depend on the semantics of the operator. Therefore, the parameters of a composite event are derived from the parameters of its component events depending on the operator.

Many event models that characterize composite events consider operators such as disjunction, conjunction and sequence. Others add the selection and negation operators. In the following paragraphs, we classify the event operators in: *binary*, *selection* and *temporal operators*. Table 1.1 synthesizes the operator families that can be used for composing event streams. Their definition is presented in Appendix 1.

The operators are used for defining well-formed algebraic expressions considering their associativity and commutability properties. By combining the estimated execution cost it is possible to propose optimization strategies for reducing event stream production.

1.4.2 Composition Techniques

Different techniques can be adopted for composing event streams, depending whether this task is done on-line or post-mortem. For an on-line composition, automata (of different types) are the most frequent adopted structure. When detected

Table 1.1 Event composition operators

FILTERING			BINARY (temporal correlation)	
Window			*Instance based*	
Time based			Disjunction	$(E_1 \mid E_2)$
	Fixed	win:within(t_b, t_e, ES$_1$)	Conjunction	(E_1 , E_2)
	Landmark	win:since(tb, ESi)	Sequence	$(E_1 ; E_2)$
	Sliding	win:sliding(tw, ts, ESi)	Concurrency	$(E_1 \parallel E_2)$
			Interval based	
Tuple based			During	$(E_2$ during $E_1)$
	Fixed size	win:batch(nb, ESi)	Ovelap	$(E_1$ overlaps $E_2)$
	Moving fixed size	win:mbatch (nb, m, ESi)	Meet	$(E_1$ meets $E_2)$
			Start	$(E_1$ starts $E_2)$
			End	$(E_1$ ends $E_2)$
Selection			TEMPORAL	
	First occurrence	(*E in H)	Temporal offset	
	History	(Times(n, E) in H)	Interval expresions	
	Negation	(Not E in H)		

event streams are continuously (i.e., recurrently) fed to nodes that process them and disseminate them to other nodes that implement composition operators. Depending on the type of automaton, different patterns can be produced and delivered to consumers. Post-mortem event streams composition, assume that it is possible to store all events streams produced during a given period, or at least a representative sample of event streams. These event histories sometimes called event traces are used to apply knowledge discovery techniques seeking to extract patterns, correlations, to understand and predict behaviour models. The following sections introduce prominent examples of these techniques.

1.4.2.1 Automata Oriented Event Composition

In current research projects, the composition process is based on the evaluation of abstractions such as *finite state automata*, *Petri nets*, *matching trees* or *graphs*.

- **Finite state automata**: Considering that composite event expressions are equivalent to regular expressions if they are not parameterized, it is possible to implement them using finite state automata. A first approach using automata has been made in the active data base system Ode [37, 45, 46]. An automaton can be defined for each event, which reaches an accepting state exactly whenever the event occurs. The event history provides the sequence of input events to the automaton. The event occurrences are fed into the automaton one at a time, in the order of their event identifiers. The current marking of an automaton determines the current stage of the composition process. If the automaton reaches an accepting state, then the composite event implemented by the automaton occurs. Nevertheless, automata are not sufficient in case of event parameters have to be supported. The automata have to be extended with a data structure that stores the event parameters of the primitive events from the time of their occurrence to the time at which the composite event is detected.

- **Petri nets** are used to support the detection of composite events that are composed of parameterized events. SAMOS [34, 47] uses the concepts of Coloured Petri nets and modifies them to so-called SAMOS Petri Nets. A Petri net consists of places, transitions and arcs. Arcs connect places with transitions and transitions with places. The places of a Petri net correspond to the potential states of the net, and such states may be changed by the transitions. Transitions correspond to the possible events that may occur (perhaps concurrently). In Coloured Petri nets, tokens are of specific token types and may carry complex information. When an event occurs, a corresponding token is inserted into all places representing its event type. The flow of tokens through the net is then determined; a transition can fire if all its input places contain at least one token. Firing a transition means removing one token from each input place and inserting one token into each output place. The parameters corresponding to the token type of the output place are derived at that time. Certain output places are marked as end places, representing composite events. Inserting a token into an end place corresponds to the detection of a composite event.
- **Trees**: Another approach to implement event composition uses matching trees that are constructed from the composite event types. The leaves represent primitive event types. The parent nodes in the tree hierarchy represent composite event types. Primitive events occur and are injected into the leaves corresponding to their event type. The leaves pass the primitive events directly to their parent nodes. Thus, parent nodes maintain information for matched events, such as mapping of event variables and matching event instances. A composite event is detected if the root node is reached and the respective event data are successfully filtered.
- **Graph-based** event composition has been implemented by several active rule systems like SAMOS [27, 28, 48], Sentinel [49] and NAOS [35]. An event graph is a Direct Acyclic Graph (DAG) that consists of non-terminal nodes (N-nodes), terminal nodes (T-nodes) and edges [27]. Each node represents either a primitive event or a composite event. N-nodes represent composite events and may have several incoming and several outgoing edges. T-nodes represent primitive events and have one incoming and possibly several outgoing edges. When a primitive event occurs, it activates the terminal node that represents the event. The node in turn activates all nodes attached to it via outgoing edges. Parameters are propagated to the nodes using the edges. When a node is activated, the incoming data is evaluated (using the operator semantics of that node and the consumption mode) and if necessary, nodes connected to it are activated by propagating the parameters of the event. If the node is marker as a final node, the corresponding composite event is signalled.

These structures are well adapted for on-line stream event composition where windows and filters are used for controlling the consumption rate of streams combined with other processing operators for causally or temporally correlating them. These structures can also be matched towards parallel programs that can make in some cases event stream composition more efficient. Having parallel programs associated to these composition structures has not yet been widely explored. The emergence of the map-reduce and data flow model and associated infrastructures can encourage the development of solutions adapted for addressing Big Data velocity and volume.

1.4.2.2 Event Correlation

The process of analysing events to infer a new event from a set of related events is defined as *event correlation*. It is mostly used to determine the root cause of faults in network systems [50]. Thus, an *event correlation system* correlates events and detects composite events. There are several methods for correlating events, including *compression*, *count*, *suppression*, and *generalization*. **Compression** reduces multiple occurrences of the same event into a single event, allowing to see that an event is recurring without having to see every instance individually. **Count** is the substitution of a specified number of similar events (not necessarily the same event) with a single event. **Suppression** associates priorities with events, and may hide a lower priority event if a higher priority event exists. Finally, in **generalization** the events are associated with a superclass that is reported rather than the specific event.

Other methods of event correlation are by *causal* relationships (i.e., event *A* causes event *B*), and by *temporal* correlations where there is a time period associated with each possible correlation, and if the proper events occur during a particular time period, they may be correlated. Event correlation techniques have been derived from a selection of computer science paradigms (AI, graph theory, information theory, automata theory) including *rule-based systems*, *model based reasoning systems*, *model traversing techniques*, *code-based systems*, *fault propagation models* and the *code-book approach*.

Rule-based systems [51, 52] are composed of rules of the form **if** condition **then** conclusion. The condition part is a logical combination of propositions about the current set of received events and the system state; the conclusion determines the state of correlation process. For example, a simple rule that correlates the event occurrences e_1 of type E_1 and e_2 of type E_2 for producing an event e_3 is: **if** e_1 and e_2 **then** e_3. The system operation is controlled by an inference engine, which typically uses a forward-chaining inference mechanism.

In [50] composite events are used for event correlation. It presents a composite event specification approach that can precisely express complex timing constraints among correlated event instances. A composite event occurs whenever certain conditions on the attribute values of other event instances become true, and is defined in the following format:

```
define composite event CE with
attributes ([NAME, TYPE], ..., [NAME, TYPE])
which occurs
whenever timing condition
TC is [satisfied | violated]
```

```
if condition
C is true
then
ASSIGN VALUES TO CE's ATTRIBUTES;
```

The rules for correlation reflect the relationship among the correlated events, such as causal or temporal relationship. If these relationships can be specified in the composite event definitions, the results of correlation are viewed as occurrences of the corresponding composite events. Thus, relationships among events for correlation, either causal or complex-temporal, are expressed as conditions on event attributes for composite events. Considering a common event correlation rule in networks with timing requirements: "when a link-down event is received, if the next link-up event for the same link is not received within 2 min and an alert message has not been generated in the past 5 min, then alert the network administrator". The composite event LinkADownAlert is defined as follows:

```
define composite event LinkADownAlert with
attributes (["Occurrence Time" : time]
       ["Link Down Time" : time])
which occurs
whenever timing condition
not LinkUp in [occTime(LinkADown),
       occTime(LinkADown)+2 min]
and not LinkADownAlert in
       [occTime(LinkADown)-3 min,
       occTime(LinkADown)+2 min]
is satisfied
if condition true is true
then {
"Link Down Time" :=occTime(LinkADown);
}
```

where LinkADown and LinkAUp correspond to the up and down events of a link A. The composite event will occur at 2 min after an occurrence of LinkADown event if no LinkAUp event occurs during 2-minute interval and no LinkADownAlert event was triggered during the past 5-minute interval.

Hence, since the composite events are used to represent the correlation rules, the correlation process is essentially the task of composite event detection through event monitoring. Therefore, if some time constraints are detected as being satisfied or violated according to the composite event definitions, the condition evaluator is triggered. The conditions on other event attributes are evaluated. Once the conditions are evaluated as true, the attribute values of the corresponding composite event are computed and their occurrences are triggered. As a result of the hard-coded system connectivity information within the rules, rule-based systems are believed to

lack scalability, to be difficult to maintain, and to have difficult to predict outcomes
due to unforeseen rule interactions.

Model-based reasoning incorporates an explicit model representing the ***structure*** (static knowledge) and ***behavior*** (dynamic knowledge) of the system. Thus,
the model describes dependencies between the system components and/or causal
relationships between events. Model-based reasoning systems [50, 53, 54] utilize
inference engines controlled by a set of correlation rules, whose conditions usually contain model exploration predicates. The predicates test the existence of a
relationship among system components. The model is usually defined using an
object-oriented paradigm and frequently has the form of a graph of dependencies
among system components.

In the **codebook** technique [55] causality is described by a causality graph whose
nodes represent events and whose directed edges represent causality. Nodes of a
causality graph may be marked as problems (P) or symptoms (S). The causality
graph may include information that does not contribute to correlation analysis (e.g.,
a cycle represents causal equivalence). Thus, a cycle of events can be aggregated into
a single event. Similarly, certain symptoms are not directly caused by any problem
but only by other symptoms. They do not contribute any information about problems
that is not already provided by these other symptoms. These indirect symptoms
may be eliminated without loss of information. The information contained in the
correlation graph must be converted into a set of codes, one for each problem in
the correlation graph. A code is simply a vector of 0 s and 1 s. The value of 1 at the
i^{th} position of a code generated for problem p_j indicates cause-effect implication
between problem p_j and symptom s_i. The *codebook* is a subset of symptoms that
has been optimized to minimize the number of symptoms that have to be analysed
while ensuring that the symptom patterns distinguish different problems.

1.4.2.3   Chronicle Recognition

A *chronicle* is a set of events, linked together by time constraints [DGG93, Gha96,
Dou96]. The representation of chronicles relies on a propositional reified logic
formalism where a set of multi-valued domain attributes are temporally qualified
by predicates such as event and hold.

The persistence of the value v of a domain attribute p during the interval
[t, t'] is expressed by the assertion:

hold(p:v, (t, t')).

An event is a change of the value of a domain attribute, the predicate event is
defined through the predicate hold:

event(p: (v1, v2), t) ≡

$\exists \tau < t < \tau' |$ hold(p:v1, (τ, t)) ^ hold(p:v2, (t, τ')) ^ (v1 ≠ v2)

A *chronicle model* represents a piece of the evolution of the world; it is composed
of four parts: (1) a set of events which represents the relevant changes of the world
for this chronicle; (2) a set of assertions which is the context of the occurrences
of the chronicle events; (3) a set of temporal constraints which relates events and

assertions between them; and (4) a set of actions which will be processed when the chronicle is recognized.

The chronicle recognition is complete as long as the observed event stream is complete. This hypothesis enables to manage context assertions quite naturally through occurrences and non-occurrences of events. Then, to process assertion hold(p:v,(t,t')), the process verifies that there has been an event(p:(v',v),t") with t"<t and such that no event p:(v,v") occurs within [t",t'].

The recognition process relies on a complete forecasting of expected events predicted by chronicle. An interval, called *window of relevance* D(e) is defined, which contains all possible occurrence times for a predicted event e of a partial instance S, in order for e to be consistent with constraints and known times of observed events in S.

A chronicle instance may progress in two ways: (1) a new event may be detected, it can be either integrated into the instance and make the remaining predictions more precise, or it may violate a constraint for an assertion and make the corresponding chronicle invalid; or (2) time passes without nothing happening and, perhaps, may make some deadline violated or some assertions constraints obsolete.

When an observed event e matches an model event e_k, the reception time r(e) = now, and either

- d(e) $\notin$ D(e_k): e does not meet the temporal constraints of the expected event e_k of S,
- d(e) $\in$ D(e_k): D(e_k) is reduced to the single point d(e).

The reduction must be propagated to other expected events, which in turn are further constrained; i.e., temporal windows are updated.

```
propagate(e_k, S)
    for all forthcoming event e_i ≠ e_k of S
        D(e_i) ← D(e_i) ∩ [D(e_k) + I(e_i - e_k)]
```

This produces a new set of non-empty and consistent D(e_i). In addition, when the internal clock is updated, this new value of now can reduce some windows of relevance D(e_i) and, in this case, it is needed to propagate it over all expected events of an instance S: D(e_i) ← D(e_i) ∩ ([t, +∞] - D(ei)). A clock update does not always require propagation, it is necessary to propagate only when a time bound is reached. Therefore, time bounds enable an efficient pruning.

When an event is integrated in a chronicle, the original chronicle instance must be duplicated before the temporal window propagation, and only the copy is updated. For each chronicle model, the system manages a tree of current instances. When a chronicle instance is competed or killed, it is removed from this tree. Duplication is needed to warranty the recognition of a chronicle as often as it may arise, even if its instances are temporally overlapping.

The size of the tree hypotheses is the main source of complexity. Using duration thresholds in a chronicle model is a strategy to reduce its size. Further knowledge restricting multiple instances of events is also beneficial. There may also be chronicles that cannot have two complete instances that overlap in time or share a common event; the user may also be interested in recognizing just one instance at a time. For both cases, when a chronicle instance is recognized, all its pending instances must be removed.

1.4.2.4 Event and Traces Mining

Data mining, also known as Knowledge-Discovery in databases (KDD) is the practice of automatically analysing large stores of data for patterns and then summarizing them as useful information. Data mining is sometimes defined as the process of navigating through the data and trying to find out patterns and finally establishing all relevant relationships. Consequently, the event-mining goal is to identify patterns that potentially indicate the production of an event within large event data sets. Event mining adopts data mining techniques for the recognition of event patterns, such as association, classification, clustering, forecasting, etc. Therefore, events within a history can be mined in a multitude of ways: unwanted events are filtered out, patterns of logically corresponding events are aggregated into one new composite event, repetitive events are counted and aggregated into a new primitive event with a count of how often the original event occurred, etc.

Event correlation approaches may be further classified as state-based or stateless. Stateless systems typically are only able to correlate alarms that occur in a certain time-window. State-based systems support the correlation of events in an event-driven fashion at the expense of the additional overhead associated with maintaining the system state.

1.4.3 Discussion

This section presented expressions of an algebra for composing events. It gave a classification of algebraic operators that can be defined depending on whether events are considered instantaneous happenings or processes with duration represented as intervals.

Event composition in large-scale systems provides a means of managing the complexity of a vast number of events. Large-scale event systems need to support event composition in order to quickly and efficiently notify relevant complex information. In addition, distributed event composition can improve efficiency and robustness of systems. Thus, event types can be related and thus denote a new complex event type. Relationships between event types can be expressed by an event composition algebra.

The different event-based approaches are characterized by their means for specifying and detecting primitive and composite events. The composition process is based on the evaluation of abstractions such as finite state automata, Petri nets, matching trees, graphs. While event tracing enables the detection of performance problems at a high level of detail, growing trace-file size often constrains its scalability on large-scale systems and complicates management, analysis, and visualization of trace data. Such strategies can cope to Big streams velocity as long as they can be efficiently used or that they can be exploited in parallel in order to ensure good performance.

1.5 Conclusion and Outlook

Typical Big Data analytics solutions such as batch data processing systems can scale-out gracefully and provide insight into large amounts of historical data at the expense of a high latency. They are hence a bad fit for online and dynamic analyses on continuous streams of potentially high velocity.

Building robust and efficient tools to collect analyse, and display large amounts of data is a very challenging task. Large memory requirements often cause a significant slow down or, even worse, place practical constraints on what can be done at all. Moreover, if when streams stem from different providers, before merging those streams into a single global one, the merge step may require a large number of resources creating a potential conflict with given infrastructure limits. Thus, the amount of event streams poses a problem for (1) management, (2) visualization and (3) analysis. The size of a stream history may easily exceed the user or disk quota or the operating system imposed file-size limit of 2 GB common on 32-bit platforms. Very often these three aspects cannot be clearly separated because one may act as a tool to achieve the other, for example, when analysis occurs through visualization.

Even if the data management problem can be solved, the analysis itself can still be very time consuming, especially if it is performed without or with only little automatic support. On the other hand, the iterative nature of many applications causes streams to be highly redundant. To address this problem, stream collection must be coupled with efficient automatic cleaning techniques that can avoid redundancy and information loss.

Existing, event stream approaches and systems seem to be adapted for dealing with velocity but do not completely scale when volume becomes big. Efficient parallel algorithms exploiting computing resources provided by architectures like the cloud can be used to address, velocity at the different phases of Big stream cycle: collection, cleaning and analysis. The huge volume of streams, calls for intelligent storage methods that can search for a balance between volume, veracity and value. Representative stream samples must be stored to support static analytics (e.g., event trace mining) while continuous on-line composition processes deal with streams and generate a real-time vision of the environment. Concrete applications are already calling for such solutions in order to build smarter environments, social and individual behaviours, and sustainable industrial processes.

Appendix 1

The events e_1 and e_2, used in the following definitions, are occurrences of the event types E_1 and E_2 respectively (with $E_1 \neq E_2$) and can be any primitive or composite event type. An event is considered as *durative*, i.e., it has a duration going from the instant when it starts until the instant when it ends [56] and its occurrence time is represented by a time interval [startI-e, endI-e].

.1 Binary Operators

Binary operators derive a new composite event from two input events (primitive or composite). The following binary operators are defined by most existing event models [35, 46, 47, 56]:

- **Disjunction**: $(E_1 \mid E_2)$
  There are two possible semantics for the disjunction operator "$\mid$": *exclusive-or* and *inclusive-or*. Exclusive-or means that a composite event of type $(E_1 \mid E_2)$ is initiated and terminated by the occurrence of e_1 of type E_1 or e_2 of type E_2, whereas inclusive-or considers both events if they are simultaneous, i.e. they occur "at the same time". In centralized systems, no couple of events can occur simultaneously and hence, the disjunction operator always corresponds to exclusive-or. In distributed systems, two events at different sites can occur simultaneously and hence, both exclusive-or and inclusive-or are applicable.

- **Conjunction**: (E_1 , E_2)
  A composite event of type (E_1 , E_2) occurs if both e_1 of type E_1 and e_2 of type E_2 occur, regardless their occurrence order. Event e_1 and e_2 may be produced at the same or at different sites. The event e_1 is the initiator of the composite event and the event e_2 is its terminator, or vice versa. Event e_1 and e_2 can overlap or they can be disjoint.

- **Sequence**: $(E_1 ; E_2)$
  A composite event of type $(E_1 ; E_2)$ occurs when an e_2 of type E_2 occurs after e_1 of type E_1 has occurred. Then, sequence denotes that event e_1 "happens before" event e_2. This implies that the end time of event e_1 is guaranteed to be less than the start time of event e_2. However, the semantics of "happens before" differs, depending on whether composite event is a local or a global event. Therefore, although the syntax is the same for local and for global events, the two cases have to be considered separately.

- **Concurrency**: $(E_1 \parallel E_2)$
  A composite event of type $(E_1 \parallel E_2)$ occurs if both events e_1 of type E_1 and e_2 of type E_2 occur virtually simultaneously, i.e. "at the same time". This implies that this operator applied to two distinct events is only applicable in global events; the events e_1 and e_2 occur at different sites and it is not possible to establish an order between them. The concurrency relation is commutative.

- **During**: (**E$_2$ during E$_1$**)
  The composite event of type (E$_2$ during E$_1$) occurs if an event e$_2$ of type E$_2$ happens during event e$_1$ of type E$_1$, i.e. e$_2$ starts after the beginning of e$_1$ and ends before the end of e$_1$.
- **Overlaps**: (**E$_1$ overlaps E$_2$**)
  The beginning of event e$_1$ of type E$_1$ is before the beginning of event e$_2$ of type E$_2$ and the end of e$_1$ is during e$_2$ or vice versa.
- **Meets**: (**E$_1$ meets E$_2$**)
  The beginning of event e$_2$ of type E$_2$ is immediately after the end of event e$_1$ of type E$_1$.
- **Starts**: (**E$_1$ starts E$_2$**)
  The beginning of event e$_1$ of type E$_1$ and e$_2$ of type E$_2$ are simultaneous. The occurrence interval of (e$_1$ starts e$_2$) is [startT-e$_1$, *latest*(endT-e$_1$, endT-e$_2$)].
- **Ends**: (**E$_1$ ends E$_2$**)
  The end of event e$_1$ of type E$_1$ and event e$_2$ of type E$_2$ are simultaneous. The ends relation is commutative. The occurrence interval of (e$_1$ ends e$_2$) is [*earliest*(startT-e$_1$, startT-e$_2$), endT-e$_2$].

.2 Selection Operators

Selection operators allow searching occurrences of an event type in the event history. The selection E$^{[i]}$ defines the occurrence of the ith element of a sequence of events of type E, i $\in$ N; where N is a natural number greater than 0, during a predefined time interval I. The following selection operators are distinguished in event models such as SAMOS [34, 47]:

- **First occurrence**: (∗E in I)
  The event is produced after the first occurrence of an event of type E during the time interval I. The event will not be produced by all the other event occurrences of E during the interval.
- **History**: (**Times(n, E) in I**)
  An event is produced when an event of type E has occurred with the specified frequency *n* during the time interval I.
- **Negation**: (**Not E in I**)
  The event is produced if any occurrence of the event type E is not produced (i.e. the event did not occur) during the time interval I.

.3Temporal Operator

A composite event can be represented by the occurrence of an event and an offset $(E + \Delta)$, for example, $E = E_1 + 00:15$ to indicate fifteen minutes before the occurrence of an event of type E_1. Thus, the occurrence time of E is $[endT-e_1, endT-e_1 + \Delta]$.

References

1. Jagadish HV, Gehrke J, Labrinidis A, Papakonstantinou Y, Patel JM, Ramakrishnan R, Shahabi C (2014) Big Data and its technical challenges. Commun ACM 57:86–94
2. Terry D, Goldberg D, Nichols D, Oki B (1992) Continuous queries over append-only databases. ACM SIGMOD Record
3. Zheng B, Lee DL (2001) Semantic caching in location-dependent query processing. In: Proceedings of the 7th international symposium on advances in spatial and temporal databases (SSTD), Redondo Beach, CA, USA
4. Urhan T, Franklin MJ (2000) Xjoin: a reactively-scheduled pipelined join operator. IEEE Data Eng Bull 23:27–33
5. De Francisci Morales G (2013) SAMOA: a platform for mining Big Data streams. In: Proceedings of the 22nd international conference on World Wide Web Companion, Geneva, Switzerland, pp 777–778
6. Adiba M, Castrejón JC, Espinosa-Oviedo JA, Vargas-Solar G, Zechinelli-Martini JL (2015) Big data management: challenges, approaches, tools and their limitations. Networking for big data
7. Abiteboul S, Manolescu I, Benjelloun O, Milo T, Cautis B, Preda N (2004) Lazy query evaluation for active xml. In: Proceedings of the SIGMOD international conference
8. Luckham D (2002) The power of events: an introduction to complex event processing in distributed systems. Addison Wesley Professional
9. Carney D, Centintemel U, Cherniack M, Convey C, Lee S, Seidman G, Stonebraker M, Tatbul N, Zdonik SB (2002) Monitoring streams: a new class of data management applications. In: Proceedings of the 28th international conference on very large data bases (VLDB), Hong Kong, China
10. Babu S, Widom J (2001) Continuous queries over data streams. SIGMOD Rec 30:109–120
11. Liu L, Pu C, Tang W (1999) Continual queries for internet scale event-driven information delivery. IEEE Trans Knowl Data Eng 11:610–628
12. Chen J, DeWitt DJ, Tian F, Wang Y (2000) NiagaraCQ: a scalable continuous query system for Internet databases. In: Proceedings of SIGMOD international conference on management of data, New York, USA
13. Dittrich J-P, Fischer PM, Kossmann D (2005) Agile: adaptive indexing for context-aware information filters. In: Proceedings of the SIGMOD international conference
14. Agarwal PK, Xie J, Yang J, Yu H (2006) Scalable continuous query processing by tracking hotspots. In: Proceedings of the 32nd international conference on very large data bases (VLDB), Seoul, Korea
15. Schreier U, Pirahesh H, Agrawal R, Mohan C (1991) Alert: an architecture for transforming a passive dbms into an active dbms. In: Proceedings international conference very large data bases
16. Cao H, Wolfson O, Xu B, Yin H (2005) Mobi-dic: mobile discovery of local resources in peer-to-peer wireless network. IEEE Data Eng Bull 28:11–18

17. Mokbel MF, Xiong X, Aref WG, Hambrusch S, Prabhakar S, Hammad M (2004) Place: a query processor for handling real-time spatio-temporal data streams (demo). In: Proceedings of the 30th conference on very large data bases (VLDB), Toronto, Canada
18. Hellerstein JM, Franklin MJ, Chandrasekaran S, Deshpande A, Hildrum K, Madden S, Raman V, Shah MA (2000) Adaptive query processing: technology in evolution. IEEE Data Eng Bull 23:7–18
19. Anicic D, Fodor P, Rudolph S, Stühmer R, Stojanovic N, Studer R (2010) A rule-based language for complex event processing and reasoning. In: Hitzler P, Lukasiewicz T (eds) Web reasoning and rule systems. Springer, Heidelberg
20. Hirzel M, Andrade H, Gedik B, Jacques-Silva G, Khandekar R, Kumar V, Mendell M, Nasgaard H, Schneider S, Soule R, Wu K-L (2013) IBM streams processing language: analyzing big data in motion. IBM J Res Dev 57:1–11
21. Zikopoulos PC, Eaton C, DeRoos D, Deutsch T, Lapis G (2011) Understanding big data. McGraw-Hill, New York
22. Yao Y, Gehrke J (2003) Query processing in sensor networks. In: Proceedings of the first biennial conference on innovative data systems research (CIDR)
23. Zadorozhny V, Chrysanthis PK, Labrinidis A (2004) Algebraic optimization of data delivery patterns in mobile sensor networks. In: Proceedings of the 15th international workshop on database and expert systems applications (DEXA), Zaragoza, Spain
24. Li H-G, Chen S, Tatemura J, Agrawal D, Candan K, Hsiung W-P (2006) Safety guarantee of continuous join queries over punctuated data streams. In: Proceedings of the 32nd international conference on very large data bases (VLDB), Seoul, Korea
25. Wolfson O, Sistla AP, Xu B, Zhou J, Chamberlain S (1999) Domino: databases for moving objects tracking. In: Proceedings of the SIGMOD international conference on management of data, Philadelphia, PA, USA
26. Avnur R, Hellerstein JM (2000) Eddies: continuously adaptive query processing. In: Proceedings of SIGMOD international conference on management of data, New York, USA
27. Chakravarthy S, Mishra D (1994) Snoop: an expressive event specification language for active databases. Data Knowl Eng 14:1–26
28. Chakravarthy S, Krishnaprasad V, Anwar E, Kim SK (1994) Composite events for active databases: semantics, contexts and detection. In: Proceedings of the 20th international conference on very large data bases (VLDB), Santiago, Chile
29. Zheng Y, Capra L, Wolfson O, Yang H (2014) Urban computing: concepts methodologies and applications. ACM Trans Intell Syst Technol 5:1–55
30. Mansouri-Samani M, Sloman M (1997) GEM: a generalized event monitoring language for distributed systems. Distrib Eng J 4:96
31. Rosenblum DS, Wolf AL (1997) A design framework for internet-scale event observation and notification. In: Proceedings of the 6th European software engineering conference, Zurich, Switzerland
32. Yuhara M, Bershad BN, Maeda C, Moss JEB (1994) Efficient packet demultiplexing for multiple endpoints and large messages. In: Proceedings of the 1994 winter USENIX conference
33. Bailey ML, Gopal B, Sarkar P, Pagels MA, Peterson LL (1994) Pathfinder: a pattern-based packet classifier. In: Proceedings of the 1st symposium on operating system design and implementation
34. Gatziu S, Dittrich KR (1994) Detecting composite events in active database systems using Petri nets. In: Proceedings of the 4th international workshop on research issues in data engineering: active database systems, Houston, TX, USA
35. Collet C, Coupaye T (1996) Primitive and composite events in NAOS. In: Proceedings of the 12th BDA Journées Bases de Données Avancées, Clermont-Ferrand, France
36. Bidoit N, Objois M (2007) Machine Flux de Données: comparaison de langages de requêtes continues. In: Proceedings of the 23rd BDA Journees Bases de Donnees Avancees, Marseille, France

37. Gehani NH, Jagadish HV, Shmueli O (1992) Event specification in an active object-oriented database. In: Proceedings of the ACM SIGMOD international conference on management of data
38. Pietzuch PR, Shand B, Bacon J (2004) Composite event detection as a generic middleware extension. IEEE Netw Mag Spec Issue Middlew Technol Future Commun Netw 18:44–55
39. Yoneki E, Bacon J (2005) Unified semantics for event correlation over time and space in hybrid network environments. In: Proceedings of the OTM conferences, pp 366–384
40. Agrawal R, Srikant R (1995) Mining sequential patterns. In: Proceedings of the 11th international conference on data engineering, Taipei, Taiwan
41. Giordana A, Terenziani P, Botta M (2002) Recognizing and discovering complex events in sequences. In: Proceedings of the 13th international symposium on foundations of intelligent systems, London, UK
42. Wu E, Diao Y, Rizvi S (2006) High-performance complex event processing over streams. In: Proceedings of the ACM SIGMOD international conference on management of data, Chicago, IL, USA
43. Demers AJ, Gehrke J, Panda B, Riedewald M, Sharma V, White WM (2007) Cayuga: a general purpose event monitoring system. In: Proceedings of the conference on innovative data systems research (CIDR), pp 412–422
44. Balazinska M, Kwon Y, Kuchta N, Lee D (2007) Moirae: history-enhanced monitoring. In: Proceedings of the conference on innovative data systems research (CIDR)
45. Gehani NH, Jagadish HV (1991) Ode as an active database: constraints and triggers. In: Proceedings of the 17th international conference on very large data bases (VLDB), Barcelona, Spain
46. Gehani NH, Jugadish HV, Shmueli O (1992) Composite event specification in active databases: model & implementation. In: Proceedings of the 18th international conference on very large data bases, Vancouver, Canada
47. Gatziu S, Dittrich KR (1993) SAMOS: an active object-oriented database system. IEEE Q Bull Data Eng Spec Issue Act Databases
48. Adaikkalavan R (2002) Snoop event specification: formalization algorithms, and implementation using interval-based semantics. MS Thesis, University of Texas, Arlington
49. Chakravarthy S (1997) SENTINEL: an object-oriented DBMS with event-based rules. In: Proceedings of the ACM SIGMOD international conference on management of data, New York, USA
50. Jakobson G, Weissman MD (1993) Alarm correlation. IEEE Netw 7:52–59
51. Liu G, Mok AK, Yang EJ (1999) Composite events for network event correlation. In: Proceedings of the 6th IFIP/IEEE international symposium on integrated network management, pp 247–260
52. Wu P, Bhatnagar R, Epshtein L, Bhandaru M, Shi Z (1998) Alarm correlation engine (ACE). In: Proceedings of the IEEE/IFIP network operation and management symposium, pp 733–742
53. Nygate YA (1995) Event correlation using rule and object based techniques. In: Proceedings of the IFIP/IEEE international symposium on integrated network management, pp 278–289
54. Appleby K, Goldszmidth G, Steinder M (2001) Yemanja – a layered event correlation engine for multi-domain server farms. Integr Netw Manag 7
55. Yemini SA, Kliger S, Mozes E, Yemini Y, Ohsie D (1996) High speed and robust event correlation. IEEE Commun Mag 34:82–90
56. Roncancio CL (1998) Towards duration-based, constrained and dynamic event types. In: Proceedings of the 2nd international workshop on active, real-time, and temporal database systems

Chapter 2
Big Data Tools and Platforms

Sourav Mazumder

Abstract The fast evolving Big Data Tools and Platforms space has given rise to various technologies to deal with different Big Data use cases. However, because of the multitude of the tools and platforms involved it is often difficult for the Big Data practitioners to understand and select the right tools for addressing a given business problem related to Big Data. In this chapter we cover an introductory discussion to the various Big Data Tools and Platforms with the aim of providing necessary breadth and depth to the Big Data practitioner so that they can have a reasonable background to start with to support the Big Data initiatives in their organizations. We start with the discussion of common Technical Concepts and Patterns typically used by the core Big Data Tools and Platforms. Then we delve into the individual characteristics of different categories of the Big Data Tools and Platforms in detail. Then we also cover the applicability of the various categories of Big Data Tools and Platforms to various enterprise level Big Data use cases. Finally, we discuss the future works happening in this space to cover the newer patterns, tools and platforms to be watched for implementation of Big Data use cases.

2.1 Introduction

The technology space in Big Data has grown in leaps and bounds in last 10 years or so with various genres of technologies attempting to address the key aspects of Big Data related problems. The characterization of 'what is Big' in Big Data is actually relative to a particular context. Today in a typical organization, the Big Data Problems are identified as the situations where the existing software tools are incapable of storing, refining, and processing targeted high volume of data ('Volume') of any arbitrary semantics and structure ('Variety') within a stipulated time ('Velocity') with required accuracy ('Veracity') and at reasonable cost ('Value') [57].

Interestingly, this challenge, that the available technologies are not good enough to solve a problem related to handling data can be traced back to as early as in

S. Mazumder (✉)
IBM Analytics, San Francisco, CA, USA
e-mail: smazumder@us.ibm.com

© Springer International Publishing Switzerland 2016
S. Yu, S. Guo (eds.), *Big Data Concepts, Theories, and Applications*,
DOI 10.1007/978-3-319-27763-9_2

1880s. In 1880, after collection of the census data, the US Census Bureau estimated that it would take 8 years to crunch the same. It was also predicted that the data generated by the 1890 census will take more than 10 years. So by the time the insight generated by the 1890 census data could be made ready for consumption it would have been already outdated by the data from 1900 census. Fortunately, that problem got solved by Herman Hollerith [109] as he developed a machine called Hollerith Tabulating Machine to bring down 10 years' worth of work needed to analyze the census data to 3 months.

The Big Data problems of modern days are driven by three fundamental shifts happened in the technology and business in the last two decades. Firstly, digital storage has become more cost effective than paper for storing contents like documents, numbers, diagrams, etc. This is also true for any other storage media for storing other humanly consumable assets like photographs, audio, video, etc. Secondly, the unprecedented rate of creation and consumption of data through web (and now with Internet Of Things [110]) using fixed or mobile devices at very large scale across various domains. Finally, the growing needs for every business to monitor and predict micro and macro level business activities to address the ever growing market pressure and competitions. These changes eventually necessitated emergence of various Big Data Tools and Platforms in the landscape of data management software in last 15 years or so. All of them were not labeled as Big Data Tools and Platforms to start with because the term 'Big Data' got popular only around beginning of this decade.

The core Big Data Tools and Platforms available today in the industry can be classified under the following broad categories of Tools and Platforms—*Hadoop Ecosystem, NoSQL Databases, In Memory Databases, Data Warehousing Appliances, Streaming Event Processing Frameworks, Search Engines, and Berkeley Data Analytics Stack (BDAS)*. Along with these core Big Data Tools and Platforms there are also technologies which can be categorized as supporting Big Data Tools and Platforms, the key ones being **Analytics & Reporting Tools** and **Data Integration & Governance Frameworks**. As in case of any other data related use cases, these two supporting technologies are needed for end to end implementation of Big Data use cases in an organization. These supporting Big Data Tools and Platforms have evolved big time over last few years to support the core Big Data Tools and Platforms. On the other hand core Big Data Tools and Platforms also have put their best effort towards the ease of integration with these supporting technologies.

The classification of Big Data Tools and Platforms mentioned above is loosely based on the fact that typically these technologies are deployed and managed separately to address different types of Big Data requirements. However, given the rapid innovations happening in the Big Data Tools and Platforms space and fast changing requirements of Big Data problems, there are overlaps within these categories.

In the rest of the sections, in this chapter, we shall discuss in details the different categories of Big Data Tools and Platforms mentioned above. We'll also highlight the overlaps wherever necessary. We shall start with the discussion of common Technical Concepts and Patterns typically used by core Big Data Tools and Platforms. Then we shall discuss the individual characteristics for each of the core Big Data Tools and Platforms in detail. Next we shall also discuss the relevant details around the supporting technologies. Afterwards we shall cover the applicability of the various categories of Big Data Tools and Platforms to various usage scenarios and their implementations in typical enterprises. Finally, we shall take a broader look on the future works happening in the space of Big Data Tools and Platforms.

While discussing the specific tools and technologies in this chapter, Open Source based tools would be discussed in greater length compared to the licensed products. This is because of the fact that the Big Data movement was primarily started and still primarily fueled by the Open Source tools and also because of the more experience and the public domain information available around them. Please note that in many places in this chapter we have used the phrase 'Big Data Technology' instead of 'Big Data Tools and Platforms' for the sake of brevity and the ease of flow of the content.

2.2 Common Technical Concepts and Patterns

The various technologies in the core Big Data Tools and Platforms space are geared towards addressing the common set of problems/challenges involved in handling Big Data. In this section we'll take a close look into the common technical concepts and patterns typically used in most of the core Big Data Tools and Platforms to address those common set of problems/challenges. The core Big Data Tools and Platforms primarily implement these concepts and patterns with appropriate variations and optimizations relevant to the primary use cases they try to solve.

We classify these Common Technical Concepts and Patterns here across following major areas—Big Data Infrastructure, Big Data Storage, Big Data Computing & Retrieval and Big Data Service Management. In the following subsections we discuss these Common Technical Concepts and Patterns in a technology agnostic way.

2.2.1 Big Data Cluster

The best way to start delving into the details of Big Data Tools and Platforms is to start with the understanding of the Big Data Clusters. The concepts around the Big Data Clusters can be divided into two major categories—Cluster Configuration & Topology and Cluster Deployment. The first one deals with the logical model of how a Big Data Cluster is divided into various types of machines/nodes with clear separation of the services they host. The second one deals with actual deployment of those nodes in physical hardware infrastructure.

2.2.1.1 Cluster Configuration & Topology

A Big Data Cluster is logically divided into two types of machines/nodes, namely the Data Nodes and the Management Nodes. These two types are very different based on the purpose they serve, their hardware configurations and typical number of them.

The Data Nodes serve two basic purposes—firstly, storing the data in a distributed fashion and secondly processing the same for transformation and access. To ensure basic scalability requirement of Big Data use cases, the golden rule used by all Big Data Technologies is to bring the processing close to data instead of getting the data to the processing layer. The same is achieved by hosting the data and running the slave processes (for processing that data) in each Data Node. The number of Data Nodes is typically high in a Big Data cluster. Some Big Data clusters in internet based companies (like Google, Yahoo, and Facebook etc.) do have thousands of Data Nodes. Even in some of the big retail, manufacturing, and financial organizations the number of Data Nodes in Big Data Cluster can go to the extent of multiple of hundred. The Data Nodes are typically heavy on disks and moderate in processor and memory capacity.

The Management Nodes serve the purpose of façade for the client applications for execution of the use cases. The client applications typically hit the master processes running on the Management Nodes which eventually triggers the slave processes in the Data Nodes and return the result back to the client application. As we go forward we'll see that the Management Nodes may run various types of master services each one corresponding to one type of component. Management Nodes also run services related to Resource Management, Monitoring, High Availability, and Security. Because Management Nodes serve all the responsibilities, a typical Big Data cluster has multiple Management Nodes. However, the number of Management Nodes in a Big Data Cluster is much lesser than Data Nodes. That number typically runs from 3 to 6 and does not proportionately increase with the increase in number of Data Nodes. Management Nodes are commonly heavy in CPU and Memory whereas very thin with respect to the disk as they don't need to store much.

Management Nodes and Data Nodes are connected over the Network, typically LAN. In the case of some Big Data Technologies, Management Nodes can be distributed over the WAN across multiple data centers for supporting disaster recovery. Some of the Management Nodes are sometimes earmarked as Edge Nodes. Edge Nodes are typically accessible over public network interface and act as a router between the Big Data cluster and end user environment. Edge nodes are not used when a routed data network is available. There can be more than one Edge Nodes in a cluster for load balancing and high availability. Edge nodes can reside within the demilitarized zone (DMZ) [221]. The rest of the Management Nodes and all Data Nodes reside inside the internal firewall of DMZ and cannot be accessed by the public network interface and only the Edge Nodes can access them.

There are two types of Networks typically defined for a Big Data cluster. The first one is the Data Network which is used by all Management Nodes and Data Nodes as private interconnect. This is used for data ingestion, data movement from one node to another during data processing, data access, etc. The second one is Management Network which is used for management of all nodes using the tools like ssh, VNC, web interface, etc. The cluster administration/management network is typically connected to the administration network of an organization. The Data Networks are typically 1 Gb or 10 Gb switch. They use link aggregate on server network adapter ports for higher throughput and high availability. In case of multi rack deployment of the nodes core switches (10 Gb or 40 Gb) are used to connect all Top of the Rack switches together. A pair of core switches is used to ensure high availability. The Management Networks are typically of 1 Gb switch without any redundancy.

2.2.1.2 Cluster Deployment

Big Data use cases largely revolve around accessing/storing very large volume of data and as we all know accessing/storing data from/to disk is the slowest process in execution of a task in a machine or cluster. Given this the Shared Nothing Architecture [222] is found to be the most efficient architecture for the deployment of Big Data Technologies. Shared Nothing Architecture ensures that there is enough disk heads available to access/store data in parallel as requested by multiple processes running concurrently. In contrast to this if a shared storage infrastructure (like SAN) is used there is a possibility that the data access/storage requests from separate processes running on separate Data Nodes may land up in single disk head. Also the latency of job execution goes up because of the protocol conversion needs to happen to move the data in and out of the storage solution and the Big Data cluster.

Hence, traditionally, Big Data Clusters are deployed on premise using Shared Nothing Architecture. However, with the advent of various new technologies and business models in the Infrastructure and Big Data space, today a Big Data Cluster can be deployed in various other ways. In a virtualized environment the Management Nodes can run on Virtual Machines with no local disk. This works well to reasonable extent as the data access happens in happening from Management Nodes is typically limited and also memory available to the Management Nodes is generally high. The Data Nodes can also be deployed in virtual machines if each virtual machine has local disk attached to the same. In the recent development in Big Data space (see discussion on Berkeley Data Analytics Stack at the later part of this chapter), all relevant data can be loaded in memory in a Big Data cluster where various parts of the data (data blocks/chunks) will reside in the memory of different Data Nodes. In this architecture it does not matter whether the data resides in SAN or a remote Cloud storage as the processes will access the data from the memory local to the Data Nodes.

Big Data Clusters can be deployed in Appliance mode too. Various Big Data Technologies are available in Appliance mode where the appliance comes with already configured Management Nodes and Data Nodes for a target set of use cases. The appliances are deployed on premise.

Instead of on premise deployment, Big Data Cluster can also be deployed in cloud in a Shared Nothing Architecture. In this option the Cloud provider provides a Shared Nothing Cluster as *Infrastructure As A Service* and the required Big Data Technology is deployed on that in the same way as that could have been done in case of on premise deployment. In cloud, Big Data Technologies are also available as *Platform As A Service* where the internal deployment architecture is completely managed by the cloud service provider. In this case the Big Data deployment architecture may or may not be Shared Nothing Architecture. The customer pays for the service and the cloud provider manages the SLAs around response time and throughput.

2.2.2 Big Data Storage Concepts

Big Data Storage is the heart of the Big Data Tools and Platforms. Unless the large volume of data of various formats is stored appropriately data computing and retrieval cannot be done efficiently. The nuances of Big Data Storage revolve around the key concepts like Data Models, Data Partitioning, Data Replication, Data Format, Data Indexing, and Data Persistence. We discuss each of them separately in the following sub-sections.

2.2.2.1 Data Models

The Big Data Technologies typically support various types of Data Models to represent the data for access and manipulation. The most popular one is the Relational Model [215] which is unquestionably the widely used model in the industry for last few decades. First proposed in 1969, by Edgar F. Codd [216], in the relational model all data is represented in terms of tuples (or records), grouped into relations (or tables) and related records are linked together with a key. The database systems with Relational Model use the Structured Query Language (SQL) [223] for defining and accessing the data. The extent of support for Relational Model and SQL provided by the Big Data Technologies varies from one to another.

However, there are Big Data Technologies which do not support Relational Model. They are knows as NoSQL Databases [228]. They support key/value based model where for any arbitrary key the value can be anything ranging from single primitive data type (like integer, character, byte etc.), blob, multi-dimensional map to complex object document structure like XML, JSON, etc.

The other interesting data model supported by Big Data Technologies is Graph data model [217] where data is represented as nodes and links or edges. The Graph data model can represent various problems such as computing distances, finding circularities in relationships, determining connectivity etc. better than the other data models discussed before in this chapter. Graph data model has applications in many real life use cases related to Social Media, Payment Transaction Network, Customer Network, etc.

Irrespective of the models, most of the Big Data Technologies are developed based on the concept of run time model definition which is also known as 'schema on read'. This helps in ingesting the data upfront without deciding on the data model first. Once the data is available in the data store, the schema (data model) is defined while reading the data. This approach is a major game changer compared to the approach used in traditional database technologies where schema has to be defined before moving the data into the platform. This idea helps fostering the notion of first bringing in the data in a common platform, without spending much of a time in analysis for defining the schema of the new or the updated (update happens very frequently these days because of continuously changing business ecosystem) data sources. Once the data is there in the Big Data store, data is filtered for the relevant information, processed to generate insights, and eventually consumed by the business processes. The unused part of original data is still kept for future needs to unearth 'known unknowns' and 'unknown unknowns'.

2.2.2.2 Data Partitioning

Every Big Data Technology needs to follow some approach to partition the data across the various Data Nodes. This is because all data cannot be stored in a single machine and also to ensure that the data processing can happen in parallel using the computing resources available in all the machines.

There are multiple approaches typically followed by various Big Data Technologies for Data Partitioning. For data modeled and accessed in the form of key/value or key/tuple the partitioning is done based on the key. Various types of schemes can be followed to achieve the required partitioning. Range partitioning—where the data is partitioned based on the range of an attribute key where keys with different range of values reside in different nodes; Hash partitioning—where the keys are assigned to a node based on the result of a hash function applied to one or more attributes; List partitioning—where the unique values of keys in each partition are specified as a List; Random partitioning—where keys are assigned to nodes in a random fashion; Round Robin partitioning—where keys are assigned to nodes using round robin mechanism; Tag based partitioning—where based one some tag on the data, the keys are grouped together to form a logical partition. For data stored and accessed in bulk without any predefined schema, Block based partitioning approach is used. In this approach each consecutive block of bytes, based on a specifically configured size of the block, is written to different nodes. For partitioning Graph data typically two approaches are used—vertex cut or edge cut depending on the problem context. Some processing algorithms also use hybrid approach which evenly distributes low-degree vertices along with their edges like edge-cut, and evenly distributes edges of high-degree vertices like vertex-cut.

Identifying a particular Data Node to allocate a partition is typically done in the following ways. The first approach is to write on the node which is local to the client program writing the data. This is typically used for Block Partitioning. In the second approach, applicable for Hash Partitioning, Round Robin Partitioning and Random Partitioning, the hash key, random key or round robin mechanism based key is used to identify the node. In the third approach, applicable for Range Partitioning, List Partitioning and Tag Partitioning, the Data Nodes can be typically earmarked beforehand based on the number of range or list or tag. There is a fourth approach too where data is collocated with other related data in the same node based on reference key/foreign key.

Partitioning also entails the aspect of occasional balancing of data within multiple Data Nodes to ensure that there are no hot spots (the situation when the client queries/processes always land up in one or few Data Nodes). This is achieved in following ways. Firstly, splitting a partition as and when it grows beyond a specific volume and secondly redistributing the entire file/table in the cluster in a scheduled fashion on daily, weekly, or monthly basis. The second approach of redistributing the entire file or table is also used when Data Nodes are added or dropped.

2.2.2.3 Data Replication

Data Replication is a common characteristic across all types of Big Data Technologies. Replication provides redundancy and thereby increases data availability and locality. With multiple copies of data on different Data Nodes, replication protects a data store from the loss of a single server because of hardware failure, service interruptions etc. With additional copies of the data, one can dedicate various copies for disaster recovery, reporting, backup, etc. Replication helps to increase the locality and availability of data for distributed query processing. The data locality helps in decreasing the processing time. In the case of high volume of concurrent read requests replication also helps to increase the read throughput.

Typically three replica of a data partition can take care of most of the failure situations. In a clustered environment, the first replica is typically put in a rack different from the one having primary replica of the same partition. The second replica can be put in different data centers in case disaster recovery is required. For selecting the right Data Nodes in different racks, the techniques similar to data partitioning are used. Many a times the different replicas of data are created in such a way that each replica represents different de-normalized view of the same data.

Data replication strategies in Big Data Technologies are many a times influenced by Dr. Eric Brewer's CAP Theorem [219]. CAP theorem says that in the case of distributed system all three of Consistency, Availability, and (Network) Partition ability cannot be achieved at the same time. While deciding on where to keep the replicas, Big Data Technologies typically either support Consistency and Availability over Partitionability (this model is known as CA) or Availability and Partitionability over Consistency (this model is known as AP). The practical implication of the first approach (CA) is that the Big Data cluster cannot have data distributed across WAN as the technology does not support Network Partitionability (Network failure across WAN). But consistency and availability of the data would be guaranteed by the target Big Data technology. In case of the second approach (AP), the Big Data cluster can be distributed over WAN with the data being always available and tolerant to Network failure across WAN. But in this case only the Eventual Consistency of the data can be supported by the target Big Data technology.

For some of the memory centric Big Data Technologies instead of data replication, Provenance (Lineage) technique [218] is used. In this case the data is recreated using the Lineage information if a particular node goes down.

2.2.2.4   Data Compression

The Big Data related problems are fundamentally about storing and processing big volume of data. Hence the considerations for compressing the data are more relevant than ever before. Data Compression helps in multiple ways. Firstly it reduces the volume of the data. That means, apart from lesser storage space required lesser over head in reading and writing the data to and from disk. Secondly this also ensures less use of network bandwidth when data processing requires moving the data from one node to another. The obvious downside of data compression is the processing time needed to compress and decompress the data while writing and reading the data respectively. Another tricky aspect in data compression is split-ability of the compressed data. As discussed before in this chapter, in Big Data, partitioning of the data is must. However, many compression techniques suffer from the limitation that once the data is compressed it cannot be split across various nodes.

Traditionally compressions techniques were proprietary where every Big Data Technology used to have its own compression scheme designed to achieve the technology specific target for throughput and response time. However, over the last decade number of generic compression techniques has emerged in the market and they can be used by any technologies. Table 2.1 provides a comparative study of some of the generic compression techniques. The compression ratio and compression number are obtained from comparison done in Yahoo [220].

2.2.2.5   Data Format

The different storage formats used to store and process data in Big Data Technologies need special discussion as that is the secret sauce of scalability and flexibility of Big Data Technologies. The formats which are widely popular today are discussed below.

- Delimited Text Files—These are the files having data in humanly readable format where records are separated using newline character '\n' and fields are commonly separated with characters like ',' '\t', etc. The examples of popular delimited files are CSV files (comma separated values), TSV files (tab separated values) etc.
- Parquet [63]—Parquet is a columnar data storage which stores the data where all values of a column are put together instead of all values of a row. Parquet was built from the ground up to support complex nested data using the record shredding and assembly algorithm (described in the Dremel [67] paper) instead of simple flattening of the nested name spaces in the complex data. Parquet can be used by any data processing framework to improve the reading, writing, and processing of data. Parquet has corresponding top level open source project in Apache.
- Optimized Row Columnar Files or ORC [64]—This is also a columnar storage format with the philosophy of storing all values of a column together instead of all values of a row. This storage format is popularly used by Hive (discussed later

Table 2.1 Comparative study of some of the common compression techniques

Tools	Algorithm	Strategy	Compression performance	Decompression performance	Compression ratio	Splitability
Gzip	Based on the DEFLATE algorithm, which is a combination of LZ77 and Huffman Coding	Dictionary based compression strategy	Low	Low	High (~60 %)	N
LZO	Uses PPM family of statistical compressors, a variant of LZ77	Dictionary based and block oriented	High	High	Less (~50 %)	Yes if indexed. It is possible to index LZO compressed files to determine split points so that LZO files can be processed efficiently in subsequent processing.
Snappy	LZ77 based	Block oriented	Highest	Highest	Low (~40 %)	Yes if used in a container format like Avro or sequence file
bzip2	Uses Burrows-Wheeler transform	Transformation based and block oriented	Lowest	Lowest	Highest (~70 %)	Yes

in this chapter). The ORC format stores the data in stripes and keeps additional information (like indexes, aggregates etc.) in the data blocks storing the stripes.

- Avro [65]—Avro is a row oriented data storage format in contrast to Parquet or ORC. Avro relies on schemas. Avro data is stored in a file with its schema so that files can be processed later by any program.
- Sequence Files [66]—Sequence Files are files consisting of binary key/value pairs. There are three types of sequence files formats—uncompressed key/value records, records where values are only compressed, and the third one is the one where keys and values are collected in 'blocks' separately and compressed. Sequence files are extensively used to store the data which are difficult to split like XML, JSON.
- Proprietary Format—As in case of compression, there are also many other storage formats which are specific and proprietary to a particular Big Data Technology. These are typically used by NoSQL Databases, In Memory Databases, and Data Warehouse Solutions where each technology tries to bring in its value add through the innovation in the Data Format. These formats also use proprietary mechanism for data compression.

Table 2.2 provides a summary of comparative characteristics of different Data Storage Formats.

Applications may have to use multiple formats for different stages of data handling. At the source side, for ingesting data from other tools/technologies to a Big Data Technology, the data would be typically in Delimited Text Format. One has to ingest it as is and then convert the same to the preferred format for the efficient processing/analytics. Some tools support direct conversion to the target data format during the data ingestion step itself. While exporting data from Big Data Technology to a target technology/tool the target data format is also typically Delimited Text format. For analytics involving Column level aggregates columnar data formats like Parquet or ORC are the best. Use of Avro makes sense if definitions of columns may change in future for a given table and most of the columns of a row are frequently used by the target use cases. Among all these formats Parquet is quickly becoming standard across various Big Data Technologies because of its generic open source back ground and efficient storage structure.

2.2.2.6 Indexing

As discussed before, in Big Data Technologies, a data file is typically partitioned in multiple chunks/blocks of data across various Data Nodes of a Big Data cluster. Indexing in Big Data serves two purposes. Firstly it is the way to identify any particular record in a file by first identifying which chunk/block of data the record belongs to. Secondly it also helps in can be also used for identifying the exact location of the record within a data block. Indexing is particularly important for random read/write use cases for randomly selecting a particular record from a very large data set. However, indexing matters for bulk data processing also for finding out the right data blocks (of a file) to process instead of processing/scanning the entire file.

Table 2.2 Comparative study of the common data formats

Characteristics	Delimited files	Parquet	ORC	Avro	Sequence files
In built schema	No	Yes	Yes	Yes	No
Columnar	No	Yes	Yes	No	No
Support for pluggable compression	Yes	Yes	Yes	Yes	Yes
Indexing information	No	No	Yes	No	No
Aggregate/Statistics	No	No	Yes	No	No
Support for complex data structure	No	Yes	Yes	Yes	No
Human readable	Yes	No	No	No	No
Typical performance	Least performant	Highest Performance	Good Performance	Not as efficient as Parquet or ORC	Slow Performance
Interoperability with other enterprise tools	Supported by most of the tools	Not much of a support outside Hadoop ecosystem	Not much of a support outside Hadoop ecosystem	Popularly used by many tools to ensure data exchange	Not much of a support outside Hadoop ecosystem

Various types of indexing mechanisms are used by different Big Data Technologies. The popular ones are B Tree [153], Inverted Index [154], Radix Tree [155], Bitmap Index [156], etc. There also exists a special type of indexing technique which is different from the regular way of locating a target record in a Data Node/Data Block. This technique does not provide information on where data exists and instead it tells where to not look for the data. The examples of such techniques are Bloom Filter [157], Zone Map [192], etc. This technique is found to be major performance booster in case of searching from big volume of data as this saves lots of disk input/output.

The popular indexing approach for bulk data processing is the use of the concept of logical partitions where each table/file is partitioned based on few partition attributes (like date, country, etc.) available in the record. The data containing same value for a partition attribute is typically kept in a separate folder. During bulk data processing specifying this partition attribute helps. The system processes the data available only in those folders which satisfy the criteria specified for the partition attribute(s) instead of scanning/processing the entire dataset.

Apart from selection of the right indexing mechanism what is also important in Big Data Technologies is storing the indexes in proper place. There are few approaches which are typically followed. In the first approach, Centralized Indexing, the index for all the data is maintained in a central place and the search is done there to identify the right location/Data Node to find the data. In the second approach, Partitioned Index, there is a centralized lookup table which keeps the list of range of data stored in a Data Node and the indexes are actually created at individual Data Node for the data residing in that particular node. In the third approach, the data is always sorted based on the primary key and the information about the range of the same is stored in a centralized lookup table. Multiple secondary indices on various attributes of the data are also supported in some of the Big Data technologies. Secondary Indexes are either created on various nodes (for data residing in that node) or they are implemented as separate Index tables.

2.2.2.7   Data Persistence

Data Persistence is one of the most important aspects of Big Data Technologies as data input/output around Disk and moving the same over Network is the major performance impediment typically faced for efficient processing and access of big volume of distributed data. At the high level, Data Persistence is tackled in two major ways. In the first approach Data Persistence is handled proprietarily by storing the data in local disk of each Data Node. In the second approach Data Persistence is handled through a generic set of Distributed File System APIs where the Distributed File System APIs can be implemented by another product/vendor ensuring all the API contracts and Quality of Service requirements are honored. This second approach is more of a rise these days as it gives more options in implementing a Big Data solution. There are two types of implementations available for Distributed File System APIs. In the more traditional option the data is primarily stored in a Shared Nothing way in the local disk of the Data Nodes (e.g. HDFS, Gluster

FS, Spectrum Scale FPO etc.). The other option, still an emerging approach, (e.g. Tachyon, Apache Ignite) is more memory centric. In this approach majority of the data is loaded in memory as distributed data blocks/chunks residing in the memory of various Data Nodes. After the processing is done the data is persisted to any pluggable data storage ranging from SAN, Cloud store like S3, NoSQL Databases, or even HDFS.

2.2.3   Big Data Computing and Retrieval Concepts

Big Data Computing and Retrieval happens in three predominant ways—processing large volume of data in rest, processing large volume of continuously streaming data, and accessing data randomly for reading/writing from/to a large volume of data in rest. The key abstractions used to address these various types of processing needs, are Distributed Processing Engines, Application Components, Data Access Interfaces, and Data Security. We discuss below each of them separately.

2.2.3.1   Distributed Processing Engine

Distributed Processing Engine is the fundamental abstraction used in the Big Data Technologies for Big Data Computing and Retrieval. In implementing this abstraction various Big Data Technologies bring in the necessary uniqueness and optimization so that they can ensure efficient processing of large volume of data. In most of the cases the Distributed Processing Engines are developed using the concepts of Massively Parallel Processing architecture [68] but with different flavor of implementations. The Distributed Processing Engines address the need for ingesting, processing, filtering, querying, modeling, exporting, and also archiving large volume of data in Big Data infrastructure. Many of the modern implementations of the Distributed Processing Engines try to exploit the SIMD (Single Instruction Multiple Datasets) [196] computation model at hardware level to execute the same instruction sequence simultaneously on a large number of discrete data sets. Another key characteristic of the Distributed Processing Engines is the ability to restart a process in the same or different node when a particular slave process fails because of any issue. Following are the typical patterns used in implementation of Distributed Processing Engines by different Big Data Technologies. They in turn cater to the three types of processing requirements mentioned before.

2.2.3.2   Directed Acyclic Graph (DAG) Based Distributed
Processing Engine

In Directed Acyclic Graph (DAG) based Distributed Processing approach [229] each job gets divided into an arbitrary set of tasks. Each vertex represents a task

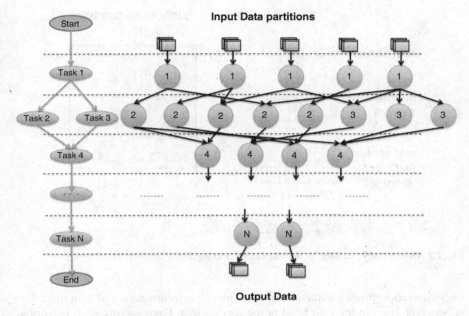

Fig. 2.1 Distributed Processing using Direct Acyclic Graph

to be executed on the data and each edge represents the flow of data between the connected vertices. Vertices can have any arbitrary number of input and output edges. Multiple vertices can execute same task but on the different parts of the same data sets. At execution time, the vertices become processes executing the task and the edges are used to transfer a finite sequence of records between the vertices. The physical implementations of the edges are typically realized by shared memory, TCP pipes, or disks. Each task gets executed in parallel on the data stored in various nodes by shipping the necessary functions to the respective Data Nodes.

Figure 2.1 shows an example detailing the execution steps involved in this approach. In this example the input data is partitioned across five Data Nodes. In each of those Data Nodes the Task 1 gets executed and the outputs from the same get distributed to either different nodes. Next the Task 2 and Task 3 get executed in eight Data Nodes and the outputs from them further get distributed in four Data Nodes. Task 4 now gets executed in four Data Nodes. This process goes on till the last task, Task N, in the DAG.

2.2.3.3   Multi Level Serving Tree (MLST) Based Distributed Processing

The multi-level serving tree based approach (popularized by Google Dremel) uses the concept of a serving tree with multiple levels to execute a job. As shown in Fig. 2.2 when a root server receives an incoming query from a client, it rewrites the

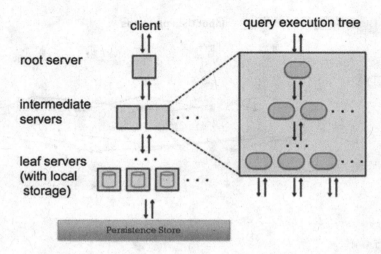

Fig. 2.2 Distributed Processing using Multi Level Serving Tree (Reproduced from [67])

query into appropriate subqueries based on metadata information and then route the subqueries down to the next level in the serving tree. Each serving level performs a similar rewriting and re-routing. Eventually, the subqueries reach the leaf servers, which communicate with the storage layer or access the data from persistent store. On the way up, the intermediate servers perform a parallel aggregation of partial results until the result of the query is assembled back in the root server.

2.2.3.4   Bulk Synchronous Parallel (BSP) Based Distributed Processing

Bulk Synchronous Parallel (BSP) based approach [50] uses the generalized graph form of a Directed Graph with cycles. Figure 2.3 shows the various steps involved in Bulk Synchronous Parallel based Distributed Processing. The input data is first partitioned using appropriate Graph partitioning techniques in multiple Data Nodes. Then the entire processing requirement of converting the input data partitions to the final outputs is divided into a set of Supersteps (or iterations). In a Superstep each Worker, running on a particular Data Node and representing a Vertex, executes a given task (part of an overall algorithm) on the data partition available at that node. After all Workers are done with their work, bulk synchronization of the outputs from each worker happens. At the end of the Superstep a vertex may modify its state or that of its outgoing edges, a vertex may also receive messages sent to it from the previous Superstep, a vertex also may send messages to other vertices (to be received in the next Superstep), or even the entire topology of the graph can get changed. This process gets repeated for the remaining Supersteps and at the end the output is produced.

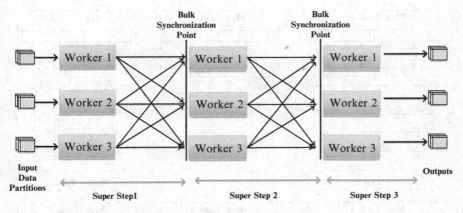

Fig. 2.3 Distributed Processing using Bulk Synchronous Parallel

2.2.3.5   Map Reduce (MR) Based Distributed Processing Engines

Map Reduce [4] is so far one of the most popular and successful approach in Distributed Processing. Google introduced Map Reduce in their distributed data processing application which was inspired by Map Reduce in functional programming model (such as LISP from 1960s). Map Reduce framework offers two interfaces, namely Map and Reduce, which can be implemented with arbitrary processing logic for processing any large volume of data. Map interface accepts any dataset as input represented by key/value pair. In the Map interface typically scalar (records level) transformations are done. The outputs from one Map are grouped by the keys. The keys and the resultant array of values associated with each key are then sorted, partitioned, and then sent to the Reducers as a list of keys to be processed. The Reduce interface is typically implemented to achieve set operations on the array of values for each key. Optionally there can be a Combiner interface too which will combine same keys from one Map process to perform the first level of reduction. Figure 2.4 depicts the steps involved in typical Map Reduce process.

It is to be noted that Map Reduce is also a specific implementation of DAG based distributed processing. In case of Map Reduce the task executed by each vertex of DAG at each stage is always either Map or Reduce instead of any arbitrary function. Many Big Data Technologies provide Map Reduce interface which end user can implement to express a given data processing requirement. However, most of the time Big Data Technologies use DAG or BSP based approach which uses Map Reduce internally. In those cases, the task in the vertex of a DAG or Superstep in BSP is implemented as Map or Reduce.

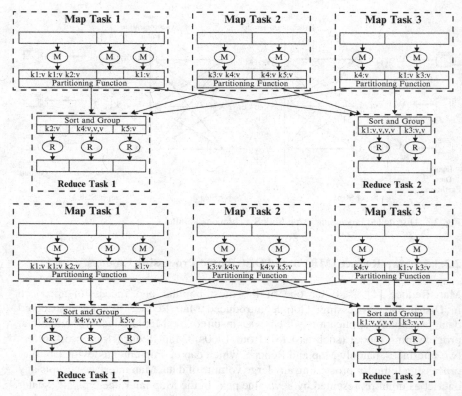

Fig. 2.4 Distributed Processing using Map Reduce (Reproduced from [13])

2.2.3.6 Long Running Shard Processes Based Distributed Processing Engine

Distributed Processing Engine using multiple Long Running Shard Processes is used for serving high throughput random Read/Write applications and Search. This is a special case of Multi Level Serving Tree based approach where instead of multi levels there are only two levels. In this model typically multiple slave daemon processes run on various Data Nodes (equivalent to the leaf nodes). Each slave process takes ownership of a partition of data and service the query requests as and when directed to the same. The master process (root server) runs on the Management Node and typically keeps track of the right Data Node where the data resides. As and when request comes from the client, master process first intercepts the same and then sends the request to the appropriate shard. Some time, once the appropriate shard is identified the master process makes the client directly connected to the shard and later on all the interaction happens between the client and the shard directly.

2.2.3.7   Producer-Consumer Agent Network Based Distributed Processing Engines

Distributed Processing Engines using Producer-Consumer Agent Network are used in Stream Event Processing. In this model multiple agents are deployed where each of them intercept a stream of events/data, process the same, and eventually push it to other agent(s). These agents are typically networked to implement multiple steps needed to process streaming events/data. Typically the starting point of the network is a data source (like tcp port, http port, message queue, file system, etc.) and the end point is another Big Data Technology (like Hadoop, NoSQL Databases, Berkeley Data Analytics Stack etc.). Multiple instances of the agents are deployed in different Data Nodes to handle scalability and availability. This model is essentially a variation of DAG based execution except the following differences. The first difference is in the case of Producer-Consumer Agent Network the DAG for the processing steps is decided at the design time by the developer/designer. The second difference is that the data movement from one task to another happens directly in producer-consumer fashion without any need of a master process.

2.2.3.8   Application Component

Application Components uses one or more Distributed Processing Engines to serve a request coming from the client. They are usually the bridge between the client application and the Distributed Processing Engine. They typically support one particular Data Access Interface (discussed later in this chapter). The client application uses the Data Access Interface supported by the Application Component to access or process the data. The Application Component translates that request from client to appropriate service call(s) to the Distributed Processing Engine. The Application Components typically manage concurrent requests from the client, security, connection pool, etc. These components are typically implemented as long running daemon processes so that they can keep on serving the incoming requests. In some cases they the implementation can be a scheduled process which runs periodically.

2.2.3.9   Data Access Interfaces

The SQL is unquestionably the widely used Data Access tool popular in the industry for last few decades. So SQL remains to be the preferred data access interface even in the Big Data Technologies. However, the extent of support for SQL varies from one technology to another. Apart from SQL based interface, Big Data Technologies support data read/write through APIs in programming languages like Java, Python, C++, Scala, etc.

Many a times Big Data Technologies with primary support for SQL interface allows User Defined Functions (UDF) for users to achieve non-relational processing. These UDFs are typically written in programming languages like C, C++, Java, etc. and made available as an executable library to the SQL processing engine. The user places these UDFs within the SQL query itself and SQL query engine executes the UDF specific libraries in appropriate place of the execution plan. The reverse approach is popular too where from a programming language SQLs are called.

Some of the Big Data Technologies like NoSQL Databases, Stream Event Processing Technologies, and Search Technologies do not support SQL interface for data access or/and processing. They support programming language API based interfaces to read/write/process data.

Many of the Big Data Technologies support creation and use of various Predictive Models. These models can be probabilistic models (where data is fitted to a model representing certain natural behavior) or Machine Learning [226] models (where the model emerges out of the data). Typically model creation and using the same for prediction are done using APIs available in different programming languages (specific to the modeling tool being used) like C++, Java, Python, Scala, R, etc.

Most of the Big Data Technologies also make data read/write possible through two widely popular platform independent generic interfaces, namely Apache Thrift [211] and REST [212]. The Apache Thrift interface combines a software stack with a code generation engine to build services that work efficiently and seamlessly across various programming languages like C++, Java, Python, PHP, Ruby, Erlang, Perl, and others. REST interface provides language independent access to data from any technology over http protocol. Thrift and REST interfaces provide immense flexibility for Big Data Technologies to interface with other tools and technologies in an enterprise.

2.2.3.10   Data Security

All Big Data Technologies provide measures for data privacy and security to variety of extents. The typical features expected are Authentication, Role Based Authorization Control, Encryption of data when it is in flight as well as at rest, and Auditing of activities related to data access.

For Authentication and Role Based Authorization Control purpose integration of the technology with enterprise directory system (LDAP) [225] is typically done. For Encryption of data in flight between the client and the Big Data Processing Component secure socket layer is used. Kerberos [224] protocol is also used in many cases (which works on the basis of 'tickets') to allow nodes communicating over a non-secure network to prove their identity to one another in a secure manner. Different Big Data Technologies typically also provide technology specific methodology to encrypt data in rest complying with any target encryption standard (like 128 bit or 256 bit encryption). Requirement for Encryption of data at rest is essential for the privacy and security regulations applicable to various industries (HIPAA for Health Care, PCI DSS for card payment, etc.). For audit capabilities technology specific approaches are available which intercepts the activities using the concept of aspect programming.

2.2.4   Big Data Service Management Concepts

The Big Data Service Management Concepts cover the patterns related to the management of services running on the Big Data cluster. Since the Big Data cluster can potentially go even beyond thousands of nodes, managing services in such a big cluster needs special attention. In this category we shall cover key major concepts, namely Resource Management, High Availability Management, and Monitoring.

2.2.4.1   Resource Management

Resource management is very important aspect for Big Data Technologies. It is needed to ensure that the computing resources (CPU, Memory, and Disk) of all nodes and the Network connecting them are reasonably utilized and shared appropriately across various types of Data Computing and Retrieval requests being serviced.

In Big Data Technologies, the key challenge of Resource Management is to manage resources between Long Running Daemon Processes and Short Lived Processes. Some technologies have Long Running Daemon Processes which continuously run on the Data Nodes and keep on accepting and executing tasks from multiple clients where the tasks are very short lived (gets done within a second or so). This type of technologies also typically supports very high number of concurrent requests (up to tens of thousands of requests per second). A variation of the same, are the technologies which have Long Running Daemon Processes and accept tasks that take some time to complete (in the range of tens of seconds to few hours). This type of technologies typically does not support more than 10–100 requests at a time. On the other hand, some technologies only support Short Lived Processes which are initiated to serve a specific task on a Data Node and when the task is done the process is destroyed. Sometimes the same process is reused across multiple tasks if all of those tasks got triggered within a specific short time window. The Long Running Daemon Processes have the advantage that there is no overhead of starting a process whenever a task/request is received. In fact they are the only way to support online applications needing data on continuous basis. The disadvantage of the same is the constant use of resource by them even when there is no request and also the complexity of registering/unregistering them with the controller/master process whenever there is a failure. On the other hand the Short Lived Processes are very easy to maintain and they do not consume any resource in continuous basis. But their downside is the extra time needed to start them whenever a request is received. There are few platforms which are geared to support all of these different types of processes within the same cluster. The resource management gets really tricky there.

Typically in Big Data Technologies Resource Management is done at the level of individual nodes as well as at the level of the entire system in a collaborative way. The common pattern is to implement a master-slave approach where each individual Data Node runs a slave process of Resource Management, The slave process reports to the master process (running in one of the Master Nodes) about the availability of the computing resources in that particular Data Node. The master process decides, using some scheduling algorithm, the requests (corresponding to respective Application Components) that are going to get those available resources. The Application Component may use those resources to serve the request. It can also refuse the same if the data needed to serve the request do not belong to that Data Node.

2.2.4.2　High Availability

In Big Data Technologies, there are three types of High Availability needs to be addressed. The first one is failover of the request when a Long Running Daemon Process (running in the Data Node) dies or the Data Node running the same goes down for some reason. The second one is rescheduling a task when a short lived process dies (or the Data Node goes down). The third one is failover of a request from an active master process (running on one of the Management Nodes) to a standby if the master process dies. The first two are typically handled by the Distributed Processing Engine as that only knows where to send the request based on the location of the data. The third one is managed by cluster level high availability service which keeps on checking whether the master process is alive.

2.2.4.3　Monitoring

In Big Data Technologies, monitoring needs to happen at multiple levels. The levels are namely Monitoring of Services, Monitoring of Requests/Loads, Monitoring of Software Resources (Thread Pool, etc.) and Monitoring of Hardware Resources. Typically all the monitoring information (metrics) is exposed using standard interfaces like JMX, SNMP, etc. The monitoring metrics are gathered and shown by the monitoring clients. Standard monitoring components like Nagios, Ganglia, etc. are used too by many of the Big Data Technologies. In many cases individual Big Data Technology provides its own monitoring interface too.

2.3　Hadoop Ecosystem

Hadoop is the single most talked about Big Data Technology Platform available today in the Big Data Technology space. The term Big Data became widely popular at the beginning of this decade because of the potential demonstrated by Hadoop technology. Hadoop is actually not a single technology but an ecosystem of a number of components (or frameworks) most of which are part of the projects developed by open source communities under Apache Software Foundations [1] and some are licensed ones developed on top of the open source components. In the last few years, Hadoop has become hugely popular for its applicability in all types of development in Big Data space, be it creation of new analytics software or development of IT applications in the enterprises. The components in Hadoop Ecosystem are in various states of maturity and are continuously evolving. Most of the components of Hadoop Ecosystem, which are widely used today, are part of Apache 'top-level-projects' [2], where as many are brewing as Apache Incubator Projects [3]. In this section we shall primarily focus on the first kind of components which have already got the status of Apache 'top-level-projects'. We'll also get into introduction to some of the incubating components which have great potential because of the amount of activities going on around them and the importance of problems space they are trying to solve.

2.3.1   Brief History of Hadoop

Hadoop was initially started by Doug Cutting and Mike Cafarella to support Nutch [62] search engine project. It was inspired by Google's papers on their Map Reduce [4] and Google File System [5]. The original goal was to develop a framework which can process a large volume of data in batch on a set of commodity hardware boxes (low cost hardware cluster) within a reasonable timeframe and cost. The framework started with two simple components—one is to store the data in distributed fashion on the multiple nodes in the cluster and the other component is to process the data using the paradigm of Map Reduce. In addition to the capabilities of storing and processing large volume of data in a low cost hardware cluster Hadoop also brought in the possibility of near linear scalability of processing time and cost. That means by merely adding more number of nodes in the hardware cluster more volume of data can be processed within similar time window. Hadoop initially was used mostly in small size companies (and startups) because of its cost effective solution. However, in last few years it has got huge traction even in enterprise world and its adoption has increased exponentially. The biggest known Hadoop cluster today is of 32,000 nodes running in Yahoo [6] which handles 26 Million jobs per month. Based on the survey conducted by Novatta in Strata + Hadoop World event in February 2015 [111], around 79 % of 66 attending organizations commented that they are successfully investing in Hadoop. In the technology front Hadoop has moved from supporting only Map Reduce to other Distributed processing Engines too. In 2015, the Open Data Platform initiative (discussed later in this section) has been started for standardization of overall Hadoop Ecosystem w.r.t. its technical components. Figure 2.5 shows the journey of Hadoop from inception of Nutch to the beginning of initiative like Open Data Platform initiative.

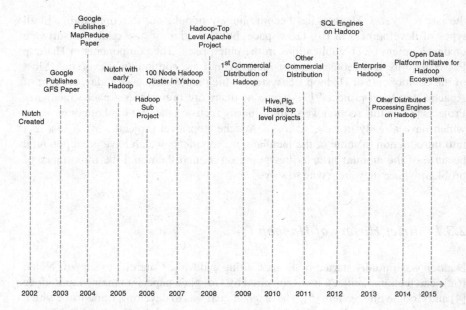

Fig. 2.5 History of Hadoop

2.3.2 Key Components of Hadoop Ecosystem

As mentioned before, Hadoop is an ecosystem of a number of components or frameworks. The components in Hadoop Ecosystem can be put together as a stack implementing various key concepts discussed previously in Common Technical Concepts and Patterns section. These components rely on each other to deliver the final outcome or use cases. These components are essentially deployed and run on a set of Data Nodes and Management Nodes in the target Hadoop cluster.

2.3.2.1 Distributed File System Component

The Distributed File System Component is the heart of Hadoop Ecosystem as all other components of Hadoop Ecosystem use the same as a mechanism to store data. Typically the Distributed File System Components can store a file of any size, storage format, and semantics in the Data Nodes of a hardware cluster. The key services provided by the Distributed File System Components are data availability and protection against data loss even if few nodes of the cluster are down. In Hadoop Ecosystem Distributed File System Components have primarily two varieties which are discussed below.

2.3.2.1.1   HDFS

Hadoop Distributed File System, commonly called as HDFS, is a module of Apache Hadoop [7] project. HDFS is an API as well as implementation of the same which comes as default as a part of the Apache Hadoop project. The HDFS implements most of the concepts of Data Storage as discussed in Common Technical Concepts and Patterns section.

The abstraction used to store data in HDFS is file. HDFS partitions any file in a set of Data Blocks of a configurable size and store them under various Data Nodes.

HDFS also replicates each Data Block. The number of replicas is configurable— the typical practice is to have three replicas. Each Data Block is replicated in such a way that it is guaranteed that at least two replicas of the Data Block will reside in two different racks. HDFS ensures the same by placing the first replica on the Data Node where the client program (writing the file) runs, the second replica on a remote rack is randomly identified and the third replica is identified on a random node of that remote rack. HDFS still does not support placing replicas across various Data Centers and thereby ensuring automatic protection in case of data center failure. The common practice today is to copy the data in another Hadoop Cluster in the other Data Center in a semi-automatic way (using DistCp [161] utility). The future work is going on to address this issue through Falcon framework (discussed later in this chapter) and the multi data center support for HDFS [160]. HDFS also supports custom placement logic for the placement of replicas of Data Blocks across various Data Nodes and racks [159]. This can be potentially used for collocating data partition for related data files to achieve better efficiency in joins. This feature can be also potentially used for the Data Block replication across multiple Data Centers.

HDFS is agnostic of Data Storage Format. It can store data of any storage format. The InputFormat, RecordReader, OutputFormat, and RecordWriter APIs can be used to read/write the data of any format. Implementations of these APIs are available for the common Data Storage Formats discussed in the Common Technical Concepts and Patterns section. In addition to that, one can also implement the same for any other custom storage format. Data stored in HDFS can be compressed also. The type of compression used mostly depends on the Data Format being used.

Unfortunately, so far, HDFS does not have any efficient way to Index the data stored in the Data Nodes. Few interesting works are going on in the industry in this regard. The researches like Adaptively Creating Clustered Indices for HDFS (LIAH, Lazy Indexing and Adaptivity in Hadoop) [162], Split-Index mechanism to store Indices for data in Hadoop in a RDBMS system [163], Multi- dimensional Indexing for data in HDFS [164], are some of them which focus on addressing this issue.

HDFS ensures that data in persisted in disk. However, there are recent developments happening in HDFS space which are geared towards more utilization of memory available in the HDFS cluster. The examples are centralized cache management in HDFS [193], support for memory as a storage medium (targeted for Apache Hadooop version 3.0) [194], etc.

Figure 2.6 depicts the key aspects of working of HDFS. The Name Node process (deployed in Management Node) of HDFS maintains the meta data (namespace)

HDFS Architecture

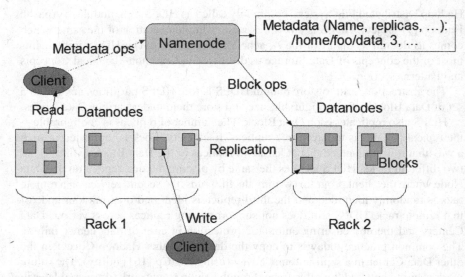

Fig. 2.6 Key aspects of HDFS Architecture (Reproduced from [20])

of the data being stored in Data Nodes. The Name Node process regulates access to data by clients, whereas the Data Node processes of HDFS are responsible for serving read and write requests for the data by the client applications. Data Node processes report all its Data Blocks to the Name Node process during the time of boot up. The Name Node process uses version number of a Data Block to check whether the Data Block is stale. While writing a file, client API contacts the Name Node process. The response of the Name Node process contains the list of Data Nodes which contain the primary and secondary replicas. Next time onwards, the client contacts the Data Node process directly without going through the Name Node process. Initially when the client pushes the changes to all Data Node processes the changes are kept in a buffer of each Data Node process. Afterwards when client sends a "commit" request to the primary, the data is committed to the primary and then to other replicas. After all secondary replicas complete the commit, the primary responses to the client about the success. All changes of Data Block distribution and metadata changes is written to an operation log file at the Management Node (where the Name Node process is running) which maintains an order list of operation. The Name Node process uses the same to recover its view after a crash. The Name Node process also regularly does check-pointing of its status to a file. In case of the Name Node process crash, the secondary Name Node process takes over after restoring the state from the last checkpoint file and replaying the operation log. While reading, the client API calculates the Data Block index based on the offset of the file pointer and requests the Name Node process for the location for the Data Block. The Name Node process replies with location of the nearest Data Node from the client which has a copy of the requested Data Block.

HDFS supports vertical partitioning of data known as HDFS Federation [195]. This HDFS Federation service uses multiple independent namespaces. The federated Name Node processed are independent and don't require coordination with each other. The Data Nodes are used as common storage for blocks by all the Name Node processes. Each Data Node process registers with all the Name Node processes in the cluster. Data Node processes send periodic heartbeats and block reports and handles commands from the Name Node processes. The other key features of HDFS are support for POSIX style file system to considerable extent, support for High Availability of the Name Node process, ability to be mounted as part of the client's local file system, support for Archival and Snapshots.

2.3.2.1.2 Other Distributed File System Implementation with POSIX Compliance

There are other Distributed File System Components available in the market which implements HDFS API. Many a times they also provide complete support for POSIX file system. The examples of the same are MapR's MapR-FS [137], IBM's Spectrum Scale FPO [138], Intel's Lusture [140], EMC's Isilon [141], Tachyon [142], and others. Any of these Distributed File Systems can be used along with other components of Hadoop Ecosystem instead of Apache HDFS implementation. These files systems comply with the HDFS API so that the rest of the components of Hadoop Ecosystem can still use the same set of HDFS services without caring for the underlying implementation.

2.3.2.2 Distributed Processing Components

The Distributed Processing Components in Hadoop Ecosystem are implementation of various types of Distributed Processing Engines discussed before in the section Common Technical Concepts and Patterns. Hadoop started with a single Distributed Processing Component, namely Hadoop Map Reduce which implements Map Reduce Distributed Processing Engine. But today Hadoop as a platform supports multiple types of Distributed Processing Components which support various types of Distributed Processing Engines. As a common execution pattern in all these Distributed Processing Components there would be a set of slave processes (either dynamically created as and when needed or run as a daemon process waiting for a request) running on the Data Nodes of a Hadoop Cluster and there would be a set of master processes running on the Master/Management nodes to coordinate the task executed by the processes running on the Data Nodes and consolidate the results generated by them. The Distributed Processing Components are used by Application Components (discussed later in this chapter).

One of the key propositions of Hadoop Ecosystem is that any type of Distributed Processing Engine can be integrated easily in Hadoop Ecosystem. This has given rise to various types of Distributed Processing Components in Hadoop Ecosystem in last few years (and more are coming in future) which implement different types of Distributed Processing Engines. The first category of Distributed Processing Components is the one which only works within Hadoop Ecosystem and is being used by multiple Application Components specific to Hadoop Ecosystem. The examples are Hadoop Map Reduce, and Tez. In the second category there are Distributed Processing Components which work only within Hadoop Ecosystem and also used by a single Application Component (mostly licensed/proprietary). The examples under this category are the Distributed Processing Components used by Cloudera Impala, IBM Big SQL, etc. In the third category we see the Distributed Processing Components which are developed to run on multiple Big Data Technologies including Hadoop, can support multiple Application Components, and are typically integrated, and packaged with other Hadoop components. The examples here are Spark and Flink. In the fourth category we see the Distributed Processing Components which are developed to run on multiple Big Data Technologies including Hadoop, support only one type of Application Component and are typically integrated, and packaged with other components of Hadoop Ecosystem. The examples under this category are Apache Drill, Apache Storm, Apache Solr, etc. Below we discuss the Distributed Processing Components from the first category. The rest of them are discussed in subsequent sections at appropriate contexts.

2.3.2.2.1 Hadoop Map Reduce

Hadoop Map Reduce [8] framework in Apache Hadoop is a Hadoop specific implementation of the generic Map Reduce model discussed previously in the Common Technical Concepts and Patterns section. The client application submits a Map Reduce job to the master/controller process. The master process invokes necessary number of Map and Reduce processes in various Data Nodes and eventually serves the result. In Hadoop Map Reduce framework each Map Process works on a single Data Block. Map Processes are pushed to the Data Nodes where one of the replicas of the input data resides. Hadoop Map Reduce supports Custom Reader and Custom Writer to read complex input data files and create output data file of desirable format. It also supports custom sorting algorithms.

2.3.2.2.2 Tez

Apache Tez [19] is a data type agnostic processing component which implements the DAG based Distributed Processing Engine. Tez allows any arbitrary complex directed-acyclic-graph (DAG) of tasks to process data in HDFS. Tez is primarily designed to be used by application developers for creating/supporting Application Components which need to process queries in near real time. Hive, Pig, and

Cascading uses Tez. Instead of using multiple Map-Reduce jobs, Tez uses single Map-Reduce-Reduce job to implement a query/processing request. It does not store the data from intermediate processing steps in HDFS and thereby enhances the performance. It also reuses resource to mitigate startup time of processes. Tez supports execution plan reconfiguration at runtime for better performance to address typical challenges like deciding on number of reducers, reduce start time, etc. Tez provides a set of APIs using which Data processing pipeline can be implemented as DAG which in turn can be run by Tez.

2.3.2.3 Application Components

The Application Components use the Distributed Processing Components to support various applications. The Application Components can be broadly categorized as SQL Components, Data Flow Components, Graph processing Components, Machine Learning Components, Streaming Components, NoSQL Components, and Search Components. As discussed in the sub-section of Distributed Processing Components, in many cases one Application Component can use multiple Distributed Processing Components (e.g. Hive uses Map Reduce, Tez also has a plan to use Spark, Hive also runs on Spark, Mahout uses Map Reduce and Spark, etc.) and reversely one Distributed Processing Component can be used by multiple Application Components (e.g. Map Reduce is used by Hive, Pig, Mahout, etc.). There are also many Application Components available from various Hadoop Distributions which work on data from HDFS but use their own native Distributed Processing Component (e.g. IBM's Big SQL [230], Cloudera Impala [231], etc.). Also there are some Application Components which are all tied to single Distributed Processing Component. The examples are the Application Components from Spark and Flink (discussed later in this chapter).

In this section we discuss the popular open source Application Components under the following categories namely SQL Components, Data Flow Components, Graph Processing Components, and Modeling Components. The Application Components those are part of other three categories, namely NoSQL, Stream Event Processing and Search are discussed separately in this chapter as they are not always part of the primary Hadoop Ecosystem (though many a times they are packaged within the same Hadoop Distribution).

2.3.2.3.1 SQL Components

SQL Components are the ones which can support ANSI SQL like interface to query and process the data. This is the group of components where majority of the innovation is happening today as SQL is a popular skill in the market for last few decades. In this sub-section we have discussed open source SQL Components. There are also vendor specific proprietary SQL components available in the market like IBM's Big SQL, Cloudera Impala, etc.).

2.3.2.4 Hive

Apache Hive [21] is the most popular component in the Hadoop ecosystem primarily because of its support for SQL. Hive is typically used for Data Warehousing use cases like ELT (extract, load, and transform), and reporting using SQL like interface. The Stinger.next [22] project for enhancement of Hive is geared towards providing all other advanced capabilities in hive like making Hive SQL 2011 compliant, adding capability to serve queries in OLAP space with sub second response time (Hive LLAP) and also transaction support (insert, update and delete). With all these Hive would be able to support more variety of use cases. Right now Hive internally uses Map Reduce Distributed Processing Component for serving the queries. However, Hive has also started using Tez for faster performance and with Hive LLAP it can provide sub second level performance. Hive also runs on Spark now [23] as of Hive 1.1.

Hive supports concurrent queries through Hive Server [30] using JDBC and ODBC interface. It also provides mechanism to impose structure on various data formats like text, columnar, ORC, Parquet, Avro etc. Hive can support any custom data format too through the use of Serializer/De-Serializer (SerDe) [28] framework of Hadoop. Hive also provides supports for User Defined Functions, User Defined Analytic Function, and User Define Table Functions to support any requirement which are typically outside SQL syntax [29]. In Hive end user has the flexibility of selecting underlying Distributed Processing Component (Map Reduce, Spark or Tez so far) to be used based on the requirement of the target use case.

2.3.2.5 Drill

Apache Drill [15] is a schema agnostic, low latency, distributed, SQL based data exploration/query engine which can help exploring data in Hadoop and any NoSQL Databases (discussed later in this chapter). Drill uses the concept of Distributed Processing Engines using Multi Level Serving Tree. It is inspired by Google's Dremel, to focus and support analytics/aggregation queries by separating out the schema and data in a data file in an optimized way.

At the core of Apache Drill [18] there is Drillbit service, which is responsible for accepting requests from the client, processing the queries, and returning results to the client. Figure 2.7 covers high level overview of Drill showing how Drillbit processes running on various Data Nodes can interact with each other to serve a query by accessing data from underlying data stores. The Drill client, any JDBC/ODBC client or Rest Client, issues a query which can be accepted by any Drillbit in the cluster. The Drillbit that accepts the query becomes the driving Drillbit node for the request. It parses the query, rewrites the same, and generates a distributed query plan optimized for fast and efficient execution. Then it contacts ZooKeeper to get a list of available Drillbit nodes in the cluster and determines the appropriate nodes to execute the various tasks in the query plan to maximize data locality. Next it schedules the execution of the tasks in the query plan on individual

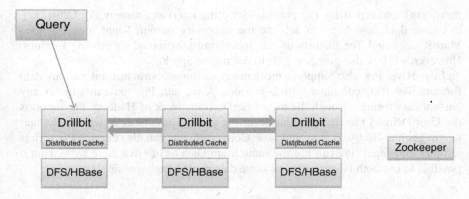

Fig. 2.7 High level processing architecture of Apache Drill (Reproduced From [16])

nodes. The individual nodes, after finishing their execution, return data to the driving Drillbit. The driving in turn returns the result back to the client.

Drill supports Dynamic Schema and Decentralized Meta Data management feature which help users to support variety of data sources. Users do not need to create and manage tables/views in a metadata repository beforehand. Instead Drill derives metadata from the storage plugins of target data sources on the fly. Users can query from multiple such data sources in a single query and then combine the same. Drill also has in built support for variety of data storage formats—CSV, TSV, Parquet, AVRO, JSON, BSON [24], and HFile (for HBase). Drill can optimize query execution with features like vectorization (which leverages SIMD processing capabilities of modern chips), distributed cache, etc.

2.3.2.5.1   Data Flow Components

Data Flow Components are the ones which allow developers to write a data flow processing pipeline that describes how the data will be transformed (such as load, filter, aggregate, join, sort, etc). Data Flow Components are not SQL based and typically have their own scripting language for interface. Data Flow Components focus on the definition of execution path of the data from start to the final state. These components are very useful for transformation of raw data to aggregates, cubes, etc. All of these Data Flow Components use the concept of Distributed Processing Engines using Directed Acyclic Graph (DAG) which internally uses Map Reduce. Here we discuss the most popular Data Flow Components available in the market which can work on data in Hadoop.

2.3.2.6   Pig

Apache Pig [31] is a very popular data Flow Component in the Hadoop ecosystem primarily used for Data Warehousing use cases like ELT (extract, load, and transform), and reporting. Pig provides scripting interface, namely Pig Latin [32], to create data flow logic to achieve the necessary output. Right now Pig uses Map Reduce and Tez majorly as the underlying Distributed Processing Engines. However, work is also going on [33] to run pig on Spark.

Like Hive, Pig also supports mechanism to impose structure on various data formats like text, columnar, ORC, Parquet, Avro, etc. Pig too can support any custom data format through the use of SerDe framework of Hadoop. Pig supports the User Defined Functions so that from Pig one can invoke code written in other languages like JRuby, Jython, and Java. Conversely one can also execute Pig scripts in other languages. Pig can use the same Meta Data as of Hive there by making it possible to use both Hive and Pig in same data processing pipeline.

2.3.2.7 Cascading

Cascading [108] is another popular Data Flow component like Pig. The sole purpose of Cascading is to enable developers to write Enterprise big data applications without the know-how of the underlying Hadoop complexity and without coding directly using the APIs form Distributed Processing Engine like Map Reduce. Instead, Cascading provides high-level logical constructs, such as *Taps*, *Pipes*, *Sources*, *Sinks*, and *Flows*. These constructs can be used as Java and Scala classes to design, develop, and deploy large-scale big data-driven pipelines. Cascading also supports Tez and Flink as the Distributed Processing Component along with Map Reduce. In future Cascading also plans to support Spark, and Storm (they are discussed later in this chapter).

2.3.2.7.1 Graph Processing Components

Graph Processing Components are useful for processing data which are better represented as Graph with vertices and edges instead of typical table, map or array like structures. The examples of such data are social networks, payment transactions, inventory meta data, etc. which can be processed more efficiently as Graph structure rather than first flattening them into a table like structure. Graph Processing Components are typically used with their own APIs. Here we discuss the open source Graph Processing Components on Hadoop. There are also few other Graph Processing tools available for Spark and Flink which can be used on data in Hadoop.

2.3.2.8 Giraph

Apache Giraph [48] is an iterative graph processing system built for scalable processing of graph data structure. Based on graph processing architecture Pregel [49], Giraph uses the concept of Bulk Synchronous Parallel (BSP) based Distributed Processing Engine. Giraph executes computation on an input graph composed of vertices and directed edges. For example in a payment transaction scenario vertices can represent accounts, and edges can represent transactions. Both vertices and edges store a *value*. The input to graph processing defines graph topology and also the initial values of vertices and edges.

2.3.2.8.1 Modeling Components

Modeling Components are the ones which can be used for the purpose of creation of predictive models on the data in Hadoop. Modeling components use traditional statistical approach for creating models as well as recent approach of creating models based on Machine Learning algorithms. Creating either of these two types of models using data distributed in different Data Nodes is a challenging task. Many a times model creation needs iterative approach too. In this section we discuss the open source modeling component available on Hadoop.

2.3.2.9 Mahout

Apache Mahout [97] is popular Modeling Component on Hadoop in the Hadoop ecosystem meant for creating Models using Machine Learning algorithms, such as classification, evaluation clustering, pattern-mining, and so on. The algorithms in Mahout are meant to be used in a Hadoop environment. Most of the machine learning algorithms implemented by Mahout internally uses Map Reduce and Spark as Distributed Processing Component. However, lately Mahout is also coming out with implementation of machine learning algorithms on top of Flink. Mahout exposes Java and Scala based APIs which are used for the purpose of machine learning model creation and prediction.

2.3.2.10 Components to run R on Hadoop

RHadoop [198] is a framework which aims to integrate popular modeling language cum platform R [197] with Hadoop. R traditionally uses memory to create models and scales vertically with more memory in a single node. RHadoop tries to address this limitation of R when integrated with data in Hadoop platform. RHadoop consists following packages—*ravro* for reading and writing files in avro format, *plyrmr* for higher level plyr like data processing for structured data, *rmr* for providing Hadoop Map Reduce functionality in R, *rhdfs* for functions providing file management of the HDFS from within R and *rhbase* for functions providing database management for the HBase.

There are few other Modeling Components available from Berkeley Data Analytics Stack on data in Hadoop (discussed later in this chapter). There are also some licensed products available in the market which deals with integrating R with Hadoop. Examples of such software are Revolution R from Revolution Analytics (subsidiary of Microsoft) [25], Big R [26], from IBM etc.

2.3.2.11 Security Components

Security is the key to any data related requirements. The requirements range from control of authentication and authorization, encryption of data at rest, and the audit requirements for different activities done by various users. Hadoop though still not completely matured in handling all types of security requirements it is marching fast in that direction.

Authentication can be done through the underlying operating system or can be delegated to an enterprise level LDAP. Hadoop also supports Kerberos for authentication of the nodes communicating over a non-secure network to prove their identity to one another in a secure manner. HDFS data at rest can be encrypted now in compliance with different regulatory requirements. The encrypted data can also be used transparently by any application accessing HDFS through various protocols like Hadoop File System Java API, Hadoop libhdfs C library, or WebHDFS REST API. Various vendors also provide necessary encryption methodologies. In Hadoop, Authorization requirements are typically handled at two levels. Firstly, the authorization can be controlled at the data level through the use of posix like (only read and write) access control features of HDFS for folders/files. Any user, trying to read or write data from/to HDFS using any application (Hive, Pig, Spark, Big SQL, etc.), can only do so if the user has necessary access to that folder/file in HDFS. The access right of user to the particular folder/file in HDFS can be integrated with enterprise level LDAP. Secondly, authorization can be also enabled at service interface access level (say REST based access, access through command line interfaces, access control at Hive Metastore level, etc.). The same can also be integrated with enterprise level LDAP. The auditing needs are typically handled by vendor provided value added services. The incubating security framework, Apache Ranger, also aims to address the same. Following components are the key security components in Hadoop Ecosystem which help dealing with various requirements around authentication, authorization, and auditing in a modular way.

2.3.2.11.1 Knox

Apache Knox [46] is a REST API based gateway for interacting with Hadoop clusters. This provides a single access point for all REST interactions with Hadoop clusters. This can help enterprises integrating Hadoop cluster with the enterprise identity management solutions and protect the details of the Hadoop cluster deployment from end users. The Knox Gateway also complements the Kerberos secured Hadoop cluster.

2.3.2.11.2 Sentry

Apache Sentry [69] is a modular system for enforcing fine grained role based authorization to data and metadata stored on a Hadoop cluster. It is currently available as incubator project in Apache Software Foundation. Sentry can provide column level access control, granular privileges to the Database statements like Create, DROP, INDEX, LOCK, etc. and support for multiple Hadoop Application Components like Hive, Impala, Search, which can be further extended to other components.

2.3.2.11.3   Ranger

Apace Ranger [70] is also an incubating project in Apache Software Foundation which is worth mentioning here. Ranger is a framework to enable, monitor, and manage comprehensive data security within the Hadoop Ecosystem. Ranger can provide centralized security administration to manage all security related tasks from a central User Interface, fine grained (Role and Attribute based) authorization to do a specific action and/or operation with any Hadoop framework/tool, standard authorization method across all Hadoop frameworks/tools, and centralized auditing of user access and administrative actions (security related) across all Hadoop Components.

2.3.2.12   Service Management Components

Service Management Components in Hadoop Ecosystem are the implementations of the Big Data Service Management concepts discussed in Common Technical Concepts and Patterns section. These are the ones which deal with management and maintenance aspects of the services deployed in a Big Data cluster. Here, below, we discuss the key Service Management Components in Hadoop Ecosystem.

2.3.2.12.1   YARN

YARN [9], Yet Another Resource Negotiator, is a generic framework which can support resource management for different types of distributed programming models on HDFS. The key motivation behind YARN was to support other Distributed Processing Components on HDFS apart from Map Reduce as Map Reduce is not suitable for all use cases (e.g. Graph Processing, Convergence oriented iterative processing typically needed in Machine Learning, Real Time or Near Real Time data access, Streaming Data processing, etc.). An analogy of YARN would be a generic purpose operating system which can support various types of concurrent processes by allocating different computing resources to them. As shown in Fig. 2.8, YARN separates the responsibilities of resource management and lifecycle management of a job across four key components—Global Resource Manager, Node Manager, Application Manager, and Pluggable Scheduler [10]. It is essentially two steps process where resource allocation is done by YARN and the application deals with the task execution.

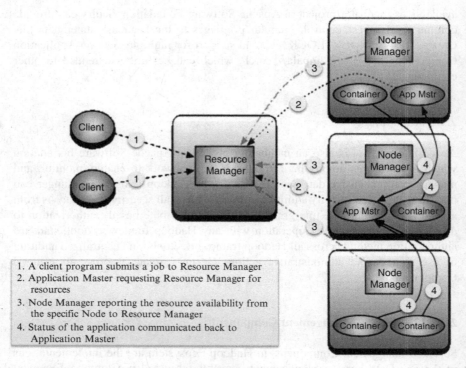

1. A client program submits a job to Resource Manager
2. Application Master requesting Resource Manager for resources
3. Node Manager reporting the resource availability from the specific Node to Resource Manager
4. Status of the application communicated back to Application Master

Fig. 2.8 High Level Architecture of YARN (Reproduced from [27])

As discussed before YARN has opened the door for other Distributed Processing Components to run on HDFS apart from Map Reduce. The most potential candidates among the various ones are Spark, Flink, Tez, Storm, Cloudera Impala, IBM Big SQL, Drill, etc. Many of them already have the integration with YARN. The remaining ones are also already moving towards that direction.

With YARN there is no need for moving data from one cluster to another cluster as it supports various types of applications on same HDFS cluster. This in turn can increase the cluster utilization and reduce the number of nodes needed to support the use cases. YARN supports application specific needs by allowing every Application to write its own Application Master. Yarn also provides reuse of computing resources like CPU and Memory across various types of applications. Yarn supports multiple versions of same applications for ease of upgrades, multi tenants needs, etc.

There are other resource management components available too in the market which can be used instead of YARN in Hadoop Ecosystem. The examples are Apache Mesos [166] (discussed later in this chapter), IBM Platform Symphony [107], etc.

2.3.2.12.2 ZooKeeper

Apache ZooKeeper [43] enables highly availability of the services running on Hadoop Cluster. It ensures reliable distributed coordination through a centralized service for maintaining configuration information, naming, providing distributed synchronization, and providing group services as aspects. Any distributed application can use all of these kinds of services through a mix of specific components of ZooKeeper and application specific conventions. ZooKeeper allows distributed processes to coordinate with each other through a shared hierarchical name space. ZooKeeper supports very high throughput and low latency needed for efficient coordination in a large distributed system. It can help avoiding single point of failure in big systems. It also supports strict ordering for sophisticated synchronization primitives to be implemented at the client.

2.3.2.12.3 Slider

Apache Slider [45], though still an incubation project, needs mention here as it aims to ease out integration of any Application Component (running on any Distributed Processing Component) with YARN to efficiently run along with other components on a single Hadoop cluster. This way Slider can help adoption of any proprietary Distributed Processing Component to run on Hadoop cluster by sharing the resources appropriately along with others. Slider supports on demand creation of applications in a YARN cluster and different versions of the same application can be run by different users in a single YARN cluster. It also helps in running different instances of same application running on the same Hadoop cluster. Slider also provides the capability to expand or shrink application instances as needed.

2.3.2.12.4 Ambari

Apache Ambari [47] provides the capabilities for provisioning, managing, and monitoring Hadoop clusters. Ambari comes with an easy-to-use web UI based on its back end REST APIs which can help system administrators in provisioning, managing, and monitoring a Hadoop cluster. On the other hand developers can use REST APIs to integrate their applications seamlessly with the management, monitoring, and provisioning capabilities of Hadoop so that everything can be managed through single interface. Ambari supports a step-by-step wizard for installing Hadoop services across any number of hosts. It also supports managing configurations of Hadoop services for the cluster. It behaves as the single component for starting, stopping, and reconfiguring Hadoop services across the entire cluster. Ambari provides a dashboard for monitoring health and status of the Hadoop cluster. Ambari has alerting capability to send emails in case of some exceptional situations (e.g., a node goes down, remaining disk space is low, etc) which are set up as triggers.

2.3.2.13   Data Integration and Governance Components

Though Data Integration and Governance components typically are external to Database Management systems, interestingly Hadoop Ecosystem also provides its own implementation of key Data Integration and Governance Components. Primarily these components take care of aspects like Meta data Management, Data Import/Export to/from of Hadoop Ecosystem, Workflow, and Taxonomy. As discussed below, some of these components are matured enough to support these requirements where as there are components which are still in proposal/evolving stage.

2.3.2.13.1   HCatalog

Apache HCatalog {34] is the meta data store for data in Hadoop which can be shared across any Application Components like Hive, Pig, etc. All DDLs executed by Hive or Pig (or other equivalent tools like Drill, Big SQL, Impala, etc.) are essentially creation/modification of records in HCatalog's meta data store. This is a very powerful framework which enables seamless execution of a hybrid data pipeline which may involve multiple tools like Hive, Pig, Big SQL, Impala etc. The meta store of Hcatalog can be implemented using any relational database like My SQL, Oracle, DB2, etc. WebHCat [35] is the REST API for HCatalog. HCatalog supports storage based authorization to check if the user has permissions on the underlying directory in HDFS before allowing the operation.

2.3.2.13.2   Sqoop

Apache Sqoop [38] is a widely popular component for import and export of data from any relational database to Hadoop and vice versa. Sqoop relies on the database to describe the schema for the data to be imported and exported back to and from Hadoop. Sqoop uses Map Reduce to import and export the data and can be configured to achieve the needed performance. Work is also going on to use Spark as back end engine for execution of Sqoop tasks. Sqoop supports variety of databases like My SQL, Microsoft SQL Server, Oracle, Netezza, and Postgress using their native connectors which ensures enhanced performance. Sqoop can be integrated with HCatalog. Sqoop also supports importing data to NoSQL solutions like HBase and Accumulo. Sqoop provides a flexible command line based interface which can be configured extensively to pass the necessary arguments.

2.3.2.13.3   Oozie

Apache Oozie [40] is a workflow scheduler which can help in stitching various types of jobs to be executed in a Hadoop cluster to implement a data processing pipeline. Oozie is essentially a java based web application which can run the DAG of actions written in HPDL—a XML Process Definition Language for Hadoop based on XPDL [41]. The actions are executed in a remote system (in this case in a Hadoop Cluster) and upon action completion, the remote systems notifies Oozie about the action completion with success and failure. Oozie supports variety of Hadoop jobs (like Java map-reduce, Streaming map-reduce, Pig, Hive, Sqoop, and Distcp as well as any arbitrary Java programs and shell scripts) out of the box through the use of parameterized workflows where one can run multiple instances of the same workflow in parallel. Jobs can be triggered either based on time or availability of data to be processed. Oozie supports JMX based monitoring of Jobs. It also supports decision points in workflow execution depending on the end status of an action.

2.3.2.13.4   Falcon

Apache Falcon [71] is a feed processing and feed management system. Though not yet used widely because of its maturity, Apache Falcon brings on to the table various interesting features. Falcon can help in defining relationship between various data and processing steps on a Hadoop environment. It supports services such as feed retention, replications across clusters, archival etc. It can also support late data handling, retry policies, etc. for ease of onboarding of new workflows/pipelines. Falcon can be integrated with HCatalog. It can support identification of Lineage information across feeds and processes. It can also notify the end customer based on availability of feed groups.

2.3.2.13.5   Atlas

Apache Atlas [72] is a governance component for data processing within Hadoop Ecosystem currently in a proposal state for Apache incubation. Promoted by Hortonworks, Aetna, Merck, Target, SAS, Schlumberger, and JPMC this framework is supposed to provide a scalable and extensible set of core foundational governance services that enables enterprises to effectively and efficiently meet their compliance requirements within Hadoop. It will also allow integration with the complete ecosystem of enterprise data management.

2.3.2.14   The Overall Hadoop Stack

The diagram below represents the relationship between various components of Hadoop Ecosystem as overall Hadoop Stack.

The various layers of overall Hadoop Stack in Fig. 2.9 are detailed below.

- The Distributed File System Components help storing and accessing the data from the nodes in the hardware cluster.

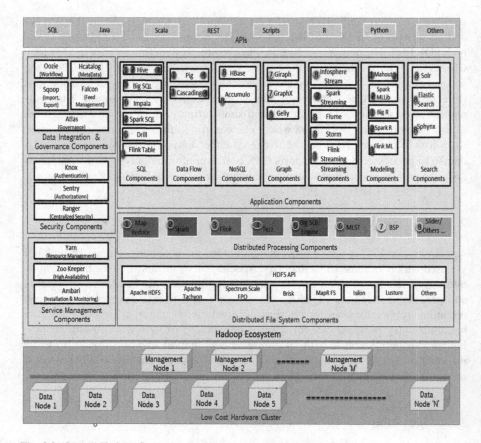

Fig. 2.9 Overall Hadoop Stack showing all components of Hadoop Ecosystem

- The Distributed Processing Components help in actual processing of the data in multiple hardware nodes by utilizing the computation power of each node in parallel.
- The Application Components provide necessary abstractions over Distributed Processing Engines so that the later can be used for different Big Data use cases around Interactive Queries, Streaming, Modeling, Search, etc. The numbered bubbles on the Application Components link an Application Component with the Distributed Processing Components (of same numbered bubble) it runs on. For example, Spark SQL has bubble with number 2 which means that it internally runs on the Distributed Processing Component Spark which also has bubble with number 2.
- The API layer is the layer which supports common interfaces like SQL, Java, R, REST, etc so that the data can be easily accessed from and integrated with other enterprise tools and technologies.

- The Service Management Components help in managing the services for high availability, dynamic resource prioritization & distribution, installation, and monitoring.
- The Security Components help in managing security related aspects like authentication, authorization, encryption, auditing, etc.
- The Data Integration and Governance Frameworks help in data import, export, data workflow, meta data management, taxonomy, etc.
- The discussions of the Distributed Computing Components and Application Components related to Spark is done later in appropriate section. However, since Spark is packaged with other components in Hadoop Ecosystem majority of the times, it is included in this diagram.
- The NoSQL Components, Streaming Components and Search Components are discussed later in this chapter in appropriate section. However, since these components are packaged with other components in Hadoop Ecosystem majority of the times, they are included in this diagram.

2.3.3   Hadoop Distributions

The various components of Hadoop Ecosystem can be directly used by obtaining the same from Apache Software Foundation in line with Apache License Version 2.0. Alternatively the same can be also obtained from commercial vendors which commonly known as Hadoop Distributions. A typical Hadoop Distribution, from a given vendor, comes with different components of Hadoop Ecosystem and value added features from the vendor as a well-tested and packaged software stack. Most of the times the Hadoop distribution from the vendor is free (i.e. no software license to be paid) if used for development purpose or in a limited set of nodes in production without any support. Sometimes the free versions are referred as Community Edition and the licensed versions are called as Enterprise Edition. An organization can always buy license from the respective vendor to avail necessary supports in production and other environments as needed. The licensing model varies from processor based model, data volume based models, user based model to mixed model.

Figure 2.10 shows the popular vendors providing Hadoop Distributions from the Forrester Wave [136]. Table 2.3 details the value added components added on top of Apache Hadoop Ecosystem by various Hadoop Distributions. The Hadoop Distributions are selected based on the best mix of latest offerings, market presence, and leadership.

2.3.3.1   Open Data Platform Initiative (ODPi) for Hadoop Ecosystem

Though most of the Hadoop Distributions today contain popular components of Hadoop Ecosystem, there is no standard available today to enforce the availability of

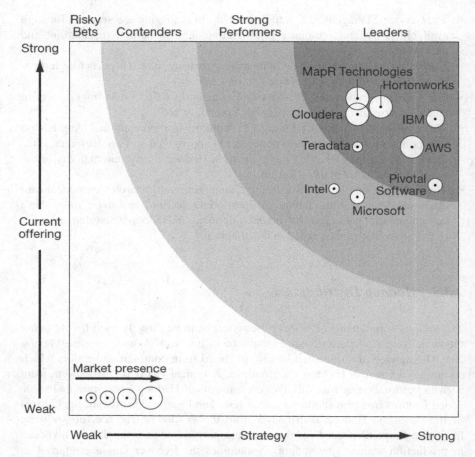

Fig. 2.10 Comparison of various Hadoop Distributions from the Forrester Wave (Reproduced from [136])

certain set of components with appropriate versions in each distribution. This makes the consumer's decision making process difficult and slows down their journey towards Big Data implementations.

The Open Data Platform initiative [73], ODPi, is a recent initiative which is aimed towards standardization of Hadoop Distributions across the vendors to minimize the fragmentation and duplication of effort within the industry. In turn this will also foster development of a more cohesive community and activities that accelerate the adoption of big data architectures using Hadoop. It is a shared initiative by various Big Data vendors, System Integrator and User Companies like Hortonworks, IBM, GE, EMC, Verizon, Infosys, Capgemini, etc.

Table 2.3 High level details of the popular Hadoop distributions

Distribution name	Vendor	URL	Key value added features on top of Apache Hadoop ecosystem
Cloudera distribution for Hadoop (CDH)	Cloudera	http://www.cloudera.com/content/cloudera/en/products-and-services/cdh.html	Cloudera Impala, Cloudera Manager, Cloudera Search, Cloudera Navigator
IBM Open Platform for Apache Hadoop (IOP)	IBM	http://www-01.ibm.com/support/knowledgecenter/SSPT3X_4.0.0/com.ibm.swg.im.infosphere.biginsights.welcome.doc/doc/welcome.html	Big SQL, Big Sheets, Big R and Scalable Machine Learning, Text Analytics, Spectrum Scale FPO, Platform Symphony
Hortonworks Data Platform (HDP)	Hortonworks	http://hortonworks.com/hdp/	HDP Search, HDP ODBC Driver, Ambari SCOM Management, Hortonworks Connector for Teradata, Quest Data Connector for Hadoop
MapR Distribution Including Apache Hadoop	MapR	https://www.mapr.com/	MapR-DB, MapR-FS, Direct Access NFS, Apache Drill

The key objectives of Open Data Platform initiative are:

- Defining a core platform, 'ODPi Core', for Hadoop Ecosystem with compatible versions of selected open source projects.
- Providing a stable base of the same through proper integration, testing and certification against which Big Data solutions providers can qualify solutions.
- Creating a set of tools and methods that enable members to create and test differentiated offerings based on the ODPi Core.

2.3.4 Hadoop as Appliance

Hadoop Ecosystem is also sometimes packaged as appliances which are essentially pre-installed and configured Hadoop Distribution on hardware racks. These preconfigured appliances can help organization to start their journey with Hadoop Ecosystem without much knowledge of the complexities involved with various frameworks of Hadoop in terms of installation and configuration for them.

The prominent offerings in this area are Oracle's Big Data Appliance [81], Avnet's Hadoop Appliance with IBM's Open Platform for Apache Hadoop [82], Microsoft's Analytics Platform System [83], Pivotal Data Computing Appliances [84], etc.

There are also few Hardware Infrastructures specially customized for running Hadoop Ecosystem and certified by various Hadoop vendors. SeaMicro SM 15,000 Fabric Compute system [85] for Hadoop is certified by Cloudera and Hortonworks. SGI InfiniteData Cluster can run any choice of Hadoop Distribution [86]. Cray CS300 cluster supercomputers have been customized for "high value" Hadoop deployments [87] and Cisco's Unified Computing System (UCS) [88] configured with reference architecture for MapR, Cloudera, and Hortonworks distributions.

2.3.5   Hadoop Ecosystem on Cloud

There are many implementations of Hadoop Ecosystem available today in cloud which can be used as Software As A Service (or alternatively Hadoop As A service). The key players in this space are Amazon's Elastic Map Reduce [74], IBM's BigInsights For Apache Hadoop on BlueMix [75], IBM's Analytics for Apache Spark, Hadoop As A Service from Qubole [76], Microsoft Azure HDInsights [77], HP Cloud with Hadoop [78], Hadoop on Google Cloud Platform [79], Hadoop As A Service from Altiscale [80], etc. The common characteristics of all of these offerings are ability to fire up a Hadoop Cluster and start running use cases in no time. They also provide various types of pricing models (data volume based, infrastructure size based, number of user based, etc.) and enterprises can choose the one suitable for the need. There is also an option to install and run Hadoop on bare metal infrastructure, Infrastructure As A Service, provided by various cloud providers like Amazon, Rackspace, IBM Softlayer, etc. The common use of this approach is to start with a development and test cluster. In overall the Hadoop Ecosystem on Cloud can be used to experiment with new use cases without much of initial time and commitment to investment and impacting any production use cases. Once the use cases are found to be meaningful the same can be implemented in cloud or on premise.

2.4   NoSQL Databases

NoSQL databases emerged in the market during the similar time when Hadoop Ecosystem started developing. The main motivation behind NoSQL movement was to develop 'built for purpose' databases instead of blindly using relational databases for all enterprise applications. The movement got predominantly fueled by the very high throughput read/write requirements of the web applications which became majorly popular as the de-facto ecommerce channel in the last decade or so. The regular relational databases were not capable of handling such high throughput read/write requirements without a lot of investment in infrastructure. That eventually resulted in various NoSQL solutions popping up in the market each trying to solve different types of data access problems.

The key characteristics of the NoSQL Databases can be summarized around four logical layers:

- Logical Data Model Layer with loosely typed extensible data schema (Map, Column Family, Document, Graph, etc.).
- Data Distribution Layer ensuring horizontal scaling on multiple nodes abiding by principles of CAP theorem. This comes along with necessary support for multiple data centers and dynamic provisioning (transparently adding/removing a node from a production cluster), a la Elasticity.
- Persistence Layer with flexibility of storing the data either in disk or memory or both; sometimes in pluggable custom stores.
- Interface Layer with support for various 'Non-SQL' interfaces (REST, Thrift, Language Specific APIs, etc) for data access without support for transaction.

Here are some popular use cases typically suitable for NoSQL Databases:

- As caching layer for data, on top of permanent data store, for very low latency data access. Example scenarios are—Product Catalogue navigation, Inventory navigation, etc.
- For intermediate storage of data to support very high throughput write requirements before storing the data in the persistent data store. This usage is suitable for the scenarios where data with Eventual Consistency is acceptable. Example scenarios are—Storing high volume of orders from online retail/travel applications, Storing of customer call data, etc.
- Storing and Mining non-transactional data. For example application logs can be stored in NoSQL Databases and then can be viewed or searched in a very fast and interactive manner.
- Serving as a store for pre-aggregated data. Data aggregated in other platforms (like Hadoop, Spark, etc.) can be pushed to NoSQL Databases. Custom Built Dashboards and also standard reporting solutions (like Jasper Soft, Tableau, etc.) can be used to access the pre-aggregated data from NoSQL databases and show the same to the end users.

Right now there are around 150 (and counting) NoSQL Databases [58] available across Open Source and Licensed Products categories. Please note that many a times other types of Big Data Technologies (like In Memory Databases, Search, etc.) are also referred as NoSQL Databases as there is no strict definition for the same. In this section we shall cover the three popular NoSQL Databases which are widely used in big enterprises as well as in small and medium size companies.

2.4.1 MongoDB

MongoDB [52] is one of the most popular Open Source NoSQL Databases that provides high performance and availability with capability to scale in an elastic way with addition of more nodes. MongoDB provides document object model for

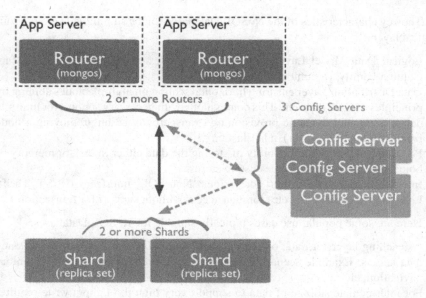

Fig. 2.11 High Level Processing Architecture of MongoDB (Reproduced from [37])

storing data which is analogous to any arbitrary object structure of the regular object oriented programming paradigm.

MongoDB supports Document Object based logical data model. Document object based data structure helps in directly storing any object available at programming level as a JSON based key/value at runtime in a Collection (analogous to a table). There is no need to define the schema at design time. Document object model also helps storing data related with each other in a de-normalized fashion within the same document object (which is equivalent to record) in the same collection (or table). This in turn ensures fast retrieval of all data related to a single key just by a single lookup at database. MongoDB stores the data in BSON (binary JSON) format and supports Snappy and Zlib compressions.

Figure 2.11 shows the high level processing architecture of MongoDB. A typical cluster in MongoDB has the key components called shards, query routers, and config servers. Shards are the independent processes where each shard owns the data in the form of chunk (or partition) of a collection (or table). MongoDB distributes data at the collection level. The process of sharding or partitioning a collection's data takes place based on the keys of the collection. A shard key is either an indexed field (on a single attribute) or an indexed compound (on multiple attributes) field that exists in every document in the collection. MongoDB divides the shard key values into chunks and distributes the chunks evenly across the shards. To divide the shard key values into chunks, MongoDB uses either range based sharding, hash based sharding, or tag aware sharding (which can be configured). MongoDB ensures a balanced sharded cluster using two background processes: the splitting and the balancing. Inserts and updates typically trigger splits. When a chunk grows beyond a specified chunk size, MongoDB splits the chunk in half without migration of the data or affecting the shards. When the distribution of a sharded collection in a cluster is uneven, the balancing process moves the chunks from the shard that has the largest number of chunks to the shard with the least number of chunks until there is a balance across the shards of the collection. Balancing process also gets kicked off after addition and deletion of a Shard.

MongoDB supports various types of indexes for ease of data access. Each shard contains a default "_id" field which itself serves as Primary Index. In addition to that secondary indices can be defined on single field, multiple fields, and arrays within the document object. MongoDB also supports geospatial index for geospatial data and text index for searching any arbitrary test string within a collection. MongoDB supports creating index as a back ground process so that the main database is available for read and write.

Query Routers, or mongos instances, interface with client applications and direct operations to the appropriate shard or shards and then returns results to the clients. There can be more than one query router to divide the load of the client request. Config servers store the cluster's metadata. This data contains a mapping of the replica sets to the shards.

In a production cluster, each Shard is equivalent to a Replica Set where each Replica set contains a configurable number (typically 3) of replications of the same data stored across different hardware nodes. In MongoDB, Replica Set is the basic mechanism for supporting High Availability. The Replica Sets can be residing in multiple machines located in different Data Center across the WAN to support disaster recovery situation. The replication can be set to be synchronous or asynchronous to ensure strict Consistency or Eventual Consistency. A Replica Set already keeps configuration, state information and so on. Drivers implement a discovery process for Replica Set members and a way to keep track of their state (up/down, primary/secondary, etc.). When failure occurs it adjusts its view of the Replica Set accordingly. For the failover of Routers, in the connection string of the driver one has to specify location/ip of multiple Routers. The driver program takes care of moving the request to the router which is up.

MongoDB does not provide any facility for managing resources and priorities across various workloads. One of the basic reason behind that is MongoDB is primarily designed to support high concurrency very short lived (milliseconds) queries. However, there is a product called Sonar Resource Management [169] from jSONAR which can be used to monitor currently running queries in MongoDB databases and can kill operations that have exceeded their quota (e.g. the operation is running for too long). This prevents runaway queries and other operations that may have been started by mistake or maliciously and that place burden on the database. MongoDB can be also run [170] on Mesos (discussed later in this chapter) for resource management purpose which can help running MongoDB with other technologies in same cluster.

MongoDB is very rich in Monitoring services. There are three methods provided by MongoDB for the same. Firstly, one can use a set of utilities distributed with MongoDB that provides real-time reporting of database activities. Secondly, there are bunch of database commands that return statistics regarding the current database state. Finally there are MongoDB Cloud Manager (a hosted service) and Ops Manager (an on premise solution) available in MongoDB Enterprise Advanced, which provide monitoring to collect data from running MongoDB deployments as well as providing visualization and alerts based on that data. These three methods are complimentary to each other and should be used in conjunction.

MongoDB provides reasonable support for enterprise Security. For authentication, all client applications need to identify themselves to MongoDB before accessing any data. This ensures that no client can access the data stored in MongoDB without being explicitly allowed. MongoDB supports two authentication mechanisms that clients can use to verify their identity: a password-based challenge and response protocol and x.509 [39] certificates. Additionally, MongoDB Enterprise also provides support for LDAP proxy authentication and Kerberos authentication. On the authorization front, MongoDB does not enable authorization by default. When authorization is enabled, MongoDB controls a user's access through the roles assigned to the user. A role consists a set of privileges, where a privilege consists actions, or a set of operations, and a resource upon which the actions are allowed. Users may have one or more roles that describe their access. MongoDB provides several built-in roles and users can construct specific roles tailored to actual requirements. The resources can be a database, collection, set of collections, or the cluster. MongoDB Enterprise includes an auditing capability for mongod and mongos instances. The auditing facility allows administrators and users to track system activity for deployments with multiple users and applications. The auditing facility can write audit events to the console, the syslog, a JSON file, or a BSON file. There are two broad classes of approaches provided by MongoDB for encrypting data at rest: Application Level Encryption and Storage Encryption. One can use these solutions together or independently. Application Level Encryption provides encryption on a per-field or per-document basis within the application layer. To encrypt document or field level data, one can use custom encryption and decryption routines or use a commercial solution such as the Vormetric [42] Data Security Platform. Storage Encryption encrypts all MongoDB data on the storage or operating system to ensure that only authorized processes can access protected data. A number of third-party libraries can integrate with the operating system to provide transparent disk-level encryption (like Linux Unified Key Setup (LUKS) [44], IBM Guardium Data Encryption [51], Vormetric Data Security Platform, Bitlocker Drive Encryption [53], etc.). For encrypting data in motion, one can use SSL (Secure Sockets Layer) to encrypt all of MongoDB's network traffic. This approach ensures that MongoDB network traffic is only readable by the intended client.

2.4.2 Cassandra

Apache Cassandra [54] is another popular Open Source NoSQL Database which also supports the need of high throughput, high availability, and low latency.

Cassandra was designed based on the principles of distributed systems technologies from Dynamo [113] and the data model from Google's BigTable [98]. Cassandra supports Eventually Consistency based on the design of Dynamo. However, the logical data model of Cassandra is Column Family oriented data structure as in BigTable.

A table in Cassandra is equivalent to multi-dimensional hash map. Within a Cassandra table, data can be stored as a set of arbitrary key/value pairs in multiple Column Families. Multiple column families can be linked together using a row key. Cassandra also supports the notion of Super Column which can be used to hold a list of columns within a column. Cassandra stores the data in a Cassandra specific data storage format. Cassandra supports various compression techniques like LZ4, Snappy, and Deflate (similar to gZip).

Like MongoDB, Cassandra's architecture also primarily revolves around the partitioning of the rows and replication of the same. Rows in a Column Family store are distributed across a cluster. The node to store a row is determined by mapping its key to a token value determined by a Partitioner. One can pick different Partitioner for each column family. Cassandra supports four types of Partitioners, namely Random Partitioner, Order Preserving Partitioner, Byte Ordered Partitioner, and Collating Order Partitioner. Cassandra uses a Distributed Hash Table (DHT) algorithm in determining how data with certain token value is stored in a node. Server token values are sorted and wrap around to form a ring. Each server is responsible for storing rows with token value range from the previous server token value to the server's own token value.

Replication in Cassandra is controlled by the replication factor. The default value is 1 which means that the data is written to only one node in the ring (no duplicated copy). Typically three replicas are recommended as in case of other Big Data Technologies. Cassandra supports both synchronous (Strict Consistency) and asynchronous (Eventual Consistency) replications providing the infrastructure designer necessary choice based on application's requirement. The replicas can be across the Data Centers over WAN to support disaster recovery situations. Cassandra provides three varieties of Replica Placement Strategies. SimpleStrategy (Default) returns the nodes that are next to each other on the ring. NetworkTopologyStrategy configures the number of replicas per data center as specified in the strategy options. OldNetworkTopologyStrategy places two replicas on different racks in the current data center and the third one in another data center.

Cassandra appends changed data (insert, update, or deletion) to commit log. The commit log acts as a crash recovery log for data. A write operation is never successful until the changed data is appended to commit log. Cassandra periodically syncs the commit log to disk every 1000 ms (this parameter is configurable). This is to ensure durability of data. Cassandra replays commit log after Cassandra restarts to recover potential data lost within 1 s before the crash. Cassandra keeps the main data to an in memory structure called Memtable. Each Column Family has a separate Memtable with data sorted by key. Once Memtable is full, the sorted data is written out sequentially to disk as SSTables (Sorted String Table). Flushed SSTable files are immutable and no changes can be done. Numerous SSTables will be created on disk for a column family. Later changes to the same key after flushing will be written to a different SSTable. SStables are merged once they reach some threshold to reduce read overhead. Cassandra depends on OS to cache SSTable files.

To process a key/column read request, Cassandra checks if the in-memory memtable cache still contain the data. If the data is not found there, Cassandra will read all the SSTables for that Column Family. For read optimization, Cassandra uses bloom Filter for each SSTable to determine whether this SSTable contains the key. Cassandra use index in SSTable to locate the data.

Primary key in Cassandra itself serves as the primary index as the Cassandra Column Family contains data sorted by the row keys. Cassandra also supports secondary index on any column. Secondary index are built in the background without blocking other operation.

In a Cassandra cluster all nodes are equal. The client driver can connect to any node in Cassandra. If a node is down, the client program has to do application level failover and try to connect to a different node. There are drivers, such as Astyanax, Hector, Pelops, etc. that can do automatic failover. Once the driver is connected to one node, that node acts as a coordinator for the query. The coordinator determines which nodes in the cluster should get the request based on the configured Partitioner and Replica Placement Strategy.

Similar to MongoDB, Cassandra does not have any in-built facility for managing resources and priorities across various workloads. One of the basic reason behind that is Cassandra is primarily designed to support high concurrency very short lived (millseconds) queries. However, like MongoDB, Cassandra also can be made to run [171] on Resource Management framework like Mesos so that it can run along with other types of Technologies in a common cluster.

Monitoring and understanding the performance characteristics of Cassandra cluster is critical to diagnosing issues and planning capacity. Cassandra exposes a number of statistics and management operations via Java Management Extensions (JMX). During normal operation, Cassandra outputs information and statistics that can be monitored using JMX-compliant tools, such as. The Cassandra nodetool utility, DataStax OpsCenter management console, or JConsole.

The security in Cassandra is limited to three basic features. First one is Authentication with feature of managing login ids and password in the database. Second one is Authorization at the table level with add/change/delete/read data for user with Grant/Revoke scheme. The third one is ability to encrypt data in flight between client and database cluster. The enterprise edition of Cassandra can use external security software like Kerberos, LDAP, etc. The same provides capability for encryption of data at rest and auditing (audit trails of all accesses, granular control on what all have to be audited, etc.).

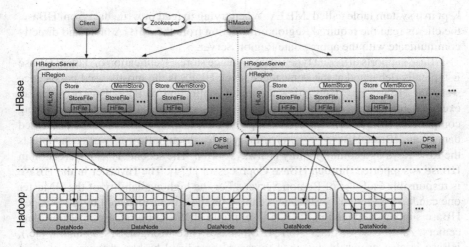

Fig. 2.12 Architecture of HBase (Reproduced from [106])

2.4.3 HBase

Apache HBase [55] is also a widely used Open Source NoSQL Database supporting
the high throughput, high availability, and low latency requirements of user facing
applications. HBase was designed based on Google's BigTable design. In contrast
to MongoDB and Cassandra, HBase can run on data in HDFS. HBase can also run
on data available in non HDFS data store though that type of implementation is not
very popular. HBase supports strict consistency.

Like Cassandra, the logical data model of HBase is Column Family oriented
data structure. HBase supports logical data model with arbitrary key/value pairs
distributed across various column families. The data in HBase is stored in a HBase
specific data storage format called HFile. HBase supports LZO, gZip, or Snappy for
data compression.

Figure 2.12 shows the scalability architecture of HBase. Typically, the HBase
cluster has one Master node, namely HMaster and multiple Region Servers namely
HRegionServer. The HMaster in the HBase is responsible for monitoring the
Cluster, assigning Regions to the Region Servers, Controlling the Load Balancing,
and Failover of Region Servers. Each Region Server contains multiple Regions,
namely HRegions. The Data in HBase Tables are stored in these Regions. Each
Region is identified by the start key (inclusive) and the end key (exclusive) and is
made up of a MemStore and multiple StoreFiles (HFile). The data lives in these
StoreFiles in the form of Column Families and eventually is stored in HDFS.
The MemStore holds in-memory modifications to the data. Each Region Server
also contains a Write-Ahead Log (called HLog or WAL) for the purpose of data
durability. When a Table becomes too big, it is partitioned into multiple Regions
automatically by the HRegionServer. The mapping of Regions to Region Server is

kept in a system table called .META. When trying to read or write data from HBase, the clients read the required Region information from the .META table and directly communicate with the appropriate Region Server.

HBase supports different types of persistence stores. Replication of data in HBase is typically delegated at the Persistence level. HDFS is the mostly used persistence store for HBase and it provides automatic replication of data. This provides an excellent integration option with processing of raw data using batch processing components (like Hive, Pig) of Hadoop and then real time access of the processed data using HBase. HBase supports primary index through Row Key of each table as the Row Keys of a column family is always sorted. The secondary index creation in HBase is supported through HBase Coprocessor [174]. The HMaster in the HBase is responsible Failover of Region Servers. For the high availability of the HMaster one can have a secondary HMaster running on the cluster managed by ZooKeeper. HBase supports replication of Data in multiple HDFS clusters across various data centers. As in case of other NoSQL Databases (like MongoDB, Cassandra, etc.), HBase is also primarily designed to serve short lived highly concurrent random access for read/write. So it does not provide a way to do resource management or query priority. However HBase can be run in Hadoop Ecosystem on YARN which can provide the necessary resource management features. HBase exposes various metrics (JMX based) for regions servers which can be used to monitor HBase. There are various tools available which can show these metrics in a GUI. HBase itself comes with a monitoring UI. The other tools like Monitis [172], Hannibal [173], etc. can be also used for this purpose.

HBase can be configured to provide User Authentication, Authorization, and Encryption for Data in rest. Authorization ensures that only valid users can communicate with HBase. This is implemented at the RPC level, and is based on the Simple Authentication and Security Layer (SASL) [114] supporting Kerberos. Since HBase depends on HDFS and ZooKeeper, secure HBase relies on a secure HDFS and a secure ZooKeeper. So HBase servers need to create a secure service session, as described above, to communicate with HDFS and ZooKeeper. All the files written by HBase are stored in HDFS. As in Unix file systems, the access control provided by HDFS is based on users, groups, and permissions. Secure HDFS adds the authentication steps that guarantee that the HBase user is trusted. ZooKeeper has an Access Control List (ACL) on each zookeeper node that allows read/write access to the users based on user information in a similar manner to HDFS. HBase also provides authorization facility using Role-based Access Control (RBAC). Using RBAC one can control the users or groups that can read and write to a given HBase resource or execute a coprocessor endpoint, using the familiar paradigm of roles. To further restrict who can read or write to certain subsets of data, one can define Visibility Labels to the cells and control access to the labelled cells. Visibility labels are stored as tags. In HBase transparent encryption of data at rest is possible on the underlying file system (both in HFiles and in the WAL).

2.4.4   Upcoming NoSQL Databases

As discussed before in this chapter more and more NoSQL Databases are coming into market to solve specific set of use cases as well as bridge the gap between regular relational databases and NoSQL. Here we discuss two upcoming NoSQL Databases which are among the promising ones.

2.4.4.1   Cockroach DB

The latest interesting addition to the NoSQL Database list is Cockroach DB [59]. Inspired by Google's Spanner [60] database, Cockroach DB promises support for distributed transaction in a geo-replicated way with read/write scalability. This makes Cockroach DB very unique compared to other NoSQL Databases. With more than 50 contributors Cockroach DB is one of the most active NoSQL projects in github right now.

2.4.4.2   Foundation DB

Another latest NoSQL Database which has generated lot of interests of late is Foundation DB [143]. The key features differentiating Foundation DB from other NoSQL Databases are support for multiple types of data models (key/value, document model, SQL type table, etc.) and the support for properties like ACID [144].

2.4.5   NoSQL Databases in Cloud

There are many cloud based NoSQL solutions available in the market today. The Amazon Dynamo DB [118], IBM's Cloudant [61], ObjectRocket (managed MongoDB and Redis service) [119], Google's Cloud BigTable [129], are few examples of managed NoSQL Database service in Cloud. Apart from that most of the Cloud providers like Amazon, Google, IBM Softlayer support running popular NoSQL Databases (like MongoDB, Cassandra etc.) on bare metal based hosted infrastructure. This approach of having NoSQL Databases in Cloud typically works well for the read only data as the data moved to NoSQL Databases are typically lesser in volume and it is the end step before the final data consumption happens. However this approach does not work that effectively if the data is also written back to the NoSQL Databases and that data has to be stored back to an on premise persistent data store. The step of pushing the data from NoSQL Databases in Cloud to on premise data store can be complex to implement and non-performant.

2.5   In Memory Databases

In-memory databases are the database management systems that primarily use main memory of a hardware node for storing and processing of data. This is in contrast to other database management systems which use a disk storage mechanism for storing the data. These databases are very fast with predictable performance as accessing data from memory eliminates disk i/o time while querying the data. These databases sometimes also provide the feature of storing the data to disk in an asynchronous fashion. One of the key design characteristics of the In Memory Databases written in Java is the use of off-heap memory instead of the memory in Java Heap. These In Memory Databases are not affected by frequent GC pauses of JVMs.

Like NoSQL Databases, In Memory Databases can also provide very high read/write throughput and can be used for online transaction processing as an intermedia temporary storage of data before the data is stored in a regular persistence store. In Memory Databases can also be used for analytics processing because they can make very high volume of memory available to the client applications. As a recent trend, the hybrid transactional and analytical processing (HTAP) applications largely use In Memory Databases.

In open source there are many options for In Memory Databases—Aerospike [115], Hazelcast [116], Terracota BigMemory [210], Gem Fire [118], Apache Ignite [120], etc. In the world of licensed software the popular ones are Oracle Coherence [121], Oracle Timesten [122], IBM Db2 Blu [123], SAP Hana [124], Exasol [125], etc.

Many popular NoSQL Databases can be configured to completely store and serve the data from memory with replication of data across multiple nodes and asynchronous persistence in disk (eventual consistency). On the other hand, many of the In Memory Databases can support NoSQL like columnar or document based data structure. That is why many a times, In Memory Database technologies are grouped along with NoSQL technologies.

Here we discuss few In Memory Databases with rich features which have open source community edition as well as commercial version for production deployment.

2.5.1   Hazelcast

Hazelcast is an In Memory Database which supports embedding instances in the application server, or instances running as separated processes on dedicated hardware. Hazelcast supports various features like Distributed and Replicated Maps, Query and Execution; Topics, Sets and Queues out of the box for data access and processing.

The key features of Hazelcast are highlighted below:

- Hazelcast supports distributed Maps. The data is partitioned using consistent hashing algorithm.
- A map can be actually multi map where a single key can have multiple values.
- The Distributed Maps can be also replicated (up to six copies) to support failover and data locality. WAN data replication across multiple data centers is possible for supporting DR.
- Hazelcast stores the key-values off-heap and the meta data in JVM heap. This helps in predictable application scaling and low latency by minimizing pauses for Java Garbage Collection.
- Hazelcast supports distributed concurrency control by use of distributed lock, distributed atomic reference, and distributed semaphore.
- Supports variety of programming clients like Java, C, C++, and REST. It also supports SQL API.
- Supports distributed computing paradigm like Map Reduce
- Supports distributed messaging paradigm like distributed Queue and Distributed Events
- Supports transactions using in-built or third party transaction management for local transactions and distributed transactions.
- Provides JMX based cluster management and monitoring capability
- Hazelcast provides an extensible, JAAS based security feature which can be used to authenticate both cluster members and clients and to perform access control checks on client operations. Access control can be done according to endpoint principal and/or endpoint address. Also supports communication between client and nodes using SSL.
- Hazelcast does not yet feature direct disk persistence, but it is planned. Hazelcast offers synchronous and asynchronous storage of data to back-end stores via a MapStore interface.

2.5.2 GemFire

Pivotal GemFire [117] stores all data in memory to avoid disk I/O time lags. Like Hazelcast in case of GemFire also instances can be embedded in the application server, or as process instances on dedicated hardware. Any member can communicate with any other in GemFire and Data is replicated across physical servers for redundancy. Gemfire supports Distributed and Replicated Maps, Query and Execution. It does not have support for Topics, Sets and Queues out of the box. Grid communication in Gemfire is based on JGroups.

The key features of GemFire are highlighted below.

- GemFire supports distributed Maps. GemFire does not support Multi Map where a key can hold multiple values.

- The Distributed Maps can be also replicated up to three replicas to support failover and data locality. Data replication across multiple data centers over WAN is possible for supporting DR
- GemFire stores the keys on-heap.
- GemFire supports distributed lock for distributed concurrency control.
- Supports variety of programming clients like Java, C, C++, and REST. It also supports SQL API
- Supports distributed computing paradigm like Map Reduce through Functions interface.
- Supports distributed messaging paradigm through Distributed Events.
- Supports transactions using in-built or third party transaction management for local transactions and distributed transactions.
- Provides JMX based cluster management and monitoring capability
- Plug-in mechanism for authentication of clients and servers and authorization of cache operations from clients. Any security infrastructure can be plugged into the system as long as the plug-in implements the required GemFire interfaces.
- Allows configuration of connections to be SSL- based separately for peer-to-peer, client, JMX, and WAN gateway connections.
- Selectively authorized cache operations by clients based on the predefined, associated roles, where the credentials are provided by the client when connecting to the server.
- Allows authorization callbacks to modify or filter data sent from the client to the server. Similarly, after the cache operations complete on the server, a post authorization callback occurs, that can filter or modify results sent to the client. However, the results cannot be modified while using function execution.
- GemFire provides direct persistence to disk.

2.5.3 BigMemory

BigMemory from Software AG is a distributed in-memory management solution for extremely low, predictable latency at any scale. BigMemory uses EhCache internally which helps in replication of data.

The key features of BigMemory are highlighted below.

- Supports distributed Maps. However, BigMemory does not support Multi Map where a key can hold multiple values.
- The Distributed Maps can be also replicated to support failover and data locality. Over the WAN data replication across multiple data centers is possible for supporting DR.
- BigMemory stores data off-heap. This helps in avoiding GC pauses of JVM.
- BigMemory supports distributed lock for distributed concurrency control.
- Supports variety of programming clients like Java, C, and C++. Support for REST is only through EhCache's support for REST. It also supports SQL API.

- Does not supports distributed computing paradigm like Map Reduce.
- Supports distributed messaging paradigm through Distributed Queues and Distributed Events.
- Supports local transactions and distributed transactions.
- Provides JMX based cluster management and monitoring capability
- Provides authentication based on LDAP. SSL is supported to for security of data in flight.
- Supports data persistence in disks and SSD.

2.5.4 In Memory Databases in Cloud

Like NoSQL Databases, there are various offerings available today for In Memory Databases in cloud. Examples are SAP Hana Cloud Platform [126], IBM DashDB [127], Exasol in Cloud [128], etc. Like NoSQL Databases, having In Memory Databases in Cloud works well if the data from In Memory Database is used in read only fashion by the consuming applications. If the data is also written back to the In Memory Databases this approach may not be appropriate especially if that data has to be stored back to an on premise persistent data store. That final step can be complex to implement and non-performant.

2.6 Data Warehouse Systems

The Data Warehouse Systems can be considered as the first generation of Big Data Technologies. They appear in the market back in early 1990s with the acquisition of Britton Lee [56] by Teradata and renaming of the same to ShareBase. These systems were designed to support the Data Warehousing use cases which had the need to support complex queries involving large volume of relational datasets with very fast response time (also known as OLAP, Online Analytical Processing, use cases).

The Data Warehouse Systems are typically built out of integrated set of servers, storage, operating system, and Database Management System in pre-installed and pre-optimized manners which are also called as Data Warehouse Appliances. In today's world there exist various Data Warehouse Systems, mostly licensed products like Teradata [131], Netezza [139], Oracle Exadata [158], Green Plum [191], etc.

The Data Warehouse Systems are typically based on relational data model and support only SQL interface. Most of the times they also support user defined functions (UDF) using which non SQL type processing can be done on the data. These functions are typically written in APIs specific to programming languages. With the growing popularity of predictive modeling, some of the Data Warehouse Systems (e.g. Teradata, Netezza, etc.) also support predictive model creation within the data store. To create the models and access the prediction from models they also support use of programming language like R. Sometimes the models are created and used through UDFs. Data Warehouse Systems also support the Stored Procedures for data processing.

Like most of the other Big Data technologies the Data Warehouse Systems implement Shared Nothing Architecture with Management Nodes hosting the Master Processes and Data Nodes running the multiple Slave Processes. Data Warehouse Systems store the data in Disks of multiple Data Nodes. The data format and compression techniques used are typically proprietary. However, for data partitioning and allocation, the approaches similar to those discussed in Common Technical Concepts and Patterns section are used.

Most of the Data Warehouse Systems use the concept of Distributed Processing Engine with Directed Acyclic Graph. In Data Warehouse Systems, each submitted query is handled by a master/coordinator process. The master process first invokes a query planner in order to generate a DAG based execution plan for the query. The DAG based execution plan breaks the query down to a set of schedulable tasks to run on the Data Nodes in the system. The master process is responsible for checking whether the plan completed successfully, and if so, transferring the results produced by the plan to the user or application that submitted the query. The execution plan may get merged with a dynamic scheduling algorithm to determine the schedule [147].

Figure 2.13 shows Distributed Processing architecture of Greenplum which is a quintessential example of Data Warehouse Systems. As shown in the diagram, the Master Process runs on the MPP Master Host (#1). It is a separate physical server (Management Node) with its own OS/CPU/storage/memory. The Master Host stores the metadata about the data. The hosts denoted as #2, #3 and #4 are the Data Nodes, referred here as Segment Hosts. As in Shared Nothing Architecture, these Segment Hosts are also individual physical servers with their own OS/CPU/storage/memory. Each of them hosts segment database, the slave process. Each segment database stores a partition of the data. The data network (interconnect switch) running between the MPP Master Host and the Segment Host is denoted as #5. Data is partitioned here across each segment database to achieve data and processing

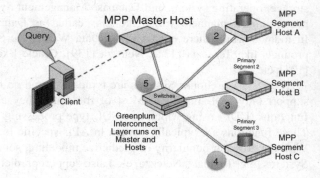

Fig. 2.13 Distributed Processing Architecture of Greenplum Data Warehouse (Reproduced from [232])

parallelism. In Greenplum one can either create hash or round-robin distribution based partitions. When the query is issued by the client, the master process generates a DAG based execution plan for the query. The DAG based execution plan breaks the query down to a set of schedulable tasks to run on the Segment Hosts where the necessary data resides (based on the where clause specified in the query). The master collates and transfers the results produced by the slaves to the client.

Data Warehouse Systems also use Replication for data availability. Typically three replica of a shard/partition can take care of most of the failure situations. In a clustered environment, the replicas are typically put in a rack different from the one having primary replica of the same partition. Replication is mostly done at the level of table partitions. This helps in query plan optimization where a small partition of a table can be broadcasted across all nodes of the other tables. Sometimes Replication is also done at the table level such that different replicas are partitioned differently. For example, one replica of the table may be hash partitioned while another may be range partitioned.

Indexing in Data Warehouse Systems are typically B tree based. However, for identifying the right Data Node for a target data entity some of the Data Warehouse Systems (like Netezza) use the approach of finding 'which nodes do not contain the data' vs 'the node containing the data'.

Data Warehouse Systems typically use a coarse-grained approach to deal with task failures. The predominant approach is to convert task failures into query failures, and then resubmit the query. If only all tasks, related to a single query, completed without failure then the query is treated as successful. Otherwise, the query is treated as failed and is rerun. This is atypical of the new generation Big Data technologies where a task failure does not mean the failure of a job/query. Instead the particular task is run again.

As in other Big Data technologies, Resource Management in Data Warehouse Systems also happens at two levels—individual nodes and at the level of the entire cluster. Configuration parameters can be set independently (e.g., size of memory buffers, maximum number of concurrent processes, and the size of log file at each node level). Resource management at the level of the entire cluster can be done through two techniques. The first one is workload differentiation. It is about distinguishing between short running and long running queries and allocating resources appropriately to meet the respective requirements of these query classes [175, 176]. The second one is setting the admission/priority control. The admission priority control limits the number of queries that can be running concurrently in the system so that every query gets some guaranteed fraction of the total resources during execution [177, 178].

Because of the maturity of Data Warehouse Systems, there are typically good tools provided by the vendors for Monitoring [179]. Typically they provide a proprietary monitoring interface using which user can figure out query performance in run time in terms of execution plan, data read, write, sorting, i/o, memory use, threads use, locking etc. Recommendations are also provided on tuning the queries.

Similar to Monitoring, in case of Security, Data Warehouse Systems are more matured compared to the new generation Big Data Technologies. Most of the Data

Warehouse Systems provide features like Authentication using enterprise LDAP, Role Based Authorization Control at the granularity of Column level, Encryption of data in flight and rest, centralized auditing capability to monitor actions by different users, etc.

2.6.1 Data Warehouse Systems in Cloud

There are few cloud based offerings of traditional Data Warehouse Systems available in the market. Amazon's Redshift [239], IBM's DashDB [127], Teradata Cloud [240] are some examples of the same. Once the data is moved to the Data Warehouse Systems in Cloud on hourly, daily, weekly basis, the same can be directly queried by the Reporting and Analytics tool typically using SQL interface. Cloud service providers manage the throughput and response time and the enterprises pay based on data volume, or infrastructure size or even based on number of users. This approach of having Data Warehouse System in Cloud is typically found to be useful because of the following reasons. Firstly, the Data warehouse System is typically the last leg of Big Data processing before the final consumption by reporting tools. The data is typically not moved out of Data Warehouse System to some other systems. Secondly, the data in Data warehouse Systems is typically much less in volume compared to the data in other systems (e.g. in Hadoop Ecosystem). And as a Third point, there is typically no write to the data in Data Warehouse Systems from the consuming applications.

2.7 Streaming Event Processing Technologies

Streaming Event Processing technologies are the ones which can support processing of very large volume of continuously incoming streaming events (or data) within sub-seconds to few seconds. The processing need may vary from simple processing (like filtering at record level) to complex processing (like aggregation and modeling of the data). All these processing typically need to happen on all the streaming events arrived with a specified time window or a micro batch.

Streaming Event Processing Technologies don't cater to the Data Storage. It is all about processing the stream of events on the fly and generating necessary alerts/actions etc. The processed data/events coming out of the Streaming Event Processing Technologies get eventually consumed by other applications in an organization. However, the same may be also used later on for modelling or other purposes. To achieve that most of the Streaming Event Processing Technologies integrate with other Big Data Technologies like Hadoop, NoSQL Databases, etc. There the final outputs from the Streaming Event Processing Technologies get persisted for future use. The Streaming Event Processing Technologies can be deployed and run in the same cluster used by technologies like Hadoop, BDAS (discussed in later section in this chapter), etc.

Streaming Event Processing Technologies typically use the concept of Producer-Consumer Agent Network where multiple Producer Agents and Consumer Agents are deployed in various nodes of the cluster. Each Producer/Consumer Agent intercepts a stream of events/data, applies a specific processing logic, and eventually pushes the result to the next Agent. The Producers and Consumers Agents are typically networked to implement multiple steps needed for overall processing of upcoming streaming events/data. The starting points of the network are various data sources and the end points are the persistence store like Hadoop or NoSQL Databases. The agents are typically Long Running Processes and can be managed by resource management frameworks like YARN or Mesos. The High Availability can be managed by using solution like ZooKeeper.

The technologies like Spark or Flink (discussed later in this chapter) provide mechanisms for Stream Event Processing inbuilt within them. In that way other use cases like SQL, Graph Processing, and Machine Learning can be run together along with Stream Processing.

Using Streaming Event Processing Technologies one can also develop capability for Complex Event Processing or CEP. CEP essentially entails ability to run a query or pattern within a set of events happened within a time window (or micro batch) and also the ability to co-relate events from different types of event streams. Currently not many of Streaming Event Processing Technologies provide CEP capabilities out of the box. But most of them have necessary building blocks in place so that these capabilities can be built up depending on the actual requirements.

There are many licensed products available to support Streaming Event processing like IBM Streams [148], Tibco Streambase [149], Software AG Apama [150], SQLStream [151], etc. Many Open Source technologies today also flourish in Stream Event Processing space—Flume, Storm, Samza, Spark Streaming, Flink Streaming, etc. Here we discuss few of those open source products for Stream Event Processing.

2.7.1   Flume

Apache Flume [36] is a Stream Event Processing Technology which can work on distributed computing resources. It can collect, aggregate, process and move large volume of streaming events or data. Originally developed for processing application logs, Flume's design has been extended for any type of streaming data or events. Flume works based on four key concepts which are simple but powerful—source, sink, channel and interceptors. The Source can be any arbitrary system behaving as origin of streaming events. The Sink can be any arbitrary system which is destination of the data. The Channel is also an arbitrary system which can hold the data in between. Finally the Interceptors are the components which help in modifying/deleting the events on the fly. Multiple sources, sinks and channels can be linked or chained together to create a sequential, parallel or mixed data flow pipeline for the processing of streaming events. Compared to the other Streaming Event

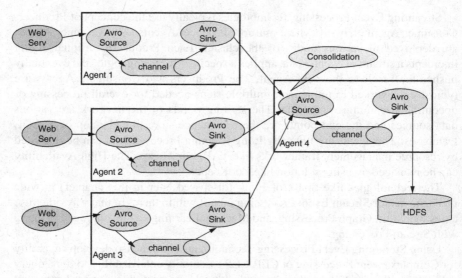

Fig. 2.14 An example of a Flume topology (Reproduced from [233])

Processing Technologies (discussed later in this chapter), Flume is better suitable for simple processing requirements of streaming events like filtering, application of regular expression, etc as these features are available out of the box. For complex processing requirements custom code has to be written. Flume is very easy to deploy, configure, and manage. Flume typically comes bundled with all Hadoop Distributions.

Figure 2.14 shows how flume can be used to build a complex topology for Stream Event Processing. An Agent is the abstraction of Flume processes running across multiple servers. An agent is typically made up of Source, Sink, Channel and Interceptor. A processing pipeline can be developed by combining multiple agents in any arbitrary way. The diagram below shows how three agents (Agent 1, Agent 2, and Agent 3) independently monitoring logs from three different web servers and then those logs are sent to Agent 4 for consolidation. Eventually those logs are stored in Hadoop after consolidation and any other necessary processing.

Flume supports variety of data sources like Spool, JMS, Thrift, etc. There is also support for defining any custom source specific to a given use case. Flume also supports variety of sinks like Thrift, IRC, HBase, HDFS, etc including custom sink. The HDFS and HBase sink helps integrating streaming data processing with Hadoop. There are options to specify various types of channels too including Memory, JDBC, File, Spillable Memory Channel, and custom Channel. Channels can be also used to store the data locally for durability of the data in case an agent is lost or the node is down. Flume also provides various simple interceptors out of the box like Timestamp, Regular Expression Filtering, Static String, etc. But there is no interceptor available for complex processing of events like aggregation, merging, etc. Custom interceptor can be created to achieve the same.

Flume supports failover through FailoverSinkProcessor which can help in failover to another sink when one sink is unavailable. Flume also provides distribution of loads to multiple agents through LoadBalanceSinkProcessor.

For Security, the HDFS sink, HBase sink, Thrift source, Thrift sink and Kite Dataset sink support Kerberos authentication. Flume also supports userid/password based authentication for JMS source. Flume supports SSL for Avro, Thrift, and HTTP sources.

Some of the Flume components report metrics to the JMX platform using MBean server. These metrics can be queried using Jconsole or any other JMX client. Flume can also report the metrics to Ganglia 3 or Ganglia 3.1 meta nodes. Flume agents can report metrics in JSON format too.

2.7.2   Storm

Storm [14] supports a distributed programming model to process high volume of unbounded streaming events in real time. Storm can support various use cases like real time analytics, online machine learning, continuous computation, etc. in a scalable and fault tolerant way with the guarantee of data processing. Storm can ingest data from variety of systems in real time and also can write the data to variety of output systems. Storm is more advanced than Flume for implementing complex processing requirements with the use of Trident API.

The core abstraction in Storm is the Stream which is an unbounded sequence of tuples. The basic primitives that provided by Storm for stream transformations are Spouts and Bolts. Spouts and Bolts have interfaces that one can implement to run application-specific logic. A Spout typically reads messages/events from a source. For example there can be a Spout which reads messages from a JMS queue and emit them as a stream or series of tuples, or there can be a Spout which connects to the Twitter API and emit a stream or tuples of tweets. A Bolt consumes any number of input streams, does some processing, and possibly emits new streams. A complex use case of stream transformations require multiple steps and thus multiple bolts. Bolts can be customized to address various types of requirements like filtering tuples, aggregation of them, joining the tuples, talk to databases, etc. Networks of Spouts and Bolts are packaged into a Topology, which is the top-level abstraction in Storm, that is submitted to Storm clusters for execution. Edges in the graph of a topology indicate the streams subscribing to various Bolts. When a Spout or Bolt emits a tuple it is sent to every Bolt that subscribes to the stream form the Spout.

Figure 2.15 shows a typical Storm cluster with the key components. There are two types of nodes in a Storm Cluster. The master node runs the Nimbus daemon process that is responsible for assigning tasks to the slave nodes, monitoring the cluster for failures, distributing the code for Storm topology, and any other customization around the cluster. On the other hand each slave node runs an instance of the Supervisor daemon. This daemon listens for work assigned (by Nimbus) to the node it runs on and starts/stops the worker processes as necessary. Each worker process executes a subset of a topology. Storm also relies on ZooKeeper to perform

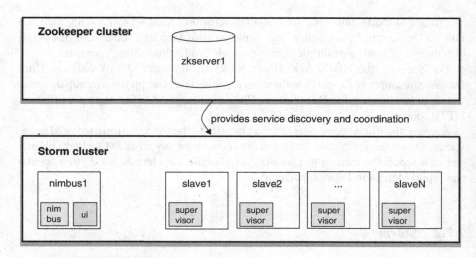

Fig. 2.15 A typical Storm cluster with the key components (Reproduced from [234])

the coordination between Nimbus and the Supervisors. Apart from using ZooKeeper for coordination purposes the Nimbus and Supervisors also store all their states in ZooKeeper or on local disk. If Nimbus process goes down it can failover to another Nimbus process. In slave node runs multiple worker processes and each worker process can run multiple threads. Each thread can execute one or more tasks specific to a Spout or a Bolt.

Storm can ingest data from various real time synchronous and asynchronous systems like JMS, Kafka, Shell, Twitter, etc. The ISpout interface of Storm can be implemented to potentially support any incoming data. Similarly Storm can write data to any output system using the concept of Bolt. The IBolt interface can be implemented to support any type of output system like JDBC (to store data to any relational database), Sequence Files, Hadoop components like HDFS, Hive, HBase, and other messaging system. Any complex processing requirement can be addressed by use of the Topology concept of Storm and Trident API. Storm supports guaranteed process of stream of events/messages. A Storm topology has a set of special Acker tasks that track the DAG of tuples created by every spout. When an acker sees that a DAG is complete, it sends a message to the spout task that created the spout tuple to acknowledge the message.

Storm can run on Resource Management Framework like YARN or Mesos which ensures proper resource allocation for Worker Processes. With the multi-tenant scheduler there is a way to isolate topologies of one tenant from another and also limit the resources that an individual user can have in the cluster. Storm can be configured to use Kerberos authentication. Storm can be also configured for automatic credential pushdown to workers and renewal of the same. Authorization can be set through different authorization plugins. Storm can be configured to run workers as the user who has launched the topology. A storm client may submit requests on behalf of another user. This is useful when another application (like

Oozie) submits a Storm topology. To ensure isolation of users in multi-tenancy situation headless users and unique group can be created in Supervisor nodes. Storm Cluster can be monitored based on various metrics at different levels. Individual topology can be monitored using Ganglia, Statsd, etc. JVM metrics like heap size, heap used, and GC time, etc. can be used too. There are also the metrics from the Storm framework itself, such as tuples per minute, latency, capacity, etc.

2.7.3   Kafka

Kafka [90] is a distributed, partitioned, replicated messaging service which is widely used as messaging system for streaming events. At a high level, the event producers send messages over the network to the Kafka cluster which in turn serves them up to event consumers. Typical example of event producers can be any online application which can continuously pass important transaction information for each transaction it is processing. The event consumers can be Storm, Spark Streaming, Flink Streaming, etc. which can further process that data by filtering, aggregating and eventually storing the results in some sink like HDFS, HBase, etc. Kafka ensures that no message is lost and also reprocesses the messages if needed.

The Kafka Architecture has three basic concepts to deal with. A stream of messages of a particular type is defined as a Topic. A Message is defined as a payload of bytes and a Topic is a category to which messages are published. A Producer is someone who publishes messages to a Topic. The published messages are then stored at a set of servers called Brokers. The Consumer is an entity which subscribes to one or more Topics and consumes the published Messages by pulling data from the Brokers. Since Kafka is distributed in nature, a Kafka cluster typically consists of multiple brokers. To balance the load, a topic is divided into multiple partitions and each broker stores one or more of those partitions. Multiple producers and consumers can publish and retrieve messages at the same time. Each partition is replicated to multiple brokers by a given replica factor. The Leader is the read/write broker for a partition. The Other brokers keep them in sync with Leader. ZooKeeper is used for managing and coordinating Kafka broker. Each Kafka broker is coordinating with other Kafka brokers using ZooKeeper. Producer and consumer are notified by ZooKeeper service about the presence of new broker in Kafka system or failure of the broker in Kafka system. Figure 2.16 shows the overall architecture of Kafka involving the key entities.

Kafka supports communication between the clients and the servers using the TCP protocol. The Kafka clients are available in many languages including Java, Scala, Python, etc. Kafka plans to support standard security features in future like authentication of client (i.e. consumer and producer) connections to brokers, authorization of the assorted operations that can take place over those connections, encrypting the connections, security principals representing interactive users, user groups, and long-running services. Kafka exposes JMX based metrics for monitoring.

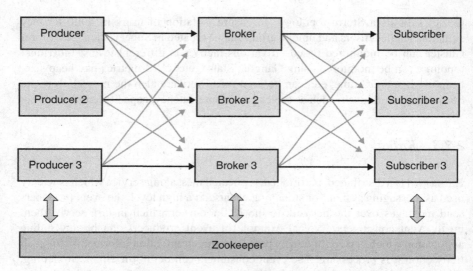

Fig. 2.16 Overall architecture of Kafka involving the key entities (Reproduced from [235])

2.7.4 Streaming Event Processing As A Service in Cloud

There are few Cloud based offerings available in Streaming Event Processing Technologies space. Few examples are Amazon's Kinesis [101], IBM's Geospatial Analytics [100], Microsoft's Stream Analytics in Azure [99], etc. The key aspects of cloud based Streaming Event Processing technologies are ability to ingest stream of events from various sources (internal and external to an enterprise) within acceptable latency, ability to push back the streaming event data to other on premise Big data stores within stipulated time, ability to pull existing data from other on premise Big data stores within reasonable timeframe, user configuration driven modeling capability for the stream processing, data security, and the pricing model (event based, infrastructure based or sometimes can be usage time based). Many a times Streaming Event Processing is implemented on Infrastructure As A Service in cloud so that the organization has full control on the technology, modeling, and integration aspects for the same. The majority of the challenges in this approach arises when there is need of merging existing data with streaming data where existing data is on premise.

2.8 Search Engines

Owing to the volume and variety of data, in the Big Data world key word(s) based Search has become a de facto standard for first level of data exploration. Various Search technologies are available in the market today in both open source world (Solr, Sphynx, Elastic, etc.) and licensed product world (IBM Watson Explorer

[241], Oracle Secure Enterprise Search [242], etc.). The heart of a search solution is indexing mechanism which can index structured and unstructured data at volume and speed. The index generated are stored in a distributed fashion in multiple nodes and a client application searches the distributed index based on the search query of the user. Few Open Source Search technologies are discussed below.

2.8.1   Apache Solr

Apache Solr [91] is an enterprise search platform built on top of the indexing engine, Apache Lucene [92]. It is a distributed indexing engine with support for load-balanced query execution, automated failover and recovery, centralized configuration and multi tenancy. Many Hadoop distributions today include Apache Solr as a part of the distribution as Solr search can be used very effectively on the data in Hadoop for initial data discovery problems.

Solr has powerful matching capabilities including phrases, wildcards, joins, grouping, etc. for any type of data Solr supports indexing of JSON, XML and CSV types of files out of the box. Solr also contains optional plugins for indexing rich content (e.g. PDFs, Word, etc.), language detection, search results clustering, etc. Solr provides large number of faceting algorithms to slice and dice data to break up search results into multiple categories, typically showing counts for each. Solr allows the user to "drill down" the search results based on those facets. Solr also provides advanced capabilities like auto-complete (type ahead search), spell checking, etc.

Figure 2.17 shows the architecture of Solr. The storage layer of Solr is used for storage of the actual Lucene index and meta data. The meta data is XML based where one can provide all the information about the data to be indexed. The indexes created can be stored in a local file system, SAN, Data Nodes of a Hadoop cluster, etc. The default Solr installation package comes with Jetty server as J2EE container. The web tier of the J2EE container provides the process space to run Solr engine to support handling multiple requests from client tier. The Solr engine, running instance of a Solr index with metadata configuration together forms the Solr core. When Solr runs in replication mode, the index replicator replicates indexes across multiple Solr cores. The master server maintains index updates, and slaves are responsible for talking with master to get them replicated. Apache Lucene core are the packages which provide core indexing functionality like reading/creating indexes, searching indexes, parsing queries, various analysis steps, ranking matched results, returning results, etc. Application layer is the web application with various UI templates based on Apache Velocity, request/response handlers, and different faceting options. Index handler handles the task of addition, updates, and deletion of data for indexing. Data Import handler integrates Solr with different data sources for indexing. To extract the contents Solr uses Apache Tika which can automatically identify the type of files (e.g. Word, Excel, or PDF) to be indexed and extracts the content. Tika can also extract document metadata such as author, title, creation

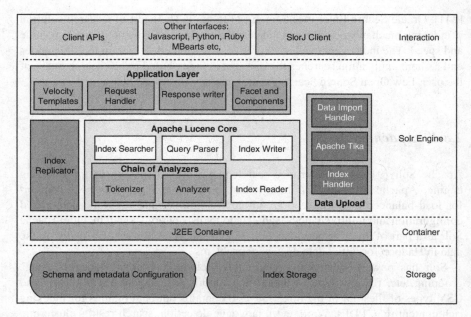

Fig. 2.17 High level architecture of Apache Solr (Reproduced from [236])

date, etc. Finally, the interaction tier provides various easy ways of interacting with Apache Solr. Apache Solr can be integrated with other various technologies using its API library and standard protocols. SolrJ, the java client for Solr enables any Java application to talk directly with Solr. JavaScript-based clients can directly integrate with Solr using JSON-based messaging. An application can also connect to an instance of Solr through HTTP.

Apache Solr provides the ability to set up a cluster of Solr servers that combines fault tolerance and high availability, called SolrCloud, The SolrCloud includes distributed indexing and search capabilities, supports central configuration for the entire cluster, automatic load balancing and fail-over for queries and ZooKeeper integration for cluster coordination and configuration. SolrCloud does not run a master node to allocate nodes, shards and replicas. Instead, it uses ZooKeeper to manage these locations, depending on configuration files and schemas. Documents can be sent to any server and ZooKeeper can figure it out.

As in case of NoSQL Databases, the Search solutions are designed for very short lived queries. So resource management is typically not part of the Search solution. However Solr can be potentially integrated with frameworks like YARN [180] and Mesos to run in the same cluster with other workloads. For Monitoring purpose Solr can expose runtime statistics as Dynamic MBeans which can be leveraged to monitor a Solr Cluster using JMX clients like Jconsole or SPM [181]. Solr does not provide any security feature either at the document level or at the communication level. Solr allows any client to add, update, search, read, and delete documents, including access to the Solr configuration, schema files and the administrative user interface. The application server containing Solr should be firewalled in a way that the only clients with access to Solr can get into the Solr cluster. Besides limiting port access to the Solr server, standard Java web security should be added by tuning the container and the configuration of the Solr web application configuration.

2.8.2   Elasticsearch

Elasticsearch [93] is a distributed, open source search and analytics engine, designed for horizontal scalability, reliability, and easy management. It is also built on top of Lucene. Elasticsearch provides features same as Solr with some additional ones like Per Operation Persistence (document changes are recorded in transaction logs on multiple nodes in the cluster to minimize the chance of any data loss), Conflict Management (Optimistic version control if needed to ensure that data is never lost due to conflicting changes from multiple processes.), Support for complex document (fields of the complex documents are indexed by default, and all the indices can be used in a single query to return complex results at a shot), etc. Elasticsearch is also integrated with various Hadoop distributions to be used for data discovery use cases.

Elastic Search provides enterprise grade capabilities for Failover. Elasticsearch clusters don't have a master node which can become single point of failure. Any node which is configured to do so (which is a default) can become a master. Thus, if a master goes down, another node will take over the role. Also, if a primary shard is not available, one replica will take over the role of the primary. For resource management in a cluster running other workloads, Elastic Search can be integrated with Mesos [183] and YARN [182]. For monitoring Elastic Search there are multiple Monitoring clients available [184].

Security solution for Elastic Search is Shield [185]. Shield is tightly integrated with Elasticsearch, verifying every request and offering the capability of user authentication and authorization. Shield supports authentication integrated with LDAP. It also lets one configure role based access control. Shield also prevents snooping or tampering by encrypting both node-to-node and client communications and also prevents unapproved hosts from joining or communicating with the cluster using IP filtering. Shield does not support encryption of data at rest. But one can use options like ecryptfs or dm-crypt to achieve that. Shield can provide complete record of all system and user activities. There by it helps to meet variety of standards related to security regulations and requirements like HIPAA, PCI DSS, FISMA, ISO, etc.

2.8.3   Sphinx Search

Sphinx Search [94] is an open source search server. Unlike Solr or Elasticsearch it uses its own indexing engine. Written in C++, Sphnyx boasts high performance and scalability numbers. It provides features similar to Solr and Elasticsearch. However it requires another database to retrieve the actual content. Sphinx Search provides

High Availability [186] and Monitoring (Sphinx Tools [187]) solution. However, Sphinx Search still does not have options for integrating with resource management tools like YARN, Mesos. For Security, Onion [188] can be used with Sphinx Search.

2.8.4 Search Technologies in Cloud

Search as a Service in Cloud is becoming a popular Software As A Service offering from various product vendors recently. The typical characteristics of this offering are around the entire lifecycle of a Search solution encompassing Uploading Content/Documents, Indexing, and Customizable user interface for Searching based on key words. Most of them also support variety of programming languages like Java, Python, .Net, etc. so that organizations can use their existing resource pool to leverage these services. The popular vendors in this area are Amazon Cloud Search [243], Elasticsearch as a Service/Found by Elastic [95], etc.

2.9 Berkeley Data Analytics Stack

Berkeley Data Analytics Stack (BDAS) [200] is comprised of a set of Big Data Frameworks that are relatively new in the industry. However, they have got vast popularity and adoption in last few years which made it worth to acknowledge them as a separate stack of promising Big Data Tools and Platforms. Primarily fueled by the research in Amp Lab in Berkeley [165], like Hadoop Ecosystem, the frameworks in BDAS are also known as Cluster Computing Frameworks. The frameworks in BDAS can provide key capabilities needed for typical Big Data requirements like fast processing of data in a cluster using memory available in various Data Nodes of cluster, storing the data in memory in a distributed fashion, management of computing resources across various types of use cases etc. Though the frameworks in BDAS implement the Big Data use cases similar to the ones addressed by Hadoop Ecosystem, BDAS frameworks are geared towards achieving the same with much smaller size of cluster and thereby reducing the cost and management overhead. Additionally, unlike Hadoop Ecosystem, BDAS can access and store data from/to local, networked or cloud based data stores (S3, NFS etc.) and other databases (Cassandra, HBase, RDBMS etc.). Also BDAS uses Analytics First approach instead of Storage First approach of Hadoop Ecosystem and other Big Data Technologies. Technologies in BDAS stack are developed ground up to support Insight creation and operationalization effort in such a way that ingested raw data first go through all complex analytics steps needed to create the Insight without requirement of any intermediate storage. The final Insight then can be stored (or pushed) to a persistent store for consumption of the same. However, many a times BDAS frameworks are also used within Hadoop Ecosystem along with other frameworks of the same. In this section we discuss the key frameworks from BDAS which are already being used in various quarts of the industry catering to the key requirements of Big Data use cases.

2.9.1   Spark

Spark is a memory based Distributed Processing Engine which can process large volume data sets with a very fast response time [11]. Spark was primarily designed for servicing iterative machine learning algorithms and interactive queries on large volume data sets [12].

The heart of Spark is the concept of Memory Based Distributed Data Sets, namely Resilient Distributed Dataset (RDD) [17] to store the data in memory. RDD is created either when data is read from underlying data store or as a result of applying any transformation logic. RDD is the collection of data partitions across various nodes along with lineage information. Data is not replicated here. Instead whenever a node goes down, Spark re-computes the data based on lineage information. Spark also can spill the data in local storage in case the memory is not sufficient. Currently work is going on in designing IndexedRDD which can support efficient fine-grained updates for RDDs. Spark exposes another high level abstraction for defining and processing data sets which is called DataFrames [199]. The DataFrame is a distributed collection of data organized into named columns. It essentially abstracts various types of RDDs depending on the context. It is conceptually equivalent to a table in a relational database or a data frame in R/Python, but with richer optimizations under the hood. DataFrames can be constructed from structured data files, tables in Hive, external databases, or existing RDDs. Spark has recently introduced another abstraction to deal with distributed data, namely Dataset. The key benefit of Datasets is the structure awareness which helps in better performance and resource utilization. Datasets represent strongly-typed, immutable collection of objects mapped to a relational schema. DataSet APIs support high level functional transformation capabilities of RDDs as well as full set of relational constructs of Dataframes. In future Datasets can potentially become the single interface in Spark for handling all types of structured data.

The key data formats supported by Spark are Delimited Files (CSV files), Parquet Format, and Sequence Files (JSON data format). Spark also supports the popular compression techniques in Hadoop Ecosystem like gZip, Snappy, LZO, etc. However, Spark's interface for reading and writing data is open enough so that anyone can easily develop data reading/writing component for Spark corresponding to any custom need. Spark supports variety of programming language interfaces like Scala, Python, Java and R. Spark provides extensive repositories of in built constructs in these languages for various types of transformation jobs. Spark also supports custom ones using the concept of passing Functions to Spark.

Spark can cater to various types of workloads namely Stream Processing, SQL, Graph Processing and also Machine Learning for Modeling within a single platform. Spark internally uses various concepts of Distributed Processing Engines like Map

Reduce, DAG based processing and Bulk Synchronous Parallel. The data processing speed of Spark is many times faster than other Distributed Processing Engines. Latest benchmarking test [135] showed that using 206 machines with around 6600 cores Daytona GraySort [134] test, which involves sorting 100 terabytes of data, can be done in Spark in 23 min. It supersedes the previous record set by Yahoo, which used a 2100-node Hadoop cluster and Map Reduce with more than 50,000 cores to complete the test (on 102.5 terabytes) in 72 min. Given these aspects Spark is becoming a very promising alternative to other Distributed Processing Engines namely Map Reduce, Tez, etc.

Though Spark can use data residing in Hadoop but it is a much generic platform which can read data from any underlying data storage like Local File Server/NFS, Cassandra, Amazon S3, etc. Spark can also run on Tachyon (discussed later in this chapter). It can also ingest streaming data from various sources like Flume, Kafka, Twitter, ZeroMQ and TCP sockets itself.

Spark can run on various resource management frameworks like YARN or Mesos (discussed later in this chapter). In addition to that, Spark can also run in a simple standalone deploy mode. By default, standalone scheduling clusters are resilient to Worker failures (as Spark itself is resilient to losing work by moving it to other workers). However, the scheduler uses a Master to make scheduling decisions, and this can create the situation of single point of failure. If the Master crashes, no new applications can be created. In order to circumvent this one can use ZooKeeper to provide leader election and some storage for states. If Spark runs on a resource management framework like YARN or Mesos (discussed later in this chapter) the high availability of scheduler is managed by the same.

Spark supports showing metrics of a running application as well as storing the same for history. Every SparkContext launches a web UI that displays useful information about the application including list of scheduler stages and tasks, summary of RDD sizes and memory usage, environmental information and information about the running executors. It is also possible to visualize the metrics of a finished application through Spark's history server, if the application's event logs exist. In addition to viewing the metrics in the UI, they are also available as JSON files. Spark has a configurable metrics system based on the Coda Hale Metrics Library. This allows users to report Spark metrics to a variety of sinks including HTTP, JMX, and CSV files. Several external tools can be used to help monitoring the performance of Spark jobs. Examples are Ganglia (can provide insight into overall cluster utilization and resource bottlenecks), OS profiling tools such as dstat, iostat, and iotop (can provide fine-grained profiling on individual nodes), JVM utilities such as jstack for providing stack traces, jmap for creating heap-dumps, jstat for reporting time-series statistics and Jconsole for visually exploring various JVM properties, etc.

Spark supports authentication between the client and server via a shared secret. The Spark UI can be secured by using the configuration at the web servlet level. Spark supports two types of ACLs for the UIs—View and Modify (to start running or killing applications). Once a user is logged into a Spark UI, Spark can decide the access right based on these ACLs. Spark supports security for the event logs stored for history server based on file permission.

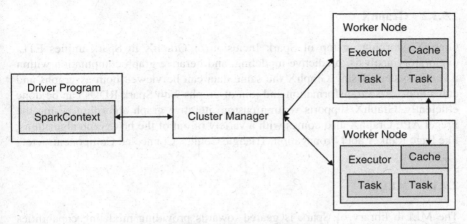

Fig. 2.18 General architecture of Spark's Distributed Processing Engine (Reproduced from [237])

Figure 2.18 shows the general architecture of Spark's Distributed Processing Engine. The Spark Context is the driver/controller program that helps the client program to connect to the Hardware Cluster where Spark is deployed. Cluster Manager creates the appropriate executor/slave processes in the Data Nodes and delegates the tasks to them.

Here are the details of various Application Components specific to Spark which are the corner stones for enterprise grade applications built on Spark.

2.9.1.1   Spark SQL

Spark SQL helps in accessing data, as a distributed dataset (Dataframe) in Spark, using SQL. The Spark SQL can be used as integrated API in Python, Scala, Java or R. This also supports execution of SQL statements from a JDBC/ODBC client. This tight integration at programming language level makes it easy to run SQL queries alongside complex analytic algorithms or stream processing or graph processing. The concept of DataFrame provides a single interface for efficiently working with various types of structured data, including Apache Hive tables, parquet files and JSON files. Spark SQL reuses the Hive front end and meta store, ensuring full compatibility with existing Hive data, queries, and UDFs.

Blink DB [204] and Sample Clean [205] are two projects currently in development which will run on Spark SQL. BlinkDB is a massively parallel, approximate query engine for running interactive SQL queries on large volume of data. It allows users to trade-off between query accuracy for response time, enabling interactive queries over massive data by running queries on data samples. Blink DB presents results annotated with meaningful error bars. Sample Clean runs on BlinkDB to automate data cleaning using the Pipeline concept. SampleClean implements a set of interchangeable and composable physical and logical data cleaning operators. This allows for quick construction and adaptation of data cleaning pipelines.

2.9.1.2 GraphX

GraphX, working on top of Spark Inclusion of GraphX in Spark unifies ETL, exploratory analysis, predictive modeling, and iterative graph computation within a single system. Using GraphX the same data can be viewed both as graphs and collections. Also transformation and join of graphs with Spark RDDs can be done efficiently. GraphX supports writing custom iterative graph algorithms using the Pregel API. GraphX also comes with a variety of out of the box graph algorithms, like Page Rank, Label Propagation, Triangle Counts, Connected Components, etc.

2.9.1.3 MLLib

The MLLib library of Spark is geared towards providing modeling capabilities on data ingested from any data store. It leverages Spark's efficiency in iterative computation. Spark MLLib supports many out of the box Machine Learning algorithms providing fast modeling capabilities because of memory based iterations for convergence. Spark MLLib can be used along with Spark SQL, Spark Graph and Spark Streaming within the same Java, Scala or Python code.

2.9.1.4 ML Pipeline

In Machine Learning, it is common to run a sequence of steps and algorithms to process and learn from data. For example, a simple text document processing workflow might include several stages like splitting each document's text into words, converting each document's words into a numerical feature vector, learning a prediction model using the feature vectors and labeling the same. Spark ML Pipeline [203] represents such workflow as a Pipeline, which consists of a sequence of Pipeline Stages (Transformers and Estimators) to be run in a specific order. An important task in Machine Learning is model selection or tuning which is essentially using the data to find the best model. ML Pipelines also facilitates this model selection process using the Cross Validation approach.

2.9.1.5 Splash

Stochastic learning algorithms are algorithms that process a large dataset by processing random samples of the datasets in sequence. Their per-iteration computation cost is independent of the overall size of the datasets. Hence stochastic learning algorithms are very efficient in the analysis of large-scale data. However, stochastic learning algorithms are difficult to parallelize as they are typically defined as sequential procedures.

The Splash [202] component running on top of Spark is a general framework for parallelizing stochastic learning algorithms on multi-node clusters. One can develop a stochastic algorithm using the Splash programming interface without worrying about issues of distributed computing. The parallelization is automatic and it is efficient.

2.9.1.6   SparkR

SparkR is an R package that provides a light-weight front end to use Apache Spark from R. SparkR provides a distributed data frame implementation that supports operations like selection, filtering, aggregation, etc. (similar to R data frames, dplyr) but on large datasets. DataFrames can be constructed from a wide array of sources such as structured data files, tables in Hive, external databases, or existing local R DataFrames. A SparkR DataFrame can also be registered as a temporary table in Spark SQL and registering a DataFrame as a table allows one to run SQL queries over its data.

2.9.1.7   System ML

Apache SystemML [227], originally from IBM Research Lab, is an open source project for Machine Learning that can run on Spark. It is an alternative to Spark's MLLib. SystemML supports flexible specification of Machine Learning algorithms in a declarative way. It also supports automatic generation of hybrid runtime plans ranging from single node in-memory computations to Distributed Processing Engines like Map Reduce or Spark. Machine Learning algorithms are expressed in an R-like syntax that includes linear algebra primitives, statistical functions, and Machine Learning specific constructs. This high-level language significantly increases the productivity of data scientists as it provides full flexibility in expressing custom analytics, and also independence from the underlying input formats and physical data representations. Automatic optimization of runtime execution plan according to the data and cluster characteristics ensures efficiency and scalability. Compared to existing Machine Learning libraries which mostly provide fixed algorithms and runtime plans, SystemML provides flexibility to define custom analytics and execution plans.

2.9.1.8   Spark Streaming

Spark Streaming [130] helps writing streaming jobs through the use of Spark's language-integrated APIs in Java, Scala and Python. Out of the box, Spark streaming provides stateful exactly-once semantics and capability to recover both lost work and operator state. As integrated with Spark ecosystem, one can run integrated code comprised of intercepting and processing streaming events, running queries on the result of processed streaming events, and also creation of predictive models on the data mashed up from processed streaming events and existing corpus of data from data stores like Hadoop. DStream is the representation of a continuous stream of data in Spark Streaming. It contains a sequence of RDDs. DStreams are createdfrom input data streams from sources. They can also be created by applying high-level operations on other DStreams. When a Spark Streaming program runs it creates a DStream after each time it gets data from the source and it generates a RDD out of that.

2.9.2 Velox

Though Velox is still an incubating project it is still worth mentioning here as Velox aims to address one of the most important aspects of Machine Learning. So far enough work has happened (and still going on) in the industry to support creation of complex models using large datasets for addressing requirements like personalized recommendations, targeted advertising, fraud management, sales prediction, etc. However, not much of work has happened for the deployment, management and serving prediction requests using the models. Velox [206], is an incubating framework in Berkeley Data Analytics Stack which aims to address this issue. It is a framework for facilitating online model management, maintenance, and prediction serving, bridging the gap between off line model creation and online prediction by the model.

2.9.3 Flink

Apache Flink [89] is another Distributed Processing Component and is very similar to Spark. Though it is not officially part of BDAS, but it can run on other frameworks of BDAS just like Spark. Flink is also a platform for distributed general-purpose data processing with programming abstractions in Java and Scala. Stream computing is fundamental to Flink's approach for distributed data processing. Every job in Flink is treated as Stream Computation, batch processing being a special case with a large Streaming window. Flink executes tasks as cyclic data flow with multiple iterations. Flink supports two iteration related operations, namely Iterator and Delta Iterator, to perform iterations while executing a task. Like Spark, Flink also supports local files, HDFS, S3, JDBC and Tachyon based persistence. The Datasets in Flink is someway equivalent to RDD in Spark. Flink can run in Standalone mode or on resource management component like YARN. The work is going on for supporting Mesos as resource management system for Flink. High Availability of Flink in Standalone mode can be ensured using ZooKeeper. The Application Components associated with Flink can be used for Graph Processing (Gelly), Machine Learning (Flink MLLib), Streaming (Flink Streaming) and Relational Queries (Table API).

2.9.4   Tachyon

Tachyon, though pretty new in the BDAS, has already generated considerable interests and adoption base across various consumer groups of Big Data Technologies. Tachyon is essentially a memory based distributed file system which enables reliable data sharing at memory-speed for Distributed Processing Components like Spark, Flink, Map Reduce, etc. Tachyon caches working set of files in memory, thereby avoiding going to disk to load datasets that are frequently read. This enables different jobs/queries from same or different technologies (Spark, Flink, Map Reduce etc.) to access and share the same data available in the memory. This also saves frameworks like Spark, Flink, Map Reduce from recreation (or replication) of the datasets in memory to address the situation of node failure as the same is handled at Tachyon's level.

Tachyon is a very active open source project with more than 60 contributors from over 20 institutions, including Yahoo, Intel, and Redhat. Tachyon is already being used in more than 50 companies, some of which have deployed Tachyon with more than 100 nodes in production. Among them the internet web service company, Baidu, is a notable example.

Tachyon distributes the data in blocks which is the unit of partition. However, instead of replicating the data Tachyon uses lineage information to reconstruct the data if a data block is lost because of node failure. Tachyon uses Edge Algorithm [190] to achieve the same which is developed based on three key ideas like checkpoints the edge of the lineage graph, favoring the high-priority files over low-priority ones for check pointing and finally, caching the datasets to avoid synchronous check pointing. Like HDFS Tachyon is also Data Format agnostic and can support all Data Formats discussed in Common Technical Concepts and Patterns section. Tachyon relies on other storage system to persist data which is called UnderFS storage system. The UnderFS storage system can be any storage system like HDFS, S3, SAN, GlusterFS etc. Tachyon provides two sets of APIs— native Java File like API and HDFS API. Fail over of master node in Tachyon is addressed by use of ZooKeeper. Tachyon does not have much support for monitoring right now apart from exposing some basic metrics around ramfs, network (client and server), worker status, block misses, etc. Tachyon reuses security infrastructure of the underlying persistence store like HDFS, S3, etc. Currently Tachyon does not support ACL but due in forthcoming version.

2.9.5   Succinct

Succinct [201] is a data store that enables efficient queries directly on a compressed representation of the underlying data. Succinct uses a compression technique that achieves compression close to that of Gzip which can still allow random access into the input data. In addition, Succinct natively supports a wide range of queries including count and search of arbitrary strings, range, and wildcard queries. Succinct supports these queries without storing any secondary indexes, without requiring data scans and without decompressing the data. All of the required information is embedded within the compressed representation and queries are performed directly on the compressed representation. As a base API, Succinct exposes a simple interface that supports above queries on flat files. Applications that perform queries on semi-structured data can extend this API to build higher-level data representations. On real-world datasets, Succinct has proven that it requires 12 times less memory compared to other similar systems. Succinct is able to push more data in memory, and hence can help in achieving lower latency in query execution up to three orders of magnitude compared to other similar systems.

2.9.6 Apache Mesos

Apache Mesos [166] is the popular resource management framework in BDAS. It is also many a times used with other Big Data Technologies like Hadoop, Search, Streaming Event Processing Technologies, etc. Mesos abstracts CPU, memory, storage, and other compute resources away from machines (physical or virtual). This helps in building and running fault tolerant distributed system with elasticity. Mesos is built using the same principles as the Linux kernel, only at a different level of abstraction. The Mesos kernel runs on every machine and provides applications (e.g., Map Reduce, Spark, Kafka, Elasticsearch, etc.) with API's for resource management and scheduling across entire datacenter and cloud environments. Mesos scalability is already proven to 10,000 s of nodes. Mesos uses ZooKeeper for high availability. The architecture of Mesos is very similar to Apache YARN. Mesos runs a master daemon that manages slave daemons running on each cluster node. The applications/frameworks (like Spark, Map Reduce etc.) run tasks on these slaves. Figure 2.19 describes the resource distribution architecture of Mesos with the examples of Slave 1 and Slave 2 serving two frameworks (same as Application Components) namely Framework 1 and Framework 2. The sequence of steps is shown as the step numbers on the arrows. In the step 1, Slave 1 informs the master availability of 4 CPUs and 4 GB memory. In step 2, Master identifies that Framework 1 should be given highest priority for utilization of the resources based on the allocation policy (obtained from Allocation Module) and offers the same. In response, Framework 1, in step 3 notifies the master to run 2 tasks on Slave 1 (one with 2 CPU and 1 GB and other with 1 CPU and 2 GB). Finally, in step 4, master launches those two tasks in Slave 1. The remaining 1 CPU and 1 GB resource available in Slave 1 is now open for Master to allocate to any other framework based on allocation policy. The framework may decide to use that resource or not based on availability of the data in that particular node. This process continuous as and when resources are available in a Slave for use by the frameworks.

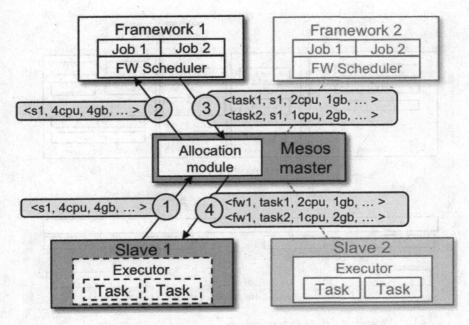

Fig. 2.19 Resource Distribution architecture of Mesos (Reproduced from [238])

2.9.7 The Overall Berkley Data Analytics Stack

The various layers of BDAS shown in Fig. 2.20 are discussed below.

- The Distributed File System Components help storing and accessing the data from various data storage solution like HDFS, S3, SAN etc. They also help multiple Distributed Processing Components (like Spark, Map Reduce, Flink etc.) to access the data stored in the memory.
- The Distributed Processing Components help in actual processing of the data in multiple hardware nodes by utilizing the computation power of each node in parallel. The prime candidates here are Spark and Flink. However in future other frameworks like Map Reduce (denoted as ** because it is future possibility) can also utilize the same as Tachyon supports complete set of HDFS APIs.
- The Application Components provide necessary abstractions over Distributed Processing Components so that the later can be used for different Big Data use cases around Interactive Queries, Streaming, Modeling, and Graph Processing, etc. The Application Components denoted as * are the ones still under development.
- The API layer is the layer which supports common interfaces like SQL, Java, R, Scala, and Python so that the data can be easily accessed from and integrated with other enterprise tools and technologies. We have discussed about the Notebooks later in this chapter.

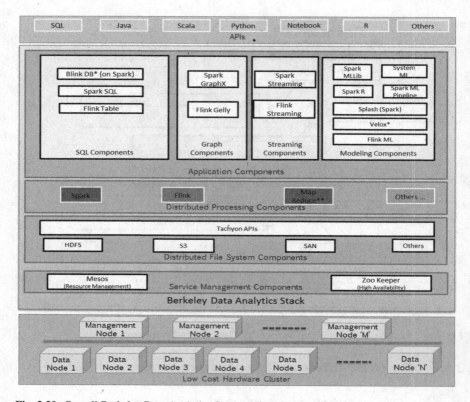

Fig. 2.20 Overall Berkeley Data Analytics Stack with all frameworks together

- The Service Management Components help in managing the services for high availability, dynamic resource prioritization, and distribution.

2.9.8 BDAS in Cloud

Among the various frameworks of BDAS so far only Spark has few implementations in cloud as 'Spark As A Service'. Front runners among those services are the service from Databricks [207] and from Qubole [208], and IBM's Analytics for Apache Spark [209]. Most of these offerings support Notebook based interface for data exploration using Spark. Use of frameworks of BDAS in Cloud is primarily advantageous from the data exploration perspective. These offerings help organizations to explore their data without the need for buying and installing multiple nodes Big Data cluster or impacting a current cluster in production. Once the data exploration is done and the target insight is defined the same can be implemented on premise.

2.10   Analytics and Reporting Tools

The business benefits of Big Data revolve around three steps. The first step is exploration of the 'known unknowns' and 'unknown unknowns' using adhoc queries, search, text extraction, and modeling techniques on small to large volume of data from various types of data sources. In the second step, the results from the first step are used to create various Aggregates, Cubes and Models commonly termed as Business Insights. Finally these insights are used in various types of Reports like Canned Reports, Adhoc Reports, and Interactive Dashboards. The technologies and tools used covering these steps are commonly termed as Analytics and Reporting tools. There are various types of Analytics and Reporting tools and technologies available in the market as discussed below.

Tools and Technologies for Data Exploration Step

- SQL clients which can be used for data exploration using SQL syntax (e.g. command line SQL tools, Toad, Eclipse, etc.)
- Spreadsheet like interface (e.g. Microsoft Excel, IBM's Big Sheets, etc.) which can connect to the Big Data Technologies using JDBC/ODBC, REST or other relevant protocols.
- Web based interfaces of Search Technologies to identify occurrences of key words in various data sources
- Using Text Extraction tools (like Gate, IBM Text Analytics, etc.) to extract relevant texts from various data sources and identify sentiment, affinity, etc. out of them.
- Modeling tools like R, Big R, SPSS, SAS, etc. to experiment with various predictive models to define the ones best applicable for the data being explored.
- Interactive shell like Spark's shell or Flink's shell which can be used to interactively explore the data
- The newest addition to this list is the web based Notebooks. Notebooks are web based interactive interface which can be used to ingest data, explore data, visualize data, creating small reports out of the results, sharing and collaborating on insights, etc. Currently Jupyter [213] Notebooks provide interface with Spark. The other incubating Notebook project is Apache Zeppelin [214] which supports Spark (Scala, Java, Python and Spark SQL), Flink, and Hive.

Tools and Technologies for Insight Creation Step

- Embedded SQLs like Stored Procedures, Custom Scripts, etc. are used to create Aggregates, Cubes etc. on regular basis. Hadoop Ecosystem provides tools like Hive, Big SQL, Pig which can be named under this category. Data Warehousing Appliances too provide features like Stored Procedures. In case of BDAS, Sprak and Flink, provide Java, Scala, Python and R interface which can be used to embed SQL in a functional programming model (this facility is something equivalent to use of stored procedures). The jobs created in this way can be run in a regular manner using a scheduler.

- Reporting Tools like SAS [244], SPSS [245], Microstrategy [246], etc. can also support creation of aggregates and cubes in their own ways.
- Modeling tools like R, Big R, SPSS, SAS, etc use data to create predictive models on regular basis as defined in Data Exploration Step

Tools and Technologies used for Reporting Step

- Tools like SAP Business Intelligence Solutions [247], IBM Cognos Software [248], Microstrategy, Tableau [249], JasperSoft [250], Pentaho [251], etc. to create Canned Reports for regular consumption of the Business Executives, Support Groups etc. and Adhoc Reports on demand based on special situational needs
- Various types of Dashboards (custom or the ones available from Reporting Tools like Business objects, Cognos, Microstrategy, Tableau, Pentaho, etc.) for Interactive data exploration with capabilities of drilling down from macro level information to micro level details.
- The tools, which bring the next generation of innovation in this area, are commonly known as Narrative Generation Platforms. These platforms have the capability to translate meaning and implications of the results from Big data Analytics to the business users. These tools and services around them typically use Natural Language Generation [102] technology on top of the Big Data Technologies. The software which are looking to be promising in this area are Quill from Narrative Science [103], Wordsmith Platform from Automated Insights [104], Arria NLG Engine from Aria, etc [105].

The Analytics and Modeling tools listed above can use data in various Big Data Technologies in multiple ways as discussed below.

2.10.1   Accessing Data from Hadoop Ecosystem

For Hadoop Ecosystem JDBC/ODBC interface is the primary means of connectivity. The JDBC/ODBC connection to Hadoop Ecosystem happens through the frameworks like Hive, Big SQL, Impala or Drill, using the JDBC/ODBC drivers provided by them. The technologies like Tableau, JasperSoft, Microstrategy, Cognos and Business Objects have already shown reasonable integration with Hadoop Ecosystem. Modeling Tools like Mahout, RHadoop, System ML, Big R, SPSS internally use Map Reduce, Spark and other Distributed Processing Engines of Hadoop Ecosystem, for creating the model on the data within the Hadoop Cluster instead of bringing the data outside. Text Extraction tools also use the Map Reduce, Spark and other Distributed Processing Components. Spreadsheet application like Big Sheets use REST based interface to internally execute data processing within Hadoop using Map Reduce and other Distributed Processing Components. Sometimes custom scripts (like Pig Scripts) are used too for this purpose.

2.10.2   Accessing Data from Berkeley Data Analytics Stack (BDAS)

The primary interface in BDAS is functional programming model (using Scala, java, Python, R) with supported APIs for processing data. Using this model one can mix multiple big data components like SQL, Streaming, Graph Processing, Machine Learning in the same program. This can be done in an interactive way through the interactive shell or web based Notebooks for data exploration purpose. Alternatively these programs can be called as jobs in a scheduled manner at regular fashion for Insight Creation or Reporting. BDAS also supports JDBC/ODBC interface as the additional means of data access and processing. The JDBC/ODBC connection to BDAS happens through the frameworks like Spark SQL, Flink Table, BlinkDB, etc. using the JDBC/ODBC drivers provided by them.

2.10.3   Accessing Data from Data Warehouse Systems

Like Hadoop Ecosystem, for Data Warehouse Applications also the primary way to connect to the data is JDBC/ODBC interface. For building Models on the data within the Data Warehousing Appliances some of the products in this category support native integration between the Modeling Tool and the Data Warehouse Systems (e.g. Netezza with SPSS and R).

2.10.4   Accessing Data from NoSQL Databases

Accessing data from NoSQL solutions using SQL is complex. For accessing data from HBase, there is SQL interface available through IBM Big SQL and Apache Phoenix [132]. The SQL connector from Simba Technologies can be used to get data from HBase, Cassandra and MongoDB using SQL. Tableau, Micro Strategy, and SAP Crystal Reports (from SAP Business Intelligence Solutions) uses the same for connecting to Cassandra and MongoDB. Other tools like Cognos, SAP Business Objects (from SAP Business Intelligence Solutions), etc. can also potentially use the same. JasperSoft has custom connectors for getting data out of HBase, MongoDB and Cassandra.

2.10.5 Accessing Data from in Memory Databases

Most of the In Memory Databases support SQL based connectivity (e.g. Hazelcast, Gem Fire, Terracota BigMemory, SAP Hana, IBM DB2 Blu, Oracle Timesten etc.). For others using language specific API is the primary way to access the data.

2.10.6 Accessing Data from Streaming Event Processing Technologies

Some of the Streaming Technologies (IBM Stream, Spark Streaming, etc.) support processing requirements like Text Extraction, Model creation, Aggregation, Filtering, etc. on streaming data for a given sliding window. Typically after processing the streaming events are stored in Hadoop Ecosystem or Data Warehouse Systems and then the data can be accessed from there using JDBC/ODBC.

2.10.7 Accessing Data from Search Technologies

For accessing data from Search Technologies the primary methodology is to use Search APIs specific to the particular Search tool using the languages like Java, Python, C++, etc.

2.10.8 Big Data Analytics As A Service

In today's market, various solution providers have offerings around different flavors of Analytics As A Service which can be used by their customers to derive analytics from their data with least effort at their side. The first variety of the offerings is where customers provide the data and the solution provider uses their tools and services to generate the insights customers are looking for. This is probably the most happening space in Big Data where solution providers are trying to provide solutions to domain specific problems using their tools and services around that. The examples of such companies are Platfora, Opera Software, Attivio, Palantir, Alpine Data labs etc. The next variation of Analytics As A Service is where typically the solution providers expose various APIs and Tools which can be used by the customers to ingest the data as well as define the custom analytics suitable to the specific needs. The examples of such companies range from big giants like Google, IBM, Microsoft to the startups like Datameer, Concurrent, WibiData, Zoom Data, DataRobot, etc. The third variation of the offerings is from system integration service companies who provide Analytics Service by selecting best suitable tools available in the market for the specific customer need. Here again the examples range from biggies like Accenture, IBM Global Service, Delloit, Infosys, Capgemini etc. to boutique companies like Impetus, Cloudwick, etc.

2.11 Data Integration and Governance Technologies

Data Integration and Governance Technologies help moving data from one Big Data Technology to another across various stages of data processing pipeline. Typically the components of this genre are used at enterprise level for any data integration and governance requirement and they are external to any Database or Data processing systems. Organization uses these components to integrate and govern the data across multiple Database systems.

For Big Data use cases the Data Integration and Governance Technologies typically cater to the following requirements.

2.11.1 Scalable and Flexible Data Movement

This requirement addresses the need to import/export data to/from various data sources or to/from one Big Data Technology to other (say from Hadoop Ecosystem or BDAS to Data Warehouse Systems) as File or directly ingesting data in a Table. The key features covered by this requirement are—UI based Data Mapping across source and target system, Ability to externalize the transformation Rules through UI framework, Ability to support transformation rules covering ANSI SQL syntax, Analytic Functions, User Defined functions, etc., Ability to support high volume of data movement in a scalable way, Ability to push down actual execution of transformation rule completely to the Big Data Technologies (like Hadoop, Data Warehousing Appliances etc.) when all data resides there, Ability to optimize the transformation process intelligently by deciding the right place to execute different steps (this is important when the data tables involved in transformation reside in multiple Big Data Technologies), Ability to support variety of relational Data Sources—Oracle, SQL Server, Informix, SAP etc as a target import/export data source, Ability to support variety of non-relational data files—XML, JSON, delimited Flat files, etc., Ability to support various protocols for data ingestion from source systems—JDBC, SFTP, REST, JMS, Custom (like SAP's custom function call), etc. and Effective error reporting.

2.11.2 Workflow

This requirement addresses the need for execution of various steps involved in an end to end data flow covering data import, data transformation and data export across various Big Data Technologies. The key features covered under this requirement are—Ability to break up workflow in multiple tasks and sub tasks, Support for scheduling, Support for execution of various types of tasks—SQL execution, REST based task execution, Command line based task execution, Effective error reporting and Restartability of a part of the Workflow.

2.11.3 Governance

This requirement addresses the need to govern the Metadata, Data Lifecycle, Policies/Rules, and Access Control. The key features covered under this requirement are—Metadata management and Lineage, Data Lifecycle Management using Policies, Business Glossary definition and management, Data Modeling capability, Data Discovery capability, Data Quality and Cleansing capability, Fine grained user access control on database objects, Fine grained exception monitoring, and Support for Detailed Activity Reports.

As discussed before in this chapter, Hadoop Ecosystem comes with its own frameworks supporting many of these requirements. However, typically an over-arching framework is needed which can address these requirements across all Big Data Technologies and other database technologies within an organization. The licensed tools like Informatica [168], IBM Information Server suits [167], Cisco Tidal [152], etc. are examples of such technologies which can cater to these requirements. In open source world Talend [145], Pentaho Community Edition [146], etc. are also popular for addressing the similar requirements. Many of these frameworks internally use the integration mechanisms supported by Hadoop Ecosystem, BDAS, Data Warehouse Systems and other Big Data Technologies. The protocols/mechanisms widely used for this purpose are JDBC/ODBC, REST, and Remote Script Execution.

2.11.4 Data Integration and Governance As A Service

Some product vendors like Informatica [112], Snaplogic [96] have started providing data integration as a service in cloud. This helps an enterprise in getting rid of overhead of managing data integration tools in terms of configuration, availability, performance etc. However, moving the data from on premise to cloud and vice-versa can be big overhead from overall performance perspective. An approach to address that problem is to have the deployment of Data Integration tool on premise of the enterprise but still being managed by the product vendor completely.

2.12 Applying Big Data Tools and Platforms in Implementation of Big Data Use Cases

At the implementation level Big Data use cases can be categorized in five different Implementation Use Cases, namely Data Ingestion, Data Exploration, Insight Creation, Data Consumption and Data Archival & Purging. Here below we discuss these Implementation Use Cases and their mapping to various core Big Data Tools and Platforms. These Implementation Use Cases are stitched together by Data Integration and Governance Technologies in various combinations to satisfy the needs of specific business use cases and eventually consumed by the Analytics and Reporting Tools.

2.12.1 Data Ingestion

This involves steps for getting the data into Big Data Technologies for storage and processing. Typically, any data, structured or unstructured, gets ingested in Hadoop Ecosystem (in HDFS as files or as Hive Table). Then the same gets transformed and aggregated with the use of tools like Hive, Pig, etc. of Hadoop Ecosystem. Alternatively, the data can also get ingested in BDAS directly and aggregates can be created there for Real Time Data analytics (also known as Fast Data Analytics). The raw data and the aggregates created in BDAS are stored back to HDFS. The aggregates created in Hadoop Ecosystem or BDAS are eventually moved to Data Warehouse Systems or NoSQL Databases or In Memory Databases based on the consumption need of the data.

There are two ways this data ingestion can happen either to Hadoop Ecosystem or BDAS. Firstly in a batch manner big files get ingested to Hadoop Ecosystem or BDAS on a regular frequency of hourly daily, weekly etc. Typically this happens through the use of the data import tools (like Sqoop, Hive's import facility, etc.) of Hadoop Ecosystem and various data ingestion adapters (like adapters for jdbc, json, parquet, etc.) of BDAS. Secondly, the streaming data (like application logs, online transaction, real time social media data from etc.) of small volume gets ingested in real time (at sub second level) or near real time (at seconds or minutes level). The streaming data first gets intercepted by Stream Processing Frameworks where data filtering, aggregation etc. happens for a given stream processing window (time based, attribute based or event based etc.). After that the result of the same gets stored in Hadoop Ecosystem (in HDFS as files or directly as Hive table). Alternatively streaming data can also get ingested to BDAS framework through Streaming Component of BDAS framework.

Please note that the data written to NoSQL Databases/In Memory Databases typically get accessed by online applications. Also data generated within these systems get ingested back to the Big Data Platform either as batch file or streaming data.

2.12.2 Data Exploration

This involves analysis and modeling of data for defining various types of insights.

This is the use case which is predominantly executed by Data Scientists/Data Analysts. This begins with the investigation of raw data to figure out what all information is there and figure out the attributes which can be used to create business insights. After that Business Insights (aggregates and models) are created on experimental basis. These experimental models and aggregates are then plugged into the business processes for serving recommendations/predictions, creating reports, showing the data in dashboard, etc. to check how useful they are.

The SQL based tools are the most widely used tools for this step. However this step can also involve search tools for key words based data exploration from structured/semi-structured/unstructured data ingested. Use of modeling tool is also prevalent for creation of experimental models for prediction/recommendation across various data sources. Before creating Predictive Models sometimes Text Extraction Tools are used to extract key words, sentiments, inclinations etc. from the unstructured/semi structured data. Those insights are further used to create the models. The Data Modeling Tools (discussed before in this chapter) can be typically used to create the models on the raw data or transformed data in Hadoop Ecosystem or BDAS without moving the data out at the level of modeling tool. Graph Processing tools are also used sometimes to support the entities which are related based on networked data structure (e.g. friends connected in social media, buyers/sellers/financial institute relationship in bidding sites, etc.).

Apart from these tools, the latest trend is the use of web based Notebooks which can be used to do all these steps from a single interface and the same also can be shared with others for validation, tuning or socialization purpose.

The data sources used in this step are the ones already ingested in Data Ingestion step. The raw data ingested in ingestion step are also sometimes merged with aggregates/models created previously for the exploration purpose. The exploration processes gets executed in Hadoop Ecosystem or BDAS.

2.12.3 Insight Creation

This involves steps for creating insights on regular basis based on the results from Data Exploration steps. The similar set of tools is used in this case as in the case of Data Exploration. However insights are created at regular basis and get used in the business process for decision making, predictions, and recommendations. The effectiveness of the insights is measured and monitored on regular basis too to ensure necessary change/tuning wherever needed. In this step, the relevant data insights are moved from Hadoop Ecosystem/BDAS to Data Warehouse Systems, NoSQL Databases, In Memory Databases and Search Technologies as required. However, many a times the data insights can be accessed from Hadoop Ecosystem/BDAS directly.

2.12.4   Data Consumption

This involves consumption of data from Big Data Technologies through various data consumption modes like Interactive Queries, Scheduled Reports, Real Time High Throughput Data Read, and Data Export which are discussed below.

The insights available in Hadoop Ecosystem (in HDFS as files or as Hive Table), Data Warehouse Systems, BDAS, NoSQL Databases or In Memory Databases can be accessed by *Interactive Queries* from Reporting tools which provide the user capability to interactively consume the data from higher to lower level of granularities in a drill down manner. Sometimes this access can even happen from other enterprise applications which need to get the data for some other needs like showing the data in a web site. The protocol of access can be SQL if the data is accessed from Hive Table, BDAS or Data Warehousing Appliances. For other databases (NoSQL or In Memory Databases) the access protocol can be non SQL ones (like database specific APIs in Java, Thrift or other languages, HTTP/Rest, R, etc.). Sometimes Reporting Tools like Dashboards can directly get data from Streaming Event Processing Technologies though Message Queues or relational databases. The response time for these implementation use cases needs to be within couple of seconds as the user actually waits for the result.

Another mode of consumption can be *Scheduled Reports*. Scheduled Reports will typically use Analytics and Reporting Tools to get the Insights (Aggregates, Cubes, and sometimes Cleaned raw Data) from Data Warehouse Systems and Hadoop Ecosystem/BDAS.

Real Time High Throughput Data Read requests (from other applications in enterprise) can access the data available in Big Data stores using SQL or non SQL APIs. For reading the data at a very high throughput NoSQL or In Memory Databases are used. The data written to the NoSQL or In memory Databases can be eventually moved to Hadoop Ecosystem (in HDFS files or as Hive Tables) or BDAS either as batch data or streaming data.

Sometimes the *Data Export* may need to happen to other systems/applications in enterprise from either of the Big Data Technologies like Hadoop Ecosystem, BDAS, NoSQL Databases, In Memory Databases, or Data Warehouse Systems. This·is typically done by using SQL based export utilities like Sqoop or any other technology specific utility.

2.12.5   Data Archival and Purging

This involves moving the old data (raw, aggregates, models) to a separate location on regular basis. Data Archival use cases typically will run on the data in Hadoop Ecosystem to move the old data from various data stores (including Hadoop) to archive folder in HDFS. The purge use case deletes the data from various data stores like Hadoop Ecosystem, Data Warehouse Systems, NoSQL Databases, etc. from time to time.

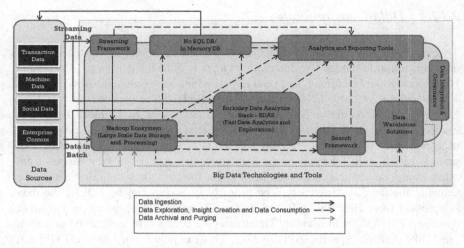

Fig. 2.21 Use cases implemented with various Big Data Tools and Platforms

Figure 2.21 depicts the points discussed above. The arrows show the data flow/access path for the various Implementation Use Cases across the different Big Data Technologies.

As one can note that there are multiple technology options available to implement a Big Data use case. Hence, one has to carefully select the right technology(ies) suitable for a particular business situation and requirements to implement the same. One has to first perform necessary due diligence to evaluate the various options and then select the technologies most suitable for the specific purpose and environment.

2.13 Future Directions

The space of Big Data Tools and Platforms is changing rapidly. It is not only getting fueled by the innovations happening in the open source world but also having support from the licensed product world in maturing those innovations for the mainstream use. The existing technologies are getting further richer in terms of features and stability every quarter. At the same time, frequent emergence of new tools and frameworks fostering different paradigms in Big Data computation, is making the existing ones stale.

In the Hadoop Ecosystem, the latest direction is to move towards establishing Hadoop as a Big Data Operating System [133]. The key proposal there is that various Distributed Processing Components and Application Components of Hadoop Ecosystem can run on top of YARN to support any type of enterprise level Big Data requirements. This can help in best utilization of the computation resources in Hadoop cluster as well as the Data available in the same. Because of the compelling promise of this vision many Big Data Technologies are coming out with a version which can run as an Application Component of Hadoop Ecosystem on top of YARN within a single Hadoop cluster. Apart from this, the other notable innovations happening in Hadoop Ecosystem are Storing data in memory in HDFS, Hive on Spark for Machine Learning capabilities, Atlas for data Governance, Ranger for centralized security with auditing capabilities, etc.

On the other hand, the Spark from Berkeley Data Analytics Stack, is emerging out as a strong competitor to various Distributed Processing Components (and corresponding Application Components) in the Hadoop Ecosystem. At the same time industry has also seen Flink, the competitor to Spark. Flink is still less matured compared to Spark and only time will say which one is going to win in this space. Tachyon is another promising technology happening in Berkeley Data Analytics Stack. Tachyon can potentially serve the purpose of distributed file system layer which is memory based as well as backed by choice of persistence store (Amazon S3, SAN, HDFS, etc.). Similarly Mesos is also a strong competition to YARN in the space of resource management framework. Also, as discussed previously, BDAS promotes the Analytics First approach (instead of Storage First approach of other Big Data Technologies) which itself is changing the philosophy behind application of different Big Data Technologies moving towards very Fast Analytics. In overall, there is a potential that, in the forthcoming days, the Berkeley Data Analytics Stack with Tachyon, Spark, Mesos and other frameworks together can be an end to end alternative of the Hadoop Ecosystem.

In NoSQL Database space technologies like Foundation DB and Cockroach DB are to be watched for. The support for acid and multiple data models can make Foundation DB choice for various use cases. On the other hand Cockroach DB is geared to solve real distributed transaction problems along with other NoSQL features.

In the In Memory Database space the products are coming out with more and more features similar to NoSQL Databases. The support for Key Value store, Document Object Model, etc. are becoming standard in In Memory Databases. In their next generation versions, Streaming Event Processing Technologies are trying to support more high level constructs for easily implementing Modeling requirements, Text Analytics, Complex Event Processing etc.

The future of Search Engines are more geared towards addition of features to support better update facility, user interface with better guided search, integration with other enterprise tools, and ability to quickly develop Search based applications, etc.

The Enterprise Data Warehouse Systems are really threatened by the price performance propositions of Hadoop Ecosystem and BDAS. However, they have started providing more features around support for Modeling without getting the data out, support for federated query to get the data from Hadoop Ecosystem transparently, better optimized appliances with lesser total cost of ownership, etc.

Analytics and Reporting Tools are coming out too with next generation features. The majority of them are focusing on seamless integration with different Hadoop Distributions and BDAS through optimized push down query processing, cubes buildings and interactive query processing. However, the most talked about future capabilities in this space is Narrative Generation Platforms. These narrative Generation Platforms not only create the numbers and insights from the Big Data but also create narrative around those to convey the meaning and implications of them to the target audiences. On the other hand, the web based Notebooks are the tools for future for agile real time data exploration and analytics.

Data Integration and Governance Tools are mainly aiming towards effectively integrating with technologies like Hadoop Ecosystem, BDAS, NoSQL Databases, etc. The key features majority of the vendors in this space implementing are ability to run on the same cluster as of Hadoop Ecosystem taking advantage of YARN platform, utilization of Spark's run time engine, achieving Push Down data processing as much as possible where the data resides, and using platform specific native integration and governance capabilities. However, their challenge is to be up to date with the changing landscape of the Big Data Technologies to integrate with.

The rapidly changing Big Data Tools and Platforms space is also a challenge for enterprise adoption of Big Data. Traditional Data Warehousing skills around SQL, ETL Tools, and Reporting Tools are challenged now. However, enterprises are also trying to move fast in creating cross platform skill base for Big Data involving SQL, Java, Web Services/REST, Python, Scala, etc. Enterprises are also participating in shaping the Big Data Technology space, the biggest example being the latest formation of the consortium Open Data Platform Initiative for Hadoop Ecosystem. The future of enterprise adoption of Big Data would be more around proving the upfront business values of both technologies and analytics use cases together. The agility to frequently try out new data products (analytics use cases) and newer Big Data Technologies in a given enterprise context, and ability to rapidly institutionalize the proven ones at enterprise level is the key to successful adoption of Big Data Tools and Platforms in enterprise space.

References

1. Apache Software Foundation. http://en.wikipedia.org/wiki/Apache_Software_Foundation. Accessed 06 Aug 2015
2. Apache Projects Directory. https://projects.apache.org/. Accessed 06 Aug 2015
3. Apache Incubator. http://incubator.apache.org/. Accessed 06 Aug 2015
4. Dean J, Ghemawat S (2004) MapReduce: simplified data processing on large clusters. In: Sixth symposium on operating system design and implementation, San Francisco, CA, December 2004
5. Ghemawat S, Gobioff H, Leung S (2003) The Google file system. In: SOSP'03 Proceedings of the nineteenth ACM symposium on operating systems principles, pp 29–43, October 19–22, 2003, Bolton Landing, New York, USA
6. Woodie A (2014) Yahoo: we run the whole company on Hadoop. In: Datanami, http://www.datanami.com/2014/06/04/yahoo-run-whole-company-hadoop/. Accessed 06 Aug 2015
7. HDFS Users Guide. https://hadoop.apache.org/docs/stable/hadoop-project-dist/hadoop-hdfs/HdfsUserGuide.html. Accessed 06 Aug 2015
8. Hadoop Map Reduce. http://hadoop.apache.org/docs/current/hadoop-mapreduce-client/hadoop-mapreduce-client-core/MapReduceTutorial.html. Accessed 06 Aug 2015

9. Saha B (2013) Philosophy behind YARN Resource Management. http://hortonworks.com/blog/philosophy-behind-yarn-resource-management/
10. Murthy A (2012) Apache Hadoop YARN – concepts and applications. http://hortonworks.com/blog/apache-hadoop-yarn-concepts-and-applications/. Accessed 06 Aug 2015
11. Apache Spark. https://spark.apache.org/. Accessed 06 Aug 2015
12. Zaharia M, Chowdhury M, Franklin MJ, Shenker S, Stoica I (2010) Spark: cluster computing with working sets. University of California, Berkeley, CA
13. Dean J, Ghemawat S (2004) Parallel execution. In: MapReduce: simplified data processing on large clusters. http://research.google.com/archive/mapreduce-osdi04-slides/index-auto-0008.html. Accessed 06 Aug 2015
14. Apache Storm. https://storm.apache.org/. Accessed 06 Aug 2015 https://storm.apache.org/documentation/Concepts.html
15. Apache Drill. http://drill.apache.org/. Accessed 06 Aug 2015
16. Apache Drill Architecture. http://drill.apache.org/architecture/. Accessed 06 Aug 2015
17. Zaharia M, Chowdhury M, Das T, Dave A, Ma J, McCauley M, Franklin MJ, Shenker S, Stoica I (2012) Resilient distributed datasets: a fault-tolerant abstraction for in-memory cluster computing. University of California, Berkeley, CA
18. Apache Drill Architecture. http://drill.apache.org/architecture/
19. Tez. http://tez.apache.org/. Accessed 06 Aug 2015
20. HDFS Architecture. In: HDFS Architecture Guide. http://hadoop.apache.org/docs/r1.2.1/hdfs_design.html. Accessed 06 Aug 2015
21. Apache Hive. https://cwiki.apache.org/confluence/display/Hive/Home. Accessed 06 Aug 2015
22. Gates A, Bains R (2014) Stinger.next: Enterprise SQL at Hadoop Scale with Apache Hive. http://hortonworks.com/blog/stinger-next-enterprise-sql-hadoop-scale-apache-hive/. Accessed 06 Aug 2015
23. Zhan X, Ho S (2015). Hive on Spark. https://cwiki.apache.org/confluence/display/Hive/Hive+on+Spark%3A+Getting+Started. Accessed 22 Jan 2016
24. Binary JSON. http://bsonspec.org/. Accessed 06 Aug 2015
25. Revolution R. http://www.revolutionanalytics.com/#homepage-section-1155. Accessed 06 Aug 2015
26. Big R. http://www-01.ibm.com/support/knowledgecenter/SSPT3X_4.0.0/com.ibm.swg.im.infosphere.biginsights.analyze.doc/doc/t_overview_bigr.html. Accessed 06 Aug 2015
27. YARN Architecture. http://hadoop.apache.org/docs/current/hadoop-yarn/hadoop-yarn-site/YARN.html. Accessed 06 Aug 2015
28. SerDe. https://cwiki.apache.org/confluence/display/Hive/SerDe. Accessed 06 Aug 2015
29. LanguageManual UDF. https://cwiki.apache.org/confluence/display/Hive/LanguageManual+UDF. Accessed 06 Aug 2015
30. HiveServer2. https://cwiki.apache.org/confluence/display/Hive/Setting+Up+HiveServer2#SettingUpHiveServer2-HiveServer2. Accessed 06 Aug 2015
31. Apache Pig. https://pig.apache.org/. Accessed 06 Aug 2015
32. Pig Latin Basics. http://pig.apache.org/docs/r0.14.0/basic.html. Accessed 06 Aug 2015
33. Pig on Spark. https://cwiki.apache.org/confluence/display/PIG/Pig+on+Spark. Accessed 22 Jan 2016
34. Apache HCatalog. https://cwiki.apache.org/confluence/display/Hive/HCatalog. Accessed 06 Aug 2015
35. Apache WebHCat. https://cwiki.apache.org/confluence/display/Hive/WebHCat. Accessed 06 Aug 2015
36. Apache Flume. https://flume.apache.org/. Accessed 06 Aug 2015
37. MongoDB Sharding. http://docs.mongodb.org/manual/core/sharding-introduction/. Accessed 06 Aug 2015
38. Apache Sqoop. http://sqoop.apache.org/. Accessed 06 Aug 2015
39. X.509. In: Wikipedia. https://en.wikipedia.org/wiki/X.509. Accessed 06 Aug 2015
40. Apache Oozie. http://oozie.apache.org/. Accessed 06 Aug 2015

41. XPDL. In: Wikipedia. http://en.wikipedia.org/wiki/XPDL. Accessed 06 Aug 2015
42. Vormetric Data Security Platform. http://www.vormetric.com/. Accessed 06 Aug 2015
43. Apache   ZooKeeper.   https://cwiki.apache.org/confluence/display/ZOOKEEPER/Index. Accessed 06 Aug 2015
44. Linux Unified Key Setup. In: Wikipedia. https://en.wikipedia.org/wiki/Linux_Unified_Key_ Setup. Accessed 06 Aug 2015
45. Apache Slider. http://slider.incubator.apache.org/. Accessed 06 Aug 2015
46. Apache Knox. https://knox.apache.org/. Accessed 06 Aug 2015
47. Apache Ambari. https://ambari.apache.org/. Accessed 06 Aug 2015
48. Apache Giraph. http://giraph.apache.org/. Accessed 06 Aug 2015
49. Malewicz G, Austern MH, Bik AJC, Dehnert JC, Horn I, Leiser N, Czajkowski G (2010). Pregel: a system for large-scale graph processing. In: Proceedings of the 2010 ACM SIGMOD international conference on management of data. http://dl.acm.org/citation.cfm?id=1807184
50. Valiant LG (1990). A bridging model for parallel computation. Commun ACM 33(8):103–111
51. IBM Infosphere Guardium Data Encryption. http://www-03.ibm.com/software/products/en/ infosphere-guardium-data-encryption. Accessed 06 Aug 2015
52. MongoDB. http://www.mongodb.com/. Accessed 06 Aug 2015
53. BitLocker Drive Encryption. http://windows.microsoft.com/en-us/windows-vista/bitlocker-drive-encryption-overview/. Accessed 06 Aug 2015
54. Apache Cassandra. http://cassandra.apache.org/. Accessed 06 Aug 2015
55. Apache Hbase. http://hbase.apache.org/. Accessed 06 Aug 2015
56. Britton Lee, Inc. In: Wikipedia. https://en.wikipedia.org/wiki/Britton_Lee,_Inc. Accessed 06 Aug 2015
57. Snijders C, Matzat U, Reips U (2012) Big data: big gaps of knowledge in the field of internet science. Int J Internet Sci 7(1):1–5
58. NoSQL. http://nosql-database.org/
59. Cockroach Labs. http://cockroachdb.org/. Accessed 06 Aug 2015
60. Corbett JC, Dean J, Epstein M, Fikes A, Frost C, Furman J, Ghemawat S, Gubarev A, Heiser C, Hochschild P, Hsieh W, Kanthak S, Kogan E, Li H, Lloyd A, Melnik S, Mwaura D, Nagle D, Quinlan S, Rao R, Rolig L, Saito Y, Szymaniak M, Taylor C, Wang R, Woodford D (2012) Spanner: Google's globally-distributed database. In: Tenth symposium on operating system design and implementation, Hollywood, CA, October 2012
61. IBM Cloudant. https://cloudant.com/. Accessed 06 Aug 2015
62. Apache Nutch. http://nutch.apache.org/. Accessed 06 Aug 2015
63. Apache Parquet. http://parquet.apache.org/. Accessed 06 Aug 2015
64. Leverenz L (2015). Language Manual of ORC. https://cwiki.apache.org/confluence/display/ Hive/LanguageManual+ORC. Accessed 06 Aug 2015
65. Apache Avro. http://avro.apache.org/docs/1.3.0/. Accessed 06 Aug 2015
66. Sequence File. http://wiki.apache.org/hadoop/SequenceFile. Accessed 06 Aug 2015
67. Melnik S, Gubarev A, Long JJ, Romer G, Shivakumar S, Tolton M, Vassilakis T (2010) Dremel: interactive analysis of web-scale datasets. In: Proceedings of the 36th international conference on very large data bases, 330–339, September 13–17, 2010, Singapore.
68. Massively   Parallel.   In: Wikipedia.   http://en.wikipedia.org/wiki/Massively_parallel_ %28computing%29. Accessed 06 Aug 2015
69. Apache Sentry. http://sentry.incubator.apache.org/. Accessed 06 Aug 2015
70. Apache Ranger. http://ranger.incubator.apache.org/. Accessed 06 Aug 2015
71. Apache Falcon. http://falcon.apache.org/index.html. Accessed 06 Aug 2015
72. Apache Atlas Proposal. https://wiki.apache.org/incubator/AtlasProposal. Accessed 06 Aug 2015
73. ODPi. https://www.odpi.org/. Accessed 22 Jan 2016
74. Amazon EMR. http://aws.amazon.com/elasticmapreduce/. Accessed 06 Aug 2015

75. IBM's BigInsight for Apache Hadoop on Bluemix. https://console.ng.bluemix.net/?ace_base=true/#/store/cloudOEPaneId=store&serviceOfferingGuid=aff58576-c0fc-4d9a-a57d-c6dd492bede1&fromCatalog=true. Accessed 06 Aug 2015
76. Qubole's Hadoop As A Service. http://www.qubole.com/hadoop-as-a-service/. Accessed 06 Aug 2015
77. HDInsight on Microsoft Azure. http://azure.microsoft.com/en-us/services/hdinsight. Accessed 06 Aug 2015
78. Big Data Computing in the HP Cloud. http://www.hpcloud.com/solutions/hadoop. Accessed 06 Aug 2015
79. Hadoop on Google Compute Engine. https://cloud.google.com/solutions/hadoop/. Accessed 06 Aug 2015
80. Altiscale Hadoop As A Service. https://www.altiscale.com/. Accessed 06 Aug 2015
81. Oracle Big Data Appliance. https://www.oracle.com/engineered-systems/big-data-appliance/index.html. Accessed 06 Aug 2015
82. Avnet Hadoop Appliance. http://news.avnet.com/index.php?s=20295&item=127070. Accessed 06 Aug 2015
83. Microsoft Analytics Platform System. http://www.microsoft.com/en-us/server-cloud/products/analytics-platform-system/Overview.aspx. Accessed 06 Aug 2015
84. EMC Data Computing Appliance. http://pivotal.io/big-data/emc-dca. Accessed 06 Aug 2015
85. SeaMicro Fabric Compute System. http://www.seamicro.com/sites/default/files/SM_DS06_v2.1.pdf. Accessed 06 Aug 2015
86. SGI InfiniteData Cluster. https://www.sgi.com/products/servers/infinitedata_cluster/. Accessed 06 Aug 2015
87. Cray Cluster Supercomputer for Hadoop. http://www.cray.com/Assets/PDF/products/cs/CS300HadoopBrochure.pdf. Accessed 06 Aug 2015
88. Cisco Unified Computing System. http://www.cisco.com/c/dam/en/us/solutions/collateral/data-center-virtualization/unified-computing/at_a_glance_c45-523181.pdf. Accessed 06 Aug 2015
89. Apache Flink. https://flink.apache.org/. Accessed 06 Aug 2015
90. Apache Kafka. http://kafka.apache.org/documentation.html#introduction. Accessed 06 Aug 2015
91. Apache Solr. http://lucene.apache.org/solr/. Accessed 06 Aug 2015
92. Apache Lucene. https://lucene.apache.org/. Accessed 06 Aug 2015
93. Elastic Search. https://www.elastic.co/products/elasticsearch. Accessed 06 Aug 2015
94. Sphynx. http://sphinxsearch.com/. Accessed 06 Aug 2015
95. Found: Elasticsearch As A Service. https://www.found.no/. Accessed 06 Aug 2015
96. Snaplogic. http://www.snaplogic.com/. Accessed 06 Aug 2015
97. Apache Mahout. http://mahout.apache.org/. Accessed 06 Aug 2015
98. Chang F, Dean J, Ghemawat S, Hsieh WC, Wallach DA, Burrows M, Chandra T, Fikes A, Gruber RE (2008) Bigtable: a distributed storage system for structured data. J ACM Trans Comput Syst (TOCS) 26(2)
99. Microsoft Azure Stream Analytics. http://azure.microsoft.com/en-us/services/stream-analytics/. Accessed 06 Aug 2015
100. IBM Geospatial Analytics. https://console.ng.bluemix.net/?ace_base=true/#/store/cloudOEPaneId=store&fromCatalog=true&serviceOfferingGuid=f5c45150-8023-4d3e-a3d4-5a3a8ca8e407. Accessed 06 Aug 2015
101. Amazon Kinesis. http://aws.amazon.com/kinesis/. Accessed 06 Aug 2015
102. Natural Language Generation. In: Wikipedia. http://en.wikipedia.org/wiki/Natural_language_generation
103. Quill. http://www.narrativescience.com/quill. Accessed 06 Aug 2015
104. Wordsmith. http://automatedinsights.com/wordsmith/. Accessed 06 Aug 2015
105. The Arria NLG Engine. http://www.arria.com/platform.php. Accessed 06 Aug 2015
106. George L (2009) HBase Architecture 101 – Storage. http://www.larsgeorge.com/2009/10/hbase-architecture-101-storage.html. Accessed 06 Aug 2015

107. IBM Platform Computing. http://www-03.ibm.com/systems/platformcomputing/products/symphony/. Accessed 06 Aug 2015
108. Cascading. http://www.cascading.org/. Accessed 06 Aug 2015
109. Herman Hollerith. Columbia University, Computing History. http://www.columbia.edu/cu/computinghistory/hollerith.html. Accessed 06 Aug 2015
110. Internet of Things. In: Wikipedia. http://en.wikipedia.org/wiki/Internet_of_Things
111. Reed J (2015) Hadoop survey offers insight into investment, adoption. DataInformed. http://data-informed.com/hadoop-survey-offers-insight-into-investment-adoption/
112. Informatica Cloud Edition. https://www.informatica.com/products/cloud-integration/editions-and-pricing/us-pricing.html#fbid=SnXuN8qeDld. Accessed 06 Aug 2015
113. DeCandia G, Hastorun D, Jampani M, Kakulapati G, Lakshman A, Pilchin A, Sivasubramanian S, Vosshall P, Vogels W (2007) Dynamo: Amazon's highly available key-value store. In: SOSP'07. http://s3.amazonaws.com/AllThingsDistributed/sosp/amazon-dynamo-sosp2007.pdf
114. Simple Authentication and Security Layer. In: Wikipedia. https://en.wikipedia.org/wiki/Simple_Authentication_and_Security_Layer. Accessed 06 Aug 2015
115. Aerospike. http://www.aerospike.com/. Accessed 06 Aug 2015
116. Hazelcast. http://hazelcast.org/. Accessed 06 Aug 2015
117. Pivotal GemFire. http://pivotal.io/big-data/pivotal-gemfire. Accessed 06 Aug 2015
118. Amazon Dynamo DB. https://aws.amazon.com/dynamodb/. Accessed 06 Aug 2015
119. ObjectRocket. http://objectrocket.com/. Accessed 06 Aug 2015/
120. Apache Ignite. https://ignite.incubator.apache.org/. Accessed 06 Aug 2015
121. Oracle Coherence. http://www.oracle.com/technetwork/middleware/coherence/overview/index-087514.html. Accessed 06 Aug 2015
122. Oracle TimesTen In-Memory Database. http://www.oracle.com/us/products/database/timesten/overview/index.html. Accessed 06 Aug 2015
123. IBM DB2 with BLU Acceleration. http://www.ibmbluhub.com/. Accessed 06 Aug 2015
124. SAP HANA. http://hana.sap.com/abouthana.html. Accessed 06 Aug 2015
125. EXASOL. http://www.exasol.com/en/products/exasolution/. Accessed 06 Aug 2015
126. SAP HANA Cloud Platform. http://hcp.sap.com/index.html. Accessed 06 Aug 2015
127. IBM DashDB Cloud Data Warehouse Service. http://www-01.ibm.com/software/data/dashdb/. Accessed 06 Aug 2015
128. EXACloud. http://www.exasol.com/en/products/exacloud/. Accessed 06 Aug 2015
129. Google Cloud Bigtable. https://cloud.google.com/bigtable/docs/. Accessed 06 Aug 2015
130. Spark Streaming. https://spark.apache.org/streaming/. Accessed 06 Aug 2015
131. Teradata. http://www.teradata.com/?LangType=1033l. Accessed 06 Aug 2015
132. Apache Phoenix. http://phoenix.apache.org/. Accessed 06 Aug 2015
133. Mazumder S, Dhar S (2015) Hadoop_as_Big_Data_Operating_System__The_Emerging_Approach_for_Managing_Challenges_of_Enterprise_Big_Data_Platform. Research Gate. http://www.researchgate.net/publication/274713261
134. Sort Benchmark Home Page. http://sortbenchmark.org/. Accessed 06 Aug 2015
135. Harris D (2014) Databricks demolishes big data benchmark to prove Spark is fast on disk, too. In: GIGAOM Research. https://gigaom.com/2014/10/10/databricks-demolishes-big-data-benchmark-to-prove-spark-is-fast-on-disk-too/. Accessed 06 Aug 2015
136. Gualtieri M, Yuhanna N, Kisker H, Murphy D (2014) The Forrester Wave™: Big Data Hadoop Solutions, Q1 2014. http://www.forrester.com/The+Forrester+Wave+Big+Data+Hadoop+Solutions+Q1+2014/fulltext/-/E-RES112461
137. Penn B (2014) Comparing MapR-FS and HDFS NFS and Snapshots. https://www.mapr.com/blog/comparing-mapr-fs-and-hdfs-nfs-and-snapshots#.VWxfXWMSknE. Accessed 06 Aug 2015
138. IBM Spectrum Scale V4.1.1 delivers software-defined storage for cloud, big data and analytics, and data-intensive technical workflows. http://www-01.ibm.com/common/ssi/cgi-bin/ssialias?infotype=an&subtype=ca&appname=gpateam&supplier=897&letternum=ENUS215-148. Accessed 06 Aug 2015

139. IBM Netezza. http://www-01.ibm.com/software/data/netezza/. Accessed 06 Aug 2015
140. Gorda B (2014) Intel® Enterprise Edition for Lustre* Software: Simpler, Smarter. http://www.intel.com/content/www/us/en/software/isc-2014-intel-enterprise-edition-lustre-software-video.html.   http://www.emc.com/collateral/hardware/solution-overview/h8319-scale-out-nas-greenplum-hd-so.pdf. Accessed 06 Aug 2015
141. Hadoop On EMC ISILON Scale-Out NAS. http://www.emc.com/collateral/software/white-papers/h10528-wp-hadoop-on-isilon.pdf. Accessed 06 Aug 2015
142. Apache Tachyon. http://tachyon-project.org/. Accessed 06 Aug 2015
143. FoundationDB. https://foundationdb.com/. Accessed 06 Aug 2015
144. ACID. In: Wikipedia. http://en.wikipedia.org/wiki/ACID. Accessed 06 Aug 2015
145. Talend. https://www.talend.com/. Accessed 06 Aug 2015
146. Pentaho. http://wiki.pentaho.com/display/COM/Community+Edition+Downloads. Accessed 06 Aug 2015
147. Lu H, Kian-Lee T (1992) Dynamic and load-balanced task- oriented database query processing in parallel systems. In: Proceedings of the 3rd international conference on extending database technology, 357–372
148. Infosphere   Streams.   http://www-03.ibm.com/software/products/en/infosphere-streams. Accessed 06 Aug 2015
149. TIBCO   StreamBase.   http://www.tibco.com/products/event-processing/complex-event-processing/streambase-complex-event-processing. Accessed 06 Aug 2015
150. Software AG APAMA. http://www.softwareag.com/corporate/products/apama_webmethods/analytics/overview/default.asp. Accessed 06 Aug 2015
151. Sqlstream. http://www.sqlstream.com/. Accessed 06 Aug 2015
152. Cisco   Tidal.   http://www.cisco.com/c/en/us/products/cloud-systems-management/tidal-enterprise-scheduler/index.html. Accessed 06 Aug 2015
153. Comer D (1979) Ubiquitous B-Tree. ACM Comput Surv (CSUR) Surv 11(2):121–137
154. Manning CD, Raghavan P, Schütze H (2008) A first take at building an inverted index. In: Introduction to information retrieval, Cambridge University Press, New York, USA
155. Binari Radix Indexes. In: Wikipedia. https://en.wikipedia.org/wiki/Radix_tree. Accessed 06 Aug 2015
156. O'Neil E, O'Neil P, Wu K (2007) Bitmap index design choices and their performance implications. In: IDEAS'07 proceedings of the 11th international database engineering and applications symposium, 72–84
157. Broder A, Mitzenmacher M (2005) Network applications of bloom filters: A survey. Internet Math 1(4):485–509
158. Oracle Exadata. https://www.oracle.com/engineered-systems/exadata/index.html. Accessed 06 Aug 2015
159. Design a pluggable interface to place replicas of blocks in HDFS. https://issues.apache.org/jira/browse/HDFS-385. Accessed 06 Aug 2015
160. Zero loss HDFS data replication for multiple datacenters. https://issues.apache.org/jira/browse/HDFS-5442. Accessed 06 Aug 2015
161. DistCp Version2 Guide. http://hadoop.apache.org/docs/r2.7.1/hadoop-distcp/DistCp.html. Accessed 06 Aug 2015
162. Dittrich J, Richter S, Schuh S (2013) Efficient OR Hadoop: why not both? Datenbank-Spektrum 13(1):17–22
163. Gankidi VR, Teletia N, Patel JM, Halverson A, DeWitt DJ (2014) Indexing HDFS Data in PDW: splitting the data from the index. Proc VLDB Endow 7(13)
164. Liao H, Han J, Fang J (2010) Multi-dimensional Index on Hadoop distributed file system. In: Fifth IEEE international conference on networking, architecture, and storage
165. Amplab. https://amplab.cs.berkeley.edu/. Accessed 06 Aug 2015
166. Apache Mesos. http://mesos.apache.org/. Accessed 06 Aug 2015
167. IBM   Information   Server   Suite.   https://www-01.ibm.com/support/knowledgecenter/SSZJPZ_11.3.0/com.ibm.swg.im.iis.productization.iisinfsv.overview.doc/topics/cisoproductsinthesuite.html. Accessed 06 Aug 2015

168. Informatica. https://www.informatica.com/. Accessed 06 Aug 2015
169. Resource Management for MongoDB. http://jsonstudio.com/resource-management-for-mongodb/. Accessed 06 Aug 2015
170. Demo: Migrating MongoDB data with Mesos and Flocker. https://mesosphere.com/blog/2015/05/21/demo-migrating-mongodb-data-with-mesos-and-powerstrip/. Accessed 06 Aug 2015
171. Nachbar E (2014) Cassandra on Mesos – Scalable Enterprise Storage. https://mesosphere.com/blog/2014/02/12/cassandra-on-mesos-scalable-enterprise-storage/. Accessed 06 Aug 2015
172. Kamenov DZ (2012) Monitoring HBase. http://www.monitis.com/blog/2012/03/28/monitoring-hbase/. Accessed 06 Aug 2015
173. Hannibal Wiki. https://github.com/sentric/hannibal/wiki. Accessed 06 Aug 2015
174. Lai M, Koontz E, Purtell A (2012) Coprocessor Introduction. https://blogs.apache.org/hbase/entry/coprocessor_introduction. Accessed 06 Aug 2015
175. Krompass S, Dayal U, Kuno HA, Kemper A (2007) Dynamic workload management for very large data warehouses: juggling feathers and bowling balls. In: Proceedings of the 33rd international conference on very large data bases, 1105–1115
176. Krompass S, Kuno HA, Wiener JL, Wilkinson K, Dayal U, Kemper A (2009) Managing long-running queries. In: Proceedings of the 13th international conference on extending database technology, 132–143
177. Pang H, Carey MJ, Livny M (1995) Multiclass query scheduling in real-time database systems. IEEE Trans Knowl Data Eng 7(4):533–551
178. Brown KP, Mehta M, Carey MJ, Livny M (1994) Towards automated performance tuning for complex workloads. In: Proceedings of the 20th international conference on very large data bases, 72–84
179. Chaudhuri S, König AC, Narasayya VR (2004) SQLCM: A continuous monitoring framework for relational database engines. In: Proceedings of the 20th IEEE international conference on data engineering, 473–484
180. Potter T (2014) Solr on YARN. In: Lucidworks. https://lucidworks.com/blog/solr-yarn/. Accessed 06 Aug 2015
181. SPM – Performance Monitoring & Alerting. http://sematext.com/spm/. Accessed 06 Aug 2015
182. Elasticsearch on YARN. https://www.elastic.co/guide/en/elasticsearch/hadoop/current/es-yarn.html. Accessed 06 Aug 2015
183. Elasticsearch on Mesos. https://github.com/mesos/elasticsearch. Accessed 06 Aug 2015
184. Health and Performance Monitoring. https://www.elastic.co/guide/en/elasticsearch/client/community/current/health.html. Accessed 06 Aug 2015
185. Shield | Security for Elasticsearch. https://www.elastic.co/products/shield. Accessed 06 Aug 2015
186. High availability – Built-in Mirroring. http://sphinxsearch.com/blog/2013/04/01/high-availability-built-in-mirroring/. Accessed 06 Aug 2015
187. Sphinx Tools beta. https://tools.sphinxsearch.com/. Accessed 06 Aug 2015
188. Security Onion. http://blog.securityonion.net/2015/05/sphinxsearch-219.html. Accessed 06 Aug 2015
189. Monitoring Tachyon. https://tachyon.atlassian.net/browse/TACHYON-84
190. Li H, Ghodsi A, Zaharia M, Shenker S, Stoica I (2014) Tachyon: reliable, memory speed storage for cluster computing frameworks. In: SoCC'14, Seattle WA, 3–5 Nov 2014
191. Pivotal Greenplum. http://pivotal.io/big-data/pivotal-greenplum-database. Accessed 06 Aug 2015
192. Klpoo R (2014) Netezza Zone Maps and I/O Avoidance. In: Database Fog Blog. http://skylandtech.net/2014/04/25/netezza-zone-maps-and-io-avoidance/
193. Centralized cache management in HDFS. https://issues.apache.org/jira/browse/HDFS-4949. Accessed 06 Aug 2015

194. Support memory as a storage medium. https://issues.apache.org/jira/browse/HDFS-5851. Accessed 06 Aug 2015
195. HDFS Federation. http://hadoop.apache.org/docs/r2.7.1/hadoop-project-dist/hadoop-hdfs/Federation.html. Accessed 06 Aug 2015
196. Sung M (2000) SIMD parallel processing. In: 6.911 Architecture Anonymous
197. R. https://www.r-project.org/about.html. Accessed 06 Aug 2015
198. RHadoop. https://github.com/RevolutionAnalytics/RHadoop/wiki. Accessed 06 Aug 2015
199. Spark DataFrames. http://spark.apache.org/docs/latest/sql-programming-guide.html#dataframes. Accessed 06 Aug 2015
200. BDAS, the Berkeley Data Analytics Stack: https://amplab.cs.berkeley.edu/software/. Accessed 06 Aug 2015
201. Succinct. http://succinct.cs.berkeley.edu/wp/wordpress/. Accessed 06 Aug 2015
202. Splash. http://zhangyuc.github.io/splash/. Accessed 06 Aug 2015
203. Spark ML Programming Guide. https://spark.apache.org/docs/latest/ml-guide.html#main-concepts. Accessed 06 Aug 2015
204. BlinkDB. http://blinkdb.org/. Accessed 06 Aug 2015
205. Sampleclean. http://sampleclean.org/. Accessed 06 Aug 2015
206. Crankshaw D (2014) Velox: models in action. https://amplab.cs.berkeley.edu/projects/velox/. Accessed 06 Aug 2015
207. Databricks Spark As A Service. https://databricks.com/product/databricks. Accessed 06 Aug 2015
208. Qubole Spark As A Service. http://www.qubole.com/apache-spark-as-a-service/. Accessed 06 Aug 2015
209. IBM Spark As A Service. http://www.spark.tc/beta/. Accessed 06 Aug 2015
210. Terracota BigMemory. http://terracotta.org/products/bigmemory. Accessed 06 Aug 2015
211. Apache Thrift. https://thrift.apache.org/. Accessed 06 Aug 2015
212. Rodriguez A (2008) RESTful Web services: the basics. In: IBM developerWorks. http://www.ibm.com/developerworks/library/ws-restful/
213. Jupyter. http://jupyter.org/. Accessed 06 Aug 2015
214. Apache Zeppelin. https://zeppelin.incubator.apache.org/. Accessed 06 Aug 2015
215. Ullman JD, Aho A (1992) The relational data model. In: Foundations of Computer Science, C edn. http://infolab.stanford.edu/~ullman/focs/ch08.pdf
216. Edgar F. Codd. In: Wikipedia. https://en.wikipedia.org/wiki/Edgar_F_Codd. Accessed 06 Aug 2015
217. Ullman JD, Aho A (1992) The graph data model. In: Foundations of computer science, C edn. http://infolab.stanford.edu/~ullman/focs/ch09.pdf
218. Simmhan YL, Plale B, Gannon D (2005) A survey of data provenance techniques. Newslett ACM SIGMOD 34(3):31–36
219. Gilbert S, Lynch NA (2012) Perspectives on the CAP theorem. Computer 45(2):30–36
220. Kamat G, Singh S (2013). Comparisons of compression. In: Hadoop Summit 2013. http://www.slideshare.net/Hadoop_Summit/kamat-singh-june27425pmroom210cv2
221. DMZ (Demilitarized Zone). In: CCM. http://ccm.net/contents/602-dmz-demilitarized-zone. Accessed 06 Aug 2015
222. Stonebraker M. The case for shared nothing. University of California, Berkeley, CA
223. Chamberlin DD, Boyce RF (1974) SEQUEL: A structured english query language. In: Proceedings of the 1974 ACM SIGFIDET workshop on Data description, access and control, 249–264
224. Kerberos: The Network Authentication Protocol. http://web.mit.edu/kerberos/. Accessed 06 Aug 2015
225. Lightweight Directory Access Protocol (LDAP). In: Wikipedia. https://en.wikipedia.org/wiki/Lightweight_Directory_Access_Protocol. Accessed 06 Aug 2015
226. Machine Learning. In: Wikipedia. https://en.wikipedia.org/wiki/Machine_learning. Accessed 06 Aug 2015
227. Apache System ML. http://systemml.apache.org/. Accessed 19 Jan 2016

228. Mazumder S (2010) NoSQL in the Enterprise. In: InfoQ. http://www.infoq.com/articles/
     nosql-in-the-enterprise. Accessed 06 Aug 2015
229. Zaman Khan RZ, Ali J (2013) Use of DAG in distributed parallel computing. Int J Appl Innov
     Eng Manag 2(11):81–85
230. Analyzing and manipulating big data with Big SQL. http://www-01.ibm.com/support/
     knowledgecenter/SSPT3X_4.0.0/com.ibm.swg.im.infosphere.biginsights.analyze.doc/doc/
     bigsql_analyzingbigdata.html. Accessed 06 Aug 2015
231. Cloudera Impala. http://www.cloudera.com/content/cloudera/en/products-and-services/cdh/
     impala.html. Accessed 06 Aug 2015
232. Introduction to Massively Parallel Processing (MPP) database. https://dwarehouse.wordpress.
     com/2012/12/28/introduction-to-massively-parallel-processing-mpp-database/. Accessed 06
     Aug 2015
233. Flume User Guide. https://flume.apache.org/FlumeUserGuide.html. Accessed 06 Aug 2015
234. Noll MG (2013) Running a Multi-Node Storm Cluster. http://www.michael-noll.com/
     tutorials/running-multi-node-storm-cluster/. Accessed 06 Aug 2015
235. Sharma A (2014) Apache Kafka: Next Generation Distributed Messaging System. http://
     www.infoq.com/articles/apache-kafka. Accessed 06 Aug 2015
236. Apache Solr Architecture. https://www.safaribooksonline.com/library/view/scaling-big-data/
     9781783281374/ch02s02.html. Accessed 06 Aug 2015
237. Spark Cluster Overview. https://spark.apache.org/docs/1.0.1/cluster-overview.html. Accessed
     06 Aug 2015
238. Mesos Architecture. http://mesos.apache.org/documentation/latest/mesos-architecture/.
     Accessed 06 Aug 2015
239. Amazon Redshift. https://aws.amazon.com/redshift/. Accessed 06 Aug 2015
240. Teradata Cloud. http://www.teradata.com/cloud-overview/?LangType=1033&LangSelect=
     true. Accessed 06 Aug 2015
241. IBM Watson Explorer. http://www.ibm.com/smarterplanet/us/en/ibmwatson/explorer.html.
     Accessed 06 Aug 2015
242. Oracle Secure Enterprise Search. http://www.oracle.com/us/products/039247.htm. Accessed
     06 Aug 2015
243. Amazon CloudSearch. https://aws.amazon.com/cloudsearch/. Accessed 06 Aug 2015
244. SAS. http://www.sas.com/en_us/software/business-intelligence.html. Accessed 06 Aug 2015
245. IBM SPSS Software. http://www-01.ibm.com/software/analytics/spss/. Accessed 06 Aug
     2015
246. Microstrategy. http://www.microstrategy.com/us/. Accessed 06 Aug 2015
247. SAP Business Intelligence Solutions. http://go.sap.com/solution/platform-technology/
     business-intelligence.html. Accessed 06 Aug 2015
248. IBM Cognos Software. http://www-01.ibm.com/software/analytics/cognos/. Accessed 06
     Aug 2015
249. Tableau Software. http://www.tableau.com/. Accessed 06 Aug 2015
250. JasperSoft Business Intelligence Software. https://www.jaspersoft.com/. Accessed 06 Aug
     2015
251. Pentaho. http://www.pentaho.com/. Accessed 06 Aug 2015.

Chapter 3
Traffic Identification in Big Internet Data

Binfeng Wang, Jun Zhang, Zili Zhang, Wei Luo, and Dawen Xia

Abstract The era of big data brings new challenges to the network traffic technique that is an essential tool for network management and security. To deal with the problems of dynamic ports and encrypted payload in traditional port-based and payload-based methods, the state-of-the-art method employs flow statistical features and machine learning techniques to identify network traffic. This chapter reviews the statistical-feature based traffic classification methods, that have been proposed in the last decade. We also examine a new problem: unclean traffic in the training stage of machine learning due to the labeling mistake and complex composition of big Internet data. This chapter further evaluates the performance of typical machine learning algorithms with unclean training data. The review and the empirical study can provide a guide for academia and practitioners in choosing proper traffic classification methods in real-world scenarios.

B. Wang
College of Computer and Information Science, Southwest University, Chongqing 400715, China
e-mail: bf_wang@163.com

J. Zhang (✉) • Z. Zhang
School of Information Technology, Deakin University, Geelong, VIC 3216, Australia

College of Computer and Information Science, Southwest University, Chongqing 400715, China
e-mail: jun.zhang@deakin.edu.au; zhangzl@swu.edu.cn

W. Luo
School of Information Technology, Deakin University, Melbourne, VIC 3125, Australia
e-mail: wei.luo@deakin.edu.au

D. Xia
College of Computer and Information Science, Southwest University, Chongqing 400715, China

School of Information Engineering, Guizhou Minzu University, Guiyang 550025, China
e-mail: gzmdxdw@swu.edu.cn

© Springer International Publishing Switzerland 2016
S. Yu, S. Guo (eds.), *Big Data Concepts, Theories, and Applications*,
DOI 10.1007/978-3-319-27763-9_3

129

3.1   Introduction

Nowadays, Internet has become a integral part of our life. Online applications in chat, gaming, shopping, work, study, and business provide immense value to everyone. However, the management and security of Internet are a big challenge to every country. Network resource control could make online transaction more efficient by considering the behavior of consumer, and serve different level bandwidth for users with different charge. In network security, the problem is that hackers can easily use security breaches of web applications to steal and tamper personal information. Moreover, network virus and crime have seriously affected people's daily life. Traffic classification is a basic technique used by Internet service providers (ISPs) and their equipment vendors [1] to manage network source and guarantee network security. In order to achieve network management and security control, network manager should be ascertain the state and principal application in the network through traffic classification. For quality of service (QoS) control, applications should be given different priority to reasonably allocate network bandwidth. Traffic classification also detect customer use of network resources that in some way contravenes the operator's terms of service [2]. In addition, security department can combine traffic classification and intrusion detection to identify suspicious traffic. More recently, the Horizon 2020 [3] clarified that network security should be regarded as a priority research field by the European Commission. Obama administration announced that secure network should be built again [4].

With the evolution of network, the technology of traffic classification changes accordingly. Traditionally, many applications were identified based on the well known port in the Internet Assigned Numbers Authority (IANA)'s list of registered ports. For example, the application will be identified as DNS if its packet derive from the 53 port number. But, more and more applications use dynamical ports, leading to the port-based technology become unreliable. To avoid total reliance on the port numbers, many commercial systems use load-based classification technology. The technology infers different applications by analysing the application layer and the signatures of the different applications. For example, Sen et al. [5] use following signatures to identify BitTorrent traffic that is a popular P2P protocol: (1) The first byte in the TCP payload is the character 19 (0x13). (2) The next 19 bytes match the string 'BitTorrent protocol'. The approach does not work well when dealing with proprietary protocols or encrypted traffic. Furthermore, direct analysis of session and application layer content may represent a breach of organisational privacy policies or violation of relevant privacy legislation [1]. To address these problems, a new traffic classification approach of using traffic's statistical characteristics (e.g., package length, byte counts, connection duration, idle time and so on) [1] is proposed. In the approach, network traffic is represented as a feature vector consisting of a few statistic characteristics. Then, the problem of traffic classification can be transformed to a machine learning problem. Internet applications are identified of using clustering or classification algorithms.

The current research of traffic classification concentrates on the application of machine learning techniques into flow statistical feature based classification methods. The feature vectors extraction is indispensable. After that, machine learning algorithms are employed to classify or cluster network traffic in a feature space. Many classic supervised machine learning algorithms were applied to classification of network traffic, such as Bayesian neural networks [7], support vector machines [8], C4.5 decision tree [9] and so on. Supervised algorithms consist of two major steps: training and testing. In the step of training, the pre-labeled training dataset is used to build a classification model. In the second step, the applications of network traffic can be identified based on the model. Besides, many researchers employ some typical unsupervised machine learning algorithms to classify network traffic, including AutoClass [10], K-means [11], DBSCAN [12], Fuzzy C-means [13]. Unsupervised algorithms aim to recognize similar traffic to same cluster. Unfortunately, it is a practical problem to map traffic clusters to the applications. Many novel approaches based on machine learning were proposed for addressing present problems of traffic classification. Literatures [14–18] proposed the new scheme for addressing the real-time problem. The approaches of literature [19–23] reduce impact of small training dataset. The literature [24] proposed a new method for classifying unknown traffic.

Network traffic is big data, which has the 5 V characteristics, i.e., Volume, Velocity, Variety, Value, and Veracity. It represents that the volume, variety, value and variety of network traffic data are increasing dramatically, and the veracity of analyzing and processing network traffic data is required. For example, the FaceBook produce about 300 million images every day, the videos of YouTube are viewed more than two billion per day, and the text messages sent by a teenager reach 4762 on Twitter in a month. It generates a large amount of network traffic for the reason of transmitting these data using Internet. However, the current technologies have difficult in processing and storing of the big data. Therefore, the new technology, Could computing, Hadoop Distributed File System (HDFS), MapReduce and Spark are applied to tackle these problem. In practice, there exist a big challenge that network traffic contain a great number of unclean traffic due to the complicate composition of network traffic. Because extracting feature vectors is essential to traffic classification based on flow statistical feature. In the process of feature extraction, the unclean traffic could bring a certain amount of error feature. In addition, unclean traffic means the transmission error or label error. When we manually process network traffic and label the applications, it is possible that the class is mislabeled due to the lack of knowledge or careless operation. For instance, the class of a feature vector should be marked HTTP is mislabelled as DNS. Unclean traffic can affect the robustness of the classification model so as to reduce the classification accuracy. Nonetheless, these above-mentioned technologies could not handle effectively the problem. This chapter will study and compare the performance of various classification algorithms on unclean traffic.

In conclusion, the chapter presents a critical review about the last decade works on network traffic classification. And, in the case of large amounts of network traffic, we will evaluate the performance of ML algorithms for classifying unclean traffic. The remainder of the chapter is organized as follow: Sect. 3.2 reviews the related work in traffic classification. In Sect. 3.3, experimental dataset, experimental methods and valuating indicators are reported in detail. Section 3.4 presents a large number of experiments and results for performance evaluation. Finally, the paper is concluded in Sect. 3.5.

3.2 Related Work

The current research of traffic classification concentrates on the application of machine learning techniques into flow statistics based methods. The methods do not rely on well-known port numbers and deeply packet inspection. Some studies are on the feature selection methods and others are about machine learning algorithms.

3.2.1 Feature Selection

Network traffic can be represented by a set of flow statistical features. In machine learning, we can learn a classification model in a high dimension feature space using the pre-labeled training set. The classification model is then applied to identify the application of testing network traffic. Table 3.1 presents the available flow statistical features [6, 7]. The quality of the feature set is crucial to the performance of traffic classification. Using irrelevant or redundant features often leads to the lower accuracy. In early works, Zander et al. [10] applied sequential forward selection (SFS) method to figure out the best feature. The method addressed the inefficiency of exhaustive search. The irrelevant and redundant features may lead to a slower training and testing process, high consumption and poor performance. Dai et al. [27] proposed a hybrid feature selection method for traffic classification using chi-squared and C4.5 algorithm (ChiSquared-C4.5) to improve computational performance. Williams et al. [28] created reduced feature sets using Correlation-based Feature Selection (CFS) and Consistency-based Feature selection (CON). Then, feature subsets were evaluated using best first and greedy search methods. Since, not all features provide good discrimination between the different applications. Erman et al. [29] employed the backward greedy feature selection method to select the best subset. Kim et al. [30] used the CFS to examine the relevance and applied a best first search to generate candidate sets of features.

There exists a problem that less popular application have a lower performance in traffic classification. To address this problem, En-Najjary et al. [31] proposed a new approach based on logistic regression to automatically select distinct, per-application features that separate effectively each application from the rest of the traffic. Wasikowski and Chen [32] found that the signal-to-noise correlation coefficient (S2N) and Feature Assessment by Sliding Thresholds (FAST) are great candidates for feature selection in imbalanced data sets. They compared three types

Table 3.1 Features description for traffic classification [7]

Features
Flow metrics(duration, packet-count, total bytes)
Packet inter-arrival time
(including mean, variance, first & third quartiles, median, minimum, maximum)
Size of TCP/IP control fields
(including mean,variance, first & third quartiles, median, minimum, maximum)
Total packets (in each direction and total for flow)
Payload size(including mean, variance, first & third quartiles, median, minimum, maximum)
Effective bandwidth based upon entropy [25]
Ranked list of top-ten Fourier-transform components of packet inter-arrival times
(for each direction)
Numerous TCP-specific values derived from tcptrace [26]
e.g., total payload bytes transmitted, total number of Pushed packets, total number of packets,
total number of ACK packets seen carrying SACK information, minimum observed segment size

of methods developed for imbalanced data classification and evaluated seven feature metrics. Later, to address the class imbalance problem, Zhang et al. [33] proposed Weighted Symmetrical Uncertainty (WSU) based on weighted entropy and designed a hybrid feature selection algorithm named WSU_AUC, which pre-filters most of features with the WSU metric and further uses a wrapper method to select features for a specific classifier with the Area Under Curve (AUC) metric. Furthermore, to avoid the impacts of dynamic traffic flows on feature selection, they propose an algorithm named SRSF that Selects the Robust and Stable Features from the results achieved by WSU_AUC.

Fahad et al. [34] proposed a novel way to identify efficiently and accurately the "best" features by first combining the results of some well-known feature selection (FS) techniques to find consistent features, and then using the proposed concept of support to select a smallest set of features and cover data optimality. Fahad et al. [35] proposed the Global Optimization Approach (GOA), to reliably identify both optimal and stable features. They used on multi-criterion fusion-based feature selection technique and an information theoretic method, and proposed a new goodness measure within a Random Forest framework to estimate the final optimum feature subset.

Feature discretization plays an important role in traffic classification. Some researchers found that the performance of Naive Bayes (NB) is dramatically affected by feature discretization. NB has been used for traffic classification in early works due to its simplicity and efficiency [36]. The recent works show NB has poor performance for traffic classification [28, 37]. Lim et al. observed that feature discretization can significantly improve the performance of NB-based traffic classification [38]. The performance of support vector machine (SVM) and K-nearest Neighbor (KNN) algorithms could also be improved by feature discretization. More interestingly, NB with feature discretization demonstrates not only significantly higher accuracy but also much faster classification speed [39].

3.2.2 Machine Learning Technology

Machine learning technology is widely used in traffic classification. Many supervised methods, unsupervised methods and Semi-supervised methods have been applied to identify the application of network traffic.

3.2.2.1 Supervised Methods

The supervised traffic classification methods require a pre-labeled training dataset. A classifier is trained in the feature space by the training set and will be applied to classify new network traffic.

A lot of works have been done to solve various problems of traffic classification using supervised methods. Moore and Zuev [36] applied the supervised Naive Bayes techniques to classify network traffic based on flow statistical features to solve the problems of payload-based traffic classification. Auld and Moore [7] used a supervised machine learning method of a Bayesian trained neural to achieve a high accuracy of traffic classification. Este et al. [8] proposed an approach based on support vector machine (SVM) to solve multi-class problems of statistical traffic classification. Li and Moore [9] identified five traffic of different types of applications by C4.5 decision tree with 99.8 % overall accuracy.

To address the problem of real-time classification, Bernaille and Teixeira [40] proposed an approach to identify network traffic using only the size of the first packets of an SSL connection. Hullar et al. [41] presented the method of analyzing only the first few bytes of the first few packets, in which a Markov model based classifier was trained to recognize P2P applications. Nguyen et al. [42] built the model of classification decision on a combination of short sub-flows at any arbitrary point in a flow's lifetime, and improved the method of classifier training to achieve a high accuracy of real-time classification. Bermolen et al. [18] studied Peer-to-Peer streaming (P2P-TV) applications, and proposed a new methodology to accurately classify P2P-TV traffic using statistics payloads and bytes in short time.

To address the problem that supervised methods are sensitive to the size of training data, Zhang et al. [19] proposed to incorporate correlated information into the classification process. In addition, they created a mathematics model based on Bayes theory and analyzed the performance of new classification approach. Glata et al. [20] proposed a classification scheme that does not require training procedure, but one-way traffic include unreachable services, scanning, peer-to-peer applications, and backscatter. Their results show that the main sources of one-way traffic derive from malicious scanning, peer-to-peer applications, and outages. Jin et al. [21] developed a lightweight modular architecture for traffic classification and combined a lot of simple linear binary classifiers to improve the accuracy. Callado et al. [22] improved the classifies to reduce this impact of sampling NetFlow in the process of classification.

There are a few works using the one-class classification algorithms for classifying network traffic. These works identify every application one by one employing one-class classification. Crotti et al. [43] proposed to build classification region for every application based normalized thresholds and statistical features of traffic. Their method only needs a single class of training data and makes a binary decision, yes or no. Xie et al. [44] adapted the method of subspace clustering to improve the performance of one-class classification.

The literature [45] discusses the challenges of big data classification in network intrusion prediction. They argue that the continuous collection of network traffic leads to the growth of volume, variety and velocity. Besides, the big data technologies, representation-learning techniques, supervised learning technologies are discussed for identifying network traffic. To process network traffic and extract dynamically network features, Singh et al. [46] build a distributed framework based on Hive. Additionally, they apply the parallel tool (Mahout) to build Random Forest model for detecting Peer-to-Peer Botnet.

3.2.2.2 Unsupervised Methods

Unsupervised methods discover internal relations in the unlabeled input data. One major unsupervised approach is clustering.

Although no class label is required in clustering, classifiers can be derived if the traffic clusters correspond to different network applications. In their early work, McGregor et al. [47] extracted simple statistical characteristics of network traffic, performed EM clustering, and manually matched the resulting clusters with network applications. Such approaches were later extended to other clustering algorithm including AutoClass [10], K-means [11], DBSCAN [12], Fuzzy C-means [13]. To avoid the manual matching of clusters and applications, Bernaille et al. [48] used a payload-analysis tool on k-means clusters. In the case of online classification, the method maps traffic to the nearest cluster according to the Euclidean distance.

To address the problem of recognizing unknown network traffic, Zhang et al. [24] proposed to extract the unknown traffic samples from mass network traffic, and built a robust binary classifier. Their experiments reduced impact of unknown application in the process of classification.

Wang et al. [49] proposed to combine flow clustering based on packet-and-flow level features, on the one hand, and application signature construction solely based on payload content, on the other hand, handle the lack of a priori knowledge. Finamore et al. [50] handled unidentified traffic by combining two types of clustering: one based on flow statistical-features and the other based on payload statistical feature. To solve the problem of mapping form flow clusters to real applications, Erman et al. [29] integrated a set of supervised training data with unsupervised learning.

3.2.2.3   Semi-Supervised Methods

Often it is difficult to get labeled data. If we use only the label data for training, the training set would be too small to fully reflect the traffic characteristics. New network applications are constantly developed, resulting in traffic data without label. Both situations cause challenges for the traditional supervised machine learning methods. To address this problem, semi-supervised machine learning method is emerging, thanks to its ability to combine supervised and unsupervised learning.

In semi-supervised learning, the training set consists of both labelled samples and unlabelled samples. First, the training set were divided into different clusters using clustering algorithm. Second, the labelled sample were used to map the clusters to applications, and the remaining clusters were assigned to a new (unknown) application [1]. Literature [51] is an early example. The training set there contains a few labelled samples and a large number of unlabelled samples. The result shows that the new method has a high precision and can recognize unknown traffic. Li et al. [52] employed a semi-supervised SVM method for classifying traffic. The method only needs a few labelled samples to achieve high accuracy.

Because a semi-supervised learning method can perform classification with only a few labeled samples and a large number of unlabelled sample classification, it reduces the cost of labelling samples and improves the performance of machine learning. However, its performance degrades with noisy traffic labels. And the method have a relatively short history. Its applied value need to more in-depth mine.

3.2.3   *Comparisons*

A number of studies compared the performance of various classification algorithms. On clustering algorithms, Erman et al. [53] compared the performance of three unsupervised clustering algorithms: K-means, DBSCAN and AutoClass, using data consisting of public trace from the University of Auckland and self-collected trace from the University of Calgary. The comparison focused on the model building time of different algorithms, but ignored other performance evaluation measurements, such as processing speed, CPU and memory usage, or the timeliness of classification.

For a comparison of unsupervised and supervised algorithms, Erman et al. [54] compared the performance of Naive Bayes classifier and AutoClass clustering algorithm. A few metrics were evaluated, including recall, precision and overall accuracy (overall accuracy is defined the same as [53] reviewed in the previous sections). Pietrzyk et al. [55] evaluated three supervised methods for an ADSL provider managing many points of presence, and the results were comparable to deep inspection solutions. Such work used parametric machine learning algorithms that require an intensive training procedure for the classifier parameters and retraining for new applications.

Williams et al. [56] provided insights of the performance of ML traffic classification. The study looked at a number of supervised ML algorithms: Naive Bayes with Discretisation (NBD), Naive Bayes with Kernel Density Estimation (NBK), C4.5 Decision Tree, Bayesian Network, and Naive Bayes. They were evaluated on the speed of classification (number of classifications per second) and the speed of model building. Lim et al. [57] studied the different supervised classification algorithms and found that the C4.5 algorithm performed best because of discretization of input features during classification. Lee et al. [58] developed benchmark software to compare the flow classification performance. The software integrated 11 existing traffic classification methods and can be used to study the effectiveness of the new method.

3.3 Comparing Classifiers with Noisy Data: Experiment Setup

The comparisons described in the last section all assume reliable class labels in the training set. In reality, such a clean-label assumption is often violated. In the following two sections, we will compare the performance of a collection of well-known classification algorithms on training data with noisy labels.

3.3.1 Experiment Workbench

Our experiments were performed with the Waikato Environment for Knowledge Analysis (WEKA) workbench. WEKA provides a comprehensive collection of machine learning algorithms and data pre-processing tools [59]. WEKA has several graphical user interfaces and programme interfaces that enable easy access to the underlying functionality. These interfaces make it easy to pre-process data and run machine learning algorithms.

3.3.2 Data Sets

Our experiment used a combined dataset [60] that consists of 638,388 traffic flows from 11 traffic classes, as shown in Table 3.2. Figure 3.1 shows the composition of different traffic classes. Features for training were based on Table 3.1. Feature selection was applied to remove irrelevant and redundant features from the feature set [61], resulting in nine features, as summarized in Table 3.3.

With this combined dataset, we performed two sets of comparisons: one for clean traffic and the other for unclean traffic.

Table 3.2 Data sets for performance evaluation

Data	Volume	Classes	Instances
Combine dataset	28.3 MB	11	638,388

Fig. 3.1 Classes composition of the combined dataset

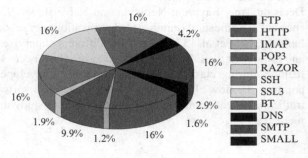

Table 3.3 Features of data set

No.	Short name	Full name
1	c2s_pkts	Client-to-server number of packets
2	c2s_psmax	Client-to-server maximum packet bytes
3	c2s_psmin	Client-to-server minimum packet bytes
4	c2s_psavg	Client-to-server average packet bytes
5	c2s_psvar	The standard deviation of client-to-server packet bytes
6	c2s_iptmin	Client-to-server minimum inter packet time
7	s2c_pkts	Server-to-client number of packets
8	s2c_psmax	Server-to-client maximum packet bytes
9	s2c_pasmin	Server-to-client minimum packet bytes

3.3.2.1 Training and Testing Dataset for Classification with Clean Labels

In order to evaluate the performance of clean traffic classification, the dataset was divided into two non-overlapping parts: a training dataset and a testing dataset. The training dataset consists of 549,013 traffic flows sampled evenly from the whole dataset to maintain the relative distribution of different classes. The remaining 89,375 traffic flows constitute the testing dataset. For faster computation, we further sampled 4 % from the training set to generate a smaller training dataset; we will refer to it as training dataset I and refer to the original testing dataset as testing dataset I.

To see the impact of training data size on clean traffic classification, we generated a sequence of training data with increasing size. This was achieved in the WEKA workbench by randomly sampling 0.1 %, 0.3 %, 0.5 %, 0.8 %, 1 %, 2 %, ..., 30 % of the training dataset I. To provide a consistent measure of classification performance, the same testing dataset I was used for different training dataset.

Table 3.4 Example of experimental data

No.	c2s_ pkts	c2s_ psmax	c2s_ psmin	c2s_ psavg	c2s_ psvar	c2s_ iptmin	s2c_ pkts	s2c_ psmax	s2c_ pasmin	Class
1	5	120	52	68.8	843.2	0.000637	4	56	52	BT
2	6	82	40	48.6667	276.267	0.000515	5	169	40	DNS
3	22	72	40	50.9091	136.468	0.000007	21	1452	52	FTP

3.3.2.2 Training and Testing Dataset for Classification with Unclean Labels

In order to evaluate the performance of unclean traffic classification, different proportion instances had their class labels randomly scrambled. For example, Table 3.4 contains three training data instances. When noise is added to the class of the first instance, its label would change from BT to, for example, DNS (or FTP).

To see the impact of noise level on classification, we generated a sequence of training sets from training dataset I with increasing portion (from 10 to 90 %) of class labels scrambled. Again, the same testing dataset I was used for all training dataset.

To see the joint effect of noise level together with training data size, we generated a sequence of training dataset sampled from the original training dataset, of the size of ranging from 1100 to 66,000. For each of the training dataset, four levels (10 %, 20 %, 30 %, 40 %) of label scrambling were applied.

3.3.3 Algorithms

A number of classification algorithms were compared.

3.3.3.1 C4.5

C4.5 is a decision tree algorithm originating from earlier implementations CLS and ID3 [62]. C4.5 aims to find out the mapped relation between the value of attribute and the class so that it could classify the new unknown instances. Given an attribute-valued dataset D, C 4.5 first grows a null set *Tree*. Then, it would compute information-theoretic criteria of each attribute a ($a \in D$). The best attribute (a_{best}) according to above computed criteria is selected as the root node. Based on a_{best}, sub-dataset D_v are induced from D. After that, we construct the sets *Tree$_V$* of different D_v, and attach *Tree$_V$* to the corresponding branch of *Tree*. Final, C 4.5 will return the result *Tree*. Selecting the best attribute rely on the value of information entropy of categorical random variable. We split to the attribute sets a in accordance with the label of classes, and computer the information entropy as following.

$$Info(D) = \sum_{i=1}^{c} -p_i \log_2 p_i \tag{3.1}$$

where c means the number of class. Then, we split to the every attribute of sets a, obtain a set of information entropy as following.

$$Info_a(D) = \sum_v \frac{|D_v|}{|D|} info(D) \tag{3.2}$$

The information gain of a attribute is defined as following.

$$Gain(a) = info(D) - info_a(D) \tag{3.3}$$

SplitInfo(a) is computed as following:

$$SplitInfo_a(D) = -\sum_v \frac{|D_v|}{|D|} \times \log_2(\frac{|D_v|}{|D|}) \tag{3.4}$$

The formula of information gain ratio is shown as following:

$$GainRatio = \frac{Gain(a)}{SplitInfo_a(D)} \tag{3.5}$$

Based on the value of GainRatio, we make the best attribute as the tree node.

3.3.3.2 Support Vector Machine

Support vector machine (SVM) aims to find out the best function to identify the sample of the two class when the dataset only includes two class [62]. The best function of classification maximize the margin of border of two classes. When the dataset could separate linearly, the classified function means the separating hyperplane that separate the data into two classes. SVM additionally finds out the best such function by maximizing the margin between the two classes.

When the dataset could not separate linearly, the SVM reflects the original data to the High dimension space using kernel function. There exists three mainly kernel function (i.e. polynomial kernel function, Gaussian kernel function and liner kernel function). In order to obtaining the maximum margin hyperplane, the SVM classifier intends to maximize the following function [62]:

$$L_p = \frac{1}{2} \left\| \vec{w} \right\| - \sum_{i=1}^{t} \alpha_i (\vec{w} \cdot \vec{x}_i + b) + \sum_{i=1}^{t} \alpha_i \tag{3.6}$$

where t means the number of training samples, and α_i, $i = 1, \ldots,$ t, are non-negative numbers such that the derivatives of L_p with respect to α_i are zero. α_i are the Lagrange multipliers and L_p is called the Lagrangian. In this equation, the hyperplane is defined by the vectors $\vec{w}$ and constant b.

3.3.3.3 Bayesian Neural Network

Bayesian neural networks (BN) employs the Bayesian framework and neural networks technology to the process of classification. First, through the input layer, a set of data $(x_1, x_2, \ldots)$ is transformed directly into the network. Subsequently, the Bayesian neural network generates an expected result in the output layer. The output depends on the architecture of the network. To predict the output, the scour depth and hidden nodes between the inputs and the output were applied to expressed more complex relationships. The transfer function relating the inputs to the i-th hidden node is given by

$$h_i = tanh(\sum_j w_{ij}^{(1)} x_j + \theta_i^{(1)})$$ (3.7)

The relationship between the hidden nodes and the output is linear, that is

$$y = \sum_i w_i^{(2)} h_i + \theta^{(2)}$$ (3.8)

The energy function is minimized adjusting the coefficient w and biases h. Because the hyperbolic function is a nonlinear function, a non-linear relationship also could be predicted using this model.

3.3.3.4 Random Forest

Random Forest (RF) trains a large number of decision trees and uses all resulting trees to generate prediction following the ensemble method [63]. The classified results depend on the vote of all trees in the ensemble. In particular, every decision tree is built based on the independent sampling training sets. All trees of random have the same distribution. Classification error depends classification ability of every tree and the correlation among them. Feature selection divides different nodes using random method, and then compare the error under different conditions. The internal estimation error, classification ability and correlation influent the number of features. Although the power of single tree may be small, after generating randomly a lot of decision trees, a testing sample can be classified according to the classified result of all trees.

3.3.3.5   K-Nearest Neighbor

K-nearest neighbor (KNN) classification aims to find k samples from the training set that are closest to the test sample. The label of test sample is identified as the most common class among all neighbors. The algorithm consists of three steps: (1) The distance or similarity metric between training sets and testing sets is computed by Euclidean distance or others. (2) The nearest k neighborhoods are selected in the accordance with the distance. (3) The class label of a testing sample are determine based on the class labels of k nearest neighbors. KNN classifiers are lazy learners, that is, models are not built explicitly unlike eager learners (e.g., decision trees, SVM, etc.).

Given a training sets D and a test sample $x = (x', y')$, the distance (or similarity) between a testing object and all the training objects $(x, y) \in D$ are computed, resulting in a nearest-neighbor list, D_z [62]. (x is a training object, while y is the value of class. Likewise, x' is a testing object and y' is the value of class.) According to the nearest-neighbor list, the test object will be recognized using the majority class of its nearest neighbors:

$$Majority\ Voting : y' = \arg\max \sum_{(x_i, y_i) \in D_z} I(v = y_i) \qquad (3.9)$$

where v is the label of a class, y_i is the label of a class for the ith nearest neighbors, and $I(\cdot)$ is an indicator function that returns the value 1 if its argument is true and 0 otherwise.

3.3.4   Evaluation Metrics

We use six metrics for classification performance. The first two, overall accuracy and F-measure, are widely used for evaluation of traffic classification. The remaining four were constructed to summarise classification performance with unclean data.

- *Overall accuracy* (Metric 1): is the ratio of the sum of all correctly classified flows to the sum of all testing flows. This metric is used to measure the accuracy of a classifier on the whole testing data.
- *F-measure* (Metric 2): is calculated by

$$F - measure = \frac{2 \times precision \times recall}{precision + recall} \qquad (3.10)$$

where precision is the ratio of correctly classified flows over all predicted flows in a class and recall is the ratio of correctly classified flows over all ground truth flows in a class. F-Measure is used to evaluate the per-class performance.

- *Unclean overall average accuracy* (Metric 3)

$$P_{uo} = \sum_{i=1}^{n} \frac{P_i}{n} \tag{3.11}$$

where n is the number of different configurations for generating unclean training data (see Sect. 3.3.2.2). P_i represents precision for the i-th configuration. Taking averaging provides a single variable to compare the noise tolerance of multiple algorithms.

- *Overall noise tolerant ratio* (Metric 4)

$$P_{ont} = \sum_{i=1}^{n} \frac{|P_0 - P_i|}{n} \tag{3.12}$$

where n and P_i has the same meaning as above, and P_0 represents the precision with the clean traffic.

- *Unclean Per-class average accuracy* (Metric 5)

$$P_{up}(j) = \sum_{i=1}^{n} \frac{P_{ij}}{n} \tag{3.13}$$

where n has the same meaning as above, but P_{ij} represents per-class precision of the i-th configuration for the class j.

- *Per-class noise tolerant ratio* (Metric 6)

$$P_{pnt}(j) = \sum_{i=1}^{n} \frac{|P_{0j} - P_{ij}|}{n} \tag{3.14}$$

where n and P_{ij} have the same meaning as above. P_{0j} represents the precision with clean traffic on the class j.

The overall accuracy, unclean overall average accuracy and overall noise tolerant ratio are applied to evaluate the overall performance. Especially, the overall noise tolerant ratio represents the ability of tolerant noise to different algorithms. The f-measure, unclean per-class average accuracy and per-class noise tolerant ratio are employed to report the per-class performance.

3.3.5 Experimental Setup

The experiment data includes nine features shown in Table 3.3. Class distribution is presented in Fig. 3.1. Parameters of all the algorithms were set to the default values of WEKA workbench. In the experiment of clean traffic, the overall accuracy and

computation time of different algorithm were measured. The experimental result
will show the classification performance on different sizes of training data. The
process was then repeated ten times. The ten results were then averaged to produce
a single estimate.

In the experiment of unclean traffic, we also applied the training dataset I and
training dataset I to run experiment. However, the training dataset was added
different proportion noise (i.e., unclean instances) from 0 to 90 % by the WEKA
workbench. The add noise means assign an incorrect label to the clean traffic
instances. Moreover, we sampled training dataset from the original training dataset,
ranging from 1100 to 66,000, maintain the noise portion (10 %, 20 %, 30 %, 40 %).
These process was then repeated ten times. Then, the ten results were averaged
to produce a single estimation. The overall accuracy and F-measure of per-class
were measured. Additionally, in the unclean traffic, the unclean overall average
accuracy, overall noise tolerant ratio, unclean per-class average accuracy and per-
class noise tolerant ratio are used to evaluate the overall and per-class performance.
Accordingly, noise tolerant of different algorithm was inferred.

3.4 Evaluation

To comprehensively evaluate the ML algorithm, the experiment results show overall
performance, computation time and per-class performance on the different size
traffic. To recap, we employed the WEKA workbench for following experiments.
First, we varied the size of clean training dataset to observe the performance of
different algorithms. Second, we varied the size of unclean training dataset to
evaluate the tolerant noise ability of different algorithms. Considering the influence
of different size of training dataset, we varied the size of training dataset based on
the fixed noise portion. The evaluation for clean traffic and unclean traffic will be
reported separately.

3.4.1 Evaluation on Clean Traffic

The overall performance was evaluated in terms of average overall accuracy against
varying training data from 0.1 %, 0.3 %, 0.5 %, ..., 1 %, 2 %, ... to 30 % per class.
Figures 3.2 and 3.3 shows the overall performance of five classification methods on
the clean network traffic.

First, a general observation is that all algorithms have a lower overall accuracy
on smaller training dataset and have a higher overall accuracy on sufficiently large
training dataset. The improvement on overall accuracy is obvious from 0.1 to
4 %. The result shows that the size of training data will be influence shapely the
accuracy of classification. The algorithm failed to build effective decision under
the extreme difficult case of very few training data. The C4.5 on the same item

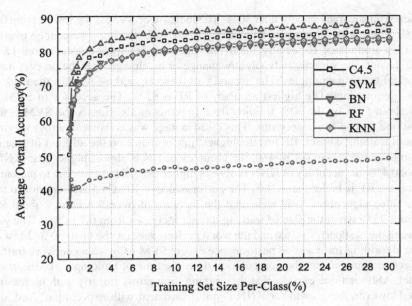

Fig. 3.2 Overall accuracy on clean traffic

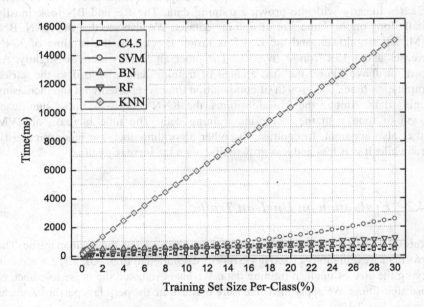

Fig. 3.3 Computation time on clean traffic

achieved an accuracy greater than 30 %. The increase of SVM is the lowest from 0.1 to 4 %. Then, with the increase of training dataset size, the improvement on overall accuracy diminishes. Especially, the overall accuracy is almost constant from 15 to 30 %. Hence, the veracity only slightly change or no change after the process have sufficient training examples. The accuracy of these algorithms reaches the peak at 30 % training data. The highest accuracy of RF is 85 %. The accuracy of SVM is only about 50 % on the 30 % training data. In terms of algorithms, the SVM is the worst one among five algorithms. This disadvantage was consistent across varying sizes of training dataset. RF has the highest performance on the all kind of size of training dataset. From 0.1 to 4 %, the accuracy of BN is almost higher than KNN. Beyond 4 %, the accuracy of KNN is always higher than BN. According to the same figure, the RF is better than C4.5. The performance of RF, C4.5 are superior to the other three algorithms. It is clear that the increase of overall accuracy about RF is about 25 % when the size of training dataset increases from 0.1 to 2 %. The gap between the best performance and the worst performance can be up to 50 %. Most of these algorithms have a good performance except SVM using clean network traffic.

Second, we consider the computation time–the time of building a classification model. Although one expects that the running time grows linearly with increasing data. However, the growth for KNN is only consistent with expectation. And, the growth for SVM showed fluctuation. For example, it took about 0.49 s on 3 %, in contrast to less than 0.41 s on 4 %. Obviously, the computation time of KNN increases linearly with the growing training data. The RF and BN took mostly equally long on the same size of training dataset. We also see that the KNN, BN, SVM, RF are slower, and the C 4.5 is faster. Especially, the runtime of KNN increases about 15 s from 1 to 30 %. The other algorithms increase slightly. As shown in above figure, the size change of training data will lead to the varied computation time. The growth of computation time is reported with the increasing training data. Among the five algorithms, the KNN reveals the most significant growth of time with the increasing training data. The time increase of SVM also is also apparent. In contrast, the other algorithms increase inconspicuously. Meanwhile, it gets less and less growth time with the increasing time.

3.4.2 *Evaluation on Unclean Traffic*

Figures 3.4 and 3.5 show the overall accuracy, time based on the unclean traffic. The performance evaluation of fixed noise ratio are reported in Figs. 3.6, 3.7, 3.8 and 3.9, varying the size of unclean training data. We also evaluated the noise tolerance of those algorithms. We apply the F-measure to illustrate the per-class performance, as shown in Fig. 3.10.

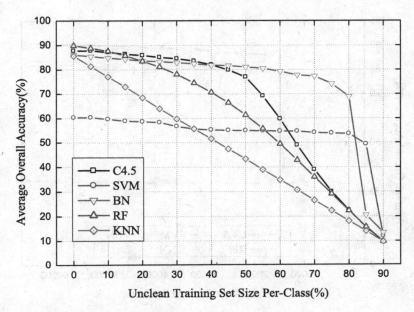

Fig. 3.4 Overall accuracy including unclean traffic

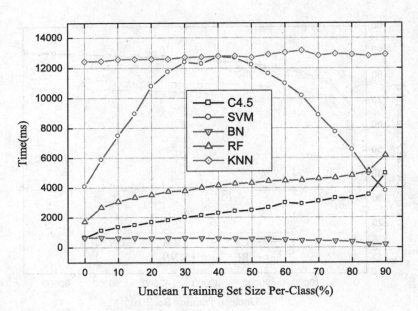

Fig. 3.5 Computation time including unclean traffic

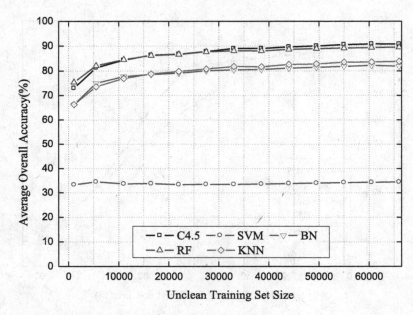

Fig. 3.6 Overall accuracy of 10 % unclean traffic training instances

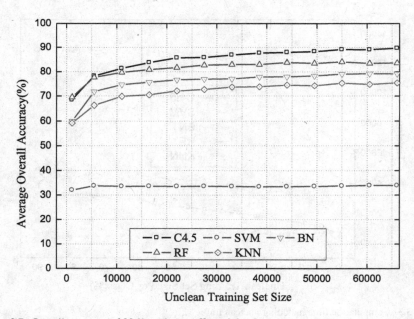

Fig. 3.7 Overall accuracy of 20 % unclean traffic training instances

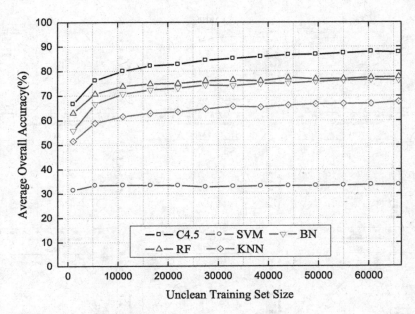

Fig. 3.8 Overall accuracy of 30 % unclean traffic training instances

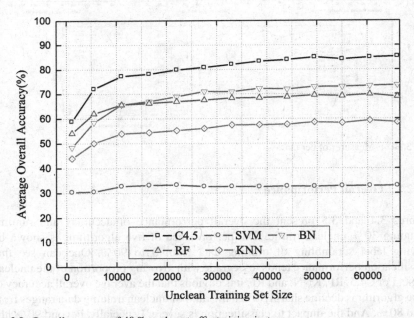

Fig. 3.9 Overall accuracy of 40 % unclean traffic training instances

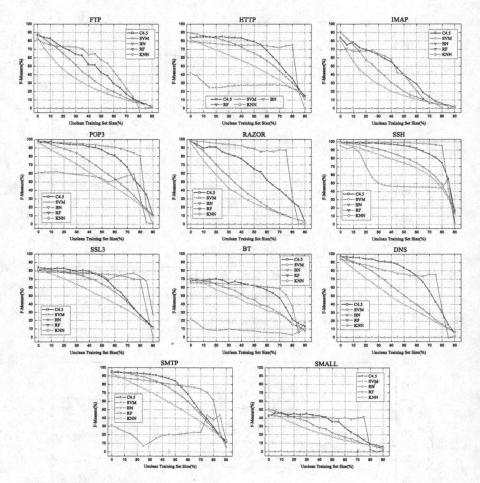

Fig. 3.10 F-Measures of per-class

3.4.2.1 Overall Performance

Figures 3.4 and 3.5 present the overall performance of accuracy and runtime
including 30 % unclean traffic. The performance of five algorithms is shown by
varying label scrambling of training data from 0 to 90 %. One can see that
classification performance tends to degrade with growing proportion of the unclean
traffic. For C4.5, RF, KNN, and RF, it is obvious that the average overall accuracy of
these algorithms decline sharply when the ratio of unclean training data ranges from
10 to 80 %. And the impact to classification is severe. Especially, beyond 90 %, the
accuracy of all algorithms are lower than 14 %. From 0 to 70 %, the decline of BN
is slow. At above 70 %, the decline of BN is clear. The overall performance of KNN
linearly decreases with the growth of size of unclean training data. In the first half,

the performance of C4.5 and RF decline slightly. In the second half, the performance declines more rapidly. The performance of SVM decreases slightly from 0 to 85 %, where the decline was about 6 %. At the same condition, the other algorithms may decrease as much as 70 %. Figure 3.5 shows that the runtime slightly changed with the growing training data. As an exception, the runtime of SVM exhibits fluctuation. Hence in conclusion, the proportion change of unclean traffic brings a significant effect on overall accuracy but little effects on runtime.

An interesting observation was the similar effect of noisy instance ratio on accuracy. Figures 3.6, 3.7, 3.8 and 3.9 all show that C 4.5 is achieved an accuracy higher than others. In contrary, the SVM have the lowest performance. Additionally, we notice the ratio of noise in Fig. 3.6 is fixed to 10 %. The results show that the accuracy slowly decrease as the size of the training data increased from 1100 to 66,000. C4.5 has the best performance at different sizes of training dataset. The next best performances are RF, BN and KNN. SVM performed lowest. C4.5 performance for 10 % unclean traffic training instances is 2 % higher than the same size of training instances with 20 % unclean traffic. And, in the same situation, the RF declines 5 %, the KNN and BN also decrease slightly. When the unclean training instances reach 30 %, the accuracy improves about 10 % from 1100 to 5500. Beyond 5500, the improvement of accuracy becomes slow. The figure suggests an order of the algorithms in terms of accuracy: C4.5, RF, BN, KNN, SVM. Inconsistent with the above three figure, Fig. 3.9 shows that BN is better than RF when the number of instances surpasses 11,000. It is concluded that the five algorithms represent similar response size changes of training data at different noisy instances ratios. There is a moderate decline in overall accuracy of mostly algorithms with the increasing noisy ratio and the same size of training data. However, SVM seems to have no change under the same condition. The results of evaluating based on metric 3, 4 are shown in Table 3.5. According to metric 3, BN has the best performance. The performance of SVM is the lowest. Metric 3 measures noise tolerance of various algorithm. The value of metric 3 for C4.5, RF and KNN are 67.0, 58.0, 50.0 % respectively which are less than the value for BN and larger than the value for SVM. Metric 3 suggests an order of the algorithms in terms of precision: BN, C4.5, RF, KNN and SVM. That is, BN shows the best performance in metric 3. Metric 4 suggests an order in terms of noise tolerance: KNN, RF, C4.5, BN, SVM. In term of metric 4, BN and SVM show the best performance. Therefore BN seems to strike a good balance between precision (metric 3) and noise tolerance (metric 4). SVM has the best noise tolerating ability. At the same time, the table reports that C4.5 also perform well in both metric 3 and metric 4. In spite of discriminative performance, it is indisputable fact the noisy traffic does reduce the classification precision.

Table 3.5 Overall performance on unclean traffic

Metrics/Algorithms	C4.5	SVM	BN	RF	KNN
Metric 3 (%)	67.0	39.0	72.0	58.0	50.0
Metric 4 (%)	18.0	10.0	10.0	29.0	34.0

3.4.2.2 Per-Class Performance

We use per-class F-measure to measure performance of these algorithms on unclean traffic training data.

Figure 3.9 shows the F-measure for 11 classes on the training data I. A general observation is that the F-measure of all algorithms have a decline trend per class. The performance of C4.5, BN, RF, KNN decrease considerably for FTP, HTTP, IMAP, POP3, RAZOR, SSH, SSL3, BT, DNS, SMTP. For SMALL, the decline was only slight. For C4.5, BN, and RF, all classes are easy to classify. POP3, SSH, SSL3, BT and DNS are easy classes, for which the F-measure of KNN is higher. In contrast, it is hard to classify RAZOR. For RAZOR, the performance declines nearly 40 % for C 4.5. For BN, HTTP, SSL3, BT and SMTP, the performance declined slowly in the first half, but rapidly in the second half. The per-class performance of above five algorithms is mostly between 70 and 100 % without noisy training data. However, five algorithms have lowest performance of about 10 % when 10 % clean traffic is available. For most of classes, the precision of BN decreases at varying rates when the proportion of noisy traffic change from 0 to 90 %. For instance, the decline is slight when the proportion of noisy traffic is less than about 75 %. Then, the decrease accelerates when the proportion of noisy traffic goes beyond 75 %. In contrast, the accuracy of SVM for 11 classes mainly reports a irregular fluctuations. The trend of per-class F-measure on other three algorithms is consistent with the trend of overall accuracy. The figure shows that SVM demonstrated good noise tolerance. The analysis reveals that the performance of each class does not always coincide with the overall performance due to the size difference of per-classes instances or other factors.

Table 3.6 represents per-class average accuracy in the unclean traffic. We observe that the BN is better than other algorithms on most classes. In contrast, the performance of SVM is lower. For FTP, BN is a better classifier and SVM is

Table 3.6 Per-class performance of unclean traffic on metric 5

Algorithms/Classes	C4.5	SVM	BN	RF	KNN
FTP (%)	36.0	0.0	61.0	27.0	17.0
HTTP (%)	68.0	46.0	67.0	62.0	54.0
IMAP (%)	32.0	0.0	62.0	24.0	15.0
POP3 (%)	71.0	55.0	78.0	60.0	54.0
RAZOR (%)	48.0	0.0	75.0	32.0	25.0
SSH (%)	82.0	42.0	86.0	74.0	69.0
SSL3 (%)	61.0	65.0	57.0	54.0	49.0
BT (%)	67.0	11.0	70.0	61.0	54.0
DNS (%)	66.0	0.0	68.0	52.0	41.0
SMTP (%)	77.0	42.0	75.0	72.0	61.0
SMALL (%)	36.0	5.0	36.0	28.0	17.0

Table 3.7 Per-class performance of unclean traffic on metric 6

Algorithms/ Classes	C4.5	SVM	BN	RF	KNN
FTP (%)	52.0	3.0	20.0	63.0	68.0
HTTP (%)	13.0	14.0	10.0	22.0	22.0
IMAP (%)	47.0	0.0	24.0	62.0	60.0
POP3 (%)	23.0	20.0	18.0	35.0	41.0
RAZOR (%)	46.0	0.0	23.0	65.0	66.0
SSH (%)	15.0	48.0	12.0	23.0	27.0
SSL3 (%)	16.0	5.0	11.0	16.0	24.0
BT (%)	13.0	10.0	14.0	24.0	25.0
DNS (%)	27.0	0.0	25.0	44.0	54.0
SMTP (%)	16.0	25.0	15.0	22.0	8.0
SMALL (%)	23.0	5.0	15.0	47.0	43.0

the worst. It is apparent that identification of HTTP, POP3, SSH and SSL3 is easy while it is hard to classify RAZOR, IMAP and SMALL. The order is similar for other traffic classes. Table 3.7 shows per-class noise tolerance, indicating that SVM and BN have better tolerance than other algorithms. The order is similar for overall performance. Meanwhile, the noise tolerance performance for HTTP, BT and SMTP is better than other classes.

3.5   Conclusion

In this chapter, we have reviewed the last decade's work on traffic classification. For researchers and practitioners, we have summarised and analysed the performance of various ML algorithms in classifying unclean traffic. Our results show that C4.5, BN, RF and KNN have higher performance on the clean network traffic. With growing portion of unclean training data, their performance decreases gradually. Such performance decline is accelerated when the unclean training data size reach a certain percentage. Although SVM performs poorly on clean data, it exhibits good tolerance of unclean data. On unclean data, in general BN is better than the other algorithms C4.5, SVM, RF, and KNN.

Acknowledgements This work was supported by National Natural Science Foundation of China (No. 61401371), Fundamental Research Funds for the Central Universities (No. XDJK2015D029), Science and Technology Foundation of Guizhou (No. LH20147386) and Natural Science Foundation of the Education Department of Guizhou Province.

References

1. Nguyen T, Armitage G (2008) A survey of techniques for internet traffic classification using machine learning. IEEE Commun Surv Tutorials 10(4):56–76
2. Xiang Y, Zhou W, Guo M (2009) Flexible deterministic packet marking: an IP traceback system to find the real source of attacks. IEEE Trans Parallel Distrib Syst 20(4):567–580
3. European Commission (2011) Horizon 2020-The framework programme for research and innovation, COM (2011) 808 final, 30 November 2011, Brussels: European Commission, available at: http://ec.europa.eu/programmes/horizon2020/en
4. United States. White House Office, Obama B (2011) International strategy for cyberspace: prosperity, security, and openness in a networked world, available at: http://www.whitehouse.gov/sites/default/files/rss_viewer/international_strategy_for_cyberspace.pdf
5. Sen S, Spatscheck O, Wang D (2004) Accurate, scalable in-network identification of P2P traffic using application signatures. In: Proceedings of the ACM WWW, pp 512–521
6. Moore AW, Zuev D (2005) Discriminators for use in flow-based classification. Intel Research Technical Report
7. Auld T, Moore A, Gull S (2007) Bayesian neural networks for internet traffic classification. IEEE Trans Neural Netw 18(1):223–239
8. Este A, Gringoli F, Salgarelli L (2009) Support vector machines for TCP traffic classification. Comput Netw 53(14):2476–2490
9. Li W, Moore AW (2007) A machine learning approach for efficient traffic classification. In: Proceedings of the 15th IEEE modeling, analysis, and simulation of computer and telecommunications systems (MASCOTS'07), pp 310–317
10. Zander S, Nguyen T, Armitage G (2005) Automated traffic classification and application identification using machine learning. In: Proceedings of the IEEE annual local computer networks, pp 250–257
11. Erman J, Mahanti A, Arlitt M (2006) Internet traffic identification using machine learning. In: Proceedings of the IEEE global telecommunications conference, pp 1–6
12. Erman J, Arlitt M, Mahanti A (2006) Traffic classification using clustering algorithms. In: Proceedings of the ACM SIGCOMM workshops, pp 281–286
13. Liu D, Lung C (2011) P2P traffic identification and optimization using fuzzy c-means clustering. In: Proceedings of the IEEE international conference on fuzzy systems, pp 2245–2252
14. Ren Y, Li G, Zhang J, Zhou W (2013) Lazy collaborative filtering for datasets with missing values. IEEE Trans Syst Man Cybern Part B 43(6):1822–1834
15. Zhang J, Chen C, Xiang Y, Zhou W (2012) Semi-supervised and compound classification of network traffic. J Secur Netw 7(4):252–261
16. Huang Y, Ma D, Zhang J, Zhao Y (2012) QDFA: query-dependent feature aggregation for medical image retrieval. IEICE Trans Inform Syst E95-D(1):275–279
17. Huang Y, Zhang J, Zhao Y, Ma D (2012) A new re-ranking method using enhanced pseudo-relevance feedback for content-based medical image retrieval. IEICE Trans Inform Syst E95-D(2):694–698
18. Zhang J, Xiang Y, Zhou W, Ye L, Mu Y (2011) Secure image retrieval based on visual content and watermarking protocol. J Comput. Oxford 54(10):1661–1674
19. Zhang J, Xiang Y, Wang Y, Zhou W, Xiang Y, Guan Y (2013) Network traffic classification using correlation information. IEEE Trans Parallel Distrib Syst 24(1):104–117
20. Glatz E, Dimitropoulos X (2012) Classifying internet one-way traffic. In: Proceedings of 12th ACM SIGMETRICS/PERFORMANCE conference on measurement and modeling of computer systems, pp 417–418
21. Jin Y, Duffield N, Erman J, Haffner P, Sen S, Zhang Z-L (2012) A modular machine learning system for flow-level traffic classification in large networks. ACM Trans Knowl Discov Data 6(1):4:1–4:34

22. Callado A, Kelner J, Sadok D, Kamienski CA, Fernandes S (2010) Better network traffic identification through the independent combination of techniques. J Netw Comput Appl 33(4):433–446
23. Carela-Espanol V, Barlet-Ros P, Cabellos-Aparicio A, Sole-Pareta J (2011) Analysis of the impact of sampling on netflow traffic classification. Comput Netw 55(5):1083–1099
24. Zhang J, Chen C, Xiang Y, Zhou W (2013) Robust network traffic identification with unknown applications. In: Proceedings of the ACM 8th symposium on information, computer and communications security (ASIA CCS), pp 405–414
25. Ostermann S (2003) tcptrace. Available at http://www.tcptrace.org
26. Zuev D, Moore AW (2005) Traffic classification using a statistical approach. In: Proceedings of the 6th passive active measurement workshop (PAM), vol 3431, pp 321–324
27. Dai L, Yun X, Xiao J (2008) Optimizing traffic classification using hybrid feature selection. In: Proceedings of the IEEE 9th conference on web-age information management (WAIM), pp 520–525
28. Williams N, Zander S, Armitage G (2006) A preliminary performance comparison of five machine learning algorithms for practical ip traffic flow classification. In: Proceedings of the SIGCOMM computer communication review, vol 36, pp 5–16
29. Erman J, Mahanti A, Arlitt M, Cohen I, Williamson C (2007) Offline/realtime traffic classification using semi-supervised learning. Perform Eval 64(9):1194–1213
30. Kim H, Claffy K, Fomenkova M, Barman D, Faloutsos M (2008) Internet traffic classification demystified: the myths, caveats and best practices. In: Proceedings of the ACM CoNEXT [Online]. Available at http://www.caida.org/publications/papers/2008/classificationndemystified/
31. En-Najjary T, Urvoy-Keller G, Pietrzyk M, Costeux JL (2010) Application-based feature selection for internet traffic classification. In: Proceedings of the IEEE 22nd conference on teletraffic congress (ITC), pp 1–8
32. Wasikowski M, Chen X (2010) Combating the small sample class imbalance problem using feature selection. IEEE Trans Knowl Data Eng 22:1388–1400
33. Zhang H, Lu G, Qassrawi MT, Zhang Y, Yu X (2012) Feature selection for optimizing traffic classification. Comput Commun 35(12):1457–1471
34. Fahad A, Tari Z, Khalil I, Habibb I, Alnuweiric H (2013) Toward an efficient and scalable feature selection approach for internet traffic classification. Comput Netw 57(9), 2040–2057
35. Fahad A, Tari Z, Khalil I, Almalawia A, Zomayab AY (2014) An optimal and stable feature selection approach for traffic classification based on multi-criterion fusion. Futur Gener Comput Syst 36:156–169
36. Moore AW, Zuev D (2005) Internet traffic classification using Bayesian analysis techniques. ACM SIGMETRICS Perform Eval Rev 33:50–60
37. Kim H, Claffy K, Fomenkov M, Barman D, Faloutsos M, Lee K (2008) Internet traffic classification demystified: myths, caveats, and the best practices. In: Proceedings of the ACM CoNEXT conference, pp 1–12
38. Lim Y-S, Kim H-C, Jeong J, Kim C-K, Kwon TT, Choi Y (2010) Internet traffic classification demystified: on the sources of the discriminative power. In: Proceedings of the 6th ACM CoNEXT conference, pp 9:1–9:12
39. Zhang J, Chen C, Xiang Y, Zhou W (2013) Internet traffic classification by aggregating correlated Naive Bayes predictions. IEEE Trans Inf Forensics Secur 8(1):5–15
40. Bernaille L, Teixeira R (2007) Early recognition of encrypted applications. In: Passive and active network measurement. Springer, Heidelberg, pp 165–175
41. Hullar B, Laki S, Gyorgy A (2011) Early identification of peer-to-peer traffic. In: Proceedings of the IEEE international conference on communications, pp 1–6
42. Nguyen T, Armitage G (2006) Training on multiple sub-flows to optimize the use of machine learning classifiers in real-world ip networks. In: Proceedings of the 31st IEEE conference on local computer networks, pp 369–376
43. Crotti M, Dusi M, Gringoli F, Salgarelli L (2007) Traffic classification through simple statistical fingerprinting. ACM SIGCOMM Comput Commun Rev 37:5–16

44. Xie G, Iliofotou M, Keralapura R, Faloutsos M, Nucci A (2012) Sub-flow: towards practical flow-level traffic classification. In: Proceedings of the IEEE INFOCOM, pp 2541–2545
45. Suthaharan S (2014) Big data classification: problems and challenges in network intrusion prediction with machine learning. ACM SIGMETRICS Perform Eval Rev 41(4):70–73
46. Singh K, Guntuku SC, Thakur A, Hota C (2014) Big data analytics framework for peer-to-peer botnet detection using random forests. Inform Sci 278:488–497
47. McGregor A, Hall M, Lorier P, Brunskill J (2004) Flow clustering using machine learning techniques. In: Passive and active network measurement. Springer, Heidelberg, pp 205–214
48. Bernaille L, Teixeira R, Akodkenou I, Soule A, Salamatian K (2006) Traffic classification on the fly. ACM SIGCOMM Comput Commun Rev 36:23–26
49. Wang Y, Xiang Y, Yu S-Z (2010) An automatic application signature construction system for unknown traffic. Concurrency Comput Pract Experience 22:1927–1944
50. Finamore A, Mellia M, Meo M (2011) Mining unclassified traffic using automatic clustering techniques. In: Proceedings of the 3rd international traffic monitoring and analysis (TMA), pp 150–163
51. Erman J, Mahanti A, Arlitt M, Cohenz I, Williamson C (2007) Semi-supervised network traffic classification. ACM SIGMETRICS Perform Eval Rev 35(1):369–370
52. Li X, Qi F, Xu D, Qiu X (2011) An internet traffic classification method based on semi-supervised support vector machine. In: Proceedings of the IEEE conference communications (ICC), pp 1–5
53. Erman J, Arlitt M, Mahanti A (2006) Traffic classification using clustering algorithms. In: Proceedings of the SIGCOMM workshop' 06, pp 281–286
54. Erman J, Mahanti A, Arlitt M (2006) Internet traffic identification using machine learning techniques. In: Proceedings of the 49th IEEE global telecommunication conference (GLOBECOM 2006), pp 1–6
55. Pietrzyk M, Costeux J-L, Urvoy-Keller G, En-Najjary T (2009) Challenging statistical classification for operational usage: the ADSL case. In: Proceedings of the 9th ACM SIGCOMM, pp 122–135
56. Williams N, Zander S, Armitage G (2006) A preliminary performance comparison of five machine learning algorithms for practical IP traffic flow classification. ACM SIGCOMM Comput Commun Rev 36(5):5–16
57. Lim Y, Kim H, Jeong J, Kim C, Kwon T, Choi Y (2010) Internet traffic classification demystified: on the sources of the discriminative power. In: Proceedings of the ACM CoNEXT conference, pp 9:1–9:12
58. Lee S, Kim H, Barman D, Lee S, Kim C, Kwon T, Choi Y (2011) Netramark: a network traffic classification benchmark. ACM SIGCOMM Comput Commun Rev 41(1):22–30
59. Hall M, Frank E, Holmes G, Pfahringer B, Reutemann P, Witten IH (2009) The WEKA data mining software: an update. SIGKDD Explor 11(1):10–18
60. Zhang J, Chen X, Xiang Y, Zhou W, Wu J (2014) Robust network traffic classification. IEEE/ACM Trans Netw 23(4):1257–1270
61. Guyon I, Elisseeff A (2003) An introduction to variable and feature selection. J Mach Learn Res 3:1157–1182
62. Wu X, Kumar V, Quinlan JR, Ghosh J, Yang Q, Motoda H, McLachlan GJ, Ng AFM, Liu B, Yu PS, Zhou Z-H, Steinbach M, Hand DJ, Steinberg D (2008) Top 10 algorithms in data mining. Knowl Inform Syst 14(1):1–37
63. Gislason PO, Benediktsson JA, Sveinsson JR (2006) Random forests for land cover classification. Pattern Recogn Lett 27(4):294–300

Chapter 4
Security Theories and Practices for Big Data

Lei Xu and Weidong Shi

Abstract Big data applications usually require flexible and scalable infrastructure for efficient processing. Cloud computing satisfies these requirements very well and has been widely adopted to provide big data services. However, outsourcing and resource sharing features of cloud computing lead to security concerns when applied to big data applications, e.g., confidentiality of data/program, and integrity of the processing procedure. On the other hand, when cloud owns the data and provides analytic service, data privacy also becomes a challenge. Security concerns and pressing demand for adopting big data technology together motivate the development of a special class of security technologies for safe big data processing in cloud environment. These approaches are roughly divided into two categories: designing new algorithms with unique security features and developing security enhanced systems to protect big data applications. In this chapter, we review the approaches for secure big data processing from both categories, evaluate and compare these technologies from different perspectives, and present a general outlook on the current state of research and development in the field of security theories for big data.

4.1 Introduction

As mentioned in previous chapters, big data has found various applications in different sectors including retailer, academia, energy, defence, etc. Big data applications require efficient and cost effective processing. Emerging cloud computing technology provides an adequate platform for these applications. For a big data application, there are three participants involved:

- Data Source. Data source provides input data for the analytic algorithm. Data source can be provided by the user or by the cloud;

L. Xu (✉) • W. Shi
University of Houston, Houston, TX, USA
e-mail: lxu13@uh.edu; larryshi@cs.uh.edu

© Springer International Publishing Switzerland 2016
S. Yu, S. Guo (eds.), *Big Data Concepts, Theories, and Applications*,
DOI 10.1007/978-3-319-27763-9_4

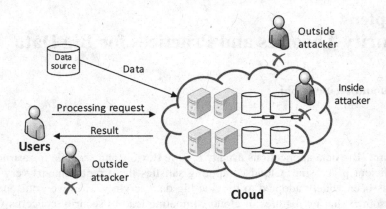

Fig. 4.1 Overview of big data processing using cloud computing technology. Data are fed into the cloud computing infrastructure for processing and the data may contain sensitive information. Both outside and inside attackers (e.g., malicious users and administrators) pose a threat to the security of the data. An outside attacker may also cause information leakage by observing the returned results when the data source is owned by cloud

- User. User retrieves big data analytic results from the cloud to improve his/her business. User can provide his/her own program to process the data or use the algorithm provided by the cloud;
- Cloud. No matter who offers the data and program, cloud carries out the computation and returns results to the user. Cloud may also provide storage service to help manage data from the data source.

Figure 4.1 summarizes the basic work flow of cloud based big data processing. Data source sends data to the cloud and user asks the cloud to process the data and retrieves corresponding results. While enabling efficient big data processing with cloud computing, it also introduces new security challenges:

1. Because of the resources sharing feature of cloud computing, different users could reside on the same infrastructure and a malicious user can cross the pre-defined boundary and access the data/results without permission. In addition, it is easy for a rogue administrator of the infrastructure with high privileges to look into the processing procedure. When the data source is provided by the user, data confidentiality is at risk. The adversaries (outside malicious users or inside rogue administrators) may also tamper the integrity of the data processing procedure;
2. When the data source is provided by the cloud and contains sensitive information, a malicious user may learn these information through requests of data analytic results.

These potential threats are depicted in Fig. 4.1.

Cryptography tools are essential for all big data security protection approaches. The cryptography community has developed its own mathematical language for scheme description and security analysis. In most cases, we will ignore the complex mathematical formulas of these cryptography tools and only provide the outlines to show how they are used to protect the big data security. More detailed information can be found in the references.

In a nutshell, big data security includes the following three aspects: confidentiality, privacy, and integrity. For some scenarios, certain aspects may play a more important role while in other cases breaching of any of these features can lead to serious consequences. In the following sections, we discuss each these security requirements separately.

4.2 Confidentiality of Big Data

When talking about big data security, confidentiality is the basic and the most common requirement for big data processing, especially in the cloud environment. In this scenario, the data source belongs to the user and the user is totally trusted. The main threats come from the inside/outside attacker on the cloud side, as showed in Fig. 4.1. Big data confidentiality requires that only the user has access to the plain content of the data while the cloud is responsible for the data processing job.

Using cloud for big data processing is a type of outsourcing computation application with its own characteristics. Most confidentiality protection techniques for outsourced computation are also applicable to big data. In the remainder of this section, we review both techniques for general outsourcing computation confidentiality protection and those specific to big data.

4.2.1 Big Data Confidentiality Protection with Cryptography for General Purpose Processing

In this section, we review two cryptography tools that are able to provide confidentiality protection for general big data applications.

4.2.1.1 Fully Homomorphic Encryption for General Purpose Big Data Processing

An intuitive way to achieve confidentiality protection is to use an encryption algorithm to encrypt the data before sending to the cloud for processing. However, classical encryption schemes (e.g., symmetric encryption scheme AES and asymmetric encryption scheme RSA) cannot help as they prevent the cloud from processing the data. Homomorphic encryption technique is developed to solve this dilemma, which can achieve confidentiality protection and data processing at the same time.

In abstract algebra, a homomorphism is a structure-preserving map between two algebraic structures such as fields, rings, and groups. Formally, let $(G_1, *)$ and $(G_2, +)$ be two algebraic structures, a function f is a homomorphism from G_1 to G_2 if $f(g_1 * g_2) = f(g_1) + f(g_2)$, where $g_1, g_2 \in G_1$ (see [34] for more details). When G_1 and G_2 are fields or rings, each of them has two operations. If the function f is a homomorphism for both of the two operations, f is called fully homomorphic as all operations on G_1 can be mapped to G_2. This idea was first extended to encryption scenario in 1978 [55], where operations on plain-text space are mapped to cipher-text space, and the results in cipher-text space can be decrypted to get corresponding results in plain-text space. When the plain-text space is defined as $\mathbb{F}_2$, corresponding operations on plain-text are equivalent to bit operations XOR and AND, which are enough to construct arbitrary circuits. If a fully homomorphic encryption scheme supports these two operations, it can support any operations on cipher-texts.

A fully homomorphic encryption (FHE) scheme consists of the following four algorithms:

- KeyGen. Given the security and public parameters, KeyGen generates a public/private key pair (pk, sk) and a evaluation public key evk. pk and evk are public while sk is kept secret;
- Encryption. Given a message m_i and public key pk, a cipher-text c is generated;
- Evaluation. Evaluation takes as input a set of cipher-texts $C = \{c_1, c_2, \cdots, c_n\}$, an evaluation function $Evl()$, and an evaluation public key evl, it outputs a cipher-text c, which is the result of encrypting output of $Evl(m_1, m_2, \cdots, m_n)$;
- Decryption. Given a cipher-text c and the private key sk, Decryption outputs the plain-text m.

Gentry developed the first FHE scheme based on idea lattices [27], and then it was extended to use other techniques for FHE scheme construction, e.g., FHE based on integer operations [68] and FHE based on learning with errors (LWE) [12]. For some schemes, evk is not necessary for Evaluation [28].

The way utilizing FHE scheme toward secure big data processing in cloud environment is straight forward:

1. Preparing and submitting the data. The user first generates a public/private key pair for FHE, and then uses the public key to encrypt the data and submits the cipher-texts to the cloud. The user also sends the evaluation function, public key, and evaluation public key to the cloud;
2. Processing and returning the results. The cloud applies the evaluation function to the received data (using the evaluation public key). The generated cipher-texts are sent back to the user;
3. Decrypting the received cipher-texts. The user uses his/her private key to decrypt the received cipher-texts and get the final results.

The advantage of using FHE scheme for confidentiality protection of big data applications is that FHE can support arbitrary operations on encrypted data and it can achieve general purpose big data processing. Furthermore, the security of FHE schemes is usually based on well studied mathematical problems. This also puts the confidentiality of the data being processed on a solid foundation.

However, using FHE schemes for confidentiality preserving big data processing also has some limitations:

1. Poor performance. Public key encryption schemes are very expensive and usually only applied for key protection. As a special type of public key encryption scheme, FHE scheme is even more expensive. Considering the amount of data need to be processed in the cloud, the user has to spend a long time to encrypt all the data. The encryption process is usually also accompanied by cipher-texts expansion, i.e., a cipher-text is much larger than the original plain-text. The expansion increases the communication cost;
2. Multiple data resources. In case there are more than one data source that is managed by different users and contributes data to the processing procedure, FHE based approach is not applicable. Users cannot use their own public key to encrypt the data because the cloud cannot operate on cipher-texts generated using different public keys;
3. Compatibility with big data processing framework. Sematic secure encryption may cause troubles for big data processing frameworks. For example, MapReduce [19] uses the values of *keys* to distribute key-value pairs to different reducers. With FHE scheme, the same *key* has different cipher-texts and the key-value pair distribution mechanism cannot work properly any more.

4.2.1.2   Secure Multi-party Computation for General Purpose Big Data Processing

The concept of secure multi-party computation (SMPC) is closely related to the idea of zero knowledge [30, 54]. For example, two millionaires can compute which one is richer without revealing their net worth. This very example was used by Yao in a 1982 paper [75] which was later named Yao's Millionaires' Problem [62]. Informally, an SMPC protocol involves n participants $P_1, P_2, \cdots, P_n$, and P_i has private data d_i. Participants want to compute the value of a public function F on n inputs $(d_1, d_2, \ldots, d_n)$. It is required that if no participant can learn more from the description of the public function F and the result of the global calculation than what he/she can learn from his/her own entry under particular conditions depending on the model used (e.g., *static corruption model* where the adversary controls a fixed set of participants, *adaptive corruption model* where the adversary can corrupt different parties during the computation).

Big data processing procedure is a special secure two-party computation. The user and the cloud are two parties, and only the user provides the input data.

Lindell and Pinkas surveyed the basic paradigms and notions of secure multiparty computation and discussed their relevance to the field of confidentiality preserving data mining [46].

Secure computation of the two-party case can be efficiently implemented by a generic protocol due to Yao [76]. Let f be the function that the user wants to evaluate. The protocol is based on expressing f as a combinational circuit with gates expressing any function $g : \{0, 1\} \times \{0, 1\} \rightarrow \{0, 1\}$ (including simple OR. AND, and NOT gates). Note that it is known that any polynomial-time function can be expressed as a combinatorial circuit of polynomial size. The input of the circuit consists of the bits of the user's input, and the output of the circuit is the evaluation result of f. The protocol is based on evaluating this circuit. The number of rounds of the protocol is constant. Its communication overhead depends on the size of the circuit, while its computation overhead depends on the number of input wires. We refer the readers to [45] for more details.

Like FHE based approach, SMPC can provide confidentiality protection for general big data application. Furthermore, SMPC based method can be easily extended to support the case of multiple data sources. Besides high cost (e.g., circuits preparation), the main disadvantage of SMPC based approach is that it requires interactions between the user(s) and cloud, which requires the user(s) to be online.

Researchers have also studied to construct SMPC protocol for special applications, we discuss applications of these protocols in big data in Sect. 4.2.2.3.

4.2.2 Big Data Confidentiality Protection with Cryptography for Special Applications

Both fully homomorphic encryption and secure multi-party computation schemes can achieve "general" confidentiality preserving big data processing at a high cost. For specific big data applications, it is possible to develop more efficient cryptography based confidentiality protection schemes.

4.2.2.1 Big Data Confidentiality Protection for Searching

Searching is one of the most common operations. In order to support searching operation while preserving the confidentiality, researchers developed a type of encryption schemes that support searching on cipher-texts. Note that the problem is trivial if we do not introduce randomness in the encryption, i.e., the same plain-text is always encrypted to the same cipher-text. But such encryption cannot meet the basic requirement of sematic security.

4.2.2.1.1   Public Key Searchable Encryption

Boneh et al. developed a public key searchable encryption scheme [10]. It consists of four algorithms:

- KeyGen. It takes a security parameter and generates a public/private key pair (pk, sk);
- PEKS. PEKS takes a public key pk and a word W to generate a searchable encryption of W;
- Trapdoor. Given a private key sk and a word W, Trapdoor produces a trapdoor T_W;
- Test. Test takes as inputs the private key sk, a searchable encryption $S =$ PEKS(pk, W'), and a trapdoor $T_W =$ Trapdoor(sk, W). If $W = W'$ it outputs 'yes', otherwise it outputs 'no'.

The encryption scheme allows the user to store encrypted data in the cloud while enabling the cloud to execute the search operation: the user first runs KeyGen to get a pair of key (pk, sk). The data are divided into words and encrypted using pk. The user sends these encrypted words to the cloud for future use (searching). If the user wants to do a search for W in the encrypted data on the cloud side, he/she generates a trapdoor T_W for W by running Trapdoor with sk and W. The cloud runs Test to search whether the word W appears in the encrypted data it possesses.

Even without considering the encryption cost, the performance of this scheme is not acceptable if the number of words is relatively large as binary search is not applicable.

4.2.2.1.2   Symmetric Key Searchable Encryption

In most cases, symmetric encryption schemes are much faster than public key encryption schemes. When the data size is large, it is desirable to have symmetric key based searchable encryption schemes.

One approach to provision symmetric encryption with search capabilities is with a so-called secure index [29]. A secure index is a data structure that allows a querier with a "trapdoor" for a word x to test in $O(1)$ time only if the index contains x. The index reveals no information about its contents without trapdoors, and trapdoors can only be generated with a secret key. For big data searching, it works as follows: the user indexes and encrypts its data and sends the secure index together with the encrypted data to the cloud. To search for a keyword w, the client generates and sends a trapdoor for w which the cloud uses to run the search operation and recover pointers to the appropriate encrypted data.

Goh designed Z-IDX that can be used for searching under the security model IND2-CKA and the scheme consists of four algorithms [29]:

- KeyGen. Given a security parameter s, outputs the master private key K_{priv};
- Trapdoor. Given the master key K_{priv} and word w, outputs the trapdoor T_w for w;

- `BulidIndex`. Given a document D and the master key K_{priv}, outputs the index I_D;
- `SearchIndex`. Given the trapdoor T_w for word w and the index I_D for document D, outputs 1 if $w \in D$ and 0 otherwise.

Reza et al. extended the work of Goh. They introduced a security model stronger than IND2-CKA and considered the situation where an arbitrary group of parties other than the owner can submit search queries [16].

4.2.2.2 Big Data Confidentiality Protection for Numerical Comparison

Big data analytics usually involve numerical data comparisons. FHE scheme can support such operations on cipher-texts but is too expensive for large amount of data and comparisons. To overcome this difficulty, more efficient order preserving encryption techniques have been developed.

Order preserving encryption keeps the orders of the numerical messages after encryption, i.e., for two messages m_1 and m_2, we have $E(m_1) \leq E(m_2)$ if and only if $m_1 \leq m_2$, where $E()$ is the encryption procedure.

Agrawal et al. developed the first order preserving encryption (OPE) scheme, which allows the cloud to do comparisons on the cipher-texts [3]. The OPES uses the same information to decrypt encoded values or encrypt new values so it is a symmetric encryption scheme. The OPES works in four steps:

1. `KeyGen`. By checking the data set, the user generates the secret key k which is used to model the data set;
2. `Model`. Given the distribution of the input data set P, the secret key k, and the target distribution, `Model` describes them as piece-wise linear splines;
3. `Flatten`. The plain-text data set P is transformed into a "flat" data set F such that the values in F are uniformly distributed;
4. `Transform`. The flatted data set F is transformed into the cipher-text set C and the values in C are distributed according to the target distribution.

Note that in this process we always have $p_i < p_j \Rightarrow f_i < f_j \Rightarrow c_i < c_j$.

Boldyreva et al. initiated the cryptographic study of order-preserving symmetric encryption in [7], which shows that it is hard for a practical OPE scheme to meet the security requirement such as IND-CPA. They developed a new security definition POPF-CCA and constructed an OPE scheme that is secure under this definition.

With OPES, the user can send cipher-texts to cloud and ask cloud to do big data analytic based on comparisons. OPES is much efficient and has been adopted by CryptDB for numerical data encryption [53]. The two main problems of OPES are:

1. Limited operation. OPES only supports comparison and it is not enough to support complex big data applications;
2. Weaker security model. Existing OPES cannot meet classical sematic security and may leak information in certain cases.

4.2.2.3 Big Data Confidentiality Protection for Special Applications with SMPC

As mentioned earlier in Sect. 4.2.1.2, one can construct a two-party SMPC protocol for any function in a general way. For special big data applications, more efficient SMPC protocols are constructed.

4.2.2.3.1 Private Set Intersection Protocol

The private set intersection (PSI) problem involves two parties, a client and a server. They want to jointly compute the intersection of their private input sets in a manner that at the end the client learns the intersection and the server learns nothing. PSI has various applications in big data. One example is DNA matching. Cloud possesses a set of DNA sequences that reflect certain illness. The user (e.g., a physician) wants to utilize the cloud to check his/her patient's DNA. With PSI, the user learns whether the suspicious DNA sequence appears in the patient's DNA while the cloud learns nothing. Cristofaro and Tsudik designed a PSI protocol with linear complexity based on RSA-OPRF [18]. Dong, Chen, and Wen proposed an efficient and scalable PSI protocol based on oblivious Bloom intersection [21].

4.2.2.3.2 Computing ID3

ID3 is a basic algorithm for constructing decision tree, which is a tool for solving the classification problem in machine learning and data mining. A decision tree is a rooted tree in which each internal node corresponds to an attribute, and the edges leaving it correspond to the possible values taken on by that attribute. The leaves of the tree contain the expected class value for transactions matching the path from the root to that leaf. Given a decision tree, one can predict the class of a new transaction by traversing the nodes from the root down. The value of the leaf at the end of this path is the expected class value of the new transaction. The ID3 algorithm is used to design a decision tree based on a given database. The tree is constructed top-down in a recursive fashion. At the root, each attribute is tested to determine how well it alone classifies the transactions. The "best" attribute is then chosen, and the remaining transactions are partitioned by it. ID3 is then recursively called on each partition, i.e., on a smaller database containing only the appropriate transactions, and without the splitting attribute [46].

Lindell and Pinkas gave an efficient SMPC protocol for computing ID3 [44]. The secure protocol is based on the observation that each node of the tree can be computed separately, with the output made public, before continuing to the next node. This is true since the assignments of attributes to each node are part of the output and may therefore be revealed. The computation starts from the root of the tree. Once the attribute of a given node has been found, both parties can separately partition their remaining transactions accordingly for the coming recursive calls.

As a result, the protocol is reduced to privately finding the attribute of a node, namely the attribute with the highest information gain.

4.2.2.4 Big Data Confidentiality Protection for Sharing

Sharing is a basic application for cloud based data management. In this scenario, there are multiple users in the system and one of the users owns the data source (owner). The owner uses the cloud to help to share the data with other users (receivers). In this process, the owner needs to ensure only selected receivers can get the data and other parties (including other users and the cloud) cannot access the data. The cloud can deploy an access control mechanism [59] to partially solve this problem. But this approach requires the user to trust the cloud and the access control system. If the user chooses to store encrypted data in the cloud to protect the confidentiality, a key distribution mechanism is required to enable data sharing.

4.2.2.4.1 Classical Public Key Approach

Classical public key encryption scheme can be used to construct confidentiality preserving data sharing in a straightforward way.

1. System setup. Each user is given a public/private key pair, and a trusted certificate authority (CA) generates certificate for each public key;
2. Data uploading. The owner encrypts the data using symmetric encryption scheme with key *dek*, and uploads the encrypted data to the cloud;
3. Data sharing. To share the data with a group of users, the owner retrieves the certificates of these users and the data owner encrypts *dek* using each of the certificate and uploads all the cipher-texts to the cloud;
4. Data retrieving. Each receiver communicates with the cloud to get the encrypted data and corresponding cipher-text of *dek*. Then the user uses its private key to decrypt to get *dek*, which is used to decrypt the data.

This approach protects the confidentiality of the shared data as the cloud can only access the encrypted data in the whole sharing process. The main disadvantage of this classical public key based data sharing is performance. The computation cost on the data owner side is linear to the number of receivers, and the owner does not leverage the cloud to help in this process.

4.2.2.4.2 Attribute Based Encryption Approach

Attribute based encryption (ABE) is an extension of identity based encryption [8] and fuzzy identity based encryption [58]. Informally, attribute based encryption schemes embed a set of attributes into the keys and cipher-texts. Only when the attributes of a key match with those of the a cipher-text, decryption can success.

There are mainly two types of attribute based encryption, cipher-text policy attribute based encryption (CP-ABE) and key policy attribute based encryption (KP-ABE).

Key policy attribute based encryption scheme [32] embeds a set of attributes into a cipher-text in the encryption process. For each user, a trusted third party generates a private key for him/her, and an access structure is associated with the private key. Only when the attributes of the cipher-text satisfy the access structure, the decryption can success. Formally, a KP-ABE scheme consists of four algorithms:

- Setup. This is a randomized algorithm that takes the security parameter and outputs the public parameters PK and a master key MK;
- Encryption. Encryption takes as input a message m, a set of attributes γ, and public parameters PK. It outputs the cipher-text c_γ;
- KeyGen. This algorithm takes an access structure A, the master key MK and the public parameters PK to produce the decryption key d_A;
- Decryption. Given the cipher-text c_γ and decryption key d_A, Decryption outputs the message m if γ satisfies A.

One way to define access structure A is using a tree where the leaves are attributes and internal nodes are logical operation. Figure 4.2 gives an example of such access structure.

Cipher-text policy attribute based encryption [5] is similar to KP-ABE and also consists of four algorithms. But for Encryption, an access structure is used to encrypt the message, and a set of attributes is used to generate the decryption key.

To apply ABE scheme for confidentiality preserving data sharing, the data owner first encrypts the data using *dek* and uses the ABE scheme to encrypt *dek*. The data owner is also responsible for generating decryption keys for other users. By embedding attributes/access structure into the cipher-texts/decryption keys, the data owner achieves similar function as attribute based access control [77].

The main problem of ABE based data sharing is that the control policy is relatively static. When the owner releases the decryption key to the receiver, the privilege is fixed. Another issue is that the cost of generating decryption key is high, and the owner needs to spend a lot of time when the number of receivers is relatively large.

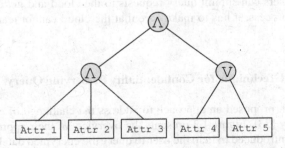

Fig. 4.2 An example of access structure. The leaves present attributes and the internal nodes are logical operations. This access structure is equivalent to expression: (Attr 1 AND Attr 2 AND Attr 3) AND (Attr 4 OR Attr 5)

4.2.2.4.3   Proxy Re-encryption based Approach

Proxy re-encryption was first studied in [6, 49], and it provides a way to convert a cipher-text encrypted using k_1 to a cipher-text of k_2 without leaking the plain-text. Formally, a proxy re-encryption scheme consists of following algorithms:

- KeyGen. Given the security and public parameters, KeyGen generates public/private key pair (pk, sk) for each user;
- ReKeyGen. This algorithm takes as input two key pair (pk_a, sk_a) and (pk_b, sk_b), and outputs a re-encryption key $rk_{a \to b}$. For some schemes, sk_b is not needed for ReKeyGen;
- Encryption. Encryption takes as input the public key pk_a and a message m. It outputs a cipher-text c_a;
- ReEncryption. With cipher-text c_a and re-encryption key $rk_{a \to b}$, the algorithm outputs a cipher-text c_b, which can be decrypted using sk_b;
- Decryption. Given cipher-text c_a (c_b) and private key sk_a (sk_b), Decrypt outputs the message m.

To apply proxy re-encryption for data sharing, ReEncryption is deployed in the cloud. Data owner encrypts the data with *dek* and *dek* is encrypted with his/her own public key. For each potential receiver, the data owner generates a re-encryption key. If the data owner wants to share the data with a specific receiver, he/she asks the cloud to re-encrypt the cipher-text of *dek* and sends to the receiver to decrypt.

The advantages of proxy re-encryption based data sharing is flexibility. The owner can change his/her sharing strategy for different files. At the same time, generation of re-encryption key is usually cheaper than ABE decryption key. The main issue of this approach is that the cloud has to be assumed to be semi-trusted.

4.2.3   Big Data Confidentiality Protection for Query

Database as a service (DaaS) is one of the killer applications of cloud based big data, and supporting SQL queries is the key component of such service. In this scenario, one of the users owns the data source (here is a database) and sends the data to the cloud. All the users can submit query requests to the cloud and get corresponding results. In this process, it has to make sure that the cloud cannot learn contents of the database.

4.2.3.1   Bucket Technique for Confidentiality Preserving Query

Hacigümüş et al. proposed an approach to address the challenge of confidentiality preserving query [33]. Figure 4.3 presents the overview of their approach, where a *secure proxy* is introduced to help the user to query the encrypted database managed by the cloud.

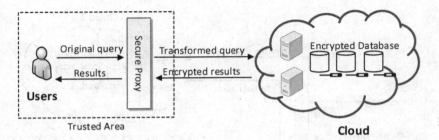

Fig. 4.3 Overview of the confidentiality preserving query. The cloud stores encrypted data and a security proxy is deployed between the end users and the cloud. The security proxy is trusted and responsible for transforming user's query and returned results from the cloud

Original Data				
eid	ename	salary	addr	did
23	Tom	70K	Maple	40
860	Mary	60K	Main	80
320	John	50K	River	50
875	Jerry	55K	Hopewell	110

Transformed Data					
etuple	eid^S	ename^S	salary^S	addr^S	did^S
110011001110010...	2	19	81	18	2
100000000011101...	4	31	59	41	4
111101000010001...	7	7	7	22	2
101010101011110...	4	71	49	22	4

Fig. 4.4 An example of bucket technique for confidentiality protection [33]. The *left table* contains the original tuples and on the *right* it is the table with protected tuples. The *first column* of the *right table* is the encryption of the original tuples, and the other columns contain the bucket IDs of the attributes

The proposed method works as follows:

1. For a given attribute, the range is divided into sub-ranges (buckets), and a random token is generated for each bucket. The original tuple is encrypted and stored together with these tokens. Figure 4.4 gives an example of processed table;
2. When a user queries the database, the query request is transformed by *secure proxy*. Specifically, all query values are replaced by corresponding bucket tokens;
3. The cloud carries out the transformed queries based on the tokens and returns the encrypted results to *secure proxy*;
4. *Secure proxy* decrypts the returned results and filter out undesirable information which are included because bucket tokens are used for the query instead of specific values. These filtered results are sent to the end user.

This approach provides a certain level of confidentiality protection because the cloud does not have access to the plain-texts of the tuples. However, bucket tokens may leak some information about the original database: frequencies that tokens appear reflect the distribution of the original attribute values.

Another issue related to this bucketization technique is performance. Because the cloud can only query with fuzzed information (bucket tokens), the returned results may contain a lot of undesirable tuples, especially for queries like Join. This wastes both communication bandwidth and computation resources on *secure proxy* side.

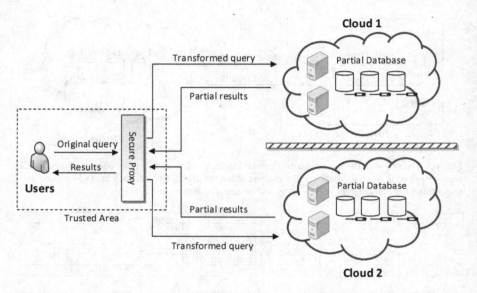

Fig. 4.5 Overview of the system that utilizes data division for confidentiality preserving query. Original database is divided into two parts and managed by two clouds, and it is supposed that the two clouds never collaborate to recover the original database

4.2.3.2   Data Decomposition for Confidentiality Preserving Query

Aggarwal et al. proposed to divide a database into two parts and use two clouds to manage each of them to achieve confidentiality preserving query [2]. Figure 4.5 shows the system overview of this method.

Let R be the attributes set of the database. The database is decomposed through attributes decomposition. A decomposition of R is denoted as $D(R) = (R_1, R_2, E)$, where R_1 and R_2 are the sets of attributes in the two fragments, and E refers to the set of attributes that are encrypted. R_1, R_2 and E satisfy that $R = R_1 \bigcup R_2$, $E \subseteq R_1$, and $E \subseteq R_2$. For a certain attribute in E, its values are encrypted with random pad: for attribute value a, a random pad r is generated, and $a_1 = a \oplus r, a_2 = r$, then a_1 and a_2 are distributed to two clouds (different ways can be used for encoding).

The confidentiality is defined using constraints $\mathscr{P}$, which is a set of subsets of R, i.e., $\mathscr{P} \subseteq 2^R$. The decomposition $D(R)$ satisfies the constraints $\mathscr{P}$ if for all $P \in \mathscr{P}$, we have $P \nsubseteq (R_1 - E)$ and $P \nsubseteq (R_2 - E)$.

4.2.4   Big Data Confidentiality Protection with Hardware

Cryptography based approaches for big data confidentiality protection usually enjoy stronger security model (they do not require the cloud to contain any trusted component) and more clear security features (security features can be formally verified). But at the same time, these schemes suffer from high cost, which seriously limits the adoption of these techniques. To offer more practical solutions, people developed hardware based approaches to protect big data confidentiality.

4.2.4.1 TPM Based Secure HDFS

Trusted platform module (TPM [66]) is one of the most widely used hardware based security protection technique which provides a secure environment for secrets storage and sensitive operations. Figure 4.6 depicts the basic components of TPM.

Cohen and Acharya designed a trusted HDFS storage system using TPM which protects the confidentiality of the data at rest [15]. HDFS is used by many big data processing frameworks for data storage. The trusted HDFS storage system uses TPM as the root of trust to manage the encryption key and does the encryption/decryption jobs. Programs must pass the TPM verification to access the decryption engine so it is hard for an attacker to compromise the confidentiality. But TPM is not designed to process huge amount of data and the performance becomes a bottle neck. The authors suggested using Intel AES instructions for encryption/decryption. This method greatly improves the performance but weakens the security level as the processor does not support security features of TPM (e.g., tamper-resistant, key sealing, etc.).

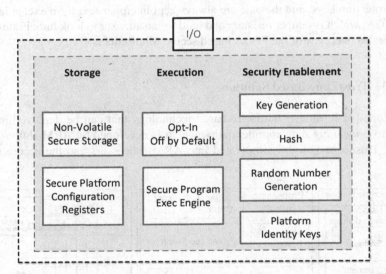

Fig. 4.6 Components of TPM [67]. Non-volatile secure storage stores persistent TPM data; secure platform configuration registers store integrity measurements; Opt-in stores TPM state information and enforces state-dependent limitations (e.g., some commands must not be executed if the TPM is disabled); secure program exec engine processes TPM commands, ensures segregation of operations and protection of secrets; security enablement provides basic cryptographic services

4.2.4.2 FPGA Based Confidentiality Preserving MapReduce

FPGAs combine some advantages of software (fast development, low non-recurring engineering costs) with those of hardware (performance, relative power efficiency). These advantages have made FPGAs an important fixture, especially for those applications that are computation intensive. Particularly, a growing body of literature has focused on applying FPGAs to accelerate MapReduce based data analytics (e.g., [61]).

Most today's FPGAs are configured with bitstreams which completely determine the functionality of the devices. Note that the bitstream is typically stored external to the FPGA in a dedicated configuration memory. Then, it is loaded into the FPGA on every power-up or reset. A disadvantage of this design is that a malicious attacker may learn the bitstream during the loading process, which may result in the compromise of intellectual property. In order to protect valuable intellectual properties of FPGA bitstream developers, many solutions have been proposed to protect the bitstreams themselves. One common approach already implemented by commercially available FPGA devices is to have a bitstream encrypted and decrypted each time when it is loaded into the FPGA. Figure 4.7 depicts the bitstream protection mechanism.

Xu et al. proposed to utilize the bitstream encryption mechanism and the tamper resistance property of FPGA for confidentiality preserving MapReduce [73, 74]. The mapper and reducer functions are securely sealed in bitstreams together with data protection keys, and the data are always kept in cipher-text form except inside the FPGA, which is tamper resistant and hard for an attacker to look into. Figure 4.8 provides an overview of the FPGA based secure MapReduce.

4.2.4.3 TrustZone Based Solution

TrustZone [4] is another hardware based technology that can be deployed in the cloud to protect big data confidentiality, which is developed by ARM (http://arm. com/). TrustZone is tightly integrated into ARM processors and the secure state

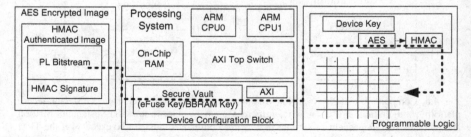

Fig. 4.7 Mechanism of bitstream encryption and authentication implemented in FPGA. In secure mode, a bitstream is encrypted with AES-CBC mode and certified using HMAC

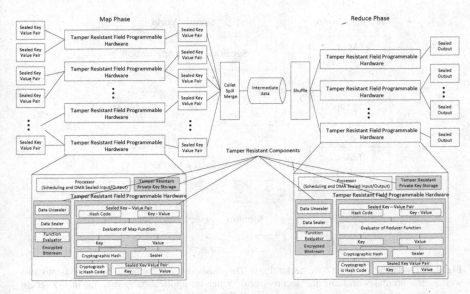

Fig. 4.8 Map and Reduce functions are distributed as encrypted and certified bitstreams. During boot, they are instantiated as programmable logic. All key-value inputs, intermediate key-value outputs, and the final results are encrypted. The cryptographic key for data encryption and decryption is only visible to the FPGA

is also extended throughout the system via specific TrustZone System IP blocks. Figure 4.9 gives an overview of the TrustZone architecture.

For a long time ARM processors were mainly used in mobile platforms because of its energy efficiency. As the electricity costs of data centers are becoming a dominant operating expense and it is expected the power cost will exceed the cost of the original capital investment [40], ARM processors are also deployed in data centers for big data processing [20, 31, 52].

Although we do not know any of existing papers discussing using TrustZone for big data applications, the basic idea of TrustZone based big data confidentiality protection is straightforward. Figure 4.10 shows the overall architecture of confidentiality preserving MapReduce using TrustZone. The input data are encrypted and only decrypted inside the secure world. The data processing functions (mapper and reducer under MapReduce framework) are also running inside the secure world so they can process the plain-texts directly. When these functions need to output some results, they always encrypt the results before sending out the secure world.

4.2.4.4 Intel SGX Based Confidentiality Preserving MapReduce

Intel Software Guard Extension (SGX) is a set of new CPU instructions that can be used by applications to set aside private regions of code and data [35]. SGX allows

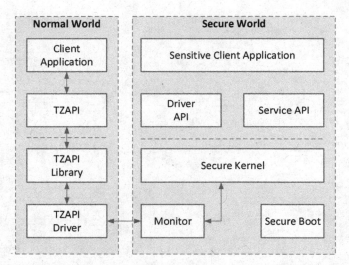

Fig. 4.9 Overview of TrustZone technology. The execution environment is divided into two worlds, the normal world and the secure world. When an application is running in the secure world, it is safely separated from others so a malicious software is unable to access the data

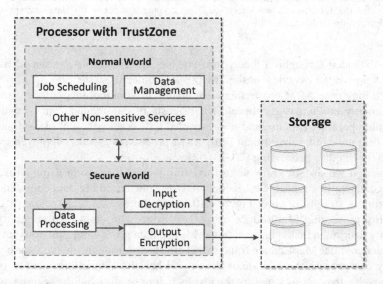

Fig. 4.10 Applying TrustZone for protection of big data confidentiality. Data are always encrypted outside the secure world. Mapper and reducer functions are executed in the secure world so they can operate on plain data

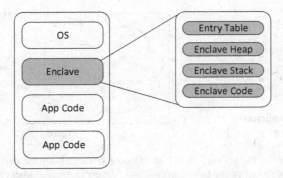

Fig. 4.11 An enclave within the application's virtual address space. Enclaves are protected by the processor: the processor controls access to enclave memory. Instructions that attempt to read or write the memory of a running enclave from outside the enclave will fail. Enclave cache lines are encrypted and integrity protected before being written out to RAM

an application to instantiate a protected container, referred to as an enclave. An enclave is a protected area in the application's address space (see Fig. 4.11), which provides confidentiality and integrity even in the presence of privileged malware. Accesses to the enclave memory area from any software not resident in the enclave are prevented [36].

Intel SGX can be deployed in the cloud environment for general purpose confidentiality preserving big data processing. Schuster et al. proposed a concrete design of secure MapReduce based on SGX [60]. The basic idea is to create enclaves for the mapper and reducer functions and the data are always kept in encrypted form outside these enclaves. Because the enclave can prevent other applications from accessing its own memory space, an attacker cannot learn the contents of the data as long as the mapper/reducer functions are trusted.

4.3   Privacy of Big Data

Although a lot of organizations have realized the value of the information extracted from big data, it is not an easy task to collect all the data. At the same time, companies like VISA and Alibaba have accumulated a huge amount of data and they have the incentive to provide analytics service based on their data to increase their revenues [71]. In this case, vendors provide both computation/storage infrastructure and source data.

Privacy is one of the main security concerns for vendors to provide such services. First, the vendors have to make sure the user only gets limited and necessary information. Otherwise the user can get the data and the vendors will lose their

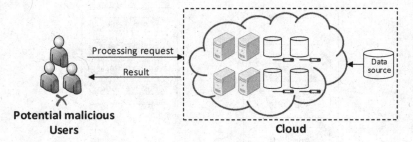

Fig. 4.12 Overview of the security model of big data privacy. Both the data source and the computation/storage infrastructure belong to the cloud. The user submits his/her processing request to the cloud, then the cloud processes the request and returns the results to the user. In this process, the cloud needs to make sure the user can only get necessary and adequate information

competitiveness. The second reason that the vendor has to control the information released to the user is that the results may contain sensitive personal information. Returning improper analytics results may violate laws such as HIPPA.

In summary, big data privacy considers the following situation:

- The cloud owns and manages not only the computatin/storage infrastructure but also the data source. As the owner of the data source, the cloud does not have the motivation to disclose the data, and we assume the cloud is trusted, i.e., the cloud will follow predefined protocols and try its best to protect the data;
- Users only provide data processing requests and get corresponding results. The user is not trusted because the data are valuable and the user may try to extract as much information as possible.

Figure 4.12 depicts the big data privacy protection scenario, and the security goal is to control the amount of information the user can get.

4.3.1 Big Data Privacy Protection Using k-Anonymity

k-anonymity provides a criterion to measure the data set being processed [65]. A data set achieves k-anonymity preserves certain level of privacy. We also review variants and extensions of k-anonymity in this section.

4.3.1.1 k-Anonymity

k-anonymity was first proposed by Sweeney [65] and it considers the following scenario: a data owner has a collection of person-specific, field structured data, and users may use these data for scientific research. In this process, the data owner has to make sure individuals who are the subjects of the data cannot be re-identified while the data remain practically useful.

First we introduce some related notations. Let $B(A_1, \cdots, A_n)$ be a table with a finite number of tuples. The finite set of attributes of B are $\{A_1, \cdots, A_n\}$. Another important concept is quasi-identifier [17]. Given a population of entities U, an entity-specific table $T(A_1, \cdots, A_n), f_c : U \to T$ and $f_g : T \to U'$, where $U \subseteq U'$. A *quasi-identifier* of T, written Q_T, is a set of attributes $\{A_i, \cdots, A_j\} \subseteq A_1, \cdots, A_n$ where $\exists p_i \in U$ such that $f_g(f_c(p_i)[Q_T]) = p_i$. The formal description of k-anonymity is given in Definition 1.

Definition 1 (k-Anonymity [65]). Let $RT(A_1, \cdots, A_n)$ be a table and QI_{RT} be the quasi-identifier associated with it. RT is said to satisfy *k-anonymity* if and only if each sequence of values in $RT[QI_{RT}]$ appears with at least k occurrences in $RT[QI_{RT}]$.

We give a concrete example to show the intuitive meaning of k-anonymity.

Example 1 ([65]). Table 4.1 provides an example of a table that adheres to k-anonymity. The quasi-identifier for the table is QI={Race, Birth, Gender, ZIP} and $k = 2$. For each of the tuples contained in the table, the values of the tuple that comprise the quasi-identifier appear at least twice.

When the operations are on the quasi-identifier set and returned results satisfy the k-anonymity feature, it is hard for an adversary to locate a certain tuple by observing the results. Sweeney also discussed several ways to attack k-anonymity, e.g., unsorted matching attack, complementary release attack, and temporal attack. We refer the readers to the original paper [65] for more detailed information.

Table 4.1 An example of k-anonymity, where $k = 2$ and QI={Race, Birth, Gender, ZIP}

Race	Birth	Gender	ZIP	Problem
Black	1965	m	0214	Short breath
Black	1965	m	0214	Chest pain
Black	1965	f	0213	Hypertension
Black	1965	f	0213	Hypertension
Black	1964	f	0213	Obesity
Black	1964	f	0213	Chest pain
White	1964	m	0213	Chest pain
White	1964	m	0213	Obesity
White	1964	m	0213	Short breath
White	1967	m	0213	Chest pain
White	1967	m	0213	Chest pain

It can be seen that for each quasi-identifier, there are at least two tuples

4.3.1.2 ℓ-Diversity

ℓ-diversity is proposed to address some weakness of k-anonymity [48]. For example, (1) an attacker can discover the values of sensitive attributes when there is little diversity in those sensitive attributes; (2) k-anonymity does not guarantee privacy against attackers using background knowledge. The formal definition of ℓ-diversity is given as follows:

Definition 2 (ℓ-Diversity [1]). Let a q^*-block be a set of tuples such that its non-sensitive values generalize to q^*. A q^*-block is ℓ-diverse if it contains at least ℓ "well-represented" values for the sensitive attribute S. A table is ℓ-diverse if every q^*-block is ℓ-diverse.

Machanavajjhala et al. gave three possible ways to define "well-presented": distinct ℓ-diversity, entropy ℓ-diversity, and recursive $(c - \ell)$-diversity [48].

4.3.1.3 t-Closeness

Li et al. found out that ℓ-diversity also has a number of limitations. In particular, it is neither necessary nor sufficient to prevent attribute disclosure. To mitigate the problem, they proposed the idea of t-closeness [43].

Definition 3 (t-Closeness [43]). An equivalence class is said to have t-closeness if the distance between the distribution of a sensitive attribute in this class and the distribution of the attribute in the whole table is no more than a threshold t. A table is said to have t-closeness if all equivalence classes have t-closeness.

4.3.2   Big Data Privacy Protection Using Differential Privacy

Differential privacy is a strong model for data privacy protection [22]. The basic idea of differential privacy is to transform the original data or add noise to the statistic result to preserve data privacy. Differential privacy ensures that adding/removing one record in the data set does not affect the processing results, and it does not depend on any assumption of the attacker's background knowledge. Differential privacy is formally described in Definition 4.

Definition 4 (Differential Privacy [22]). A randomized function K gives ϵ-differential privacy if for all data sets D_1 and D_2 differing on at most one element, and all $S \subseteq Range(K)$,

$$Pr[K(D_1) \in S] \leq exp(\epsilon) \times Pr[K(D_2) \in S]. \tag{4.1}$$

Differential privacy captures the essence of data privacy protection. An algorithm K satisfying Definition 4 addresses concerns about the leakage of sensitive information x: even if x is removed from the data set, no outputs (and thus consequences of outputs) would become significantly more or less likely. For example, if the database were to be consulted by an insurance provider before deciding whether or not to insure a certain customer, then the presence or absence of the customer in the database will not significantly affect his/her chance of receiving coverage.

Differential privacy has two useful properties [50]:

Property 1 (Sequential Composition). Given n random algorithms $A_1, A_2, \cdots, A_n$ and a data set D, if $A_i(1 \leq i \leq n)$ gives ϵ_i-differential privacy, then the combination of $\{A_1, A_2, \cdots, A_n\}$ gives ϵ-differential privacy on D, where $\epsilon = \sum \epsilon_i$.

Property 2 (Parallel Composition). Let algorithm A provides ϵ-differential privacy, and D_i be arbitrary disjoint subsets of a data set D. The sequence of A on D_i provides ϵ-differential privacy.

There are mainly two types of big data privacy protection frameworks that utilize differential privacy:

- Interactive framework. Interactive framework (or online query framework) works in the following way: the user submits a query Q to the cloud and the cloud generates a new Q' from Q that satisfies the differential privacy. Then the cloud applies Q' to its managed data set and returns the result O' to the user. Interactive framework usually only allows limited number of queries;
- Noninteractive framework. In noninteractive framework (or offline publish framework), the cloud publishes statistical information about the data set it manages. The released information satisfy differential privacy requirement and the user can query the released information directly.

A lot of work has been done to develop big data applications that support differential privacy. PINQ is a interactive system supports tasks such as aggregation query, join query, and clustering while providing differential privacy [50]. GUPT provides a noninteractive data analytics system supporting k-means clustering, regression analysis, and clustering [51]. Airavat integrates differential privacy with MapReduce to offer clustering function [56].

4.3.3   Big Data Privacy Protection on User Side

According to security assumptions in the scenario of big data privacy protection, the cloud is trusted and provides both the data and the processing service, so there is no need to deploy any hardware based protection mechanism on cloud side. On the user side, it is useful to have systematic approaches that can control the spreading of results retrieved from the cloud. This idea is similar to digital right management (DRM), which is an effective way to control executing, viewing, copying, and altering of works or devices on the user side [24].

Basically, DRM is an aggregation of security technologies to protect the interests of content owners so that they may maintain persistent ownership and control of their content [41]. In the case of big data privacy, big data processing results are treated as contents that the cloud sends to the user. Although the user has the right to use these results, the cloud wants to ensure the user does not distribute these information to others. In the following, we briefly review two types of techniques for data spreading control.

4.3.3.1 Software Based Data Distribution Control

The cloud can choose to encrypt the results before sending to the user, and the user needs a special software installed to decrypt the results. In order to distribute the received data without limitations, the user has to either extract the decryption key embedded in the software or share the whole software package with others. To prevent these threats, the software usually has the components showed in Fig. 4.13.

White-box implementation of decryption algorithm [14, 70] plays a key role in this software based data spreading control approach. Nearly all existing encryption schemes such as AES, DES, and RSA suppose the encryption/decryption process as an atomic operation. If classical implementation is used for decryption of received data, the user can look into the decryption process and extract the key easily, which compromises the whole spreading control mechanism. White-box implementation merges the operations involved key with other operations and adds hiding operations to prevent an attacker from learning the key information by observing the decryption process.

The software based data distribution control does not require special hardware and prevents an adversary from distributing received analytic results freely because he/she needs to break the white-box encryption mechanism to extract the key or disable the unauthorized copy prevention module to run the software on other

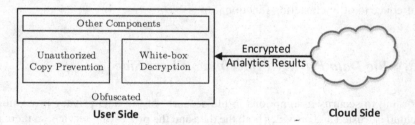

Fig. 4.13 Sketch of the software based data spreading control system. Unauthorized copy prevention component verifies the execution environment before running and it is hard for the user to reinstall it in different computers. The white-box decryption [14] component allows the decryption running in a malicious environment while preserving the confidentiality of the key used in this process. Obfuscation is applied so the user cannot separate each component

machines. The main disadvantage of the software based approach is that the security of the system is based on white-box cryptography and obfuscation, which is hard to evaluate.

4.3.3.2 Hardware Based Data Distribution Control

We mentioned several hardware based security techniques in Sect. 4.2 that are useful for protecting the confidentiality of big data, i.e., TPM [66], FPGA [74], ARM TrustZone [4], and Intel SGX [35]. These techniques can also be deployed on the user side for big data privacy protection by controlling data distribution. The way to use these hardware based approaches is similar to the software based method. The main difference is that those components related to information distribution control (i.e., decryption module to get plain data analytic results and execution environment detection module to prevent running the software in another machine) are put in a hardware based secure environment.

Hardware based data distribution control is usually more expensive than software based approach but it usually provides a higher level of security. The only concern is that hardware has to be carefully designed and does not have any vulnerabilities.

4.4 Integrity of Big Data

Integrity is an important aspect of security, and it involves maintaining the consistency, accuracy, and trustworthiness of data over its entire life cycle [11]. Big data application usually involves distributed, multiple steps processing. In this process, data must not be changed during transition, and pre-defined procedures must be followed to ensure that the data are not altered or modified by unauthorized parties. Integrity is critical for big data applications because the conclusions drawn from the data are usually used by the user to support decision making. By tampering the integrity, an attacker may lead the user to wrong directions.

4.4.1 General Big Data Processing Integrity Protection with Digital Signature

Digital signature is the most common approach for integrity protection, and it has lots of variants with special properties. Here we briefly discuss applying these techniques for general purpose big data processing integrity protection.

4.4.1.1 Classical Digital Signature and MAC for Processing Integration Protection

Classical digital signature usually requires a PKI system and has been standardized (e.g., the digital signature standard [25] and the elliptic curve version digital signature standard [37]). A digital signature scheme consists of three algorithms:

1. `Initialization`. A party is given a public/private key pair (pk, sk). sk is kept as a secret and pk is published as a certificate;
2. `Signature generation`. Given a message m, the signer uses sk to calculate a signature sig for m;
3. `Signature verification`. Given a message m, a signature sk and a certificate contains public key pk, the verifier can verify whether sig is generated using m and corresponding private key sk.

The way to use classical digital signature for big data integrity protection is as follows: each party participating in the computation is given a pair of public/private key, and the PKI issues a certificate for each public key. Whenever one party finishes processing of one piece of data, it will generate a digital signature of the output with its private key and attach the signature to the result. The party receiving the result can use the corresponding certificate (which has the public key embedded) to verify the integrity of the result. To prevent an attacker from discarding or replaying intermediate results, the sender can embed a sequence number to each result before generating the signature. As long as the private keys are not leaked, it is hard for an adversary to tamper the big data processing process because any modification of the intermediate results will lead to failure of signature verification. Figure 4.14 depicts big data processing integrity protection using classical digital signature.

This approach achieve the goal of integrity protection but suffers from the following shortcomings:

1. High cost. PKI is usually believed to be expensive and not scalable [64]. The signature generation/verfication are also not cheap, especially considering the number of these operations in the scenario of big data processing;

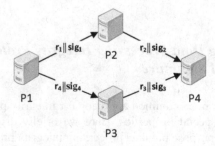

Fig. 4.14 Using classical digital signature for integrity protection in big data scenario. At each step, the previous signature is verified and a new signature is generated for the new result

2. Untraceable. One party can only verify the integrity of result of the last step. If there is something wrong, it is very hard to track back to find out the malicious party;
3. Strong assumption. This approach assumes that the data processing and signature generation functions are executed in a trust environment. Otherwise an adversary can output a wrong result with a valid signature, which is impossible to be detected by the receiver of the result.

To remove the PKI and reduce the cost of integrity protection, one can use HMAC [26] or CMAC [23] instead of classical digital signature. HMAC/CMAC involves a secret key for both integrity tag generation and verification procedures, so each receiver needs to share a secret key with corresponding sender. Generation/verification of HMAC/CMAC are usually much faster than digital signature but the disadvantage is also obvious: every party involved needs to share some secret keys with others. If one party reveals this secret key, the whole system will fail.

4.4.1.2   Homomorphic Signature

Using digital signature/HMAC/CMAC for integrity protection requires the processing parties to access the private key or secret key. Otherwise it cannot generate the signature/HMAC/CMC. If the party is compromised, it is easy for the adversary to modify the output result and generate a corresponding valid signature/HMAC/CMC.

Homomorphic signature is a powerful tool that can address this problem. We first give the definition of homomorphic encryption and then discuss the way to use it for big data integrity protection. The formal definition of homomorphic signature is given in Definition 5. In the definition, M is the message space, K is the private key set, K' is the public key set, and Y is the signature space.

Definition 5 (Homomorphic Signature [38]). For a signature scheme Sig : $K \times M \to Y$, Vrfy : $K' \times M \times Y \to \{bad, ok\}$ and a binary operation $\odot : M \times M \to M$. We say that Sig is homomorphic with respect to $\odot$ if it comes with an efficient family of binary operations $\otimes_{k'} : Y \times Y \to Y$ so that $y \otimes_{k'} y' = \mathrm{Sig}(x \odot x')$ for all x, x', y, y' satisfying $\mathrm{Vrfy}(x, y) = \mathrm{Vrfy}(x', y') = \mathrm{ok}$.

Big data integrity protection using homomorphic signature works in the following way:

1. Key generation. The owner (user manages the data source) generates a homomorphic signature public/private key pair. The public key is shared with the cloud;
2. Data initialization. The owner divides the data into units and generates a signature for each unit. Both the data and the signatures are provided to the cloud;
3. Processing. At each step, the cloud operates on the data as well as on the corresponding signatures. Both the result and its newly generated signature are passed to the next step. Note that in this process, only public key is required;
4. Verification. At any stage of data processing, the user and the cloud can verify the integrity of the (intermediate)results by verifying the signatures.

Using homomorphic signature for big data integrity protection still depends on the security of nodes in the cloud system. Although a compromised node cannot learn the private key, it can still generate wrong results with valid signatures. Another problem with this approach is performance. When the size of the data being processed is large, generation of signatures is usually too expensive.

4.4.2 Big Data Query Integrity Protection

As mentioned before, database query is one of the common big data applications. When the cloud manages the database and answer users' queries on the data set, it is necessary to have a mechanism to guarantee the intact results are returned instead of partial results or results with some items replaced.

4.4.2.1 Integrity Preserving Query with Dual Encryption

Wang et al. proposed a dual encryption method to guarantee the integrity of the returned results [69]. Before sending the database to the cloud, the entire database is encrypted at tuple level using a primary key k, and a small selected part of the database is encrypted using another key k' (these tuples work as check points). User queries are transformed by a secure proxy before sending to the cloud for processing, this secure proxy is also responsible for checking the integrity of returned results. More specifically, given a batch of queries $Q = < q_1, q_2, \cdots, q_u >$, the secure proxy encrypts each query using primary key k and sends $Q^k = < q_1^k, q_2^k, \cdots, q_u^k >$ to the cloud. The secure proxy also encrypts Q using key k' to get $Q^{k'} = < q_1^{k'}, q_2^{k'}, \cdots, q_u^{k'} >$. $Q^{k'}$ is also sent to the cloud. After getting query results of both Q^k and $Q^{k'}$, the secure proxy can compare corresponding results to see whether they are consistent.

If the encryption scheme used is semantic secure, an adversary cannot distinguish whether a tuple in the database is encrypted using k or k'. So the proposed mechanism can detect integrity tampering with a probability. For example, if the returned results of query $q_1, q_1^{k'}$ are denoted as R_{q_1} and $R_{q_1^{k'}}$ respectively, the secure proxy checks whether $R_{q_1^{k'}} \subset R_{q_1}$. If it is not true, the secure proxy can confirm the integrity is tampered. But if an attacker can modify R_{q_1} and $R_{q_1^{k'}}$ correspondingly, the secure proxy cannot detect the integrity tampering.

While the dual encryption scheme can help to prevent an attacker from modifying the returned results, it also introduces extra costs: (1) Part of the database has to be stored twice in the cloud; (2) For a single query request, an extra query for integrity protection is required. This also introduces extra communication burden.

4.4.2.2 Integrity Preserving Query with Extra Records

Xie et al. proposed to insert a small amount of records into the outsourced data set to guarantee the query integrity [72]. The basic idea is to have a set of inserted tuples stored on both the user side and cloud side, and the cloud cannot separate these tuples from others.

The integrity protection scheme requires all tuples are kept encrypted on the cloud side and the user generates a tag for each tuple (including both original and inserted):

$$a_h = \begin{cases} H(tid||a_1|| \cdots ||a_n), & t \text{ is original tuple;} \\ H(tid||a_1|| \cdots ||a_n) + 1, & t \text{ is inserted tuple.} \end{cases}$$

a_h is used by the user to determine whether an received tuple is original or inserted for integrity protection because the user can decrypt an tuple and evaluate the hash function H. When the user submits a query to the cloud and gets corresponding results, he/she checks whether the related inserted tuples are included to determine the integrity of the query results. Xie et al. proposed a deterministic algorithm to generate the inserted tuples, which can reduce the storage cost on the user side compared with random tuple generation [72].

4.4.2.3 Integrity Preserving Query in Dynamic Environment

Most of the query results integrity protection techniques consider the scenario where the data set is fixed. Li et al. discussed the situation where the user may update the data and introduced the concept of "freshness", which is another aspect of integrity [42].

When the user updates the database, the cloud may still retain an old version and answer the query with old information, which compromises the "freshness" property. Li et al. proposed a data structure named embedded Merkle tree and utilized signature aggregation technique [9] to protect the freshness of the query results.

4.4.3 Big Data Storage Integrity Protection

The integrity of the big data itself is the basis for other aspects of integrity of big data applications. Because it is unrealistic for the owner to ask the cloud to send back all the data to verify the integrity of the remote data, more efficient methods are developed to solve this problem.

Juels and Kaliski proposed the concept of "proofs of retrievability" (POR [39]). In their scheme the verifier stores only a single cryptographic key—irrespective of the size and number of the files whose retrievability it seeks to verify—as well as a small amount of dynamic state for each file. Briefly, the POR protocol works as follows:

1. The user encrypts file F and randomly embeds a set of randomly-valued check blocks called *sentinels*. The use of encryption guarantees that the sentinels indistinguishable from other file blocks;
2. The user challenges the cloud by specifying the positions of a collection of sentinels and asking the cloud to return the associated sentinel values. If the cloud has modified or deleted a substantial portion of F, then with high probability it will also have suppressed a number of sentinels.

The key function of the POR protocol is to process the file F and embed sentinels, which are further divided into four steps:

1. Error correction. The file F is carved into k-blocks chunks. The user applies an error correction code to each chunk and yield a file F';
2. Encryption. The user uses a symmetric encryption scheme to encrypt each chunk of F' to get F'';
3. Sentinel creation. The user uses a one-way function to create a set of sentinels and appends these sentinels to F'' to get F''';
4. Permutation. The user uses a pseudorandom permutation [47] to permute blocks of F''' to get the final file and sends to cloud to store.

The POR protocol allows the user to check the integrity of the data stored in the cloud without downloading the whole file and can correct some random errors. One of the main limitations of the POR approach is that it can only support a limited number of challenges.

Chang and Xu proposed the remote integrity check (RIC) model [13], which is similar to POR but does not consider the capability of recovery.

4.4.4 Big Data Integrity Protection with Hardware

In most cases, hardware based approaches for big data confidentiality protection mentioned in Sect. 4.2.4 are also applicable for integrity protection by replacing encryption/decryption operations with signature generation/verification operations. There are also other possibilities to utilize hardware to protect big data integrity.

4.4.4.1 TPM Based Integrity Protection Through Software Protection

One of TPM's main functions is to provide attestation service, a mechanism for software to prove its identity [63]. The goal of attestation is to prove to a remote party that a program is intact and trustworthy.

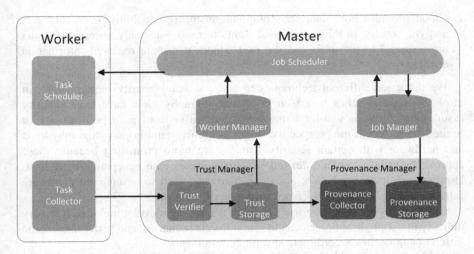

Fig. 4.15 Overview of TMR [57]. *Trust Collector* is added to the worker node to generate trust evidence (i.e., the attestation tickets) and provides the remote attestation service. *Trust Manager* and *Provence Manager* are added to master node. *Trust Manager* uses *Trust Verifier* to connect *Trust Collector* on workers to perform attestations. *Provenance Manager* uses *Provenance Collector* to gather the security properties of worker nodes and binds them with corresponding tasks

Ruan and Martin constructed a trusted MapReduce infrastructure TMR using TPM [57]. This method achieves the goal of integrity protection by protecting the integrity of the MapReduce software stack (Fig. 4.15).

4.5 Conclusion and Discussion

Big data plays an important role in different sectors and data is becoming valuable assets. Cloud computing provides scalable computation/storage capability and is widely adopted for efficient big data processing. Because two parties (cloud and user) are involved in the big data processing procedure and they do not trust each other, security becomes a concern for both of them. Basically, the scenarios are divided into two classes:

1. User provides data and cloud provides computation/storage capability. In this case, there are two security requirements:
   - Confidentiality. While utilizing cloud for data processing, the user does not want to expose the plain data to cloud;
   - Integrity. The user wants to make sure the processing procedure is not tampered, e.g., modifying/deleting the intermediate results, or inserting fake message into the process.

2. Cloud provides both data and computation/storage capability, user only gets analytic results. In this case, cloud wants to make sure only necessary results are returned to the user, and the user cannot distribute received information arbitrarily.

We discussed different techniques to address these security requirements. In most cases, approaches based on novel cryptography tools have least security assumptions and enjoy solid foundations, but suffer from poor performance or limited scope. From the perspective of practicability, combing cryptography tools and hardware with certain security features are more promising because these approaches usually provide desired security features with acceptable extra cost. However, protection schemes based on hardware need to assume the hardware satisfy certain properties, which are hard to verify or prove.

In summary, big data security protection is a rapidly developing area. It is very unlikely that a single approach can fit into different scenarios, and better to combine different approaches according to specific requirements.

References

1. Aggarwal CC, Philip SY (2008) A general survey of privacy-preserving data mining models and algorithms. Springer, Berlin
2. Aggarwal G, Bawa M, Ganesan P, Garcia-Molina H, Kenthapadi K, Motwani R, Srivastava U, Thomas D, Xu Y (2005) Two can keep a secret: a distributed architecture for secure database services. In: Second biennial conference on innovative data systems research - CIDR 2005, pp 186–199
3. Agrawal R, Kiernan J, Srikant R, Xu Y (2004) Order preserving encryption for numeric data. In: ACM international conference on management of data - SIGMOD 2004. ACM, New York, pp 563–574
4. ARM (2009) ARM security technology building a secure system using TrustZone technology
5. Bethencourt J, Sahai A, Waters B (2007) Ciphertext-policy attribute-based encryption. In: IEEE symposium on security and privacy - S&P 2007. IEEE Computer Society, Silver Spring, MD, pp 321–334
6. Blaze M, Bleumer G, Strauss M (1998) Divertible protocols and atomic proxy cryptography. In: Goos G, Hartmanis J, van Leeuwen J (eds) Advances in cryptology - EUROCRYPT 1998. Lecture notes in computer science, vol 1403. Springer, Berlin, pp 127–144
7. Boldyreva A, Chenette N, Lee Y, O'Neill A (2009) Order-preserving symmetric encryption. In: Joux A (ed) Advances in cryptology - EUROCRYPT 2009. Lecture notes in computer science, vol 5479. Springer, Berlin, pp 224–241
8. Boneh D, Franklin M (2001) Identity-based encryption from the weil pairing. In: Kilian J (ed) Advance in cryptology - CRYPTO 2001. Lecture notes in computer science, vol 2139. Springer, Berlin, pp 213–229
9. Boneh D, Gentry C, Lynn B, Shacham H et al (2003) A survey of two signature aggregation techniques. RSA Cryptobytes 6(2):1–10
10. Boneh D, Crescenzo GD, Ostrovsky R, Persiano G (2004) Public key encryption with keyword search. In: Advances in cryptology - EUROCRYPT 2004. Lecture notes in computer science, vol 3027. Springer, Berlin, pp 506–522
11. Boritz JE (2005) IS practitioners' views on core concepts of information integrity. Int J Account Inf Syst 6(4):260–279

12. Brakerski Z, Vaikuntanathan V (2011) Efficient fully homomorphic encryption from (standard) LWE. In: Ostrovsky R (ed) IEEE 52nd annual symposium on foundations of computer science - FOCS 2011. IEEE Computer Society, Silver Spring, MD, pp 97–106
13. Chang EC, Xu J (2008) Remote integrity check with dishonest storage server. In: Jajodia S, López J (eds) 13th european symposium on research in computer security – ESORICS 2008. Lecture notes in computer science, vol 5283. Springer, Berlin, pp 223–237
14. Chow S, Eisen P, Johnson H, Van Oorschot PC (2003) A white-box des implementation for drm applications. In: Digital rights management. Springer, Berlin, pp 1–15
15. Cohen JC, Acharya S (2014) Towards a trusted HDFS storage platform: mitigating threats to hadoop infrastructures using hardware-accelerated encryption with TPM-rooted key protection. J Inf Secur Appl 19(3):224–244
16. Curtmola R, Garay J, Kamara S, Ostrovsky R (2006) Searchable symmetric encryption: improved definitions and efficient constructions. In: Proceedings of the 13th ACM conference on computer and communications security - CCS 2006. ACM, New York, pp 79–88
17. Dalenius T (1986) Finding a needle in a haystack or identifying anonymous census records. J Off Stat 2(3):329
18. De Cristofaro E, Tsudik G (2010) Practical private set intersection protocols with linear complexity. In: Sion R (ed) 14th International conference financial cryptography and data security - FC 2010. Lecture notes in computer science, vol 6052. Springer, Berlin, pp 143–159
19. Dean J, Ghemawat S (2008) Mapreduce: simplified data processing on large clusters. Commun ACM 51(1):107–113
20. Delplace V, Manneback P, Pinel F, Varette S, Bouvry P (2013) Comparing the performance and power usage of GPU and ARM clusters for MapReduce. In: Third international conference on cloud and green computing - CGC 2013. IEEE, New York, pp 199–200
21. Dong C, Chen L, Wen Z (2013) When private set intersection meets big data: an efficient and scalable protocol. In: Proceedings of the 20th ACM conference on computer and communications security - CCS 2013. ACM, New York, pp 789–800
22. Dwork C (2006) Differential privacy. In: Automata, Languages and Programming - ICALP 2006. Lecture notes in computer science, vol 4052. Springer, Berlin, pp 1–12
23. Dworkin M (2011) NIST SP 800-38A recommendation for block cipher modes of operation: the CMAC mode for authentication
24. Fetscherin M (2002) Present state and emerging scenarios of digital rights management systems. Int J Media Manag 4(3):164–171
25. FIPS 186-2 (2000) Digital signature standard (DSS)
26. FIPS 198-1 (2008) The keyed-hash message authentication code (HMAC)
27. Gentry C (2009) Fully homomorphic encryption using ideal lattices. In: Mitzenmacher M (ed) Proceedings of the 41st annual ACM symposium on theory of computing - STOC 2009. ACM, New York, pp 169–178
28. Gentry C, Sahai A, Waters B (2013) Homomorphic encryption from learning with errors: conceptually-simpler, asymptotically-faster, attribute-based. In: Canetti R, Garay JA (eds) Advances in cryptology – CRYPTO 2013. Lecture notes in computer science, vol 8043. Springer, Berlin, pp 75–92
29. Goh EJ (2003) Secure indexes. IACR cryptology ePrint archive. http://eprint.iacr.org/2003/216.pdf
30. Goldwasser S, Micali S, Rackoff C (1985) The knowledge complexity of interactive proof-systems. In: Proceedings of the 7th annual ACM symposium on theory of computing - STOC 1985. ACM, New York, pp 291–304
31. Goodacre J, Cambridge A (2013) The evolution of the ARM architecture towards big data and the data-centre. In: Proceedings of the 8th workshop on virtualization in high-performance cloud computing - VHPC 2013. ACM, New York, p 4
32. Goyal V, Pandey O, Sahai A, Waters B (2006) Attribute-based encryption for fine-grained access control of encrypted data. In: Juels A, Wright RN, di Vimercati SDC (eds) Proceedings of the 13th ACM conference on computer and communications security - CCS 2006. ACM, New York, pp 89–98

33. Hacigümüş H, Iyer BR, Li C, Mehrotra S (2002) Executing SQL over encrypted data in the database-service-provider model. In: Franklin MJ, Moon B, Ailamaki A (eds) Proceedings of the ACM international conference on management of data - SIGMOD 2002. ACM, New York, pp 216–227
34. Herstein IN (1990) Abstract algebra. Macmillan, New York
35. Hoekstra M, Lal R, Pappachan P, Phegade V, Del Cuvillo J (2013) Using innovative instructions to create trustworthy software solutions. In: Proceedings of the 2nd international workshop on hardware and architectural support for security and privacy - HASP 2013. ACM, New York
36. Intel Software Guard Extensions Programming Reference (2014). https://software.intel.com/sites/default/files/managed/48/88/329298-002.pdf
37. Johnson D, Menezes A, Vanstone S (2001) The elliptic curve digital signature algorithm (ECDSA). Int J Inf Secur 1:36–63
38. Johnson R, Molnar D, Song D, Wagner D (2002) Homomorphic signature schemes. In: Preneel B (ed) Topics in cryptology – CT-RSA 2002. Lecture notes in computer science, vol 2271. Springer, Berlin, pp 244–262
39. Juels A Jr, BSK (2007) Pors: proofs of retrievability for large files. In: Ning P, di Vimercati SDC, Syverson PF (eds) Proceedings of the 2007 ACM conference on computer and communications security - CCS 2007. ACM, New York, pp 584–597
40. Koomey JG, Belady C, Patterson M, Santos A, Lange KD (2009) Assessing trends over time in performance, costs, and energy use for servers. Lawrence Berkeley National Laboratory, Stanford University, Microsoft Corporation, and Intel Corporation, Technical Report
41. Ku W, Chi CH (2004) Survey on the technological aspects of digital rights management. In: Zhang K, Zheng Y (eds) 7th international conference on information security - ISC 2004. Lecture notes in computer science, vol 3225. Springer, Berlin, pp 391–403
42. Li F, Hadjieleftheriou M, Kollios G, Reyzin L (2006) Dynamic authenticated index structures for outsourced databases. In: Proceedings of the 2006 ACM international conference on management of data - SIGMOD 2006. ACM, New York, pp 121–132
43. Li N, Li T, Venkatasubramanian S (2007) t-closeness: Privacy beyond k-anonymity and ℓ-diversity. In: IEEE 23rd international conference on data engineering - ICDE 2007, pp 106–115. doi:10.1109/ICDE.2007.367856
44. Lindell Y, Pinkas B (2000) Privacy preserving data mining. In: Bellare M (ed) Advances in cryptology - CRYPTO 2000. Lecture notes in computer science, vol 1880. Springer, Berlin, pp 36–54
45. Lindell Y, Pinkas B (2009) A proof of security of Yao's protocol for two-party computation. J Cryptol 22(2):161–188
46. Lindell Y, Pinkas B (2009) Secure multiparty computation for privacy-preserving data mining. J Priv Confid 1(1):5
47. Luby M, Rackoff C (1988) How to construct pseudorandom permutations from pseudorandom functions. SIAM J Comput 17(2):373–386
48. Machanavajjhala A, Kifer D, Gehrke J, Venkitasubramaniam M (2007) ℓ-diversity: privacy beyond k-anonymity. ACM Trans Knowl Discov Data 1(1). doi:10.1145/1217299.1217302. http://doi.acm.org/10.1145/1217299.1217302
49. Mambo M, Okamoto E (1997) Proxy cryptosystems: delegation of the power to decrypt ciphertexts. IEICE Trans Fundam Electron Commun Comput Sci E80-A:54–63
50. McSherry FD (2009) Privacy integrated queries: an extensible platform for privacy-preserving data analysis. In: Çetintemel U, Zdonik SB, Kossmann D, Tatbul N (eds) Proceedings of the ACM SIGMOD international conference on management of data - SIGMOD 2009. ACM, New York, pp 19–30
51. Mohan P, Thakurta A, Shi E, Song D, Culler D (2012) Gupt: privacy preserving data analysis made easy. In: Proceedings of the ACM SIGMOD international conference on management of data - SIGMOD 2012. ACM, New York, pp 349–360
52. Ou Z, Pang B, Deng Y, Nurminen JK, Yla-Jaaski A, Hui P (2012) Energy-and cost-efficiency analysis of ARM-based clusters. In: 12th IEEE/ACM international symposium on cluster, cloud and grid computing - CCGrid 2012. IEEE, New York, pp 115–123

53. Popa RA, Redfield C, Zeldovich N, Balakrishnan H (2011) CryptDB: protecting confidentiality with encrypted query processing. In: Proceedings of the 23rd ACM symposium on operating systems principles - SOSP 2011. ACM, New York, pp 85–100

54. Quisquater JJ, Quisquater M, Quisquater M, Quisquater M, Guillou L, Guillou MA, Guillou G, Guillou A, Guillou G, Guillou S (1990) How to explain zero-knowledge protocols to your children. In: Menezes A, Vanstone SA (eds) Advances in cryptology – CRYPTO89 Proceedings. Lecture notes in computer science, vol 537. Springer, Berlin, pp 628–631

55. Rivest RL, Adleman L, Dertouzos ML (1978) On data banks and privacy homomorphisms. Found Secure Comput 4(11):169–180

56. Roy I, Setty ST, Kilzer A, Shmatikov V, Witchel E (2010) Airavat: security and privacy for mapreduce. In: USENIX symposium on networked systems design & implementation - NSDI 2010, USENIX, vol 10, pp 297–312

57. Ruan A, Martin A (2012) TMR: towards a trusted MapReduce infrastructure. In: IEEE eighth world congress on services - SERVICES 2012. IEEE, New York, pp 141–148

58. Sahai A, Waters B (2005) Fuzzy identity-based encryption. In: Cramer R (ed) Advances in cryptology - EUROCRYPT 2005. Lecture notes in computer science, vol 3494. Springer, Berlin, pp 457–473

59. Sandhu RS, Coyne EJ, Feinstein HL, Youman CE (1996) Role-based access control models. Computer 29(2):38–47

60. Schuster F, Costa M, Fournet C, Gkantsidis C, Peinado M, Mainar-Ruiz G, Russinovich M (2015) VC3: trustworthy data analytics in the cloud using SGX. In: 36th IEEE symposium on security and privacy - S&P 2015. IEEE, New York

61. Shan Y, Wang B, Yan J, Wang Y, Xu N, Yang H (2010) FPMR: MapReduce framework on FPGA. In: Cheung PYK, Wawrzynek J (eds) Proceedings of the 18th annual ACM/SIGDA international symposium on field programmable gate arrays - FPGA 2010. ACM, Monterey, CA, pp 93–102

62. Sheikh R, Mishra DK, Kumar B (2011) Secure multiparty computation: from millionaires problem to anonymizer. Inform Secur J A Glob Perspect 20(1):25–33

63. Shi E, Perrig A, Van Doorn L (2005) Bind: a fine-grained attestation service for secure distributed systems. In: 26th IEEE symposium on security and privacy - S&P 2005. IEEE, New York, pp 154–168

64. Slagell A, Bonilla R, Yurcik W (2006) A survey of PKI components and scalability issues. In: 25th IEEE international on performance, computing, and communications conference - IPCCC 2006. IEEE, New York, pp 475–484

65. Sweeney L (2002) k-anonymity: a model for protecting privacy. Int. J. Uncertainty Fuzziness Knowledge Based Syst 10(05):557–570

66. TCG (2011) TPM Main Specification. http://www.trustedcomputinggroup.org/resources/tpm_main_specification

67. Trusted Platform Module (TPM) Summary (2008). Technical Report, Trusted Computing Group

68. van Dijk M, Gentry C, Halevi S, Vaikuntanathan V (2010) Fully homomorphic encryption over the integers. In: Gilbert H (ed) Advances in cryptology - EUROCRYPT 2010. Lecture notes in computer science, vol 6110. Springer, Berlin, pp 24–43

69. Wang H, Yin J, Perng CS, Yu PS (2008) Dual encryption for query integrity assurance. In: Proceedings of the 17th ACM conference on information and knowledge management. ACM, New York, pp 863–872

70. Wyseur B (2009) White-box cryptography. Katholieke Universiteit, Arenbergkasteel, B-3001 Heverlee, Belgium

71. Xiaoxiao L (2014) Alibaba has big hopes for new big data processing service. http://english.caixin.com/2014-07-17/100705224.html

72. Xie M, Wang H, Yin J, Meng X (2007) Integrity auditing of outsourced data. In: Koch C, Gehrke J, Garofalakis MN, Srivastava D, Aberer K, Deshpande A, Florescu D, Chan CY, Ganti V, Kanne CC, Klas W, Neuhold EJ (eds) Proceedings of the 33rd international conference on Very large data bases - VLDB 2007, VLDB Endowment, pp 782–793

73. Xu L, Pham KD, Kim H, Shi W, Suh T (2014) End-to-end big data processing protection in cloud environment using black-box: an FPGA approach. Int J Cloud Comput
74. Xu L, Shi W, Suh T (2014) PFC: privacy preserving FPGA cloud - a case study of MapReduce. In: 7th IEEE international conference on cloud computing
75. Yao AC (1982) Protocols for secure computations. In: IEEE 23th annual symposium on foundations of computer science - FOCS 1982. IEEE, New York, pp 160–164
76. Yao ACC (1986) How to generate and exchange secrets. In: IEEE 27th annual symposium on foundations of computer science - FOCS 1986. IEEE, New York, pp 162–167
77. Yuan E, Tong J (2005) Attributed based access control (abac) for web services. In: Proceedings of 2005 IEEE International Conference on Web Services - ICWS 2005. IEEE, New York

Chapter 5
Rapid Screening of Big Data Against Inadvertent Leaks

Xiaokui Shu, Fang Liu, and Danfeng (Daphne) Yao

Abstract Keeping sensitive data from unauthorized parties in the highly connected world is challenging. Statistics from security firms, research institutions, and government organizations show that the number of data-leak instances has grown rapidly in the last years. Deliberately planned attacks, inadvertent leaks, and human mistakes constitute the majority of the incidents. In this chapter, we first introduce the threat of data leak and overview traditional solutions in detecting and preventing sensitive data from leaking. Then we point out new challenges in the era of big data and present the state-of-the-art data-leak detection designs and algorithms. These solutions leverage big data theories and platforms—data mining, MapReduce, GPGPU, etc.—to harden the privacy control for big data. We also discuss the open research problems in data-leak detection and prevention.

5.1 Introduction: Data Leaks in the Era of Big Data

The exposure of sensitive data has become a severe threat to organizational and personal security. For a period of 5 years from 2010 to 2014, RiskBasedSecurity, a cyber security firm, reported a ten times growth of leaked records. These leaked records include credit card numbers, medical records, classified documents, etc. The total number of leaked records in 2014 reached a record high of 1.1 billion through 3014 incidents [53]. Kaspersky Lab estimated the average damage cost by an incident to be $720,000 [35], and FBI warned retailers about the increasing threat of data leaks in 2014 [20].

To understand data leaks and find defenses against the threat, we classify data-leak incidents into two categories by their causes:

- *Intentional leaks* include both external and internal threats such as network intrusion, phishing, espionage, virus, etc.
- *Inadvertent leaks* include accidental data sharing by employees, transmitting confidential data without proper encryption, etc.

X. Shu (✉) • F. Liu • D. (Daphne) Yao
Department of Computer Science, Virginia Tech, Blacksburg, VA 24060, USA
e-mail: subx@cs.vt.edu; fbeyond@cs.vt.edu; danfeng@cs.vt.edu

© Springer International Publishing Switzerland 2016
S. Yu, S. Guo (eds.), *Big Data Concepts, Theories, and Applications*,
DOI 10.1007/978-3-319-27763-9_5

Recent intentional data-leak incidents include SONY Picture, Home Depot, Target, Neiman Marcus, P.F. Chang, and Michaels and Aaron Brother. They hit the headlines of newspapers and Internet media for their data breaches during the last 2 years (2013–2014). For instance, the Target Corporation's network was breached between November 27 and December 18, 2013. 40 million credit and debit card numbers and 70 million records of personal information were stolen in this single incident. Months later, this number was surpassed by the Home Depot breach and the SONY Picture breach.

Many inadvertent leaks, e.g., forwarding a confidential email outside the company, are widely seen in companies and organizations. Such incidents can be found in 29 % of all 4438 data leaks reported by Kaspersky Lab during a 12-month period from 2013 to 2014 [35]. Although inadvertent leaks do not result in explicit economic loss of a company, they can be further exploited to launch effective attacks through these implicit leaking channels.

Encrypting data in the storage is one of the most basic methods preventing sensitive data from leaking, and it is effective against external leaks if used properly. It nullifies data leaks by preserving data in encrypted forms even when the data is stolen. However, encryption does not prevent sensitive data from leaking when the data is decrypted and consumed by processes in memory. In this case, software vulnerabilities and other internal threats can still cause data leaks even they are properly encrypted.

Besides general security mechanisms that enforce organizational security and privacy to prevent data leaks, specific solutions countering data leaks can be deployed to detect data-leak events and perform countermeasures against the events. Data-leak detection (DLD) is a solution that reveals data-leak events in a single device or among a network of devices. The detection usually combines a multitude of techniques that target different causes of data leaks.

Traditional virus detection, firewalls, and intrusion detection are basic elements to detect and prevent intentional leaks. A proper combination of these basic systems provides a comprehensive detection against sophisticated attack vectors, such as advanced persistent threats (APT), which are responsible for many significant data breach incidents.

Data tracking [15, 26, 44, 69] is an approach against both intentional and inadvertent data leaks. The basic idea is to track the flow of sensitive data within a single device or a network so that unauthorized data flows are prohibited or stopped. The detection tracks every segment of memory that the sensitive data is stored. Data tracking approach may incur heavy overhead at runtime. In addition, it may require a network-wide memory tracking solution across distributed systems/devices.

Content screening is an approach to detect data leaks at critical sites in a device (e.g., a network interface) or in a network (e.g., a gateway), but not to track the flow of sensitive data anywhere, anytime. It inspects data flows at critical sites (e.g., data flow boundaries) and recognizes sensitive data in the content if any. It is practical that detection-related computations are only performed at specific sites in a device or a network. Several commercial data-leak detection solutions are based on the content screening approach [23, 24, 28, 62]. The key of content screening for detection is the **recognition of sensitive data**. The detection system is deployed at critical data flow boundaries. It extracts the content from intercepted data flows and seeks the trace of sensitive data in the content. Although this strategy is practical and costs less than sensitive data tracking, it does not detect stealthy intentional data leaks that could be privately encrypted by an attacker. Therefore, this technique is mostly used for detecting inadvertent data leaks.

A basic technique to *recognize sensitive data* from data flow content is to compute the set intersection rate between the set of n-grams from the content and the set of n-grams from the sensitive data. The use of n-grams preserves local features of sensitive data and reduces false positives. The set-intersection-based detection is versatile, capable of analyzing both text and some binary-encoded context (e.g., Word or pdf files). The method has been used to detect similar documents on the web [8], shared malicious traffic patterns [10], malware [30], as well as email spam [40]. Set intersection based detection is simple to implement, and can be found in several commercial products for data-leak detection [23, 24, 28, 62].

However, the era of big data brings new challenges for data-leak detection.

- *Scalability Challenge* A naive implementation of the set intersection procedure requires $O(nm)$ complexity, where n and m are sizes of the two sets A and B, respectively. If the sets are relatively small, then a faster implementation is to use a hashtable to store set A and then testing whether items in B exist in the hashtable or not, giving $O(n + m)$ complexity. However, if A and B are both very large, a naive hashtable may have hash collisions that slow down the computation. Increasing the size of the hashtable may not be practical due to memory limitation and thrashing.
- *Accuracy Challenges* As the size of sensitive data increases, the accuracy of the detection is heavily affected by two accuracy challenges.
  - *Transformed Data Leaks.* The exposed data in the content may be unpredictably transformed or modified by users or applications, and it may no longer be identical to the original sensitive data, e.g., insertions of metadata or formatting tags, substitutions of characters for formatting purposes. It reduces the accuracy of set-intersection-based approaches.
  - *Partial Data Leaks.* The exposed data in the content may be a consecutive segment of sensitive documents instead of entire pieces of sensitive data. It is an extreme case of deletion (one kind of transformation in general) where most of sensitive data is removed. It is listed as a separate challenge since it completely nullifies set-intersection-based approaches.

- *Privacy Challenge* Cloud computing is one of the key infrastructures in the era of big data, which enables the storage and processing of large volumes of data. However, conventional set intersection operations require the possession of the sensitive data. The requirement makes it improper to outsource data-leak detection procedures to a third party, i.e., the DLD provider. Simply hashing sensitive n-grams does not solve the problem, because the DLD provider can learn the sensitive data from data flows that contain data leaks.

In this chapter, we describe two detection solutions in details that are specifically designed to address the big data challenges for data-leak detection.

5.1.1 MR-DLD: Privacy-Preserving Data-Leak Detection Through MapReduce Collection Intersection

MR-DLD leverages MapReduce [17], a programming model for distributed data-intensive applications, to realize collection intersection operations in parallel and perform data-leak detection. The detection is distributed and parallel, capable of screening massive amount of content for exposed information.

The advantage of MR-DLD is its scalability and privacy-preserving features. Because of the intrinsic $\langle key, value \rangle$ organization of items in MapReduce, the worst-case complexity of MR-DLD is correlated with the size of the leak (specifically a $\gamma \in [0, 1]$ factor denoting the size of the intersection between the content collection and the sensitive data collection). This complexity reduction brought by the γ factor is significant because the value is extremely low for normal content without a leak. In MR-DLD, items not in the intersection (non-sensitive content) are quickly dropped without further processing. Therefore, the MapReduce-based algorithms have a lower computational complexity compared to the single-host collection-intersection implementation.

The data privacy protection is realized using fast one-way transformation. This transformation requires the pre- and post-processing by the data owner for hiding and precisely identifying the matched items, respectively. Both the sensitive data and the content need to be transformed and protected by the data owner before it is given to the MapReduce nodes for the detection. In the meantime, such a transformation has to support the equality comparison required by the collection intersection. In addition, the one-way transformation is updated with new key for each detection session. The periodical updates prevent an adversary from learning frequency information from content digests and performing frequency analysis. This technique provides strong privacy guarantee for the data owner, in terms of the low probability for a MapReduce node to recover the sensitive data.

5.1.2 AlignDLD: Data-Leak Detection Through Alignment

AlignDLD solves the challenge of transformed and partial data-leak detection through a specially designed sequence alignment algorithm. *The alignment is between the sampled sensitive data sequence and the sampled content being inspected.* The alignment produces scores indicating the amount of sensitive data contained in the content.

The advantage of AlignDLD is its accuracy and scalability. AlignDLD measures the order of n-grams. It also handles arbitrary variations of patterns without an explicit specification of all possible variation patterns. Experiments show that AlignDLD substantially outperforms the collection-intersection-based methods in terms of detection accuracy in a multitude of transformed data-leak scenarios.

The scalability issue is solved in AlignDLD by sampling both the sensitive data and content sequences before aligning them. This procedure is enabled by a *comparable* sampling algorithm and a *sampling-oblivious* alignment algorithm in a pair. The comparable sampling algorithm yields constant samples of a sequence wherever the sampling starts and ends. The sampling-oblivious alignment algorithm infers the similarity between the original unsampled sequences with sophisticated traceback techniques through dynamic programming. The algorithm infers the lost information (i.e., sampled-out elements) based on the matching results of their neighboring elements. Evaluation results show that AlignDLD boosts the performance, yet only incurs a very small amount of mismatches.

The rest of the chapter is organized as follows. We first formalize the basic set intersection model for conventional data-leak detection in Sect. 5.2. In the next two sections, we detail the two data-leak detection solutions solving big data challenges in Sects. 5.3 and 5.4, respectively. Then we give the literature review on data-leak detection and related techniques in Sect. 5.5. We discuss the open problems in the field and conclude the chapter in Sects. 5.6 and 5.7.

5.2 Model and Background

In a typical content-screening data-leak detection model, two types of sequences, i.e., sensitive data sequence and content sequence, are analyzed.

- *Content sequence* is the sequence to be examined for leaks. The content may be extracted from file systems on personal computers, workstations and servers, or from payloads extracted from network traffic.
- *Sensitive data sequence* contains the information (e.g., customers' records, proprietary documents) that needs to be protected and cannot be exposed to unauthorized parties. The sensitive data sequence should not be known to the analysis system if it is not secure and trustworthy (e.g., detection is performed by cloud or DLD provider).

5.2.1 Security Model

We classify data leaks into two categories according to their causes:

- Case I *Inadvertent data leak*: The sensitive data is accidentally leaked in the outbound traffic by a legitimate user. This chapter focuses on detecting this type of accidental data leaks over supervised network channels. Inadvertent data leak may be due to human errors such as forgetting to use encryption, carelessly forwarding an internal email and attachments to outsiders, or due to application flaws (such as described in [33]). A supervised network channel could be an unencrypted channel or an encrypted channel where the content in it can be extracted and checked by an authority. Such a channel is widely used for advanced NIDS where MITM (man-in-the-middle) SSL sessions are established instead of normal SSL sessions [31].

- Case II *Intentional data leak*: A rogue insider or a piece of stealthy software may steal sensitive personal or organizational data from a host. Because the malicious adversary can use strong private encryption, steganography or covert channels to disable content-based traffic inspection, this type of leaks is out of the scope of the network-based solution. Host-based defenses (such as detecting the infection onset [67]) need to be deployed instead.

In this chapter, we describe data-leak detection solutions against Case I, the inadvertent data leaks over supervised network channels. In other words, the detection techniques in this chapter aim to discover sensitive data appearance in network traffic over supervised network channels. We assume that: (1) plaintext data in supervised network channels can be extracted for inspection; (2) the data owner is aware of legitimate data transfers; and (3) whenever sensitive data is found in network traffic, the data owner can decide whether or not it is a data leak. Network-based security approaches are ineffective against data leaks caused by malware or rogue insiders as in Case II, because the intruder may use strong encryption when transmitting the data, and both the encryption algorithm and the key could be unknown to the detection system.

5.2.2 Basic Solution

The basic approach for detecting data leak is based on computing the similarity between content sequences and sensitive data sequences, specifically **the intersection of two collections of shingles**. A shingle (q-gram) is a fixed-size sequence of contiguous bytes. For example, the 3-gram shingle set of string abcdefgh consists of six elements {abc, bcd, cde, def, efg, fgh}. Local feature preservation is accomplished through the use of shingles. Therefore, the basic approach can tolerate sensitive data modification to some extent, e.g., inserted tags, a small amount of character substitution, and lightly reformatted data. The use of shingles for finding duplicate web documents first appeared in [7, 8].

One collection consists of shingles obtained from the content sequence and the other collection consists of shingles from the sensitive sequence. Collection intersection differs from set intersection, in that it also records duplicated items in the intersection, which is illustrated in Fig. 5.1. Recording the frequencies of

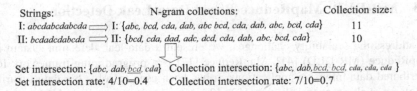

Strings: N-gram collections: Collection size:
I: *abcdabcdabcda* ⟹ I: {*abc, bcd, cda, dab, abc bcd, cda, dab, abc, bcd, cda*}   11
II: *bcdadcdabcda* ⟹ II: {*bcd, cda, dad, adc, dcd, cda, dab, abc, bcd, cda*}   10

Set intersection: {*abc, dab, bcd, cda*}   Collection intersection: {*abc, dab, bcd, bcd, cda, cda, cda* }
Set intersection rate: 4/10=0.4   Collection intersection rate: 7/10=0.7

Fig. 5.1 An example illustrating the difference between set intersection and collection intersection in handling duplicates for 3-grams

intersected items achieves more fine-grained detection. Thus, collection intersection is preferred for data-leak analysis than set intersection.

Formally, given a content collection C_c and a sensitive data collection C_s, the detection algorithms aim to compute the intersection rate $Irate \in [0, 1]$ defined in (5.1), where $Inum$ is the occurrence frequency of an item i in the intersection $C_s \cap C_c$. The sum of frequencies of all items appeared in the collection intersection is normalized by the size of the sensitive data collection (assuming $|C_s| < |C_c|$), which yields the intersection rate $Irate$. The rate represents the percentage of sensitive data that appears in the content. $Irate$ is also referred to as the *sensitivity score* of a content collection.

$$Irate = \frac{\sum\limits_{i \in \{C_s \cap C_c\}} Inum_i}{|C_s|} \qquad (5.1)$$

Existing commercial products for data-leak detection/prevention are likely based on the basic solution introduced above in Sect. 5.2.2. These products include Symantec DLP [62], IdentityFinder [28], GlobalVelocity [23], and GoCloud-DLP [24]. Data-leak detection techniques used in the literature include keyword searching [36], data tracking [26, 44, 69], watermarking [2, 46], etc.

The most severe problem with these techniques in big data era is that they are not able to process massive content data in time. In addition, none of them address the privacy challenges, meaning that the person or company who performs detection is possible to learn about the sensitive data.

MapReduce has been used to address the scalability challenge in data mining [78], machine learning [45], database [4, 64], and bioinformatics [43]. It is also recently used in security areas such as log analysis [22, 68], spam filtering [12, 13] and malware detection [21, 49, 79]. Privacy-preserving techniques are also widely invented for secure multi-party computation [70]. Shingle with Rabin fingerprint [50] is also used for collaborative spam filtering [40], worm containment [10], virus scan [25], and fragment detection [52].

These techniques laid the foundation for the two new approaches below on detecting data leak in massive content.

5.3   MR-DLD: MapReduce-Based Data-Leak Detection

To address the scalability challenges, we present a data-leak detection system in MapReduce (MR-DLD) [41]. MapReduce [17] is a programming framework for distributed data-intensive applications. It has been used to solve big data security problems such as spam filtering [12, 13], Internet traffic analysis [39] and log analysis [4, 42, 68]. MapReduce algorithms can be deployed on nodes in the cloud or in local computer clusters.

The detection also provides privacy enhancement to preserve the confidentiality of sensitive data during the outsourced detection. Because of this privacy enhancement, the MapReduce algorithms can be deployed in distributed environments where the operating nodes are owned by third-party service providers. Applications of the MR-DLD system include data-leak detection in the cloud and outsourced data-leak detection.

5.3.1   Threat Model

In this model, two parties participate in the large-scale data-leak detection system: data owner and data-leak detection (DLD) provider.

- *Data owner* owns the sensitive data and wants to know whether the sensitive data is leaked. It has the full access to both the content and the sensitive data. However, it only has limited computation and storage capability and needs to authorize the DLD provider to help inspect the content for the inadvertent data leak.
- *DLD provider* provides detection service and has unlimited computation and storage power when compared with data owner. It can perform offline inspections on big data without real-time delay. However, the DLD provider is honest-but-curious (aka semi-honest). That is, it follows the prescribed protocol but may attempt to gain knowledge of sensitive data. The DLD provider is not given the access to the plaintext content. It can perform dictionary attacks on the signature of sensitive data records.

The goal of MR-DLD is to offer DLD provider the solution to scan massive content for sensitive data exposure and minimize the possibility that the DLD provider learns about the sensitive information.

5.3.2   Confidentiality of Sensitive Data

Naive collection-intersection solutions performing on *shingles* provide no protection for the sensitive data. The reason is that MapReduce nodes can easily reconstruct sensitive data from the shingles. MR-DLD utilizes several methods for the data owner to transform shingles before they are released to the MapReduce nodes. These transformations, including specialized hash function, provide strong-yet-efficient confidentiality protection for the sensitive information. In exchange for these privacy guarantees, the data owner needs to perform additional data pre- and post-processing operations.

In addition to protecting the confidentiality of sensitive data, the pre-processing operations also need to satisfy the following requirements:

- Equality-preserving: the transformation operation should be deterministic so that two identical shingles within one session are always mapped to the same item for comparison.
- One-wayness: the function should be easy to compute given any shingle and hard to invert given the output of a sensitive shingle.
- Efficiency: the operation should be efficient and reliable so that the data owner is able to process very large content.

The collection intersection (in Sect. 5.3.4) is computed on one-way hash values of n-grams, specifically Rabin fingerprints. Rabin fingerprint is a fast one-way hash function, which is computational expensive to invert. In addition, Rabin fingerprints can be computed in linear time [7]. The computation can be implemented with fast XOR, shift and table lookup operations.

Specifically, Rabin fingerprint of a n-bit shingle is based on the coefficients of the remainder of the polynomial modular operation with an irreducible polynomial $p(x)$ as the modulo as shown in (5.2), where c_{n-i+1} is the i-th bit in the shingle C.

$$f(C) = c_1 x^{n-1} + c_2 x^{n-2} + \ldots + c_{n-1} x + c_n \bmod p(x) \qquad (5.2)$$

To meet the privacy requirements, the MR-DLD approach expands the Rabin fingerprint and presents a new "keyed-hash" operation as shown in (5.3), where K is data owner selected secret session key and S is the input shingle.

$$f(K, p(x), S) = K \oplus (s_1 x^{n-1} + s_2 x^{n-2} + \ldots + s_{n-1} x + s_n \bmod p(x)) \quad (5.3)$$

The difference between the expanded operation and Rabin fingerprint is that $p(x)$ and K change periodically as parameters. Different from a regular keyed-hash method, the "key" in the MR-DLD operation is used to keep updating the fingerprint method. In this chapter, we refer to the expanded operation as Rabin fingerprint. Section 5.3.5 presents the security analysis of the MR-DLD approach especially on the confidentiality of sensitive data.

5.3.3   Technical Requirements and Design Overview

In this section, we introduce MapReduce and the specific challenges when performing data-leak detection with MapReduce. We further present the workflow of the MR-DLD detection framework and the overview of the collection intersection algorithm used in the framework.

5.3.3.1   MapReduce-Based Design and Challenges

MapReduce is a programming model for processing large-scale data sets on clusters. With an associated implementation (e.g., Hadoop), MapReduce frees programmers from handling program's execution across a set of machines. It takes care of tasks scheduling, machine failures and inter-machine communication. A MapReduce algorithm has two phases: map that supports the distribution and partition of inputs to nodes, and `reduce` that groups and integrates the nodes' outputs. MapReduce data needs to be in the format of ⟨*key, value*⟩ pair, where *key* serves as an index and the value represents the properties corresponding to the key/data item. Programmer usually only needs to specify the `map` and `reduce` function to process the ⟨*key, value*⟩ pairs. Figure 5.2 illustrate the process of a MapReduce program execution.

The input big data in distributed file system is split and pre-processed by RECORDREADER. The output of RECORDREADER is a set of ⟨*key, value*⟩ pairs, which are sent to `map`. Each programmer specified map processes a ⟨*key, value*⟩ pair and generates a list of new ⟨*key, value*⟩ pairs. In Fig. 5.2, the first map generates three ⟨*key, value*⟩ pairs. The output ⟨*key, value*⟩ pairs are redistributed with the keys as indexes. All the pairs with key *K1* in Fig. 5.2 is processed by the first `reduce`. `Reduce` analyzes the group of values with the same key and writes the result back to distributed file system.

A significant of real world problems are able to be expressed by this model. A complex problem may require several rounds of map and reduce operations, requiring redefining and redistributing ⟨*key, value*⟩ pairs between rounds. New large-scale processing models are also proposed. For example, Google's Percolator [48] focuses on incrementally processing updates to a large data set. Muppet [38] provides a MapReduce-style model for streaming data. The collection intersection problem cannot be represented by the Percolator model. Although Muppet is able to perform collection intersection with streaming content, it cannot be used here due to its memory-heavy feature.

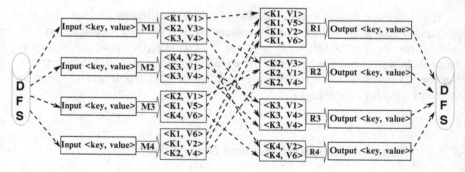

Fig. 5.2 Overview of MapReduce execution process. map takes each ⟨*key, value*⟩ pair as input and generates new ⟨*key, value*⟩ pairs. The output ⟨*key, value*⟩ pairs are redistributed according to the *key*. Each `reduce` processes the list of *values* with the same key and writes results back to DFS

There exist several MapReduce-specific challenges when realizing collection-intersection based data-leak detection.

1. **Complex data fields** Collection intersection with duplicates is more complex than set intersection. This requires the design of complex data fields for ⟨*key, value*⟩ pairs and a series of map and reduce operations.
2. **Memory and I/O efficiency** The use of multiple data fields (e.g., collection size and ID, shingle frequency) in ⟨*key, value*⟩ pairs may cause frequent garbage collection and heavy network and disk I/O when processing big data.
3. **Optimal segmentation of data streams** While larger segment size allows the full utilization of CPU, it may cause insufficient memory problem and reduced detection sensitivity.

The MR-DLD data-leak detection algorithms in MapReduce addresses these technical challenges in MapReduce framework and achieves the security and privacy goals. The MR-DLD approach has well designed structured-yet-compact representations for data fields of intermediate values, which significantly improves the efficiency of the detection algorithms. The prototype also realizes an additional post-processing partitioning and analysis, which allows one to pinpoint the leak occurrences in large content segments. The MR-DLD approach is experimentally evaluated to test the impact of segment sizes on the detection throughput and identify the optimal segment size for performance.

5.3.3.2 Workload Distribution and Detection Workflow

The details of how the workload is distributed between data owner and DLD provider is as follows and shown in Fig. 5.3:

1. Data owner has m sensitive sequences $\{S_1, S_2, \cdots, S_m\}$ with average size $\mathscr{S}'$ and n content segments $\{C_1, C_2, \cdots, C_n\}$ with average size $\mathscr{C}'$. It obtains shingles from the content and sensitive data respectively. Then it chooses the parameters $(n, p(x), K, L)$, where n is the length of a shingle, $p(x)$ is the irreducible

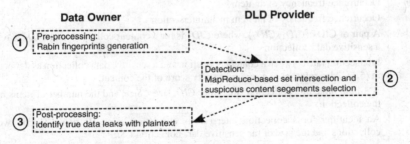

Fig. 5.3 Workload distribution for DLD provider and data owner

polynomial and L is the fingerprint length. The data owner computes Rabin fingerprints with (5.2) and releases the sensitive collections $\{C_{S1}, C_{S2}, \cdots, C_{Sm}\}$ and content fingerprint collections $\{C_{C1}, C_{C2}, \cdots, C_{Cn}\}$ to the DLD provider.

2. DLD provider receives both the sensitive fingerprint collections and content fingerprint collections. It deploys MapReduce framework and compares the n content collections with the m sensitive collections using two-phase MapReduce algorithms. By computing the intersection rate of each content and sensitive collections pair, it outputs whether the sensitive data was leaked and reports all the data-leak alerts to data owner.

3. Data owner receives the data-leak alerts with a set of tuples $\{(C_{Ci}, C_{Sj}), (C_{Ck}, C_{Sl}), \cdots\}$. The data owner maps them to suspicious content segments and the plain sensitive sequences tuples $\{(C_i, S_j), (C_k, S_l), \cdots\}$. The data owner consults plaintext content to confirm that true leaks (as opposed to accidental matches) occur in these content segments and further pinpoint the leak occurrences.

To compute the intersection rate of two fingerprint collections $Irate$, the MR-DLD approach has two MapReduce algorithms, DIVIDER and REASSEMBLER, each of which has a map and a reduce operation. Map and reduce operations are connected through a redistribution process. During the redistribution, outputs from map (in the form of $\langle key, value \rangle$ pairs) are sent to reducer nodes, as the inputs to the reduce algorithm. The key value of a record decides to which reducer node the it is forwarded. Records with the same key are sent to the same reducer.

Notations used in the algorithms introduced below are shown in Table 5.1, including collection identifier CID, size CSize (in terms of the number of items), occurrence frequency $Snum$ of an item in one collection, occurrence frequency $Inum$ of an item in an intersection, and intersection rate $Irate$ of a content collection with respect to some sensitive data.

Table 5.1 Notations used in the MapReduce algorithms

Syntax	Definition
CID	An identifier of a collection (content or sensitive data)
$CSize$	Size of a collection
$Snum$	Occurrence frequency of an item
$Inum$	Occurrence frequency of an item in an intersection
$CSid$	A pair of CIDs $\langle CID_1, CID_2 \rangle$, where CID_1 is for a content collection and CID_2 is for a sensitive data collection
$Irate$	Intersection rate between a content collection and a sensitive data collection as defined in (5.1). Also referred to as the sensitivity score of the content.
ISN	A 3-item tuple of a collection $\langle$identifier CID, size $CSize$, and the number of items in the collection$\rangle$
CSS	An identifier for a collection intersection, consisting of an ID pair $CSid$ of two collections and the size of the sensitive data collection $CSize$

1. DIVIDER takes the following as inputs: fingerprints of both content and sensitive data, and the information about the collections containing these fingerprints. Its purpose is to count the number of a fingerprint's occurrences in a collection intersection (i.e., *Inum* in (5.1)) for all fingerprints in all intersections.

   In map operation, it re-organizes the fingerprints to identify all the occurrences of a fingerprint across multiple content or sensitive data collections. Each map instance processes one collection. This reorganization traverses the list of fingerprints. Using the fingerprint as the key, it then emits (i.e., redistributes) the records with the same key to the same node.

   In reduce, for each fingerprint in an intersection the algorithm computes the *Inum* value, which is its number of occurrences in the intersection. Each reduce instance processes one fingerprint. The algorithm outputs the tuple $\langle CSS, Inum \rangle$, where *CSS* is the identifier of the intersection (consisting of IDs of the two collections and the size of the sensitive data collection.[1]) Outputs are written to MapReduce file system.

2. REASSEMBLER takes as inputs $\langle CSS, Inum \rangle$ (outputs from Algorithm DIVIDER). The purpose of this algorithm is to compute the intersection rates (i.e., *Irate* in (5.1)) of all collection intersections $\{C_{c_i} \cap C_{s_j}\}$ between a content collection C_{c_i} and a sensitive data collection C_{s_j}.

   In map, the inputs are read from the file system and redistributed to reducer nodes according to the identifier of an intersection *CSS* (key). A reducer has as inputs the *Inum* values for all the fingerprints appearing in a collection intersection whose identifier is *CSS*. At reduce, it computes the intersection rate of *CSS* based on (5.1).

In the next section, we present the algorithms for realizing the collection intersection workflow with one-way Rabin fingerprints. Section 5.3.5 explains why the privacy-preserving technique is able to protect the sensitive data against semi-honest MapReduce nodes.

5.3.4 Collection Intersection in MapReduce

We present the collection-intersection algorithm in the MapReduce framework to screening large content data. The algorithm computes the intersection rate of two collections as defined in (5.1). Each collection consists of Rabin fingerprints of n-grams generated from a sequence (sensitive data or content).

RECORDREADER is a (standard) MapReduce class. It is customized to read initial inputs into the detection system and transform them into the $\langle key, value \rangle$ format required by the map function. The initial inputs of RECORDREADER are content fingerprints segments and sensitive fingerprints sequences. For the DIVIDER

---

[1] The sensitive data collection is typically much smaller than the content collection.

Algorithm 1 DIVIDER: To count the number of a fingerprint's occurrences in a collection intersection for all fingerprints in all intersections

Input: Output of RECORDREADER in a format of ⟨*CSize, Fingerprint*⟩ as ⟨*key, value*⟩ pair.
Output: ⟨*CSS, Inum*⟩ as ⟨*key, value*⟩ pair, where *CSS* contains content collection ID, sensitive data collection ID and the size of the sensitive data collection. *Inum* is occurrence frequency of a fingerprint in the collection intersection.

```
 1: function DIVIDER::MAPPER(CSize, Fingerprint)
 2:     ▷ Record necessary information for the collection.
 3:     ISN ← CID, CSize and Snum
 4:     Emit⟨Fingerprint, ISN⟩
 5: end function
 1: function DIVIDER::REDUCER(Fingerprint, ISNlist[c₁, . . . , cₙ])
 2:     j = 0, k = 0
 3:     ▷ Divide the list into a sensitive list and a content list
 4:     for all cᵢ in ISNlist do
 5:         if cᵢ belongs to sensitive collections then
 6:             SensList[++j] ← cᵢ
 7:         else
 8:             ContentList[+ + k] ← cᵢ
 9:         end if
10:     end for
11:     ▷ Record the fingerprint occurrence in the intersection
12:     for all sens in SensList do
13:         for all content in ContentList do
14:             Size ← sens.CSize
15:             Inum ← Min(sens.Snum, content.Snum)
16:             CSS ← ⟨content.CID, sens.CID, Size⟩
17:             Emit ⟨CSS, Inum⟩
18:         end for
19:     end for
20: end function
```

algorithm, the RECORDREADER has two tasks: (1) to read in each map split (e.g., content segment) as a whole and (2) to generate ⟨*CSize, fingerprint*⟩ pairs required by the map operation of DIVIDER algorithm.

5.3.4.1 DIVIDER Algorithm

DIVIDER is the most important and computational intensive algorithm in the system. Pseudocode of DIVIDER is given in Algorithm 1. In order to count the number of a fingerprint's occurrences in a collection intersection, the map operation in DIVIDER goes through the input ⟨*CSize, fingerprint*⟩ pairs, and reorganizes them to be indexed by fingerprint values. For each fingerprint in a collection, map records its origin information (e.g., *CID, CSize* of the collection) and *Snum* (fingerprint's frequency of occurrence in the collection). These values are useful for later intersection-rate computation. The advantage of using the fingerprint as the index (key) in the map's outputs is that it allows the reducer to quickly identify non-intersected items.

After redistribution, entries having the same fingerprint are sent to the same reducer node as inputs to the reduce algorithm.

Reduce algorithm is more complex than map. It partitions the occurrences of a fingerprint into two lists, one list (*ContentList*) for the occurrences in content collections and the other for sensitive data (*SensList*). It then uses a double for-loop to identify the fingerprints that appear in intersections. Non-intersected fingerprints are not analyzed, significantly reducing the computational overhead. This reduction is reflected in the computational complexity analysis in Table 5.2, specifically the $\gamma \in [0, 1]$ reduction factor representing the size of the intersection.

The for-loops also compute the occurrence frequency *Inum* of the fingerprint in an intersection. The output of the algorithm is the $\langle CSS, Inum \rangle$ pairs, indicating that a fingerprint occurs *Inum* number of times in a collection intersection whose identifier is *CSS*.

5.3.4.2   REASSEMBLER Algorithm

The purpose of REASSEMBLER is to compute the intersection rates *Irate* of all collection-and-sensitive-data intersections. Pseudocode of REASSEMBLER is in Algorithm 2. The map operation in REASSEMBLER emits (i.e., redistributes) inputs

---

Algorithm 2 REASSEMBLER: To compute the intersection rates *Irate* of all collection intersections $\{ C_{c_i} \cap C_{s_j} \}$ between a content collection C_{c_i} and a sensitive data collection C_{s_j}

Input: Output of DIVIDER in a format of $\langle CSS, Inum \rangle$ as $\langle key, value \rangle$ pairs.
Output: $\langle CSid, Irate \rangle$ pairs where *CSid* represents a pair of a content collection ID and a sensitive collection ID, while *Irate* represents the intersection rate between them

```
1: function REASSEMBLER::MAPPER(CSS, Inum)
2:     Emit⟨CSS, Inum⟩
3: end function
```

```
1: function REASSEMBLER::REDUCER(CSS, Inum[n₁, ..., nₙ])
2:     intersection ← 0
3:     ▷ Add up all the elements in Inum[]
4:     for all nᵢ in Inum[] do
5:         intersection ← intersection + nᵢ
6:     end for
7:     CSid ← CSS.CSid
8:     ▷ Compute intersection rate
9:     Irate ← |intersection| / CSS.CSize
10:    Emit ⟨CSid, Irate⟩
11: end function
```

⟨*CSS, Inum*⟩ pairs according to their key *CSS* values to different reducers. The reducer can then compute the intersection rate *Irate* for the content and sensitive data collection pair. I.e., this redistribution sends all the intersected items between a content collection C_{c_i} and a sensitive data collection C_{s_j} to the same reducer.

5.3.4.3 Example of the Algorithms

Steps of the MapReduce algorithms are illustrated with an example (on four MapReduce nodes) in Fig. 5.4. The example has two content collections C_1 and C_2, and two sensitive data collections S_1 and S_2. The four data collections are generated by the data owner and sent to DLD provider. The sizes of the corresponding collections are 3, 4, 3 and 3, respectively. Each element (e.g., *a*) in the collections represents a fingerprint. The items after the steps indicate how the operations compute.

Step 1 Before the algorithms, the customized RECORDREADER reads the collections and sends ⟨*key, value*⟩ pairs to maps. In node 1, RECORDREADER parses collection C_1 by generating a ⟨*key, value*⟩ whenever it encounters an element. The key is the collection size 3 for C_1 and the value is the element it encounters.

- Node1: $\{a, b, c\} \Rightarrow \{⟨3, a⟩, ⟨3, b⟩, ⟨3, c⟩\}$
- Node2: $\{a, h, c, h\} \Rightarrow \{⟨4, a⟩, ⟨4, h⟩, ⟨4, c⟩, ⟨4, h⟩\}$
- Node3: $\{a, b, d\} \Rightarrow \{⟨3, a⟩, ⟨3, b⟩, ⟨3, d⟩\}$
- Node4: $\{d, h, h\} \Rightarrow \{⟨3, d⟩, ⟨3, h⟩, ⟨3, h⟩\}$

Step 2 For the element *a* in node 1, map in DIVIDER outputs the pair ⟨*a*, $(C_1, 3, 1)$⟩, indicating that fingerprint (key) *a* is from content collection C_1 of size 3 and occurs once in C_1. The outputs are redistributed according the key values. All occurrences of fingerprint *a* are sent to node 1, including two occurrences

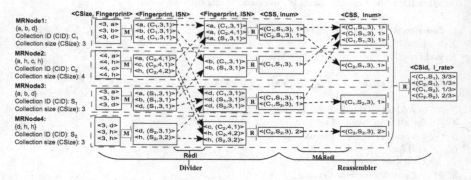

Fig. 5.4 An example illustrating DIVIDER and REASSEMBLER algorithms, with four MapReduce nodes, two content collections C_1 and C_2, and two sensitive data collections S_1 and S_2. **M, R, Redi** stand for map, reduce, and redistribution, respectively. ⟨key, value⟩ of each operation is shown at the *top*

from content collections C_1 and C_2, one occurrence from sensitive data collection S_1. Similar process applies to all the other fingerprints. The items below shows how a is manipulated in different nodes.

- a in node1: $\langle 3, a \rangle \Rightarrow \langle a, (C_1, 3, 1) \rangle$
- a in node2: $\langle 4, a \rangle \Rightarrow \langle b, (C_2, 4, 1) \rangle$
- a in node3: $\langle 3, a \rangle \Rightarrow \langle c, (S_1, 3, 1) \rangle$

Step 3 Reduce in DIVIDER computes the intersection of content and sensitive collections for each fingerprint. In node 1, given the list of collections that fingerprint a exists, reduce algorithm uses a double for-loop and identifies that a appears in intersection $C_1 \cap S_1$ and intersection $C_2 \cap S_1$. The intersections are set as keys. The occurrence frequencies of fingerprint a are set as values. In node 1, a appears once in $C_1 \cap S_1$ and once in $C_2 \cap S_1$.

- Node1: $\langle a, \{(C_1, 3, 1), (C_2, 4, 1), (S_1, 3, 1)\} \rangle \Rightarrow \{\langle (C_1, S_1, 3), 1 \rangle, \langle (C_2, S_1, 3), 1 \rangle\}$
- Node2: $\langle b, \{(C_1, 3, 1), (S_1, 3, 1)\} \rangle \Rightarrow \{\langle (C_1, S_1, 3), 1 \rangle\}$
- Node3: $\langle d, \{(C_1, 3, 1), (S_1, 4, 1), (S_2, 3, 1)\} \rangle \Rightarrow \{\langle (C_1, S_1, 3), 1 \rangle, \langle (C_1, S_2, 3), 1 \rangle\}$
- Node4: $\langle c, \{(C_2, 4, 1)\} \rangle \Rightarrow NULL$; $\langle h, \{(C_2, 4, 2), (S_2, 3, 2)\} \rangle \Rightarrow \{\langle (C_2, S_2, 3), 2 \rangle\}$

Step 4 In REASSEMBLER, the outputs of DIVIDER are redistributed. All the pairs with the same intersection are sent to the same node. In node 1, all the occurrence frequencies of fingerprints in intersection $C_1 \cap S_1$ are collected. The total number of fingerprints shared by C_1 and S_1 is 3. The intersection rate is 1.

- Node1: $\langle (C_1, S_1, 3), \{1, 1, 1\} \rangle \Rightarrow \langle (C_1, S_1), 3/3 \rangle$
- Node2: $\langle (C_2, S_1, 3), \{1\} \rangle \Rightarrow \langle (C_2, S_1), 1/3 \rangle$
- Node3: $\langle (C_1, S_2, 3), \{1\} \rangle \Rightarrow \langle (C_1, S_2), 1/3 \rangle$
- Node4: $\langle (C_2, S_2, 3), \{2\} \rangle \Rightarrow \langle (C_2, S_2), 2/3 \rangle$

With the outputs of all the nodes, we can get the intersection rates of all the intersections. The intersection rates are used to determine which content collections are suspicious.

5.3.4.4 Complexity Analysis

The computational and communication complexities of various operations of the algorithm are shown in Table 5.2. The average size of a sensitive data collection is denoted by $\mathscr{S}$, the average size of a content collection by $\mathscr{C}$, the number of sensitive data collections by m, the number of content collections by n, and the average intersection rate by $\gamma \in [0, 1]$. In real world detection, the size of $\mathscr{C}m$ could be very large. Without loss of generality, it is assumed that $|\mathscr{S}| < |\mathscr{C}|$ and $|\mathscr{S}m| < |\mathscr{C}n|$. Post-processing is not included in complexity analysis.

Table 5.2 Computation and communication complexity of each phase in the MR-DLD MapReduce algorithm and that of the conventional hashtable-based approach

Algorithm	Computation	Communication
Pre-processing of MR-DLD	$O(\mathscr{C}n + \mathscr{S}m)$	$O(\mathscr{C}n + \mathscr{S}m)$
Divider of MR-DLD::Mapper	$O(\mathscr{C}n + \mathscr{S}m)$	$O(\mathscr{C}n + \mathscr{S}m)$
Divider of MR-DLD::Reducer	$O(\mathscr{C}n + \mathscr{S}mn\gamma)$	$O(\mathscr{S}mn\gamma)$
Reassembler of MR-DLD::Mapper	$O(\mathscr{S}mn\gamma)$	$O(\mathscr{S}mn\gamma)$
Reassembler of MR-DLD::Reducer	$O(\mathscr{S}mn\gamma)$	$O(mn)$
Total of MR-DLD	$O(\mathscr{C}n + \mathscr{S}mn\gamma)$	$O(\mathscr{C}n + \mathscr{S}mn\gamma)$
Hashtable	$O(\mathscr{C}n + \mathscr{S}mn)$	N/A

The average size of a sensitive data collection is denoted by $\mathscr{S}$, the average size of a content collection by $\mathscr{C}$, the number of sensitive data collections by m, the number of content collections by n, and the average intersection rate by $\gamma \in [0, 1]$

The total communication complexity $O(\mathscr{C}n + \mathscr{S}mn\gamma)$ covers the number of records ($\langle key, value \rangle$ pairs) that all operations output. For a hashtable-based (non-MapReduce) approach, where each content collection is stored in a hashtable (total n hashtables of size $\mathscr{C}$ each) and each sensitive data item (total $\mathscr{S}m$ items) is compared against all n hashtables, the computational complexity is $O(\mathscr{C}n + \mathscr{S}mn)$.

5.3.5 Security Analysis and Discussion

MapReduce nodes that perform the data-leak detection may be controlled by honest-but-curious providers (aka semi-honest), who follow the protocol, but may attempt to gain knowledge of the sensitive data information (e.g., by logging the intermediate results and making inferences). The security and privacy guarantees provided by the MR-DLD data-leak detection system is analyzed in this subsection. We also point out the limitations associated with the collection intersection based DLD approach.

5.3.5.1 Privacy Guarantee

The privacy goal of the MR-DLD system is to prevent the sensitive data from being exposed to DLD provider or untrusted nodes. Let f_s be the Rabin fingerprint of sensitive data shingle s. Using the algorithms in Sect. 5.3.4, a MapReduce node knows fingerprint f_s but not shingle s of the sensitive data. Attackers are assumed to be not able to infer s in polynomial time from f_s. This assumption is guaranteed by the one-way Rabin fingerprinting function [51].

In addition, to prevent DLD provider from performing frequency analysis, the data owner chooses a different irreducible polynomial $p(x)$ for each session. To be specific, the data owner needs to:

1. Divide the content into multiple blocks. Each block is assigned to a session.
2. Select a new irreducible polynomial $p(x)$ for each session.
3. Divide each session (block) into several subsessions. Select a new secret session key K for each subsession. We assume that the data in each subsession is small enough, without providing useful frequency information.
4. For each subsession, pre-process the content block and a copy of sensitive data with the polynomial $p(x)$. XOR all the fingerprints of the subsession with session key K and send the result to DLD provider.

This above transformation preserves the equality comparison (as required in Sect. 5.3.2). It ensures that the same shingles are mapped to the same fingerprint within a session).

Following the above steps, the same shingle is mapped to different fingerprints in multiple sessions. The advantage of this design is the increased randomization in the fingerprint computation, making it more challenging for the DLD provider to correlate values and infer preimage. DLD provider cannot have enough frequency information to infer sensitive information. This randomization also increases the difficulty of dictionary attacks.

In MR-DLD system, the irreducible polynomials need to be only known to the data owner. As Rabin fingerprint is not designed to be a keyed hash, DLD provider may still be able to infer the polynomial from fingerprints. However, the privacy of sensitive data is still guaranteed even if $p(x)$ is known to DLD provider. Let f_1 be the Rabin fingerprint of shingle c_1 in block B_1 and f_2 be the Rabin fingerprint of shingle c_2 in block B_2. B_1 uses irreducible polynomial $p(x)_1$ and $B2$ uses irreducible polynomial $p(x)_2$. DLD provider can merge the frequency information of block B_1 and block B_2 only if it knows whether f_1 and f_2 are generated from the same shingle. However, this is computational impossible because DLD provider does not know the session keys for the two blocks, thus needs to resort to brute-force guessing, which is expensive.

To perform successful frequency analysis, the DLD provider needs to have a large content block, which is transformed with one key K and one $p(x)$. The transformation breaks large content into smaller ones, with each encoded with different key K and $p(x)$. As the DLD provider cannot merge frequency information of multiple blocks, the combination usage of XOR and $p(x)$ can help increases the difficulty of successful frequency analysis.

5.3.5.2   Detection Accuracy

We discuss the sources of possible false negatives—data-leak cases being over-looked and false positives—legitimate content misclassified as data leak in the detection.

Collisions Collisions may be due to where the legitimate content happens to contain the partial sensitive-data fingerprints by coincidence. The collisions may increase with shorter shingles, or smaller numbers of partial fingerprints, and may decrease if additional features such as the order of fingerprints are used for detection. A previous large-scale information-retrieval study empirically demonstrated the low rate of this type of collisions in Rabin fingerprint [8], which is a desirable property suggesting low unwanted false alarms in our DLD setting. Using 6 shingles of 8 bytes each on 200 million documents, researchers found that the probability for two documents that share more than a certain number of shingles to significantly differ from each other is quite low [8]. For example, the probability that two documents having resemblance greater than 97.5 % do not share at least two features is less than 0.01; and the probability that two documents with less than 77 % resemblance do share two or more shingles is less than 0.01 [8]. Collisions due to two distinct shingles generating the same fingerprint are proved to be low [7] and are negligible.

Modified data leak The underlying shingle scheme of the basic approach has limited power to capture heavily modified data leaks. False negatives (i.e., failure to detect data leak) may occur due to the data modification (e.g., reformatting). The new shingles/fingerprints may not resemble the original ones, and cannot be detected. As a result, a packet may evade the detection. The modified data-leak detection problem is a general problem for all comparison-based data-leak detection solutions. More advanced content comparison techniques than shingles/fingerprints are needed to fully address the issue.

Selective fragments leak The partial disclosure scheme may result in false negatives, i.e., the leaked data may evade the detection because it is not covered by the released fingerprints. This issue illustrates the tradeoff among detection accuracy, privacy guarantee and detection efficiency.

5.3.6   Evaluation

The algorithms are implemented with Java in Hadoop, which is an open-source software system implementing MapReduce. The length of fingerprint and shingle is set to 8 bytes (64 bits). This length was previously reported as optimal for robust similarity test [8], as it is long enough to preserve some local context and short enough to resist certain transformations. The prototype also implements an additional IP-based post-processing analysis and partition focusing on the suspicious content. It allows the data owner to pinpoint the IPs of hosts where leaks occur. The outputs are the suspicious content segments and corresponding hosts.

Several technical measures are made to reduce disk and network I/O. Sequence-File (structured) format is used as the intermediate data format. The size of ⟨key, value⟩ pairs is also minimized. E.g., the size of *value* after map in DIVIDER is 6 bytes on average. COMBINATION classes are also implemented to significantly reduce the amount of intermediate results written to the distributed file systems (DFS). This reduction in size is achieved by aggregating same ⟨key, value⟩ pairs. This method reduces the data volume by half. Hadoop compression is also enabled, giving as high as 20-fold size reduction.

The algorithms are deployed in two different 24-node Hadoop systems, a local cluster and Amazon Elastic Compute Cloud (EC2). For both environments, one node is set as the master node and the rest as slave nodes.

- *Amazon EC2:* 24 nodes each having a c3.2xlarge instance with eight CPUs and 15 GB RAM.
- *Local cluster:* 24 nodes each having two quad-core 2.8 GHz Xeon processors and 8 GB RAM.

Enron Email Corpus, including both email header and body, are used to perform the performance experiments. The entire dataset is used as content and a small subset of it is used as the sensitive data.

The experiments aim to answer the following questions.

1. How does the size of content segment affect the analysis throughput? (Sect. 5.3.6.1)
2. What is the throughput of the detection on Amazon EC2 and the local clusters? (Sect. 5.3.6.2)
3. How does the size of sensitive data affect the detection performance? (Sect. 5.3.6.3)

5.3.6.1 Optimal Size of Content Segment

Content volume is usually overwhelmingly larger than sensitive data, as new content is generated continuously in storage and in transmission. Thus, the throughput of different sizes and numbers of content segments is evaluated in order to find the optimal segment size for scalability on DLD provider's side. A content segment with size $\hat{C}$ is the original sequence that is used to generate the n-gram content collection. A sensitive sequence with size $\hat{S}$ is the original sequence that is used to generate the n-gram sensitive collection.

Fig. 5.5 DLD provider's throughput with different sizes of content segments. For each setup (*line*), the size of the content analyzed is 37 GB

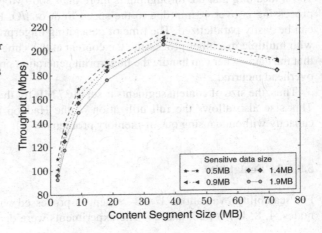

Fig. 5.6 Data owner's
pre-processing overhead on a
workstation with different
sizes of content segments.
The total size of content
analyzed is 37 GB

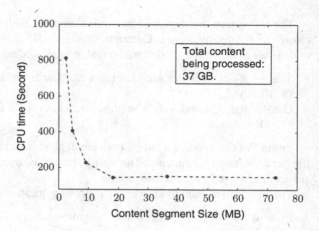

The total size of content analyzed is 37 GB, which consists of multiple copies of Enron data. Detection performance under different content segment sizes (from 2 to 80 MB) is measured. The size of sensitive data is varied from 0.5 to 2 MB. The results are shown in Fig. 5.5.

We can observe that when $\hat{C} < 37$ MB, the throughput of the analysis increases with the size $\hat{C}$ of content segment. When $\hat{C}$ becomes larger than 37 MB, the throughput begins to decrease. The reason for this decrease is that more computation resources are spent on garbage collection with larger $\hat{C}$. There are over 16 processes running at one node at the same time. Each process is assigned 400 MB to process 37×8 MB shingles.

Data owner's overhead of generating fingerprints is also evaluated with the same datasets. The experiment is performed on a quad-core 3.00 GHz Xeon processor and 8 GB RAM machine running Ubuntu 14.04.1. The results are shown in Fig. 5.6. We observe that the CPU time of generating fingerprints falls off quickly with the content segment size increasing. When $\hat{C} > 20$ MB, the CPU time is less than 100 s, meaning that the throughput is more than 3000 Mbps. The total time of pre-processing is over 40 min due to the speed limit of I/O. However, pre-processing can be easily parallelized. The time of generating fingerprints is linearly decreased with multiple machines processing the content at the same time. This fact indicates that the data owner can handle the fingerprint generation process without significant overhead incurred.

Thus, the size of content segments is set to 37 MB for the rest of the experiments. This size also allows the full utilization of the Hadoop file system (HDFS) I/O capacity without causing out-of-memory problems.

5.3.6.2 Scalability

For scalability evaluation, 37 GB content is processed with different numbers of nodes, 4, 8, 12, 16, 20, and 24. The experiments were deployed both on the local

Fig. 5.7 Throughput with different number of nodes on a local cluster or Amazon EC2

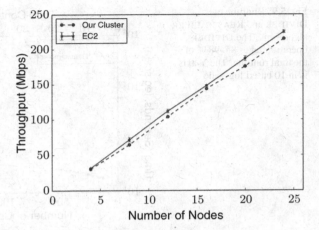

Fig. 5.8 Throughput with different amount of content workload. Each content segment is 37 MB

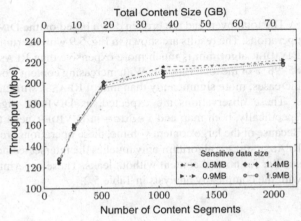

cluster and on Amazon EC2. The results are shown in Fig. 5.7. The system scales well, as the throughput linearly increases with the number of nodes. The peak throughput observed is 215 Mbps on the local cluster and 225 Mbps on Amazon EC2. EC2 cluster gives 3–11 % performance improvement. This improvement is partly due to the larger memory. The standard error bars of EC2 nodes are shown in Fig. 5.7 (from three runs). Variances of throughputs on the local cluster are negligible.

The throughput is also evaluated under a varying number of content segments n, i.e., workload. The results are shown in Fig. 5.8, where the total size of content analyzed is shown at the top X-axis (up to 74 GB). Throughput increases as workload increases as expected.

In the experiments above, the size of sensitive data is small enough to fit in one collection. The larger size of sensitive data increases the computation overhead, which explains the slight decrease in throughput in Figs. 5.5 and 5.8.

Fig. 5.9 Runtime of
DIVIDER and REASSEMBLER
algorithms. The DIVIDER
operation takes 85–98 % of
the total runtime. The Y-axis
is in 10 based log scale

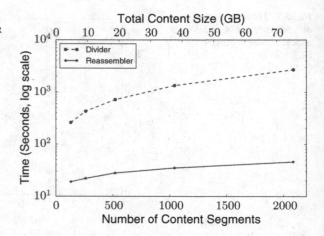

The total overhead are broken down based on the DIVIDER and REASSEMBLER operations. The results are shown in Fig. 5.9 with the runtime (Y-axis) in a log scale. DIVIDER algorithm is much more expensive than REASSEMBLER, accounting for 85–98 % of the total runtime. With increasing content workload, DIVIDER's runtime increases, more significantly than that of REASSEMBLER.

These observations are expected, as DIVIDER algorithm is more complex. Specifically, both map and `reduce` in DIVIDER need to touch *all* content items. Because of the large content volume, these operations are expensive. In comparison, REASSEMBLER algorithm only touches the intersected items, which is substantially smaller for normal content without leaks. These experimental results are consistent with the complexity analysis in Table 5.2.

5.3.6.3 Performance Impact of Sensitive Data

The performance results in Fig. 5.5 are reorganized so that the sizes of sensitive data are shown at the X-axis. The new figure is Fig. 5.10, where each setup (line) processes 37 GB data and differs in their size for content segment. There are a few observations. First, smaller content segment size incurs higher computational overhead, e.g., for keeping tracking the collection information (discussed in Sect. 5.3.6.1).

The second observation is that the runtime increases as the size of sensitive data increases, which is expected. Experiments with the largest content segment (bottom line in Fig. 5.10) have the smallest increase, i.e., the least affected by the increasing volume of sensitive data.

This difference in intercept is explained next. The total computation complexity is $O(\mathscr{C}n + \mathscr{S}mn\gamma)$ (Table 5.2). In $O(\mathscr{C}n + \mathscr{S}mn\gamma)$, $n\gamma$ serves as the coefficient (i.e., intercept), as the total size $\mathscr{S}m$ of sensitive data increases, where n is the number of content segments. When 37 GB content is broken into small segments,

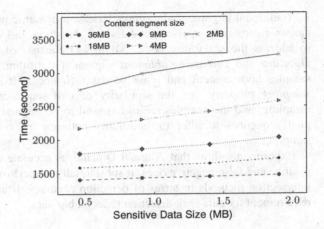

Fig. 5.10 Runtime with a varying size of sensitive data. The content volume is 37.5 GB for each setup. Each setup (*line*) has a different size for content segments

n is large. A larger coefficient magnifies the increase in sensitive data, resulting in more substantial overhead increase. Therefore, the line at the bottom of Fig. 5.10 represents the recommended configuration with a large 37 MB content segment size.

Summary The experimental findings are summarized as below.

1. The MR-DLD approach linearly scale on big data with the number of nodes. it achieves 225 Mbps throughput on Amazon EC2 cluster and a similar throughput on the local cluster. *Divider* algorithm accounts for 85–98 % of the total runtime.
2. Larger content segment size $\hat{C}$ (up to 37 MB) gives higher performance. This observation is due to the decreased amount of bookkeeping information for keeping track of collections, which results in significantly reduced I/O overhead associated with intermediate results. Data owner can also handle the fingerprint generation process without significant overhead incurred.
3. When the content segment size $\hat{C}$ is large (37 MB), the increase in the amount of sensitive data has a relatively small impact on the runtime. Given the content workload, larger $\hat{C}$ means fewer number of content segments, resulting in a smaller coefficient.

5.4 AlignDLD: Data-Leak Detection Through Alignment

To address the detection accuracy challenges, i.e., transformed data leaks and partial data leaks, we present *AlignDLD*, a data-leak detection solution with alignment techniques [58]. The key to the detection of transformed data leaks is a specialized sequence alignment algorithm, which handles arbitrary variations of patterns without an explicit specification of all possible variation patterns.

AlignDLD conducts an alignment between the sampled sensitive data sequence and the sampled content being inspected. The alignment produces a score indicating the amount of sensitive data contained in the content.

Traditional alignment algorithms based on dynamic programming is slow and cannot be directly applied to data-leak detection tasks on big data. In order to address the scalability issue, AlignDLD consists of a *comparable* sampling algorithm and a *sampling oblivious* alignment algorithm. The sampling algorithm samples both content and sensitive data sequences. It satisfies the *comparable sampling* property that the similarity of two sequences is preserved through sampling, and the samples are meaningful to be aligned. AlignDLD aligns sampled sequences to infer the similarity between the original sequences before sampling.

Experiments show that AlignDLD achieves accurate detection with low false positive and false negative rates. It substantially outperforms traditional collection-intersection methods in terms of detection accuracy. It also meets the scalability requirement for data-leak detection tasks on big data.

5.4.1 Models and Overview

Traditional collection-based data-leak detection models face two challenges toward accurate data-leak detection.

High detection specificity: the ability to distinguish true leaks from coincidental matches, which can cause false alarms. Existing collection-based detection is orderless, where the order of matched patterns (*n*-grams) is ignored. Orderless detection can result in false positives as shown below.

Sensitive data	abcdefg
3-grams of the sensitive data	abc, bcd, cde, def, efg
Content stream (false positive)	...efg...cde...abc...

Pervasive and localized modification. Sensitive data could be modified before it is leaked out. The modification can occur throughout a sequence (pervasive modification). The modification can also only affect a local region (local modification). We describe some modification examples:

- Character replacement, e.g., WordPress replaces every space character with a + in HTTP POST requests.
- String insertion: HTML tags inserted throughout a document for formatting or embedding objects.
- Data truncation or partial data leak, e.g., one page of a two-page sensitive document is transmitted.

We present AlignDLD, a data-leak detection model using efficient sequence comparison techniques to analyze a large amount of content. A diagram illustrating the security model of AlignDLD is shown in Fig. 5.11.

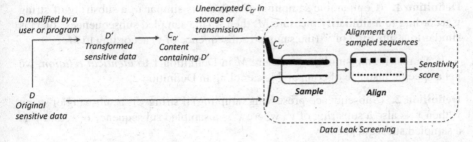

Fig. 5.11 A schematic drawing showing the two types of sequences in transformed data-leak detection model, their relations, and the workflow of the detection

AlignDLD consists of a special **sampling algorithm** and a corresponding **alignment algorithm** working on preprocessed n-grams of sequences. The pair of algorithms computes a quantitative similarity score between sensitive data and content. Local alignment, as opposed to global alignment, is used to identify similar sequence segments, enabling the detection of partial data leaks.

The workflow includes EXTRACTION, PREPROCESSING, SAMPLING, ALIGNMENT, and DECISION operations.

EXTRACTION   collects the content sequences.
PREPROCESSING   prepares the sequences of n-grams for content/sensitive data.
SAMPLING   generates samples from the preprocessed content/sensitive sequences.
ALIGNMENT   performs local alignment between the two sampled sequences.
DECISION   confirms and reports leaks according to the sensitive data sharing
    policy.

5.4.2   Comparable Sampling

We formally define the new sampling requirement needed in data-leak detection and present the comparable sampling algorithm used in AlignDLD.

5.4.2.1   Definitions

One great challenge in aligning sampled sequences is that the sensitive data segment can be exposed at an arbitrary position in a network traffic stream or a file system. The sampled sequence should be deterministic despite the starting and ending points of the sequence to be sampled. Moreover, the leaked sensitive data could be inexact but similar to the original string due to unpredictable transformations. We define the capability of giving comparable results from similar strings in Definition 1.

Definition 1. (Comparable sampling) if string x is similar to a substring of string y according to a similarity measure M, then x' (the sampled subsequences[2] of x) is similar to a substring of y' (the sampled subsequence of y) according to M.

If we restrict the similarity measure M in Definition 1 to *identical relation*, we get a specific instance of comparable sampling in Definition 2.

Definition 2. (Subsequence-preserving sampling) if string x is a substring of string y, then x' is also a substring of y', where x' is a sampled subsequence of x, and y' is a sampled subsequence of y.

Because a subsequence-preserving sampling procedure is a restricted comparable sampling, so the subsequence-preserving sampling is deterministic, i.e., the same input always yields the same output. The vice versa may not be true.

5.4.2.2   Comparable Sampling Algorithm

We present a comparable sampling algorithm, the advantage of which is its **context-aware selection**, i.e., the selection decision of an item depends on how it compares with its surrounding items according to a selection function. As a result, the sampling algorithm is *deterministic* and *subsequence-preserving*.

The comparable sampling algorithm takes in $\mathscr{S}$, an input list of items (n-grams of sensitive data or content), and outputs $\mathscr{T}$, a sampled list of the same length; the sampled list contains null values, which correspond to items that are not selected. The null regions in $\mathscr{T}$ can be aggregated, and $\mathscr{T}$ can be turned into a *compact representation* $\mathscr{L}$. Each item in $\mathscr{L}$ contains the value of the sampled item and the length of the null region between the current sampled item and the preceding one.

$\mathscr{T}$ is initialized as an empty list, i.e., a list of null items. The algorithm runs a small sliding window w on $\mathscr{S}$ and utilizes a selection function to decide what items in w should be selected for $\mathscr{T}$. The selection decision is made based on not only the value of that item, but also the values of its neighboring items in w. Therefore, unlike a random sampling method where a selection decision is stochastic, Algorithm 3 satisfies the subsequence-preserving and comparable sampling requirements.

In Algorithm 3, without loss of generality, we describe the sampling method with a specific selection function $f = \min(w, N)$. f takes in an array w and returns the N smallest items in w. f is *deterministic*. It selects items without bias when items (n-grams) are preprocessed using Rabin's fingerprint.[3] f can be replaced by other functions that have the same properties. The selection results at each sliding window position determine what items are chosen for the sampled list. The parameters N and $|w|$ determine the sampling rate. The directional collection difference operation

---

[2]Subsequence (with gaps) is a generalization of substring and allows gaps between characters, e.g., `lo-e` is a subsequence of `flower` (- indicates a gap).

[3]Rabin's fingerprint is min-wise independent.

Algorithm 3 A subsequence-preserving sampling algorithm

Require: an array $\mathscr{S}$ of items, a size $|w|$ for a sliding window w, a selection function $f(w, N)$ that
    selects N smallest items from a window w, i.e., $f = \min(w, N)$
Ensure: a sampled array $\mathscr{T}$
  1: initialize $\mathscr{T}$ as an empty array of size $|\mathscr{S}|$
  2: $w \leftarrow \text{read}(\mathscr{S}, |w|)$
  3: let $w.head$ and $w.tail$ be indices in $\mathscr{S}$ corresponding to the higher-indexed end and lower-
    indexed end of w, respectively
  4: collection $m_c \leftarrow \min(w, N)$
  5: **while** w is within the boundary of $\mathscr{S}$ **do**
  6:     $m_p \leftarrow m_c$
  7:     move w toward high index by 1
  8:     $m_c \leftarrow \min(w, N)$
  9:     **if** $m_c \neq m_p$ **then**
10:        item $e_n \leftarrow \text{collectionDiff}(m_c, m_p)$
11:        item $e_o \leftarrow \text{collectionDiff}(m_p, m_c)$
12:        **if** $e_n < e_o$ **then**
13:           write value e_n to $\mathscr{T}$ at $w.head$'s position
14:        **else**
15:           write value e_o to $\mathscr{T}$ at $w.tail$'s position
16:        **end if**
17:     **end if**
18: **end while**

`collectionDiff` in Algorithm 3 (lines 10 and 11) is similar to the set difference operation, except that it does not eliminate duplicates, i.e., identical items are kept in the results.

$\mathscr{T}$ output by Algorithm 3 takes the same space as $\mathscr{S}$ does. Null items can be combined, and $\mathscr{T}$ is turned into a *compact representation* $\mathscr{L}$, which is consumed by the sampling-oblivious alignment algorithm in the next phase.

5.4.2.3 Sampling Algorithm Analysis

The complexity of Algorithm 3 using the $\min(w, N)$ selection function is $O(n \log |w|)$, or $O(n)$ where n is the size of the input, $|w|$ is the size of the window. The factor $O(\log |w|)$ comes from maintaining the smallest N items within the window w.

The sampling rate $\alpha \in [\frac{N}{|w|}, 1]$ approximates $\frac{N}{|w|}$ for random inputs. For arbitrary inputs, the actual sampling rate depends on the characteristics of the input space and the selection function used.

A sufficient number of items need to be sampled from sequences to warrant an accurate detection. The empirical result in Sect. 5.4.4 shows that sampling with $\alpha = 0.25$ can detect as short as 32-byte-long sensitive data segments.

5.4.3 Sampling Oblivious Alignment

We present a specialized alignment algorithm that runs on compact sampled sequences $\mathscr{L}^{a\cdot}$ and $\mathscr{L}^b$ to infer the similarity between the original sensitive data sequence $\mathscr{S}^a$ and the original content sequence $\mathscr{S}^b$. It needs to satisfy a new requirement **sampling oblivion**, i.e., the result of an alignment on sampled sequences $\mathscr{L}^a$ and $\mathscr{L}^b$ should be consistent with the alignment result on the original $\mathscr{S}^a$ and $\mathscr{S}^b$.

Regular local alignment without the sampling oblivion property may give inaccurate alignment on sampled sequences. However, because values of unselected items are unknown to the alignment, the decision of match or mismatch cannot be made solely on them during the alignment. The described algorithm infers the comparison outcomes between null regions based on (1) the comparison outcomes between items surrounding null regions and (2) sizes of null regions, because leaked data region is usually consecutive, e.g., spans at least dozens of bytes. For example, given two sampled sequences a-b and A-B, if a == A and b == B, then the two values in the positions of the null regions are likely to match.

5.4.3.1 Dynamic Programming Components

The presented sample-oblivious alignment algorithm is based on dynamic programming. A string alignment problem is divided into three prefix alignment subproblems: the current two items (from two sequences) are aligned with each other, or one of them is aligned with a gap. In the algorithm, comparison outcomes between null regions are inferred based on their non-null neighboring values and their sizes/lengths. The comparison results include *match*, *mismatch* and *gap*, and they are rewarded (match) or penalized (mismatch or gap) differently for sampled items or null regions according to a weight function $f_w()$.

We present the recurrence relation of the dynamic program alignment algorithm in Algorithm 4. For the i-th item $\mathscr{L}_i$ in a sampled sequence $\mathscr{L}$ (the compact form), the field $\mathscr{L}_i.value$ denotes the value of the item and a new field $\mathscr{L}_i.span$ denotes the size of null region between that item and the preceding non-null item. The algorithm computes a non-negative score matrix H of size $|\mathscr{L}^a|$-by-$|\mathscr{L}^b|$ for the input sequence $\mathscr{L}^a$ and $\mathscr{L}^b$ and returns the maximum alignment score with respect to a weight function. Each cell $H(i,j)$ has a score field $H(i,j).score$ and two extra fields recording sizes of neighboring null regions, namely $null_{row}$ and $null_{col}$. $null_{row}$ and $null_{col}$ fields for all three cell candidates h^{up}, h^{left}, h^{dia} are initialized as 0.

The weight function $f_w()$ takes three inputs: the two items being aligned (e.g., $\mathscr{L}_i^a$ from sensitive data sequence and $\mathscr{L}_j^b$ from content sequence) and a reference cell c (one of the three visited adjacent cells $H(i-1,j-1)$, $H(i,j-1)$, or $H(i-1,j)$), and outputs a score of an alignment configuration. One of $\mathscr{L}_i^a$ and $\mathscr{L}_j^b$ may be a gap (−) in the alignment. The computation is based on the penalty given to mismatch and gap conditions and reward given to match condition. $f_w()$ in Algorithm 4 differs

---

Algorithm 4 Recurrence relation in dynamic programming

Require: A weight function f_w, visited cells in H matrix that are adjacent to $H(i,j)$: $H(i-1, j-1)$, $H(i, j-1)$, and $H(i-1, j)$, and the i-th and j-th items $\mathscr{L}_i^a$, $\mathscr{L}_j^b$ in two sampled sequences $\mathscr{L}^a$ and $\mathscr{L}^b$, respectively.

Ensure: $H(i,j)$

1: $h^{up}.score \leftarrow f_w(\mathscr{L}_i^a, -, H(i-1, j))$
2: $h^{left}.score \leftarrow f_w(-, \mathscr{L}_j^b, H(i, j-1))$
3: $h^{dia}.score \leftarrow f_w(\mathscr{L}_i^a, \mathscr{L}_j^b, H(i-1, j-1))$
4: $h^{dia}.null_{row} \leftarrow \begin{cases} 0, & \text{if } \mathscr{L}_i^a = \mathscr{L}_j^b \\ H(i-1, j).null_{row} + \mathscr{L}_i^a.span + 1, & \text{else} \end{cases}$
5: $h^{dia}.null_{col} \leftarrow \begin{cases} 0, & \text{if } \mathscr{L}_i^a = \mathscr{L}_j^b \\ H(i, j-1).null_{col} + \mathscr{L}_j^b.span + 1, & \text{else} \end{cases}$
6: $H(i,j) \leftarrow \arg\max_{h.score} \{h^{up}, h^{left}, h^{dia}\}$
7: $H(i,j).score \leftarrow \max\{0, H(i,j).score\}$

---

from the typical weight function in Smith-Waterman algorithm [59] in its ability to infer comparison outcomes for null regions. This inference is done accordingly to the values of their adjacent non-null neighboring items.

5.4.3.2 Alignment Algorithm Analysis

The complexity of the presented alignment algorithm is $O(|\mathscr{L}^a||\mathscr{L}^b|)$, where $|\mathscr{L}^a|$ and $|\mathscr{L}^b|$ are lengths of compact representations of the two sampled sequences. The alignment complexity for a single piece of sensitive data of size l is the same as that of a set of shorter pieces with a total size l, as the total amounts of matrix cells to compute are the same.

In a real-world deployment, the overall sensitive data sequence $\mathscr{S}^a$ is usually close to a fixed length, and more attention is commonly paid to the length of the content sequence $\mathscr{S}^b$. In this case, the complexity of the alignment is $O(|\mathscr{L}^b|)$ where $\mathscr{L}^b$ is the sampled list of $\mathscr{S}^b$.

The alignment of two sampled sequences achieves a speedup in the order of $O(\alpha^2)$, where $\alpha \in (0, 1)$ is the sampling rate. There is a constant damping factor due to the overhead introduced by sampling. The expected value is 0.33 because of the extra two fields, besides the score field, to maintain for each cell in H. The damping factor is experimentally verified in Sect. 5.4.4.

5.4.4 Detection Accuracy Evaluation

We present the detection results of AlignDLD against transformed data leaks and partial data leaks in this section. AlignDLD is compared with Coll-Inter, a standard collection-intersection method. Parallel versions of the prototype are discussed in Sect. 5.4.5 to demonstrate the detection capability in processing big data.

- *AlignDLD:* the sample-and-align data-leak detection method with sampling parameters $N = 10$, $|w| = 100$, 3-grams and 32-bit Rabin's fingerprints.[4]
- *Coll-Inter:* a data-leak detection system based on collection intersection, which is widely adopted by commercial tools such as GlobalVelocity and GoCloudDLP. Standard 8-grams and 64-bit Rabin's fingerprints are used.

5.4.4.1 Detecting Modified Leaks

Data-leak detection are performed via AlignDLD and Coll-Inter on three types of data leaks listed below.

1. Content without any leak, i.e., the content does not contain any sensitive data.
2. Content with unmodified leak, i.e., genuine sensitive data appears in the content.
3. Content with modified leaks caused by `WordPress`, which substitutes every space with "+" in the content.

The content and sensitive data in this experiment are selected emails from *Enron* dataset, which consists of 517,424 real emails from 150 users [34]. The content without leak consists of 950 randomly chosen Enron emails, and the sensitive data consists of 50 randomly chosen ones. We compute the sensitivities of the content according to (5.4).

$$\mathbb{S} = \frac{\xi}{r \times \min\left(|\mathscr{S}^a|, |\mathscr{S}^b|\right)} \tag{5.4}$$

The results of the detection are presented in Fig. 5.12. The table to the right of each figure summarizes the detection accuracy under the best threshold. Both methods perform as expected in the scenarios of no-leak (dotted lines on the left) and unmodified leak (dashed lines on the right).

The solid lines in Fig. 5.12 represent the detection results of leaks with `WordPress` modifications. AlignDLD in Fig. 5.12a gives much higher sensitivity scores to the transformed data leak than Coll-Inter. With a threshold of 0.2, **all the email messages with transformed leaks are detected,** i.e., it achieves 100 % recall. The false positive rate is low. In contrast, Coll-Inter in Fig. 5.12b yields a significant overlap between messages with no leak and messages with transformed leaks. Its best detection yields a 63.8 % recall and a ten times higher false positive rate.

---

[4]Rabin's fingerprint is used for unbiased sampling (Sect. 5.4.2).

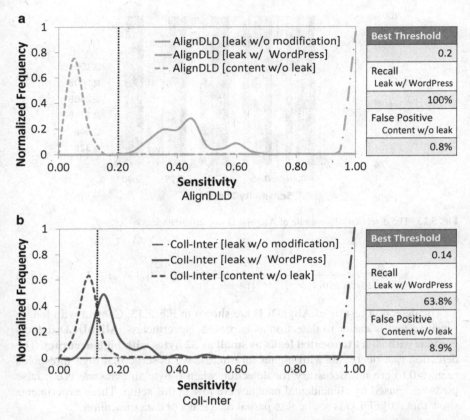

Fig. 5.12 Detection comparison of the leak through WordPress using AlignDLD (**a**) and collection intersection (**b**). *Solid lines* show the sensitivity distribution of the modified leaks via WordPress

5.4.4.2 Partial Data Leaks

In data truncation or partial data-leak scenarios, consecutive portions of the sensitive data are leaked. In this experiment, a content sequence contains a portion of sensitive text. The total length of the sensitive text is 1 KB. The size of the leaked portion in the content ranges from 32 bytes to 1 KB. Each content sequence is 1 KB long with random padding.

We measure the *unit sensitivity* $\tilde{S} \in [0, 1]$ on segments of content sequences. Unit sensitivity $\tilde{S}$ is the normalized *per-element* sensitivity value for the aligned portion of two sequences. It is defined in (5.5), where $\tilde{\xi}$ is the maximum local alignment score obtained between aligned segments $\mathscr{S}^a$ and $\mathscr{S}^b$, which are sequence segments of sensitive data D and content $C_{D'}$. The higher $\tilde{S}$ is, the better the detection is. Threshold l is a predefined length describing the shortest segment to invoke the measure. $l = 16$ in the experiments.

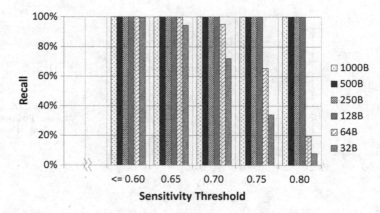

Fig. 5.13 The detection success rate of AlignDLD in partial data leaks

$$\tilde{\mathbb{S}} = \frac{\tilde{\xi}}{r \times \min\left(|\tilde{\mathscr{S}^a}|, |\tilde{\mathscr{S}^b}|\right)} \quad \text{where } \min\left(|\tilde{\mathscr{S}^a}|, |\tilde{\mathscr{S}^b}|\right) \geq l \qquad (5.5)$$

The detection results of AlignDLD are shown in Fig. 5.13. Content with longer sensitive text is easier to detection as expected. Nevertheless, **AlignDLD detects content with short truncated leaks as small as 32 bytes with high accuracy.** The detection rate decreases with higher thresholds. We observe that high thresholds (e.g., >0.6) are not necessary for detection when 8-byte shingles are used; false positives caused by coincidental matches are low in this setup. These experiments show that AlignDLD is resilient to partial data leaks or data truncation.

5.4.5 Parallelization and Evaluation

The capability of processing large amounts of content and sensitive data is demonstrated with multithreading CPU and GPU prototypes of AlignDLD.[5]

In the multithreading CPU prototype, both SAMPLING and ALIGNMENT procedures are paralleled with `pthread` library. Long streams are split into multiple substrings, which are sampled in parallel by different threads and then assembled for output. ALIGNMENT is the most time-consuming procedure and is made parallel on both CPU and GPU. A parallelized score matrix filling method is used to compute a diagonal of cells at the same time. This method consumes linear space.

We evaluate the performance of the most time-consuming ALIGNMENT procedure on the Tesla GPU. Times of speedup in detecting sensitive data of types `txt`,

---

[5]The GPU prototype is realized on one NVIDIA Tesla C2050 with 448 GPU cores.

Table 5.3 Times of speedup in AlignDLD's alignment operation. [P] represents a parallel version

Traffic	Enron			MiscNet		
data	txt	png	pdf	txt	png	pdf
CPU	1.00	1.00	1.00	1.00	1.00	1.00
CPU[P]	3.59	3.29	3.40	2.78	3.18	2.82
GPU[P]	44.36	47.93	47.98	34.60	42.51	41.59

Table 5.4 Throughput (in Mbps) of the Alignment operation on GPU

Sensitive data size (KB)	250	500	1000	2500
Sampling rate				
0.03	426	218	110	44
0.12	23	11	5	2

png, or pdf against *Enron* or *MiscNet* (miscellaneous 500 MB network traffic), respectively, are shown in Table 5.3. The GPU AlignDLD prototype achieves over 40 times of speedup over the CPU version on large content datasets. The prototype achieves a throughput of over 400 Mbps against 500 MB misc network traffic (*MiscNet*) shown in Table 5.4. This throughput is comparable to that of a moderate commercial firewall. More optimizations on data locality and memory usage can be performed in real-world detection products.

5.5   Other Defenses Against Data Leaks

In this section, we present other data-leak detection and prevention techniques. Most of them are not designed to analyze leaks in big data. In addition, we introduce the state-of-the-art techniques that could be used in data-leak detection.

5.5.1   Other Data-Leak Detection Techniques

Existing commercial data-leak detection/prevention solutions include Symantec DLP [62], IdentityFinder [28], GlobalVelocity [23], and GoCloudDLP [24]. All solutions are likely based on *n*-gram set intersection. IdentityFinder searches file systems for short patterns of numbers that may be sensitive (e.g., 16-digit numbers that might be credit card numbers). Symantec DLP is based on *n*-grams and Bloom filters. The advantage of Bloom filter is space saving. However, filter membership testing is based on unordered *n*-grams, which generates coincidental matches and false alarms. Most of these commercial detection solutions do not have the privacy-preserving feature and cannot be outsourced. GoCloudDLP [24] is a little different, which allows its customers to outsource the detection to a fully honest DLD provider.

Borders and Prakash [6] presented a network analysis based approach for estimating information leak in the outbound traffic. The method identifies the anomalous and drastic increase in the amount of information carried by the traffic. The method was not designed to detect small-scale data leak. Croft and Caesar [16] compared two logical copies of network traffic to control the movement of sensitive data. The work by Papadimitriou and Garcia-Molina [46] aims at finding the agents that leaked the sensitive data. Blanton et al. [5] proposed a solution for fast outsourcing of sequence edit distance and secure path computation, while preserving the confidentiality of the sequence.

Examples of host-based approaches include Auto-FBI [80] and Aquifer [44]. Auto-FBI guarantees the secure access of sensitive data on the web. It achieves this guarantee by automatically generating a new browser instance for sensitive content. Aquifer is a policy framework and system. It helps prevent accidental information disclosure in OS.

Another approach to the detection of sensitive data leak is to track the data/metadata movement. Several tools are developed for securing sensitive information on mobile platforms [26, 44, 69]. Nadkarni and Enck described an approach to control the sharing of sensitive files among mobile applications [44]. File descriptors (not the content) are stored, tracked and managed. The access control on files is enforced through policies. Yang et al. presented a method aiming at detecting the transmission of sensitive data that is not intended by smartphone users via symbolic execution analysis [69]. Hoyle et al. described a visualization method for informing mobile users of information exposure [26]. The information exposure may be caused by improper setting or configuration of access policies. The visualization is through an avatar apparel approach. Croft and Caesar expand the data tracking from a single host to a network and use shadow packets to distinguish normal traffic from leaks [15]. The security goals and requirements in all these studies are very different from ours, leading to different techniques developed and used.

iLeak is a system for preventing inadvertent information leaks on a personal computer [36]. It takes advantages of the keyword searching utility present in many modern operating systems. iLeak monitors the file access activities of processes and searches for system call inputs that involve sensitive data. Unlike the general data-leak detection approach, iLeak is designed to secure personal data on a single machine, and its detection capability is restricted by the underlying keyword searching utility, which is not designed for detecting either transformed data leaks or partial data leaks.

Bertino and Ghinita addressed the issue of data leaks in the database from the perspective of anomaly detection [2]. Normal user behaviors are monitored and modeled in DBMS, and anomalous activities are identified with respect to potential data-leak activities. Bertino also discussed watermarking and provenance techniques used in data-leak prevention and forensics [2], which is investigated in details by Papadimitriou and Garcia-Molina in [46].

5.5.2 Existing Privacy-Preserving Techniques

There have been several advances in understanding the privacy needs [37] or the privacy requirement of security applications [66]. In this chapter, we identify the privacy needs in an outsourced data-leak detection service and provide a systematic solution to enable privacy-preserving DLD services.

Shingle with Rabin fingerprint [50] was used previously for identifying similar spam messages in a collaborative setting [40], as well as collaborative worm containment [10], virus scan [25], and fragment detection [52].

There are also other privacy-preserving techniques invented for specific processes, e.g., DNA matching [63], or for general purpose use, e.g., secure multi-party computation (SMC). Similar to string matching methods discussed above, [63] uses anonymous automata to perform the comparison. Shu and Yao presented privacy-preserving methods for protecting sensitive data in a non-MapReduce based detection environment [57]. SMC [70] is a cryptographic mechanism, which supports a wide range of fundamental arithmetic, set, and string operations as well as complex functions such as knapsack computation [71], automated troubleshooting [27], network event statistics [9, 65], private information retrieval [74], genomic computation [32], private database query [73], private join operations [11], and distributed data mining [29]. The provable privacy guarantees offered by SMC comes at a cost in terms of computational complexity and realization difficulty.

5.5.3 Applications and Improvements of MapReduce

MapReduce framework was used to solve problems in data mining [78], machine learning [45], database [4, 64], and bioinformatics [43]. MapReduce algorithms for computing document similarity (e.g., [1, 18, 76]) involve pairwise similarity comparison. Similarity measures may be Hamming distance, edit distance or Jaccard distance. MapReduce was also used by security applications, such as log analysis [22, 68], spam filtering [12, 13] and malware and botnet detection [21, 49, 79] for scalability. The security solutions proposed by Bilge et al. [3], Yang et al. [68] and Yen et al. [72] analyzed network traffic or logs with MapReduce, searching for malware signatures or behavior patterns. None of the existing MapReduce solutions addresses data-leak detection problem.

Several techniques have been proposed to improve the privacy protection of MapReduce framework. Such solutions typically assume that the cloud provider is trustworthy. For example, Pappas et al. [47] proposed a data-flow tracking method in cloud applications. It audits the use of the sensitive data sent to the cloud. Roy et al. [54] integrate mandatory access control with differential privacy in order to manage the use of sensitive data in MapReduce computations. Yoon and Squicciarini [75] detected malicious or cheating MapReduce nodes by correlating different nodes' system and Hadoop logs. Squicciarini et al. [60] presented techniques that prevent information leakage from the indexes of data in the cloud.

There exist MapReduce algorithms for computing the set intersection [4, 64]. They differ from the collection intersection algorithms, as explained in Sect. 5.2.2. Collection intersection algorithm requires new intermediate data fields and processing for counting and recording duplicates in the intersection. Several techniques were developed for monitoring or improving MapReduce performance, e.g., to identify nodes with slow tasks [14], GPU acceleration [19] and efficient data transfer [42]. These advanced techniques can be applied to further speed up MR-DLD.

5.6 Conclusions

In this chapter, we introduced the background of data-leak detection and presented two techniques in detail, both of which are able to rapidly screen big content for inadvertent data exposure.

MR-DLD is a MapReduce based system for detecting the occurrences of sensitive data patterns in massive-scale content in data storage or network transmission. It provides privacy enhancement to minimize the exposure of sensitive data during the outsourced detection. MR-DLD was also deployed and evaluated with the Hadoop platform on Amazon EC2 and a local cluster, and it achieved 225 Mbps analysis throughput.

AlignDLD is based on aligning two sampled sequences for similarity comparison. The main feature of this solution is its ability to detect transformed or modified leaks. This approach consists of a comparable sampling algorithm and a specialized alignment algorithm for comparing two sampled sequences. The unique design of the two algorithms enables its accuracy and scalability. The extensive experimental evaluation with real-world data and leak scenarios confirms that this method has a high specificity (i.e., low false alarm rate) and detects transformed data leaks much more effectively than collection-intersection methods.

5.7 Future Work

The MR-DLD approach could be improved by being deployed on hybrid cloud environments, which consist of private machines owned by the data owner and public machines owned by the cloud provider. It is another general approach that secures computation with mixed sensitive data. The MapReduce system in the hybrid cloud is installed across public cloud and private cloud (e.g., [77]). It may require much more computation capacity for data owner when compared with our specific architecture. The use of hybrid cloud infrastructure will likely improve the efficiency of the detection system.

Alignment algorithm on MapReduce has been studied in bioinformatics for DNA sequence read mapping (e.g., [55, 56]). The AlignDLD approach could also be implemented on MapReduce, improving its privacy-preserving ability and scalability. Each mapper and reducer could be sped up with the MapReduce on GPU cluster framework (e.g., [61]). By combining the AlignDLD approach and the MR-DLD approach with these latest techniques, future data-leak detection approaches can achieve higher detection accuracy and scalability.

Acknowledgements This work has been supported by NSF S^{2}ERC Center (an I/UCRC Center) and ARO YIP grant W911NF-14-1-0535.

References

1. Baraglia R, Morales GDF, Lucchese C (2010) Document similarity self-join with MapReduce. In: 2010 IEEE 10th international conference on data mining (ICDM). IEEE Computer Society, Sydney, Australia, pp 731–736
2. Bertino E, Ghinita G (2011) Towards mechanisms for detection and prevention of data exfiltration by insiders: keynote talk paper. In: Proceedings of the 6th ACM symposium on information, computer and communications security, ASIACCS '11, pp 10–19
3. Bilge L, Balzarotti D, Robertson W, Kirda E, Kruegel C (2012) Disclosure: detecting botnet command and control servers through large-scale netflow analysis. In: Proceedings of the 28th annual computer security applications conference, ACSAC '12. ACM, New York, NY, pp 129–138. doi:10.1145/2420950.2420969. http://doi.acm.org/10.1145/2420950.2420969
4. Blanas S, Patel JM, Ercegovac V, Rao J, Shekita EJ, Tian Y (2010) A comparison of join algorithms for log processing in MapReduce. In: Proceedings of the 2010 ACM SIGMOD international conference on management of data, SIGMOD '10. ACM, New York, NY, pp 975–986 doi:10.1145/1807167.1807273. http://doi.acm.org/10.1145/1807167.1807273
5. Blanton M, Atallah MJ, Frikken KB, Malluhi QM (2012) Secure and efficient outsourcing of sequence comparisons. In: Computer security - ESORICS 2012 - 17th European symposium on research in computer security, Proceedings, Pisa, 10–12 Sept 2012, pp 505–522. doi:10.1007/978-3-642-33167-1_29. http://dx.doi.org/10.1007/978-3-642-33167-1_29
6. Borders K, Prakash A (2009) Quantifying information leaks in outbound web traffic. In: IEEE symposium on security and privacy. IEEE Computer Society, San Jose, CA, USA, pp 129–140
7. Broder AZ (1993) Some applications of Rabin's fingerprinting method. In: Capocelli R, De Santis A, Vaccaro U (eds) Sequences II. Springer, New York, pp 143–152. doi:10.1007/978-1-4613-9323-8_11. http://dx.doi.org/10.1007/978-1-4613-9323-8_11
8. Broder AZ (2000) Identifying and filtering near-duplicate documents. In: Proceedings of the 11th annual symposium on combinatorial pattern matching, pp 1–10
9. Burkhart M, Strasser M, Many D, Dimitropoulos X (2010) Sepia: privacy-preserving aggregation of multi-domain network events and statistics. In: Proceedings of the 19th USENIX Security Symposium, pp 15–15
10. Cai M, Hwang K, Kwok YK, Song S, Chen Y (2005) Collaborative Internet worm containment. IEEE Secur Priv 3(3):25–33
11. Carbunar B, Sion R (2010) Joining privately on outsourced data. In: Secure data management. Lecture notes in computer science, vol 6358. Springer, Berlin, pp 70–86
12. Caruana G, Li M, Qi, H (2010) SpamCloud: a MapReduce based anti-spam architecture. In: Seventh international conference on fuzzy systems and knowledge discovery. IEEE, Yantai, Shandong, China, pp 3003–3006

13. Caruana G, Li M, Qi M (2011) A MapReduce based parallel SVM for large scale spam filtering. In: Eighth international conference on fuzzy systems and knowledge discovery. IEEE, Shanghai, China, pp 2659–2662

14. Chen Q, Liu C, Xiao Z (2014) Improving MapReduce performance using smart speculative execution strategy. IEEE Trans Comput 63(4):954–967. doi:10.1109/TC.2013.15

15. Croft J, Caesar M (2011) Towards practical avoidance of information leakage in enterprise networks. In: Proceedings of the 6th USENIX conference on hot topics in security, HotSec'11, pp 7–7

16. Croft J, Caesar, M (2011) Towards practical avoidance of information leakage in enterprise networks. In: 6th USENIX workshop on hot topics in security, HotSec'11. USENIX Association

17. Dean J, Ghemawat S (2008) MapReduce: simplified data processing on large clusters. Commun ACM 51(1):107–113

18. Elsayed T, Lin JJ, Oard DW (2008) Pairwise document similarity in large collections with MapReduce. In: ACL (Short Papers). The Association for Computer Linguistics, pp 265–268

19. Fang W, He B, Luo Q, Govindaraju NK (2011) Mars: accelerating MapReduce with graphics processors. IEEE Trans Parallel Distrib Syst 22(4):608–620

20. FBI Cyber Division (2014) Recent cyber intrusion events directed toward retail firms

21. François J, Wang S, Bronzi W, State R, Engel T (2011) BotCloud: detecting botnets using MapReduce. In: IEEE international workshop on information forensics and security. IEEE, Iguacu Falls, Brazil, pp 1–6

22. Fu X, Ren R, Zhan J, Zhou W, Jia Z, Lu G (2012) LogMaster: mining event correlations in logs of large-scale cluster systems. In: IEEE 31st symposium on reliable distributed systems. IEEE, Irvine, CA, USA, pp 71–80

23. Global Velocity Inc (2015) Global velocity inc. http://www.globalvelocity.com/. Accessed Feb 2015

24. GTB Technologies Inc (2015) GoCloudDLP. http://www.goclouddlp.com/. Accessed Feb 2015

25. Hao F, Kodialam M, Lakshman T, Zhang H (2005) Fast payload-based flow estimation for traffic monitoring and network security. In: Proceedings of the 2005 symposium on architecture for networking and communications systems, pp 211–220

26. Hoyle R, Patil S, White D, Dawson J, Whalen P, Kapadia A (2013) Attire: conveying information exposure through avatar apparel. In: Proceedings of the 2013 conference on computer supported cooperative work companion, CSCW '13, pp 19–22

27. Huang Q, Jao D, Wang HJ (2005) Applications of secure electronic voting to automated privacy-preserving troubleshooting. In: Proceedings of the 12th ACM conference on computer and communications security, pp 68–80

28. Identifyfinder (2015) Identity finder. http://www.identityfinder.com/. Accessed Feb 2015

29. Jagannathan G, Wright RN (2005) Privacy-preserving distributed k-means clustering over arbitrarily partitioned data. In: Proceedings of the 11th ACM SIGKDD international conference on knowledge discovery in data mining, pp 593–599

30. Jang J, Brumley D, Venkataraman S (2011) BitShred: feature hashing malware for scalable triage and semantic analysis. In: Proceedings of the 18th ACM conference on computer and communications security, CCS '11, pp 309–320

31. Jang Y, Chung S, Payne B, Lee W (2014) Gyrus: a framework for user-intent monitoring of text-based networked applications. In: Proceedings of the 23rd USENIX security symposium, pp 79–93

32. Jha S, Kruger L, Shmatikov V (2008) Towards practical privacy for genomic computation. In: Proceedings of the 29th Ieee symposium on security and privacy, pp 216–230

33. Jung J, Sheth A, Greenstein B, Wetherall D, Maganis G, Kohno T (2008) Privacy oracle: a system for finding application leaks with black box differential testing. In: Proceedings of the 15th ACM conference on computer and communications security, pp 279–288

34. Kalyan C, Chandrasekaran K (2007) Information leak detection in financial e-mails using mail pattern analysis under partial information. In: Proceedings of the 7th WSEAS international conference on applied informatics and communications, vol 7, pp 104–109

35. Kaspersky Lab (2014) Kaspersky lab IT security risks survey 2014: a business approach to managing data security threats
36. Kemerlis VP, Pappas V, Portokalidis G, Keromytis AD (2010) iLeak: a lightweight system for detecting inadvertent information leaks. In: Proceedings of the 6th European conference on computer network defense
37. Kleinberg J, Papadimitriou CH, Raghavan P (2001) On the value of private information. In: Proceedings of the 8th conference on theoretical aspects of rationality and knowledge, pp 249–257
38. Lam W, Liu L, Prasad S, Rajaraman A, Vacheri Z, Doan A (2012) Muppet: Mapreduce-style processing of fast data. Proc VLDB Endow 5(12):1814–1825. doi:10.14778/2367502.2367520. http://dx.doi.org/10.14778/2367502.2367520
39. Lee Y, Kang W, Son H (2010) An internet traffic analysis method with MapReduce. In: Network operations and management symposium workshops (NOMS Wksps), 2010 IEEE/IFIP, pp 357–361. doi:10.1109/NOMSW.2010.5486551
40. Li K, Zhong Z, Ramaswamy L (2009) Privacy-aware collaborative spam filtering. IEEE Trans Parallel Distrib Syst 20(5):725–739
41. Liu F, Shu X, Yao D, Butt AR (2015) Privacy-preserving scanning of big content for sensitive data exposure with mapreduce. In: Proceedings of the 5th ACM conference on data and application security and privacy, CODASPY 2015, San Antonio, TX, 2–4 Mar 2015, pp 195–206
42. Logothetis D, Trezzo C, Webb KC, Yocum K (2011) In-situ MapReduce for log processing. In: USENIX annual technical conference. USENIX Association
43. Matsunaga AM, Tsugawa MO, Fortes JAB (2008) Cloudblast: combining MapReduce and virtualization on distributed resources for bioinformatics applications. In: eScience. IEEE Computer Society, Indianapolis, IN, USA, pp 222–229
44. Nadkarni A, Enck W (2013) Preventing accidental data disclosure in modern operating systems. In: ACM conference on computer and communications security. ACM, Berlin, Germany, pp 1029–1042
45. Panda B, Herbach JS, Basu S, Bayardo RJ (2009) Planet: massively parallel learning of tree ensembles with MapReduce. Proc VLDB Endow 2(2):1426–1437. doi:10.14778/1687553.1687569. http://dx.doi.org/10.14778/1687553.1687569
46. Papadimitriou P, Garcia-Molina H (2011) Data leakage detection. IEEE Trans Knowl Data Eng 23(1):51–63
47. Pappas V, Kemerlis V, Zavou A, Polychronakis M, Keromytis A (2013) Cloudfence: enabling users to audit the use of their cloud-resident data. In: Research in attacks, intrusions, and defenses. Lecture notes in computer science, vol 8145. Springer, Berlin, pp 411–431. doi:10.1007/978-3-642-41284-4_21. http://dx.doi.org/10.1007/978-3-642-41284-4_21
48. Peng D, Dabek F (2010) Large-scale incremental processing using distributed transactions and notifications. In: Proceedings of the 9th USENIX conference on operating systems design and implementation, OSDI'10. USENIX Association, Berkeley, CA, pp 1–15. http://dl.acm.org/citation.cfm?id=1924943.1924961
49. Provos N, McNamee D, Mavrommatis P, Wang K, Modadugu N (2007) The ghost in the browser: analysis of web-based malware. In: First workshop on hot topics in understanding botnets. USENIX Association
50. Rabin MO (1981) Fingerprinting by random polynomials. Technical Report TR-15-81, The Hebrew University of Jerusalem
51. Rabin MO (1981) Fingerprinting by random polynomials. Technical Report TR-15-81, Harvard Aliken Computation Laboratory
52. Ramaswamy L, Iyengar A, Liu L, Douglis F (2004) Automatic detection of fragments in dynamically generated web pages. In: Proceedings of the 13th international conference on world wide web, pp 443–454
53. RiskBasedSecurity (2015) Data breach quickview: 2014 data breach trends
54. Roy I, Setty STV, Kilzer A, Shmatikov V, Witchel E (2010) Airavat: security and privacy for MapReduce. In: Proceedings of the 7th USENIX symposium on networked systems design and implementation, pp 297–312. USENIX Association

55. Schatz MC (2008) Blastreduce: high performance short read mapping with mapreduce. University of Maryland. http://cgis.cs.umd.edu/Grad/scholarlypapers/papers/MichaelSchatz. pdf

56. Schatz MC (2009) Cloudburst: highly sensitive read mapping with mapreduce. Bioinformatics 25(11):1363–1369. doi:10.1093/bioinformatics/btp236. http://bioinformatics.oxfordjournals. org/content/25/11/1363.abstract

57. Shu X, Yao D (2012) Data leak detection as a service. In: Proceedings of the 8th international conference on security and privacy in communication networks (SecureComm), Padua, pp 222–240

58. Shu X, Zhang J, Yao D, Feng W (2015) Rapid and parallel content screening for detecting transformed data exposure. In: Proceedings of the third international workshop on security and privacy in big data (BigSecurity). Hongkong, China

59. Smith TF, Waterman MS (1981) Identification of common molecular subsequences. J Mol Biol 147(1):195–197

60. Squicciarini AC, Sundareswaran S, Lin D (2010) Preventing information leakage from indexing in the cloud. In: IEEE international conference on cloud computing, CLOUD 2010, Miami, FL 5–10 July. IEEE, Miami, FL, USA, pp 188–195. doi:10.1109/CLOUD.2010.82. http://dx.doi.org/10.1109/CLOUD.2010.82

61. Stuart JA, Owens JD (2011) Multi-gpu mapreduce on gpu clusters. In: Proceedings of the 2011 ieee international parallel & distributed processing symposium, IPDPS '11. IEEE Computer Society, Washington, DC, pp 1068–1079. doi:10.1109/IPDPS.2011.102. http://dx.doi.org/10. 1109/IPDPS.2011.102

62. Symantec (2015) Symantec data loss prevention. http://www.symantec.com/data-loss-prevention. Accessed Feb 2015

63. Troncoso-Pastoriza JR, Katzenbeisser S, Celik M (2007) Privacy preserving error resilient DNA searching through oblivious automata. In: Proceedings of the 14th ACM conference on computer and communications security, pp 519–528

64. Vernica R, Carey MJ, Li C (2010) Efficient parallel set-similarity joins using MapReduce. In: Proceedings of the 2010 ACM SIGMOD international conference on management of data, SIGMOD '10. ACM, New York, NY, pp 495–506. doi:10.1145/1807167.1807222. http://doi. acm.org/10.1145/1807167.1807222

65. Williams P, Sion R (2008) Usable PIR. In: Proceedings of the 13th network and distributed system security symposium

66. Xu S (2009) Collaborative attack vs. collaborative defense. In: Collaborative computing: networking, applications and worksharing. Lecture notes of the Institute for Computer Sciences, Social Informatics and Telecommunications Engineering, vol 10. Springer, Berlin, pp 217–228

67. Xu K, Yao D, Ma Q, Crowell A (2011) Detecting infection onset with behavior-based policies. In: Proceedings of the 5th international conference on network and system security, pp 57–64

68. Yang SF, Chen WY, Wang YT (2011) ICAS: an inter-VM IDS log cloud analysis system. In: 2011 IEEE international conference on cloud computing and intelligence systems (CCIS), pp 285–289. doi:10.1109/CCIS.2011.6045076

69. Yang Z, Yang M, Zhang Y, Gu G, Ning P, Wang XS (2013) AppIntent: analyzing sensitive data transmission in Android for privacy leakage detection. In: Proceedings of the 20th ACM conference on computer and communications security

70. Yao ACC (1986) How to generate and exchange secrets. In: Proceedings of the 27th annual symposium on foundations of computer science, pp 162–167

71. Yao D, Frikken KB, Atallah MJ, Tamassia R (2008) Private information: to reveal or not to reveal. ACM Trans Inf Syst Secur 12(1):6

72. Yen TF, Oprea A, Onarlioglu K, Leetham T, Robertson W, Juels A, Kirda E (2013) Beehive: large-scale log analysis for detecting suspicious activity in enterprise networks. In: Proceedings of the 29th annual computer security applications conference, ACSAC '13. ACM, New York, pp 199–208. doi:10.1145/2523649.2523670. http://doi.acm.org/10.1145/2523649.2523670

73. Yi X, Kaosar MG, Paulet R, Bertino E (2013) Single-database private information retrieval from fully homomorphic encryption. IEEE Trans Knowl Data Eng 25(5):1125–1134
74. Yi X, Paulet R, Bertino E (2013) Private information retrieval.   Synthesis lectures on information security, privacy, and trust. Morgan & Claypool Publishers
75. Yoon E, Squicciarini A (2014) Toward detecting compromised mapreduce workers through log analysis. In: 2014 14th IEEE/ACM international symposium on cluster, cloud and grid computing (CCGrid), pp 41–50. doi:10.1109/CCGrid.2014.120
76. Yuan P, Sha C, Wang X, Yang B, Zhou A, Yang S (2010) XML structural similarity search using MapReduce. In: 11th international conference, web-age information management. Lecture notes in computer science, vol 6184. Springer, New York, pp 169–181
77. Zhang C, Chang EC, Yap R (2014) Tagged-MapReduce: a general framework for secure computing with mixed-sensitivity data on hybrid clouds.   In: 2014 14th IEEE/ACM international symposium on cluster, cloud and grid computing (CCGrid), pp 31–40. doi:10.1109/CCGrid.2014.96
78. Zhao W, Ma H, He Q (2009) Parallel k-means clustering based on MapReduce. In: Cloud computing, first international conference, CloudCom 2009. lecture notes in computer science, vol 5931. Springer, Berlin. pp 674–679
79. Zhuang L, Dunagan J, Simon DR, Wang HJ, Osipkov I, Tygar JD (2008) Characterizing botnets from Email spam records. In: First USENIX workshop on large-scale exploits and emergent threats, LEET '08. USENIX Association
80. Zohrevandi M, Bazzi RA (2013) Auto-FBI: a user-friendly approach for secure access to sensitive content on the web. In: Proceedings of the 29th annual computer security applications conference, ACSAC '13. ACM, New York, NY, pp 349–358. doi:10.1145/2523649.2523683. http://doi.acm.org/10.1145/2523649.2523683

Chapter 6
Big Data Storage Security

Mi Wen, Shui Yu, Jinguo Li, Hongwei Li, and Kejie Lu

Abstract The demand for data storage and processing is increasing at a rapid speed in the big data era. The management of such tremendous volume of data is a critical challenge to the data storage systems. Firstly, since 60 % of the stored data is claimed to be redundant, data deduplication technology becomes an attractive solution to save storage space and traffic in a big data environment. Secondly, the security issues, such as confidentiality, integrity and privacy of the big data should also be considered for big data storage. To address these problems, convergent encryption is widely used to secure data deduplication for big data storage. Nonetheless, there still exist some other security issues, such as proof of ownership, key management and so on. In this chapter, we first introduce some major cyber attacks for big data storage. Then, we describe the existing fundamental security techniques, whose integration is essential for preventing data from existing and future security attacks. By discussing some interesting open problems, we finally expect to trigger more research efforts in this new research field.

M. Wen (✉)
College of Computer Science and Technology, Shanghai University of Electric Power, Room 405, Fenjin Building, 2103 Pingliang Rd., Shanghai 200090, China
e-mail: miwen@shiep.edu.cn

S. Yu
School of Information Technology, Deakin University, T2.04.3, 221 Burwood HWY, Burwood, VIC 3125, Australia
e-mail: shui.yu@deakin.edu.au

J. Li
College of Computer Science and Technology, Shanghai University of Electric Power, Room 417, 2103 Pingliang Rd., Shanghai 200090, China
e-mail: lijg@shiep.edu.cn

H. Li
School of Computer Science & Engineering, University of Electronic Science and Technology of China, 2006 Xiyuan Rd., Chengdu 610054, China
e-mail: hongweili@uestc.edu.cn

K. Lu
Department of Electrical and Computer Engineering, University of Puerto Rico at Mayagüez, Call Box 9000, Mayagüez 00681, Puerto Rico
e-mail: kejie.lu@upr.edu

© Springer International Publishing Switzerland 2016
S. Yu, S. Guo (eds.), *Big Data Concepts, Theories, and Applications*,
DOI 10.1007/978-3-319-27763-9_6

6.1   Introduction

With the rapidly increasing amounts of data produced worldwide, the amount of data to be processed continues to witness a quick increase. According to a recent report from Center for Democracy and Technology (CDT), more than 2.5 quintillion bytes of data are generated every day [1]. To contain such a massive amount of data, storage continues to grow at an explosive rate (52 % per year) [2]. By the end of 2015, the size of the total generated data will surpass 7.9 ZB. This number is expected to reach 40 ZB in 2020 [3] with very high increasing speed. Consequently, big data era is more than just a matter of data size. Big data also represents the increasing complexity of the data handling process. Instead of sitting in one archive storage, data is now typically distributed among different locations.

For instance, outsourcing data to cloud servers, as shown in Fig. 6.1, is a promising approach to relieve data owners from the burden of such a large amount of data storage and maintenance. In this approach, users can store their data on cloud servers and execute computation and queries using the servers' computational capabilities [4]. As users tend to use as much space as they can and vendors constantly look for techniques aiming to minimize redundant data and maximize space savings. With the fact that 80 % of generated data is claimed to be unstructured. Hadoop [5] is emerging as the most popular big data platform to manage and structure data for further analysis. However, the replication mechanism of Hadoop generates a lot of duplicate data, which occupy both disk space and network bandwidth. Moreover, there may be several smart devices monitoring the same area, duplicated copies of data can be generated [6]. Redundancy in big data workloads becomes even higher in the case of dynamic updating data sets in social network and bioinformatics networks.

Data deduplication [7, 8] is a technique for storing only a single copy of redundant data, and providing links to that copy instead of storing other actual

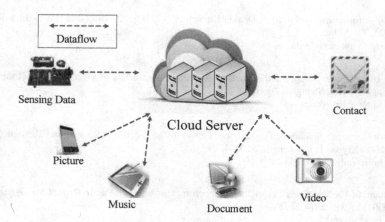

Fig. 6.1 Cloud storage service for big data

copies of this data. Data deduplication is widely used in data storage systems to reduce cost and save space in data centers. Deduplication is not only used in backups and archives, but also increasingly adopted in primary workloads [9]. SNIA white paper reports that the deduplication technique can save up to 90 % storage for backup applications [10] and up to 90 % in standard file systems [11]. Most of the commercial cloud storage systems, such as Dropbox, have been applying deduplication to save the network bandwidth and the storage cost with data deduplication [12].

However, cloud servers might be untrusted, and intentionally share sensitive data with the third parties for commercial purposes. To protect the confidentiality of sensitive data while supporting deduplication, data should be encrypted before outsourcing to the cloud server [13, 14]. While cryptography makes ciphertext indistinguishable from theoretically random data, i.e., encrypted data are always distributed randomly, so identical plaintext encrypted by randomly generated cryptographic keys will very likely have different ciphertexts, which cannot be deduplicated. To solve the conflict, convergent encryption and proof of ownership are used in data deduplication schemes. Also, to prevent the information leaked by data deduplication, some countermeasures for the leakage risk are proposed.

In this chapter, we address the key security issues for big data storage. The remainder of this chapter is organized as follows. In Sect. 6.2 we describe the desirable properties and system architecture of big data storage, followed by the existing cyber attacks in Sect. 6.3. Next, we introduce the security fundamentals in Sect. 6.4. Finally, we draw our summary and future works in Sect. 6.5.

6.2 System Architecture for Big Data Storage

In this section, we will introduce the desirable security and efficiency properties, as well as the system architecture, for big data storage in cloud environment.

6.2.1 Desirable Properties

In the cloud storage environment, the storage server may be honest but curious, and data owners are honest as well. However, there exists an adversary $\mathscr{A}$ in the system intending to eavesdrop and invade the database on cloud servers to pry into the file content. In addition, $\mathscr{A}$ can also launch some active attacks to threaten the data confidentiality and privacy.

Therefore, in order to prevent $\mathscr{A}$ from learning the files' content and to reduce storage space and upload bandwidth, the following properties should be achieved for big data storage.

- *Efficiency*: Since the amount of data is very large, the storage service providers tend to minimize redundant data and maximize space savings, thus, the most important metric for big data storage is the storage efficiency. Further, the data communication costs much more bandwidth when outsourcing data to the cloud server, so the transmission efficiency should be achieved.
- *Data Confidentiality*: The data owner can encrypt the file F before outsourcing, and successfully prevent the unauthorized entities, including eavesdroppers and cloud servers, from prying into the outsourced data.
- *Data Privacy*: Any partial information of the data content cannot be leaked during any operations except for decryption by authorized users. For example, $\mathscr{A}$ cannot get any information about the data when someone query over the encrypted data or anyone uploading other data files with data deduplication.
- *Key Confidentiality*: Data should not be accessed by unauthorized users or illegal data owners. It means that only legal data owners can get the convergent key, hence, decrypt the encrypted file F.
- *Data Availability*: Data availability means that the big data can be accessed by legal users from anywhere. The data can also be on-demand shared among a group of trusted users, such as partners in a collaboration team or employees in the enterprise organization.

6.2.2 System Architecture

In big data era, cloud storage service is becoming more and more popular. In this chapter, to reduce the redundant data and improve the transmission efficiency, we consider an outsourcing system architecture with cross-user client-side deduplication. The system consists of some data owners (called clients), who may have data files ($F_i, i = 1, \cdots, n$); and a cloud storage server as shown in Fig. 6.2. To upload a

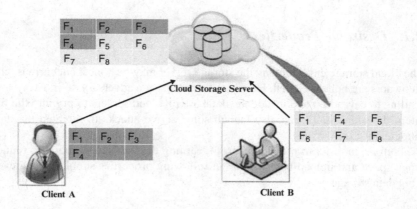

Fig. 6.2 System model for big data outsourcing with cross-user deduplication

file, the client first generates a file tag to perform the file-level duplicate check. If the file is a duplicate, then all its blocks must be duplicates as well; otherwise, the client further performs the block-level duplicate check and identifies the unique blocks. Then, the client encrypts the unique blocks by using the convergent key, which is derived by computing the hash value of the original file. Further, the convergent key also will be encrypted to be uploaded. Each data copy is also associated with a tag for the duplicate check. The encrypted data, encrypted convergent key and the data tag all will be uploaded to the cloud.

The client (data owner) is responsible for outsourcing data copies to the cloud storage server. In a data deduplication system, only the first client of a file needs to upload while the following clients of the same file does not require to upload the duplicate copies any more. The cloud server has two types of storage systems: a rapid storage system for storing the tags for efficient duplicate checks, and a database system for storing both encrypted data copies and encrypted convergent keys. Furthermore, the server will also perform duplicate check before the data owners upload their files. If there is identical content stored in server, the owner is not required to upload the file again, which can reduce the storage cost at the server side and save the upload bandwidth at owner side.

6.3 Cyber Attacks for Big Data Storage

From a user's perspective, big data outsourcing raises security and privacy concerns [12]. We must trust third-party cloud providers to properly enforce confidentiality, integrity checking, and access control mechanisms against insider and outsider attacks. Therefore, one of the major concerns of users and organizations outsourcing their data to cloud providers is the issue of data integrity and privacy. Another concern is the network availability attack, which aims to use up or overwhelm the communication and computational resources of network and to result in delay or failure of communication. As a result, the big data availability may be hindered.

Furthermore, data deduplication can lead to information leakage to dishonest users. They can observe whether a certain file or block was deduplicated. This can be done by either examining the amount of data transferred over the network, or by observing the log of the storage software. Harnik et al. [15] describe three types of side channel attacks on cloud storage services. Now, we will discuss the security concerns in the following subsections.

6.3.1 Attack I: Network Availability

A network availability attack takes place in the form of denial of service (DoS). Its objectives are to use up or overwhelm the communication and computational resources of the network, resulting in delay or failure of data communications.

For example, an adversary may flood a storage server with false information at very high frequency such that the storage server spends most of the time verifying the authenticity of the information and is not able to timely respond to legitimate network traffic. Communication and control in some real-time applications are time critical. A delay of a few seconds may cause irreparable damage to them. A network availability attack must be handled effectively.

6.3.2 Attack II: Confirmation of a File

In the attack of Confirmation of a File (COF), an attacker who already knows the full plaintext of a file, can check if a copy of that file has already been stored. If the attacker is the cloud provider or an insider, he might also learn which users are the owners of that file (e.g. illegally stored a movie or a song). Depending on the content of the file, this type of information leakage can be dangerous. For instance, assume an attacker Alice wants to learn information about Bob, a cloud storage service user. Obviously, if Alice suspects that Bob has some specific sensitive file F that is unlikely to be in the possession of any other user, she can use deduplication to check whether this conjecture is true. All Alice needs to do is to try to back up a copy of F and check whether deduplication occurs. For example, there is a file proving some illegal activity, such as recording of a violent event or material related to child trafficking gangs. Once law enforcement authorities get a copy of this file, they can upload it to different cloud storage providers and identify the storage services storing copies of the file. They can then request an authority to ask the service provider to reveal the identities of users who uploaded the file.

6.3.3 Attack III: Learning the Contents of Files

Attack II only lets the attacker check whether a specific file is stored in the cloud storage service. In Learning the Contents of Files (LCF) attack, the attacker can disclose highly sensitive information. They already knows most of a file and tries to guess the unknown parts by checking if the result of the encryption matches the observed ciphertext. This is the case when those documents have a predefined template and a small part of variable content. For instance, Alice and Bob work in the same company, which uses a cloud backup service to back up all of its employees' machines. Their salary slips are backed up monthly. If Alice wants to know Bob's salary, which is probably in the 6000–20,000 range. All Alice needs to do is generating a template of Bob's salary slip, with Bob's name and the date of payday, and then generate a copy of the salary slip for each possible salary. She then uploads each one of her forged copies. Bob's actual salary will be revealed when deduplication occurs.

This attack can be applied whenever the number of possible versions of the target file is moderate. It seems relevant for a corporate environment in which files are often small variations of standard templates. Suppose both Alice and Bob participate in an auction that requires bidders to submit their bids on some standard form containing their name and bid. If Alice can guess Bob's most likely bids, she can use the same brute-force attack to find Bob's actual bid and then set her bid accordingly.

6.3.4 Attack IV: A Covert Channel

Covert channel is a hidden communication model which aims to exchange information bypassing security policies [16]. Cross-user data deduplication opens a back door for information to be leaked from one user to another through covert channels. Recently, several researchers have identified a single-bit covert channel that can be established by making use of the cross-user deduplication [17].

In a single-bit covert channel, suppose there is a sender Alice installed some malicious software on Bob's machine. Alice has a receiving program at her attacking computer. Alice might wish to hide the communication between the malicious software and its receiving program. If Bob is using an online storage service that uses cross-user deduplication, Alice can use the deduplication attack to establish a covert channel from the malicious software to a receiving program that she runs. Now, assume, the malicious software generates one of two versions of a file, X_0 or X_1, and saves it on Bob's machine. If the Bob wants to send X_1, it will upload the file X_1 to the cloud. Otherwise, it will upload the X_0 file. Alice then retrieves the message by loading both files to the cloud. If Alice finds out the uploading time of the file X_1 is much faster than the time needed to transmit file X_0, it can infer that deduplication on file X_1 has been conducted and Bob must have tried to send X_1. Similarly, Alice can infer whether Bob tried to send X_0.

That is, she learns what message the software sent. Alice can use the covert channel to transfer arbitrarily long messages by having the software save more than a single file and by using more than two options for each file's contents. A detailed performance analysis of this method can reference to [18, 19].

6.4 Security Fundamentals

6.4.1 Data Deduplication

Data deduplication is a specialized data compression technique for eliminating duplicate copies of repeating data in big data storage. The technique is used to improve storage utilization and can also be applied to reduce the number of bytes that must be sent. Based on different criteria, data deduplication can be classified into different types, as shown in Fig. 6.3. According to the data granularity [20], deduplication strategies can be categorized into two main categories: file-level deduplication [21] and block-level deduplication [22], which is nowadays the most common strategy. For file level deduplication, it eliminates duplicate copies of the same file. In block-based deduplication, duplicate blocks of data will be eliminated in non-identical files. Further, the block size can either be fixed or variable [23].

Another categorization criteria is the location at which deduplication is performed: if data are deduplicated at the client, then it is called client-side (or source-based) deduplication, otherwise server-side (or target-based) deduplication. In the server-side approach, the target data storage device or service handles deduplication, and the client is unaware of any deduplication that might occur. This technology improves storage utilization, but doesn't save bandwidth. Traditional deduplication technique (i.e. [24–26]) is the server-side deduplication. In client-side deduplication, the client first hashes each data segment he wishes to upload and sends these results to the storage provider to check whether such data are already stored; thus only "undeduplicated" data segments will be actually uploaded by the user. Thus, deduplication at the client side can achieve both bandwidth and storage savings, it unfortunately can make the system vulnerable to side-channel attacks [15]. The attackers can immediately discover whether a certain data is stored or not. On the contrary, by deduplicating data at the server-side, the system is protected against side-channel attacks but the communication overhead in such solution does not saved.

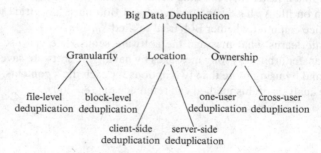

Fig. 6.3 Categories of big data deduplication

According to the data ownership [20], deduplication strategies can be categorized into another two categories: one-user deduplication or cross-user deduplication. In particular, if data deduplication is performed across different user accounts, we classifies it into cross-user deduplication; otherwise, it is one-user deduplication. At the could environment, the cross-user deduplication often takes place at the client where the data is located, thus, it can be called "cross-user client-side" deduplication. As expected, the cross-user source-based approach offers better storage and bandwidth utilization.

6.4.2 Convergent Encryption

Although data deduplication brings a lot of benefits, security and privacy concerns arise as users' sensitive data are susceptible to both insider and outsider attacks. To protect the confidentiality of outsourced data, various cryptographic solutions have been proposed in the literatures (e.g., [27, 28]). Their ideas build on traditional encryption, in which each user encrypts data with an independent secret key. However, deduplication and encryption, to a great extent, conflicts with each other [29]. Deduplication takes advantage of data similarity in order to achieve storage reduction. While cryptography makes ciphertext indistinguishable from theoretically random data, i.e., encrypted data are always distributed randomly, so identical plaintext encrypted by randomly generated cryptographic keys will have different ciphertexts which cannot be de-duplicated.

To solve the above conflict, Douceur et al. proposed convergent encryption [24] to enforce data confidentiality while making deduplication feasible. The main idea of the convergent encryption is that each data owner encrypts his data by using a convergent key K with symmetric encryptions. The convergent key is computed from the corresponding data file by using some hash functions. To support deduplication, a tag is also computed for the file and used to detect duplicate by the cloud storage server. If two data copies are the same, then their tags are the same. Note that, both the convergent key and the tag are independently derived, and the tag cannot be used to deduce the convergent key and compromise data confidentiality, as shown in Fig. 6.4. Especially, a convergent encryption scheme includes four phases:

1. Key Generation: A convergent key K is generated from the original data file. We can use a hash function $H_1(F) = K$ as the computation of convergent encryption key. H_1 can be any widely used hash functions, such as SHA-1 etc.
2. Data Encryption: A symmetric encryption algorithm, such as AES-256, can be used to do the data encryption. The algorithm takes both the convergent key K and the data copy F as inputs and then outputs a ciphertext $C = Enc(K, F)$.
3. Data Decryption: The decryption algorithm can be chosen according to the encryption algorithm. It takes both the ciphertext C and the key K as inputs and then outputs $F = Dec(K, C)$.

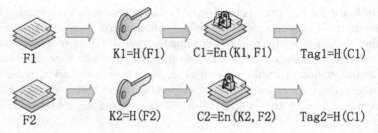

Fig. 6.4 The convergent encryption framework

4. Tag Generation: Tag generation algorithm can be defined as another hash function of F, for example, $T(F) = H_2(F)$, which will be stored on the CSS with its corresponding encrypted data.

However, convergent encryption suffers from some weaknesses which have been widely discussed in literatures [26, 30]. As the encryption key depends on the value of the plaintext, an attacker who has gained access to the storage can launch the "dictionary attacks" by comparing the ciphertexts resulting from the encryption of well-known plaintext values from a dictionary with the stored ciphertexts. Indeed, even if encryption keys are encrypted with users' private keys and stored somewhere else, the potentially malicious cloud provider, who has no access to the encryption key but has access to the encrypted chunks, can easily perform offline dictionary attacks and discover predictable files. Furthermore, the information leakage in such encryption scheme can be unacceptable [31]. What's worse, the convergent encryption gives one deterministic transform from a particular plaintext to the ciphertext, which exposes more vulnerability. In the context of side channel attack examination, the use of convergent encryption doesn't solve the security risks because users can still identify the occurrence of deduplication [15].

6.4.3   Proof of Ownership

To prevent unauthorized access, Halevi et al. [32] propose a secure proof of ownership protocol (PoW) for deduplication systems, such that a user needs to provide the proof that he/she indeed owns the same file when a duplicate is found. After the proof, subsequent users with the same file will be provided a pointer from the server without needing to upload the same file. A user can download the encrypted file with the pointer from the server, which can only be decrypted by the corresponding data owners with their convergent keys. Thus, convergent encryption allows the cloud to perform deduplication on the ciphertexts and the proof of ownership prevents the unauthorized user to access the file.

6.4.3.1 Baseline Approach with MACs

A straightforward approach to construct PoW is to compute fresh MACs (i.e. Message Authentication Code) online. For example, to prove the ownership of a file F, the prover can compute a MAC over F with a random key k_i, where k_i is chosen by the verifier. To verify the correctness of this MAC value, the verifier needs to re-compute the MAC value of F under the same key. This approach is secure, but sometime it cannot be applied for two reasons: one is that in some applications of PoW, the verifier does not have access to the file F; the other is that the stringent requirement on efficiency (including disk IO efficiency) does not allow verifier to access entire file F during the interactive proof.

Given another scenario, if the MACs are pre-computed offline, in the verifying phase, t number of keys $k_1, \cdots, k_t$ are randomly chosen and t number of MAC values $MAC_{k_i}(F)$ are computed correspondingly. In the ith proof session, the verifier sends the MAC key k_i to the prover and expects $MAC_{k_i}(F)$ as response. This approach is not secure in the setting of PoW [32], since a single malicious adversary could consume up all of t pre-computed MACs easily by impersonating or colluding with t distinct cloud users.

6.4.3.2 Proofs of Retrievability

Some instances of Proofs of Retrievability (POR) [33, 34] can serve as PoW. Several PoW constructions are just the Merkle Hash Tree based POR scheme (MHT-POR) [32], which combines error erasure code and Merkle Hash Tree proof method. The server stores root of the Merkle hash tree. When proof is needed, the server asks client to present paths to t random leaves. The drawback of this approach is that, the relatively expensive error erasure code is applied over the whole input file, which is very bad for large files. In [35], error erasure code is applied over the output of the randomness extractor, which is much shorter than the whole input file. Recently, Zheng and Xu [36] attempts to equip proofs of storage with deduplication capability. However, their work is not in the leakage setting of Halevi et al. [32].

6.4.3.3 Some Projection Approaches

Gabizon et al. [37] proposed a randomness extractor for input under bit-fixing distribution. Halevi et al. [32] also use the pairwise independent hash family to project files' hash values. A large input file is hashed into a constant size (e.g. 3T = 3 – 64 MB) hash value and then apply the merkle hash tree proof method over the hash value. This construction is secure, but very inefficient in both computation and randomness complexity. Furthermore, large random seed also implies large communication cost required to share this seed among all owners of the same file. Pietro and Sorniotti [38] propose another efficient PoW scheme by choosing the projection of a file onto some randomly selected bit-positions as the file proof. Pietro and Sorniotti treat a projection $(F[i_1], \ldots, F[i_t])$ of file F onto t randomly chosen bit-positions $(i_1, \ldots, i_t)$ as the "proof" of ownership of file F. Similar to the "hash-as-a-proof" method, this work is extremely efficient but insecure in the bounded leakage setting.

Note that all the above schemes do not consider data privacy. Recently, Ng et al. [39] extend PoW for encrypted files, but they do not address how to minimize the key management overhead.

6.4.4 Key Management

Although convergent encryption has been extensively adopted for secure deduplication, a critical issue of making convergent encryption practical is to efficiently and reliably manage a huge number of convergent keys [40].

6.4.4.1 Original Approach

The original convergent key management idea is that, a data copy is first encrypted with a convergent key derived by the data copy itself, and then the convergent key is encrypted by a master key that will be kept locally and securely by each user. The encrypted convergent keys are then stored, along with the corresponding encrypted data copies, in cloud storage. The master key can be used to recover the encrypted keys and hence the encrypted files. In this way, each user only needs to keep the master key and the metadata about the outsourced data.

However, the original approach is infeasible, as it will generate an enormous number of keys with the increasing number of users. Specifically, each user must associate an encrypted convergent key with each block of its outsourced encrypted data copies, so as to later restore the data copies. Although different users may share the same data copies, they must have their own set of convergent keys so that no other users can access their files. Thus, the original approach's overhead becomes more prominent if fine-grained block-level deduplication is needed, which is both inefficient and unreliable.

6.4.4.2 Secret Sharing Based Approach

For the purpose of achieving efficient and reliable key management in secure deduplication. Dekey [29] is proposed, in which users do not need to manage any keys on their own but instead securely distribute the convergent key shares across multiple servers. Specifically, Dekey uses the Ramp secret sharing scheme (RSSS) [41, 42] to store convergent keys. The (n, k, r)-RSSS ($n > k > r \geq 0$) generates n shares from a secret such that the secret can be recovered from any k shares but

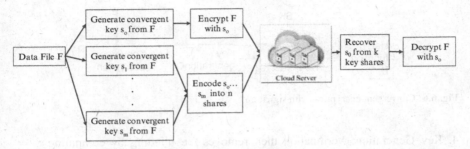

Fig. 6.5 Convergent key management with (n, k, r)-RSSS

cannot be recovered from fewer than k shares, as shown in Fig. 6.5. Only the first user who uploads the data is required to compute and distribute such secret shares, while all other users who own the same data copy need not to compute and store these shares again. To recover data copies, a user must access a minimum number of key servers through authentication and obtain the secret shares to reconstruct the convergent keys. In other words, the secret shares of a convergent key will only be accessible by the authorized users who own the corresponding data copy. This significantly reduces the storage overhead of the convergent keys and makes the key management reliable against failures and attacks.

6.4.4.3 Server-Aided Approach

Since the encryption processes in convergent encryption are public, which means that anyone having access to the data can perform the encryption and produce valid ciphertext, the adversary can easily obtain one bit of information. For instance, whether a ciphertext is the encryption of a message from a small set. This can be a serious leakage. DupLESS [43], attempts to solve the problem. It introduces another secret key, denoted SK, held by a key server (KS). Data is encrypted with a key that is derived from both the data and SK. Encryption is thus not public anymore. This disables dictionary attacks.

DupLESS builds from RSA blind signatures [44, 45]. Especially, the encryption key generation details are as following:

1. Initialization: Randomly select a public RSA exponent e. Given e and a large integer N, the secret key d can be computed such that $ed \equiv 1 mod\phi(N)$, where $\phi(N)$ is the Euler function of N. Modulus N is the product of two distinct primes of roughly equal length and $N < e$. Then, (N, e) is published as the public key and $SK = d$ is the secret key.
2. Hash Blinding: The client uses a hash function $H : \{0, 1\}^* \rightarrow Z_N$ to first hash the message M to an element $h = H(M)$, and then blinds h with a random group element $r \in Z_N$ as: $x = hr^e mod N$. x is sent to the KS.
3. Sever-Aided Signature: The KS signs it by computing $y = x^d mod N$, and sends back y.

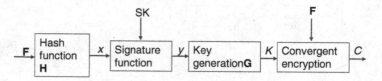

Fig. 6.6 Convergent encryption with signature

4. Key Generation: Verification then removes the blinding by computing $z = yr^{-1} mod N$, and then ensures that $z^e mod N$ is indeed equal to $H(M)$. Finally, the encryption key is computed as $G(z)$, where $G : Z_N \rightarrow \{0,1\}^k$ is another hash function.

DupLESS provides a better possible security than the original convergent encryption for secure deduplication. However, its reliance on a dedicated key server not only makes it difficult to deploy in a less managed setting such as *P2P* systems, but also impairs its security, as compromising a single key server reduces its protection to that of convergent encryption.

6.4.4.4 Encryption with Signature

To escape the deployment and security vulnerability of server-aided approach, Duan et al. [46] propose an efficient, deterministic and non-interactive threshold signature, which is built upon Shoup's RSA-based threshold signature scheme [47], as shown in Fig. 6.6. The deterministic nature of the scheme ensures the convergence property. It is also non-interactive, and is essentially as efficient as possible: the workload for generating a signature share is roughly equivalent to computing a single RSA signature.

1. Initialization: Randomly select system parameters (p, q, p', q', e). (N, e) is the public key and d is the secret key. Let $m = p'q'$. The private key d is shared using a random degree t polynomial $f(X)$. Let n be the total number of signers. The secret key of signer i is $s_i = f(i)$ mod m. The dealer chooses a random $v \in Q_N$ and computes $v_i = v^{s_i}$ for $i = 1, \cdots, n$, where Q_N is the subgroup of squares in Z_N^*. The dealer sends (v, v_i) to signer i.
2. Signature Shares: Given $x = H(M)$ from message M, the signature share of signer i is: $x_i = x^{2\Delta s_i} \in Q_N$, $\Delta = n!$. In this subsection, H and H' are two different hash functions. Then, a proof of correctness (z, c) is computed as:

$$v' = v^r, \tilde{x} = x^{4\Delta}, x' = \tilde{x}^r,$$
$$c = H'(v, \tilde{x}, v_i, x_i^2, v', x'), z = s_i c + r.$$

where, $r \in Z_{2L(N)+2L_1}$, L_N is the bit length of N and L_1 a secondary security parameter.

6 Big Data Storage Security

3. Signature Verification: The client verify the received signature by checking if the following equation is correct. If so, the signature would be correct, otherwise, it is not.

$$v^z v_i^{-c} = v',$$
$$\tilde{x}^z x_i^{-2c} = x'.$$

4. Combining Shares: After the client collecting $t + 1$ valid shares from a set S of players, the final signature can be produced as follows.

$$\lambda_{0,i}^S = \Delta \frac{\Pi_{j \in S \setminus \{i\}} j}{\Pi_{j \in S \setminus \{i\}} (j - i)} \in Z,$$

$$w = \prod_{j \in S} x_i^{2\lambda_{0,i}^S}.$$

When we get w, the signature y can be computed as $y = w^a x^b$, where $y^e = x$ and a, b are integers such that $e'a + eb = 1$ for $e' = 4\Delta^2$. a, b can be computed using extended Euclidean algorithm on e' and e.

6.4.5 Randomized Solution

A cloud storage provider can prevent clients from identifying the occurrence of deduplication by running deduplication always at the servers. However, this approach eliminates some of deduplication's advantages, such as transforming time and bandwidth savings. Now, how to weaken the correlation between deduplication and the existence of files in the storage service while preserving the data deduplication advantages is challenging.

Harnik et al. [15] suggest that set a random threshold for every file and perform deduplication only if the number of copies of the file exceeds this threshold. The details of this solution is as follows. For every file F, the storage server randomly chooses a threshold $t_F \in [2, d]$ store this value privately, where d is a parameter that might be public (e.g. $d = 20$). No one but the server should be able to compute t_F, even if the contents of F are known. Alternatively, the server could use a secret key s and compute the threshold as a function of the file contents, or of the file's hash value, and of the secret key s. That means, $t_F = F(F, s)$. In this case, there's no need to explicitly store the threshold of F because the server can easily recompute it.

1. Initialization: For every file F, the server keeps a counter c_F of the number of clients that have previously uploaded copies of F.
2. File Uploading: When a new copy of the file is uploaded, the server will check if $c_F \geq t_F$ or if the client has previously uploaded F. If so, the data will be deduped at the client side; Otherwise, no deduplication occurs. Here, the

minimum number of copies for which deduplication can occur is 2, because it is impossible to perform deduplication when the first copy of the file is uploaded. In this manner, the occurrence of deduplication from users is hid during the first $t_F - 1$ times that F is uploaded because the file is uploaded as if no copy of it is available at the server.

However, once the multiple data copies are transferred to the server side, the system can perform deduplication. Thus, the overall disk space savings are the same as in the server-based approach. The only drawback is that the bandwidth utilization is smaller because $(t_F - 1)$ more copies of the file are uploaded. In real applications, the server can optimize the random threshold for every file based on the files' content sensitivity. Lee et al. [48] analyze the solutions performance when d equals to different values, the results show that their proposed solution offers outstanding security than existing alternatives.

6.4.6   Query Over Encrypted Data

To protect the confidentiality of sensitive data while supporting deduplication, the convergent encryption technique has been proposed to encrypt the data before uploading to the server. However, from efficient data utilization point of view, the issue of keyword search over convergent encrypted data in deduplication storage system has to be addressed. Li and Chen et al. [49] propose a secure deduplication storage systems with keyword search for effective data utilization. However, the encrypted data tag and the search trapdoor are constructed by the same secret key; and thus, except the data owners, the encrypted data cannot be shared or searched by other users. Wen and Lu et al. [50] propose an efficient scheme, BDO-SD, for big data outsourcing with secure deduplication. Their scheme considers both data deduplication and keyword search over encrypted data. Data owner can outsource its data by using convergent encryption. Data users can get matched files by giving file tag or file keywords to the cloud server.

6.5   Summary and Future Works

In this article, we have studied the network architecture for big data storage and discussed the basic cyber attack behaviors in big data storage environment. Also, several fundamental approaches to resist these behaviors are offered. Following, we conclude the article by discussing several open problems and possible solutions, in accordance with the fundamental security techniques introduced previously. Our objective is to shed more light on the data deduplication security and privacy issues and to trigger more research efforts along this emerging research area.

In the further, one of the challenging issues is how to manage the outsourced data in a storage-efficient way when users encrypt data for preserving privacy and frequently update it. When the data is updated, file-level deduplication makes entire copy of updated file although there are small modifications. Block-level deduplication solves this problem, but it requires metadata larger than the outsourced blocks. To address this problem, Koo and Yoon [51] propose a hybrid deduplication scheme that minimizes storage overhead. Their scheme performs file-level deduplication along with isolation of only updated blocks with augmented metadata. However, the data security of [51] should be improved to support dynamic encrypted data updates.

Furthermore, how to get a trade off between deduplication and encryption under different security requirements, such as protecting information leakage, lowering performance overhead for dynamic update, key management for shared data chunks among large groups of users etc., also need to be discussed in the future.

Acknowledgements This work is supported by the National Natural Science Foundation of China under Grant (No. 61572310, No. 61572311); Innovation Program of Shanghai Municipal Education Commission (No. 14YZ129, No. 14ZZ150).

References

1. Park N, Lilja, DJ (2010) Characterizing datasets for data deduplication in backup applications. In: 2010 IEEE international symposium on workload characterization (IISWC). IEEE, Washington, pp 1–10
2. Zikopoulos PC, Eaton C, DeRoos D, Deutsch T, Lapis G (2012) Understanding big data. McGraw-Hill, New York
3. O'Driscoll A, Daugelaite J, Sleator RD (2013) 'Big data', hadoop and cloud computing in genomics. J Biomed Inform 46(5):774–781
4. Wang C, Wang Q, Ren K, Lou W (2010) Privacy-preserving public auditing for data storage security in cloud computing. In: INFOCOM, 2010 proceedings IEEE. IEEE, San Diego, pp 1–9
5. Shvachko K, Kuang H, Radia S, Chansler R (2010) The hadoop distributed file system. In: 2010 IEEE 26th symposium on mass storage systems and technologies (MSST). IEEE, Incline Village, pp 1–10
6. Luan TH, Cai LX, Chen J, Shen X, Bai F (2014) Engineering a distributed infrastructure for large-scale cost-effective content dissemination over urban vehicular networks. IEEE Trans Veh Technol 63(3):1419–1435
7. Russell D (2010) Data deduplication will be even bigger in 2010. https://www.gartner.com/doc/1297513/data-deduplication-bigger-
8. Stanek J, Sorniotti A, Androulaki E, Kencl L (2014) A secure data deduplication scheme for cloud storage. In: Financial cryptography and data security. Springer, Heidelberg, pp 99–118
9. Srinivasan K, Bisson T, Goodson GR, Voruganti K (2012) iDedup: latency-aware, inline data deduplication for primary storage. In: FAST, vol 12, pp 1–14
10. Dutch M (2008) SNIA: understanding data de-duplication ratios. http://www.snia.org/sites/default/files/Understanding_Data_Deduplication_Ratios-20080718.pdf
11. Costa LB, Al-Kiswany S, Lopes RV, Ripeanu M (2011) Assessing data deduplication trade-offs from an energy and performance perspective. In: 2011 international green computing conference and workshops (IGCC). IEEE, Orlando, pp 1–6

12. Li J, Li Y, Chen X, Lee PP, Lou W (2014) A hybrid cloud approach for secure authorized deduplication. IEEE Trans Parallel Distrib Syst 26(5):1206–1216, 2015
13. Wen M, Lu R, Lei J, Li H, Liang X, Shen XS (2013) SESA: an efficient searchable encryption scheme for auction in emerging smart grid marketing. Secur Commun Netw 7(1):234–244
14. Wen M, Lu R, Zhang K, Lei J, Liang X, Shen X (2013) PaRQ: a privacy-preserving range query scheme over encrypted metering data for smart grid. IEEE Trans Emerg Top Comput 1(1):178–191
15. Harnik BPD, Shulman-Peleg A (2010) Side channels in cloud services: deduplication in cloud storage, IEEE Security & Privacy 8(6):40–47
16. Ju S, Song X (2004) On the formal characterization of covert channel. In: Content computing. Springer, Heidelberg, pp 155–160
17. Mulazzani M, Schrittwieser S, Leithner M, Huber M, Weippl E (2011) Dark clouds on the horizon: using cloud storage as attack vector and online slack space. In: USENIX security symposium
18. Millen JK (1987) Covert channel capacity. In: 2012 IEEE symposium on security and privacy. IEEE Computer Society, Oakland, p 60
19. Berk V, Giani A, Cybenko G, Hanover N (2005) Detection of covert channel encoding in network packet delays. Rapport technique TR536, de lUniversité de Dartmouth
20. Puzio P, Molva R, Onen M, Loureiro S (2013) Cloudedup: secure deduplication with encrypted data for cloud storage. In: 2013 IEEE 5th international conference on cloud computing technology and science (CloudCom), vol 1. IEEE, Bristol, pp 363–370
21. Wilcox-O'Hearn Z, Warner B (2008) Tahoe: the least-authority filesystem. In: Proceedings of the 4th ACM international workshop on storage security and survivability. ACM, New York, pp 21–26
22. Cox LP, Murray CD, Noble BD (2002) Making backup cheap and easy. In: Proceeding of the 5th symposium on operating systems design and implementation
23. Rabin MO et al (1981) Fingerprinting by random polynomials. Center for Research in Computing Techn., Aiken Computation Laboratory, Univ.
24. Douceur JR, Adya A, Bolosky WJ, Simon P, Theimer M (2002) Reclaiming space from duplicate files in a serverless distributed file system. In: Proceedings of 22nd international conference on distributed computing systems, 2002. IEEE, Washington, pp 617–624
25. Storer MW, Greenan K, Long DD, Miller EL (2008) Secure data deduplication. In: Proceedings of the 4th ACM international workshop on storage security and survivability. ACM, New York, pp 1–10
26. Bellare M, Keelveedhi S, Ristenpart T (2013) Message-locked encryption and secure deduplication. In: Advances in cryptology–EUROCRYPT 2013. Springer, Heidelberg, pp 296–312
27. Kamara S, Lauter K (2010) Cryptographic cloud storage. In: Financial cryptography and data security. Springer, Heidelberg, pp 136–149
28. Wang Q, Wang C, Ren K, Lou W, Li J (2011) Enabling public auditability and data dynamics for storage security in cloud computing. IEEE Trans Parallel Distrib Syst 22(5):847–859
29. Li J, Chen X, Li M, Li J, Lee PP, Lou W (2014) Secure deduplication with efficient and reliable convergent key management. IEEE Trans Parallel Distrib Syst 25(6):1615–1625
30. Perttula D, Warner B, Wilcox-O'Hearn Z (2008) Attacks on convergent encryption. https://tahoe-lafs.org/hacktahoelafs/drew_perttula.html
31. Clements AT, Ahmad I, Vilayannur M, Li J et al (2009) Decentralized deduplication in san cluster file systems. In: USENIX annual technical conference, pp 101–114
32. Halevi S, Harnik D, Pinkas B, Shulman-Peleg A (2011) Proofs of ownership in remote storage systems. In: Proceedings of the 18th ACM conference on computer and communications security. ACM, New York, pp 491–500
33. Shacham H, Waters B (2008) Compact proofs of retrievability. In: Advances in cryptology-ASIACRYPT 2008. Springer, Heidelberg, pp 90–107
34. Dodis Y, Vadhan S, Wichs D (2009) Proofs of retrievability via hardness amplification. In: Theory of cryptography. Springer, Heidelberg, pp 109–127

35. Xu J, Zhou J (2014) Leakage resilient proofs of ownership in cloud storage, revisited. In: Applied cryptography and network security. Springer, Heidelberg, pp 97–115
36. Zheng Q, Xu S (2012) Secure and efficient proof of storage with deduplication. In: Proceedings of the second ACM conference on data and application security and privacy. ACM, New York, pp 1–12
37. Gabizon A, Raz R, Shaltiel R (2006) Deterministic extractors for bit-fixing sources by obtaining an independent seed. SIAM J Comput 36(4):1072–1094
38. Di Pietro R, Sorniotti A (2012) Boosting efficiency and security in proof of ownership for deduplication. In: Proceedings of the 7th ACM symposium on information, computer and communications security. ACM, New York, pp 81–82
39. Ng WK, Wen Y, Zhu H (2012) Private data deduplication protocols in cloud storage. In: Proceedings of the 27th annual ACM symposium on applied computing. ACM, New York, pp 441–446
40. Kavade MMA, Lomte A (2014) A literature survey on secure de-duplication using convergent encryption key management. Int J Eng and Comput Sci, 3(11):9201–9204
41. Blakley GR, Meadows C (1985) Security of ramp schemes. In: Advances in cryptology. Springer, Heidelberg, pp 242–268
42. De Santis A, Masucci B (1999) Multiple ramp schemes. IEEE Trans Inf Theory 45(5): 1720–1728
43. Bellare M, Keelveedhi S, Ristenpart T (2013) Dupless: server-aided encryption for deduplicated storage. In: Proceedings of the 22nd USENIX conference on security. USENIX Association, Berkeley, pp 179–194
44. Camenisch J, Neven G et al (2007) Simulatable adaptive oblivious transfer. In: Advances in cryptology-EUROCRYPT 2007. Springer, Heidelberg, pp 573–590
45. Bellare M, Namprempre C, Pointcheval D, Semanko M et al (2003) The one-more-rsa-inversion problems and the security of Chaum's blind signature scheme. J Cryptol 16(3):185–215
46. Duan Y (2014) Distributed key generation for encrypted deduplication: achieving the strongest privacy. In: Proceedings of the 6th edition of the ACM workshop on cloud computing security. ACM, New York, pp 57–68
47. Shoup V (2000) Practical threshold signatures. In: Advances in cryptology-EUROCRYPT 2000. Springer, Heidelberg, pp 207–220
48. Lee S, Choi D (2012) Privacy-preserving cross-user source-based data deduplication in cloud storage. In: 2012 international conference on ICT convergence (ICTC). IEEE, Jeju Island, pp 329–330
49. Li J, Chen X, Xhafa F, Barolli L (2015) Secure deduplication storage systems supporting keyword search. J Comput Syst Sci 81(8):1532–1541
50. Wen M, Lu K, Lei J, Li F, Li J (2015) BDO-SD: an efficient scheme for big data outsourcing with secure deduplication. In: Proceedings of the third international workshop on security and privacy in big data. IEEE, Hong Kong, pp 243–248
51. Koo D, Hur J, Yoon H (2014) Secure and efficient deduplication over encrypted data with dynamic updates in cloud storage. In: Frontier and innovation in future computing and communications. Springer, Heidelberg, pp 229–235

Chapter 7
Cyber Attacks on MapReduce Computation Time in a Hadoop Cluster

William Glenn and Wei Yu

Abstract In this chapter, we addressed the security issue in a Hadoop cluster when some nodes are compromised. We investigated the impact of attacks on the completion time of a MapReduce job when a node is compromised in a Hadoop cluster. We studied three attack methods: (1) blocking all incoming data from the master node except for the special messages that relay the status of the slave node, (2) delaying the delivery of packets that are sent to the master node, and performing an attack such as denial-of-service attack against the master node. To understand the impact of these attacks, we implemented them on different cluster settings that consist of three, six, and nine slave nodes and a single mater node in our testbed. Our data shows these attacks can affect the performance of MapReduce by increasing the computing time of MapReduce jobs.

7.1 Introduction

Big data has become a popular topic in the research community recently. The ability to analyze what is known as big data has a variety of uses across multiple fields. It has great uses in sciences fields such as biology, astronomy, and particle physics, in various organizations to provide useful information such as increased performance and effectiveness of the operations, cutting retail costs, etc. [1]. In the recent past, more and more attentions have been being brought to big data research and development due to its applicability and potential use in many fields. Thus, it is important to address cyber security concerns that may be applied to big data, which is the focus of this study.

The definition of "big data" is still up to debate. The authors in [1] suggested a definition of involving data which cannot "be perceived, acquired, managed, and processed by traditional information technology and software/hardware tools within

W. Glenn • W. Yu (✉)
Department of Computer and Information Sciences, Towson University,
Towson, MD 21252, USA
e-mail: wglenn2@students.towson.edu; wyu@towson.edu

© Springer International Publishing Switzerland 2016
S. Yu, S. Guo (eds.), *Big Data Concepts, Theories, and Applications*,
DOI 10.1007/978-3-319-27763-9_7

257

a tolerable time". Authors in [2] defined big data through three specific terms: volume, velocity, and variety [2]. Volume refers to as the amount of data that is typically identified with being "big", while velocity is concerned about how fast the data must be analyzed and processed in order to stay relevant to what it is meant to represent. Because there is no strict format or type of data that big data comes in, variety is considered as a characteristic of big data, meaning that it can include documents, geographic coordinates, videos, images, or any other type. A later definition includes value, meaning that there is some important information to be gained by analyzing the data in question [3].

Obviously, a problem that arises with these definitions is how much data there needs to be in order for the information to be considered big. If one were to gather data gigabyte by gigabyte, at what point is the collection of data to be considered "big data"? For example, Facebook collects at least half a petabyte of data per day, but this pales in comparison to Google, which processes over 20 petabytes in the same period of time [4]. Thus, we can see that a single instance of big data consists of a vast amount of individual bytes, which is going to increase. Particularly, according to a study by IBM in 2011, 90 % of the total data available to humanity had been created only in the last 2 years at the writing of the study and that each day, 2,500,000 terabytes of data were generated [5]. The total amount of data that we will generate is expected to double every few years. Nonetheless, as technology becomes more powerful over time in terms of both storage and computing speed, the amount of data that can easily be handled also changes over time. This means that what is considered an extremely large amount of data in terms a computer system's ability to analyze will also change, making big data a "moving target" when time progresses [6].

To get around the issue of the amount of data increasing while technology lags behind, it was found that numerous cheaper machines can be linked together to make fast computations [7]. By running computations in parallel, massive amounts of data can be analyzed simultaneously through the use of cheap resources, but still run efficiently. To this end, Hadoop is a framework developed by Apache that uses the idea of creating clusters of commodity machines in order to process large amounts of data [8]. It was originally based on the work by Google, in which a distributed file system and MapReduce implementation were constructed [9]. It has become a very popular solution for carrying out big data analytics, being used by Yahoo and Facebook, with a Hadoop cluster available for data processing even being offered as a service by Amazon [10, 11]. As of 2014, Yahoo has a single Hadoop cluster containing 4500 machines, with many other clusters along with this one but of smaller sizes [12]. Hadoop may not be able to handle real-time processing, but it is able to efficiently analyze large amounts of data via batch processing supported by its massively parallel nature [13].

Nonetheless, there are some security issues in big data, which could be raised by the distributed processing and the storage of the sensitive information on a non-trustworthy environment. It found that there are security problems in Hadoop [14].

It is worth noting that Hadoop was original designed solely for its ability to process large datasets. Security has only recently become a concern for Apache and users of Hadoop and because of this, many security issues have come to light [15]. Due to its widespread usage, it is critical to investigate these security issues and understand their implications.

To address this issue, in this chapter, we conducted a case study of Hadoop by determining how the time it takes for a cluster to process some amount of data can be affected if a node within the cluster is compromised by an adversary who could launch various attacks. Notice that value and velocity are important parts of big data processing [3, 4]. Due to the velocity property, the value of a big data can decrease until the information that can be gleaned from it is no longer relevant. Thus, big data must be processed promptly in order to retain most of its meaning. Particularly, in this case study, we considered three different attacks that could increase the time taken for a Hadoop MapReduce job to complete. In our experiments, the number of slave nodes used in clusters were three, six, and nine, all of which stored the same data and were subjected to the same attacks so as to assess how the completion time is affected by cluster size. The first attack blocks all the input from the master node except for a few special ports, making the compromised slave node unable to communicate with the master node. The second attack delays all the packets sent from the compromised node, but still allows the communication to complete. Lastly, the third attack directly targets the master node with a SYN flooding to attempt a denial-of-service attack. We implemented these attacks and compared the results with the normal operation to understand the impact of attacks on a Hadoop cluster.

The remainder of the chapter is organized as follows: In Sect. 7.2, we review Hadoop. In Sect. 7.3, we present the attacks used against Hadoop, as well as the tools and techniques used to implement these attacks in detail. In Sect. 7.4, we show the experiment results. In Sect. 7.5, we discuss some issues. In Sect. 7.6, we present the literature review. In Sect. 7.7, we give the final remarks.

7.2   Review of Hadoop

In this section, we give an overview of Hadoop. There are three key components in Hadoop, including the Hadoop Distributed File System (HDFS), Hadoop's version of MapReduce (called Hadoop MapReduce), and YARN, along with the set of libraries provided by Hadoop Common [8]. Each of these components can be controlled through configuration files within each installation, allowing customization [16]. Hadoop also offers web interfaces that can be used to perform activities such as monitoring nodes or jobs, navigating the distributed file system, and seeing what nodes are storing, and others. In the following, we describe how these three components function to enable the processing of big data.

7.2.1 HDFS

The idea behind Hadoop is to distribute a very large amount of data among hundreds or thousands of machines. To do so, it needs some sort of way to keep track of the data, which is performed through a distributed file system such as HDFS. It splits files up into segments (called blocks) of a certain size (usually 64 MB) and then stores these segments onto one or more machines [17]. When the same segments are stored on machines, such a type of data redundancy enables the capability of recovering files if failures occur. The obvious trade-off here is the extra space needed, but because commodity machines are being used the extra space should be affordable. Duplicating blocks makes HDFS and Hadoop in general fault tolerant.

In the structure of HDFS, there is typically one master computer (or node) that keeps track of the various files that are divided into a number of data blocks. The master computer is also called the NameNode and manages access to these files. It enables the adding of files to the file system by dividing a file into blocks and sending each of these blocks to other machines. Deleting files requires the deletion of all of these blocks. The rest of the machines in the cluster are the slave machines, which are also called DataNodes. The DataNodes store all of these files in the form of blocks. DataNodes can take commands from the NameNode to manage all of the stored blocks. All communication is done through TCP/IP, where daemons of both DataNodes and the NameNode run on their respective machines [17].

The NameNode stores the current state of its file system in a file, which it is able to load when it starts. Because it can be costly to constantly load and change the file whenever the file system is updated, it only tracks the changes to the system in a log file while the NameNode is running. Then later on, when it starts up again, all changes in the file recorded the log files are applied and the newly updated state is recorded [17]. In addition, there is a secondary NameNode, which could apply these changes at regular intervals to make sure the log file does not get too large [18].

Because of the chance of failure of any of the machines that store the data, Hadoop has a way of monitoring which systems are active through the use of what it calls "Heartbeat" messages [17]. If a DataNode sends its Heartbeat message, the NameNode knows that this DataNode is still active. If it fails to do so for a long period of time, this node is marked as a dead node. In addition, DataNodes send "Blockreport" messages to let the NameNode know the file blocks that are currently on that particular DataNode. Using this information, the NameNode can replicate blocks if needed or mark a file as corrupted or incomplete if there are missing blocks for a given file [17]. Figure 7.1 illustrates the basic HDFS structure [17].

7.2.2 MapReduce

The MapReduce algorithm is a core piece of the Hadoop framework, which makes it feasible to easily and efficiently process a large set of data by using a number

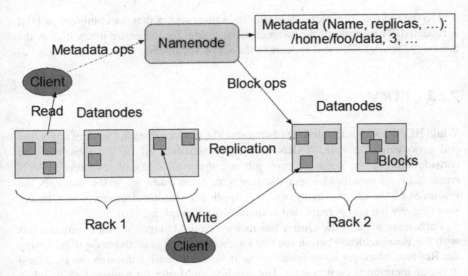

Fig. 7.1 HDFS structure [17]

of commodity machines. It works in conjunction with HDFS to distribute the computation tasks amongst the various nodes, which store the corresponding data. A specific instance of running a MapReduce algorithm is called a job [19]. When a job is run, it is first split into various maps. The purpose of these maps depends on the exact job in question, but in general it runs the first half of processing on the data stored in each of the individual blocks of the files being analyzed. Because these blocks are split amongst multiple nodes, the maps all run in unison on each of these individual nodes. When these maps are complete, their outputs will be processed by one or more reduces. A reduce begins to accumulate and combines the sorted output of each map once an individual map is complete. The reduce part of the algorithm could perform further analysis, which is dependent upon the specific MapReduce job being run. The input and output of all of the parts of a MapReduce job are comprised of various key-value pairs, which are used to transfer data between maps and reduces. MapReduce jobs can be implemented in several different languages. By default, Hadoop provides all the necessary libraries to accomplish this in Java. Because Hadoop is a customizable framework, the specific implementation of the MapReduce algorithm can be chosen by the user, as well as the number of maps and reduces used [19].

In the example discussed by Apache, a specific MapReduce job is used to count the number of words in a set of text documents [19]. Here, each map of the algorithm determines each individual word in the block that is assigned to cover. In this specific job, a combiner is used as well. A combiner is run after the map and before the reduce and can be used to affect the map output in some way. In this example, it adds up the number of instances that each word occurs in that block so that each word has only one number associated with it. The output of the combiner is then sent to the reducer, in which essentially the same process that the combiner just did is repeated. The output of the reducer is the output for the entire job, which is the number of times each word appears in the set of documents.

7.2.3 YARN

While HDFS handles the storage of data and MapReduce does the work of analyzing and processing the data, YARN is used to schedule all of the jobs with the consideration of the needs of each job and the availability of resources. YARN consists of a ResourceManager daemon that, as its name suggests, manages the resources of the cluster, along with an ApplicationMaster daemon, which makes sure that any job that is requested is successfully completed [20].

Each slave node in the cluster has its own NodeManager, which communicates with the ResourceManager on the master about the status of the node (e.g., letting the ResourceManager know whether the node is still active through the Heartbeat message mentioned earlier, etc.). The ApplicationMaster for a given task or job is also located within the slave nodes. The nodes with ApplicationMaster are managed by the ApplicationManager, a part of the ResourceManager. This part of the ResourceManager daemon assign the job to be completed to the ApplicationMaster, which actually perform the job by acquiring the resources needed.

The Scheduler is the other half of the ResourceManager daemon. This is the part of the ResourceManager that not only schedules job to be completed, but it is also what the ApplicationMaster communicates with in order to acquire any resources that it may need. Resources (e.g., CPU time, the amount of memory available on a system, etc.) are represented through Container objects [20]. It is through YARN that MapReduce jobs are able to be completed through the job scheduling and resource allocation. Figure 7.2 depicts how YARN works [20].

7.3 Approach

In accord with the classic CIA triad of computer security, the attacks mentioned in this paper affect the availability of the services provided by Hadoop whilst leaving the others intact. The availability is disrupted through the prolongation of the process, through which any new information is extracted from a set of big data. Considering the time-sensitive nature of big data, this can have repercussions for any that wish to use the information they have gathered effectively. In the consumer goods industry, the interests of consumers may change and new products may be released. In government, if big data is used for national security, a delaying of valuable information could have malefic consequences. Thus, in many circumstances, the timely analysis of big data is crucial to the value of the information it may contain and when the ability to obtain this information swiftly is compromised, a range of negative consequences may occur.

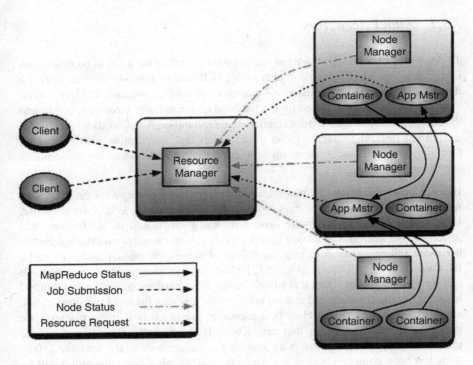

Fig. 7.2 YARN overall structure [20]

Due to the increased security issues in Hadoop, some defensive features have been developed in Hadoop, such as Kerberos for enabling the authentication [21] among others. By enabling authentication feature, Hadoop starts in secure mode and results in only authorized users who can run a task on Hadoop. Data can be encrypted before being transferred over a network, which helps to prevent any sniffing that may be taking place. Nonetheless, if the adversary has gained root access, this security mechanism can be easily bypassed. New to Hadoop is the ability to not only encrypt the data that is being transferred, but also the data that is stored on the disk. "Encryption zones" were added to encrypt the data using a single key [22]. HDFS does not have access to the key to decrypt the data, so theoretically it can only be done by an authorized user, who has access to the key. From this aspect, even root access, which compromises the previous security mechanism, does not allow for a decrypted view of the data. The importance of addressing the Hadoop security problems was highlighted in [15]. In addition, some security vulnerabilities in Hadoop's encryption scheme were shown in [23]. In our study, we assume that the adversary has gained the full control of a slave node in the cluster and can disrupt the operation of Hadoop by considering a goal of increasing the time taken for a job to complete. Our work can be extended to investigate other attacks such as collusive one that the adversary controls multiple slaves and master. In the following, we first present attack scenarios and then show the implementation.

7.3.1 Attack Scenarios

To determine how an adversary can impact the time taken for a job to complete, we first review how MapReduce completes the job. Recall that the slave nodes store the data blocks for a Hadoop cluster and master node sends commands to slaves about how to process the data. Based on the received command, the slave nodes complete the computation and send the data back to the master node. Thus, to affect the overall computing time, the adversary can either affect the computation resources (e.g., CPU) on the slave nodes, or disrupt the communication between the slave nodes and the master node.

Block Communication To block communication, one strategy for an adversary is to turn off the machine or make it unusable. Nonetheless, as discussed earlier, Hadoop is resilient to hardware failure so that there would be no fundamental difference between the adversary making the machine unusable and the machine's hardware failing. After detecting the failure of slaves, the master node can make the correction by replicating blocks [17]. One way that an adversary can overcome this failure mitigation scheme is to only allow the Heartbeat messages transmitted between the master node and a slave node, while all other forms of communication are disabled. Note that the Heartbeat messages are the way that the master node keeps track of slave nodes that are active. If the Heartbeat messages can be transmitted successfully, there is no way for the master node to tell whether a slave node has been compromised or not. Even though all other communication will be blocked, the master node will still attempt to send the tasks for MapReduce jobs to the compromised node to complete. Nonetheless, none of these messages will actually reach the compromised node, leading to the disruption of job completion and thus the completion time will be extended. If the distributed file system is setup to use replication, any task sent to be completed on blocks on the compromised node can still be sent to the normally functioning nodes. This will allow for overall job completion despite some blocks being unavailable on the compromised node.

Delay Communication Another way that an attack can affect the completion time of a MapReduce job is to delay the communication between the master node and the compromised slave node. Because communication is done through TCP, this means delaying individual TCP packets [17]. By making this delay a sufficiently large time, the completion time should have a noticeable increase as the master node will have to wait for all of these delayed responses. Because each can potentially send many individual TCP packets, delaying packets can severely affect the time taken to complete the assigned job depending what this delay is. All of the packets can still reach each individual machine successfully, so there should be no disruption of the job actually completing. If this delay is made to be an extremely large amount, it may be possible that this any number of timeouts such as those in the configuration files may come into play [24–27]. This could possibly make this attack almost equivalent to the previous described one. Heartbeat messages are also still able to be sent and thus the node will still be marked functioning properly.

Denial-of-Service Against Master Node   The aforementioned attacks focus solely on affecting the communication between the master node and the individual compromised node directly. Another way to affect the completion time is to distrupt the master node directly. Because all slaves nodes need to communicate with the master node, this is a change in dynamics from the previous attacks. SYN floods have been a form of denial-of-service attack used against connections that communicate through TCP. Since TCP is a reliable transport layer protocol, Hadoop clusters always use. Generally speaking, a SYN flood is an attack that affects a target's ability to handle TCP connections with other peers. TCP connections are established through a three-way handshake, consisting of a SYN packet sent from the one attempting to establish a connection, a SYN-ACK packet sent back that confirms the request, as well as an ACK to complete the connection. By overwhelming the target machine with an enormous number of SYN packets without fully establishing a connection, the adversary could fill up the memory of the target machine until it has not resource to accept new connections [28]. The idea here is to use the compromised node to perform this SYN flood attack against the master node, thereby affecting the rate at which communication from every slave node is able to actually reach and be processed by the master node.

Manipulating Data Stored on Slave Node   While not an attack against the completion time of a job, there was something interesting discerned in the course of searching for ways to affect a Hadoop cluster. Each slave node stores a number of blocks associated with files, where each of these blocks has one file associated with it. The file has the same name as the block that it is associated with, along with a few extra numbers in the name that follow the pattern 1001, 1002, 1003, etc., preceded by an underscore. The other file also has the .*meta* extension, presumably storing extra data about that block. Based on our experiments, we found that if two blocks are the same size (as they should be as they are all to be stored as the same size with the exception of the last block as there is likely not enough data left in the file), one can switch their names and the names of their meta files while the cluster continue to function as normal. The state of the filesystem can be checked with Hadoop's *fsck* tool [18]. We tested this with blocks associated with text files, bitmap images, and jpeg images. As shown in Figs. 7.3 and 7.4, the images were left corrupted if the blocks are switched with text files, but Hadoop did not detect any issue with any of the changed files. Two text files can also have their texts changed if their blocks are switched. The switching of blocks actually changes the files themselves. Thus, by performing this action, the output of MapReduce jobs can be manipulated.

7.3.2   Implementation

In our experiment, Hadoop 2.6.0 was downloaded from http://hadoop.apache.org/releases.html and set up with one master node and a varying number of slave nodes, going from three, to six, and finally nine. Considering the popularity of Hadoop,

Fig. 7.3 Image before blocks are switched with text file blocks

Fig. 7.4 Result of switching image blocks with text file blocks (new image file downloaded via the Hadoop web interface)

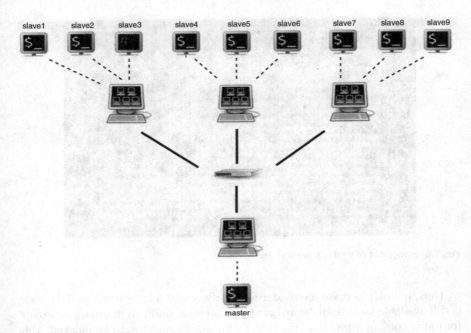

Fig. 7.5 Experiment setup

there are a number of online resources available, which describe how to set up the environment, including the one on the Apache website itself [16, 29]. In our experiments, a virtual machine (VM) was used on one computer for the master node, and a separate computer was used for each set of three slave nodes, all running on VMs. Thus, for the cluster with nine slave nodes, one VM on one machine was the master while three more separate computers each had three VMs running on them for a total of nine slave nodes. The computer used were all PCs running Windows 7 64-bit with Intel Core i5-2500 processors and 16 GB of RAM. All the VMS ran Ubuntu 14.04. Each VM ran Ubuntu 14.04 with 3 GB of RAM, with Hadoop being run in its default mode (not secure mode). This setup can be seen below in Fig. 7.5, where slave 3 represents the compromised node.

Block Communication To implement the attack that blocks communication, the network traffic was examined using the tcpdump tool. By performing the traffic analysis, we found that there was constant traffic between the master node and the slave nodes on the master node ports of 7255 (a value which depends upon each individual configuration of Hadoop) and 8031 (default resource tracker port) [24]. Interestingly, examining the contents of packets on both of these ports reveals that both of them have involve the Heartbeat messages. An example of some of the recorded traffic is illustrated in Fig. 7.6.

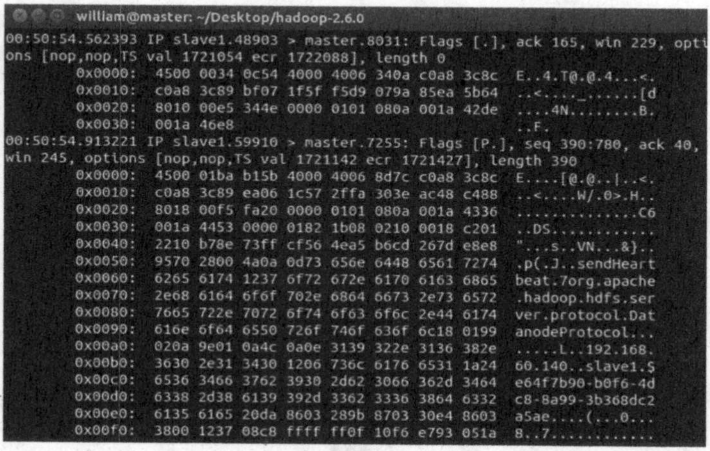

Fig. 7.6 Screenshot of tcpdump network traffic capture

Thus, in order to make the master node believe that a compromised slave node is still available to perform the assigned task, all input traffic to this machine except for traffic coming from these two ports on the master nodes must be blocked. This was conducted using a firewall rule added through the *iptables* tool. By launching this attack, we found that the effected slave node could no longer participate in MapReduce jobs while the master node would continue to send it tasks to complete despite this fact. Notice that if a replication factor of 1 is used, it would make sense that a MapReduce job would never be able to fully complete due to the fact that there is no other blocks on the cluster that matches the data stored on the compromised DataNode. In our experiment, a replication factor of 3 was used so that jobs could always be completed. Figure 7.7 shows the status of the nodes through the web interface for Hadoop. One can also navigate to the Datanodes section of the web interface and confirm that the nodes are still frequently in contact with the NameNode.

Delay Communication The attack that delays communication involves the delaying the network traffic sent from the compromised node, which was implemented through the *tc* tool [30]. This tool, which comes by default on *Ubuntu*, allows one to manipulate network traffic in a variety of ways including delaying the data transmission as desired here. In our experiment, this tool was used to postpone every packet leaving the compromised node by adding an extra 1.5 s delay. In our test environment, pinging the master VM from the compromised VM results in a round trip time of around 0.5 ms in the normal condition. Thus, adding 1.5 s to each packets results in an enormous increase in time taken for a packet to arrive.

Denial-of-Service Against Master Node The third attack, the SYN flood, was implemented using the *hping3* tool, which allows for many different types of packets to be sent and can be used for penetration testing purpose. Nonetheless, this tool was

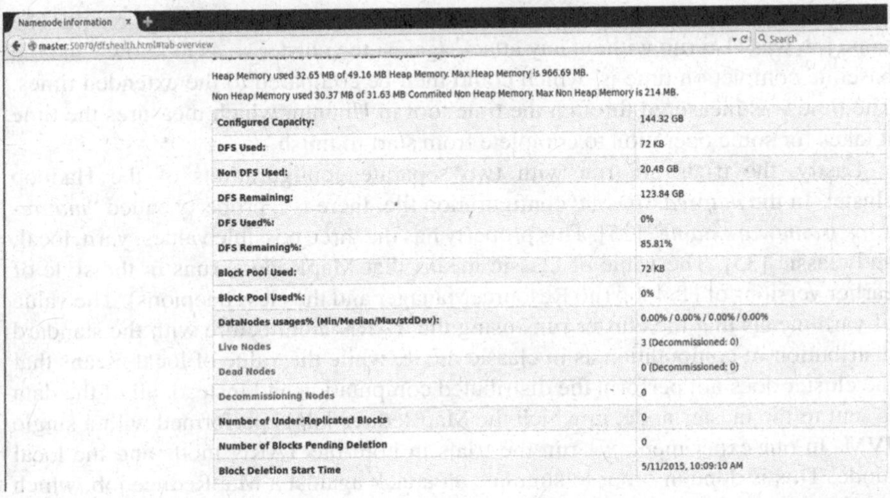

Heap Memory used 32.65 MB of 49.16 MB Heap Memory. Max Heap Memory is 966.69 MB.

Non Heap Memory used 30.37 MB of 31.63 MB Commited Non Heap Memory. Max Non Heap Memory is 214 MB.

Configured Capacity:	144.32 GB
DFS Used:	72 KB
Non DFS Used:	20.48 GB
DFS Remaining:	123.84 GB
DFS Used%:	0%
DFS Remaining%:	85.81%
Block Pool Used:	72 KB
Block Pool Used%:	0%
DataNodes usages% (Min/Median/Max/stdDev):	0.00% / 0.00% / 0.00% / 0.00%
Live Nodes	3 (Decommissioned: 0)
Dead Nodes	0 (Decommissioned: 0)
Decommissioning Nodes	0
Number of Under-Replicated Blocks	0
Number of Blocks Pending Deletion	0
Block Deletion Start Time	5/11/2015, 10:09:10 AM

Fig. 7.7 Node status on web interface

not included by default on the *Ubuntu* version that we use. It is worth noting with root access, an adversary can download this tool, install it or a similar one on the system, or implement his or her own on the system [31]. Port 50070 (the port for the web interface of the NameNode) on the master node was targeted with a flood of SYN packets of random IP addresses and 50 extra bytes added to each packet, which can be used to help bypass any default security [16, 32].

To measure the impact of these attacks, we need to perform a MapReduce job and record the completion time of the designated job when each of attacks is in place. We choose a large file to perform the experiments. We found that Wikipedia offers dumps of its webpages in HTML, so a file created from the data in one of these dumps was used as input for the MapReduce job here. Specifically, the ceb folder from September 2007 was used in the calculation in our experiments [33]. This folder contains thousands of files with very little information, which was found to be suboptimal for Hadoop as this framework cannot process a large number of small files such as these efficiently [34]. Thus, this realization leads to the collection of the contents of some of these files into a single large file, which could then easily be added into the distributed file system. The end result of this collection and combination was a single file of 385.157 MB. The block size was also changed to 10 MB in order to simulate larger Hadoop clusters, which would have many blocks per node.

The specific MapReduce job run in the Hadoop cluster was the WordMean job, which comes with the Hadoop program. It is located within the *hadoop-mapreduce-examples-2.6.0.jar* in the *share/hadoop/mapreduce* directory within the Hadoop directory. This program analyzes the contents of the files that are specified in order to compute the average length of all the words in each file. For each Hadoop cluster, each attack was performed three times in order to produce an average result. The same job was also run without any attack against the cluster so as to know what the baseline completion time is, which could then be compared to the extended times. The time was measured through the time tool in Ubuntu, which measures the time it takes for some operation to complete from start to finish.

Lastly, the trials are run with two separate configurations of the Hadoop cluster. In the *mapred-site.xml* configuration file, there is a property called "*mapreduce.framework.name*" [25]. This property has the three possible values: yarn, local, and classic [35]. The value of classic means that MapReduce runs in the style of earlier versions of Hadoop (no ResourceManager and thus less daemons). The value of yarn means that the cluster runs using the YARN architecture with the standard distribution of computation as in classic mode, while the value of local means that the cluster does not perform the distributed computation and instead, all of the data is sent to the master node, in which the MapReduce job is performed with a single JVM. In our experiment, we run the trials in both the YARN mode and the local mode. This is done in order to simulate an attack against a MapReduce job, which would require more heavy communication or output than the MapReduce job used, as well as simulate the result of running these attacks against tasks such as printing a file to the standard output on the master node. This MapReduce job should not require many packets to be sent as it is only reporting the mean, but other types of jobs may require much more communication and thus these attacks could work more effectively against them. The local configuration here requires that the entire file to be given to the master node in order to complete the job, thus allowing for these attacks to be simulated against MapReduce jobs with more communication required or against printing or displaying the file. Figure 7.8 displays some typical output after running the WordMean job with the time tool against the file used in this experiment.

7.4   Evaluation Results

Tables 7.1, 7.2, and 7.3 show the results for the experiment results with the YARN configuration and each attack, where each table represents a different cluster size. The corresponding results for the local value of mapreduce.framework.name can be seen in Tables 7.4, 7.5, and 7.6.

The completion times for the normal runs of the MapReduce job in the local configuration are shown in Tables 7.4, 7.5, and 7.6. The results are expected. This is because this configuration does not actually do any of the distributed computation, as mentioned earlier.

We can observe that all of these attacks resulted in an increase in completion time for both configurations. Nonetheless, it is interesting to see that for the YARN configuration, not only does the blocking of the input ports lead to extreme variability in the completion time with a cluster size of three slave nodes, but this

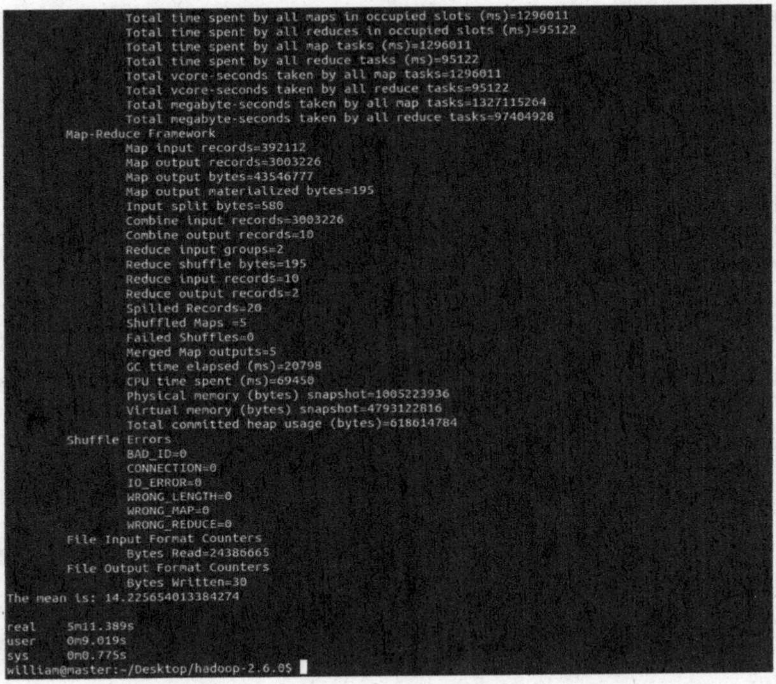

```
		Total time spent by all maps in occupied slots (ms)=1296011
		Total time spent by all reduces in occupied slots (ms)=95122
		Total time spent by all map tasks (ms)=1296011
		Total time spent by all reduce tasks (ms)=95122
		Total vcore-seconds taken by all map tasks=1296011
		Total vcore-seconds taken by all reduce tasks=95122
		Total megabyte-seconds taken by all map tasks=1327115264
		Total megabyte-seconds taken by all reduce tasks=97404928
	Map-Reduce Framework
		Map input records=392112
		Map output records=3003226
		Map output bytes=43546777
		Map output materialized bytes=195
		Input split bytes=580
		Combine input records=3003226
		Combine output records=10
		Reduce input groups=2
		Reduce shuffle bytes=195
		Reduce input records=10
		Reduce output records=2
		Spilled Records=20
		Shuffled Maps =5
		Failed Shuffles=0
		Merged Map outputs=5
		GC time elapsed (ms)=20798
		CPU time spent (ms)=69450
		Physical memory (bytes) snapshot=1005223936
		Virtual memory (bytes) snapshot=4793122816
		Total committed heap usage (bytes)=618614784
	Shuffle Errors
		BAD_ID=0
		CONNECTION=0
		IO_ERROR=0
		WRONG_LENGTH=0
		WRONG_MAP=0
		WRONG_REDUCE=0
	File Input Format Counters
		Bytes Read=24386665
	File Output Format Counters
		Bytes Written=30
The mean is: 14.225654013384274

real	5m11.389s
user	0m9.019s
sys	0m0.775s
william@master:~/Desktop/hadoop-2.6.0$
```

Fig. 7.8 Last part of output from MapReduce WordMean application along with a time command output

Table 7.1 Results for MapReduce job to complete in seconds with three DataNodes (YARN configuration)

	Attack used			
Experiments	Control (no attack)	Input ports blocked	Packet delay	SYN flood
1	132.625	751.999	293.535	153.755
2	107.982	180.929	284.534	153.718
3	121.134	1701.505	296.641	148.237
Average	120.580	878.144	291.570	151.903
Variance	152.049	589,972.3	39.541	10.082

variability decreases significantly as the cluster size increases. In contrast to the local configuration, the increase in time caused by this method also falls behind the increase in time caused by the delay of packets in the latter two cluster sizes. In the local configuration, the blocking of ports always causes the highest increase in completion time. In fact, for a cluster size of three slave nodes in the local configuration, the completion time increased by around 3682 % on average, while for six slave nodes the increase was around 1852 % and for nine slave nodes about

Table 7.2 Time for MapReduce job to complete in seconds with six DataNodes (YARN configuration)

| Experiments | Attack used | | | |
	Control (no attack)	Input ports blocked	Packet delay	SYN flood
1	80.163	130.648	173.460	106.782
2	73.703	132.532	141.867	108.653
3	70.567	130.360	167.251	96.718
Average	74.811	131.180	160.859	104.051
Variance	23.942	1.392	280.170	41.205

Table 7.3 Time for MapReduce job to complete in seconds with nine DataNodes (YARN configuration)

| Experiments | Attack used | | | |
	Control (no attack)	Input ports blocked	Packet delay	SYN flood
1	76.033	130.601	187.551	101.942
2	73.646	128.599	163.322	101.649
3	76.707	69.308	96.822	113.430
Average	75.462	109.503	149.232	105.674
Variance	2.587	1212.710	2206.841	45.142

Table 7.4 Time for MapReduce job to complete in seconds with three DataNodes (local configuration)

| Experiments | Attack used | | | |
	Control (no attack)	Input ports blocked	Packet delay	SYN flood
1	35.790	1417.207	277.499	258.538
2	36.011	1297.238	328.618	273.589
3	35.852	1357.365	304.687	229.863
Average	35.884	1357.270	303.601	253.997
Variance	0.0130	3598.147	654.172	492.459

Table 7.5 Time for MapReduce job to complete in seconds with six DataNodes (local configuration)

| Experiments | Attack used | | | |
	Control (no attack)	Input ports blocked	Packet delay	SYN flood
1	36.083	876.425	198.615	194.556
2	36.053	755.852	292.499	190.655
3	34.789	454.971	219.493	184.169
Average	35.642	695.749	236.968	189.793
Variance	0.546	47,115.12	2429.995	27.529

Table 7.6 Time for MapReduce job to complete in seconds with nine DataNodes (local configuration)

Experiments	Attack used			
	Control (no attack)	Input ports blocked	Packet delay	SYN flood
1	35.958	455.992	202.337	202.452
2	34.758	695.594	166.288	201.888
3	35.866	635.676	196.209	216.969
Average	35.527	595.754	188.278	207.103
Variance	0.446	15,547.6	372.058	73.083

1577 %. In the YARN configuration, the three slave node cluster has too high of a variability for its average increase in completion time to hold much meaning. Nonetheless, for six and nine slave nodes, there was only in increase by 75 % and 45 %, respectively.

We observe that the amount of affected completion time for a cluster of a given size through the blocking of ports is largely dependent upon the timeout for the connection to the slave node. After altering the values for the timeout properties through Hadoop's four configuration files in both the YARN and local type clusters, there did not seem to be a change in amount of time that leads to a timeout in the MapReduce job [24–27]. It is possible that in order to change the timeout setting as it applies to the completion of a job, the Hadoop source code must be changed.

It can also be seen that, for both configurations, the first two attacks (the blocking of ports and packet delay), both of which focus on the traffic coming from a single slave node, have the declined computation time as the cluster size increases. This is in contrast to the third attack, the SYN flood, which always has relatively the same impact on completion time. For example, the average difference in time for the YARN configuration with three and six slave nodes with the first attack is 757.564 and 56.360 s, respectively. For the second attack, these values were 170.99 and 86.048 s, while the third attack had differences of 31.323 and 30.212 s. The first two attacks had differences that decreased by 92.56 % and 49.68 %, while the third attack had a decrease in difference of only 3.55 %. These same computation done on the local configuration show similar results for the first two attacks, but the SYN flood completion time increase seems to fluctuate more. It can be said that it does not have a strict tendency to decrease as the cluster size increases because the completion time for this attack does actually increase significantly when the cluster size is increased from six to nine, even though it decreased from three to six. In addition to this, the SYN floods seem to have been less effective on the standard YARN setup and did not extend the completion time to a large due.

The reason why these first two attacks decrease in severity as the cluster size increases is because as it increases, each individual DataNode has less blocks that it needs to store if each cluster is given the same file or files. Since each node has less blocks, it has less to compute and thus will possibly communicate less with the master node. With not as much communication going on, the master node no longer has to wait on the compromised node as long for the contents of a file or for its results. This means that as the number of blocks that the compromised node must analyze relative to the total number of blocks to be analyzed for a single job decreases, the less effective attacks that focus on communication interference between the compromised node and the master node are. Because the SYN flood attack focuses more on the master node, which is involved indirectly in every computation through the assigning of jobs and must communicate with every node involved in a job, it is likely that this attack would always cause some noticeable increase in time no matter what the size of the cluster is (if there are no defenses that stop the attack).

In general, it is clear from these results that attacks focused on the disruption of communication between the master node and one or more slave nodes are less effective on a YARN configuration than a local configuration. In turn, this suggests these attacks are more effective against a task that involves larger amounts of communication, such as displaying the contents of a large file to the user or a MapReduce job that has a large output. This is because, in the YARN configuration, there is not much communication that needs to take place as compared to the latter one. In the latter configuration, all the contents of a file must be sent to the master node for analysis. This is similar to what happens when a user displays a file stored in Hadoop's distributed file system; the entire contents of the file must be sent to the master node from across the cluster from various nodes. In a cluster configured to use YARN properly, the master node would only send some instructions to the slave nodes that they would then execute, meaning that the master node would spend more time waiting for their responses than actively communicating with them (except for the Heartbeat messages). Because there are less packets sent, the disruption of these packets has less of an effect on the completion time.

An interesting result from this experiment is how increasing the number of slaves nodes from six to nine in the truly computation-distributed YARN configuration of the cluster did not seem to alter the completion time significantly. In fact, the average completion time actually went up, albeit not very much and is most likely just a small anomaly. The reason for this lack of change in completion time may have to do with the jobs being scheduled poorly or the data not being spread out very well when it was added to the distributed file system. It may also be due to differences in the time it takes for the VMs to create processes based on the map and reduce tasks they are assigned. This result may be indicative of the fact that adding more nodes to a cluster is not necessarily the best way to reduce completion time; there are many potential factors that can influence this time [36].

7.5   Discussion

Due to the fact that there are many different configurations for an individual Hadoop cluster, making general deductions or inferences from a specific set of data can be difficult. Hadoop allows for much customization of various parameters for an individual cluster, including altering the number of map and reduce tasks per job, the amount of memory available to the heap for each individual JVM created, the number of threads available to certain JVMs, and the intervals between status checks of different parts of the framework [24–27]. Given all of these parameters available to each Hadoop cluster, the results seen in this experiment may differ somewhat depending on the configuration (the setup used here consisted of only the default settings).

It may be possible that there is more potential in the impact of computation time completion through the delaying of packets to the master node. By increasing this delay even more, it will take a significant amount of time for individual packets to reach the master node, albeit communication will still be taking place so the connection should theoretically not be shut down. More experiments could be conducted in a very large Hadoop cluster in order to see how these methods work in these conditions, along with experiments that increase this delay by a much larger amount as well.

While the results here show that the completion time is extended by a large amount in comparison to the original time where an attack is not launched, and thus viable against small clusters, our work can be extended to a very large Hadoop cluster. For the YARN setting, the average time increase for the packet delay method went from 170.990 s to 86.048 s when the cluster size was increased from three to six slave nodes. Thus, it may be that for clusters with many slave nodes, attacks that focus only on a single node may continue this trend to the point where the increase is a negligible amount. It is worth noting that because there are many factors that can affect the completion time of a MapReduce job subject to these attacks, including the number of blocks stored on the compromised node, how much communication takes place, and the delay setting, these attacks should still be tested against a large cluster to draw conclusive evidence.

With new technologies come ways to exploit these technologies. A Hadoop cluster is an interesting target due to the information it can potentially store and because of how businesses and organizations can use it in order to make decisions based off of the results it produces. Nonetheless, all of these attacks here as well as many others can be prevented in the first place by making sure that the slave nodes (and also the master since it is so preeminent in the cluster, as mentioned before) are securely controlled, thereby severely limiting the ways in which an adversary could gain control of any of these nodes. The nature of Hadoop splitting files and spreading them across machines, as well as its resilience to hardware failure, may offer some inherent protection against malicious machinations that an adversary may induce and seek to affect the completion time of a MapReduce job though. It is important to continue to respond to security threats to Hadoop as it is still popular and important to many organizations, especially these threats only recently become higher important to the development of Hadoop.

7.6 Related Work

Most of the prominent security issues surrounding big data in general have been concerned with privacy and securing this data from outside influence [37, 38]. Collections of big data could potentially contain much information about many different individuals, which could be used to identify these individuals along with various information about them. Not only is this straightforward information a concern, but any information that can be extrapolated from the data is also of concern. For example, creating a social graph of users as the authors of [39] have done to determine the relationships between different people could be possible. Both information collected by government organizations and private businesses such as those that provide social media services are of concern [37]. These issues can be addressed through encryption of data, anonymization, and through access control to only allow certain authorized users to access sensitive data. Also how to leverage the rich resources in cloud computing to improve the cyber operation is a related issues [40–42].

When it comes to Hadoop specifically, as mentioned previously, several security issues have been raised. For example, Sharma and Navdeti have summarized these issues in [15]. As described by the authors in that paper, Hadoop has many problems with arbitrary users being able to access data they should not, sniffing data being transferred, and executing any code they choose. By default, Hadoop provides little to no security. The authors of [15] describe solutions to these problems, including the use of the Kerberos protocol, access control, encryption, etc. Fortunately, Apache has begun to address these issues by offering a secure mode for Hadoop, which now includes many of these security mechanisms previously mentioned [21]. Because of this relatively new inclusion of security features into Hadoop, more research should be done to make sure that these features are implemented effectively and that there is no longer great security risks to using this software.

7.7 Final Remarks

Based on the experiment data, the more blocks that are stored on a compromised slave node that seeks to inhibit the communication from itself to the master node retains most of its effectiveness when that slave node has a large portion of the total amount of blocks that are to be processed. It can also be seen that in a standard Hadoop cluster using distributed computing through YARN, the slave nodes may not have to communicate with the master node as much in order to complete their job if that job does not require it, such as the one used here. This is in comparison to a task such as displaying a file on the master node (simulated through the local configuration of MapReduce). This means that these methods of disrupting communication are much more effective during a task such as the latter because of the higher amount of communication required, though it is unclear how this effective these methods would be in Hadoop clusters with a very large number of machines.

It is also worthy to note that attacks that focus on the master node instead of a single slave node always seem to be more consistent in their results. This is because of the master node's centrality to the entire Hadoop cluster and its vital role in its operations. The problem here is that, for this particular setup, this type of attack did not seem to add much time to the total completion time for any of the cluster sizes, especially for the YARN configuration. Clusters with thousands of machines that only do a large amount of processing with little output may not experience much of a setback with the attacks used here; more data gathered from large clusters such as these would be needed in order to determine the efficacy of these attacks on a cluster of this type. Potential future work includes extending the attacks used here to Hadoop clusters of larger sizes, trying larger packet delay amounts, and determining whether or not a cluster has been compromised through examination of computation time.

Acknowledgement This work was also supported in part by US National Science Foundation (NSF) under grants: CNS 1117175 and 1350145. Any opinions, findings and conclusions or recommendations expressed in this material are those of the authors and do not necessarily reflect the views of the funding agencies.

References

1. Chen M, Mao S, Liu Y (2014) Big data: a survey. Mob Netw Appl 19:171–209. doi:10.1007/s11036-013-0489-0, Available: http://mmlab.snu.ac.kr/~mchen/min_paper/BigDataSurvey2014.pdf. [Accessed 1 May 2015]
2. Laney D (2001) 3-D data management: controlling data volume, velocity, and variety. META Group Original Research Note. [Online] Available: http://blogs.gartner.com/doug-laney/files/2012/01/ad949-3D-Data-Management-Controlling-Data-Volume-Velocity-and-Variety.pdf. Accessed 1 May 2015
3. Mayer-Schönberger V, Cukier K (2013) Big data: a revolution that will transform how we live, work, and think. John Murray, London
4. Hendler J (2013) Broad data: exploring the emerging web of data. Mary Ann Liebert, Inc., publishers. [Online]. doi: 10.1089/big.2013.1506. Available: http://online.liebertpub.com/doi/full/10.1089/big.2013.1506. Accessed 1 May 2015
5. Monreal-Feil L (2011) IBM study: digital era transforming CMO's agenda, revealing gap in readiness. IBM. [Online]. Available: http://www-03.ibm.com/press/us/en/pressrelease/35633.wss. Accessed 1 May 2015
6. Kaisler S, Armour F, Espinosa JA, Money W (2013) Big data: issues and challenges moving forward. In: Proceedings of 46th Hawaii international conference on system sciences. [Online]. Available: http://www.cse.hcmut.edu.vn/~ttqnguyet/Downloads/SIS/References/Big%20Data/%282%29%20Kaisler2013%20-%20Big%20Data-%20Issues%20and%20Challenges%20Moving%20Forward.pdf. Accessed 2 May 2015
7. Dorband JE, Raytheon JP, Ranawake U (2002) Commodity computing clusters at Goddard Space Flight Center. In: Proceedings of Earth Science Technology Conference 2002. [Online]. Available: http://esto.nasa.gov/conferences/estc-2002/Papers/A6P6%28Dorband%29.pdf. Accessed 2 May 2015
8. Welcome to Apache™ Hadoop®! (2015) The Apache Software Foundation. [Online]. Available: http://hadoop.apache.org/. Accessed 2 May 2015

9. EMC Education Services (2015) Data science and big data analytics: discovering, analyzing, visualizing, and presenting data. Wiley, Indianapolis
10. Henschen D (2014) 16 top big data analytics platforms. InformationWeek. [Online]. Available: http://www.informationweek.com/big-data/big-data-analytics/16-top-big-data-analytics-platforms/d/d-id/1113609. Accessed 2 May 2015
11. Amazon EMR. Amazon Web Services. [Online]. Available: http://aws.amazon.com/elasticmapreduce/. Accessed 2 May 2015
12. Asay M (2014) Why the world's Hadoop installation may soon become the norm. TechRepublic. [Online]. Available: http://www.techrepublic.com/article/why-the-worlds-largest-hadoop-installation-may-soon-become-the-norm/. Accessed 10 May 2015
13. Sagiroglu S, Sinanc D (2013) Big data: a review. In: 2013 International conference on collaboration technologies and systems, San Diego, CA, pp 42–47
14. Tankard C (2012) Big data security. Netw Secur 2012(7):5–8
15. Sharma PP, Navedti CP (2014) Securing big data Hadoop: a review of security issues, threats, and solution. Int J Comput Sci Inform Technol 5(2):2126–2131. [Online]. Available: http://www.ijcsit.com/docs/Volume%205/vol5issue02/ijcsit20140502263.pdf. Accessed 4 May 2015
16. Hadoop cluster setup (2014) The Apache Software Foundation. [Online]. Available: https://hadoop.apache.org/docs/stable/hadoop-project-dist/hadoop-common/ClusterSetup.html. Accessed 2 May 2015
17. HDFS architecture (2014) The Apache Software Foundation. [Online]. Available: http://hadoop.apache.org/docs/r2.6.0/hadoop-project-dist/hadoop-hdfs/HdfsDesign.html. Accessed 2 May 2015
18. HDFS users guide (2014) The Apache Software Foundation [Online]. Available: http://hadoop.apache.org/docs/r2.6.0/hadoop-project-dist/hadoop-hdfs/HdfsUserGuide.html. Accessed 4 May 2015
19. MapReduce tutorial (2014) The Apache Software Foundation. [Online]. Available: http://hadoop.apache.org/docs/r2.6.0/hadoop-mapreduce-client/hadoop-mapreduce-client-core/MapReduceTutorial.html. Accessed 2 May 2015
20. Apache Hadoop nextgen MapReduce (YARN) (2014). The Apache Software Foundation. [Online]. Available: http://hadoop.apache.org/docs/r2.6.0/hadoop-yarn/hadoop-yarn-site/YARN.html. Accessed 2 May 2015
21. Hadoop in secure mode (2014) The Apache Software Foundation. [Online]. Available: http://hadoop.apache.org/docs/r2.6.0/hadoop-project-dist/hadoop-common/SecureMode.html. Accessed 10 May 2015
22. Transparent encryption in HDFS (2014) The Apache Software Foundation. [Online]. Available: http://hadoop.apache.org/docs/r2.6.0/hadoop-project-dist/hadoop-hdfs/TransparentEncryption.html. Accessed 10 May 2015
23. Diaz A. (2015) Hadoop 2.6 and native encryption-at-rest. DZone. [Online]. Available: http://java.dzone.com/articles/hadoop-encryption-rest. Accessed 10 May 2015
24. The Apache Software Foundation. [Online]. Available: https://hadoop.apache.org/docs/r2.6.0/hadoop-yarn/hadoop-yarn-common/yarn-default.xml. Accessed 3 May 2015
25. The Apache Software Foundation. [Online]. Available: http://hadoop.apache.org/docs/r2.6.0/hadoop-mapreduce-client/hadoop-mapreduce-client-core/mapred-default.xml. Accessed 3 May 2015
26. The Apache Software Foundation. [Online]. Available: http://hadoop.apache.org/docs/r2.6.0/hadoop-project-dist/hadoop-common/core-default.xml. Accessed 3 May 2015
27. The Apache Software Foundation. [Online]. Available: https://hadoop.apache.org/docs/r2.6.0/hadoop-project-dist/hadoop-hdfs/hdfs-default.xml. Accessed 3 May 2015
28. Eddy WM (2015) Defenses against TCP SYN flooding attacks. Cisco. [Online]. Available: http://www.cisco.com/web/about/ac123/ac147/archived_issues/ipj_9-4/syn_flooding_attacks.html. Accessed 10 May 2015

29. Jay (2014) How to install Hadoop on Ubuntu 13.10. DigitalOcean. [Online]. Available: https://www.digitalocean.com/community/tutorials/how-to-install-hadoop-on-ubuntu-13-10. Accessed 2 May 2015
30. Linux Foundation (2009) netem. Linux Foundation. [Online]. Available: http://www. linuxfoundation.org/collaborate/workgroups/networking/netem. Accessed 2 May 2015
31. blackMORE Ops. (2015) Denial-of-service attack – DoS using hping3 with spoofed IP in Kalix Linux. blakcMore Ops. [Online]. Available: http://www.blackmoreops.com/2015/04/21/denial-of-service-attack-dos-using-hping3-with-spoofed-ip-in-kali-linux/. Accessed 3 May 2015
32. TCP SYN packet with data. Cisco. [Online]. Available: http://tools.cisco.com/security/center/viewIpsSignature.x?signatureId=1314&signatureSubId=0&softwareVersion=6.0&releaseVersion=S272. Accessed 3 May 2015
33. Index of /other/static_html_dumps/September_2007/ceb/. (2007) Wikimedia. [Online]. Available: http://dumps.wikimedia.org/other/static_html_dumps/September_2007/ceb/. Accessed 18 April 2015
34. Dean A (2013) Dealing with Hadoop's small file problem. Snowplow Analytics Limited. [Online]. Available: http://snowplowanalytics.com/blog/2013/05/30/dealing-with-hadoops-small-files-problem/. Accessed 18 April 2015
35. Venner J, Wadkar S, Siddalingaiah M (2014) Pro Apache Hadoop. Apress, New York
36. Hansen CA (2015) Optimizing Hadoop for the cluster. Institute for Computer Science, University of Tromsø, Norway. [Online]. Available: http://citeseerx.ist.psu.edu/viewdoc/download?doi=10.1.1.486.1265&rep=rep1&type=pdf. Accessed 2 June 2015
37. Kaisler S, Armour F, Espinosa J. A, Money W (2013) Big data: issues and challenges moving forward. In: 2013 46th Hawaii international conference on system sciences (HICSS), IEEE. [Online]. Available: http://www.computer.org/csdl/proceedings/hicss/2013/4892/00/4892a995.pdf. Accessed 10 Jul 2015
38. Lafuente G (2015) The big data security challenge. Netw Secur 2015(1):12–14
39. Chen S, Wang G, Jia W (2015) κ-FuzzyTrust: efficient trust computation for large-scale mobile social networks using a fuzzy implicit social graph. Inf Sci 318:123–143
40. Ge L, Zhang H, Xu G, Yu W, Chen C, Blasch EP (2015) Towards MapReduce based machine learning techniques for processing massive network threat monitoring data, to appear in networking for big data. CRC Press & Francis Group, USA
41. Xu G, Yu W, Chen Z, Zhang H, Moulema P, Fu X, Lu C (2015) A cloud computing based system for network security management. Int J Parallel Emergent Distrib Syst 30(1):29–45
42. Yu W, Xu G, Chen Z, Moulema P (2013) A cloud computing based architecture for cyber security situation awareness. In: Proceedings of 4th international workshop on security and privacy in cloud computing (SPCC), Washington DC, USA

Chapter 8
Security and Privacy for Big Data

Shuyu Li and Jerry Gao

Abstract Security and privacy is one of the critical issues for big data and has drawn great attention of both industry and research community. Following this major trend, in this chapter we provide an overview of state-of-the-art research issues and achievements in the field of security and privacy of big data, by highlighting recent advances in data encryption, privacy preservation and trust management. In section of data encryption, searchable encryption, order-preserving encryption, structured encryption and homomorphic encryption are respectively analyzed. In section of privacy preservation, three representative mechanisms including access control, auditing and statistical privacy, are reviewed. In section of trust management, several approaches especially trusted computing based approaches and trust and reputation models are investigated. Besides, current security measures for big data platforms, particularly for Apache Hadoop, are also discussed. The approaches presented in the chapter selected for this survey represent only a small fraction of the wide research effort within security and privacy of big data. Nevertheless, they serve as an indication of the diversity of challenges that are being addressed.

8.1 Introduction

Big data is believed to play a critical role in the future of our lives. The era of big data has ushered in a wealth of opportunities for discovering new values, helping us to gain an in-depth understanding of the hidden values. Yet these opportunities bring with them increasing challenges related to data security and privacy. For example, on one hand, data sharing across different parties and for different purposes is crucial for many applications, the availability of big data technologies makes it possible to quickly analyze huge data sets and is thus further pushing the massive collection of data. On the other hand, the combination of multiple datasets may allow parties

S. Li (✉)
Shaanxi Normal University, Xi'an, China
e-mail: lishuyu@snnu.edu.cn; lishuyu1978@163.com

J. Gao
San Jose State University, San Jose, CA, USA
e-mail: jerry.gao@sjsu.edu

© Springer International Publishing Switzerland 2016
S. Yu, S. Guo (eds.), *Big Data Concepts, Theories, and Applications*,
DOI 10.1007/978-3-319-27763-9_8

holding these datasets to infer sensitive information. If a security breach occurs to big data, it would potentially affect a much larger number of people and result in even more serious legal repercussions and reputational damage than at present.

The collection, aggregation, analysis and sharing of large scale heterogeneous data are now possible. Security and privacy concerns are growing as big data becomes more and more accessible. These concerns are magnified by the 5Vs (volume, velocity, variety, veracity and value) of big data. Security and privacy of Big Data has drawn great attention of both industry and research community.

Several challenges of security and privacy for big data are listed as follows:

- Currently, how to provide data security and privacy according to 5Vs of big data, lacks a fundamental but comprehensive understanding.
- Existing traditional technological approaches to security and privacy are inadequate for big data and increasingly being breached.
- The platforms, tools and technologies that are being developed to manage these massive data sets are often not designed to take security and privacy measures in mind.
- How to efficiently identify sensitive fragments of data that are stored within the large scale data set, especially within the unstructured/semi-structured data set.
- As data outsourcing becomes more popular, cloud users lack of immediate data control and find it difficult to fully trust cloud-based services because cloud-based data storage and protection methods are largely user transparent.
- How to use these massive data sets efficiently while ensuring privacy, new privacy preservation approaches are strongly needed.

To address these challenges, service providers increasingly are adopting new techniques, including the use of a third-party auditor to verify the integrity of data stored in the cloud, and access control based on data attributes and semantics, etc. Current research on security and privacy issues for big data is still in the early stages, and no universal model or set of techniques has yet emerged.

Big data also have security advantages. When organizations categorize knowledge, they control data according to specified by the regulations such as imposing store periods. This allows organizations to select data that has neither little value nor any need to be kept so that it is no longer available for theft [1]. Besides, the deployment of big data for security intelligence is very attractive and useful to many organizations, since large scale data sets can be mined or analyzed in the early stages for threats such as evidence of malware, anomalies, or fraud.

The needs and challenges for privacy and security of big data causes that both industry and the research community must re-thinking and re-designing methodologies for big data. In what follows we highlight some recent advances that can enhance security and privacy of big data. The rest of this chapter is organized as follows: Sect. 8.2 reviews different recently proposed encryption approaches which are good candidates to support big data security since encryption is the widely accepted standard technique for big data and cloud services, including searchable encryption, order-preserving encryption, structured encryption and homomorphic encryption. Section 8.3 discusses privacy issues and the three related privacy protection mechanisms which are access control, auditing, and statistical privacy. Section 8.4 analyzes trust management in big data and cloud environment, mainly focusing on trusted computing based approaches and trust and reputation models. Section 8.5 presents security concerns of big data platforms and presents the recent security improvement for Hadoop. Finally, the conclusion is included in Sect. 8.6.

8.2 Data Encryption

To protect the confidentiality of sensitive private data stored in the cloud, encryption is the widely accepted standard technique. Big data brings about challenges to data encryption due to its large scale and high diversity. The performance of previous encryption methods on small and medium-scale data could not meet the demands of big data, developing novel cryptography approaches and efficient algorithms for structured/semi-structured/unstructured big data are very important for secure data management. In this section, recent advances in encryption methodology including searchable encryption, order-preserving encryption, structured encryption and homomorphic encryption, are reviewed respectively. Scheme classification of these encryption approaches is depicted in the Fig. 8.1.

8.2.1 Searchable Encryption

In recent years, searchable encryption (SE) has emerged as an important problem at the intersection of cryptography, cloud computing and big data.

Searchable encryption is a cryptographic primitive which allows a, user to securely search over encrypted data via keywords without first decrypting it. Some SE schemes implement this via a ciphertext that allows searching, but most SE schemes in the literature employ the approach of building a searchable index, which is encrypted in such a way that its content is hidden to the server unless it is given appropriate tokens or trapdoors. Here the trapdoor can only be generated via authorized secret keys.

A definition of the index-based searchable encryption is given as follows:

An index-based Searchable Encryption (SE) scheme is a tuple of six algorithms

$$SE = (KeyGen, BuildIndex, Encryption, Query, Search, Decryption)$$

- $KeyGen(1^\lambda)$: the key generation algorithm takes a security parameter λ as input, it outputs a secret key K.
- $BuildIndex(D)$: the index building algorithm takes a document collection $D = \{D_1, \ldots, D_2\}$ as input, it outputs an index $\mathscr{L}$.

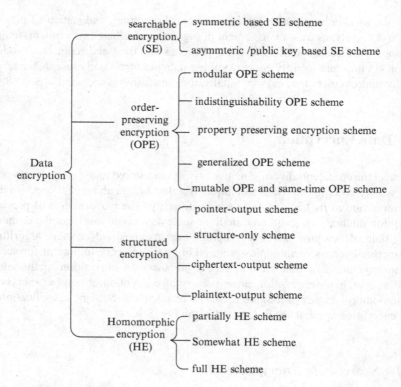

Fig. 8.1 Scheme classification

- *Encryption*$(D, \mathscr{L}, K)$: the encryption algorithm takes a document collection D, an index $\mathscr{L}$ and a secret key K as input, it outputs an encrypted document collection $C = \{c_1, \ldots, c_2\}$ and a secure index $\mathcal{SL}$.
- *Query*(ω, k): the query algorithm takes a keyword ω and a secret key K as input, it outputs an encrypted query q_ω.
- *Search* $(q_\omega, \mathcal{SL})$: the search algorithm takes a query q_ω and a secure index $\mathcal{SL}$ as input, it outputs a collection of document identifiers whose corresponding data file containing the keyword ω, which denoted as $R(\omega) = \{id(\omega, 1), \ldots id(\omega, p)\}$ where $id(\omega, i)$ $(1 \le i \le \rho)$ denotes the i-th identifier in $R(\omega)$.
- *Decryption*(C_i, K): the decryption algorithm takes an encrypted data file $C_i \in C$ and a secret key K as input, it outputs D_i.

SE schemes are built on the client/server model, where the server stores encrypted data on behalf of one or more clients (i.e., the writers). To request content from the server, one or more clients (i.e., readers) are able to generate trapdoors for the server, which then searches on behalf of the client [2]. Thus SE schemes can be divided into the following four SE architectures: single writer/single reader (S/S), multi-writer/single reader (M/S), single writer/multi-reader (S/M) and multi-writer/multi-reader (M/M). The first one is suitable for the scenario of data outsourcing and the others are suitable for the scenario of data sharing.

Two types of searchable encryption schemes have been developed so far, namely symmetric key based and public key based searchable encryption. Each one has specific application scenarios and different efficiency/query expressiveness/security tradeoffs. Detailed summarization of existing searchable encryption schemes can be found in [2].

(1) **Symmetric Searchable Encryption**: symmetric searchable encryption (SSE) can be properly utilized in the application setting where the entity that generates the data and the ones that search over it share the same secret key(s).

SSE was first introduced by Song et al. [3], in their work, the queries can be performed via sequential scanning or indexes. The sequential scan is inefficient since the server needs to scan through all documents while the indexes are incomplete. Due to this, Goh [4] proposes a data structure formally known as secure indexes. The technique, which is based on Bloom filters, improves on search efficiency. Building on Goh's proposal, Chang and Mitzenmacher [5] suggest stronger security model based on their observations of information leakage in Goh's secure indexes. However, this comes with a tradeoff on computation efficiency. Improved security notions on symmetric searchable encryption schemes are then proposed by Curtmola et al. [6], the main contribution is the notion of non-adaptive and adaptive chosen-keyword attacks.

To provide better query expressiveness of the SSE scheme, some solutions for extended query have been proposed. For example, conjunctive keyword search of Golle et al. [7] and Cash et al. [8], fuzzy search of Adjedj et al. [9] and Li et al. [10]. Cash et al. [8] propose a sub-linear SSE construction supporting conjunctive queries for arbitrarily structured data. The idea is based on inverted index and to query for the estimated least frequent keyword first and then filter the search results for the other keywords. The search protocol is interactive in the sense that the server replies to a query with encrypted document IDs. The client has to decrypt these IDs before retrieving the corresponding documents. Li et al. [10] propose a search scheme for fuzzy keyword searches based on pre-specified similarity semantics using the edit distance (number of operations such as substitution, deletion and insertion required to transform one word into another). The idea is to pre-compute fuzzy keyword sets with edit distance per keyword and store them encrypted on the server. The trapdoors are generated in the same manner, so that the server can test for similarity.

To support update of documents, Kamara et al. [11] propose a dynamic SSE scheme, to allow efficient updates (add, delete, and modify documents) of the database. The idea is to add a deletion array to keep track of the search array positions that need to be modified in case of an update. In addition, they use homomorphically encrypted array pointers to modify the pointers without decrypting. To add new documents, the server uses a free list to determine the free positions in the search array. Recently, new dynamic SSE schemes, such as the works of Naveed et al. [12] and of Stefanov et al. [13], have been proposed by achieving better index size and update time with less information leakage compared to [11].

(2) **Asymmetric Searchable Encryption/Public Key based Searchable Encryption**: asymmetric searchable encryption (ASE) is also known as public key based searchable encryption (PKSE), is appropriate for application setting of data sharing. Boneh et al. [14] present the first public key based searchable encryption scheme with keyword search. Constructions of the proposed scheme are based on bilinear maps and trapdoor permutation. Improved definitions on ASE are given by Abdalla et al. [15].

As attempts to enrich query expressiveness of ASE, conjunctive keyword search [7], subset [16] and range queries [17] over encrypted data have also been proposed in ASE settings. For example, Boneh and Waters [16] develop an ASE scheme for conjunctive keyword searches from a generalization of Anonymous Identity Based Encryption. The idea is to use hidden vector encryption for searching in encrypted data. The proposed scheme supports equality, comparison, general subset queries, and arbitrary conjunctions of those. The authors also present a general framework for analyzing and constructing SE schemes. Bao et al. [18] propose a multi-user scheme, where each user has a distinct secret key to insert his or her own encrypted data to the database, while each user is allowed to query the whole database. The idea is to use a bilinear map to make sure that users using different query keys still generate the same index for a keyword. The system allows one to dynamically add and revoke users without the distribution of new keys. The index generation and data encryption are interactive algorithms.

Compared with ASE, SSE is more efficient because it is based on fast symmetric cryptographic primitives. The searchable index of most SSE today is built upon a collection of inverted lists, associating the trapdoor of each individual keyword with an encrypted set of related file identifiers. Such efficient data structure allows that the work performed by the server per returned file is constant, but index update still needs more improvement. While ASE is its flexibility to supports complex search request with low efficiency. This is because almost all known ASE schemes are built upon the expensive evaluation of pairing operations on elliptic curves, which is much slower than symmetric cryptographic primitives like block ciphers or hash functions.

The tradeoff of schemes among efficiency, security, and query expressiveness must be carefully taken into consideration.

8.2.2 Order-Preserving Encryption

Order-Preserving Encryption (OPE) is an encryption method whose ciphertexts preserve order of plaintexts. OPE was originally studied heuristically in the database community by Agrawal et al. [19].

Formally, an order-preserving symmetric encryption scheme with plaintext-space $[M]$ and ciphertext space $[N]$ is a tuple of algorithms $OPE = (Kg, Enc, Dec)$ where:

- The randomized key-generation algorithm Kg outputs a key K.
- The deterministic encryption algorithm Enc on inputs a key K and a plaintext m outputs a ciphertext c.
- The deterministic decryption algorithm Dec on inputs a key K and a ciphertext c outputs a plaintext m.

In addition to the usual correctness requirement that

$$Dec\,(Enc\,(K, m)) = m$$

for every plaintext m and key K, we require that

$$m_1 \leq m_2 \text{ if and only if } Enc\,(K, m_1) \leq Enc\,(K, m_2)$$

for all plaintexts m_1, m_2 and every key K.

OPE is appealing because systems can perform order operations on ciphertexts in the same way as on plaintexts: for example, numerous fundamental database operations: sorting, simple matching, range queries, and SQL operations. This property results in good performance and requires minimal changes to existing software, making it easier to adopt. For example, two notable works on building database systems that run queries over encrypted data are CryptDB and Monomi. Both of them use an OPE scheme as one of their main encryption strategies that allows to execute database queries efficiently.

The ideal security goal for an order-preserving scheme is *IND-O-CPA* (indistinguishability under ordered CPA attack), which means reveal no additional information about the plaintext values besides their order. Indeed, *IND-O-CPA* was not only unachievable but it was shown that any OPE under this notion is broken with overwhelming probability if the OPE scheme has a super-polynomial size message space. In other words, OPE cannot ensure this naturally defined indistinguishability at all or has to have a very small message space (to a point of losing its utility). Thus OPE is an inherently "leaky" method, an OPE scheme has to reveal something about plaintexts other than their order: i.e., information about the distance between the two plaintexts.

To minimize information leakage and increase the security, a large body of improvement works on OPE schemes are proposed.

Modular OPE is a promising extension to OPE [20, 21]. The idea behind Modular OPE is simple: a secret modular offset j is included in the secret key and the encryption of x becomes MOP $E(x) = OPE\,(x + j)$, where OPE is the underlying OPE scheme. Based on notion of modular OPE, Boldyreva et al. [20] settle on a weaker security guarantee that was later shown to leak at least half of the plaintext bits. Recently, Mavroforakis et al. [21] extends security definitions of those introduced by [20] to capture both the location privacy (how much about the plaintext location is revealed) and distance privacy (how much about the pair wise distances between the plaintexts is revealed). Two new query execution algorithms for Modular OPE are proposed.

Indistinguishability OPE is proposed by Malkin et al. [22]. This new indistinguishability-based security notion for OPE is based on two known security notions for OPE, namely, $(r, q + 1) - WoW$ (Window One-Wayness) [20] and *IND-O-CPA*, which can ensure secrecy of lower bits of a plaintext under essentially a random ciphertext probing setting.

Property Preserving Encryption is a variant of the OPE whose encryption function preserve some given property [23]. The security notions for this scheme can be considered as those for OPE. However, almost the same attack as that of [24] can break any OPE scheme under these security notions when the scheme has a super-polynomial size message space.

Generalized OPE is introduced by Xiao and Yen [25], also achieve a stronger security by changing the model of OPE. But their schemes can be used in the very restrictive cases where the message space size is less than polynomial in the security parameter, or all encryption queries are within some polynomial size interval.

Mutable OPE and same-time OPE is proposed by Popa et al. [26] to achieve ideal security. The mutability of ciphertexts indicates a small number of ciphertexts of already-encrypted values to change as new plaintext values are encrypted (e.g., it is straightforward to update a few ciphertexts stored in a database).

Intuitively, mutable OPE works by building a balanced search tree containing all of the plaintext values encrypted by the application. The order-preserving encoding of a value is the path from the root to that value in the search tree. The search tree can be stored on the same untrusted server that stores the encrypted data, and the trusted client encrypts values by inserting them into the tree using an interactive protocol. The length of the path encoding is equal to the depth of the tree, so to ensure ciphertexts do not become arbitrarily long, the search tree maybe rebalanced when needed. Based on notion of mutable OPE, a stronger definition of same-time OPE security is proposed which requires that an adversary only learns the order of items present in the database at the same time. These protocols can be run without revealing any information about plaintexts except their order. However, they are more specializing than the original OPE, since they are interactive and they employ stateful encryption functions.

Remarkably, it has recently been shown that *IND-O-CPA* security can even be achieved in the non-interactive setting by a "generalized" form of OPE that allows an arbitrary comparison operation on ciphertexts, but such schemes are far from practical.

8.2.3 Structured Encryption

Large portions of online data are not stored in a simple text form; rather they have rich data structures. For example, graphs have been increasingly used to model complicated data, such as social network graphs and personal images. Structured encryption is proposed by Chase and Kamara to handle access to this type of data in encrypted form [27].

A structured encryption scheme encrypts structured data in such a way that it can be queried through the use of a query-specific token that can only be generated with knowledge of the secret key. Structured encryption can be seen as a generalization of index-based searchable symmetric encryption (SSE).

Formally, an symmetric structured encryption scheme is a tuple of five polynomial-time algorithms $\sum = (Gen, Enc, Token, Query, Dec)$ where

- **Gen** is a probabilistic algorithm that generates a key K with input 1^k;
- **Enc** is a probabilistic algorithm that takes as input K, a data structure δ and a sequence of private and semi-private data M and outputs an encrypted data structure γ and a sequence of ciphertexts c;
- **Token** is a (possibly probabilistic) algorithm that takes as input K and a query q and outputs a search token τ;
- **Query** is a deterministic algorithm that takes as input an encrypted data structure γ and a search token τ and outputs a set of pointers $J \subseteq [n]$ and a sequence of semi-private data $V_1 = (V_i)_{i \in I}$, where $I = \pi^{-1}[J]$;
- **Dec** is a deterministic algorithm that takes as input K and a ciphertext c_j and outputs a message m_j.

There are several different definitions of structured encryption, namely:

- Structure only, which only considers the encryption of data structures, not the data items associated with it.
- Ciphertext output, where the scheme takes γ, τ and c as inputs according to the model described above. However, different from the above model, the ciphertext output scheme returns a set of ciphertexts (containing the results of the query) rather than a set of pointers.
- Plaintext output, is strictly least secure than above types, since the algorithm, while taking γ, τ and c as inputs, returns data items in plaintext, exposing the data to the party performing the query.

Kamara and Wei [28] use structured encryption for designing special-purpose garbling circuits. The main idea of their approach essentially reduces the problem of designing special-purpose garbled circuits to the problem of designing structured encryption schemes. Consequently, improvements in either the efficiency or functionality of structured encryption can lead to similar improvements in the design of special-purpose two-party protocols in the semi-honest model and other cryptographic primitives that rely on input-private garbled circuits. A 2-dimensional scheme based on the 1-dimensional construction of structured scheme and pseudo-random synthesizers is proposed by Naor and Reingold [29]. The utility of their approach is demonstrated by applications of online social networks.

Poh and Mohamad et al. [30] propose a Message Query (MeQ) scheme with *CQA2-security* (Chosen Queries Attack) for searching encrypted knowledge, where the knowledge is represented in a well-established formalism known as basic conceptual graphs (CG). The MeQ scheme that is based on structured encryption, can query an encrypted document database and retrieves encrypted document matching the query. The query is a CG. In other words, given a phrase (or a sentence) structured as a CG as the query, the scheme returns multiple documents that contain the query, phrases and sentences related to the query.

Besides, trying to use structured encryption under the active adversary setting, Mohamad and Poh [31] also propose a verifiable structured encryption and its security under the notion of reliability similar to verifiable SSE, but with difference on how a tag for verifiability is defined. Reliability means the search result can be verified to contain exactly the documents containing the input keyword. Reliability must be preserved for both the data and the semi-private data. And taking the same approach as Kurosawa and Ohtaki [32], this is accomplished by computing an authentication tag that binds together the index pointers to data in the data structure, and the semi-private data that is indexed under the same pointers. A verifiable structured encryption scheme has similar characteristics of a structured encryption scheme. That is, induced permutation is used and the scheme is associative and chainable. Its differences from the definition of the usual structured encryption scheme lie in the inclusion of a verify function and the authentication token Tags. They prove that the verifiable structured encryption schemes achieve (L_1, L_2)-security under adaptive chosen keyword attack and reliability under chosen keyword attack. Besides, they provide two verifiable variants of the label and labeled graph schemes proposed by Chase and Kamara [27].

8.2.4 Homomorphic Encryption

Homomorphic encryption (HE) can be formally defined as follows:

A homomorphic (public-key) encryption scheme $HE = (Keygen, Enc, Dec, Eval)$ is a quadruple of probabilistic polynomial-time algorithms as follows.

- Key generation. The algorithm $(ph, evh, sh) \leftarrow Keygen(1^h)$ takes a unary representation of the security parameter and outputs a public encryption key ph, a public evaluation key evh and a secret decryption key sh.
- Encryption. The algorithm $c \leftarrow Enc_{ph}(\mu)$ takes the public key ph and a single bit message $\mu \in \{0, 1\}$ and outputs a ciphertext c.
- Decryption. The algorithm $\mu^* \leftarrow Dec_{sh}(c)$ takes the secret key sh and a ciphertext c and outputs a message $\mu^* \in \{0, 1\}$.
- Homomorphic evaluation. The algorithm $c_f \leftarrow Eval_{evh}(f, c_1, \ldots, c_l)$ takes the evaluation key evh, a function f: $\{0, 1\}^l \rightarrow \{0, 1\}$ and a set of l ciphertexts $c_1, \ldots, c_l$, and outputs a ciphertext c_f.

HE can be divided into three sub types:

- Partially HE (PHE): is HE scheme where only one type of operations (multiplication or addition) is possible;
- Somewhat HE (SHE): is HE scheme that can do a limited number of additions and multiplications;
- Fully HE (FHE): is HE scheme that can perform an infinite number of additions and multiplications. In a nutshell, a FHE scheme is an encryption scheme that allows evaluation of arbitrarily complex programs on encrypted data.

In 2009, the first fully homomorphic encryption was proposed by Gentry [33]. But constructing an FHE scheme requires managing the remaining random part called noise by keeping it under a certain limit to ensure decryption. One way to solve this noise problem is called bootstrapping. The main idea of bootstrapping is to modify a somewhat FHE scheme so it can homomorphically run its own decryption procedure. Including the public key an encryption of the secret key, bootstrapping allows the transformation of a given ciphertext into a new ciphertext that encrypts the same bit but has lower noise. Unfortunately, bootstrapping implies a growth of the public key and the procedure to transform the ciphertexts is prohibitively heavy.

A variety of optimizations and variations have been published. The works of Dijk et al. [34], Brakerski and Vaikuntanathan [35] follow Gentry's idea and presented a SHE schemes which apply squashing to make scheme bootstrappable and thus leveled FHE (scheme that can evaluate *depth-L* arithmetic circuits) could be obtained. Gentry and Halevi [36] propose a FHE scheme without squashing and showed how the sparse subset sum assumption can be replaced by either the (decisional) Die-Hellman assumption or an ideal lattice assumption, by representing the decryption circuit as an arithmetic circuit with only one level of (high fan-in) multiplications.

Gentry et al. [37] recently show how to achieve a FHE scheme that does not require additional auxiliary information for the homomorphic evaluation. This scheme uses matrices for ciphertexts instead of vectors.

Brakerski et al. [38] construct a leveled FHE scheme without bootstrapping. Main idea of their work is to use modulus reduction in an "iterative" way to carefully manage the growth of noise in the ciphertext, and ultimately achieve leveled FHE.

The leveled FHE scheme that can be parameterized to compute homomorphically multivariate polynomials of bounded degree d, where d can be virtually chosen as large as needed. Since leveled FHE scheme are less complex than the FHE ones and are able to process a number of multiplications that are sufficient for most applications, they are considered today as the most promising schemes for practical applications [39].

For (leveled) FHE schemes, there are two versions of the cryptosystem: one dealing with integer vectors, the security of which is linked with the hardness of the learning with errors (LWE) problem [40]; and the other one with integer polynomials, the security of which is linked with the hardness of the ring-learning with errors $(R) - LWE$ problem. The latter one can be expected to contribute significantly to the performance improvements required to make homomorphic encryption based computations a practical reality.

At present, a few implementations of FHE schemes have been realized and the efficiency of implementing FHE scheme also gained much attention. For example, Gentry and Halevi [41] conduct a study on reducing the complexity of implementing the scheme. More detail about this topic can be referred to [42].

On one hand, due to high overhead of FHE schemes (huge algorithmic complexity, large key size, and ciphertext expansion), current FHE schemes remain not efficient and are difficult to use in practice. On the other hand, progress in FHE has been fast-paced, and it can now be reasonably said that practical homomorphic encryption-based computing will become a reality in the near future.

8.3 Privacy Preservation

The concept of privacy is very different in different countries, cultures or jurisdictions. One popular definition adopted by Organization for Economic Cooperation and Development (OECD) is "any information relating to an identified or identifiable individual (data subject)." Generally speaking, privacy is associated with the collection, analysis, storage, and destruction of personal data. With the exploding use of online services and proliferation of mobile devices, the privacy concern about access to and sharing of personal information is growing. Increasing volume and variety of data sets also highlight the need for control of access privacy to the data. With advanced data analysis and some outside knowledge, it is often possible to discover a lot of private information from the published data. Despite significant accomplishments of privacy research in areas including privacy-preserving data publish and privacy-preserving data mining, privacy remains one of the major challenges for big data.

In this section, we survey the three representative mechanisms which are access control, auditing, and statistical privacy for protecting privacy. Our goal in this section is to learn the basic ideas and recent advances of these techniques and understand the privacy performance tradeoffs they made.

8.3.1 Access Control

Access control is the process of limiting access to system resources for only authorized people, programs, processes, or other system components, which plays an important role in the field of information security. Unfortunately, traditional access control approaches are only applicable to systems in which data owners and the service providers are within the same trusted domain. While in cloud and big data environment, data owners and service providers are usually not in the same trusted domain.

In the big data environment, there are several emerging challenges for access control. One of these challenges is how to perform access control while at the same time maintaining the privacy of the user personal and context information. Besides, access control is developing from a centralized approach towards access and usage control techniques for open environments that allow policy to travel with the data that needs to be protected. Policy enforcement with decentralized control in distributed environments and the cloud with key and identity management, update management, and revocation remain to be very challenging. Flexible and fine-grained access control is also strongly desired in the service-oriented cloud computing model.

From the view of access control models, a lot of works have been done.

Almutairi et al. [43] propose the architecture for the cloud to address problems of distributed access control, side-channel attacks and noninterference in the presence of multi-tenancy, and resource virtualization. An XML-based declaration of access control policies is used in this architecture. Hu et al. [44] abstract a general big data process model based on general distributed processing environment, and presented a access control scheme that is focused on authorization to protect big data processing and data from insider attacks in the big data cluster, under the assumption that authentication is already established. The proposed general purpose scheme still stayed in the theoretical level. Zeng et al. [45] proposed content based access control (CBAC) model that is suitable for content-centric information sharing of big data. CBAC makes access control decisions based on the semantic similarity (Top-K similarity) between the requester's credentials and the content of the data. Oracle's Virtual Private Database (VPD) is used to implement enforcement mechanism of CBAC. Oulmakhzoune et al. [46] propose a privacy-aware access control model (PrivOrBAC) that allows for the definition of fine-grained privacy policies and preferences for each data element, using a query rewriting algorithm to enforce privacy preferences. Mazurek et al. [47] propose Penumbra—a file-system access-control architecture that provides a policy model combining semantic policy specification with logic-based credentials. Penumbra's design supports distributed file access, private tags, tag disagreement between users, decentralized policy enforcement, and unforgeable audit records. A prototype implementation is also presented.

Li et al. [48] review a series of extended role-based access control (RBAC) schemes and their application in cloud environment. Extended RBAC mechanisms for cloud computing are discussed elaborately. Basic RBAC extension based on PKI and domain information includes: d-RBAC (distributed role-based access control) using restriction policy, coRBAC (cloud optimized RBAC) using role ontology, and E-RBAC (efficient RBAC) incorporating dynamic characteristic. A-RBAC (Attribute Role-Based Access Control) enforces RBAC policies on encrypted data using a hybrid cloud infrastructure. Comparisons around those schemes are also provided.

In the field of attribute based access control, Nabeel et al. [49] propose an attribute-based fine-grained access control model that allows one to enforce access control policies taking into account identity information about users for data stored in a public cloud without requiring this information to be disclosed to the cloud, thus preserving user privacy.

Sahani et al. [50] introduce the concept of Attribute based Encryption (ABE) in which an encrypted ciphertext is associated with a set of attributes, and the private key of a user reflects an access policy over attributes. The user can decrypt if the ciphertext's attributes satisfy the key's policy. Goyel et al. [51] improve expressibility of ABE which supports any monotonic access formula and Ostrovsky [52] enhances it by including non-monotonic formulas.

ABE schemes are classified into key-policy ABE (KP-ABE) [53] and ciphertext-policy ABE (CP-ABE) [54], depending on how attributes and policy are associated with ciphertexts and users' decryption keys. In KP-ABE, attributes are used to describe the encrypted data and policies are built into user's keys; while in CP-ABE, the attributes are used to describe a user's credential, and an encryptor determines a policy on who can decrypt the data. KP-ABE falls short of flexibility in attribute management and lacks scalability in dealing with multiple-levels of attribute authorities. While CP-ABE is conceptually closer to traditional access control models and seems to be well suited for access control due to its expressiveness in describing access control policies. However, basic CP-ABE schemes are far from enough to support access control in cloud environments. In a CP-ABE scheme, decryption keys only support user attributes that are organized logically as a single set, so users can only use all possible combinations of attributes in a single set issued in their keys to satisfy policies. To solve this problem, Bobba et al. [55] introduce ciphertext-policy attribute-set-based encryption (ASBE). ASBE is an extended form of CP-ABE which organizes user attributes into a recursive set structure.

Several other works examine different ABE schemes. Hur et al. [56] presented an attribute-based access control scheme to enforce fine-grained access control on the outsourced data. The proposed scheme uses dual encryption protocol exploiting the combined features of CP-ABE and group key management algorithm, and efficient attribute and user revocation capability is supported. Wang et al. [57] propose hierarchical attribute-based encryption (HABE) to achieve fine-grained access control in cloud storage services by combining hierarchical identity-based encryption (HIBE) and CP-ABE. Compared with ASBE, this scheme cannot support compound attributes efficiently and does not support multiple value assignments. Wan et al. [58] propose a hierarchical attribute-set-based encryption (HASBE) scheme for access control in cloud computing. The HASBE scheme incorporates a hierarchical structure of system users by applying a delegation algorithm to ASBE. The scheme provides support for hierarchical user grant, file creation, file deletion, and user revocation.

8.3.2   Data Auditing

Instead of enforcing correct behavior through restrictions, auditing deters individuals from misbehaving by creating an indisputable log of their actions. In a cloud environment, auditing will also enable the correct assigning responsibility.

To enable privacy-preserving public auditing in big data environment, auditing protocol should satisfy following security and performance requirements:

- Low overhead cost. Data auditing shall be lightweight and maintain low overhead—in terms of both communication and computation costs for service providers and users.
- Public auditability. Allowing third party auditor (TPA) to verify the correctness of the data on demand without retrieving a copy of the whole data or introducing additional on-line burden to users.
- Privacy preserving. Any data auditing protocol should therefore be capable of verifying the correctness of encrypted files while still maintaining data privacy during the auditing process.
- Dynamic Data Support. As data owners are subject to dynamically updating their data via various application purposes. The design of auditing protocol should incorporate this important feature of data dynamics in big data and cloud environment.
- Batch auditing support. Multiple client representatives occasionally might need to verify data at the same time. Therefore, the auditing protocol should support batch auditing.

While traditional auditing protocols fail to meet these requirements, new techniques are proposed and evolving to meet the above needs. These include Information Flow Tracking based approach and probabilistic approach.

Recently, there has been several works on incorporating Information Flow Tracking (IFT) mechanisms into cloud environments with the goal of enforcing end-to-end information flow policies that are set by individual applications instead of a central way. Ganjali [59] proposes H-one, an auditing mechanism for cloud that logs information leakage by tracking data using information flow tracking techniques to implement efficient and privacy-preserving logs that will enable the auditing of the administrators of the cloud infrastructure. Pappas et al. [60] introduce CloudFence—a data flow tracking framework based on runtime binary instrumentation that supports byte-level data tagging and tag propagation. CloudFence supports auditing for both service providers (confining data propagation within well-defined domains) and users (independently auditing their cloud-resident data). A prototype implementation of CloudFence is also presented.

From the view of probabilistic methodology, researchers have proposed two basic approaches called Provable Data Possession (PDP) [61] and Proofs of Retrievability (POR) [62]. The main difference between PoR and PDP is the notion of security that they achieve. A PoR audit guarantees that the server maintains knowledge of all of the client data, while a PDP audit only ensures that the server is storing most of the client data. On a technical level, the main difference in most prior PDP/PoR constructions is that PoR schemes store a redundant encoding of the client data on the server. Besides, PDP provides much weaker security guarantees than PoR.

Ateniese et al. [61] first propose the PDP model for ensuring possession of files on untrusted storages. They provided a RSA-based scheme for the static case and also provided a publicly verifiable version to allow anyone challenge the server for data possession. Their protocol is defined for static file and cannot be extended to dynamic data storage without introducing security loopholes easily.

Various PDP schemes have been recently proposed. To support dynamic data operations such as insertion and modification, Scalable PDP [63] and Dynamic PDP [64] are proposed. Scalable PDP [63] is a lightweight PDP scheme based on cryptographic Hash function and symmetric key encryption, but the server can deceive the owner by using the previous metadata or responses due to lack of the randomness in the challenge. The number of updates and challenges is limited and fixed in a priori. Also, one cannot perform block insertions anywhere. Based on this work, Erway et al. [64] introduce two Dynamic PDP schemes with a Hash function tree to realize the $O(\log n)$ communication and computational costs for a file consisting of n blocks. Zhu et al. [65] propose a collaborative PDP (CPDP) scheme without compromising data privacy in hybrid clouds. Collaborative PDP is based on homomorphic verifiable responses and hash index hierarchy, public verification and dynamic scalability is also supported by this scheme. Besides, Zhu et al. [66, 67] also propose an interactive PDP protocol for public auditability. The proposed interactive PDP protocol can prevent not only the fraudulence of prover (soundness property) but also the leakage of verified data (zero-knowledge property). The soundness and zero-knowledge properties of this scheme are proved by constructing a polynomial-time knowledge Extractor, having rewindable black-box access to the prover, under the Computational Diffie–Hellman (CDH) assumption. The performance of auditing is also improved with respect to probabilistic queries and periodic verification. Wang et al. [68] combine the public key based homomorphic authenticator with random masking to achieve the privacy-preserving public auditing. To support efficient batch auditing, they further explore the technique of bilinear aggregate signature to extend the auditing system into a multi-user setting, where TPA can perform multiple auditing tasks simultaneously.

Juels and Kaliski [62] present a POR scheme that permits detection of tampering or deletion of a remotely located file or relegation of the file to storage with uncertain service quality. The proposed scheme relies largely on preprocessing steps the client conducts before sending a file to cloud service provider and suffers from the lack of support for dynamic operations. Shacham and Waters [69] propose an improved version of this protocol called Compact POR which uses homomorphic property to aggregate a proof into $O(1)$ authenticator value and $O(t)$ computation cost for t challenge blocks, but their solution is also static and exists the leakage of data blocks in the verification process. Wang et al. [70] present a privacy preserving dynamic PDP scheme with $O(\log n)$ cost by integrating the above Compact POR scheme and Merkle Hash Tree (MHT) in dynamic PDP. Furthermore, several POR schemes and models have been proposed recently including [71, 72]. Since the response of challenges has homomorphic property, the above schemes can leverage the PDP construction in hybrid clouds. Cash et al. [73] propose a dynamic POR solution for outsourced data and users can execute an audit protocol (with poly-logarithmic computation and communication complexity) to ensure that the server maintains the latest version of their data. The proposed solution splits up the data into small blocks and redundantly encodes each block of data individually, so that an update inside any data block only affects a few codeword symbols. To improve efficiency, codeword symbols are stored on the server and the algorithmic technique of oblivious RAM is used when accessing codeword symbols. Due to the black-box application of oblivious RAM, the proposed dynamic POR scheme offers access pattern privacy. A recent work of Stefanov et al. [74] consider PoR for dynamic data as part of a cloud-based file system called Iris, but in a more complex setting where an additional trusted "portal" performs some operations on behalf of the client, and can cache updates for an extended period of time. Although reads and writes in Iris are quite efficient, the complexity of the updates and the audit in that work is proportional to square-root of the data size. Shi et al. [75] propose a publicly verifiable and dynamic PoR scheme that achieves comparable bandwidth overhead and client-side computation with a standard Merkle Hash Tree (MHT). The proposed scheme provides the much stronger PoR guarantees, roughly at the same practical and asymptotic overhead as dynamic PDP schemes. Yuan [76] proposes an efficient POR scheme with constant communication cost and public verifiability, which is achieved by tailoring and uniquely combining techniques such as constant size polynomial commitment and homomorphic linear authenticators. The security of proposed scheme is proved based on the Computational Diffie–Hellman Problem, the Strong Diffie–Hellman assumption and the Bilinear Strong Diffie–Hellman assumption.

Besides, Liu et al. [77] propose a public auditing scheme based on Boneh–Lynn–Shacham (BLS) signature with support of fine-grained updates (arbitrary-length of data block instead of fixed size can be updated) over variable-sized file blocks. In addition, an authentication process between the client and TPA is also proposed to prevent TPA from endless challenges, thereby cut the possibility of attacks over multiple challenges from source.

A detailed comparison of various PDP scheme and POR scheme can be referred to [78, 79]. And the strengths and weaknesses of these techniques are roughly summarized in [80]. Currently, no single proposed auditing protocol meets all of above requirements. Thus, a full auditing protocol that maintains data integrity and privacy in big data environment remains a challenge for future research.

8.3.3 Statistical Privacy

Statistical privacy is the art of designing a privacy mechanism that transforms sensitive data into data that are simultaneously useful and non-sensitive.

To guarantee privacy, source data can be processed for anonymization. Many data anonymization techniques have been developed, including perturbation [81], K-anonymity [82] which in turn led to other models such as, ℓ-diversity [83], (α, K)-anonymization [84], t-closeness [85], (k, e)-anonymity [86] and (c, k)-safety [87].

In perturbation, the original data is modified by adding noise, or generalized to less accurate values, etc. In K-anonymity, the original data is modified such that a given data is not distinguishable from at least k other data. ℓ-diversity requires that the distribution of a sensitive attribute in each equivalence class has at least ℓ well-represented values. Wong et al. [85] propose a new privacy model called (α,

K)-anonymization by integrating both K-anonymity and confidence bounding into a single privacy model.

Among those models, K-anonymity has been widely studied because of its conceptual simplicity. Li et al. [88] propose a method to model an adversary's background knowledge by mining negative association rules, which is then used in the anonymization process. Kisilevich et al. [89] propose K-anonymity of classification trees using suppression, in which multi-dimensional suppression is performed by using a decision tree to achieve K-anonymity. Matatov et al. [90] propose anonymizing separate projections of a dataset instead of anonymizing the entire dataset by partitioning the underlying dataset into several partitions that satisfy K-anonymity. A classifier is trained on each projection and then classification tasks are performed by combining the classification of all such classifiers. Tassa et al. [91] improve the quality of K-anonymity by introducing new models: $(K, 1)$-anonymity, $(1, K)$-anonymity, and (K, K)-anonymity and K-concealment. They argue that $(K, 1)$-anonymity, $(1, K)$-anonymity, and (K, K)-anonymity do not provide the same level of security as K-anonymity. K-concealment, on the other hand, provides the comparable level of security that guarantees that every record is computationally indistinguishable from at least K-1 others with higher quality. In their work, anonymity is typically achieved by means of generalizing the database entries until some syntactic condition is met.

Each of these techniques has some problems when applied to big data. The popular K-anonymity methods can no longer anonymize the data without losing an unacceptable amount of information. The algorithms become impractical because the underlying problem is NP-hard. The perturbation methods become less effective because it is possible to estimate the original data from the perturbed data when the data volume becomes large. Besides, the anonymized data could be could be cross-referenced with other available data following de-anonymization techniques. These privacy preserving techniques still have much to achieve in order to render sensitive information of users truly private.

Recently, research on the differential privacy [92] has gained much interest. Intuitively, differential privacy guarantees that adding or removing a record from the data will have little effect on the output of a privacy mechanism M. Differential privacy provides each participant in a dataset with a strong guarantee and makes no assumptions about the prior knowledge of attackers. Since its introduction, differentially private algorithms have been developed for a wide range of data mining and analysis tasks, for both tabular data and networked data.

Differential privacy satisfies an important property called composability. If M_1 and M_2 are two mechanisms that satisfy differential privacy with parameters ε_1 and ε_2, releasing the outputs of M_1 and M_2 together satisfies differential privacy with parameter $\varepsilon_1 + \varepsilon_2$. Other known privacy measures (like K-anonymity and ℓ-diversity) do not satisfy composability.

A lot of research has been carried on with differential privacy problem. In [93], the degradation of the differential privacy level under adaptive interactions was characterized. In [94], for any statistical estimator and input distribution satisfying a regularity condition, it was proved that there is a differentially private estimator with the same asymptotic output distribution. In [95], the methods were developed to approximate a filter by its differentially private version. Lu [96] considers the problem of estimating parameters for the exponential random graph model (ERGM) under differential privacy. The proposed solution firstly uses (ε, δ)-differentially private algorithms for estimating two key statistics: alternating k-triangle and alternating k-twopath, noise is proportionally added to a high-likelihood bound on the local sensitivity of the statistics. Then the solution runs an improved Bayesian method for ERGM parameter estimation according to the noisy sufficient statistics. A survey of the differential privacy in machine learning was given in [97]. Relations between different formalisms for statistical inference privacy were discussed in [98].

Since most data analysts are not experts in differential privacy, they cannot benefit from its strong guarantees unless they have access to suitable tools.

Currently, several tools have been developed for certifying that a given query is differentially private. For example, Reed and Pierce [99] propose a functional programming language, Fuzz, for writing differentially private queries. Fuzz uses linear types to track sensitivity and a probability monad to express randomized computation, and differential privacy guarantee follows directly from the soundness theorem of the type system. But Fuzz only supports the sensitivity analysis based on static values. To solve this problem, Gaboardi et al. [100] present Dependent Fuzz (DFuzz), an extension of Fuzz with a combination of linear indexed types and lightweight dependent types. This combination allows a richer sensitivity analysis that is able to certify a larger class of queries as differentially private, including ones whose sensitivity depends on runtime information. PINQ [101] is an SQL-like differentially private query language embedded in C#. Airavat [102] is a MapReduce-based solution using a modified Java VM. Both PINQ and Airavat check privacy at runtime, while Fuzz and DFuzz use a static check. Another language-based solution is CertiPriv [103], which is a machine-assisted framework for reasoning about differential privacy. CertiPriv can certify many queries at the cost of much higher complexity.

In summary, k-anonymity enables general-purpose data publication with reasonable utility at the cost of some privacy weaknesses, for example, it is vulnerable to attacks based on the possible lack of diversity of the non-anonymized confidential attributes or on additional background knowledge available to the attacker. On the contrary, differential privacy is rigorous privacy model and offers robust privacy guarantee at the cost of substantially limiting the generality and/or utility of anonymized outputs [104]. Some researchers also argue that differential privacy does not sufficiently capture the diversity in the privacy-utility trade-off space. For instance, recent work has shown two seemingly contradictory results. In certain applications (e.g., social recommendations) differential privacy is too strong and does not permit sufficient utility. Next, when data are correlated (e.g., when constraints are known publicly about the data, or in social network data) differentially private mechanisms may not limit the ability of an attacker to learn sensitive information [105].

To achieve success in big data environment, two important problems need to be taken into consideration. One important problem is ensuring the privacy of linked data, reasoning about privacy in such data is tricky since information about individuals may be leaked through links to other individuals. Besides, Due to 5Vs of big data, we need techniques that protect privacy while guaranteeing utility. When producing information for big data, understanding balance between privacy and utility is another important problem for research.

8.4 Trust Management

Trust is highly related to security and privacy since ensuring system security and user privacy is a necessity to gain trust. Although trust has been studied in many disciplines including sociology, psychology, economics, and computer science, it still lacks a uniform and generally accepted definition. In general, trust is a measure of confidence that an entity will behave in an expected manner, despite the lack of ability to monitor or control the environment in which it operates [106]. Risk and interdependence are two important factors characterizing a trust relationship. The source of risk is the uncertainty regarding the intention of the other party. Interdependence is characterized by the fact that the interests of the two parties are related and cannot be achieved without relying on each other. The relationship is not a trust relationship if these two conditions do not exist [107].

Trust is an important concept for users in the cloud to select cost effective and trustworthy services. Trust is also important for service providers to decide on the infrastructure provider that can comply with their needs, and to verify if the infrastructure providers maintain their agreements during service deployment [108]. In cloud environment, different attributes that are often available from multiple sources need to be taken into account in order to ensure reliable decision making for trust assessment.

In cloud environment, it's important to consider two major types of trust: hard trust and soft trust. Hard trust approaches consider the service platforms trusted if the existence of necessary security primitives is provable, trust value is commonly calculated based on techniques like encryptions, audits and certificates. Soft trust is a subjective term involving aspects such as intrinsic human emotions, perceptions, interaction experiences including user feedbacks and reviews. Trusted computing based approaches are examples of hard trust while trust and reputation models are examples of soft trust. Trusted computing based approaches and trust and reputation models are discussed in detail as follows.

Trusted computing technology provides the hardware support needed to bootstrap trust in a computer. Trusted Platform Module (TPM) is the core component of trusted computing. The TPM chip contains an endorsement private key that uniquely identifies the TPM (thus, the physical host), and some cryptographic functions that cannot be modified. The respective manufacturers sign the corresponding public key to guarantee the correctness of the chip and validity of the key. The TPM chip can either work stand-alone by measuring the loaded software stack from boot time in a procedure called static root of trust, or works with mechanisms for dynamically launching and measuring protected execution environments, this procedure is called the dynamic root of trust.

Several proposals [109, 110] have advocated leveraging trusted computing technology to make cloud services more resilient to security concerns. Those proposals mainly rely on TPM chip deployed on every node in the cloud. Each TPM chip would store a strong identity (unique key) and a fingerprint (hash) of the software stack that booted on the cloud node. TPMs could then restrict the upload of customer data to cloud nodes whose identities or fingerprints are considered trusted. This capability offers a building block in the design of trusted cloud services by securing data confidentiality and integrity against insiders, or confining the data location to a desired geographical or jurisdictional boundary [111]. To ensure cloud infrastructure trustworthy, Krautheim et al. [112] propose security architecture for cloud computing named Private Virtual Infrastructure (PVI), using a trust model to share the responsibility of security between the service provider and users. Schiman et al. [113] propose a hardware based attestation mechanism to provide assurance regarding data processing protection in the cloud for users.

However, current trusted computing technology is ill-suited to the cloud for three main reasons: first, TPMs are difficult to use in a multi-node environment due to its nature of stand-alone configuration; second, TPMs exposes the internal details of cloud infrastructure by revealing the identity and software fingerprint of individual cloud nodes; third, the current implementation of TPMs is inefficient and lacks flexibility and scalability to cloud services.

To address the limitations (such as standalone configuration and low efficiency) of trusted computing applied in cloud environment, Santos et al. [111] present Excalibur system to enable the design of trusted cloud services. Excalibur provides a new trusted computing abstraction which uses ciphertext-policy attribute-based encryption (CP-ABE), called policy-sealed data, that lets data be encrypted and then unencrypted only by nodes whose configurations match the policy. Excalibur has been incorporated into the Eucalyptus open-source cloud platform to demonstrate its practicality. To ensure the confidentiality and integrity of data outsourced to Infrastructure as a Service (IaaS) services, Santos et al. [114] propose a trusted cloud computing platform (TCCP), providing a closed box execution environment that guarantees confidential execution of user virtual machines. Moreover, it allows users to attest to the IaaS provider and determine whether or not the service is secure before they launch their virtual machines.

In the field of trust and reputation models, various trust models have been proposed in the literature and several classification methods have been presented.

Depending on the detailed implementation techniques, these trust models can be classified into:

- Statistical and machine learning based model: has a sound mathematical foundation for trust management. Bayesian systems, belief models, Artificial Neural Networks (ANNs) and Hidden Markov Models (HMMs) are the major techniques for computing and predicting trust. Taking Bayesian systems as an example, binary ratings (honest or dishonest) are commonly used in Bayesian systems to assess trust by statistically updating the beta probability density functions.

- Heuristics based model: focuses on defining an easy to understand and practical model for constructing robust trust management systems.
- Behavior based model: focuses on user behavior in the community such as social network. For example, Adali et al. [115] evaluate trust based on the communication behavior of members in a social network. They further divide behavioral trust into two types of trust: conversation trust which specifies how long and how frequently two members communicate with each other, and propagation trust which refers to the propagation of information.
- Hybrid model: is composed by at least two models mentioned above. For example, Malik et al. [116] present a hybrid solution defining key heuristics and HMM for reputation assessment.

According to different trust management techniques adopted in the literature, Noor et al. [117] classify these trust models into four different categories: Policy, Recommendation, Reputation, and Prediction.

- Policy as a trust management technique: uses a set of policies, each of which assumes several roles that control authorization levels and specifies a minimum trust threshold in order to authorize access. The trust thresholds are based on the trust results or the credentials.
- Recommendation as a trust management technique: recommendations take advantage of participant's knowledge about the trusted parties, especially given that the party at least knows the source of the trust feedback. Recommendations can appear in different forms such as the explicit recommendation or the transitive recommendation.
- Reputation as trust management technique: reputation is what is generally said or believed about a person's or thing's character or standing [118]. Reputation is important because the feedback of the various cloud service consumers can dramatically influence the reputation of a particular cloud service either positively or negatively. Reputation can have direct or indirect influence on the trustworthiness of a particular entity.
- Prediction as a trust management technique: prediction is very useful, especially when there is no prior information regarding the cloud service's interactions (e.g., previous interactions, history records). Prediction can be used to refine the trust results and to increase the credibility of trust feedback.

In cloud environment, reputation based trust systems have received a lot of attention. Ferrer et al. [119] use multiple factors including trust, risk, eco-efficiency and cost for service providers to evaluate the infrastructure providers for their service. Hwang et al. [120] identifies several realistic vulnerabilities in the existing cloud services providers and proposes an architecture to reinforce the security and privacy in the cloud applications. A hierarchy of P2P reputation system is provided to protect cloud resources. Alhamad et al. [121] proposes a trust model for cloud computing based on the usage of SLA information. This work describes the requirements and benefits of using SLA for trust modeling, provides a high level architecture capturing major functionalities required, and provides a protocol for the trust model. To evaluate the trustworthiness of infrastructure providers performed by the service providers, Pawar et al. [108] propose a reputation based trust model, which calculates trust values based on three different parameters, namely compliance of SLA parameters, service and infrastructure providers satisfaction ratings, and service and infrastructure provider behavior. For each of the different parameters above, trust values are calculated based on an extension of the Josang's opinion model [122]. The opinion is expressed in terms of belief, disbelief, uncertainty and base rate which is used in conjunction with the subjective logic.

Besides, there is a few notable works focusing on trust management in cloud environment from different views. Habib et al. [123] propose a multi-faceted trust management system for cloud computing marketplaces, which can identify trustworthy cloud providers in terms of different attributes. The proposed trust management system is implemented by using the Consensus Assessment Initiative Questionnaire (CAIQ) as one of the sources of trust information. Using concepts from the Cloud Accountability Life Cycle [124], Ryan et al. [125] present a conceptual framework—TrustCloud, trying to address accountability and trust in cloud computing. Three abstraction layers is proposed in the concept model: the system layer that performs file-centric logging, the data layer that supports the data abstraction and facilitates data-centric logging, while the workflow layer focusing on the audit trails and the audit-related data found in the software services in the cloud. The framework exploits a centralized architecture, detective controls, and monitoring techniques for achieving trusted cloud services.

In inter-cloud environment, computing constitutes collaboration between independently owned autonomous clouds, establishment of trust is even more important and complex, as besides the users, cloud providers must trust each other and the trust of a cloud provider affect other cloud providers. The concept of trust federations can be used in this regard. Trust federation is a combination of technology and policy infrastructure that allows organizations to trust each other's verified users to enable the sharing of information, resources, and services in a secure and distributed way [126].

In the inter-cloud environment, providers may have different levels of trust in each other, which makes all-or-nothing trust model (an entity is either trusted or non-trusted) is not appropriate, Bernstein and Vij [127] suggest a dynamic trust-level model layered on top of the public key infrastructure (PKI). Abawajy [128] proposes a distributed reputation-based trust management system that allows parties to determine the trustworthiness of other entities and enables a service requester to obtain the trustworthiness of the service. Building a trusted context is also crucial for inter-cloud environment. In the trusted context, providers must be able to access each other's services while they still adhere to their internal security policies. Celesti et al. [129] use eXtensible Access Control Markup Language (XACML) and Security Assertion Markup Language (SAML) to build a customized trusted context for cross-cloud federation.

In big data environment, trust management plays an important role for reliable data collection and analysis, qualified services, and enhanced user privacy and data security. Though trust in connection with big data has received little attention so far, several surveys from different domains have been conducted trying to bridge the gap.

Sherchan et al. [107] review the definitions and measurements of trust from the prism of different disciplines, with a focus on social networks. In their work, the social capital of an online community is defined as the density of interactions that is beneficial to the members of the community and social trust is derived from social capital. And recent works on addressing social trust is also discussed from three aspects: trust information collection, trust evaluation, and trust dissemination. Yan et al. [130] present a comprehensive literature review about Internet of Things (IoT) trust management technologies regarding trust properties and holistic trust management objectives and propose a research model in order to achieve comprehensive trust management in IoT and direct future research. Govindan and Mohapatra [131] present a survey on various trust computing approaches that are geared towards mobile adhoc networks (MANETs), and analyze different literature on the trust dynamics including trust propagation, trust aggregation and trust prediction. Noor et al. [117] survey the main techniques and research prototypes that efficiently support trust management of services in cloud environments, and present a generic analytical framework that assesses existing trust management research prototypes in cloud computing and relevant areas using a set of assessment criteria. Sanger et al. [132] distinguish two branches for the research in trust and big data, namely big data for trust and trust in big data. The former addresses questions of how to use big data for trust assessment whereas the latter discusses possibilities and challenges to create trust in big data. In each of these branches, they raise several research questions and provide information on current research efforts that are promising for answering them.

The developments in the era of big data enable the utilization of more data sources than ever before. However, this implies the need for verifying their trustworthiness and especially for evaluating the quality of the input data [132]. A number of issues about trust for big data, such as trust in different big data life cycle stages, including: collection, process, analysis and usage; trust relationship evaluation and evolution, etc. should receive more attention and need to be extensively studied.

8.5 Security for Big Data Platforms

Currently, a lot of platforms and tools for big data are emerging. However, the platforms and tools that are being developed to manage these massive data sets are often not designed to incorporate adequate security or privacy measures. Most state of art big data platforms tend to rely on traditional firewalls or implementations at the application layer to restrict access to the data.

Taking Amazon Simple Storage Service (S3) as an example, S3 is the data storage and management infrastructure for Amazon's Elastic Compute Cloud (EC2), the users can decide how, when and to whom the information stored in Amazon Web Services is accessible. Amazon S3 API provides access control lists (ACLs) for write and delete permissions on both objects and objects containers, denoted buckets. However, no high-level security mechanism is available to protect the environment from complex attacks, such as the ones that cannot be prevented by authentication mechanisms [133].

Presently, Hadoop is widely used in big data applications in the industry and considerable academic research is also based on Hadoop. But Hadoop, like many open source technologies, was not created with security in mind. Hadoop's core specifications are still being developed by the Apache community and, thus far, do not adequately address enterprise requirements for robust security, policy enforcement, and regulatory compliance. Security matters are more complicated, since Hadoop is not a single technology, but an entire eco-system of applications including Hive, HBase, Zookeeper, Oozie, and Job Tracker.

Hadoop platform now supports some security features through the current implementation of Kerberos, the use of firewalls, and basic HDFS permissions. Hadoop Distributed File System (HDFS) implements security as a rudimentary file and directory permission mechanism, and uses Kerberos [134] as the underlying authentication system. The Kerberos implementation utilized the token-based framework to support a flexible authorization enforcement engine. But Kerberos is not a mandatory requirement for a Hadoop cluster, making it possible to run entire clusters without deploying any security. Kerberos is also difficult to install and configure on the cluster, and to integrate with Active Directory (AD) and Lightweight Directory Access Protocol (LDAP) services. This makes security problematic to deploy, and thus constrains the adoption of even the most basic security functions for users of Hadoop. Besides, HDFS lacks of encryption technique. Even if a typical user does not have full access to the file system, HDFS is vulnerable to various attacks that it cannot detect, such as Denial of Service. A malicious developer could easily write code to impersonate users' Hadoop services; a malicious user could read arbitrary data blocks from data nodes, bypassing access control restrictions, or writing garbage data to data nodes. Further, anyone could submit a job to a Job Tracker and it could be arbitrarily executed [44].

Some efforts have been made to improve security of Hadoop platform.

Apache Accumulo is a distributed key-value store with multi-level access control based on Google's BigTable [135] design and built on top of Apache Hadoop. It improves the BigTable design in the form of cell-based mandatory and attribute-based access control capabilities and a server-side programming mechanism that can modify key-value pairs in the data management process. Similarly, BigSecret [136] enables secure querying of cell-level encrypted data in HBase. SecureMR [137] provides a decentralized replication-based integrity verification scheme for MapReduce job execution.

Roy et al. [102] propose Airavat, a MapReduce-based system which provides strong security and privacy guarantees for sensitive data, using a combination of mandatory access control and differential privacy. Airavat employs SELinux [138] and adds SELinux-like mandatory access control to the MapReduce distributed file system. To prevent leaks through the output of the computation, Airavat enforces differential privacy using modifications to the Java Virtual Machine and the MapReduce framework. Data providers control the security policy for their sensitive data, including a mathematical bound on potential privacy violations. Users without security expertise can perform computations on the data, but Airavat confines these computations, preventing information leakage beyond the data provider's policy. If a MapReduce computation is differentially private, the security level of its result can be safely reduced.

Zhao et al. [139] design and implement a security framework for the G-Hadoop. G-Hadoop is an extension of the Hadoop MapReduce framework with the functionality of allowing the MapReduce tasks to run on multiple clusters. The proposed framework simplifies user authentication and job submission process of the current G-Hadoop implementation with a single-sign-on (SSO) approach. Under this framework, privacy of user information is invisible at the side of the slave nodes and access control mechanism confines users only have the right to access the resource of a cluster that he can access with an SSH connection. In addition, the designed security framework provides a number of different security mechanisms (such as proxy credentials and user session) to protect the G-Hadoop system from the most common attacks, such as MITM attack.

Ulusoy et al. [140] develop Vigiles2, a fine grained access control enforcement mechanism for MapReduce systems without requiring any modification to MapReduce system source code. Vigiles2 realizes policy enforcement as a middleware layer that rewrites the cloud's front-end API with reference monitors (RM). The cloud-resident RMs filter the outputs of data accesses, preventing unauthorized access to policy prohibited key-values at runtime. Policies are expressed as user-specific, computable predicates over records.

Zettaset Company provides Orchestrator [141], a security solution for big data that is embedded in the data cluster itself. The aim of Orchestrator is to simplify the integration of Hadoop clusters into an existing security policy framework. Zettaset Company claim that Orchestrator has several key capabilities: support fine grained access control based on RBAC, policy management with support for LDAP and AD, compliance support for reporting and forensics by providing centralized configuration management, logging, and auditing. This also enhances security by maintaining tight control of ingress and egress points in the cluster and history of access to data.

Many security professionals of industry have highlighted challenges related to Hadoop's security model, and as a result there has been an explosive growth in security-focused tools that complement Hadoop offerings, with products like Cloudera Sentry, IBM InfoSphere Optim Data Masking, Intel's secure Hadoop distribution, DataGuise for Hadoop, etc.

Although a number of interesting approaches have been developed, these methods are not generally known and not in widespread use in industry. This dearth of well-developed security mechanisms in big data systems has emerged as an important hindrance for widespread adoption. Attempts are needed to make them better known and to bring them to practice.

8.6 Conclusion

We have entered an era of big data. Through better analysis of the large scale of data that are becoming available, there is the potential to improve the efficiencies of enterprises and improve the quality of our lives. However, due to its extraordinary scale, there are a number of security and privacy challenges that must be addressed to allow us to exploit the full potential of big data, such as efficient encryption and decryption algorithms, privacy preservation mechanisms, reliability and integrity verification of big data.

This review covers several distinct topics within security and privacy of big data, we hope this discussion inspires additional curiosity about the technical nature of security and privacy of big data. Fundamental research towards addressing these challenges must be supported and encouraged if we are to achieve the promised benefits of big data.

References

1. Sagiroglu S, Sinanc D (2013) Big data: a review. In: International conference on collaboration technologies and systems (CTS). IEEE, pp 42–47
2. Bösch C, Hartel P, Jonker W, Peter A (2014) A survey of provably secure searchable encryption. ACM Comput Surv (CSUR) 47(2):18
3. Song DX, Wagner D, Perrig A (2000) Practical techniques for searches on encrypted data. In: Proceedings of the IEEE symposium on security and privacy (SP). IEEE, pp 44–55
4. Goh E-J (2003) Secure indexes. IACR Cryptology ePrint Archive 2003:216
5. Chang Y-C, Mitzenmacher M (2005) Privacy preserving keyword searches on remote encrypted data. In: Ioannidis J, Keromytis A, Yung M (eds) Applied cryptography and network security. Springer, Heidelberg, pp 442–455
6. Curtmola R, Garay J, Kamara S, Ostrovsky R (2006) Searchable symmetric encryption: improved definitions and efficient constructions. In: Proceedings of the 13th ACM conference on computer and communications security. ACM, pp 79–88
7. Golle P, Staddon J, Waters B (2004) Secure conjunctive keyword search over encrypted data. In: Jakobsson M, Yung M, Zhou J (eds) Applied cryptography and network security. Springer, Heidelberg, pp 31–45
8. Cash D, Jarecki S, Jutla C, Krawczyk H, Roşu M-C, Steiner M (2013) Highly-scalable searchable symmetric encryption with support for boolean queries. In: Canetti R, Garay JA (eds) Advances in cryptology–CRYPTO 2013. Springer, Heidelberg, pp 353–373
9. Adjedj M, Bringer J, Chabanne H, Kindarji B (2009) Biometric identification over encrypted data made feasible. In: Prakash A, Gupta IS (eds) Information systems security. Springer, Heidelberg, pp 86–100
10. Li J, Wang Q, Wang C, Cao N, Ren K, Lou W (2010) Fuzzy keyword search over encrypted data in cloud computing. In: Proceedings of INFOCOM 2010, IEEE, pp 1–5
11. Kamara S, Papamanthou C, Roeder T (2012) Dynamic searchable symmetric encryption. In: Proceedings of the 2012 ACM conference on computer and communications security. ACM, pp 965–976

12. Naveed M, Prabhakaran M, Gunter C (2014) Dynamic searchable encryption via blind storage. In: IEEE symposium on security and privacy (SP). IEEE, pp 639–654
13. Stefanov E, Papamanthou C, Shi E (2013) Practical dynamic searchable encryption with small leakage. IACR Cryptol ePrint Arch 2013:832
14. Boneh D, Di Crescenzo G, Ostrovsky R, Persiano G (2004) Public key encryption with keyword search. In: Cachin C, Camenisch J (eds) Advances in cryptology-Eurocrypt 2004. Springer, Heidelberg, pp 506–522
15. Abdalla M, Bellare M, Catalano D, Kiltz E, Kohno T, Lange T, Malone-Lee J, Neven G, Paillier P, Shi H (2005) Searchable encryption revisited: consistency properties, relation to anonymous IBE, and extensions. In: Shoup V (ed) Advances in cryptology–CRYPTO 2005. Springer, Heidelberg, pp 205–222
16. Boneh D, Waters B (2007) Conjunctive, subset, and range queries on encrypted data. In: Vadhan SP (ed) Theory of cryptography. Springer, Heidelberg, pp 535–554
17. Shi E, Bethencourt J, Chan TH, Song D, Perrig A (2007) Multi-dimensional range query over encrypted data. In: IEEE symposium on security and privacy (SP'07). IEEE, pp 350–364
18. Bao F, Deng RH, Ding X, Yang Y (2008) Private query on encrypted data in multi-user settings. In: Chen L, Mu Y, Susilo W (eds) Information security practice and experience. Springer, Heidelberg, pp 71–85
19. Agrawal R, Kiernan J, Srikant R, Xu Y (2004) Order preserving encryption for numeric data. In: Proceedings of the 2004 ACM SIGMOD international conference on management of data. ACM, pp 563–574
20. Boldyreva A, Chenette N, O'Neill A (2011) Order-preserving encryption revisited: improved security analysis and alternative solutions. In: Rogaway P (ed) Advances in cryptology–CRYPTO 2011. Springer, Heidelberg, pp 578–595
21. Mavroforakis C, Chenette N, O'Neill A, Kollios G, Canetti R (2015) Modular order-preserving encryption, Revisited. pp 763–777. doi:10.1145/2723372.2749455
22. Malkin T, Teranishi I, Yung M (2013) Order-preserving encryption secure beyond one-wayness. IACR Cryptol ePrint Arch 2013:409
23. Pandey O, Rouselakis Y (2012) Property preserving symmetric encryption. In: Pointcheval D, Johansson T (eds) Advances in cryptology–EUROCRYPT 2012. Springer, Heidelberg, pp 375–391
24. Boldyreva A, Chenette N, Lee Y, O'neill A (2009) Order-preserving symmetric encryption. In: Joux A (ed) Advances in cryptology-EUROCRYPT 2009. Springer, Heidelberg, pp 224–241
25. Xiao L, Yen I-L, Huynh D (2012) A note for the ideal order-preserving encryption object and generalized order-preserving encryption. IACR Cryptol ePrint Arch 2012:350
26. Popa RA, Li FH, Zeldovich N (2013) An ideal-security protocol for order-preserving encoding. In: IEEE symposium on security and privacy (SP). IEEE, pp 463–477
27. Chase M, Kamara S (2010) Structured encryption and controlled disclosure. In: Abe M (ed) Advances in cryptology-ASIACRYPT 2010. Springer, Heidelberg, pp 577–594
28. Kamara S, Wei L (2013) Garbled circuits via structured encryption. Springer, Heidelberg
29. Naor M, Reingold O (1995) Synthesizers and their application to the parallel construction of pseudo-random functions. In: Proceedings of the 36th annual symposium on foundations of computer science. IEEE, pp 170–181
30. Poh GS, Mohamad MS, Z'aba MR (2012) Structured encryption for conceptual graphs. In: Hanaoka G, Yamauchi T (eds) Advances in information and computer security. Springer, Heidelberg, pp 105–122
31. Mohamad MS, Poh GS (2013) Verifiable structured encryption. In: Kutylowski M, Yung M (eds) Information security and cryptology. Springer, Heidelberg, pp 137–156
32. Kurosawa K, Ohtaki Y (2012) UC-secure searchable symmetric encryption. In: Keromytis AD (ed) Financial cryptography and data security. Springer, Heidelberg, pp 285–298
33. Gentry C (2009) Fully homomorphic encryption using ideal lattices. In: STOC. pp 169–178
34. Van Dijk M, Gentry C, Halevi S, Vaikuntanathan V (2010) Fully homomorphic encryption over the integers. In: Gilbert H (ed) Advances in cryptology–EUROCRYPT 2010. Springer, Heidelberg, pp 24–43

35. Brakerski Z, Vaikuntanathan V (2011) Fully homomorphic encryption from ring-LWE and security for key dependent messages. In: Rogaway P (ed) Advances in cryptology–CRYPTO 2011. Springer, Heidelberg, pp 505–524

36. Gentry C, Halevi S (2011) Fully homomorphic encryption without squashing using depth-3 arithmetic circuits. In: IEEE 52nd annual symposium on foundations of computer science (FOCS). IEEE, pp 107–109

37. Gentry C, Sahai A, Waters B (2013) Homomorphic encryption from learning with errors: conceptually-simpler, asymptotically-faster, attribute-based. In: Canetti R, Garay JA (eds) Advances in cryptology–CRYPTO 2013. Springer, Heidelberg, pp 75–92

38. Brakerski Z, Gentry C, Vaikuntanathan V (2012) (Leveled) fully homomorphic encryption without bootstrapping. In: Proceedings of the 3rd innovations in theoretical computer science conference. ACM, pp 309–325

39. Aguilar-Melchor C, Fau S, Fontaine C, Gogniat G, Sirdey R (2013) Recent advances in homomorphic encryption: a possible future for signal processing in the encrypted domain. IEEE Signal Process Mag 30(2):108–117

40. Brakerski Z, Vaikuntanathan V (2014) Efficient fully homomorphic encryption from (standard) LWE. SIAM J Comput 43(2):831–871

41. Gentry C, Halevi S (2011) Implementing Gentry's fully-homomorphic encryption scheme. In: Paterson KG (ed) Advances in cryptology–EUROCRYPT 2011. Springer, Heidelberg, pp 129–148

42. Fau S, Sirdey R, Fontaine C, Aguilar-Melchor C, Gogniat G (2013) Towards practical program execution over fully homomorphic encryption schemes. In: Eighth international conference on P2P, parallel, grid, cloud and internet computing (3PGCIC). IEEE, pp 284–290

43. Almutairi AA, Sarfraz MI, Basalamah S, Aref WG, Ghafoor A (2011) A distributed access control architecture for cloud computing. IEEE Softw 2:36–44

44. Hu VC, Grance T, Ferraiolo DF, Kuhn DR (2014) An access control scheme for big data processing. In: International conference on collaborative computing: networking, applications and worksharing (CollaborateCom). IEEE, pp 1–7

45. Zeng W, Yang Y, Luo B (2013) Access control for big data using data content. In: IEEE international conference on big data. IEEE, pp 45–47

46. Oulmakhzoune S, Cuppens-Boulahia N, Cuppens F, Morucci S, Barhamgi M, Benslimane D (2014) Privacy query rewriting algorithm instrumented by a privacy-aware access control model. Ann Telecommun 69(1–2):3–19

47. Mazurek ML, Liang Y, Melicher W, Sleeper M, Bauer L, Ganger GR, Gupta N, Reiter MK (2014) Toward strong, usable access control for shared distributed data. In: Proceedings of the 12th USENIX conference on file and storage technologies. USENIX Association, pp 89–103

48. Li H, Wang S, Tian X, Wei W, Sun C (2015) A survey of extended role-based access control in cloud computing. In: Proceedings of the 4th international conference on computer engineering and networks. Springer, pp 821–831

49. Nabeel M, Shang N, Bertino E (2013) Privacy preserving policy-based content sharing in public clouds. IEEE Trans Knowl Data Eng 25(11):2602–2614

50. Sahai A, Waters B (2005) Fuzzy identity-based encryption. In: Cramer R (ed) Advances in cryptology–EUROCRYPT 2005. Springer, Heidelberg, pp 457–473

51. Goyal V, Pandey O, Sahai A, Waters B (2006) Attribute-based encryption for fine-grained access control of encrypted data. In: Proceedings of the 13th ACM conference on computer and communications security. ACM, pp 89–98

52. Ostrovsky R, Sahai A, Waters B (2007) Attribute-Based encryption with non-monotonic access structures. In: CCS Proceedings of ACM conference on computer & communications security

53. Yu S, Wang C, Ren K, Lou W (2010) Achieving secure, scalable, and fine-grained data access control in cloud computing. In: INFOCOM, 2010 Proceedings IEEE, pp 1–9

54. Bethencourt J, Sahai A, Waters B (2007) Ciphertext-policy attribute-based encryption. In: IEEE symposium on security and privacy (SP'07). IEEE, pp 321–334

55. Bobba R, Khurana H, Prabhakaran M (2009) Attribute-sets: a practically motivated enhancement to attribute-based encryption. In: Backes M, Ning P (eds) Computer security–ESORICS 2009. Springer, Heidelberg, pp 587–604

56. Hur J, Noh DK (2011) Attribute-based access control with efficient revocation in data outsourcing systems. IEEE Trans Parallel Distrib Syst 22(7):1214–1221

57. Wang G, Liu Q, Wu J (2010) Hierarchical attribute-based encryption for fine-grained access control in cloud storage services. In: Proceedings of the 17th ACM conference on computer and communications security. ACM, pp 735–737

58. Wan Z, Liu JE, Deng RH (2012) HASBE: a hierarchical attribute-based solution for flexible and scalable access control in cloud computing. IEEE Trans Inf Forensics Secur 7(2): 743–754

59. Ganjali A, Lie D (2012) Auditing cloud management using information flow tracking. In: Proceedings of the seventh ACM workshop on scalable trusted computing. ACM, pp 79–84

60. Pappas V, Kemerlis VP, Zavou A, Polychronakis M, Keromytis AD (2013) CloudFence: data flow tracking as a cloud service. In: Stolfo SJ, Stavrou A, Wright CV (eds) Research in attacks, intrusions, and defenses. Springer, Heidelberg, pp 411–431

61. Ateniese G, Burns R, Curtmola R, Herring J, Kissner L, Peterson Z, Song D (2007) Provable data possession at untrusted stores. In: Proceedings of the 14th ACM conference on computer and communications security. ACM, pp 598–609

62. Juels A, Kaliski Jr BS (2007) PORs: Proofs of retrievability for large files. In: Proceedings of the 14th ACM conference on computer and communications security. ACM, pp 584–597

63. Ateniese G, Di Pietro R, Mancini LV, Tsudik G (2008) Scalable and efficient provable data possession. In: Proceedings of the 4th international conference on security and privacy in communication networks. ACM, p 9

64. Erway CC, Küpçü A, Papamanthou C, Tamassia R (2015) Dynamic provable data possession. ACM Trans Inf Syst Secur (TISSEC) 17(4):15

65. Zhu Y, Hu H, Ahn G-J, Han Y, Chen S (2011) Collaborative integrity verification in hybrid clouds. In: 7th International conference on collaborative computing: networking, applications and worksharing (CollaborateCom). IEEE, pp 191–200

66. Zhu Y, Hu H, Ahn G-J, Yau SS (2012) Efficient audit service outsourcing for data integrity in clouds. J Syst Softw 85(5):1083–1095

67. Zhu Y, Wang H, Hu Z, Ahn G-J, Hu H (2011) Zero-knowledge proofs of retrievability. Sci China Inf Sci 54(8):1608–1617

68. Wang C, Wang Q, Ren K, Lou W (2010) Privacy-preserving public auditing for data storage security in cloud computing. In: INFOCOM, 2010 Proceedings IEEE, pp 1–9

69. Shacham H, Waters B (2008) Compact proofs of retrievability. In: Pieprzyk J (ed) Advances in cryptology-ASIACRYPT 2008. Springer, Heidelberg, pp 90–107

70. Wang Q, Wang C, Li J, Ren K, Lou W (2009) Enabling public verifiability and data dynamics for storage security in cloud computing. In: Backes M, Ning P (eds) Computer security– ESORICS 2009. Springer, Heidelberg, pp 355–370

71. Bowers KD, Juels A, Oprea A (2009) HAIL: a high-availability and integrity layer for cloud storage. In: Proceedings of the 16th ACM conference on computer and communications security. ACM, pp 187–198

72. Dodis Y, Vadhan S, Wichs D (2009) Proofs of retrievability via hardness amplification. In: Reingold O (ed) Theory of cryptography. Springer, Heidelberg, pp 109–127

73. Cash D, Küpçü A, Wichs D (2013) Dynamic proofs of retrievability via oblivious ram. In: Johansson T, Nguyen P (eds) Advances in cryptology–EUROCRYPT 2013. Springer, Heidelberg, pp 279–295

74. Stefanov E, van Dijk M, Juels A, Oprea A (2012) Iris: A scalable cloud file system with efficient integrity checks. In: Proceedings of the 28th annual computer security applications conference. ACM, pp 229–238

75. Shi E, Stefanov E, Papamanthou C (2013) Practical dynamic proofs of retrievability. In: Proceedings of the 2013 ACM SIGSAC conference on computer & communications security. ACM, pp 325–336

76. Yuan J, Yu S (2013) Proofs of retrievability with public verifiability and constant communi-cation cost in cloud. In: Proceedings of the 2013 international workshop on security in cloud computing. ACM, pp 19–26
77. Liu C, Chen J, Yang LT, Zhang X, Yang C, Ranjan R, Rao K (2014) Authorized public auditing of dynamic big data storage on cloud with efficient verifiable fine-grained updates. IEEE Trans Parallel Distrib Syst 25(9):2234–2244
78. Küpçü A (2010) Efficient cryptography for the next generation secure cloud: protocols, proofs, and implementation. Lambert Academic Publishing
79. Liu C, Ranjan R, Zhang X, Yang C, Georgakopoulos D, Chen J (2013) Public auditing for Big Data storage in cloud computing—a survey. In: 16th international conference on Computational Science and Engineering (CSE). IEEE, pp 1128–1135
80. Wei DS, Murugesan S, Kuo S-Y, Naik K, Krizanc D (2013) Enhancing data integrity and privacy in the cloud: an agenda. IEEE Comput 46(11):87–90
81. Aggarwal CC, Philip SY (2008) A general survey of privacy-preserving data mining models and algorithms. Springer
82. Samarati P, Sweeney L (1998) Generalizing data to provide anonymity when disclosing information. In: PODS. p 188
83. Machanavajjhala A, Kifer D, Gehrke J, Venkitasubramaniam M (2007) l-diversity: privacy beyond k-anonymity. ACM Trans Knowl Discov Data (TKDD) 1(1):3
84. Wong R, Li J, Fu A, Wang K (2009) (α, k)-anonymous data publishing. J Intell Inf Syst 33(2):209–234
85. Li NH, Li TC, Venkatasubramanian S(2007) t-closeness: privacy beyond k-anonymity and l-diversity. In: IEEE 23rd international conference on data engineering (ICDE 2007). IEEE, pp 106–115
86. Zhang Q, Koudas N, Srivastava D, Yu T (2007) Aggregate query answering on anonymized tables. In: IEEE 23rd international conference on data engineering (ICDE 2007). IEEE, pp 116–125
87. Martin DJ, Kifer D, Machanavajjhala A, Gehrke J, Halpern JY (2007) Worst-case background knowledge for privacy-preserving data publishing. In: IEEE 23rd international conference on data engineering (ICDE 2007). IEEE, pp 126–135
88. Li T, Li N (2008) Injector: mining background knowledge for data anonymization. In: IEEE 24th international conference on data engineering (ICDE 2008). IEEE, pp 446–455
89. Kisilevich S, Rokach L, Elovici Y, Shapira B (2010) Efficient multidimensional suppression for k-anonymity. IEEE Trans Knowl Data Eng 22(3):334–347
90. Matatov N, Rokach L, Maimon O (2010) Privacy-preserving data mining: a feature set partitioning approach. Inform Sci 180(14):2696–2720
91. Tassa T, Mazza A, Gionis A (2012) k-concealment: an alternative model of k-Type anonymity. Trans Data Priv 5(1):189–222
92. Dwork C (2011) Differential privacy. In: Encyclopedia of cryptography and security. Springer, Heidelberg, pp 338–340
93. Oh S, Viswanath P (2013) The composition theorem for differential privacy. Preprint. arXiv:13110776
94. Smith A (2011) Privacy-preserving statistical estimation with optimal convergence rates. In: Proceedings of the 43rd annual ACM symposium on theory of computing. ACM, pp 813–822
95. Le Ny J, Pappas GJ (2014) Differentially private filtering. IEEE Trans Autom Control 59(2):341–354
96. Lu W, Miklau G (2014) Exponential random graph estimation under differential privacy. In: Proceedings of the 20th ACM SIGKDD international conference on knowledge discovery and data mining. ACM, pp 921–930
97. Ji Z, Lipton ZC, Elkan C (2014) Differential privacy and machine learning: a survey and review. Preprint. arXiv:14127584
98. Barber RF, Duchi JC (2014) Privacy and statistical risk: formalisms and minimax bounds. Preprint, arXiv:14124451

99. Reed J, Pierce BC (2010) Distance makes the types grow stronger: a calculus for differential privacy. ACM Sigplan Not 45(9):157–168
100. Gaboardi M, Haeberlen A, Hsu J, Narayan A, Pierce BC (2013) Linear dependent types for differential privacy. In: ACM SIGPLAN Notices, vol 1. ACM, pp 357–370
101. McSherry FD (2009) Privacy integrated queries: an extensible platform for privacy-preserving data analysis. In: Proceedings of the 2009 ACM SIGMOD international conference on management of data. ACM, pp 19–30
102. Roy I, Setty ST, Kilzer A, Shmatikov V, Witchel E (2010) Airavat: security and privacy for MapReduce. NSDI 10:297–312
103. Barthe G, Köpf B, Olmedo F, Zanella Béguelin S (2012) Probabilistic relational reasoning for differential privacy. In: ACM SIGPLAN Notices, vol 1. ACM, pp 97–110
104. Soria-Comas J, Domingo-Ferrer J, Sanchez D, Martinez S (2013) Improving the utility of differentially private data releases via k-anonymity. In: 12th IEEE international conference on trust, security and privacy in computing and communications (TrustCom). IEEE, pp 372–379
105. He X, Machanavajjhala A, Ding B (2014) Blowfish privacy: tuning privacy-utility trade-offs using policies. In: Proceedings of the 2014 ACM SIGMOD international conference on management of data. ACM, pp 1447–1458
106. Singh S, Bawa S (2007) A privacy, trust and policy based authorization framework for services in distributed environments. Int J Comput Sci 2(2):85–92
107. Sherchan W, Nepal S, Paris C (2013) A survey of trust in social networks. ACM Comput Surv (CSUR) 45(4):47
108. Pawar PS, Rajarajan M, Nair SK, Zisman A (2012) Trust model for optimized cloud services. In: Dimitrakos T, Moona R, Patel D, McKnigh DH (eds) Trust management VI. Springer, Heidelberg, pp 97–112
109. Kannan J, Maniatis P, Chun B-G (2011) Secure data preservers for web services. In: Proceedings of the Second USENIX conference on web application development. pp 25–36
110. Raj H, Robinson D, Tariq TB, England P, Saroiu S, Wolman A (2011) Credo: trusted computing for guest VMs with a commodity hypervisor. Technical Report MSR-TR-2011-130, Microsoft Research
111. Santos N, Rodrigues R, Gummadi KP, Saroiu S (2012) Policy-sealed data: a new abstraction for building trusted cloud services. In: USENIX security symposium. pp 175–188
112. Krautheim FJ (2009) Private virtual infrastructure for cloud computing. In: Proceedings of HotCloud
113. Schiffman J, Moyer T, Vijayakumar H, Jaeger T, McDaniel P (2010) Seeding clouds with trust anchors. In: Proceedings of the 2010 ACM workshop on Cloud computing security workshop. ACM, pp 43–46
114. Santos N, Gummadi KP, Rodrigues R (2009) Towards trusted cloud computing. In: Proceedings of the 2009 conference on hot topics in cloud computing. San Diego, CA, pp 3–3
115. Adali S, Escriva R, Goldberg MK, Hayvanovych M, Magdon-Ismail M, Szymanski BK, Wallace W, Williams G (2010) Measuring behavioral trust in social networks. In: IEEE international conference on Intelligence and Security Informatics (ISI). IEEE, pp 150–152
116. Malik Z, Akbar I, Bouguettaya A (2009) Web services reputation assessment using a hidden Markov model. In: Bares L, Chi C-H, Suzuki J (eds) Service-oriented computing. Springer, Heidelberg, pp 576–591
117. Noor TH, Sheng QZ, Zeadally S, Yu J (2013) Trust management of services in cloud environments: obstacles and solutions. ACM Comput Surv (CSUR) 46(1):12
118. Jøsang A, Ismail R, Boyd C (2007) A survey of trust and reputation systems for online service provision. Decis Support Syst 43(2):618–644
119. Ferrer AJ, HernáNdez F, Tordsson J, Elmroth E, Ali-Eldin A, Zsigri C, Sirvent R, Guitart J, Badia RM, Djemame K (2012) OPTIMIS: a holistic approach to cloud service provisioning. Futur Gener Comput Syst 28(1):66–77
120. Hwang K, Kulkareni S, Hu Y (2009) Cloud security with virtualized defense and reputation-based trust management. In: Eighth IEEE international conference on dependable, autonomic and secure computing (DASC'09). IEEE, pp 717–722

121. Alhamad M, Dillon T, Chang E (2010) Sla-based trust model for cloud computing. In: 13th international conference on network-based information systems (NBiS). IEEE, pp 321–324
122. Jøsang A (2001) A logic for uncertain probabilities. Int J Uncertainty Fuzziness Knowledge Based Syst 9(03):279–311
123. Habib SM, Ries S, Mühlhäuser M, Varikkattu P (2014) Towards a trust management system for cloud computing marketplaces: using CAIQ as a trust information source. Secur Commun Netw 7(11):2185–2200
124. Ko RK, Lee BS, Pearson S (2011) Towards achieving accountability, auditability and trust in cloud computing. In: Abraham A et al (eds) Advances in computing and communications. Springer, Heidelberg, pp 432–444
125. Ko RK, Jagadpramana P, Mowbray M, Pearson S, Kirchberg M, Liang Q, Lee BS (2011) TrustCloud: A framework for accountability and trust in cloud computing. In: IEEE World Congress on Services (SERVICES). IEEE, pp 584–588
126. Toosi AN, Calheiros RN, Buyya R (2014) Interconnected cloud computing environments: challenges, taxonomy, and survey. ACM Comput Surv (CSUR) 47(1):7
127. Bernstein D, Vij D (2010) Intercloud security considerations. In: IEEE second international conference Cloud Computing Technology and Science (CloudCom). IEEE, pp 537–544
128. Abawajy J (2009) Determining service trustworthiness in intercloud computing environments. In: 10th international symposium on pervasive systems, algorithms, and networks (ISPAN). IEEE, pp 784–788
129. Celesti A, Tusa F, Villari M, Puliafito A (2010) How to enhance cloud architectures to enable cross-federation. In: IEEE 3rd international conference cloud computing (CLOUD). IEEE, pp 337–345
130. Yan Z, Zhang P, Vasilakos AV (2014) A survey on trust management for internet of things. J Netw Comput Appl 42:120–134
131. Govindan K, Mohapatra P (2012) Trust computations and trust dynamics in mobile adhoc networks: a survey. IEEE Commun Surv Tutorials 14(2):279–298
132. Sanger J, Richthammer C, Hassan S, Pernul G (2014) Trust and big data: a roadmap for research. In: 25th international workshop on database and expert systems applications (DEXA). IEEE, pp 278–282
133. Băsescu C, Carpen-Amarie A, Leordeanu C, Costan A, Antoniu G (2011) Managing data access on clouds: a generic framework for enforcing security policies. In: IEEE international conference on advanced information networking and applications (AINA). IEEE, pp 459–466
134. Neuman BC, Ts'O T (1994) Kerberos: an authentication service for computer networks. IEEE Commun Mag 32(9):33–38
135. Chang F, Dean J, Ghemawat S, Hsieh WC, Wallach DA, Burrows M, Chandra T, Fikes A, Gruber RE (2008) Bigtable: a distributed storage system for structured data. ACM Trans Comput Syst (TOCS) 26(2):4
136. Pattuk E, Kantarcioglu M, Khadilkar V, Ulusoy H, Mehrotra S (2013) Bigsecret: a secure data management framework for key-value stores. In: IEEE sixth international conference on cloud computing (CLOUD). IEEE, pp 147–154
137. Wei W, Du J, Yu T, Gu X (2009) Securemr: a service integrity assurance framework for mapreduce. In: Computer security applications conference (ACSAC'09). Annual. IEEE, pp 73–82
138. Mccarty B (2004) SELinux: NSA's open source security enhanced linux. Oreilly & Associates, Cambridge
139. Zhao J, Wang L, Tao J, Chen J, Sun W, Ranjan R, Kołodziej J, Streit A, Georgakopoulos D (2014) A security framework in G-Hadoop for big data computing across distributed cloud data centres. J Comput Syst Sci 80(5):994–1007
140. Ulusoy H, Kantarcioglu M, Pattuk E, Hamlen K (2014) Vigiles: fine-grained access control for mapreduce systems. In: 2014 IEEE international congress on big data (BigData Congress). IEEE, pp 40–47
141. Rahul P, GireeshKumar T (2015) A novel authentication framework for Hadoop. In: Artificial intelligence and evolutionary algorithms in engineering systems. Springer, pp 333–340

Chapter 9
Big Data Applications in Engineering and Science

Kok-Leong Ong, Daswin De Silva, Yee Ling Boo, Ee Hui Lim, Frank Bodi, Damminda Alahakoon, and Simone Leao

Abstract Research to solve engineering and science problems commonly require the collection and complex analysis of a vast amount of data. This makes them a natural exemplar of big data applications. For example, data from weather stations, high resolution images from CT scans, or data captured by astronomical instruments all easily showcase one or more big data characteristics, i.e., volume, velocity, variety and veracity. These big data characteristics present computational and analytical challenges that need to be overcame in order to deliver engineering solutions or make scientific discoveries. In this chapter, we catalogued engineering and science problems that carry a big data angle. We will also discuss the research advances for these problems and present a list of tools available to the practitioner. A number of big data application exemplars from the past works of the authors are discussed with further depth, highlighting the association of the specific problem and its big data characteristics. The overview from these various perspectives will provide the reader an up-to-date audit of big data developments in engineering and science.

K.-L. Ong (✉) • D. De Silva • D. Alahakoon
La Trobe Business School, ASSC, La Trobe University, Melbourne, Australia
e-mail: kok-leong.ong@latrobe.edu.au; d.desilva@latrobe.edu.au; d.alahakoon@latrobe.edu.au

Y.L. Boo
School of Business IT and Logistics, RMIT University, Melbourne, Australia
e-mail: yeeling.boo@rmit.edu.au

E.H. Lim • F. Bodi
Thiess Services Pty Ltd, 25-37 Huntingdale Road, Burwood, Victoria, Australia, 3125
e-mail: elim@thiess.com.au; fbodi@thiess.com.au

S. Leao
School of Built Environment, University of Salford, Lancashire, UK
e-mail: s.zarpelonleao@salford.ac.uk

© Springer International Publishing Switzerland 2016
S. Yu, S. Guo (eds.), *Big Data Concepts, Theories, and Applications*,
DOI 10.1007/978-3-319-27763-9_9

315

9.1 Introduction

There is no doubt that many fields of engineering and science are highly driven by data or have a lot of data that is ripe to be taken advantage of. The engineering and science domain is possibly one of the most immediate domain that comes to mind when discussing big data given the evidence-driven nature of these two fields. And as such, many of us easily find mentions of engineering and science applications as examples in the research literature or when the characteristics of big data is being discussed [40, 46, 55], i.e., volume, velocity, variety and occasionally, value or variability [118]. In fact on many occasions, the very problems in these fields often drive new innovations and not surprisingly, the same can be said for engineering and sciences' contribution to the advances in big data technologies.

There are now more sources of data than ever before (e.g., documents, websites, social media, IoT) and with more means to capture data (smartphones, sensors, RFID) too. What this means is that the sheer volume and complexities of the data has resulted in new developments, where different big data problems demand new solutions [16, 20, 95]. As the reader will discover in the discussion of this chapter, there are a lot of challenges and difficulties [3] in the areas of data capture, storage, searching, sharing, analysis, and visualisation. These challenges will need to be addressed in order to realise the value proposition posed by big data as a problem. This has led to some [42] calling big data in the specific area of engineering and science the "fourth science paradigm for scientific discoveries". The key idea is that the large amount of data that needs to be computed requires serious computing power [41] rooted in theory of distributed computing. By creating a large scalable computing framework, some believe that solutions can be found for problems in particle physics, bio-informatics, earth sciences, and so on.

This correlation of large amount of data and computing power is however simplistic. As noted in [46], the characteristics itself does not singularly define the complexity of the problem. It is also about the analysis required, and the amount of time one can afford to wait for the result. On the last point, this refers to both the (1) "window of opportunity" that the analytical insights is of value and (2) the amount of interaction a user needs with the analytical process in order to answer an analytical question. Ultimately, all these variables are to be considered before one can determine when there is a big data problem (and when it's not).

Interestingly when we restrict ourselves to just problems in engineering and science, the big data problem is a lot more pronounce and naturally it should be—these problems would push the limits of every variables that [46] has discussed, making engineering and science problems compelling big data exemplars. In this chapter, we aim to give a broad survey of the big data problems and solutions already reported in the existing literature. This informal audit of where the state-of-the-art is will provide the reader a clearer picture on the following

- Which areas of engineering and science have reported advances in the research literature;
- What type of big data problems have been investigated;

- What is available to a practitioner to solve big data problems (i.e., tools); and
- What are some exemplars of everyday engineering and science problems that face big data problems and thus, require big data solutions.

9.2 Big Data Advances in Engineering and Science

To provide a reasonable snapshot of the developments, we undertook a literature survey exercise using the key phrase "big data" across major digital libraries. The results are then manually refined by identifying literature that is deemed to belong to the engineering and science domains focusing on recent developments between 2013–2015 whenever possible. From this subset, we categorise them into various industries and listed a few representatives as shown in Fig. 9.1. Complementing this figure is an overview of the industries which will be discussed next and additional examples are listed in Fig. 9.1 under the "related articles" column. Flowing from this overview, we will discuss two specific problems that align with the theme of this book, i.e., weather forecasting and astronomical data analysis.

9.2.1 Overview

Urbanisation has caused issues, such as traffic congestion, energy consumption, and pollution. Zheng et al. [117] believe that urban computing will provide solutions to overcoming these issues through the big data that have been generated in cities. In fact urban computing connects urban sensing, data management, and data analytics into a recurrent process for an unobtrusive and continuous improvement of people's lives, city operation systems, and the environment. According to predictions, cities in the future will generate over 4.1 TB per day per square kilometre of urbanised land area by 2016. To address the data management aspect of this vision, Dobre and Xhafa [29] discussed CAPIM, a platform that automates the process of collecting and aggregating context information on a large scale. CAPIM integrates services designed to collect context data such as, location and a user's profile. It was used in the implementation of an intelligent transportation system (ITS) to assist users and city officials understand traffic problems in large cities.

Shi and Abdel-Aty [87] also studied the traffic problem where they proposed a microwave vehicle detection system (MVDS) used in an expressway network in Orlando. The purpose of MVDS is to reduce congestion and crash risk in the network. To achieve this, the system uses 275 detectors that spans 75 miles of the expressway network. These detectors are spaced less than 1 mile apart, with each generating a lot of data in real-time to the MVDS. Every minute, these detectors report comprehensive traffic flow parameters of each expressway lane. The dense deployment of the detection system on the scale of the expressway network presents a big data problem for the MVDS.

Industry	Examples of applications	Data types and examples	Related articles
Urbanization and city planning	Urbanization	This industry considers data from areas such as geographical, traffic, cell phone signals, commuting, environmental monitoring, economy and energy.	[117, 30]
	Pervasive computing	Data collected from RFID sensors, and annotation tools and also GPS/GIS.	[6]
	Geographical information systems (GIS)	Locational data prepared by ArcGIS 10.0.	[77]
Transportation	Transportation	Statistical data of city economy, construction, population, and different energy parameters.	[26, 35, 89, 103]
Environmental science	Earth	Locational and geospatial data.	[8, 41, 68, 94]
Computer engineering/science	Cloud and network	PeMS traffic datasets	[61, 74]
	Optimization	Data collected from UCI machine learning and gene microarray dataset.	[11]
	Pattern recognition	Data collected from FIMI and UCI repositories.	[60]
	Social networking	Textual data	[79, 83]
	Natural Language Processing (NLP)	Textual data	[2]
Electricity	Smart meter	Data appeared on the bills and consist of hourly measurements of energy consumption. Also some data about the buildings, the floor area and the year of construction were of particular interest for the present study.	[5, 87, 116]
	Electrical matters (e.g., pricing, Consumption pattern, Transformation)	German forecasting data	[45, 47, 65]
		Electricity information collected from smart meter of special transformer users of a city in Henan Province.	
Medical science and biology	Pharmacogenomics	Gene expression dataset	[36]
	Biology	Data generated through genome-wide association, transcriptome, epigenome, microbiome, and metabolome studies.	[17, 71]
	Healthcare	Locational attributes of disease data such as, m-Health, Google Earth.	[22, 52, 95]
	Genomics	Gene expression dataset	[10, 73, 75, 104]
	Patient monitoring	Data collected from medical and biological sensors. Electronic health information about an individual patient and also clinical dataset.	[19, 80, 81, 109]
Decision science	Business intelligence (BI)	Different sorts of data collected through surveys, observations, or interviews. Also data collected from digital devices such as Google glass, sensors and etc.	[37]
	Business analytics (BA)		[31]
Social science	Digital media	Textual and in general audio-visual data.	[66]
	Journalism		[34]

Fig. 9.1 Big data applications seen in the literature in areas of engineering and science

Away from roads and cities, climate researchers are also using more data than ever before to understand climate change. Steed et al. [92] for example has introduced a new system called exploratory data analysis environment (EDEN) to facilitate analysis of data from complex earth simulation. Using visual analytics, they showed that the large amount of simulation data can be better analyse to improve critical comprehension of earth system processes. Baumann et al. [8] meanwhile has addressed gaps in earth scientific data through a new data analysis engine call EarthServer. The data analysis engine enables large volume of data (from different data sources) to be assimilated and analysed in an ad-hoc manner using a peer network of data centres worldwide.

Among these data sources, text documents are increasingly becoming a prominent and important data source. As more organisations become interested in analysing the textual information they have either internally or from external outlets like social media, big data solutions for text analytics becomes necessary by the natural sheer volume of these documents and the amount of preprocessing required. Agerri et al. [2] showcase an example of developing a distributed architecture to scale up text analytics. Unlike basic parallel frameworks, it runs a complete chain of linguistic processors (NLP) on several virtual machines. This provides an interesting and nice complement to other massively parallel text processing systems that are no publicly available, such as YouTube's transcription and translation APIs.

In some cases, it is necessary to process textual data as a two-dimensional data set. To model textual data in this form, the issue of high-dimensionality and spareness in the data set needs to be dealt with. In some cases, evolutionary algorithms are required because of its superior exploration features for optimisation problems. Of course, evolutionary algorithms are a controversy in the context of big data, which suggest the exponential increase in the search complexity rendering a solution untenable. Nevertheless, it may not be time to write evolutionary algorithms off in the big data space just yet. Bhattacharya et al. [11] for example has reported an evolutionary algorithm with enhanced ability to deal with the problems of high dimensionality and sparseness of big data. In addition to an informed exploration of the solution space, this technique balances exploration and exploitation using a hierarchical multi-population approach.

In the electricity domain, the deployment of smart meters has created a new source of data that needs to be captured, managed and analysed. To handle this issue, a lightweight architecture capable of collecting an ever-increasing amount of meter data from various metering systems was proposed in [116]. The architecture is capable of cleaning, aggregating and analysing the smart meter data to support various smart-grid applications. To handle the big data aspect of the problem, high performance design such as concurrency processing techniques were implemented in the proposed prototype. Another big data application in this area is the management of peak load within a smart electricity grid [114]. The aim is to reduce peak-valley load difference and improve load rate effectively in the grid. The large amount of data is analysed in real-time to understand consumers' electricity usage patterns and the insights are then used to manage the peak load shift in real-time.

Last but not least, medical applications and remote monitoring technologies are increasing the volume of health data available for analysis. These remote medical and biological sensors emit information about individual patients and occurs at short interval resulting in a large amount of data quickly becoming available. With a lot of patients, the total amount of data to monitor quickly grows. More importantly, the data from these remote sensors are often only meaningful for a short period of time only, especially in areas of patient care. Big data solutions customised for such purposes are thus being studied. Paez et al. [75] for example used big data processing techniques to monitor vital signs for patients who are outdoors. The information is transmitted via a mobile phone that is paired with a Web-based system that captures and manages the patient data. The analytics behind then looks at the vital signs data triggering emergency alarms to the relevant care givers without delays that may be life-threatening. Similar works are also presented in [19, 22, 50].

In this overview, we briefly presented a breadth of big data problems across a range of engineering and science areas. This overview highlights the omni-presence of big data in everyday problems which we can expect a contribution of advances in the technology as solutions are built for these problems. To also align with the common theme present in this book, the next two sections discusses two problems in more detail: (1) weather forecasting and (2) astronomical data processing.

9.2.2 Weather Forecast

One very interesting science problem with big data characteristics is weather forecasting. More profound and impactful than it is immediately obvious to most, weather plays a significant role in many aspects of our lives. Bad weather for example affects the activities people undertake, creates traffic chaos, sways the consumers' purchase decision, affect energy consumption, and much more. When the weather conditions get severely worse, it can even cause serious damage to assets, the economy and ultimately, the loss of human lives. Extreme weather events such as the 2012 Hurricane Sandy has caused more than $50 billion in damages and left more than 8.5 million people without power [94]. These severe weather storms also took significant number of lives including the 2004 Sumatra, Indonesia tsunami that tallied more than 230,000 deaths; more recently in 2011, the loss of more than 18,000 lives from the tsunami event at the north pacific coast of Japan.[1]

To avoid or minimise the impact that these weather events can cause, simulation models are developed to forecast the weather in the future, e.g., [1, 59, 101]. With increased and improved data collection capabilities and access to powerful computers, weather modelling is now significantly more accurate and predicts weather conditions further into the future than before. From the data perspective, we now have more data and more variables available to include for analysis. Apart from the data collected by weather stations, we now have access to satellite data about the earth's electro-magnetic radiation, and also temperature and wind data (direction and speed) from airplanes. Combine these with historical data from model simulations, environmental measurements, historical damage and outage data, etc., it is not hard appreciate the impact of volume characteristics in weather modelling and simulation. One of the more recent and ambitious weather research project by [65] talks about data volume in the exa-scale range with up to 10,240 ensemble data sets for running complex simulations on powerful computers with the aim to model weather changes down to 30 second-interval resolutions. Such fine resolution modelling is important as severe weather such as a tsunami event could develop deliver a full impact in less than 10 min.

Besides the opportunity to run large scale complex simulations, researchers in the last decade have explored the use of weather data to develop predictive models using machine learning and data mining techniques. In [109] for example, satellite remote

---

[1]http://goo.gl/lxuUib.

sensing images were used to forecast the presence of heavy rainfall using a custom spatial data mining technique. The system identifies the correlations and causalities between mesoscale convective systems (MCS) and possible heavy rainfall occurrences, yielding results that are up-to-date and consistent for forecasting. This was something that meteorologists were unable to do because of the sheer volume of remote sensing data sets that they have to manually go through—a process that was referred to as "expert-eye-scanning" technique. And because the analysis rely on the expertise of the individual, the forecast can also be inconsistent.

While [109] uses analytics to reduce analysis time and improve forecast consistency, [100] explore the use of machine learning techniques to improve forecast accuracy. The traditional way to improve accuracy is to create a localised weather forecast model (usually a regression model) by considering a subset of the data relevant to a given region. This means considering only data such as air temperature, moisture, surface pressure and wind in the spatial locality where the forecast is to be made. Most weather prediction centres produces this localised regression model for forecast using a technique call 'statistical downscaling". To improve forecast accuracy, neural networks or fuzzy logic could be used to learn the data points following a statistical downscale. These machine learning approaches improve forecast accuracy because of their inherent ability to deal with the natural uncertainty and randomness of weather patterns. In fact, [18] went further by creating a custom solution that uses both neural networks and fuzzy logic to achieve an even higher accuracy!

As computational power increases and access to more data sources become viable with the presence of sensor networks, forecasters can now increasingly work through more data than ever to create highly accurate forecast models. As this accuracy is being achieved, the development heads into forecasting further ahead into the future. This is now possible because the analysis is been made possible with big data technologies. EarthRisk Technologies[2] for example touts its ability to develop predictive models that can forecast weather up to 40 days in advance.[3] In this case, the model is created from over 82 billion calculations and 60 years of weather data.

It isn't hard to appreciate how some refer to weather data as one of the original big data problems. According to Information Week,[4] the national oceanic and atmospheric administration (NOAA) collects over 80 TB of data each day (velocity), with these data coming from various sources (variety) including different sensors, models and historical data sets. So to analyse all that data over a period of time, the amount of processing that we are looking at is massive (volume). Nevertheless, the importance of tackling this big data problem is obvious for the reasons already mentioned above but the motivation goes beyond just the prevention of asset or live losses.

---

[2]http://earthrisktech.com.

[3]http://goo.gl/jJ8Qr.

[4]http://goo.gl/S2bxQ0.

Increasingly, knowing how the weather will behave allows companies to know how their consumers may behave because weather has a proven influence on *purchase psychology*. This knowledge simply reflects the well known case where "stores sell hot soups and umbrellas on a cold wet day". More importantly, knowing how a weather may turn out the following day means businesses can now forecast what they sell, how much both in terms of quantity and price to sell, and ultimately maximise business opportunities both in the physical world and also the online world. It also means that an insurance company will be able to price their premiums profitably, and that road authorities can better prepare for bad weather conditions that cause traffic chaos. Construction companies can better schedule work while energy companies can forecast energy demand that in turn, allow fund managers to play the futures market accordingly (e.g., buying and selling of gas for heating).

9.2.3 Big Universe, Big Data

Long before the terms such as "big data" and "data science" comes into discussion, astronomy scientists have been collecting large amounts of astronomical data and trying to analyse it [80]. In fact, it is possibly one of the domains where data was acquired far more rapidly than the rate at which the collective group of scientists can analyse. With advances in technology, this problem is likely to become more acute. To give an idea of how fast astronomical data is growing, consider when the Sloan digital sky survey (SDSS[5]) project that first started in 2000. Within the first few weeks of its commission, it has collected more data than all data collected in the history of astronomy. By 2016 when the large synoptic survey telescope (LSST[6]) becomes operational, it will just take less than a week to amass the amount of data that took the SDSS 15 years to achieve.[7] The rate and amount of data that these equipment generates comfortably reflect the big data characteristics of volume, velocity and variety, e.g., images, optical spectra, infrared spectra, etc.

Astronomy scientists collect this massive amount of data for one purpose. That is to search for answers to the questions they have about the universe. If indeed the answers is to be found in the data, then the next question is "how to process them quickly, at least in pace with the rate at which they are collected". For a long time, astronomy scientists have this big data problem. They have more data than their computers can ever process fast enough. Before big data solutions, scientists have sought to tap into massive amount of computing power from expensive super-computers to 'free' distributed computing via public participation

---

[5]http://www.sdss.org.

[6]http://www.lsst.org.

[7]http://www.economist.com/node/15557443.

(e.g., SETI@home project,[8] which uses internet-connected computers to analyse radio telescope data to find extra-terrestrial intelligence).

The bulk of big data tools will simply provide an alternative form of access to large amount of computing power but it is the 'built-in' machine learning and data mining components in big data products that is likely to change the way astronomy scientists analyse the data they already have [47]. For example, the big data setup to analyse the astronomical data could run a clustering algorithm to identify star clusters and super-clusters, and then a classification algorithm to tag these clusters as Types I or II supernovae, Types I or II Cepheid variable stars, etc. Other examples include the search for special objects or rare phenomena that is of interest to astronomy scientists [31], classification of solar activities, regression models for stellar physical parameter measurement, and more. For readers interested in a good recent overview of the various applications of analytics to astronomical data, we recommend [13, 113] to the reader. Of course, other examples of applications of analytics can also be found in [4, 98, 115].

Besides the core analytics that big data tools have, the ability for scientists to interact with the data is equally important. After all, the analytics and processing done in the backend is worthless unless the results are conveyed to the scientists via visualisation and interaction with the model such that insights are then discovered. Research wise, a lot of focus has been on the multi-dimensionality of astronomical data sets. This includes scalable visualisation techniques (e.g., [74]), user interface design [27] as well as feature reduction [115]. In fact, so much of these works revolve around data that within the study of astronomy, a new branch of research call "Astroinformatics" has emerged. Researchers in this area tout it as a new discipline that will drive research to address the challenges of processing large amounts of data coming quickly from next generation telescopes. Borne et al. [14] suggests that it should be seen as another recognised research methodology within astronomy to the likes of bioinformatics.

Since then, we are seeing new outlets sharing new advances in this area. Some relevant to the theme of this chapter includes Schutter and Shamir's [82] work on using unsupervised machine learning to learn the similarities between galaxy morphological types and to automatically deduce the morphological sequence of galaxies. This work is interesting in the sense that it combines computer vision with a custom-built quantitative method that evaluates similarity using an algorithm call *Weighted Nearest Distance* to deduce the network similarities between the different morphological types in galaxy images. It's an exemplar of how big data analytics can potentially achieve the level of analysis that human experts are unable to do so efficiently. This is because morphological analysis has been carried out mostly through visual inspection by trained experts and so, does not scale to a large number of galaxy images. A different approach undertaken in [28] is to develop a deep neural network model for the task. By exploiting translational and rotational

---

[8]http://setiathome.ssl.berkeley.edu.

symmetry, their model was able to achieve a high degree of accuracy. The model is then deployed to only forward challenging images to the experts for manual analysis.

From what we have seen in the literature, we see that a lot of the work in this area focused on the initial phase of making the data collected available in a manageable fashion to the scientist. For example, the high resolution images from the telescopes isn't exactly what concerns scientists but rather it is the information embedded in those high resolution images that scientists want to know about that matters. The state of the art in this area this focus on how big data analytics will help manage that "information overload", such as the examples mentioned above where morphological sequences in images are extracted and analysed for the scientists. It's such information that will enable scientists to discover what we do not yet know about the universe. As "astroinformatics" continues to gain momentum, we can expect the nuggets of insights extracted today to become the building blocks for making discoveries tomorrow.

9.3 Data Management and Analytics for Engineering and Science

Having covered the research literature, it is also worthwhile to undertake an audit of what big data products are available for adoption in practice. In this section, we will present a brief discussion of the first generation big data tools where most of the products outlined in appendix are developed from. This list is compiled in such a ways that it also categorises products according to their relevance within the KDD process (i.e., selection, preprocessing, transformation, data mining, interpretation/evaluation). For the practitioner, this list will be useful in helping identify key products to start working with depending on the KDD task at hand.

Before data can be analysed, it needs to be captured in storage. There have been studies into whether commercial relational database management systems are suitable for processing extremely large amount of data [49]. Besides the volume factor, there is also the need to deal with new data types beyond the structured data sets brought about by ER data models. This motivated the need for NoSQL (short for *not only SQL*). NoSQL is clearly non-relational so it handles unstructured data sets as a complement to the RDBMS. A key design characteristics of the NoSQL is its flexible schema allowing data of different formats to be captured and managed. Common formats of NoSQL databases include key-value pairs, column oriented, graph oriented, or document oriented stores [12]. The very first version of NoSQL was offered as an open-source solution but there are now many commercial versions available with its own enhancements.

From the storage, data can then be retrieved for processing. In the big data suite of tools, the most well-known would be the Hadoop framework implementing the MapReduce setup over a computer cluster. As a framework, Hadoop presents a suite of components including programs, tools, connection utilities, etc., to enable distributed processing of massive amount of data. Hadoop is optimised for adjacent read requests (streaming reads), where each element needs to be processed in the same way (e.g., applying the same operation over every data element). As a result, the total compute time depends on the complexity of each operation, the volume of data and the time window where all the data must finish its processing. Fortunately balancing these factors is easily achieved within the MapReduce model, allowing massive scalability to be achieved [89] by simply adding more compute nodes performing the same operation to cater to the volume of the data. The simplicity of the Hadoop framework quickly gained extensions to improve its massive processing capabilities. G-Hadoop [102] for example, allows MapReduce tasks to run on different clusters while HaoLap [90] integrates Hadoop and online analytical processing (OLAP) executing OLAP operations on the MapReduce framework to allow OLAP operations on massive amount of data.

Of course, not everyone will have access to a dedicated distributed computing infrastructure. Hence, cloud providers for these services would be ideal. OpenNebula, OpenStack and Eucalyptus [96] are examples of cloud-based computing tools that provisions the big data infrastructure required by ad-hoc users. OpenNebula [105] is an open source project aimed at building an industry standard open source cloud computing tool. OpenNebula manages the complexity and heterogeneity of large and distributed infrastructures and offers a lot of rich features, flexibility and better interoperability to build private, public or hybrid clouds. OpenStack is similar to OpenNebula but it is a collection of open source software project instead. Lastly, we have Eucalyptus [68] which is another similar cloud computing framework but is commonly available to academia for experimental instrumentation and study.

Besides these generic infrastructures, there are also domain specifics such as the one proposed by Kramer and Senner [53], which is a commercial software architecture for processing of large-volume geospatial data in the cloud. Another example is a new tool for traffic information mining, called RTIC-C [112]. It builds on top of Hadoop and HBase by adding specific traffic mining applications and providing a RESTful web services to support third party integration. These extensions from private vendors over the open source versions will deliver new features and improvements, leading to the products we see in appendix. Such transitions represent the maturity of the research in big data, with the technology transferring over to the industry as commercial products. This change is important for the technology to reach critical mass and for many customers who already have data in established RDBMS, they would expect their vendor to provide that natural transition to accessing big data technologies.

9.4 Application Exemplars

As research outcomes get commercialised into big data products, the next step is the adoption of these tools by "everyday problems" so as to reach big data ubiquity. In this section, we present three big data exemplars that are projects that the authors have worked on previously. While some are not on the same grand scale to the likes of analysing extraterrestrial signals in massive TB of data, they represent the problems that could benefit from big data technologies. Hopefully by showcasing these applications, we will motivate readers to adopt big data solutions on a wider range of problems.

9.4.1 Clinical Decision Support

The need to acquire, manage and analyse healthcare big data is becoming commonplace in clinical decision-support (CDS). Financial savings, quality assurance, workflow optimisation, error prevention, facilitation of best practices and clinical research are some of the major benefits of big data management and analytics in CDS. This exemplar will explore the complexities of applying big data analytics to healthcare data, propose a solution to address these complexities and review outcomes generated by the solution.

CDS has evolved from medical data processing tools to complex decision support frameworks and infrastructure for clinical knowledge management. Two prominent taxonomies for CDS architectures are presented in [83, 108]. Wright and Sittig [108] define architecture as the form of interaction between related systems, with four distinct CDS phases; standalone, integrated, standards-based and the service model. The phases are evolutionary but it is not uncommon to find systems from the first phase in contemporary clinical environments. Standalone systems would take clinical parameters as input and make suggestions of diagnoses or therapy; they were confined to a single area of medicine. In the integration phase CDS were incorporated into clinical information systems (CIS) resulting in proactive systems with more streamlined data entry. The requirements of inter-organisational and government policy-driven information exchange led to the next phase, the use of standards to represent, encode, store and share clinical knowledge. The more recent phase, the service model, separates CIS from CDS and provides interfaces for communication between the two. This allows a broad range of information interchange possibilities across departments and even hospitals, as well as other organisations concern. Despite obvious challenges and the need for agreed standards for information exchange, such a model also provides wide opportunities for further clinical knowledge creation through data analytics from various sources while recognising multi-dimensionality of the users. Sen et al. [83] explore CDS architectures in the context of the underlying technology. The authors highlight the need for an overarching architecture that integrates three existing architectures. These three, which are identified in terms of the underlying technology, are information management, data analytics and knowledge management. Convergence into a single overarching architecture is further justified as it can then address many of the grand challenges of CDS stated in [88].

This convergence of CDS is largely driven by the generation/accumulation of big data and the increasing need to incorporate big data analytics (BDA) outcomes into the healthcare decision-making process. Granular data accumulation, temporal abstraction, multimodality, unstructured data and integration of multi-source data are complexities to the application of BDA to healthcare data. These complexities (presented below) will be explored bottom-up so that low-level explanations contribute to understanding of high-level requirements.

Granular data accumulation   A variety of clinical information systems capture patient information, ranging from a patient demographic record on a desktop application to cardiac monitors in an emergency room. This information exists at different levels of granularity, in diverse formats and recorded at varying frequency. For instance, sensor readings from a cardiac monitor are well-defined in terms of grain, format and frequency, however blood glucose measurements, although in the same format, can vary in terms of grain and frequency. A patient can record blood glucose levels at different times during the day when at home whereas a clinic may capture a single measurement but derive a different measure (glycated haemoglobin) to determine the three month average. This difference in granularity can be an extra dimension of information for BDA when paired with medication, demographic or behavioural information. Another example is recording medication information along with medical imaging. BDA can be used to identify changes in medical images and relate these to changes in medications or dosage. BDA is not limited by volume, velocity or variety so it is pertinent to capture and accumulate information at all levels of granularity.

Granular data accumulation also extends to capturing outcomes and feedback. Outcomes from a specific exercise routine, dietary modifications or change of medication needs to be captured and recorded. Completeness of medical data from start to end of the patient lifecycle is crucial for successful BDA in translational research. It is equally important to capture patient feedback as this reflects their own experience of the medical condition. BDA can be used to identify associations between outcomes, feedback, symptoms, medication and behavioural changes but the quality of the findings is heavily dependent on the completeness of the data accumulated.

Temporal abstraction   Time and granularity are the key dimensions for patient information collected over time. Temporal abstraction (TA) is defined [84] as a process which takes in a set of time-stamped parameters, external events and abstraction goals to generate abstractions of the data to be used for interpretation of past/present data. The intention is to transform temporal data from a simple, numerical form to informative and qualitative descriptions which can be understood by clinicians. A comprehensive review of techniques used in clinical data analysis systems was presented in [91]. They highlight several inadequacies, such as confinement to temporal trends and level shifts, limited dimensionality of abstraction output and lack of integration with other analysis outcomes. Complex TA is a further development to represent higher-level abstractions not directly from the data but from intermediate TA outcomes. Keravnou [51] defines complex TAs as compound time objects with a repeating element, a repeating pattern and progression pattern, where the repeating element itself could be periodic. Bellazzi et al. [9] developed a complex TA in the domain of diabetes monitoring to detect two overlapping interval abstractions and also the successive increase and decrease of blood glucose levels. Another well-researched approach to complex TAs is to represent the changing nature of a timer series using characters and words as symbols. Sharshar et al. [86] separated a data stream into trend and stability for each data point and applied rules to convert the signal into transient, decrease, increase or constant categories. A further abstraction was applied when individual characters, defining the state of the signal, are merged to form words. These 'words' can be mined for clinically relevant associations and projections. TA and complex TA effectuate summarisation of highly granular data to abstract clinically relevant representations recorded over time for conventional data mining techniques. However with the advent of BDA the clinical knowledge embedded into TA of the same becomes equally useful to navigate the large space of granular data accumulation.

Multimodality   Multiple contexts/modes can be found in a clinical environment to represent and also identify a patient. Modes such as demography, behaviour, symptoms, diagnosis, blood-gas measurements and medication are indicative of the patient's condition, disease trajectory and future well-being. CDS greatly benefits from this multimodal representation of the patient's state. Capturing the multiple modes of an entire sample of patients is an equally rich resource for inference and prediction in translational research. Multimodality in business analytics is frequently addressed by data warehousing technologies. Despite its prevalence in many industries, its adoption by medical organisations has been limited. Early implementations of clinical data warehousing (CDW) were aimed at solving specific clinical problems. There are still a few recent case studies that demonstrate the applicability of data warehouse concept in medical domain. For example, [107] describe the use of a data warehouse for hospital infection control. It was populated with data from three hospitals and demonstrated to be useful for measurement of antimicrobial resistance, antimicrobial use, the cost of infections, and detection of antimicrobial prescribing errors. Chute et al. [23] present a review of the Enterprise Data Trust at the Mayo Clinic, which is a collection of all electronic data organised to support information management, analytics and high-level decision-making. In recent research endeavours, [44, 62] have proposed and implemented data warehousing solutions to address the information needs of translational research. Hu et al. [44] developed a data warehouse integrating pathology and molecular data with a clinical data model to support a breast cancer translational research program. STRIDE (Stanford Translational Research Integrated Database Environment) is an informatics platform for clinical and translational research. It consists of a data management system, a CDW and a development framework for new applications. The complexity with healthcare data arises when designing a suitable dimensional model to encompass the variety of information (demographic to clinical) and type of information (structured and unstructured) accumulated.

Unstructured data   Healthcare data is inundated with unstructured content consisting mainly of textual records ranging from clinician comments to patient feedback. Textual records of this nature can exist at all levels of granularity noted earlier. Patient feedback can be collected before and after a surgery, during a period of new medication or a behavioural change. In addition to text, other unstructured formats include images, audio/video recordings and associative datasets. Given the inherent structure of the discipline, a majority of clinical text can be associated with well-formed ontologies. However, textual records received from patients need to be interpreted using a trusted knowledge base. The design and development of such a user-warrant ontology becomes a complex task given the variety of terms that can be used to refer to medical conditions and symptoms. Nguyen et al. [67] and Prakasa and Silva [77] have studied the extraction of an ontology from end-user feedback in healthcare. Many of the big data technologies have been developed to address the complexities of unstructured data. The central data models are key-value pair (KVP), column family stores, document databases and graph databases [21]. The lack of a fixed schema makes these data models flexible and scalable, however they do not follow standard properties found in relational databases. Each type of unstructured data can be analysed independently for patterns of interest, however complexities arise when outcomes from such disparate sources needs to be integrated, in part or whole.

Information fusion This is a widely researched field as seen in [15] who surveyed many definitions for information fusion in order to propose their own. According to Bostrm et al.'s [15] definition, it an efficient method for automatically or semi-automatically transforming information from different sources and different points in time into a representation that provides effective support for human or automated decision making. Focus is largely on the transformation of information, which includes means for combining and aggregating to infer as well as reduce information. Much research has been conducted on multi-sensor fusion [52], image fusion [37] and web information fusion [111]. Independently, intelligent fusion techniques have been developed based on post-perceptual integration phenomena [97] and cross-modal influence strategy [24]. In healthcare, levels of granularity and the temporal factor need to be well-aligned with the purpose of information fusion. Structured and unstructured healthcare data accumulated at different levels of granularity will be processed by BDA within the mutually exclusive modals to generate analytics outcomes. Although these outcomes are beneficial on their own, they can be further fused to create a comprehensive account of a patient (for clinical decision support) or a medical condition (for translational research). The computational requirements of such large-scale information fusion can be efficiently handled by big data technologies, however the complexities of the data model for effective information fusion is largely unaddressed.

A prototypical trial was conducted on data accumulated by the diabetes screening complications research initiative (DiScRi) run at a regional Australian university [48]. It is a diabetes complications screening program in Australia where members of the general public participate in a comprehensive health review. The screening clinic has been collecting data for over 10 years and includes close to a hundred

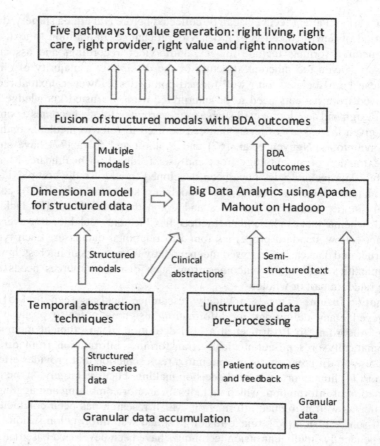

Fig. 9.2 Big data analytics (BDA) solution—the diabetes screening complications research initiative (DiScRi) experiment

features including demographics, socio-economic variables, education background, clinical variables such as blood pressure, body-mass-index (BMI), kidney function, sensori-motor function as well as blood glucose levels, cholesterol profile, pro-inflammatory markers, oxidative stress markers and use of medication. The dataset is reflective of typical big data accumulation in a clinical environment to be used for both clinical decision support and translational research. Figure 9.2 illustrates the solution used to address the stated complexities to BDA.

At the lowest layer, data is accumulated at varied grains. High level data such as patient demographics and diagnosis are recorded by medical practitioners while low level blood glucose measurements, blood pressure, body mass index and others are recorded by lab technicians at the screening clinic and by patients and carers in their own homes. Structured data is maintained in a relational database while unstructured data, mainly free-flow text such as patient feedback and clinician notes, is saved in flat files. Clinical scientists derive standard statistics (patient numbers, average age, average clinician visits etc.) from the granular data for routine reporting. In the secondary layer, time-series data is fed into temporal abstraction techniques in order to embed clinical knowledge into the sequence of data points. Blood pressure recordings, blood glucose levels and sensori-motor function data are transformed in this manner. Free flow text is pre-processed to a format suitable for analysis; stop word removal, lemmatisation and named entity recognition are conducted in this phase. Optionally, a verified ontology as specified by Nguyen et al. [67] and Prakasa and Silva [77] can be used to add context to patient comments and feedback. The third layer consists of two functions, dimensional modelling and the actual BDA. Temporal abstraction generates structured information with embedded clinical knowledge. This inherent structure can be captured in a dimensional model and implemented as a data warehouse.

BDA is the second function. The primary input is semi-structured text data containing patient feedback and clinician notes. Clinical abstractions and granular data form the secondary input. The analytics outcomes from BDA range from clustering, classification, association rules, predictions, summarisation and visualisation. This primary output is fused with the outputs from clinical abstractions and models of structured information. For instance, the association of patient age with feedback provided can be understood by fusing the BDA outcome with the demographic dimension in the warehouse. Similarly, fusion of other structured with the unstructured information leads to expedient insights on patients and their conditions. These insights can lead to the five pathways of value generation in healthcare, right living, right care, right provider, right value and right innovation [38].

The nature of data and expectations of the healthcare professional has led to complexities when developing BDA in a clinical context. This exemplar showcase the key information challenges of a modern science problem and presented a potential solution for Diabetes screening. The fusion of structured and unstructured big data is a major challenge in a breadth of applications and is likely to be an issue of interest to the research community and practitioners in the short to medium term as more turn towards building a BDA platform.

9.4.2   Managing the Life Cycle Replacement Program for Telecommunication Power Systems Equipment

Telecommunication technology has revolutionised almost all aspect of human development history. Both individuals and organisations rely heavily on telecommunication technology for daily activities such as withdrawing cash from ATM, calling someone with mobile phone, completing online business transactions, and so on. Consequently, it would be 'catastrophic' for many if telecommunication failed because of power loss to the transmission and network equipment. To ensure reliability, telecommunication operators typically ensure redundant backup power supply (e.g., backup generator, standby batteries or Uninterruptible Power Supply) are available to the critical systems to ensure stable power availability during mains outage. It is vital for the operators to ensure that the telecommunication infrastructures are able to provide services that are constantly connected, reliable and excellent for supporting daily operations. Undoubtedly, the most important physical asset to telecommunication operators is their infrastructure. It is an expensive business as a high capital expenditure (CAPEX) is required not only the expansion of telecommunication networks but also the maintenance and management of the life cycle replacement program for network and power equipment.

Silcar/Thiess is an Australia-based company that manages and operates the telecommunication power assets for telecommunication operators. The company manages around one million lead-acid battery cells in telecommunications service comprising more than 300 different types of makes and models and around 100,000 rectifier modules comprising more than 200 rectifier types. The lead-acid battery cells are the major component of the telecommunication power backup system, which provide power to the network and transmission equipment during any mains outage or power equipment failure. Given the many types of facilities (e.g., exchange buildings, mobile huts and shelters, roadside cabinets and customer installations), their environment across vast geographic distribution (e.g., in metropolitan and regional areas with different climate conditions, different housing types—underground *vs* air-conditioned *vs* non-air-conditioned building), the complexity generated in managing replacement decisions is considerable. Moreover, the replacement decision-making process is complex and difficult due to information overload and is made worse by the variety of data being generated on a regular basis. This irregular emission of data results in a high volume, high velocity and inevitably a low veracity data source. The penalty of not addressing this complexity manifests at one end of the scale as reduced network reliability and at the other, as increased CAPEX costs. Therefore, it is imperative to leverage the data collected for addressing the complexity of replacement decisions as well as for designing an effective and preventive policy tailored for life cycle replacement.

9.4.2.1 The Complexity of Telecommunications Data

To contextualise the scenario of what type of data and how certain data is collected or generated at Silcar/Thiess, a typical business process or workflow involving field data collection is depicted in Fig. 9.3. The replacement decisions are made based on one of the input data sources, namely field data source, which is recorded by field technicians mainly during preventive maintenance and reactive maintenance. Preventive maintenance is "scheduled maintenance" in which normal performance data from battery and rectifier modules is collected periodically. Specifically, field technicians will conduct discharge testing to determine the degradation of battery capacity and/or collect conductance measurements. In addition, any defects on battery and rectifier modules picked up by field technicians during preventive maintenance are also recorded. Reactive maintenance arises from ad-hoc requests

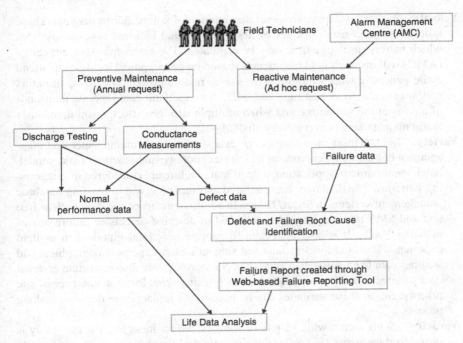

Fig. 9.3 The business process or workflow of field technicians for field data collection

that are system generated lodgements at the alarm management centre. Issues such as loss of mains supply may be noted in defect reports and recorded. Such reactive maintenance may be undertaken many times for each system. It is a mandatory requirement for field technicians to create failure reports for defective equipment through a web-based failure reporting tool. Subsequently, life data analysis for battery is performed based on the input data sources from field data originated from full discharge testing and failure reporting.

With the challenges encountered from the management perspective and also the complexity of data generated or collected in a typical business process or workflow, the complexity of data in Silcar/Thiess exhibits big data properties.

Volume There are about one million battery cells as part of the power system network that supply to the telecommunication equipment in which data such as date of manufacture, date of install, manufacture make/model, battery type, installation housing type, environmental control option, etc., are required for asset modelling and for optimised replacement policy. Millions of data points are also collected annually from preventative maintenance which includes the end of discharge voltage, discharge time, conductance values, float voltage and temperature for each battery cell. In the data warehouse, there are hundreds of GB of data collected, which are used by different stakeholders throughout Silcar/Thiess. In addition, there are new systems added to the database as the telecommunication network grows.

Velocity   Battery systems may generate a number of failure alarms per year. These failure alarms consist of a set of alarm points and incident timestamps from which battery discharge time may be estimated. The alarm management centre (AMC) will dispatch field technicians (based on geographical location) to attend a site generally with a mobile generator to restore power. The AMC monitors nationwide alarms in real time and 24/7. A single fault can generate thousands of alarms at the same time and when multiple sites are affected simultaneously alarm management becomes very challenging.

Variety   Silcar/Thiess uses a variety of data sources in its maintenance and management of batteries. Features such as the technology, manufacturer make/model, batch, environment, application, date of manufacture are considered in categorising batteries. The data may be structured and recorded within existing database management systems in Silcar/Thiess. In addition, unstructured data such as free text and SMS messages are also collected to describe defects or failure modes of battery cells. It is also important to capture anecdotal inputs such as field experience from field technicians and subject matter experts. Geographical and weather data from Australian Bureau of Meteorology are also important external data sources as well as site data such as housing type, location site access, site priority, etc. as these attributes can be used in the replacement decision making process.

Veracity   With such a wide variety of sources, the business process inevitably is prone to data errors (Fig. 9.3). For example, field technicians may incorrectly diagnose the cause of battery failure choosing an incorrect option on the failure reporting tool. Similarly, there are situations where the external impact on batteries (e.g., high temperature at the environment) has been overlooked. The field technicians may forget to report important information and therefore missing values are created. These factors lead to low veracity in the data collected at Silcar/Thiess. .

9.4.2.2   Equipment Reliability Analysis

An equipment reliability analysis (ERA) program [61] for telecommunication power equipment life cycle replacement has been developed and implemented to systematically address the complexity in maintaining and managing life cycle replacement decisions from its big data sources. Prior to the ERA program, the sheer volume of different types of equipment made it difficult to manage beyond a simplistic set of rules applied collectively.

The ERA program was a result of field testing its operation for more than 2 years. It has shown improvements in the replacement decisions resulting in longer term planning capabilities leading to better and more effective CAPEX management. Focusing on life data analysis for rectifiers and batteries specifically, [61] details the continuous improvement process in the ERA program which has helped improve the transparency of on-line access to equipment replacement decisions. .

The development of the ERA system at Silcar/Thiess has proven to overcome a number of difficulties in managing a diverse and large telecommunication power asset base. Firstly improved transparency by making the big data digestible for stakeholders created evidence to support CAPEX-based equipment replacement decisions. Secondly, the ERA system allows for consistent grouping of similar equipment to facilitate risk management and "whole of life" asset management. This means that the company is now able to control its risk exposure to failure that arise from ageing batteries while operating under tight budget constraints. This is possible through the risk modelling created from the data enabling risks to be quantified across a large diversity of asset types and applications. Using this model, the company is able to defer battery replacements while minimising and managing any impact that may arise.

As mentioned, remote monitoring of equipment health statistics will generate a large increment of data and the ERA program will need to be upgraded to handle the increased volume and to provide the real time analytics of equipment condition. From the big data perspective, the existing ERA program has already captured and demonstrated the handling of different characteristics of big data. As the program scales up even more, more powerful big data management tools and analytics will be required. On this note, the industry trend towards big data and analytics is developing and in turn, that has resulted in an unprecedented offering of big data solutions as seen in appendix.

9.4.3 Participatory Sensing for Noise Analytics

With most of the world's population living in metropolitan areas, many are exposed to excessive levels of noise as a result of night traffic that can have a detrimental impact on their sleep. According to [56, 106], constant exposure of environmental noise at night (above 42 db(A)) disturbs a person's sleep and can lead to health conditions such as hypertension, arteriosclerosis, and myocardial infarction. In the state of Victoria within Australia, an established suburb must be exposed to above 68 db(A) during the day before intervention is considered. At such high thresholds, the chances of the public receiving intervention is low and consequently, no mitigation strategy is in place to protect residents from night time noise exposure above 42 db(A). This significant gap between the mitigation threshold and the WHO's recommended level of noise for adequate rest also means little data has been collected to understand noise levels affecting the well-being of residents.

Given that the noise level at night is what really affects ones' health condition, mitigation should ideally occur as soon as excessive traffic noise complaints are received. Unfortunately, this is often not the case because

- The state does not have a night noise threshold and the daytime threshold of 68 db(A) is no where near the WHO's recommended 42 db(A)
- Intervention is always assumed to be government initiated but political interests and access to public funds would often take priority over any set threshold

This noise traffic issue was particularly pronounce in a group of ten suburbs managed by the City of Boroondara council. As affluent suburbs, it has access to an excellent transport network including two freeways bordering the north and south regions where about 800 households are within close distance to either freeway. For a long time, residents have complained about the traffic noise and despite scientific evidence [106], council investigation [56] and resident protests, there was no action from the state government. The council then decided to undertake a different approach by drawing inspiration from participatory sensing research [54] to create a community-driven solution.

The 2Loud? project aims to turn the mobile phones of residents into noise sensors so as to collect scientifically accurate noise readings on a large scale. The detailed noise readings from within households at night will allow (1) the council to be adequately informed when discussing matters with road authorities and (2) residents can learn about their noise situation within their homes.

The app,[9] as the fabric for the entire project, first connect disperse individuals who are curious or affected by traffic noise near their homes. When they can assess their noise situation, it gave stakeholders a sense of empowerment and immediate impact. For residents whom are affected by traffic noise, the app shows strategies that residents can action themselves. For the council, the setup efficiently and effectively collect large amounts of objective data that they need but more importantly, the project sends a message that the council is addressing the community's problems.

9.4.3.1 Handling Large Volume of Noise Data Streams

As shown in Fig. 9.4, 2Loud? is made up of (1) the app that participants use as sensors to capture noise data; (2) a set of scalable computing resources in the cloud; and (3) a set of data analysis algorithms that process and export the data into GIS and acoustic software tools. Using these tools, we were able to analyse and visualise the results to understand the noise situation in the individual homes and identify patterns across an entire region.

While the most tangible component for residents is the app, it was the technology that worked behind the scene that enable the project to deliver on the council's goals. Individually, each app sends a stream of noise readings to the server for storage which is conceptually straightforward. Implementing this however was the major challenge in the project. First, the data captured and collated across residents who participated require further analysis and processing. The types of analysis on the noise was collectively refer to as "noise analytics" and includes

- Linking various data pieces to the unique participants;
- Processing the cell-level readings;
- Obtaining the engineering readings (LAeq) recognised by the road authorities;

---

[9]https://itunes.apple.com/au/app/2loud/id645246491?mt=8.

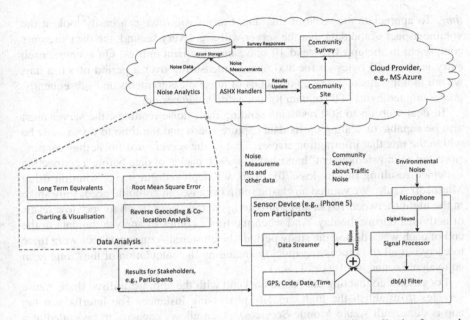

Fig. 9.4 System architecture of the entire participatory system from mobile application front-end to the data processing backend in the Microsoft Azure cloud

- Preparing the data for ArcGIS for visualisation; and
- Linking the data for analysis for feedback on mitigation strategies.

To enable noise analytics, the app must transmit the appropriate information back to the servers. This is called a noise measurement entry and it includes the measured sound level in db(A), the user's ID, the geo-location, data and time. The geo-location was recorded to make sure that a measurement was taken at the right location, i.e., within a given address and indoor. The geo-location information is also used to eliminate any measurements that may have been taken out-side of the designated region thus, ensuring that the measurements obtained from the smartphone were not only accurate but also within the defined 'indoor' areas.

On the phone, this means transmitting 10 noise measurements every second to the server. In each entry, the db(A) reading needs to be processed by performing Fourier Transform on the raw SPL reading from the microphone to obtain the selected energy levels within the frequency spectrum of the A-weighted scale.[10] To achieve this over a sustained a 9 h period each day, the app must compute efficiently and sends the data to the server quickly.

On the server side, the data received must be quickly stored and an acknowledgement issued. The challenge is when we need to design for a maximum of 800 participants who will be sending their data stream to the server *at the same*

[10]http://www.engineeringtoolbox.com/decibel-d_59.html.

time. To appreciate the scale of this data transmission, we can easily look at the volume aspect of the data that the server will see. Every second, the data streamer component in the app will send 10 noise measurement entries. On average, each entry is about 50 bytes so for 800 phones measuring over a period of 9 h a day, we are looking at streaming up to 12 GB of noise measurements and subsequently, processing terabytes (TB) of data for the entire study period.

To deal with up to 800 residents sending their noise readings, the server must also be capable of scaling up its data capture speed and the time to do so must be within the rate that information arrives. That is, the server must finish the "capture, store and acknowledgement" handshake for each packet of data before a connection is denied resulting in data loss. To do so, we deployed our server solution using Microsoft Azure. We wanted an elastic setup because our compute needs only spike in the night (between 10 pm and 7 am) and generally goes down to very low levels of activities during the day. And when the times comes to analyse the data at the end of each week during the study period, the clustered Azure instances were there to carry out all the processing quickly, including the calculation of the "long term equivalent" sound levels (i.e., LAeq).

For ease of connecting the Azure backend with the app, we utilised three Azure services to establish the high-capacity processing instance. The interface to the app is done with Azure Mobile Services, which allows capacity to be scaled at a scheduled time or by the number of calls being made to the service. Up to 10 unit counts can be provisioned to handle the incoming HTTP requests (which carried the noise measurement readings). The mobile service is tied to an SQL database to hold the interim readings, which was also configured to be scalable to handle the varying load. Finally, an Azure website instance was created with ASPX handlers coded in .NET/C# to realise the various data post-processing and analysis. We went with this particular option as our stakeholders at the time were unfamiliar with new big data tools on the market. They felt it was better to go with something that their team also felt confident of and hence, the choice of such a setup that a more sophisticated tool today easily handles.

9.4.3.2 Summary

Public participation has always been an important aspect of ensuring sustainable development of cities [7]. With advances in technology, urbanisation and increased awareness of democratic rights, participatory sensing has seen significant growth [25] to become a preferred means of collating public opinions to reveal insights and patterns across a large spatial region [36]. As technology progresses and the public becoming proficient with their technology, participatory sensing will underpin many new systems to come especially in the creation of smart-cities. These new systems will have large data streams that feed into reasoning systems such as those suggested by Valle et al. [99], or into analytical services such as Amazon Kinesis for creating near real-time dashboards, alerts and reports. The 2loud? project is an example of such an initiative with the work already receiving interests from overseas.

In November 2014, the project [57, 71] was chosen to be included in the European Commission of Science for Environment Policy,[11] which has a large readership of influential readers including politicians, European academics and policy makers. The work has since then performed well in the Altmetric measurement[12] illustrating significance of using big data for "everyday problems".

9.5   Conclusions

The development of big data tools is both challenging and exciting in the current times. While research has advanced the ability to process massive amount of data quickly, the broader use-case for the new technology remains limited by the fact that there are many more problems that are *not* big data in nature. Nevertheless, the scope for more data being captured and utilised will likely increase rather than not for two reasons. First as big data tools mature, the ease of use will make the technology a lot more accessible. This reinforces the case for more data collection especially given the lowering storage cost. Second, as adoption increases and understanding of the technology gains traction in the wider community, more business value propositions will be established. Again this will feed the desired for more data and hence, more polished big data tools going forward.

This chapter looks at the state of the art in big data research and outlined the tools that are currently available to the reader. More than just an attempt to index the tools, it also seeks to provide a categorisation of the tool and a position of the tool within the KDD framework as given in the appendix. The table in the appendix will thus provide a good starting point for practitioners search for the right tool to do a particular analytical task. Finally, three completed projects were discussed as exemplars of big data applications in engineering and science. The first was a recent completion demonstrating the timing of the project to ride the big data wave as seen in its solution. The second is an example of a problem on the crux of benefitting from the maturity of the technology. The last example showcases how big data problem was solved using Microsoft Azure's built in elastic scalability, making it an ideal candidate to move to the next step of the big data technology evolution.

Appendix: Big Data and Analytical Tools

A non-exhaustive table of currently available big data tools, open-sourced and commercial versions.

---

[11]http://goo.gl/Xh8T1Q.

[12]http://www.altmetric.com/details/2470954.

Category	Product name	KDD framework positioning	URL
Data Grid	GridGain	Selection, transformation	www.gridgain.com
	IBM eXtreme Scale		www.ibm.com/software/products/en/webphere-extreme-scale
	VMware GemFire		www.vmware.com/products/vfabric-gemfire/overview
	GiaSpaces XAP		www.gigaspaces.com
	Hazelcast		www.hazelcast.com
	Oracle Coherence		www.oracle.com/technetwork/middleware/coherence
	CloudTran		www.coludTran.com
	ScaleOut Software		www.scaleoutsoftware.com
Data caching	InfiniSpan	Selection	www.infinispam.org
	Ehcache		www.Ehcache.org
	Memcached		www.memcached.org
Data caching and "as a services"	Amazon Elastic Mapreduce	Selection, pre-processing, transformation, data mining	www.aws.amazon.com/elasticmapreduce
	IronCache		www.iorn.io/cache
	Garantia Data Memcached Cloud		www.redislabs.com
	MemCashier		www.memcashier.com
Data management in the cloud	Amazon RDS		www.aws.amazon.com/rds
	Rackspace Cloud Database		www.rackspace.com.au/cloud-hosting
	Google Cloud SQL		www.hpcloud.com/products-services/relational-database
	HP cloud RDB		www.fathomdb.com
	FathomDB		www.fathomdb.com
	www.Database.com		www.database.com
	SQL Azure		www.azure.microsoft.com
	ClearDB		www.cleardb.com
	SAP Sybase ASE		www.sap.com/pc/tech/database/software/adaptive-server-enterprise
	Xeround		www.xeround.com

Category	Name	Description	URL
Analytics including "as a service".	Teradata	Selection, pre-processing, transformation, data mining, evaluation	www.teredata.com.au
	Google BigQuery		www.cloud.google.com/bigquery
	Kognitio		www.kognitio.com
	TempoDB		www.angel.co/tempodb
	Amazon Redshift		www.aws.amazon.com/redshift
	1010data		www.1010data.com
	BitYota		www.bityota.com
	Inforbright	Data mining, evaluation	www.inforbright.com
	Actian		www.actian.com
	Metamarkets Druid		www.metamarkets.com/what-we-do/technology
	EMC Greenplum		www.emc.com/campaign/global/greenplumdca
	HP Vertica		www.vertica.com
	SAP Sybase IQ		www.sap.com/australia/pc/tech/database/software/sybase-iq-big-data-management/index.html//
New SQL Database	Percona	Selection	www.percona.com
	SQLFire		www.vmware.com/au/products/vfabricsqlfire/overview
	Translattice		www.translattice.com
	JustOneDB		www.justonedb.com
	MemSQL		www.memsql.com
	Datomic		www.datomic.com
	Akiban		www.akiban.com
	FairCom		www.faircom.com
	VoltDB		www.voltdb.com
	NuoDB		www.nuodb.com
	Drizzle		www.drizzle.com
	Clustrix		www.clustrix.com
	ScaleDB		www.scaledb.com
	ScaleBase		www.scalebase.com

	Product	Activities	URL
High performance and clustered dada management	ScaleArc		www.scalearc.com
	Tesora		www.tesora.com
	TokuMX, TokuDB		www.tokutek.com
	CodeFutures	Selection, pre-production, transformation, evaluation	www.codefutures.com
	Continuent	Selection, transformation	www.continuent.com
	Postgres SQL		www.postgressql.com
	Oracle Exalytics	Selection, pre-production, transformation, data mining, evaluation	www.oracle.com/engineered-systems/exalytics
	IBM Netezza		www.ibm.com/software/au/data/netezza
	SAP HANA	Selection, pre-production, transformation, data mining, evaluation	www.hana.sap.com
	Exadata	Selection, transformation, pre-production, evaluation	www.oracle.com/engineered-systems/exadata
	Galera		www.galeracluster.cim/products
	EnterpriseDB		www.enterprisedb.com
	Xtreme Data		www.xtremedata.com
	ParSteam		www.parsteam.com
	Exasol		www.exasol.com/en
	Oracle TimesTen		www.oracle.com/technetwork/database/database-technologies/timesten/overview/index.html
	IBM SolidDB		www.ibm.com/software/data/soliddb–departure
	Firebird		www.firebird.org
	Actian Ingres		www.ibm.com/products/operational-database
	Informix		www.ibm.com/software/au/data/informix

Category	Product	Function	URL
	IBM DB2		www.ibm.com/DB2_BLU_comparsion
	Oracle Database		www.oracle.com/database
	MySQL		www.mysql.com
	MariaDB		www.mariadb.org
	Postgre SQL		www.postgresql.org
Large scale unstructured data management	InterSystems Catch	Selection, transformation	www.intersystems.com
	Versant		www.versant.com
	McObject		www.mcobject.com
	Progress ObjectStore		www.objectstore.com
	WakandaDB		www.wakanda.org/events/seattle-js-creating-web-apps-wakandadb
	IBM IMS		www.ibm.com/software/au/data/ims
	Adabas		www.softwareag.com/corporate/products/adabas_natural/adabas/overview/default.asp
	UniData		www.unidata
	Documentum xDB		www.developer.emc.com/docs/document/xdb/manual
	Tamino XML Server		www.xml.com/pub/p/119
	Ipedo XML database		www.xml.coverpages.org/ipedoXMLDatabase.html
	Splice Machine	Selection, transformation, pre-processing, data mining	www.splicemachine.com
	Drawn to Scale	Selection, transformation, pre-processing	www.crunchbase.com/organization/drawn-to-scale
	markLogic	Selection, transformation	www.marklogic.com

		Selection, transformation, pre-processing	
Document, key-value NoSQL management	Handlerscoket		www.percona.com/doc/percona-server/5.5/performance/handlersocket.html
	LevelDB		www.leveldb.com
	Oracle NoSQL		www.oracle.com/us/products/database/nosql
	Voldemort		www.project-voldemort.com/voldemort/javadoc/all/overview-summary.html
	RavenDB		www.ravendb.net
	CouchDB		www.couchdb.apache.org
	RethinkDB		www.rethinkdb.com
Parallel storage engines	Accumulo		www.accumlo.apache.org
	HBase		www.hbase.apache.org/0.94/apidocs/overciew-summary.html
	Hypertable		www.hypertable.org
Graph database management	Giraph		www.giraph.apache.org
	FlockDB		www.github.com/BGehrels/FlockDB-Client
	AffinityDB		www.affinitydb.cfapps.io
	YarcData		www.dbms2.com/2012/07/02/yarcdata
	DEX		www.sparsity-technologies.com
	Nero4j		www.nero4j.com

Category	Product	Function	URL
Index-based data management	Attivio	Selection	www.attivio.com/enterprise-search
	IBM InfoSphere Data Explorer		www.ibm.com/Big_Data
	Oracle Endeca Server		www.oracle.com/technetwork/middleware/endeca/server/overview/index.com
	HP-Autonomy		www.autonomy.com
	Lucene/Solr		www.lucene.apache.org/solr
	Elasticsearch		www.elastic.co
	LucidWorks Big Data		www.lucidWorks.com/solutions/enterprise
	NADATA	Selection, data mining	www.ngdata.com
Hadoop and large scale analytics	Microsoft HDInsight	Data mining, pre-processing, transformation, evaluation	www.azure.microsoft.com/en-gb/services/hdinsight
	Qubole		www.qubole.com
	Treasure Data		www.treasuredata.com
	Infochimps		www.infochimps.com
	Mortar Data		www.mortardata.com

References

1. Gómez I, Caselles V, Estrela MJ (2014) Real-time weather forecasting in the Western Mediterranean Basin: An application of the RAMS model. Atmos Res 139:71–89
2. Agerri R, Artola X, Beloki Z, Rigau G, Soroa A (2014) Big data for natural language processing: a streaming approach. Knowledge-Based Systems
3. Ahrens J, Hendrickson B, Long G, Miller S, Ross R, Williams D (2011) Data-intensive science in the us doe: case studies and future challenges. Comput Sci Eng 13(6):14–24
4. Al-Jarrah OY, Yoo PD, Muhaidat S, Karagiannidis GK, Taha K (2015) Efficient machine learning for big data: a review. Big Data Res 2(3):87–93. Big data, analytics, and high-performance computing
5. Alahakoon D, Yu X (2015) Smart electricity meter data intelligence for future energy Systems: a survey. IEEE Trans Ind Inf 99
6. Amato A, Di Martino B, Venticinque S (2014) Big data processing for pervasive environment in cloud computing. In: International conference on intelligent networking and collaborative systems (INCoS). IEEE, pp 598–603
7. Banisar D, Parmar S, De Silva L, Excell C (2012) Moving from principles to rights: rio 2012 and access to information, public participation and justice. Sustainable Development Law & Policy 12(3):8–14
8. Baumann P, Mazzetti P, Ungar J, Barbera R, Barboni D, Beccati A, Bigagli L, Boldrini E, Bruno R, Calanducci A, Campalani P, Clements O, Dumitru A, Grant M, Herzig P, Kakaletris G, Laxton J, Koltsida P, Lipskoch K, Mahdiraji AR, Mantovani S, Merticariu V, Messina A, Misev D, Natali S, Nativi S, Oosthoek J, Pappalardo M, Passmore J, Rossi AP, Rundo F, Sen M, Sorbera V, Sullivan D, Torrisi M, Trovato L, Veratelli MG, Wagner S (2014) Big data analytics for earth sciences: the EarthServer approach. Digital Earth 1–27. doi:10.1080/17538947.2014.1003106
9. Bellazzi R, Larizza C, Magni P, Montani S, Stefanelli M (2000) Intelligent analysis of clinical time series: an application in the diabetes mellitus domain. Artif Intell Med 20(1):37–57
10. Bhardwaj R, Sethi A, Nambiar R (2014) Big data in genomics: an overview. In: IEEE international conference on big data. IEEE, pp 45–49
11. Bhattacharya M, Islam R, Abawajy J (2014) Evolutionary optimization: a big data perspective. J Netw Comput Appl 59:416–426
12. Bhogal I, Choksi J (2015) Handling big data using NoSQL. In: Advanced information networking and applications workshops. IEEE
13. Borne K (2009) Scientific data mining in astronomy. Taylor & Francis/CRC, Boca Raton, pp 91–114
14. Borne K, Accomazzi A, Bloom J, Brunner R, Burke D, Butler N, Chernoff DF, Connolly B, Connolly A, Connors A, Cutler C, Desai S, Djorgovski G, Feigelson E, Finn LS, Freeman P, Graham M, Gray N, Graziani C, Guinan EF, Hakkila J, Jacoby S, Jefferys W, Kashyap R, Kelly B, Knuth K, Lamb DQ, Lee H, Loredo T, Mahabal A, Mateo M, McCollum B, A. Muench, Pesenson M, Petrosian V, Primini F, Protopapas P, Ptak A, Quashnock J, Raddick MJ, Rocha G, Ross N, Rottler L, Scargle J, Siemiginowska A, Song I, Szalay A, Tyson JA, Vestrand T, Wallin J, Wandelt B, Wasserman IM, Way M, Weinberg M, Zezas A, Anderes E, Babu J, Becla J, Berger J, Bickel PJ, Clyde M, Davidson I, van Dyk D, Eastman T, Efron B, Genovese C, Gray A, Jang W, Kolaczyk ED, Kubica J, Loh JM, Meng X-L, Moore A, Morris R, Park T, Pike R, Rice J, Richards J, Ruppert D, Saito N, Schafer C, Stark PB, Stein M, Sun J, Wang D, Wang Z, Wasserman L, Wegman EJ, Willett R, Wolpert R, Woodroofe M (2009) Astroinformatics: a twenty first century approach to astronomy. In: Astro2010: the astronomy and astrophysics decadal survey. ArXiv Astrophysics e-prints, vol. 2010, p. 6P
15. Bostrm H, Andler SF, Brohede M, Johansson R, Karlsson A, Van Laere J, Niklasson L, Nilsson M, Persson A, Ziemke T (2007) On the definition of information fusion as a field of research. Technical Report, University of Skövde

16. Bryant RE (2011) Data-intensive scalable computing for scientific applications. Comput Sci Eng 13(6):25–33
17. Bunyavanich S, Schadt EE (2015) Systems biology of asthma and allergic diseases: a multiscale approach. J Allergy Clin Immunol 135(1):31–42
18. Chang F-J, Chiang Y-M, Tsai M-J, Shieh M-C, Hsu K-L, Sorooshian S (2014) Watershed rainfall forecasting using neuro-fuzzy networks with the assimilation of multi-sensor information. J Hydrol 508:374–384
19. Chawla NV, Davis DA (2013) Bringing big data to personalised healthcare: a patient-centered framework. J Gen Intern Med 28(3):660–665
20. Chen CLP, Zhang C-Y(2014) Data-intensive applications, challenges, techniques and technologies: A survey on big data. Inf Sci 275:314–347
21. Chen H, Chiang RHL, Storey VC (2012) Business intelligence and analytics: from big data to big impact. MIS Q 36(4):1165–1188
22. Chen H, Compton S, Hsiao O (2013) DiabeticLink: a health big data system for patient empowerment and personalised healthcare. Springer, Heidelberg, pp 71–83
23. Chute CG, Beck SA, Fisk TB, Mohr DN (2010) The enterprise data trust at mayo clinic: a semantically integrated warehouse of biomedical data. J Am Med Inform Assoc 17(2):131–135
24. Coen MH (1999) Cross-modal clustering. In: Proceedings of the national conference on artificial intelligence, vol 20. AAAI/MIT, Menlo Park/Cambridge/London, p 932
25. Conrad C, Hilchey K (2011) A review of citizen science and community-based environmental monitoring: issues and opportunities. Environ Monit Assess 176(1–4):273–291
26. Cottrill CD, Derrible S (2015) Leveraging big data for the development of transport sustainability indicators. J Urban Technol 22(1):45–64
27. de Souza RS, Ciardi B (2015) AMADA: analysis of multidimensional astronomical datasets. Astron Comput 12:100–108
28. Dieleman S, Willett KW, Dambre J (2015) Rotation-invariant convolutional neural networks for galaxy morphology prediction. Mon Not R Astron Soc 450(2):1441–1459
29. Dobre C, Xhafa F (2014) Intelligent services for big data science. Futur Gener Comput Syst 37:267–281
30. Duan L, Xiong Y (2015) Big data analytics and business analytics. J Manag Anal 2(1):1–21
31. Dutta H, Giannella C, Borne K, Kargupta H (2007) Distributed top-k outlier detection from astronomy catalogs using the demac system. In: SIAM international conference on data mining. Society for Industrial and Applied Mathematics
32. Fairfield J, Shtein H (2014) Big data, big problems: emerging issues in the ethics of data science and journalism. J Mass Media Ethics 29(1):38–51
33. Faizrahnemoon M, Schlote A, Maggi L, Crisostomi E, Shorten R (2015) A big data model for multi-modal public transportation with application to macroscopic control and optimisation. Control 88(11):2354–2368 (just-accepted)
34. Fan J, Liu H (2013) Statistical analysis of big data on pharmacogenomics. Adv Drug Deliv Rev 65(7):987–1000
35. Fan S, Lau RYK, Zhao JL (2015) Demystifying big data analytics for business intelligence through the lens of marketing mix. Big Data Res 2(1):28–32
36. Goldman J, Shilton K, Burke J, Estrin D, Hansen M, Ramanathan N, Reddy S, Samanta V, Srivastava M, West R (2009) Participatory sensing: a citizen-powered approach to illuminating the patterns that shape our world. Report
37. Goshtasby AA, Nikolov S (2007) Image fusion: advances in the state of the art. Inf Fusion 8(2):114–118
38. Groves P, Kayyali B, Knott D, Van Kuiken S (2013) The big data revolution in healthcare. McKinsey Q. https://www.google.com.au/url?sa=t&rct=j&q=&esrc=s&source=web&cd=1&cad=rja&uact=8&ved=0ahUKEwitjMO8grfKAhVFk5QKHVBjAgYQFggcMAA&url=https%3A%2F%2Fwww.mckinsey.com%2F~%2Fmedia%2Fmckinsey%2Fdotcom%2Fclient_service%2FHealthcare%2520Systems%2520and%2520Services%2FPDFs%2FThe_big_data_revolution_in_healthcare.ashx&usg=AFQjCNEQMv70t52p6Lc8T8LwNDnQldB-tA

39. Guo H (2014) Digital earth: big earth data. Int J Digital Earth 7(1):1–27
40. Hashem IAT, Yaqoob I, Anuar NB, Mokhtar S, Gani A, Khan SU (2015) The rise of big data on cloud computing: Review and open research issues. Inf Syst 47:98–115
41. Heer J, Mackinlay J, Stolte C, Agrawala M (2008) Graphical histories for visualization: Supporting analysis, communication, and evaluation. IEEE Trans Vis Comput Graph 14(6): 1189–1196
42. Hey AJG, Tansley S, Tolle KM (2009) The fourth paradigm: data-intensive scientific discovery, vol 1. Microsoft Research, Redmond
43. Horn M, Mirzatuny M (2013) Mining big data to transform electricity. Springer, New York pp 47–58
44. Hu H, Correll M, Kvecher L, Osmond M, Clark J, Bekhash A, Schwab G, Gao D, Gao J, Kubatin V (2011) Dw4tr: a data warehouse for translational research. J Biomed Inform 44(6):1004–1019
45. Huang J, Niu L, Zhan J, Peng X, Bai J, Cheng S (2014) Technical aspects and case study of big data based condition monitoring of power apparatuses. In: IEEE PES Asia-Pacific power and energy engineering conference (APPEEC). IEEE, pp 1–4
46. Jacobs A (2009) The pathologies of big data. Commun ACM 52(8):36–44
47. Jagadish HV (2015) Big data and science: myths and reality. Big Data Res 2(2):49–52. Visions on Big Data
48. Jelinek HF, Wilding C, Tinely P (2006) An innovative multi-disciplinary diabetes complications screening program in a rural community: a description and preliminary results of the screening. Aust J Prim. Health 12(1):14–20
49. Ji C, Li Y, Qiu W, Awada U, Li K (2012) Big data processing in cloud computing environments. In: Proceedings of the international symposium on parallel architectures, algorithms and networks, I-SPAN
50. Keh H-C, Hui L, Chou K-Y, Cheng Y-C, Yu P-Y, Huang N-C (2014) Big data generation: application of mobile healthcare. Springer, Switzerland pp 735–743
51. Keravnou ET (1997) Temporal abstraction of medical data: deriving periodicity. Springer, Berlin, pp 61–79
52. Khaleghi B, Khamis A, Karray FO, Razavi SN (2013) Multisensor data fusion: a review of the state-of-the-art. Inf Fusion 14(1):28–44
53. Krmer M, Senner I (2015) A modular software architecture for processing of big geospatial data in the cloud. Comput Graph 49:69–81
54. Lane N, Miluzzo E, Lu H, Peebles D, Choudhury T, Campbell A (2010) A survey of mobile phone sensing. IEEE Commun 48(9):140–150
55. Laney D (2001) 3d data management: controlling data volume, velocity and variety. Technical Report, META Group Research Note
56. Leao S, Peerson A, Elkadhi H (2012) Effects of exposure to traffic noise on health. In: Proceedings of the 5th healthy cities: working together to achieve liveable cities conference, Geelong
57. Leao S, Ong K-L, Krezel A (2014) 2loud?: community mapping of exposure to traffic noise with mobile phones. Environ Monit Assess 186(10):6193–6202
58. Leung CK.-S., Jiang F (2014) A data science solution for mining interesting patterns from uncertain big data. In: 2014 IEEE fourth international conference onBig data and cloud computing (BdCloud), IEEE, pp 235–242.
59. Li X, Plale B, Vijayakumar N, Ramachandran R, Graves S, Conover H (2008) Real-time storm detection and weather forecast activation through data mining and events processing. Earth Sci Inf 1(2):49–57
60. Li L, Su X, Wang Y, Lin Y, Li Z, Li Y (2015) Robust causal dependence mining in big data network and its application to traffic flow predictions. Transp Res C Emerg Technol 58(B):292–307
61. Lim EH, Bodi F (2012) Managing the complexity of a telecommunication power systems equipment replacement program. In: 2012 IEEE 34th international telecommunications energy conference (INTELEC), pp 1–9

62. Lowe HJ, Ferris TA, Hernandez PM, Weber SC (2009) STRIDE–An integrated standards-based translational research informatics platform. In: AMIA Annual Symposium Proceedings, vol. 2009, American Medical Informatics Association, p 391

63. Ludwig N, Feuerriegel S, Neumann D (2015) Putting big data analytics to work: feature selection for forecasting electricity prices using the lasso and random forests. J Decis Syst 24(1):19–36

64. Mahrt M, Scharkow M (2013) The value of big data in digital media research. J Broadcast Electron Media 57(1):20–33

65. Miyoshi T, Kondo K, Imamura T (2014) The 10,240-member ensemble Kalman filtering with an intermediate AGCM. Geophys Res Lett 41(14):5264–5271. doi:10.1002/2014GL060863

66. Nativi S, Mazzetti P, Santoro M, Papeschi F, Craglia M, Ochiai O (2015) Big data challenges in building the global earth observation system of systems. Environ Model Softw 68:1–26

67. Nguyen BV, Burstein F, Fisher J (2014) Improving service of online health information provision: a case of usage-driven design for health information portals. Inf Syst Front 17(3):493–511

68. Nurmi D, Wolski R, Grzegorczyk C, Obertelli G, Soman S, Youseff L, Zagorodnov D (2009) The eucalyptus open-source cloud-computing system. In: 9th IEEE/ACM international symposium on cluster computing and the grid, 2009 (CCGRID'09), IEEE, pp 124–131

69. Oberg AL, McKinney BA, Schaid DJ, Pankratz VS, Kennedy RB, Poland GA (2015) Lessons learned in the analysis of high-dimensional data in vaccinomics. Vaccine 33(40):5262–5270

70. ODriscoll A, Daugelaite J, Sleator RD (2013) big data, hadoop and cloud computing in genomics. J Biomed Inform 46(5):774–781

71. Ong K-L, Leao S, Krezel A (2014) Participatory sensing and education: helping the community mitigate sleep disturbance from traffic noise. Pervasive Comput Commun 10(4):419–441

72. Palmieri F, Fiore U, Ricciardi S, Castiglione A (2015) Grasp-based resource re-optimization for effective big data access in federated clouds. Futur Gener Comput Syst 54:168–179

73. Peise E, Fabregat-Traver D, Bientinesi P (2014) High performance solutions for big-data GWAS. Parallel Comput 42:75–87

74. Perkins S, Questiaux J, Finniss S, Tyler R, Blyth S, Kuttel MM (2014) Scalable desktop visualisation of very large radio astronomy data cubes. New Astron 30:1–7

75. Pez DG, Aparicio F, De Buenaga M, Ascanio JR (2014) Chronic patients monitoring using wireless sensors and big data processing. In: 2014 Eighth International Conference on Innovative mobile and internet services in ubiquitous computing (IMIS), IEEE, pp 404–408

76. Pijanowski BC, Tayyebi A, Doucette J, Pekin BK, Braun D, Plourde J (2014) A big data urban growth simulation at a national scale: configuring the GIS and neural network based land transformation model to run in a high performance computing (HPC) environment. Environ Model Softw 51:250–268

77. Prakasa A, De Silva D (2013) Development of user warrant ontology for improving online health information provision. In: 24th Australasian conference on information systems (ACIS), RMIT University, pp 1–12

78. Procter R, Vis F, Voss A (2013) Reading the riots on twitter: methodological innovation for the analysis of big data. Int J Soc Res Methodol 16(3):197–214

79. Raghupathi W, Raghupathi V (2014) Big data analytics in healthcare: promise and potential. Health Inf Sci Syst 2(1):3

80. Schraml J (1978) On-line and real-time processing in radio astronomy. Comput Phys Commun 15(5):347–349

81. Schroeder R, Taylor T (2015) Big data and wikipedia research: social science knowledge across disciplinary divides. Inf Commun Soc 18(9):1039–1056

82. Schutter A, Shamir L (2015) Galaxy morphology an unsupervised machine learning approach. Astron Comput 12:60–66

83. Sen A, Banerjee A, Sinha AP, Bansal M (2012) Clinical decision support: Converging toward an integrated architecture. J Biomed Inform 45(5):1009–1017

84. Shahar Y (1994) A knowledge-based method for temporal abstraction of clinical data. Ph.D. Dissertation program in medical information sciences, Stanford University School of Medicine, Stanford

85. Shahrokni H, Levihn F, Brandt N (2014) Big meter data analysis of the energy efficiency potential in Stockholm's building stock. Energy Build 78:153–164
86. Sharshar S, Allart L, Chambrin M-C (2005) A new approach to the abstraction of monitoring data in intensive care. Springer, Berlin, pp 13–22
87. Shi Q, Abdel-Aty M (2015) Big data applications in real-time traffic operation and safety monitoring and improvement on urban expressways. Transp Res C Emerg Technol
88. Sittig DF, Wright A, Osheroff JA, Middleton B, Teich JM, Ash JS, Campbell E, Bates DW (2008) Grand challenges in clinical decision support. J Biomed Inform 41(2):387–392
89. Sivaraman E, Manickachezian R (2014) High performance and fault tolerant distributed file system for big data storage and processing using hadoop. In: 2014 international conference on intelligent computing applications (ICICA), IEEE, pp 32–36
90. Song J, Guo C, Wang Z, Zhang Y, Yu G, Pierson J-M (2014) HaoLap: a hadoop based OLAP system for big data. J Syst Softw 102:167–181
91. Stacey M, McGregor C (2007) Temporal abstraction in intelligent clinical data analysis: a survey. Artif Intell Med 39(1):1–24
92. Steed CA, Ricciuto DM, Shipman G, Smith B, Thornton PE, Wang D, Shi X, Williams DN (2013) Big data visual analytics for exploratory earth system simulation analysis. Comput Geosci 61:71–82
93. Stevens KB, Pfeiffer DU (2015) Sources of spatial animal and human health data: casting the net wide to deal more effectively with increasingly complex disease problems. Spatial and Spatio-temporal Epidemiology 13:15–29
94. Sullivan K, Uccellini L (2013) Service assessment: Hurricane/post-tropical cyclone sandy. National oceanic and atmospheric administration, National Weather Service, May 2013
95. Szalay A (2011) Extreme data-intensive scientific computing. Comput Sci Eng 13(6):34–41
96. Tang W, Feng W (2014) Parallel map projection of vector-based big spatial data: coupling cloud computing with graphics processing units. Comput Environ Urban Syst. http://www.sciencedirect.com/science/article/pii/S019897151400012X
97. Torra V (2003) On some aggregation operators for numerical information. Springer, Berlin, pp 9–26
98. Valds JJ, Bonham-Carter G (2006) Time dependent neural network models for detecting changes of state in complex processes: applications in earth sciences and astronomy. Neural Netw 19(2):196–207. Earth Sciences and Environmental Applications of Computational Intelligence.
99. Valle ED, Ceri S, van Harmelen F, Fensel D (2009) It's a streaming world! reasoning upon rapidly changing information. IEEE Intell Syst 24(6):83–89
100. Valverde MC, Araujo E, Velho HC (2014) Neural network and fuzzy logic statistical downscaling of atmospheric circulation-type specific weather pattern for rainfall forecasting. Appl Soft Comput 22:681–694
101. Van Wart J, Grassini P, Yang H, Claessens L, Jarvis A, Cassman KG (2015) Creating long-term weather data from thin air for crop simulation modeling. Agric For Meteorol 209–210:49–58
102. Wang L, Tao J, Ranjan R, Marten H, Streit A, Chen J, Chen D (2013) G-hadoop: mapreduce across distributed data centers for data-intensive computing. Futur Gener Comput Syst 29(3):739–750
103. Wang M, Wang J, Tian F (2014) City intelligent energy and transportation network policy based on the big data analysis. Procedia Comput Sci 32:85–92
104. Ward RM, Schmieder R, Highnam G, Mittelman D (2013) Big data challenges and opportunities in high-throughput sequencing. Syst Biomed 1(1):29–34
105. Wen X, Gu G, Li Q, Gao Y, Zhang X (2012) Comparison of open-source cloud management platforms: openstack and opennebula. In: 2012 9th international conference onFuzzy systems and knowledge discovery (FSKD), IEEE, pp 2457–2461
106. WHO Regional Office for Europe (2010) Burden of disease from environmental noise: practical guidance. Report, World Health Organisation

107. Wisniewski MF, Kieszkowski P, Zagorski BM, Trick WE, Sommers M, Weinstein RA, Chicago Antimicrobial Resistance Project (2003) Development of a clinical data warehouse for hospital infection control. J Am Med Inform Assoc 10(5):454–462

108. Wright A, Sittig DF (2008) A four-phase model of the evolution of clinical decision support architectures. Int J Med Inform 77(10):641–649

109. Yang Y, Lin H, Guo Z, Jiang J (2007) A data mining approach for heavy rainfall forecasting based on satellite image sequence analysis. Comput Geosci 33(1):20–30

110. Yang J-J, Li J, Mulder J, Wang Y, Chen S, Wu H, Wang Q, Pan H (2015) Emerging information technologies for enhanced healthcare. Comput Ind 69:3–11

111. Yao, JT, Raghavan VV, Wu Z (2008) Web information fusion: a review of the state of the art. Inf Fusion 9(4):446–449

112. Yu J, Jiang F, Zhu T (2013) RTIC-C: a big data system for massive traffic information mining. In: 2013 international conference on cloud computing and big data (CloudCom-Asia), IEEE, pp 395–402

113. Zhang Y, Zhao Y (2015) Astronomy in the big data era. Data Sci J 14(11):1–9

114. Zhang X, Li D, Cheng M, Zhang P (2014) Electricity consumption pattern recognition based on the big data technology to support the peak shifting potential analysis. In: IEEE PES Asia-Pacific power and energy engineering conference, pp 1–5

115. Zheng H, Zhang Y (2008) Feature selection for high-dimensional data in astronomy. Adv Space Res 41(12):1960–1964

116. Zheng J, Li Z, Dagnino A (2014) Speeding up processing data from millions of smart meters. In: Proceedings of the 5th ACM/SPEC international conference on performance engineering, ACM, pp 27–37

117. Zheng Y, Capra L, Wolfson O, Yang H (2014) Urban computing: concepts, methodologies, and applications. ACM Trans Intell Syst Technol (TIST) 5(3):38

118. Zikopoulos P, Eaton C (2011) Understanding big data: analytics for enterprise class Hadoop and streaming data. McGraw-Hill Osborne Media, New York

Chapter 10
Geospatial Big Data for Environmental and Agricultural Applications

Athanasios Karmas, Angelos Tzotsos, and Konstantinos Karantzalos

Abstract Earth observation (EO) and environmental geospatial datasets are growing at an unprecedented rate in size, variety and complexity, thus, creating new challenges and opportunities as far as their access, archiving, processing and analytics are concerned. Currently, huge imaging streams are reaching several petabytes in many satellite archives worldwide. In this chapter, we review the current state-of-the-art in big data frameworks able to access, handle, process, analyse and deliver geospatial data and value-added products. Operational services that feature efficient implementations and different architectures allowing in certain cases the online and near real-time processing and analytics are detailed. Based on the current status, state-of-the-art and emerging challenges, the present study highlights certain issues, insights and future directions towards the efficient exploitation of EO big data for important engineering, environmental and agricultural applications.

10.1 Introduction

The current generation of space-borne sensors are generating nearly continuous streams of massive earth observation (EO) datasets. Shortly, high-resolution multispectral images will be available almost once a week and in some regions twice per week. In addition to open data satellite missions from national and European organizations (mostly by USA and EU), space industry and startup companies are increasing significantly as launches get cheaper and technology gets smaller. Several operating small inexpensive satellites (will) make geospatial data widely available for several applications. This new generation of interconnected satellites capture and transmit Remote Sensing (RS) data with a sub-meter resolution daily, allowing the monitoring of earth surface changes with greater frequency than ever before. Satellite-based earth observation industry is witnessing an impressive growth, with around 260 satellite launches expected over the next decade. Moreover, recent regulatory relaxations regarding the sell and purchase of very high-resolution

A. Karmas (✉) • A. Tzotsos • K. Karantzalos
Remote Sensing Laboratory, National Technical University of Athens, Zographou Campus, 15780 Athens, Greece
e-mail: thanasis.karmas@gmail.com; tzotsos@gmail.com; karank@central.ntua.gr

© Springer International Publishing Switzerland 2016
S. Yu, S. Guo (eds.), *Big Data Concepts, Theories, and Applications*,
DOI 10.1007/978-3-319-27763-9_10

satellite imagery data has paved the way for further expansion where new industry participants can enter and provide diverse on-demand services which will lead not only to new market sectors but also to novel applications, products and services, and even new business models.

These huge EO streams which are received through satellite downlink channels at gigabit rates, increase as a consequence at astonishing rates, reaching currently several petabytes in many satellite archives [19, 57, 68, 74]. According to the statistics of the Open Geospatial Consortium (OGC), the global archived observation data would exceed the one Exabyte during 2015.

However, it is estimated that most of datasets in existing satellite imaging archives have never been accessed and processed [65] apart from certain supercomputer centers. Therefore, in order to harness the full potential of these massive earth and environmental datasets, sophisticated methods for organizing and analyzing them are required [27, 46, 68, 87] and processing power, people and tools need to be brought to the data [6, 28, 47, 56].

Therefore, harvesting valuable knowledge and information from EO big data turns out to be extremely challenging [50, 57, 58, 72], while the increasing data volumes are not the only consideration. As the wealth of data increases, the challenge of indexing, searching and transferring increases exponentially as well. Open issues include the efficient data storage, handling, management and delivery, the processing of multimodal and high-dimensional datasets as well as the increasing demands for real-time (or near real-time) processing for many critical geospatial applications [73, 74, 87].

Moreover, RS datasets are multi-modal, acquired from multispectral, radar, lidar, etc. sensors. It is estimated that the archives of NASA include nearly 7000 types of EO datasets. The high dimensional ones (e.g., hyperspectral imagery) contain hundreds of different wavelength data and therefore, tons of information must be stored, processed, transmitted and analysed towards harnessing the potential of these diverse and multi-dimensional datasets.

The development of novel geospatial web services [50, 85, 91] for on-demand remote sensing analysis is a key issue. Geospatial web services enable users to leverage distributed geospatial data and computing resources over the network in order to automate geospatial data integration and analysis procedures. These services should be interoperable and allow for collaborative processing of geospatial data for information and knowledge discovery. The aforementioned features can be accomplished through the utilization of the service computing and workflow technologies [37, 84].

All the aforementioned aspects are actively and intensively discussed in the scientific community and industry towards building innovative solutions and providing cutting-edge technology. To this end, in the present chapter we review the current state-of-the-art on big data frameworks able to handle, process, analyse and deliver geospatial data and value-added products. Certain operational services are detailed featuring efficient implementations and architectures allowing in certain cases the online and near real-time processing and analytics. In particular, the tasks of storing, handling, retrieving, analyzing and publishing geospatial data pose significant challenges for several aspects of the state-of-the-art processing systems, including system architectures, parallel programming models, data managing on multilevel memory hierarchy and task scheduling. Current dominating system architectures for data-intensive environmental and agricultural applications are reviewed. Recently developed cutting-edge geospatial tools for cluster-based high performance computing, cloud-based platforms, parallel file systems and databases are described. Examples featuring valuable environmental and agricultural geospatial products are also presented. Last but not least, based on the current status and state-of-the-art and simultaneously considering the emerging challenges, the present study highlights certain issues, insights and future directions towards the efficient exploitation of EO big data for important engineering, environmental and agricultural applications.

10.2   Geospatial Big Data

Geospatial data (or geodata) possess qualitative and/or quantitative information along with explicit positioning and location details, such as a road network from a Geographic Information System (GIS) or a geo-referenced satellite image. Geospatial data may include additional attribute data that describe particular features found in a dataset. Geospatial data are mainly available in two formats i.e., vector (Sect. 10.2.2) and raster (Sect. 10.2.3). The vast majority of geospatial datasets tend to exhibit certain properties that classify them in the most important, interesting and challenging category of datasets, namely, Big Data. In the following sections, various geospatial big data examples are discussed (Sect. 10.2.1) in order to establish this perspective. Moreover, the development and usage of open geospatial standards for geospatial content, services, GIS data processing and data sharing (Sect. 10.2.4) is presented.

10.2.1   Multi-V Geospatial Data

Big Data are characterised by what is often referred to as a multi-V model. In particular, focusing on geospatial data, this model encapsulates five fundamental properties of EO Big Data [54]:

- **Volume:** Big datasets are the ones that occupy very large sizes in terms of storage needed.
- **Velocity:** This property accounts for the rapidness not only of the arrival of new data to a system for insertion and processing but also to how quickly a system is able to respond to processing queries on the data submitted by the users.
- **Variety:** With the term variety the different data types, non-aligned data structures as well as inconsistent data semantics are represented.
- **Veracity:** Veracity refers to how much the data can be trusted given the reliability of its source [83].

- **Value:** This property corresponds the monetary worth that a company can derive from employing Big Data computing.

Although the choice of Vs used to explain Big Data is often arbitrary and varies across technical reports and articles across the Web—e.g. as of writing viability is becoming a new V—variety, velocity, and volume [77, 92] are the items most commonly mentioned.

A goal of this study is to position the multi-V model that characterizes Big Data in regard to geospatial data. This is achieved through the presentation of use case examples derived from real world applications and challenges. This study aims to address both forms of geospatial data i.e. raster and vector data models.

Raster geospatial datasets [14] exhibit all of the properties of the multi-V model that characterizes Big Data. More specifically, raster data form big volume datasets. There is an abundance of examples that uphold this statement. In social networks there are cases of tables of incidences that their size is close to $10^8 \times 10^8$. In the earth sciences field, ESA[1] plans to host 10^{12} images that their sizes range from 500 MB to 2 GB or even beyond. Moreover, the velocity of raster data is tremendous. NASA's instrument MODIS (or Moderate Resolution Imaging Spectroradiometer) that is on board satellites Terra[2] and Aqua[3] captures and transmits daily almost 1 TB of raster data. The distributed sensors used in radio astronomy (LOFAR: distributed sensor array farms for radio astronomy) collect 2–3 PB of data per year. Furthermore, the variety of raster data is vast as we obtain data from various sensors that have different properties and operational functionalities. Furthermore, the veracity of raster data plays an important role in their use as the collected and calculated information that is derived from these datasets need to be accompanied with quality metadata. Usually, predefined procedures are used for the calculation of faults in these datasets. However, there are cases where this is happening, and a serious issue in terms of avoiding error propagation exists.

Vector geospatial datasets are also involved in a wide range of application fields that exhibit the properties of the multi-V model. Apart from simple geospatial applications that involve vector data, the most challenging one is the management and exploration of mobility data. Mobility data [70] is ubiquitous, particularly due to the automated collection of time-stamped location information from GPS-equipped devices, from everyday smartphones to dedicated software and hardware in charge of monitoring movement in land (e.g. automobiles), sea (e.g. vessels) and air (e.g. aircrafts). Such wealth of data, referenced both in space and time, enables novel classes of applications and services of high societal and economic impact, provided that the discovery of consumable and concise knowledge out of these raw data collections is made possible. These data collections form big datasets. The numbers speak for themselves as for example the tracking of 933 vessels sailing in

---

[1] www.esa.int.

[2] http://terra.nasa.gov.

[3] http://aqua.nasa.gov.

the Aegean sea during a 3 days period resulted in 3 million GPS recordings. All these valuable data need innovative solutions in order to be analysed. Real-time analysis of geospatial big data for the provision of alerts and alternates in case of emergency situations is of critical importance. To this end, several challenges are determined that must me tackled in order to be able to utilise geospatial data and create innovative, sustainable and useful geospatial data applications and services.

10.2.2 Vector Data

Many geospatial data are available in the form of vector data structures. Vector data structures are constructed from simple geometrical primitives that are based on mathematical expressions and consist of one or more interlinked nodes to represent images in computer graphics. One node determines a location in space through the use of two or three axes. In the context of geospatial data a location in space is usually determined from its geographical coordinates (i.e. longitude, latitude) and its height from sea level. The geometrical primitives can be a point, a line segment, a polyline, a triangle as well as other polygons in 2 dimensions and a cylinder, a sphere, a cube and other polyhedrons in 3 dimensions.

Vector data provide a way for the representation of entities of the real world. An entity can be anything that exists in a place. Trees, houses, roads and rivers are all entities. Each of these entities, apart from its location, has additional information—attributes that describe it. This information can be either in textual or numerical form.

Map data are usually represented in vector form. Roads for example are usually represented from polylines. Other geographical entities such as lakes or even civil entities such as provinces and countries are represented from complex polygons. Some entities can be represented by more than one geometrical primitive depending on the context of the representation. For example a river can be represented by either a curve or a polygon depending on the importance of keeping the river's width.

Utilizing the vector form to represent geospatial data has several advantages [23]. Two of the most important ones are the following:

- Vector data exhibit small demands in terms of storage sizes as the size of their disk footprint does not depend on the dimensions of the object that is represented.
- The focus (zoom in) in a vector data representation can be arbitrary high without altering the visual result of the representation.

10.2.3 Raster Data

Raster data are the other common form in which geospatial data are created and delivered. Raster data model defines space as an array of equally sized cells (i.e. bitmaps or pixels) arranged in rows and columns and composed of single or multiple bands. Each pixel [86] covers an area of fixed size and contains a value produced by a sensor that describes the conditions for the area covered. A satellite image is a typical example of a 2 dimensional raster image.

Apart from the values of each pixel the data include the area covered by the raster image that is determined for example from the geographical coordinates (i.e. longitude, latitude) of its corner pixels, the spatial resolution of the image that is determined by the total number of pixels that the image is composed or more often, as far as geospatial data are concerned, by the total area covered by a single pixel and finally the spectral resolution of the image that is determined from the number of spectral bands for which the image contains information.

The larger the spatial resolution of an image, the better its quality but the cost in storage space increases proportionally. This is in contrast with the vector data model: in order to achieve better image quality more storage resources are needed. Another disadvantage in comparison to vector data is that if one wants to achieve increased zoom quality, the pixel based model imposes limitations: pixel edges appear after a certain zoom level. As a result, the perception of continuity is lost and the various objects that are depicted are not easily distinguished.

Raster data on the other hand are extremely useful [23] when there is need to present information that is continuous in an area and as a result it cannot easily be separated in entities speaking with terms of vector data. For example a valley that has great variety in colors and vegetation density is very difficult to be represented through the vector data model. Either a very simple representation would be utilized, losing valuable information as a result of the simplification, or a very complex one would be utilized so as to digitize every single detail, a task that would require a lot of time and effort. Raster data is therefore the intended solution when we need to represent areas with homogeneous characteristics as the human eye is very capable of interpreting images and distinguishing small details that would be difficult to digitise sufficiently due to their large numbers.

Raster data are not only suitable for representing real world surfaces but can also represent more abstract concepts. For example they can display the rainfall tendencies or the danger for fire manifestation in an area. In such applications every pixel of the raster image represents a different value. In the example with the fire manifestation danger every pixel can contain a value in scale from 1 to 10 for the danger in a particular area.

The common case in geospatial data applications and mainly in their presentation, is to utilize together vector and raster data as it is evident that the two representations complete one another as far as their advantages are concerned. It is common to use raster data as base layers of information and overlay them with information that is derived from vector layers.

10.2.4 Open Geospatial Standards

The vision of the research community [31] is that all available geospatial data should be accessible through the Web and that the Web consists a "place" where geospatial data are in an easy and straightforward way published, interconnected and processed towards the extraction of knowledge and information through interoperable web services and data formats. Towards this direction, the Open Geospatial Consortium (OGC) has standardized several procedures for the analysis of geospatial data through the Web. The most important and popular standards are presented in the following sections (Sect. 10.2.4.2).

10.2.4.1   Open Geospatial Consortium (OGC)

OGC organization [67] was established in 1994 in order to promote collaboration between the various GIS systems and secure interoperability among them. The idea of an open GIS system is to withdraw from the model of developing GIS systems as monolithic software modules and advance towards designing and implementing a modular system that would include many and different software system modules. OGC is the result of the cooperation based on a consensus between public and private sector vendors and organizations, dedicated to the creation and management of an industrial scale architecture towards the interoperable processing of geospatial data. OGC's technical goals [17] are the following:

- A universal space-time data model as well as a processing model on these data that would cover all existing and potential space-time applications. This model is called "OGC data model".
- The definition of the specifications that would apply to all of the important database programming languages in order to enable them to implement the OGC data model.
- The definition of the specifications for each of the most widespread distributed computing environments in order to enable them to implement the OGC processing model.

OGC's technical activities span three different categories. These are the development of abstract specifications, the development of implementation specifications as well as the process of revising all existing specifications.

According to the goals that OGC has set, the purpose of the development of abstract specifications [66] is the creation and documentation of a conceptual model responsible for the creation of implementation specifications. Abstract specifications consist of two models: the essential model that establishes the conceptual connection between software and the real world and the abstract model that defines a final software system in a neutral way as far as its implementation is concerned (meaning that the actuals protocols needed are not defined). This gives the potential to data servers and their clients which run processing algorithms to communicate in various environments such as through the Internet, across Intranets or even in the same workstation. Technical specifications which implement the abstract specifications in each of the most widespread distributed computing environments (e.g. CORBA—Common Object Request Broker Architecture environment, DCOM and Java) are available.

All the models that are included in the abstract specifications documents and in the documents of implementation specifications are developed with UML (Unified Modeling Language). The main entity of the OGC model is the "feature" that has a certain type and geometry both of which are defined by OGC itself under the "well-known structures".

10.2.4.2 OGC Open Standards

OGC's standards[4] are technical documents that define meticulously interfaces and encodings. Software engineers use these documents to construct or integrate open interfaces and encodings in their products and services. These standards are the main products of OGC that have been developed by the community with the purpose of addressing specific interoperability challenges. Ideally, when OGC standards are integrated in products or online services that were the result of the work of two software engineers who worked independently, the produced system components can function immediately in cooperation with each other without the need for any additional work (plug and play). OGC standards along with the technical documents that define them are available to everyone at no cost. The most popular and important interface standards of OGC are presented briefly in the following paragraphs.

10.2.4.2.1   WCS

OGC's WCS (Web Coverage Service) interface standard [12], defines a standard interface and functionalities that allow for the interoperable access in geospatial data that are in the form of grid coverages. The term coverage typically describes data such as remote sensing images, digital terrain models (DTM) as well as other phenomena that can be represented by numerical values at measurement points. WCS standard is in essence a web data service. It defines a service for accessing data that allows for the retrieval of grid coverages, such as DTMs, through the HTTP protocol. The response of a dedicated web server in a WCS request includes both grid coverage's metadata and the actual data that are encoded in a specific digital image format such as GeoTIFF or NetCDF image formats.

10.2.4.2.2   WFS

OGC's WFS (Web Feature Service) interface standard [82], defines web functionalities for retrieving and processing vector data. This standard defines procedures that allow for the discovery of available sets of features (GetCapabilities), the description of geographic features (DescribeFeatureType), the retrieval of part of

---

[4]www.opengeospatial.org/standards.

the data through the use of a filter (GetFeature) as well as the addition, the updating or the removal of features (Transaction). All WFS services support data input and output through the utilization of the Geography Markup Language (GML) standard. Some WFS services support additional encodings such as GeoRSS and shapefiles. Users typically interact with WFS services through web browsers or GIS software. These allow them to gain access to data layers from various data sources through the Web.

10.2.4.2.3   WMS

OGC's WMS (Web Map Service) interface standard [24], provides a simple HTTP interface for the request and retrieval of georeferenced images and maps from one or more distributed spatial databases. The response of the database server to a WMS request is one or more images (in JPEG, PNG, etc. formats) that can be easily presented from either any web browser or from desktop applications running on a personal workstation.

10.2.4.2.4   CSW

OGC's CSW (Catalog Service for the Web) interface standard [62], specifies a design pattern for defining interfaces to publish and search collections of descriptive information (metadata) about geospatial data, services and related information objects. Providers of resources, such as content providers, use catalogues to register metadata that conform to the provider's choice of an information model; such models include descriptions of spatial references and thematic information. Client applications can then search for geospatial data and services in very efficient ways.

10.2.4.2.5   WPS

OGC's WPS (Web Processing Service) interface standard [80], provides rules for the modelling of input and output data (requests and responses) for geospatial processing services and also describes the access to spatial processing functions through the Web. These functions can include all kinds of algorithms, calculations or models that have been designed to operate on geospatial data that follow either the vector data model or the raster data model. A WPS service can perform simple calculations such as the intersection of two polygons or the addition of two digital images as well as more complex ones such as the implementation of a model for the global climate change. WPS standard defines three basic functionalities through which all processing is performed:

- **GetCapabilities**: This functionality requests from a WPS server to respond with the features of the provided service which include the service's metadata as well as the metadata that describe all available processing functions.

- **DescribeProcess**: This functionality requests from a WPS server the description of a WPS function that is available by the service. By the provision of a particular parameter (identifier) the function that will be described is determined while there is potential for requesting the description of more than one functions.
- **Execute**: This functionality submits a request to a WPS server so as to execute a certain processing function with the provided input values and the desired output data. The request, which is an XML file, can be submitted to the server either with the GET method or with the POST method of the HTTP protocol.

WPS interface standard is extremely useful as it provides an abundance of possibilities. Some of them are the reduction of the complexity of the entire procedure of data processing, the creation of processing chains, the simplification of the management of the processing functions as well as the interoperable access to processing functions of great complexity.

10.2.4.2.6 WCPS

OGC's WCPS (Web Coverage Processing Service) interface standard [11], defines a high level query language that allows for the server-side processing of complex queries that are applied on multidimensional raster data. This language functions as an interface between various clients and a server and can be characterized as the SQL language for data that are in the form of a coverage. WCPS allows for the submission of on demand processing queries to the server aiming at the ad-hoc processing of coverages in order to extract various types of results such as the calculation of a variety of quality indices, the determination of statistical evaluations as well as the creation of various types of charts such as histograms. It is a functional programming language which means that it has no side effects and uses declarative semantics which leaves room for many optimizations on the server side during query execution. This language has been designed to be safe in evaluation, which means that any valid query written in WCPS is guaranteed to terminate in a finite amount of time. This property is very important in client-server environments as it ensures that the system is secured against Denial of Service (Dos) attacks at the level of one isolated processing query. The preservation of this property (i.e. safe in evaluation) means that the language loses some capabilities as it has limited expressive power. Explicit use of iteration (e.g. for-loop) and recursion are prohibited. These design choices have been taken as a client should not have unlimited power to determine what is executed on the server-side. Even though the potential for certain calculations is lost, a wide range of processing queries are still supported. For instance, transposing a matrix might not be possible but algorithms like general convolutions are still expressible.

10.3 Geospatial Big Data Frameworks

The increasing amount of geospatial datasets [53] is outstripping the current systems' capacity of exploring and interpreting them. The tasks of storing, handling, retrieving, analyzing and publishing geospatial big data [59] pose significant challenges and create opportunities for several aspects of the state-of-the-art geospatial big data frameworks Fig. 10.1. Several components are included like cloud-based infrastructure, interoperability standards, parallel systems and programming models, Database Management Systems (DBMS) on multilevel memory hierarchy and task scheduling. Furthermore, the growing amount and resolution of geospatial data from remote sensing platforms and traditional geospatial information systems

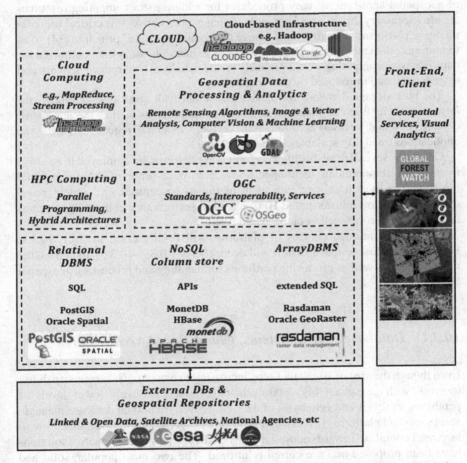

Fig. 10.1 The current dominating architecture and technology for geospatial big data and analytics

(GIS), as well as the geospatial data from new data sources such as social media and Internet of Things datasets, provide great opportunities to answer new and bigger questions from a geospatial perspective.

The emergence of geospatial big datasets is revolutionizing the techniques for analyzing and extracting valuable insights from these vastly expanding geospatial data streams. Rapid processing of geospatial big data with increasing volumes and complexity forms a great challenge for the existing big data frameworks. There is an urgent need for novel advances in system architecture, especially towards achieving inherent scalability of the underlying hardware and software. In particular, these data-intensive systems should exhibit potential for linear scaling in order to accommodate the processing of geospatial data at almost any volume.

For the purpose of meeting the near real-time processing requirement of some of geospatial applications, easy procedures for adding extra computing resources are also necessary. From a performance efficiency perspective, it is critical for data-intensive platforms to abide by the "move the code to the data" principle [34] so as to minimize data movement. Therefore, a storage hierarchy of system optimized for data-intensive computing would probably reside data locally to reduce network and system overhead introduced by data transferring.

The bulk storage demands for databases, the need for array storage models for large-scale scientific computations and large output files as well as the aggressive concurrency and per server throughput [21] are essential requirements for the applications on highly scalable computing clusters.

Currently, several available high performance platforms are employed in an effort to meet the requirements mentioned above and make sense of these geospatial big data. The most dominant choices of platforms concentrate on, namely, novel database platforms, cluster-based HPC (i.e. high performance computing) systems or supercomputers as well as cloud-based platforms.

The aforementioned choices of platforms will be discussed in Sect. 10.3.1. Following this discussion, an effort will occur (Sects. 10.3.2–10.3.5), to present the most popular as well as promising platforms for handling and processing geospatial big data.

10.3.1 Databases, HPC systems, Cloud-Based Architectures

Even though the size of Big Data keeps increasing exponentially, current capability to work with geospatial big datasets is only in the relatively lower levels of petabytes, exabytes and zettabytes of data. Moreover, traditional database management tools and platforms [21] are unable to process geospatial datasets that grow so large and complex. Towards addressing this challenge new and innovative solutions have been proposed and are currently utilized. The two most popular, solid and robust ones are Database Management Systems (DBMS) that implement the array data model on the one hand and NoSQL (Not Only SQL) database management platforms on the other.

Array DBMSs are built specifically for serving big raster datasets. As raster datasets consist of pixels forming a regular grid of one, two, or more dimensions, the array data structure is the most appropriate one for modelling geospatial big raster data. Array DBMSs implement the array data model that supports arrays as first class citizens. The model is based on an array algebra [9] developed for database purposes that introduces the array as a new attribute type to the relational model. On top of the model a query language is implemented that extends standard SQL and is enriched with array operators for raster data retrieval and processing. Array DBMSs in essence store and manage structured data. Known array DBMS implementations include *Rasdaman*, MonetDB/SciQL, PostGIS, Oracle GeoRaster and SciDB database platforms.

NoSQL [36] is a current approach for large and distributed data management and database design. A NoSQL database provides a mechanism for storage and retrieval of data that is modelled in means other than the tabular relations used in relational databases. NoSQL systems are either entirely non-relational or simply avoid selected relational functionality such as fixed table schemas and join operations. The reason why mainstream big data platforms adopt NoSQL is to break and surpass the rigidity of normalized relational DBMS schemas. Many NoSQL database platforms though, still use SQL in its database systems, as SQL is a more reliable and simpler query language with high performance in stream big data real-time analytics.

NoSQL database platforms store and manage unstructured data in a way that is contrary to relational databases as it separates data storage and management into two independent parts instead of dealing with these issues simultaneously. This design gives NoSQL databases systems a lot of advantages. The main advantages are the potential for scalability of data storage with high-performance as well as flexibility for data modelling, application developing and deployment [36]. Most NoSQL databases are schema-free. This property enables applications to quickly modify the structure of data without needing to rewrite any tables. Moreover, it allows for greater flexibility when structured data are heterogeneously stored. Well-known NoSQL implementations that serve geospatial data include MongoDB, Google BigTable, Apache HBASE and Cassandra. Companies that use NoSQL database platforms include Google, Facebook, Twitter, LinkedIn and NetFlix.

Apart from database platforms a wide variety of cluster-based HPC systems including grid computing, cluster computing and ubiquitous computing are used to process geospatial big datasets and extract meaningful information. A cluster platform [73, 74] normally performs a large computational problem by the collaborative work of multiple computers (nodes) while offering a single-system image. Currently, cluster platforms are the mainstream architecture for high performance computing and large scale scientific applications. Major organizations and enterprises such as NASA [55] and Google [7] have built large cluster systems consisting of many individual nodes for the processing of geospatial data. This kind of system [59] is able to offer high-level of data capacity, throughput, and availability by virtue of the software fault tolerance, data backup and optimized system management.

HPC systems are evolving towards hybrid and accelerator-based architectures featuring multicore CPUs as well as GPUs [35]. Moreover, they are equipped with high performance Infiniband computing network with high bandwidth for achieving low latency communication between system nodes. HPC systems though, are compute-intensive oriented and both the system architecture and tools are not optimized for data-intensive applications where data availability is the main concern. Thus, in spite of the massive computational capabilities of HPC systems, effective processing of geospatial big data on existing cluster-based HPC systems still remains a challenge. Towards confronting this issue a transition to systems that are arranged in multiple hierarchical levels is taking place. These systems have a higher dimensional connection topology and multilevel storage architecture as well. As far as performance efficiency is concerned it is of critical importance to take data locality into account. Programming for these multiple levels of locality and routes for a certain dimensionality is yet very challenging and there is a long way down to reaching viable solutions.

The development of virtualization technologies [59] have made supercomputing more accessible and affordable through the utilization of commodity hardware instead of very expensive HPC systems. Powerful computing infrastructures hidden behind virtualization software make systems behave like a true physical computer, enriched with the potential of flexibility on the specification of virtual system's details such as number of processors, memory, disk size and operating system. The use of these virtual computers is known as cloud computing [30], which has been one of the most robust Big Data techniques [78].

For real-time geospatial big data applications timeliness of system response when the volume of data is very large, is at the top priority. Cloud computing [1, 29, 81] integrates software, computations and user data to provide remote services through aggregation of multiple different workloads into a large cluster of processors. Cloud computing [21] not only delivers applications and services over the Internet but also has been extended to provide infrastructure as a service (IaaS), for example, Amazon EC2, platform as a service (PaaS), such as Google AppEngine and Microsoft Azure and software as a service (SaaS). Moreover, storage in cloud computing infrastructure provides a tool for storing Big Data with good scalability potential.

Cloud computing is a highly feasible technology and has attracted a large number of researchers to develop it and try to apply its solutions to Big Data problems. There is a need for software platforms and respective programming models that would take full advantage of the cloud computing principles and potential for storage and processing of big data. Towards this direction Apache Hadoop is one of the most well-established software platforms that support data-intensive, distributed and parallel applications. It implements the computational paradigm named Map/Reduce. Apache Hadoop platform consists of the Hadoop kernel, Map/Reduce and Hadoop distributed file system (HDFS) that offers strategic layouts and data replication for fault tolerance and better accessing performance, as well as a number of related projects that on top of it including Apache Hive, Apache HBase, Apache Spark, etc.

Map/Reduce [25] is a programming model and an execution scheme for processing and generating large volume of data sets. It was originally introduced and developed by Google and after its release it was also developed by Yahoo and other companies. Map/Reduce is based on the divide and conquer algorithm design paradigm and works by recursively breaking down a complex problem into many sub-problems (i.e. Map step), until they are scalable for solving directly. Then the sub-problems are solved in separate and parallel ways (i.e. Reduce step). The solutions to the sub-problems are then combined to give a complete solution to the original problem.

All of the well-known companies are utilising cloud computing in order to provide their services. Apart from Google, recently Yahoo has deployed its search engine on a Hadoop cluster. Moreover, Facebook and eBay also develop their large applications at a scale of exabyte with Hadoop. In addition, for large-scale geospatial data processing, search and accessing, the Hadoop-GIS [3] framework is also built upon the Hadoop system.

10.3.2   Rasdaman

Rasdaman is a universal (i.e. domain-independent) Array DBMS [8, 10, 15] which offers features for big raster data storage, manipulation and processing. Domain independent means that *Rasdaman* can act as the host database platform in wide range of database applications including online analytical processing (OLAP), statistics, earth and space sciences, medical imagery, wind channels, simulations and multimedia.

Rasdaman supports multi-dimensional arrays of very large sizes and arbitrary number of dimensions that span a remarkably rich manifold of information. From 1-D time series and 2-D images to OLAP data cubes with dozens of dimensions. Due to its design aims and capabilities the system can inherently handle big satellite imaging data. *Rasdaman*'s architecture is based on a transparent array partitioning, called tiling. Conceptually, there is no size limitation for *Rasdaman* as a central DBMS of raster datasets. It features a rich and powerful query language (i.e. RasQL) that resembles SQL but is specifically designed and implemented for serving raster datasets. RasQL is a general-purpose declarative query language enriched with internal execution, storage and transfer optimizations. Additionally, *Rasdaman* features parallel server architecture that offers a scalable, distributed environment to efficiently process very large numbers of concurrent client requests and serve distributed datasets across the Web.

Rasdaman has proven[5] [13, 48–50, 68] its efficiency and effectiveness due to its powerful query language, the transparent array partitioning that nullifies a single object's size limitations and allows for scalability as well as the feature of internally supported tile compression for reduced database size.

Moreover, *Rasdaman* implements several OGC standards towards achieving interoperability with other systems. In particular, for WCPS interface standard

---

[5]http://www.copernicus-masters.com/index.php?kat=winners.html&anzeige=winner_t-systems2014.html.

Rasdaman is the reference implementation [11]. WCPS interface standard defines a query language that allows for retrieval, filtering, processing and fast subsetting of multi-dimensional raster coverages such as sensor, simulation, image, and statistics data.

WCPS queries are submitted to the *Rasdaman* database server through PetaScope component [2]. PetaScope is a java servlet package which implements OGC standard interfaces thus allowing on demand submission of queries that search, retrieve, subset and process multidimensional arrays of very large sizes. Moreover, it adds geographic and temporal coordinate system support towards leveraging *Rasdaman* into a complete and robust geospatial big data server. The *Rasdaman Community* license releases the server under the GPL license and all client parts in LGPL, thereby allowing the use of the system in any kind of license environment.

10.3.3 MonetDB

Another framework that has been successfully used in EO applications is MonetDB which is an is an open source column-oriented DBMS. MonetDB [61] was designed to demonstrate high performance when executing complex queries against very large databases. For example when combining tables with hundreds of columns and multi-million rows. MonetDB has been applied in a wide range of high-performance applications such as OLAP, data mining, GIS, streaming data processing, text retrieval and sequence alignment processing. It was employed successfully as a database back-end in the development of a real-time wildfire monitoring service that exploits satellite images and linked geospatial data (Sect. 10.4.1).

MonetDB's architecture [43] is represented in three layers, each with its own set of optimizers. The front-end is the top layer and provides query interfaces for SQL, SciQL and SPARQL general-purpose programming languages. Queries are parsed into domain-specific representations, like relational algebra for SQL, and are then optimized. The generated logical execution plans are then translated into MonetDB Assembly Language (MAL) instructions, which are passed to the next layer. The middle or back-end layer provides a number of cost-based optimizers for the MAL. The bottom layer is the database kernel, which provides access to the data stored in Binary Association Tables (BATs). Each BAT is a table consisting of an Object-identifier and value columns, representing a single column in the database.

MonetDB's internal data representation also relies on the memory addressing ranges of contemporary CPUs using demand paging of memory mapped files, and thus departing from traditional DBMS designs involving complex management of large data stores in limited memory.

Its architecture is indeed pioneering and also integrates query recycling. Query recycling [44] is an architecture for reusing the byproducts of the operator-at-a-time paradigm in a column store DBMS. Recycling makes use of the generic idea of storing and reusing the results of expensive computations and uses an optimizer to pre-select instructions to cache. The technique works in a self-organizing fashion and is designed to improve query response times and throughput.

Moreover, MonetDB was one of the first databases to introduce Database Cracking. Database Cracking [42] is an incremental partial indexing and/or sorting of the data. It directly exploits the columnar nature of MonetDB. Cracking is a technique that shifts the cost of index maintenance from updates to query processing. The query pipeline optimizers are used to massage the query plans to crack and to propagate this information. The technique allows for improved access times and self-organized behaviour.

Furthermore, MonetDB features the MonetDB/SQL/GIS module which comes with an interface to the Simple Feature Specification of the OGC and thus supports all objects and functions defined in the specification. This opens the route to host geospatial data and thus develop GIS applications. Spatial objects can, however, for the time being only expressed in the Well-Known Text (WKT) format. WKT includes information about the type of the object and the object's coordinates. The implementation of the Simple Feature Specification gives the potential to MonetDB to function as a geospatial database server.

10.3.4   MrGeo

The National Geospatial-Intelligence Agency (NGA) [63] in collaboration with DigitalGlobe,[6] recently released as open source an application that simplifies and economizes the storage and processing of large-scale raster data, reducing the time it takes analysts to search, download, preprocess and format data for analysis.

MapReduce for Geospatial, or MrGeo, is a geospatial toolkit designed to provide raster-based geospatial capabilities (i.e. storage and processing) performable at scale by leveraging the power and functionality of cloud-based architecture. The software use, modification, and distribution rights are stipulated within the Apache 2.0 license. NGA has a vision for MrGeo to become the standard for storing, enriching and analyzing massive amounts of raster data in a distributed cloud environment.

MrGeo can ingest and store global datasets in the cloud in an application-ready format that eliminates several data pre-processing steps from production workflows thus freeing the user from all the heavy data logistics previously required in downloading and preprocessing the data on traditional desktop GIS systems. This allows the user to ask bigger questions of the data in the cloud, and receive just the calculated answers for their areas of interest, instead of having to pre-process all the stored data for obtaining the result.

MrGeo provides a general yet robust engine of MapReduce analytics for the processing of georeferenced raster data such as digital elevation models and multispectral as well as hyperspectral satellite and aerial imagery. It also provides a user-friendly command line syntax called Map Algebra interface that enables the development of custom algorithms in a simple scripting API and allows for

---

[6]https://www.digitalglobe.com.

algebraic math operations, focal operations(i.e. slope) and graph operations (e.g. cost distance) in order to chain basic operations into pipelines so as to create higher level analytic outputs.

MrGeo [64] is built upon the Hadoop ecosystem to leverage the storage and processing of hundreds of commodity hardware. An abstraction layer between the MapReduce analytics and storage methods provides a diverse set of cloud storage options such as HDFS, Accumulo, HBASE etc. Functionally, MrGeo stores large raster datasets as a collection of individual tiles stored in Hadoop to enable large-scale data and analytic services. The data storage model that maintains data locality via spatial indexing along with the co-location of data and analytics offers the ·advantage of minimizing the movement of data in favour of bringing the computation to the data; a standard principle when designing Big Data systems. It features a plugin architecture that facilitates modular software development and deployment strategies. Its data and analytic capabilities are provisioned by OGC and REST service end points.

MrGeo has been used to store, index, tile, and pyramid multi-terabyte scale image databases. Once stored, this data is made available through simple Tiled Map Services (TMS) and/or Web Mapping Services (WMS). Even though, MrGeo is primarily built for serving raster datasets, new features have been recently added that allow for vector data storage and processing.

10.3.5 CartoDB

There is a current need for flexible and intuitive ways to create dynamic online maps and design web geospatial applications. CartoDB is an open source tool that allows for the storage and visualization of geospatial data on the web and aims to become the next generation mapping platform for Big Data that follow the vector data model.

CartoDB [20] is a Software as a Service (SaaS) cloud computing platform that provides GIS and web mapping tools for displaying vector data in a web browser. CartoDB was built on open source software including PostGIS and PostgreSQL. The tool uses JavaScript extensively in the front end web application, in the back end through Node.js based APIs as well as for implementing client libraries. CartoDB platform offers a set of APIs and libraries to help users create maps, manage their data, run geospatial analytics tasks, and other functions through REST services or with client developed libraries.

CartoDB is split into four components. The first is the web application, where users can manage data and create custom maps. Users who are not technically inclined can use an intuitive interface to easily create custom maps and visualizations. Advanced users can access a web interface to use SQL to manipulate data and apply map styles using a cartography language similar to CSS (i.e. CartoCSS). The second component is a Maps API that acts as a dynamic tile service, which creates new tiles based on client requests. In addition to the Maps API, a SQL API is provided, where PostgreSQL-supported SQL statements can be used to retrieve data from the database. The SQL API serves data in various formats including JSON, GeoJSON, and CSV. Finally, there is the CartoDB.js library, which can be used for wrapping the Maps and SQL APIs into complete visualizations or for integrating data into other web applications [75].

CartoDB users can use the company's free platform or deploy their own instance of the open source software. With CartoDB, it is easy to upload geospatial data in various formats (e.g. Shapefiles, GeoJSON, etc.) using a web form and then make it public or private. After it is uploaded, one can visualize the data in a table or on a map, search it using SQL and apply map styles using CartoCSS. It is also possible to access it using the CartoDB API and SQL API, or export it to a file.

Known users of the CartoDB platform for the production of dynamic online maps include major organizations and powerful stakeholders in the technology world such as NASA, Nokia [32] and Twitter.

10.4   Geospatial Environmental and Agricultural Services

Following the discussion about Geospatial Big Data and Geospatial Big Data Frameworks in the previous sections, here we will try to present the big picture about the research goal and direction of the developed and developing technology for geospatial data.

The goal is to put together geospatial big data repositories along with geospatial big data frameworks and create novel, sustainable, useful and cost-effective services. There have been intense efforts from a variety of vendors, organizations, institutions and companies to create Geospatial Environmental and Agricultural Services for a wide range of scientific and industrial fields. Delivery of reliable services through the utilization of big datasets is the main issue nowadays. This is the case as there is an abundance of geospatial data from ubiquitous and various types of sensors as well as several developed geospatial frameworks and programming models towards their efficient handling, processing and extraction of meaningful information. Most of research funding opportunities in the field of geospatial data are turning towards design and implementation of novel services in an effort to motivate the exploitation of all these huge streams of data.

Several projects administered by global partnerships are currently developing innovative Geospatial Environmental and Agricultural Services. For example, the EarthServer project[7] in its phase 1 is creating an on-demand online open access and ad-hoc analytics infrastructure for massive (100+ TB) Earth Science data based on leading-edge Array Database platform and OGC WCPS standard. EarthServer establishes several, so-called, lighthouse applications, each of which poses distinct challenges on Earth Data analytics. These are Cryospheric Science, Airborne

---

[7]www.earthserver.eu.

Science, Atmospheric Science, Geology, Oceanography and Planetary Science. In particular, for Planetary Science, PlanetServer application is being developed.

PlanetServer[8] [68], is an online visualization and analysis service for planetary data that demonstrates how various technologies, tools and web standards can be used so as to provide big data analytics in an online environment. PlanetServer focuses on hyperspectral satellite imagery and topographic data visualization and analysis, mainly for mineralogical applications. Apart from the big data analytics part PlanetServer could aid in collaborative data analysis, as it is capable of sharing planetary data hosted on a database server and querying them from either any web client through any supported web browser or from any online processing service that adheres to OGC standards. Currently, phase 2 of EarthServer is starting with the ambitious goal that each of the participating data centers will provide at least 1 Petabyte of 3-D and 4-D datacubes. Technology advance will allow real-time scaling of such Petabyte cubes, and intercontinental fusion. This power of data handling will be wrapped into direct visual interaction based on multi-dimensional visualization techniques, in particular: NASA WorldWind.

In addition, the European Space Agency (ESA) leads a global partnership towards developing, Geohazard Supersites,[9] an earth observation platform involved in monitoring the dynamic and complex solid-earth system as well as the assessment of geohazards and ultimately focusing on earthquake and volcano research. Its mission is to support the Group of Earth Observation (GEO) in the effort to reduce loss of life and property caused by the natural disasters of earthquakes and volcano eruptions. The Geohazard Supersites project relies on cutting-edge computing facilities that feature more than 350 CPUs in about 70 nodes, 330 TB of local online storage and internal as well as external connection of 1 Gbps LAN in an effort to advance scientific understanding of the physical processes which control earthquakes and volcanic eruptions as well as earth surface dynamics. The Geohazard Supersites platform will provide an open source, unified e-infrastructure for enabling secure solid earth data sharing on the cloud and international collaboration that will eventually result in improved data products for solid earth monitoring, better scientific understanding of geo-hazards and combination of information extracted from different sources (e.g. satellite & in-situ).

In this section, innovative Geospatial Environmental and Agricultural Services that span a wide range of activities will be presented in an effort to make more comprehensible the combination of geospatial data and processing platforms of different orientation towards the creation, design and implementation of geospatial services and applications.

---

[8]www.planetserver.eu.

[9]http://www.helix-nebula.eu/usecases/esa-ssep-use-case.

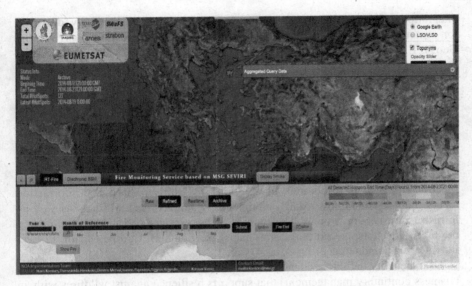

Fig. 10.2 The user interface of the FIREHUB service (accessed 31 July 2015)

10.4.1   FireHub

The developed FIREHUB[10] project proposes a fully transferable to all sites of Europe fire detection and monitoring service and provides large-scale burn scar mapping capabilities during and after wildfires as well as hourly fire-smoke dispersion forecasting [52]. It is currently fully covering the Greek territory and has already been used by emergency managers for the monitoring of wildfires (Fig. 10.2).

The service has been developed following a database approach to the development of EO applications using scientific database management and linked data technologies and is implemented on top of MonetDB as the central DBMS and Strabon which is a semantic spatiotemporal RDF store. It utilizes SciQL [89] an SQL-based query language for scientific applications with arrays as first class citizens. SciQL allows MonetDB to effectively function as an array database. SciQL is used together with the Data Vault technology, providing transparent access to large scientific data repositories [90].

Data Vault is a database-attached external file repository for MonetDB, similar to the SQL/MED standard. The Data Vault technology allows for transparent

---

[10]http://www.copernicus-masters.com/index.php?kat=winners.html&anzeige=winner_bsc2014.
html.

integration with distributed/remote file repositories. It is specifically designed for remote sensing data exploration and mining [45]. There is support for the GeoTIFF (Earth observation), FITS (astronomy), MiniSEED (seismology) and NetCDF formats. The data is stored in the file repository, in the original format, and loaded in the database in a lazy fashion, only when needed. The system can also process the data upon ingestion, if the data format requires it. As a result, even very large file repositories can be efficiently analyzed, as only the required data is processed in the database. Data Vaults map the data from the distributed repositories to SciQL arrays, allowing for improved handling of spatio-temporal data in MonetDB [45].

FIREHUB depends on the real-time processing of satellite images of different spectral and spatial resolutions in combination with auxiliary geo-information layers (land use/land cover data, administrative boundaries and roads as well as infrastructure networks data). The outputs of the service are validated fire-related products (e.g. hotspot and burnt area maps) for Southern Europe (Spain, France, Italy, Portugal and Greece).

User benefits include evidence-based decision making (in civil protection and business continuity management) that supports resilience against wildfires with an eye towards societal and economic welfare as well as protection of human lives, private property, and ecosystems.

10.4.2 Global Forest Watch

Another geospatial platform is the Global Forest Watch Service[11] [38] which is a milestone online framework powered by Google Earth Engine towards the quantification of global forest change which has been lacking despite the recognized importance of forest ecosystem services. It forms a dynamic online forest monitoring and alert system which exploits satellite technology, open data and crowdsourcing to guarantee access to timely and reliable information about forest status globally (Fig. 10.3).

In particular, Global Forest Watch (GFW) is an interactive online forest monitoring and alert system designed to empower people everywhere with the information they need to better manage and conserve forest landscapes. GFW uses cutting edge technology and science to provide the timeliest and most precise information about the status of forest landscapes worldwide, including near-real-time alerts showing suspected locations of recent tree cover loss. GFW is free and simple to use, enabling anyone to create custom maps, analyze forest trends, subscribe to alerts, or download data for their local area or the entire world. Users can also contribute to GFW by sharing data and stories from the ground via GFW's crowdsourcing tools, blogs, and discussion groups. Special 'apps' provide detailed information for

---

[11]http://www.globalforestwatch.org/.

Fig. 10.3 The user interface of the Global Forest Watch platform powered by the Google Earth Engine (accessed 31 July 2015)

companies that wish to reduce the risk of deforestation in their supply chains, users who want to monitor fires across Southeast Asia, and more. GFW serves a variety of users including governments, the private sector, NGOs, journalists, universities, and the general public.

Global Forest Watch hosts a wealth of data relating to forests. Some data have been developed by the World Resources Institute or by GFW partner organizations. Other data are in the public domain and have been developed by governments, NGOs, and companies. The data vary in accuracy, resolution, frequency of update, and geographic coverage. Global Forest Watch was launched on February 20, 2014, convening government and corporate leaders to explore how governments, businesses and communities can halt forest loss. Recent reported results based on GFW and earth observation satellite data were used to map global forest loss (2.3 million square kilometers) and gain (0.8 million square kilometers) from 2000 to 2012 at a spatial resolution of 30 m. The tropics were the only climate domain to exhibit a trend, with forest loss increasing by 2101 square kilometers per year.

10.4.3 RemoteAgri

In recent decades, EO and RS scientific fields have provided valuable insights into agronomic management [39, 76]. Along with geospatial technology, they continue to evolve as an agronomic tool of significant importance which provides information to scientists, consultants and farmers about the status of their crops towards

Fig. 10.4 The user interface of the *RemoteAgri* platform (accessed 31 July 2015)

improved and optimal management decisions [88]. By precisely measuring the way in which agricultural fields reflect and emit electromagnetic energy in different spectral regions, EO satellites can quantitatively assess agronomic parameters by monitoring a wide range of variables including surface temperature, photosynthetic activity, soil moisture and weed or pest infestations (Fig. 10.4).

Agricultural maps produced from RS data are useful at several stages in the agricultural value chain and allow the farmer to make rational and comprehensive decisions when planning, planting and growing new crops. Geospatial products and EO information deliver direct benefits in the agriculture sector which stem from: (1) cost reductions through optimizing the application of field inputs, (2) profitability through increased yield and (3) potential competitive advantages through ameliorating crop quality and optimal decisions on crop type, variety and land cover/use. In addition, by reducing field inputs, the run-off of fertilizers and pesticides is reduced and therefore benefit the environment.

Towards this direction, a framework for the online, on the server-side analysis of EO data has been designed and developed [47] for precision agriculture applications. In particular, the core functionality consists of the *Rasdaman* Array DBMS for storage, and the OGC WCPS for data querying. Various WCPS queries have been designed and implemented in order to access and process multispectral satellite imagery. The WebGIS client, which is based on the OpenLayers and GeoExt javascript libraries, exploits these queries enabling the online ad-hoc spatial and spectral multispectral data analysis. The developed queries, which are focusing on agricultural applications, can efficiently estimate vegetation coverage, canopy and water stress over agricultural and forest areas. The online delivered remote sensing products have been evaluated and compared with similar processes performed from standard desktop remote sensing and GIS software.

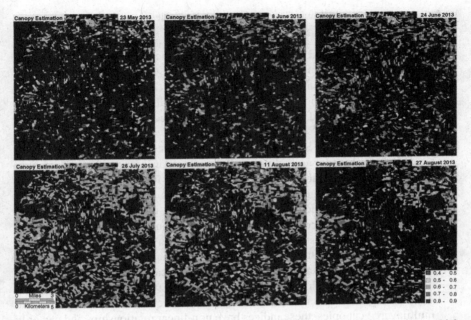

Fig. 10.5 Multitemporal canopy greenness levels after the application of the developed geospatial service over an agricultural area near Larissa at the Thessaly region, Greece

10.4.3.1 Agricultural Services

The developed services, which have been implemented through WCPS queries, are addressing important tasks like vegetation detection, canopy greenness estimation (green foliage density) and land surface temperature mapping (Fig. 10.5).

Standard vegetation indices have been employed which have been proven highly successful in assessing vegetation condition, foliage, cover, phenology, and processes such as evapotranspiration (ET), primary productivity and fraction of photosynthetically active radiation absorbed by a canopy [4, 71]. Vegetation indices represent, in general, composite properties of the leaf area index (LAI) and canopy architecture, since plant canopy reflectance integrates the contributions of leaf optical properties, plant canopy architecture and the reflectance of underlying materials like soil, plant litter, and weeds [33, 39]. Therefore, the system calculates certain standard broadband indices towards optically measuring and mapping the canopy greenness which can be considered as a composite property of leaf chlorophyll content, leaf area, green foliage density, canopy cover and structure.

In particular, the following services have been developed and validated in *RemoteAgri*:

(1) **Color Composites and Vegetation Indices:** For the purpose of visualizing the stored earth observation data the creation of color composites upon a request is possible. Apart from natural color composites (e.g., RGB432 for Landsat 8), the online calculation of other composites is also available like RGB543 and RGB654. Standard broadband vegetation indices are also calculated upon request.

(2) **Vegetation detection:** Since the different AOIs that the user can indicate (from single fields to broader agricultural areas) may contain areas with no vegetation, this service is responsible for classifying a certain image into two classes i.e., vegetation and not vegetation. This information is derived through a specific query based on the calculation of NDVI against a threshold value or through a more complex and computationally intensive multiclass classification. The result is delivered and stored in a binary imaging format.

(3) **Canopy greenness:** Based on vegetation detection and NDVI computation, this service delivers canopy greenness maps. Optical observations on LAI can be well correlated with vegetation indices like NDVI for single plant species which are grown under uniform conditions. However, for mixed, dense and multilayered canopies, these indices have non-linear relationships and can only be employed as proxies for crop-dependent vegetation parameters such as fractional vegetation cover, LAI, albedo and emissivity. The service proceeds with a further classification for those areas that have been detected to contain vegetation towards estimating the different canopy greenness levels which can be associated with the vegetative canopy vigour, biomass, leaf chlorophyll content, canopy cover and structure.

(4) **Crop-field Surface Temperature:** Various studies have demonstrated the relationship between satellite thermal data and actual rates of ET towards quantifying water consumption on specific, individually-irrigated and rainfed fields [18, 41]. Evaporation, in general, cools surfaces, so lower surface temperatures are typically associated with wetter soil and greater ET rates. In-season irrigation issues and patterns can be detected early enough before the symptoms are visually apparent in the canopy. This service calculates surface temperature using narrow band emissivity and corrected thermal radiance towards the quantification of the water use on a field-by-field basis. In particular, precision irrigation requires accurate spatial and temporal monitoring of the actual water use in order to infer water stress for irrigation decisions, aid in yield and assessment of drought conditions. Focusing on a simplified query structure and based on the detected vegetation regions, the information from the available satellite thermal band (e.g., Landsat 8 TIRS) is employed. For practical and visualization purposes, the temperature values are transformed into Celsius degrees and are then classified into 6 to 8 categories with non-overlapping intervals.

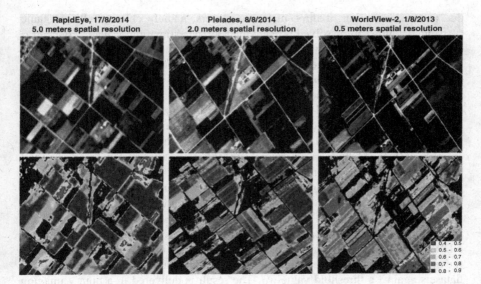

Fig. 10.6 Canopy greenness estimation on the Vegora agricultural region from different satellite sensors (i.e., RapidEye, Pleiades, WorldView-2) and spatial resolutions. The natural color composites are shown in the *top* and the estimated canopy greenness levels from the developed system, on the *bottom*

In Fig. 10.6, the canopy greenness maps are shown based on different satellite sensors (i.e., RapidEye, Pleiades, WorldView-2) and spatial resolutions. Although, acquired at different dates, the information about the spatial in-field variability increases with the level of spatial detail. More specifically, for the vineyards located in this particular area (PDO zone of Amynteo where the Xinomavro variety is dominating) canopy greenness maps, with a spatial resolution between 0.5 and 5 m, can depict the spatial variability that is associated with the vegetative canopy vigour, biomass, leaf chlorophyll content, canopy cover and structure.

10.4.4   RemoteWater

Water quality is a fundamental aspect of global freshwater resources. Information about water quality is needed to assess baseline conditions and to understand trend for water resource management. Therefore, the importance of evaluating and monitoring water quality in terrestrial reservoirs is clear and self-evident. The most commonly used methodology to examine the quality of water is through in-situ sampling and chemical analysis. In-situ sampling leads to accurate estimations but lacks in several other areas.

Therefore, reliable and low cost monitoring methods and techniques are becoming more and more essential. However, natural inland waters are optically complex due to the interaction of three main parameters, namely chlorophyll, inorganic suspended solids and dissolved organic matter. The estimation of water concentrations in sensitive shallow systems through the use of multispectral remote sensing imagery can be hindered due to possible errors in consistent correlation. The optical complexity poses many challenges to the accurate retrieval of biogeochemical parameters. The depth of the lake and the aquatic vegetation levels is of significant importance. Many standard chlorophyll-a retrieval algorithms, which are optically dominated by phytoplankton and their breakdown products, tend to fail when applied to more turbid inland and coastal waters whose optical properties are strongly influenced by non-covarying concentrations of non-algal particles and coloured dissolved organic matter [40, 69, 79].

Based on a similar framework like the aforementioned *RemoteAgri* tool, a geospatial service able to monitor the quality of inland water was developed. More specifically, the calculation of the Normalized Difference Water Index (NDWI) is the first component of the *RemoteWater* service. Based on the calculation of the NDWI the detection of water bodies can be performed upon request. In particular, the query performs water detection based on the calculation of NDWI on the stored datasets against a threshold value *wd*. The result is delivered in a binary imaging format (Fig. 10.7).

Moreover, the concentration of the photosynthetic green pigment chlorophyll-*a* in inland water bodies is a proven indicator of the abundance and biomass of microscopic plants (phytoplankton) such as unicellular algae and cyanobacteria. Chlorophyll data are useful over a range of spatial scales for monitoring the water quality and environmental status of water bodies. Both the Blue and the Coastal spectral bands, as well as the Green one for lower absorption rates have

Fig. 10.7 The user interface of the RemoteWater platform (accessed 31 July 2015)

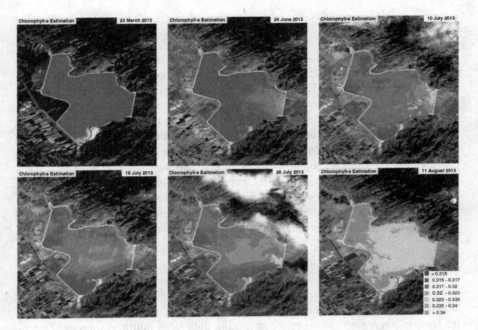

Fig. 10.8 Multitemporal chlorophyll concentrations after the application of the Chlorophyll Estimation geospatial service

been employed. For visualisation purposes the output is determined by zoning the different estimated chlorophyll levels.

Experimental results from six different acquisition dates are demonstrated for the Chlorophyll Estimation service (in Fig. 10.8). In particular, Fig. 10.8 pictures a sensitive and shallow inland water body i.e., Lake Karla in Magnesia Prefecture, Greece. One can observe that from early spring the Chlorophyll levels are gradually increasing with a peak during the summer period. In particular, during just a 20 days period (from middle July to middle August) Chlorophyll concentrations have increased significantly. This is in accordance with the in-situ measurements which are periodically performed according to the EU water directives. More dates and results of these particular two services can be found here: http://users.ntua.gr/karank/Demos/BigGeoServices.html.

10.5   Current Challenges

In this section, current challenges in regard to geospatial big data and particularly the specific issue of their management for performing analytics are discussed.

10.5.1   Data Volume

How to handle an always increasing volume of geodata? This challenge is the
most fundamental in the field of Big Data, since this is the determinant property
of this kind of datasets. The two most common ways to address this issue is
through either data partitioning or remote processing of geospatial data. In the
first case, geodata are partitioned in smaller, distributed pieces of data, processed
in a parallel environment and the results are then gathered and combined so as
to perform final analysis. In the second case, when data cannot be partitioned (in
cases when the study problem includes global features/characteristics that have
to be calculated and shared globally between processes, e.g. knowledge-based
classification, image understanding through context information etc.), the solution
is to bring the processing to the data, through remote execution of algorithms, and
very high code optimization and robust processing algorithms.

10.5.2   Data Variety

When the data is unstructured, how to quickly extract meaningful content out of
it? How to aggregate and correlate streaming data from multiple sources? Due to
the vast variety of the original data, big data experts usually employ knowledge
discovery methods which refer to a set of activities designed to extract new
knowledge from complex datasets. Methods like multi-modal data fusion for raster
data, help remote sensing experts to extract information from multi-sensor imagery.
In a similar way, advanced methods for spatial indexing (like adaptive map tiling
schemes within n-dimensional data arrays) is the way forward towards performing
very complex spatial queries to both raster and vector datasets.

10.5.3   Data Storage

How to efficiently recognise and store important information extracted from
unstructured data? How to store large volumes of information in a way it can be
timely retrieved? Are current file systems optimised for the volume and variety
required by analytics? If not, what are the new capabilities that are needed? How to
store information in a way that it can be easily migrated/ported between data centres
and/or cloud providers? Although data storage is becoming gradually cheaper and
more efficient, robust distributed systems are required with the ability to partition
data efficiently, duplicate information, search and retrieve data in extremely high
speeds. Such state-of-the-art systems are currently evolving, but for geospatial
datasets (especially raster) these systems are not yet optimized to handle huge
geospatial files in a distributed environment. Recent systems involving storage of
Landsat 8 and MODIS imagery show that scalability of storage has not yet reached
a satisfying level. Cloud storage systems like the RADOS (reliable autonomic

distributed object store) Block Device[12] and GlusterFS[13] will become even more efficient in the near future, especially with spatial extensions, in order to smartly distribute information on storage based on spatial information.

10.5.4   Data Integration

New protocols and interfaces for the integration of information that are able to manage data of different nature (structured, unstructured, semi-structured) and sources are required. In this area, the work done by open standards in the spatial world is in an optimal direction. Through open standardisation procedures, new efficient standards emerge, like GeoJSON, Vector Tiles, Irregular tiles in n-array databases, which are all under some kind of standardization process (either in OGC or under an open source license on GitHub). Given that there is ongoing work in spatial indexes, even for unstructured data (like SOLR spatial indexing or spatial extensions of CouchDB), the challenge of integrating geospatial big data seems to be anticipated and addressed by current and future technology.

10.5.5   Data Processing and Resource Management

New programming models optimised for streaming and/or multidimensional data; new backbend engines that manage optimised file systems; engines able to combine applications from multiple programming models (e.g. MapReduce, workflows, and bag-of-tasks) on a single solution/abstraction are among the current challenges. The way to optimise resource usage in such complex system architectures is, also, an open matter. These challenges can fairly be considered as the harder ones to tackle and in particular for geospatial big data. Either by predicting the nature of data or by robust algorithms which can efficiently extract the required information, a system architect must optimize the workflows for data retrieval, data preprocessing, distribution of storage and finally utilization of services and delivery of analytics and value-added geospatial maps.

10.5.6   Visualisation and User Interaction

There are important research challenges in the field of big data visualisation, especially for geospatial data, mainly due to their dimensionality. Firstly, more

---

[12]http://ceph.com/docs/master/rbd/rbd/.

[13]http://www.gluster.org/.

efficient data processing techniques are required in order to enable real-time visualisation. To this end, Choo and Park [22] appoint some techniques that can be employed such as the reduction of spatial accuracy, the processing at coarser scales in relation to the screen/device resolution, reduced convergence, and data scale confinement. Methods considering each of these techniques could be further expanded. Visualisation approaches for the management of computer networks and software analytics [60] is also an area that is attracting attention by researchers and practitioners for its extreme relevance to management of large-scale infrastructure (such as cloud-based systems) and software, with implications in global software development, open source software development, and software quality improvements.

The aforementioned challenges reflect the currently main open issues, however the list above is not exhaustive [5, 16, 26].

10.6 Future Perspectives

Current geospatial big data technologies are working towards, scalability, efficiency of storage and delivery of geospatial analytics in order to deliver spatial analysis information not only to a large audience of GIS professionals but also to users of mobile applications, social media and open data initiatives. The main goal is to move from simple monitoring and reporting on events to a collection of high-end spatial services that can provide useful analytics to every-day requirements from end-users and professionals involved in spatial information applications like agriculture, environment, forestry etc. More specifically, we are in anticipation of a move from data analytics and real-time applications not only to the monitoring of changes in real time but also to the prediction of changes through robust modelling, artificial intelligence and machine learning.

Furthermore, in geospatial big data, a paradigm shift to every-day monitoring of the entire planet not only through micro-satellites, in a spatial resolution of a few meters (in the raster world), but also with hyperspectral imagery from drones and satellites is expected in the following years. Moreover, significant attention will gain the upcoming technology of video streaming from earth observation satellites [51] which will introduce a huge evolution of available spatial data from space, with concurrent explosion in data storage needs and compression rates from new algorithms.

In RS, the introduction of low-cost drones, is expected to boost the acquisition of remote sensing data with ultra high spatial resolution i.e., 10 cm or less. This imposes more challenges on the amount of image processing resources and requires more effort and tools towards automation, especially for the interpretation of raw data to calibrated and validated information. To this end, machine learning techniques like deep learning approaches can provide robust frameworks for image classification and object recognition.

In addition, location-based geospatial services form new perspectives in the framework of Smart Cities and the Internet-of-Things. Cutting-edge technology gradually makes possible the accurate and quick in-door positioning, navigation and 3D reconstruction. The potential for integrating 3D maps, geospatial analytics and services with front-end systems provide the necessary boost for R&D along with a new range of applications.

Last but not least, by merging maps and reconstructed objects with the real world augmented reality can form the way we perceive the world. To this end, personalized maps based on the rapid and real-time integration of user requests, perceived, extracted or predicted geometry with geodata are among the future directions. From a computational cartography aspect creating personalized mapping services depends on the level that the structure of geospatial information allows for its automatic processing. Further advances in semantics can offer an adequate ontology for such an automated geospatial analysis.

References

1. Adamov A (2012) Distributed file system as a basis of data-intensive computing. In: 2012 6th International conference on application of information and communication technologies (AICT), pp 1–3. doi:10.1109/ICAICT.2012.6398484
2. Aiordachioaie A, Baumann P (2010) Petascope: An open-source implementation of the ogc wcs geo service standards suite. In: Gertz M, Ludascher B (eds) Scientific and statistical database management. Lecture Notes in Computer Science, vol 6187, Springer, Berlin/Heidelberg, pp 160–168
3. Aji A, Wang F, Vo H, Lee R, Liu Q, Zhang X, Saltz J (2013) Hadoop gis: A high performance spatial data warehousing system over mapreduce. Proc VLDB Endowment 6(11):1009–1020. doi:10.14778/2536222.2536227, http://dx.doi.org/10.14778/2536222.2536227
4. Asrar G, Kanemasu E, Yoshida M (1985) Estimates of leaf area index from spectral reflectance of wheat under different cultural practices and solar angles. Remote Sens Environ 17:1–11
5. Assuncao MD, Calheiros RN, Bianchi S, Netto MA, Buyya R (2014) Big data computing and clouds: trends and future directions. J Parallel Distrib Comput. doi:http://dx.doi.org/10.1016/j.jpdc.2014.08.003, http://www.sciencedirect.com/science/article/pii/S0743731514001452
6. Babaee M, Datcu M, Rigoll G (2013) Assessment of dimensionality reduction based on communication channel model; application to immersive information visualization. In: 2013 IEEE international conference on big data, pp 1–6. doi:10.1109/BigData.2013.6691726
7. Barroso L, Dean J, Holzle U (2003) Web search for a planet: the google cluster architecture. IEEE Micro 23(2):22–28. doi:10.1109/MM.2003.1196112
8. Baumann P (1994) Management of multidimensional discrete data. Int J Very Large Data Bases 4(3):401–444
9. Baumann P (1999) A database array algebra for spatio-temporal data and beyond. In: Next generation information technologies and systems, pp 76–93
10. Baumann P (2009) Array databases and raster data management. In: Ozsu T, Liu L (eds), Encyclopedia of database systems. Springer, New York
11. Baumann P (2010) The OGC web coverage processing service (WCPS) standard. GeoInformatica 14(4):447–479. doi:10.1007/s10707-009-0087-2
12. Baumann P (2012) OGC WCS 2.0 Interface Standard-Core: Corrigendum (OGC 09-110r4)

13. Baumann P (2014) rasdaman: array databases boost spatio-temporal analytics. In: 2014 fifth international conference on computing for geospatial research and application (COM.Geo), pp 54–54
14. Baumann P, Nativi S (2012) Adding big earth data analytics to geoss. Group on Earth Observations Ninth Plenary Session – GEO-IX. Brazil, 22–23 November
15. Baumann P, Dehmel A, Furtado P, Ritsch R, Widmann N (1998) The multidimensional database system rasdaman. In: Proceedings of the 1998 ACM SIGMOD international conference on management of data. ACM Press, New York, pp 575–577
16. Begoli E, Horey J (2012) Design principles for effective knowledge discovery from big data. In: 2012 joint working IEEE/IFIP conference on IEEE software architecture (WICSA) and European conference on software architecture (ECSA), pp 215–218
17. Buehler K, McKee L (2006) The openGIS guide (third edition). In: Technical Committee, version 1, Engineering Specification Best Practices, OGIS TC Doc. 96-001
18. Cammalleri C, Anderson M, Gao F, Hain C, Ku W (2014) Mapping daily evapotranspiration at field scales over rainfed and irrigated agricultural areas using remote sensing data fusion. Agr Forest Meteorol 186(0):1–11
19. Cappelaere P, Sanchez S, Bernabe S, Scuri A, Mandl D, Plaza A (2013) Cloud implementation of a full hyperspectral unmixing chain within the nasa web coverage processing service for EO-1. IEEE J Sel Top Appl Earth Obs Remote Sens 6(2):408–418. doi:10.1109/JSTARS.2013.2250256
20. CartoDB (Retrieved 2015) https://cartodb.com/platform
21. Chen J, Chen J, Liao A, Cao X, Chen L, Chen X, He C, Han G, Peng S, Lu M, Zhang W, Tong X, Mills J (2014) Global land cover mapping at 30m resolution: a POK-based operational approach. Int J Photogr Remote Sens. doi:http://dx.doi.org/10.1016/j.isprsjprs.2014.09.002
22. Choo J, Park H (2013) Customizing computational methods for visual analytics with big data. Computer Graphics and Applications, IEEE 33(4):22–28
23. Davis B (1996) GIS: A Visual Approach. OnWord Press
24. de la Beaujardiere J (2006) OpenGIS Web Map Server Implementation Specification (OGC 06-042)
25. Dean J, Ghemawat S (2008) Mapreduce: Simplified data processing on large clusters. Commun ACM 51(1):107–113. doi 10.1145/1327452.1327492, http://doi.acm.org/10.1145/1327452.1327492
26. Demchenko Y, Zhao Z, Grosso P, Wibisono A, De Laat C (2012) Addressing big data challenges for scientific data infrastructure. In: 2012 IEEE 4th international conference on cloud computing technology and science (CloudCom). IEEE, New York, pp 614–617
27. Espinoza-Molina D, Datcu M (2013) Earth-observation image retrieval based on content, semantics, and metadata. IEEE IEEE Trans Geosci Remote Sens 51(11):5145–5159. doi:10.1109/TGRS.2013.2262232
28. Evangelidis K, Ntouros K, Makridis S, Papatheodorou C (2014) Geospatial services in the cloud. Comput. Geosci. 63(0):116–122. doi:http://dx.doi.org/10.1016/j.cageo.2013.10.007, http://www.sciencedirect.com/science/article/pii/S0098300413002719
29. Foster I, Zhao Y, Raicu I, Lu S (2008) Cloud computing and grid computing 360-degree compared. In: Grid computing environments workshop, 2008 (GCE '08), pp 1–10. doi:10.1109/GCE.2008.4738445
30. Furht B, Escalante A (2011) Handbook of cloud computing. Springer, New York
31. Garcia-Rojas A, Athanasiou S, Lehmann J, Hladky D (2013) Geoknow: leveraging geospatial data in the web of data. In: Open data on the web workshop, http://jens-lehmann.org/files/2013/odw_geoknow.pdf
32. gigaomcom (Retrieved 2015) Can you predict future traffic patterns? Nokia thinks it can. https://gigaom.com/2013/07/02/living-cities-lights-up-traffic-in-5-cities-with-interactive-data-visualization/

33. Glenn EP, Huete AR, Nagler PL, Nelson SG (2008) Relationship between remotely-sensed vegetation indices, canopy attributes and plant physiological processes: what vegetation indices can and cannot tell us about the landscape. Sensors 8(4):2136. doi:10.3390/s8042136, http://www.mdpi.com/1424-8220/8/4/2136

34. Gray   J   (2008)   Distributed   computing   economics.   Queue   6(3):63–68. doi:10.1145/1394127.1394131, http://doi.acm.org/10.1145/1394127.1394131

35. Habib S, Morozov V, Frontiere N, Finkel H, Pope A, Heitmann K (2013) Hacc: Extreme scaling and performance across diverse architectures. In: Proceedings of the international conference on high performance computing, networking, storage and analysis (SC '13). ACM, New York, pp 6:1–6:10. doi:10.1145/2503210.2504566, http://doi.acm.org/10.1145/2503210.2504566

36. Han J, Haihong E, Le G, Du J (2011) Survey on nosql database. In: 2011 6th international conference on pervasive computing and applications (ICPCA), pp 363–366. doi:10.1109/ICPCA.2011.6106531

37. Han W, Yang Z, Di L, Yue P (2014) A geospatial web service approach for creating on-demand cropland data layer thematic maps. Transactions of the ASABE 57(1):239–247. doi:http://dx.doi.org/10.13031/trans.57.10020

38. Hansen MC, Potapov PV, Moore R, Hancher M, Turubanova SA, Tyukavina A, Thau D, Stehman SV, Goetz SJ, Loveland TR, Kommareddy A, Egorov A, Chini L, Justice CO, Townshend JRG (2013) High-resolution global maps of 21st-century forest cover change. Science 342(6160):850–853. doi:10.1126/science.1244693

39. Hatfield JL, Prueger JH (2010) Value of using different vegetative indices to quantify agricultural crop characteristics at different growth stages under varying management practices. Remote Sens 2(2):562. doi:10.3390/rs2020562, http://www.mdpi.com/2072-4292/2/2/562

40. Hunter PD, Tyler AN, Présing M, Kovács AW, Preston T (2008) Spectral discrimination of phytoplankton colour groups: the effect of suspended particulate matter and sensor spectral resolution. Remote Sens Environ 112(4):1527–1544. doi:http://dx.doi.org/10.1016/j.rse.2007.08.003, http://www.sciencedirect.com/science/article/pii/S0034425707004051, remote Sensing Data Assimilation Special Issue

41. Hwang K, Choi M (2013) Seasonal trends of satellite-based evapotranspiration algorithms over a complex ecosystem in East Asia. Remote Sens Environ 137(0):244–263

42. Idreos S, Kersten ML, Manegold S (2007) Database cracking. In: CIDR 2007, Third biennial conference on innovative data systems research, Asilomar, CA, January 7-10, 2007, Online Proceedings, pp 68–78, http://www.cidrdb.org/cidr2007/papers/cidr07p07.pdf

43. Idreos S, Groffen F, Nes N, Manegold S, Mullender S, Kersten M (2012) Monetdb: two decades of research in column-oriented database architectures. IEEE Data Eng Bull 35(1):40–45

44. Ivanova MG, Kersten ML, Nes NJ, Gonçalves RA (2010) An architecture for recycling intermediates in a column-store. ACM Trans Database Syst 35(4):24:1–24:43. doi:10.1145/1862919.1862921, http://doi.acm.org/10.1145/1862919.1862921

45. Ivanova M, Kersten M, Manegold S (2012) Data vaults: A symbiosis between database technology and scientific file repositories. In: Ailamaki A, Bowers S (eds) Scientific and statistical database management. Lecture notes in computer science, vol. 7338. Springer, Berlin/Heidelberg, pp 485–494. doi:10.1007/978-3-642-31235-9_32, http://dx.doi.org/10.1007/978-3-642-31235-9_32

46. Karantzalos K, Bliziotis D, Karmas A (2015) A scalable web geospatial service for near real-time, high-resolution land cover mapping. IEEE J Sel Top Appl Earth Obs Remote Sens Special Issue on 'Big Data in Remote Sensing' 8(10):4665–4674

47. Karantzalos K, Karmas A, Tzotsos A (2015) RemoteAgri: processing online big earth observation data for precision agriculture. In: European conference on precision agriculture

48. Karmas A, Karantzalos K (2015) Benchmarking server-side software modules for handling and processing remote sensing data through rasdaman. In: (WHISPERS) IEEE workshop on hyperspectral image and signal processing: evolution in remote sensing

49. Karmas A, Karantzalos K, Athanasiou S (2014) Online analysis of remote sensing data for agricultural applications. In: OSGeo's European conference on free and open source software for geospatial

50. Karmas A, Tzotsos A, Karantzalos K (2015) Scalable geospatial web services through efficient, online and near real-time processing of earth observation data. In: (BigData Service 2015) IEEE international conference on big data computing service and applications
51. Kopsiaftis G, Karantzalos K (2015) Vehicle detection and traffic density monitoring from very high resolution satellite video data. In: IEEE international geoscience and remote sensing symposium (IGARSS 2015)
52. Koubarakis M, Kontoes C, Manegold S (2013) Real-time wildfire monitoring using scientific database and linked data technologies. In: 16th international conference on extending database technology
53. Kouzes R, Anderson G, Elbert S, Gorton I, Gracio D (2009) The changing paradigm of data-intensive computing. Computer 42(1):26–34. doi:10.1109/MC.2009.26
54. Laney D (Retrieved 6 February 2001) 3d data management: controlling data volume, velocity and variety. Gartner
55. Lee C, Gasster S, Plaza A, Chang CI, Huang B (2011) Recent developments in high performance computing for remote sensing: a review. IEEE J Selected Top Appl Earth Obsand Remote Sens 4(3):508–527. doi:10.1109/JSTARS.2011.2162643
56. Liu B, Blasch E, Chen Y, Shen D, Chen G (2013) Scalable sentiment classification for big data analysis using Naive Bayes Classifier. In: 2013 IEEE international conference on big data, pp 99–104. doi:10.1109/BigData.2013.6691740
57. Ma Y, Wang L, Liu P, Ranjan R (2014) Towards building a data-intensive index for big data computing - a case study of remote sensing data processing. Information Sciences. doi:http://dx.doi.org/10.1016/j.ins.2014.10.006
58. Ma Y, Wang L, Zomaya A, Chen D, Ranjan R (2014) Task-tree based large-scale mosaicking for massive remote sensed imageries with dynamic dag scheduling. IEEE Trans Parallel Distrib Syst 25(8):2126–2137. doi:10.1109/TPDS.2013.272
59. Ma Y, Wu H, Wang L, Huang B, Ranjan R, Zomaya A, Jie W (2014) Remote sensing big data computing: challenges and opportunities. Futur Gener Comput Syst. doi:http://dx.doi.org/10.1016/j.future.2014.10.029, http://www.sciencedirect.com/science/article/pii/S0167739X14002234
60. Menzies T, Zimmermann T (2013) Software analytics: so what? IEEE Softw 30(4):31–37
61. MonetDB (Retrieved 2015) https://www.monetdb.org/home/features
62. Nebert D, Whiteside A, Vretanos P (2007) OpenGIS Catalogue Services Specification (OGC 07-006r1)
63. NGA (2014) Digitalglobe application a boon to raster data storage, processing
64. NGA (Retrieved 2015) https://github.com/ngageoint/mrgeo/wiki
65. Nikolaou C, Kyzirakos K, Bereta K, Dogani K, Giannakopoulou S, Smeros P, Garbis G, Koubarakis M, Molina D, Dumitru O, Schwarz G, Datcu M (2014) Big, linked and open data: applications in the German aerospace center. In: The semantic web: ESWC 2014 satellite events. Lecture notes in computer science. Springer International Publishing, New York, pp 444–449. doi:10.1007/978-3-319-11955-7_64, http://dx.doi.org/10.1007/978-3-319-11955-7_64
66. OGC (Retrieved 20 June 2015) OGC abstract specifications. http://www.opengeospatial.org/standards/as
67. OGC (Retrieved 20 June 2015) OGC history. http://www.opengeospatial.org/ogc/historylong
68. Oosthoek J, Flahaut J, Rossi A, Baumann P, Misev D, Campalani P, Unnithan V (2013) Planetserver: innovative approaches for the online analysis of hyperspectral satellite data from Mars. Adv Space Res pp 219–244. doi:http://dx.doi.org/10.1016/j.asr.2013.07.002
69. Palmer SC, Hunter PD, Lankester T, Hubbard S, Spyrakos E, Tyler AN, Présing M, Horváth H, Lamb A, Balzter H, Tóth VR (2015) Validation of envisat {MERIS} algorithms for chlorophyll retrieval in a large, turbid and optically-complex shallow lake. Remote Sens Environ 157(0):158–169. doi:http://dx.doi.org/10.1016/j.rse.2014.07.024, http://www.sciencedirect.com/science/article/pii/S0034425714002739, [special Issue: Remote Sensing of Inland Waters]

70. Pelekis N, Theodoridis Y (2014) Mobility data management and exploration. Springer, New York
71. Pettorelli N, Vik J, Mysterud A, Gaillard J, Tucker C, Stenseth N (2005) Using the satellite-derived ndvi to assess ecological responses to environmental change. Trends Ecol Evol 20:503–510
72. Pijanowski BC, Tayyebi A, Doucette J, Pekin BK, Braun D, Plourde J (2014) A big data urban growth simulation at a national scale: configuring the GIS and neural network based land transformation model to run in a high performance computing (HPC) environment. Environ Model Software 51(0):250–268. doi:http://dx.doi.org/10.1016/j.envsoft.2013.09.015
73. Plaza AJ (2009) Special issue on architectures and techniques for real-time processing of remotely sensed images. J Real-Time Image Proc 4(3):191–193
74. Plaza AJ, Chang CI (2007) High performance computing in remote sensing. Chapman & Hall/CRC Press, New York
75. Repository CC (Retrieved 2015) https://github.com/cartodb/cartodb.js
76. Rouse JW Jr, Haas RH, Schell JA, Deering DW (1974) Monitoring vegetation systems in the great Plains with Erts, vol.351. NASA Special Publication, Washington p 309
77. Russom P (2011) Big data analytics. TDWI best practices report, The Data Warehousing Institute (TDWI) Research
78. Sakr S, Liu A, Batista D, Alomari M (2011) A survey of large scale data management approaches in cloud environments. IEEE Commun Surv Tutorials 13(3):311–336. doi:10.1109/SURV.2011.032211.00087
79. Sass G, Creed I, Bayley S, Devito K (2007) Understanding variation in trophic status of lakes on the boreal plain: a 20 year retrospective using landsat {TM} imagery. Remote Sens Environ 109(2):127–141
80. Schut P (2007) OpenGIS web processing service (OGC 05-007r7)
81. Vouk M (2008) Cloud computing 2014; issues, research and implementations. In: 30th international conference on information technology interfaces, 2008 (ITI 2008), pp 31–40. doi:10.1109/ITI.2008.4588381
82. Vretanos PPA (2010) OpenGIS Web Feature Service 2.0 Interface Standard (OGC 09-025r1 and ISO/DIS 19142)
83. Yu P (2013) On mining big data. In: Wang J, Xiong YH (ed) Web-age information management. Lecture notes in computer science. Springer, Berlin, Heidelberg
84. Yue P, Gong J, Di L, Yuan J, Sun L, Sun Z, Wang Q (2010) Geopw: laying blocks for the geospatial processing web. Trans GIS 14(6):755–772. doi:10.1111/j.1467-9671.2010.01232.x, http://dx.doi.org/10.1111/j.1467-9671.2010.01232.x
85. Yue P, Di L, Wei Y, Han W (2013) Intelligent services for discovery of complex geospatial features from remote sensing imagery. ISPRS J Photogramm Remote Sens 83(0):151–164. doi:http://dx.doi.org/10.1016/j.isprsjprs.2013.02.015, http://www.sciencedirect.com/science/article/pii/S0924271613000580
86. Zeiler M (1999) Modeling our world: the ESRI guide to geodatabase design. ESRI Press, Redlands
87. Zell E, Huff A, Carpenter A, Friedl L (2012) A user-driven approach to determining critical earth observation priorities for societal benefit. IEEE J Sel Top Appl Earth Obs Remote Sens 5(6):1594–1602. doi:10.1109/JSTARS.2012.2199467
88. Zhang X, Seelan S, Seielstad G (2010) Digital northern great plains: a web-based system delivering near real time remote sensing data for precision agriculture. Remote Sens 2(3):861. doi:10.3390/rs2030861, http://www.mdpi.com/2072-4292/2/3/861
89. Zhang Y, Kersten M, Ivanova M, Nes N (2011) Sciql: bridging the gap between science and relational dbms. In: Proceedings of the 15th symposium on international database engineering & Applications (IDEAS '11). ACM, New York, NY, pp 124–133. doi:10.1145/2076623.2076639, http://doi.acm.org/10.1145/2076623.2076639
90. Zhang Y, Scheers B, Kersten MNN Mand Ivanova (2011) Astronomical data processing using sciql, an sql based query language for array data. In: Astronomical data analysis software and systems XXI, vol 461, p 729

91. Zhao P, Foerster T, Yue P (2012) The geoprocessing web. Comput Geosci 47(0): 3–12. doi:http://dx.doi.org/10.1016/j.cageo.2012.04.021, http://www.sciencedirect.com/science/article/pii/S0098300412001446, towards a Geoprocessing Web
92. Zikopoulos P, Eaton C (2012) Understanding big data: analytics for enterprise class hadoop and streaming data. McGraw-Hill Companies, Inc., New York

Chapter 11
Big Data in Finance

Bin Fang and Peng Zhang

Abstract Quantitative finance is an area in which data is the vital actionable information in all aspects. Leading finance institutions and firms are adopting advanced Big Data technologies towards gaining actionable insights from massive market data, standardizing financial data from a variety of sources, reducing the response time to real-time data streams, improving the scalability of algorithms and software stacks on novel architectures. Today, these major profits are driving the pioneers of the financial practitioners to develop and deploy the big data solutions in financial products, ranging from front-office algorithmic trading to back-office data management and analytics.

Not only the collection and purification of multi-source data, the effective visualization of high-throughput data streams and rapid programmability on massively parallel processing architectures are widely used to facilitate the algorithmic trading and research. Big data analytics can help reveal more hidden market opportunities through analyzing high-volume structured data and social news, in contrast to the underperformers that are incapable of adopting novel techniques. Being able to process massive complex events in ultra-fast speed removes the roadblock for promptly capturing market trends and timely managing risks.

These key trends in capital markets and extensive examples in quantitative finance are systematically highlighted in this chapter. The insufficiency of technological adaptation and the gap between research and practice are also presented.

To clarify matters, the three natures of Big Data, volume, velocity and variety are used as a prism through which to understand the pitfalls and opportunities of emerged and emerging technologies towards financial services.

B. Fang, Ph.D.
QuantCloud Brothers Inc., Setauket, NY 11733, USA
e-mail: bin.fang@quantcloudtech.com

P. Zhang, Ph.D. (✉)
Stony Brook University, Stony Brook, NY 11794, USA
e-mail: peng.zhang@stonybrook.edu; pzhang99@gmail.com

© Springer International Publishing Switzerland 2016
S. Yu, S. Guo (eds.), *Big Data Concepts, Theories, and Applications*,
DOI 10.1007/978-3-319-27763-9_11

11.1 Overview

Just a decade ago, finance was a small-data discipline. The data scarcity is the main reason. Most exchanges provided only Open, High, Low, Close (OHLC) four prices per instrument per day. Intraday data beyond what was required by the regulations was not kept even for the biggest market markers. For example, commodity trading floors kept no more than 21 days of intraday history until 6 years ago [1].

Today, the proliferation of data has changed the financial industry dramatically, not only in portfolio analysis and risk management, but also in retail banking and credit scoring. Along with the ever-increasing volume, velocity and variety (3V's) of financial data, capital firms have been investigating in ways to make Big Data more manageable and to condense enormous amount of information into actionable insights, in order for keeping their competitive edges in the business.

11.1.1 Quick View of the Financial Industry

Financial industry encompasses a broad range of businesses that manage money, including commercial banks, investment banks, credit card companies, insurance companies, consumer finance companies, stock brokerages, investment funds and some government-run institutions. The businesses can range from as big as JPMorgan Chase, which has more than 250,000 employees globally, to as small as a proprietary trading shop consisting of couple of individuals. However, the essence is the same, which is to maximize the profit, minimize the risk and position themselves for ongoing success, by gaining insights into market opportunities, customers and operations.

The context of the insights is various depending on the individual businesses. For an investment company, it can be a multi-factor relation which determines how one specific stock goes within a certain time of period. For instances, a major factor of the long-term stock price movement of XOM (ExxonMobil) would be its earnings and cash flow, which in turn are determined by the global crude oil price and inventory. However for a high-frequency propriety trading shop, the insights for the short-term price movement of the same XOM would be the liquidity in the markets, short-term buy/sell pressure, the sector momentum, and crude oil future movement.

Besides the context, another perspective is the insights are ever-changing. Unlike gravitational force depending solely on mass and distance in physics, or water molecules consisting of two hydrogen and one oxygen in chemistry, finance is an area that essentially dealing with people, instead of nature. We are changing day-by-day, so are the insights people trying to gain. Back to the XOM long-term stock price example we mentioned earlier, the technology revolution of shale oil extraction has become a very important factor to be added in, which significantly affected OPEC policy, global oil inventory and price. Sometime this change can be abrupt. One good example is that on January 15th 2015, without any pre-notification, the Swiss

National Bank (SNB) unexpectedly abandoned the euro cap at 1.20, introduced in September 2011. This made Swiss franc soared as much as 30 % in chaotic trade. Any strategies based on this 1.2 Swiss franc/Euro cap assumption became invalid immediately.

To some extent, it is quite like how information and technology play the role in modern battlefields. In order to win in financial markets, institutions need to examine large pools of data, extract value from complicated analysis in a timely manner. Take the trading MSFT (Microsoft) for example. Because MSFT traded in different markets, data from all these markets are needed in order to get a global view of the stock. MSFT has very tight relations with, let's say AAPL (Apple), IBM, INTL(Intel), DJI (Dow Jones Indices) and etc. we need to get those data as well, even though we are interested only in trading MSFT. The more data we have, the more complicated analysis can be practiced, which usually means more time needs to be devoted. However the transient market opportunities don't give us this leisure. The speed to transform big data into actionable insights distinguishes the profitable from the losing. This problem is exactly what the modern big data techniques are designed to handle.

11.1.2 3V's in Financial Markets

The principal characteristics of Big Data, including the volume, variety and velocity (3V's), have been embodied in all aspects of financial data and markets.

11.1.2.1 Volume

Data volume in financial markets has been growing at a tremendous rate. As algorithmic trading becomes a main stream on Wall Street during the past decade, capital markets stepped into Big Data era as well. For example, High Frequency Trading (HFT), as a primary form of quantitative trading, using proprietary trading strategies carried out by computers to move in and out of positions in seconds or fractions of a second, represents 2 % of the approximately 20,000 firms operating today, however accounted for 60–73 % of all US equity trading volume as of 2009, with that number falling to approximately 50 % in 2012 [2, 3].

For the big picture, although the total shares changed hand is only tenfold of 20 years ago, the total number of transactions was increased by 50 times, with this number being more than 120 times during the financial crisis (Fig. 11.1). If L1 quotes are counted in, the number would be one order of magnitude more than the trades averagely; and if L2 quotes are included as well, prepare to double or quadruple the amount one more time.

Not only structured data from dozens of exchanges, banks and data vendors, but also unstructured data from news, twitters, even social media have been used by the industry in daily practice for various purposes, for instances, to supplement for investment decisions making, to tailor products per customer basis in retail banking,

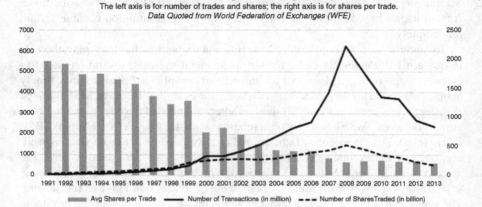

Fig. 11.1 The number of transactions and number of shares traded in NYSE and NASDAQ. *Source:* World Federation of Exchanges

to have a holistic view of individual's creditworthiness, and so on. This part of data accounts for another big portion of the volume.

11.1.2.2 Velocity

One decade ago, the stocks OHLC prices were reported the following day (on the T + 1 basis). In current financial market, a stock can experience about 500 quote changes and about 150 trades in 1 ms, 1800 quotes and 600 trades in 100 ms, 5500 quotes and 700 trades in 1 s [4]. To catch high frequency data consolidated from dozens of markets and venues and to submit orders nationally or even globally with ultra-low latency, various infrastructures, hardware and software techniques have been designed and deployed by different vendors, such as microwave/optic fiber data transition, FPGA, and ASIC. The reason that firms, especially the ones practicing HFT, have been willing to spend tens of millions dollars for these infrastructures or technologies to gain tiny increments of speed is that 'milliseconds mean millions'.

Not only for professional investment, but the increase of speed is also happening in everyone's regular life. The use of web and mobile devices has dramatically increased the speed and frequency of transaction to everybody. People order Starbucks, Taco Bell by clicking several keys; people check in, check out, asking for room service all on your smart phone; people also make deposit, pay bills through mobile apps in just seconds. All these represent challenges and opportunities to financial institutions. Analytics and the ability to efficiently and effectively exploit the big data technology stack, advanced statistical modeling, and predictive analytics in support of real-time decision making across business channels and operations will distinguish those companies that flourish in uncertain markets from those that misstep.

11.1.2.3 Variety

Financial data mainly consists of structured and unstructured data.

Structured data is the information having fixed structure and length. In financial industry, most of structured data are in the form of time series. There are various structured data in the markets. Based on the types of instruments, it has equities, futures, options, ETFs and OTCs. Different markets and venues usually have different formats even for the same instrument. Various data vendors provide consolidated data with various highlights, some of which being focusing on the latency of interconnection among several data sources by providing state-of-the-art network infrastructures, i.e., Pico Quantitative Trading, and some of which marketed as global feed coverage by offering a uniformed format, i.e., Reuters.

Unstructured data is information that is unorganized and does not fall into a pre-determined model. This includes data gathered from social media sources, such as news articles, weather reports, twitters, emails or even audio and video, which help institutions to deliver greater insights into customers' needs, fraud transactions, and market sentiment. Although complicated, strategies based on unstructured data have widely been utilized by professional traders for years, a good example is the Hash Crash on April 23, 2013 [5], in which event-driven trading algorithms responded to the hijacked Associated Press @AP Twitter feed and briefly wiping $121 billion off the value of companies in the S&P 500 index, before recovering minutes later [6].

To process both the unparalleled amount of structured and unstructured data feeds, big data technologies are definitely needed, since it is no longer possible for traditional relational database and data warehousing technologies to handle them efficiently.

11.1.3 Big Data in Context

The concept of "big" in financial industry context is different from what it is in scientific or retail contexts. In retail businesses, for example, the analysis of profiling of customers mainly involves analysis of unstructured data from social media sources. However, financial markets primarily deal with structured data collected from a limited set of sources, such as exchanges and data vendors. Although unstructured data sets have been used with firms for sentiment analysis and trading, these have not traditionally been the data sets of primary importance to the business.

In financial markets, big data problems are not considered as being represented by any of the three V's alone. Regarding the volume, technologies that are good at handling the high volume of tick data, which has always been the biggest data set, have already been deployed in a structured manner for years. Although not perfect, these technologies have been able to scale up to meet increased electronic flows of data resulting from increased market activities. In terms of velocity, HFT has adequately dealt with much higher velocity of data, squeezing the feed/order latency from microsecond to nanosecond and to near the hardware theoretical limits. But this is not traditionally considered as big data technologies. Complicated analysis have already been used in like OTC derivatives using various sets of data for quite some time even before big data concept exists. So it is not suitable to say that variety or complexity of data alone can be tagged as a big data problem.

Big data challenges in financial context are usually referred to projects that involve multiple factors, such as high volumes of complex data that must be cross-referenced in a specific timeframe. Although not necessarily required to be performed in real time, current tasks are tend to be consolidating different data sets from various sources, structured and unstructured, from heterogeneous asset class and risk information, deploying complex data aggregations for ad hoc regulatory reports, credit analysis, trading signal generation or risk management for instances, while reducing the latencies of data aggregation and increasing the effectiveness of data management.

Today, real-time streaming data is widely available. The proliferation of data is significantly changing business models in financial firms, whether in market making or long-term portfolio management. Even long-only portfolio managers nowadays add screens of data-driven signals to their portfolio selection models in order to abstract volatility and noise, and realize pure returns for their investors. On the other hand, portfolio managers ignoring or under-studying the multitude of available data are adding a considerable risk to their investment portfolios.

11.2   Applications of Big Data Technologies

By consolidating data management in traditional silos, financial firms are able to manage portfolio, analyze risk exposure, perform enterprise-level analytics, and comply with regulations from a more holistic point of view. The ever-growing volumes of data and the requirements to fast access, aggregate, analyze and act on them within a limited time frame make traditional technologies such as Relation Database Management Systems (RDBMS) impossible to accomplish these advanced analytics for most of the times. The emerging big data technologies, however, become invaluable in their abilities to meet the elasticity to the rapidly-changing requirements. They can ultimately help firms to discover many innovative and strategic directions that firms couldn't get before.

Based on a recent research, SunGard identified ten trends shaping big data initiatives across all segments of the financial industry [7]:

1. Larger market data sets containing historical data over longer time periods and increased granularity are required to feed predictive models, forecasts and trading impacts throughout the day.
2. New regulatory and compliance requirements are placing greater emphasis on governance and risk reporting, driving the need for deeper and more transparent analyses across global organizations.

3. Financial institutions are ramping up their enterprise risk management frameworks, which rely on master data management strategies to help improve enterprise transparency, auditability and executive oversight of risk.
4. Financial services companies are looking to leverage large amounts of consumer data across multiple service delivery channels (branch, web, mobile) to support new predictive analysis models in discovering consumer behavior patterns and increase conversion rates.
5. In post-emergent markets like Brazil, China and India, economic and business growth opportunities are outpacing Europe and America as significant investments are made in local and cloud-based data infrastructures.
6. Advances in big data storage and processing frameworks will help financial services firms unlock the value of data in their operations departments in order to help reduce the cost of doing business and discover new arbitrage opportunities.
7. Population of centralized data warehouse systems will require traditional ETL processes to be re-engineered with big data frameworks to handle growing volumes of information.
8. Predictive credit risk models that tap into large amounts of data consisting of historical payment behavior are being adopted in consumer and commercial collections practices to help prioritize collections activities by determining the propensity for delinquency or payment.
9. Mobile applications and internet-connected devices such as tablets and smartphone are creating greater pressure on the ability of technology infrastructures and networks to consume, index and integrate structured and unstructured data from a variety of sources.
10. Big data initiatives are driving increased demand for algorithms to process data, as well as emphasizing challenges around data security and access control, and minimizing impact on existing systems.

Big data has been emerging to be driving business analytics in the enterprise level to help with innovation and decision-making in today's financial industry. These analytics include, but not limited to, portfolio management, trading opportunities hunting, execution analysis, risk management, credit scoring, regulatory compliance, security and fraud management. The ability to efficiently and effectively deploy the big data technologies to support real-time decision making across whole business will widen the gap between successful companies and those misstep.

11.2.1 Retail Banking

Online and mobile banking has reshaped today's banking institutions, making them different from a decade ago. Over the years, channel growth has had enormous impacts on retail banking, as customers began using alternate channels more frequently. The use of web and mobile channels has led to a decrease in face-to-face interactions between the customers and the banks, and in the meantime led to an increase in virtual interactions and increasing volume of customer data. The data that banks hold about their customers is much bigger in volume and much more diverse in variety than ever before. However, only a small portion of them gets utilized for driving successful business outcomes. Big data technologies can make effective use of customer data, helping develop personalized products and services, like most e-commerce companies already did.

Customers have expectations about similar experiences from the retail banking as they have in popular e-commerce destinations, such as Amazon and EBay. However, banks are often unable to deliver effective personalized service. The main reason is the low level of customer intelligence. Without deep know-how about their customers, banks may not be able to meet these expectations. Big data analytics help banks goldmine and maximize the value of their customer data, to predict potential customer attrition, maximize lead generation and unlock opportunities to drive top line growth before their competitors can [8].

There are certain things that retail banks can do to advance the level of customer intelligence [7]:

- Leverage big data to get a 360° view of each customer.
- Drive revenues with one-to-one targeting and personalized offers in real-time.
- Reduce business risk by leveraging predictive analytics for detecting fraud.
- Achieve greater customer loyalty with personalized retention offers.
- Employ the power of big data without worrying about complexities and steep learning curves.

As an example, before big data was tamed by technology, Bank of America took the usual approach to understanding customers—it relied on sample. Now, it can increasingly process and analyze data from its full customer set. It has been using big data to understand multi-channel customer relationships, by monitoring customer 'journeys' through the tangle of websites, call centers, tellers, and other branch personnel to have a holistic view of the paths that customers follow through the bank, and how those paths affect attrition or the purchase of particular financial services. The bank also uses transaction and propensity models to determine which customers have a credit card or mortgage that could benefit from refinancing at a competitor and then makes an offer when the customer contacts the bank through online, call center or branch channels [9].

US bank, the fifth largest commercial bank in the United States, shows another good example of archiving more effective customer acquisition with the help of big data solutions. The bank wanted to focus on multi-channel data to drive strategic decision-making and maximize lead conversions. It deployed an analytics solution that integrates data from online and offline channels and provides a unified view of the customer. This integrated data feeds into the bank's CRM solution, supplying the call center with more relevant leads. It also provides recommendations to the bank's web team on improving customer engagement on the bank's website. As an outcome, the bank's lead conversion rate has improved by over 100 % and customers receive an personalized and enhanced experience [10].

A mid-sized European bank used data sets of over 2 million customers with over 200 variables to create a model that predicts the probability of churn for each customer. An automated scorecard with multiple logistic regression models and decision trees calculated the probability of churn for each customer. Through early identification of churn risks, the bank saved itself millions of dollars in outflows it otherwise could not have avoided [8].

11.2.2 Credit Scoring

The conventional methodology for loan and credit scoring that financial institutions have been using is based on a five component composite score, including (1) past loan and credit applications, (2) on time payments, (3) types of loan and credit used, (4) length of loan and credit history and (5) credit capacity used [7]. Until the big data scoring services become available, this approach has seen little innovation in making scoring a commodity.

With big data technologies, for instance machine learning algorithms, loan and credit decisions are determined in seconds by automated processes. In some cases, the technology can use million-scale data points to asses customers' credit scores in real-time.

The variety of data that can be used for credit scoring has expanded considerably. With this invaluable data, the new technologies can give financial companies the capability to make the observation of shopping habits look downright primitive. The information gathered from social media, e-commerce data, micro geographical statistics, digital data brokers and online trails is used to mathematically determine the creditworthiness of individuals/groups, or to market products specifically targeted to them.

Such technologies give a 360-degree comprehensive view of any prospective customer, based on his relatives, his colleagues and even his web browsing habits. This ultimately helps to expand the availability of credit to those who struggle to obtain fair loans. Research has shown that everything, ranging from users' political inclination to sexual orientation can now be accurately predicted by parsing publicly available information on social networks such as Facebook and Twitter, as shown in Fig 11.2.

The biggest barrier of adopting Big Data in Credit Scoring, however, is the fear of regulatory scrutiny. When it comes to big data, there is no clear prohibition on using data for underwriting. With the technologies, financial companies are capable of predicting lots of things that's illegal to use for lending and are regarded as discrimination. "Because big data scores use undisclosed algorithms, it is impossible to analyze the algorithm for potential racial discriminatory impact," the National Consumer Law Center wrote in a recent paper on big data [11]. It can become a fair lending issue, if the use of that data results in disproportionate negative outcomes for members of a protected class.

It is this fear of regulatory scrutiny that has left many big banks and credit card companies reluctant to dive completely into the new world of non-traditional

Personal characteristics can be predicted by social media data

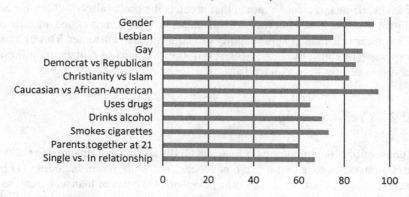

Fig. 11.2 Success rate of using Facebook 'likes' to predict personal characteristics (%). *Source:* Kosinski, Stillwell and Graepel for the National Academy of Sciences of the USA

credit information. For many lenders, non-traditional data is regarded as augment or supplements to traditional scoring methods that still rely largely on historical information. Instead, a lot of start-ups have been actively using non-traditional information, with their goals being to use the variety of information now available to extend credit in a more efficient way, or to those lacking traditional credit information.

One of the successful start-ups by leveraging new techniques is Big Data Scoring, which is a European provider of credit scoring solutions based on social media. It was founded in 2013 and is aimed to provide services to banks and consumer lending companies. Their credit scoring model based purely on information from Facebook, with Gini coefficient of 0.340. In order to build the model, Facebook data about individuals was collected in various European countries with prior permission from the individuals. This data was then combined with the actual loan payment information for the same people and the scoring models were built using the same tools used in building traditional credit scoring models. According to the company's website, this new underwriting model provides on average 25 % improvement over the current best-in-class scoring models. For a lender, this translates directly into better credit quality and more clients. Use of big data can save money on credit losses, while at the same time increase revenue through expanding the potential client base.

11.2.3 Algorithmic Trading

In early 1990s, the largest exchanges adopted electronic "matching engine" to bring together buyers and sellers. In 2000, decimalization changed the minimum tick size from 1/16 of a dollar to US$0.01 per share. Both of the facts encouraged algorithmic trading in the past 2 decades, and at its peak in 2009, more than 70 % of the US equity trading volume was contributed by quantitative trading [12]. Even conventional traders nowadays increasingly started to rely on algorithms to analyze market conditions and supplement their trading and execution decisions.

Algorithmic trading mainly uses huge historical data to calculate the success ratio of the algorithms being written. Algorithms evaluate thousands of securities with complex mathematical tools, far beyond human capacity. They also combine and analyze data to reveal insights that are not readily apparent to the human eye. This is where true innovation happens—there is a seemingly endless amount of data available to us today, and with the right tools financial modeling becomes limited only by the brain power and imagination of the quant at work. Big data techniques are the right tools that can facilitate the alpha-generation cycle of development-deployment-management, which is the process every serious investor has been taking. Base on functionalities, the process can be categorized as Data Management, Strategy Development and Product Deployment, where various big data techniques could be deployed.

- Data management: markets are more complex and interconnected and information traverses the connections more rapidly than a decade ago. One cannot get a comprehensive view of a portfolio with just one source of data any more. Capital firms need to store and stream in various types and enormous amount of data, and effectively link disparate data together to get an actionable insight. Big data technologies provide solutions for effective data management, such as the column based database like NoSQL, and in-memory database.
- Strategy development: when identifying and tuning trading strategies, different algorithms, various combinations of parameters, disparate sets of symbols and various market conditions are needed to be experimented to find the most profitable strategies with least drawdown. This process is an extremely computation-intensive and data-intensive task. Big data techniques such as MapReduce, which has been widely used in other industries, are not quite suitable for algorithmic trading, because instead of batch processing, real-time streaming/analytics are of more needs. Complex Event Processing (CEP) has been widely adopted for real-time analysis.
- Product deployment: a comprehensive series of risk checks, verifications, market exposure checks and control actions in accordance with regulations is required to be done before any order populated to execution gateways. These measures provide protection to both the markets and the funds themselves. Ideally these checks do not introduce much unwanted latency to the live trading system. An accurate, concise, real-time trading monitoring system is a necessary tool for traders, portfolio managers to have a comprehensive view of portfolios/accounts, and to provide human intervention capabilities.

Big Data is an invaluable tool to allow for better visibility, faster alpha-generation cycles and improved control over risks in algorithm trading. Big Data strategies can also be used to fast gather and process information to create a clear understanding of market in order to drive front office trading strategies, as well as to determine the valuation of individual securities. Traders are able to determine whether various market participants, including those on Twitter or blogs, are bullish or bearish and formulate investment strategies accordingly.

11.2.4 Risk Management

Risk management has been a high-priority focus area for most financial institutions [13, 14]. Post-crisis, financial institutions face new demands and challenges. More detailed, transparent and increasingly sophisticated reports are required from the regulators. Comprehensive and regular stress tests across all asset classes are required for banks. Improved risk modeling and real-time risk monitoring are expected by the industry because of the recent money laundering scandals and 'rogue trader'.

As institution becomes more concentrated, markets become more interconnected and information traverses the connections more rapidly, complexity has grown across every aspects of the industry. In the meantime, risks increase with complexity. The demands to improve monitoring of risk, risk coverage, and more predictive power of risk models have never been such high. Big Data technologies, accompanied with thousands of risk variables, can allow banks, asset managers and insurance institutions to proactively detect potential risks, react more efficiently and more effectively, and make robust decisions. Big Data can be targeted to an organization's particular needs and applied to enhance different risk domains.

- Credit risk: big data can aggregate information not only from conventional structured database, but also from mobile devices, social media and website visit, etc. to gain greater visibility into customers behavior and to monitor closer borrowers for real-time events that may increase the chances of default.
- Liquidity risk: banks finance the longer-term instruments, which are sold to their customers by borrowing via short-term instruments. That leverage can be lost quickly as funding is withdrawn. It has been a known difficulty to model and forecast liquidity crises. Big data has the capability of linking superficially unrelated events in real time, which could presumably precede a liquidity crisis such as widening credit spreads.
- Counterparty credit risk. To calculate Credit Valuation Adjustment (CVA) at portfolio level or fully simulate potential exposure for all path-dependent derivatives as structured products, banks need to run 10–100 K Monte Carlo scenarios, to which in-memory and GPU technologies allow enormous amount of data to be processed at incredibly high speeds, and let the derivatives be traded at better level than the competitors.
- Operational Risk. New technologies have the capability of collecting data from anywhere. Not only does it include trading systems, social media and emails, but also computer access log files and door swipe card activities. A fully comprehensive, integrated data analysis can detect fraud before the damage has hit disastrous levels.

Numerous institutions have already begun to implement big data projects for risk management. An example is the UOB bank from Singapore. It successfully tested a risk system based on big data, which makes the use of big data feasible with the help of in-memory technology and reduces the calculation time of its VaR (value at risk) from about 18 h to only a few minutes. This will make it possible in future to carry out stress tests in real time and to react more quickly to new risks. Another success example is Morgan Stanley. The bank developed its capacities in processing big data and thus optimized its portfolio analysis in terms of size and result quality. It is expected that these processes will lead to a significant improvement of financial risk management, thanks to automated pattern recognition and increased comprehensibility [15].

"Whether it's guarding against fraud or selling something new, being able to pull data from 80 different businesses enables us to get ahead of problems before they're problems," says Wells Fargo Chief Data Officer Charles Thomas [13].

11.2.5 Regulatory Compliance

After the financial crisis of 2008, stringent regulatory compliance laws have been passed to improve operational transparency, increasing the visibility into consumer actions and groups with certain risk profiles. Today's financial firms are required to be able to access years of various types of historical data in response to the requests from regulators at any given time.

The requirements and purposes vary from law to law. For instances,

- Dodd-Frank Act, which is for the authority to monitor the financial stability of major firms whose failure could have a major negative impact on economy, requires firms to hold historical data for at least 5 years;
- Basel III, the third Basel Accord, which is for authorities to have a closer look at the banks' capital cushion and leverage levels, requires retention of transaction data and risk information for 3–5 years;
- FINRA/Tradeworx Project is a comprehensive and consolidated audit trail by FINRA to monitor real-time transactions, in order to detect potentially disruptive market activity caused by HFT. Tick data set (quotes, updates, cancellations, transactions, etc.) and a real-time system by Tradeworx are included.

Not only is the amount of data required to be held much more, but also some ad-hoc reports are required to be more comprehensive and time sensitive. For examples, information from unstructured data of emails, twitters, voice mails are required to be extracted; and in some cases, this information is again required to be cross referenced to key sets of structured data of transactions in order to facilitate trade reconstruction and reporting. Linking data sets across a firm can be particularly challenging, especially for a top-tier firm with dozens of data warehouses storing data sets in a siloed manner. The speed of report generation is also critical. A good example is that the trade reconstruction reports under Dodd-Frank is required to respond within 72-hour period and needs to cope with data including audio records, text records and tagged with legal items too.

To assist the firms in resolving this matter, IBM and Deloitte have developed a system that can parse complex government regulations related to financial matters, and compare them to a company's own plans for meeting those requirements. The work is aimed to help financial firms and other organizations use advanced big data analysis techniques to improve their practices around risk management and regulatory compliances. The service draws on Deloitte's considerable experience in regulatory intelligence, and uses IBM's cloud capabilities and big data-style analysis techniques. Basically, it will use IBM's Watson-branded cognitive computing services to parse written regulations paragraph by paragraph, allowing organizations to see if their own frameworks are meeting the mandates described in the regulatory language. This analysis could help cut costs of meeting new regulatory guidelines [16].

11.3 Hurdles to Adopting Big Data

The importance of big data deployments highlights that actionable information and insight are equally pegged with scalability for future data volume increases [17]. Over 60 % of financial institutions in North America, believe that big data analytics provides a significant competitive advantage, and over 90 % believe that successful big data initiatives will determine the winners of the future [18]. However, the majority of firms active in the capital markets do not have a big data strategy in place at an enterprise level. For instance, according to a research, less than half of banks analyze customers' external data, such as social media activities and online behavior. Only 29 % analyze customers' share of wallet, one of the key measures of a bank's relationship with its customers [19]. Moreover, only 37 % of capital firms have hands-on experience with live big data deployments, while the majority are still focusing on pilots and experiments [20]. The reasons for this gap between willingness and realities will be summarized in this section.

11.3.1 Technological Incompatibilities

Big data in financial industry pay attention to data flows as opposed to stocks. Many failures of big data projects in the past were because of the lack of compatibility between financial industry needs and the capabilities of big data technologies. Big data originally came from the practices of scientific research and online searching. Hadoop implementation via MapReduce has been one of the successful big data strategies for parallel batch processing with good flexibility and easy migration. However, these technologies have sometimes been unsuccessful in capital markets, because it relies on offline batch processing, which is not suitable for real-time analytics. Moreover, resource management and data processing are tightly coupled together by Hadoop, so it is not possible to prioritize tasks when running multiple applications simultaneously.

11.3.2   Siloed Storage

Traditional data management typically distributes data across systems focusing on specific functions such as portfolio management, mortgage lending, etc. Thus firms are either lack of a seamless holistic view of customers/markets or have big overlap of data across dozens of legacy data warehouses. For example, from the front office to the back office, Deutsche bank has been collecting petabytes of data, which are stored across 46 data warehouses, where there is 90 % overlap of data [21]. The data storage strategy needs to be changed via the addition of a focus on tiered storage, placing the data sets of most importance on faster devices and other sets be less readily accessible but more cheaply stored. In the meantime, data retention needs a more proactive approach to retire and delete data after the end of the retention timeframe reaches. Data storage transition can be extremely challengeable with decades of years of traditional siloed storage.

11.3.3   Inadequate Knowledge

New skill sets to benefit from big data analytics are needed. These skills include programming, mathematical, statistical skills and financial knowledge, which go beyond what traditional analytics tasks require. The individuals with all these knowledge are what people usually called "data scientists", who need to be not only well versed in understanding analytics and IT, but should also have the ability to communicate effectively with decision makers. However, the biggest issue in this regard is finding employees or consultants that understand both the business and the technology [22]. Some firms have chosen to hire a team with the combined skills of a data scientist due to the lack of a single available individual with all of the required capabilities [17].

11.3.4   Security and Privacy Concern

By distributing business sensitive data across systems, especially by storing them in Cloud, security risk is an unavoidable concern for financial firms. Protecting a vast and growing volume of critical information and being able to search and analyze it to detect potential threats is more essential than ever. Research indicates that 62 % of bankers are cautious in their use of big data due to privacy and security issues

[23]. When executive decisions to be made for big data strategies deployment, senior management may decide against handling over sensitive information to cloud, especially public cloud providers, because if anything goes wrong, the reputational damage to the brand or the cutting-edge intellectual property loss would far outweigh any possible benefits. With regard to the concern, private clouds tend to be the norm for top-tier capital firms.

11.3.5 Culture Shift

Culture shift from a 'Data as an IT asset' to a 'Data as a Key Asset for Decision-Making' is a must. Most traditional role of IT adheres to standards and controls on changes, views data from a static/historic perspective, and analytics has been more of an afterthought. Big data analytics is largely aimed to be used in a near real-time basis to reflect and mine the constantly data changing, and to react quickly and intelligently [22]. The traditional networks, storages and relational databases can be swamped by big data flows. Consequently, attempts to replicate and scale the existing technologies will not keep up with big data demands. The technologies, skills and traditional IT culture have been changed by big data.

Data managers, once considered to be primarily in the back office and IT, are now increasingly considered to be a vital source of value for the business. Data Scientists as well need to be organized differently than analytical staff was in the past, to be closer to products and processes within firms. Dislike the traditional analytical tasks, data scientists are focused on analyzing information from numerous disparate sources with the objective of unlocking insights that will either create value or provide a solution to a business problem. The job of a data scientist goes beyond just analytics to include consultancy services, research, enterprise-wide taxonomy, automating processes, ensuring the firm keeps pace with technology development and managing analytics vendors [17].

11.4 Technology and Architecture

Different from traditional data management technologies, a number of characteristics of big data technologies are specifically developed for the need of handling enormous volume of data, large variations of feed sources, and high-speed and processing real-time data. To this end, technologies such as Hadoop, column-oriented databases, in-memory database and complex event processing (CEP) are most often cited as examples of big data in action.

11.4.1 Hadoop

Apache's Hadoop is open-source software originally designed for online searching engine to grab and process information from all over the internet. It has two well-known components, MapReduce and Hadoop Distributed File System (HDFS). It was designed to distribute blocks of subdivided data across different file systems and run data processing in parallel, with the name of the first stage called "Map"; then consolidates the processed output to one single server to accomplish the second stage called "Reduce".

One successful use case in financial services is that BNP Mellon Corp. credited Hadoop for allowing it to provide clients real-time visibility into when their trades are executed at the Hadoop Summit in June 2014 [24]. BNY Mellon gets trade instructions from its clients—portfolio advisors and investment managers—and handles those trades and the after-trade processing. Some number of days later, depending on the type of financials, clients receive a confirmation back saying this trade was executed and the paper is being held in a specific repository. It used to be not giving a lot of visibility into what's happened in the financial system. However, with Hadoop, the bank found a much cheaper way to process and store data. Now the company can start to give clients real-time visibility into what's happening with the business the bank handles for them.

11.4.2 Column-Oriented and In-Memory Databases

Traditional Relational Database Management System (RDBMS) is a database management system (DBMS) that is based on the relational model. It has been used by the industry for decades. Given the fact it is row-oriented, RDBMS have the properties of Atomicity, Consistency, Isolation, Durability (ACID), which are ideal for transactions processing. In current financial industry, however, enormous structured and unstructured data are needed for market sentiment analysis, real-time portfolio analysis, credit scoring analysis etc. The data stored are not frequently modified and mostly read-only, such as market tick data set; however the amount is big and is queried more frequently and repeatedly, so instead scalability and distributed processing capabilities are required.

Column-oriented databases, however, store mostly time-series and focus on supporting data compression, aggregation and quick query. The downside to these columnar databases is that they will generally only allow batch updates and therefore have a much slower update time than traditional models. However, in most practices of financial services, the time series are read-only. There are couple of commercial column-oriented-database products in the markets which were designed for high-speed access to market and tick data for analysis and trading, with KDB+ being the most prevalent example. In addition to column oriented, in-memory database has been started utilizing in the industry for high-speed applications and scale linearly up or down on the fly based on memory requirements.

11.4.3 Complex Event Processing

The need for fast actions and timely responses is of paramount importance in financial industry, and traditional databases apparently don't provide these capabilities. Thus, complex event processing (CEP) emerged. Complex event processing is a general category of technology designed to analyze streams of data flowing from live sources to identify patterns and significant business indicators. CEP enables firms to analyze and act upon rapidly changing data in real time; to capture, analyze and act on insight before opportunities are lost forever; and to move from batching process to real-time analytics and decisions.

Imagine a business decision that combines all information sources to render a real-time action. Information could include: current event, static information about entities involved in the event, information about past events correlated to the current event and entity, information relating to the entity and current event, and trends about the likely futures, derived from predictive models. This complex analysis is possible with CEP, which can address the following requirements:

- Low latency: typically less than a few milliseconds, but sometimes less than 1 millisecond, between the time that an event arrives and it is processed;
- High throughput: typically hundreds or a few thousand events processed per second, but burst may happen into millions of events per second;
- Complex patterns and strategies: such as patterns based on temporal or spatial relationships.

The financial services industry was an early adopter of CEP technology, using complex event processing to structure and contextualize available data so that it could inform trading behavior, specifically algorithmic trading, by identifying opportunities or threats that indicate traders or automatic trading systems buy or sell. For example, if a trader wants to track MSFT price move outside 2 % of its 10-minute-VWAP, followed-by S&P moving by 0.5 %, and both within any 2 min time interval, CEP technology can track such an event. Moreover, it can trigger action upon the happening of the event to buy MSFT, for example. Today, a wide variety of financial applications use CEP, including risk management systems, order and liquidity analysis, trading cost analysis, quantitative trading and signal generation systems, and etc.

11.5 Cloud Environment

In other industries, big data is often closely connected with the Cloud computing. The obvious advantage of using cloud is to save up front cost of IT investment, but the majority of the capital firms are very cautions of public cloud in commercial sensitive areas. Small companies have been enjoying 'pay-as-you-go' model for cloud services, but the giant firms are not, especially when data control, data protection, and risk management are major concerns. Providing cloud services to major financial institutions is no longer so much about the arguments for or against any particular cloud model. Instead, it's about changing culture [25]. In this section, we briefly present the benefits, challenges, practical solutions of cloud usage in financial industry.

11.5.1 Benefits

Ever since the financial crisis, the rise of cloud services in financial industry, especially global Tier one financial institutions, have been mainly and undoubtedly driven by the increasing demands from customers and regulators, as well as the pressure of cutting expenses and shrinking margins. Obviously, cloud providers can make business processes more efficient, enabling banks to do more with less and reducing the immense cost of in-house IT. By using cloud, businesses are able to scale up or down on a 'pay-as-you-go' basis, rather than being reliant on internal IT resources. For examples, Commonwealth Bank of Australia reduced expenditure on infrastructure and maintenance from 75 % of total outgoings to just 25 % by being a partnership with Amazon Web Services (AWS). Another example is that by utilizing cloud, BankInter in Spain was able to reduce the time needed for risk analysis from 23 h to less than 1 h [25].

11.5.2 Challenges

Inevitably there are headwinds for cloud deployment in financial industry. These include concerns over the possible reputation damage the banks might suffer, loss of competitive edge from proprietary technology and strategies for hedge funds if its security is breached, government intrusion to data privacy, and loss of direct control over IT. As the cost of storage has gone down, cloud storage of data actually seems not particularly useful or beneficial, because the cost saving may not be able to offset the risk of security breach and damage which could do to the firms. If something goes wrong, the reputation damage, or proprietary technology stolen would far outweigh any possible benefits.

Another big problem with cloud is one of the hardest to resolve: extraterritoriality. Whose rules should apply to a cloud service that serves one country but hosted in another? What if the cloud is being used by an international organization—a large, global Tier One bank such as J.P. Morgan, for instance? With differing rules between North America, Europe and Asia, the only way round the problem is to understand exactly where the data is at all times. This way, a bank can work out how to deal with rules that have a cross-border implication. For instance, the US FATCA legislation applies to any bank that interacts with a US taxpayer. But providing the IRS with details of US customers may inadvertently contravene local rules in other countries which demand that customer data is protected and not shared with third parties.

11.5.3 Hybrid Cloud

To resolve the security concern, a good workaround solution is to use hybrid cloud. More innovative things can go on private cloud, while less sensitive can go public. The scale, power, and flexibility of the Hybrid Cloud provides financial companies with significant benefits, particularly the ability to extend existing infrastructure without incurring a large capital outlay for capacity while retaining sensitive data/code on-premises as appropriate or mandatory by regulations. While in general terms most businesses expect a private cloud to be more expensive than a public cloud, the private cloud is actually cheaper for a big institution above a certain scale, because to use a public cloud the firm would have to implement such stringent security that any cost saving would be eaten away in any case.

"We are very slow as an industry to understand big data," said Alastair Brown, head of e-channels, Global Transaction Banking at RBS. But when we have worked out the best way to use it, "it will almost certainly be unaffordable to run the algorithms without using cloud capabilities." Cloud is part of the future, it provides a competitive advantage, and it is moving from a buzzword to real implementation [25].

11.6 The Future

Finance is no longer a small data discipline. The ability to process enormous amount of information on the fly separates winners from losers in today's financial markets. Being aware of latest big data finance tools and technology is a necessity for every prudent financial service professional.

Big data in financial industry is still at the start of its journey. It has yet been across the industry alone as a whole. Some top-tier financial firms have acted as early adopters but they usually do not have comprehensive big data strategies in place, instead focusing on some specific areas such as risk management, trade analytics, etc. The frontrunners that have already been aware of the benefits of big data are certainly going to extend their usage of these strategies. However, these implementations will likely remain piecemeal for the near future.

The focusing areas of future big data investment will be extended toward client analytics. Current investments in big data has been largely focusing on revenue generations in the front office, such as trading opportunities mining and portfolio management, but the future is likely to be more on client acquisition and retention to enhance and personalize customer experience. Client analytics have been proven to be able to benefit both acquisition and retention. Research showed that banks that apply analytics to customer data have a four-percentage point lead in market share over banks that do not. The difference in banks that use analytics to understand customer attrition is even starker at 12-percentage points [26].

The future growth of big data as a strategy in the industry relies on the continued education of internal staffs about its uses and advantages. Most of the financial firms using big data tend to hire experts in order to grow their internal knowledge base [17]. However, this will open up to key person risk if the big data knowledge and skills are not disseminated wider among internal staffs. Plus same as other technologies, after initiative, the big data needs constant refinement and evolvement to adapt the dynamic market conditions. Firms also need to invest continually in training their analytics staff on new techniques and their business personnel to enhance decision-making. The continued in-house education will be a key to future successful deployments and maintenance of big data strategies and technologies over time.

References

1. Aldridge I (2015) Trends: all finance will soon be big data finance
2. Iati R (2009) The real story of trading software espionage. WallStreet and Technology. Available: AdvancedTrading.com
3. (2012) Times Topics: high-frequency trading. The New York Times
4. Lewis M (2014) An adaption from 'Flash Boys: A Wall Street Revolt', by Michael Lewis, The New York Times
5. Egan M (2013) Survey: 'Hash Crash' didn't seriously erode market structure confidence, FoxBusiness
6. Kilburn F (2013) 2013 review: social media, 'Hash Crash' Are 2013's trendingtopics
7. Gutierrez DD (2015) InsideBIGDATA guide to big data for finance
8. (2014) Big data: profitability, potential and problems in banking, Capgemini Consulting
9. Groenfeldt T (2013) Banks use big data to understand customers across channels, Forbes
10. Zagorsky V (2014) Unlocking the potential of Big Data in banking sector
11. Yu P, McLaughlin J, Levy M (2014) Big Data, a big disappointment for scoring consumer creditworthiness. National Consumer Law Center, Boston
12. Algorithmic trading
13. (2014) Retail banks and big data: big data as the key to better risk management, A report from the Economist Intelligence Unit
14. Arnold Veldhoen SDP (2014) Applying Big Data To Risk Management: transforming risk management practices within the financial services industry
15. Andreas Huber HH, Nagode F (2014) BIG DATA: potentials from a risk management perspective
16. Jackson J (2015) IBM and Deloitte bring big data to risk management, Computerworld
17. O'Shea V (2014) Big Data in capital markets: at the start of the journey, Aite Group Report (commissioned by Thomson Reuters)
18. M a Celent (2013) How Big is Big Data: big data usage and attitudes among North American financial services firms
19. (2013) BBRS 2013 banking customer centricity study
20. Jean Coumaros JB, Auliard O (2014) Big Data alchemy: how can banks maximize the value of their customer data? Capgemini Consulting
21. (2013) Deutsche bank: big data plans held back by legacy systems, Computerworld UK
22. (2012) How 'Big Data' is different, MIT Sloan Management Review and SAS

23. C. P. Finextra research, NGDATA (2013) Monetizing payments: exploiting mobile wallets and big data
24. King R (2014) BNY Mellon finds promise and integration challenges with Hadoop. Wall Street J
25. Holley E (2014) Cloud in financial services – what is it not good for?
26. Aberdeen (2013) Analytics in banking

Chapter 12
Big Data Applications in Business Analysis

Sien Chen, Yinghua Huang, and Wenqiang Huang

Abstract How can service providers turn their big data into actionable knowledge that drives profitable business results? Using the real-world case of China Southern Airlines, this chapter illustrates how big data analytics can help airline companies to develop a comprehensive 360-degree view of the passengers. This chapter introduces a number of data mining techniques, including Weibo customer value modeling, social network analysis, website click-stream analysis, customer activity analysis, clustering analysis, Recency-Frequency-Monetary (RFM) analysis, and principle component analysis. Using the sample dataset provided by the airline company, this chapter demonstrates how to apply big data techniques to explore passengers' travel pattern and social network, predict how many times the passengers will travel in the future, and segment customer groups based on customer lifetime value. In addition, this chapter introduces a multi-channel intelligence customer marketing platform for airlines. The findings of this study provide airline companies useful insights to better understand the passenger behavior and develop effective strategies for customer relationship management.

12.1 Introduction

While many companies are aware of the significant value of big data, they are struggling in using appropriate data analytical methods to figure out useful insights from the mountains of real-time structured and unstructured data. How can service providers turn their big data into actionable knowledge that drives profitable business results? Using the real-world case of China Southern Airlines,

S. Chen (✉)
Xiamen University, Xiamen Xindeco Ltd, Xiamen, China
e-mail: sandy80@vip.sina.com

Y. Huang
San Jose State University, San Jose, CA, USA
e-mail: yinghua.huang@sjsu.edu

W. Huang
China Southern Airlines, Guangzhou, China
e-mail: hwq@csair.com

© Springer International Publishing Switzerland 2016
S. Yu, S. Guo (eds.), *Big Data Concepts, Theories, and Applications*,
DOI 10.1007/978-3-319-27763-9_12

this chapter illustrates how big data analytics can help airline companies to develop a comprehensive 360-degree view of the passengers, and implement consumer segmentation and relationship marketing.

Known as the "people industry", the transportation and tourism industries have been faced with the challenges of providing personalized service and managing customer relationships for a long time. As the number of international and domestic travelers keeps growing rapidly, the transportation and tourism industries generate a massive amount of consumer behavioral data through both online and offline service delivery processes, which convey important information about the customers and their value to the service providers. In this new era of business intelligence, data itself has become a critical strategic and competitive asset for every company [1].

Focusing on the passenger's travel history and webtrends data, this chapter introduces a number of data mining techniques to investigate passenger behavior. Weibo customer value modeling, social network analysis, website click-stream analysis, customer activity analysis, cluster analysis, Recency-Frequency-Monetary (RFM) analysis, and principle component analysis are applied in analyzing passenger profiles and managing customer relationships. In addition, this chapter introduces a multi-channel intelligence customer marketing platform, and explains how airlines companies can use this platform to collect passenger data and create analytical reports to inform business decision making.

Using the data mining results from the passenger database of China Southern Airlines, this chapter further discusses the marketing implications of big data analytics. The data mining results reveal passenger travel patterns, preference, travel social networks and other aspects of purchase behavior. This chapter explains how airline companies can design corresponding marketing segmentation and promotion strategies (e.g., cross-sell and up-sell) based on data mining results. This chapter sheds new light on airline precision marketing and customer relationship management.

12.2 Big Data Challenge in Airline Industry

Faced with the increasingly fierce competition in the aviation market, domestic and international airline companies have shifted their attention to customer relationship management [2]. They have come to realize that customer resource are the most valuable for competition. Nowadays, airline companies have a vast amount of data about every step that their customers take during the travel cycle. To a certain extent, airline companies take control of big data about their customers [3]. The passenger data are tremendous in the customer relationship management system. However, these data are usually only used to support specific operational procedures, rather than to develop business intelligence. The passenger databases contain many data descriptions, but data are not shared between different departments. In other words, passenger data storage and management are in a mess.

Therefore, how to utilize these unorganized data for developing business values, is the challenge faced by many airline companies. The effective big data production

Table 12.1 Travel life cycle and amount of data

Travel life cycle phase	How customer generates data?	Where is that data found?
Searching: This phase is usually applicable in case of leisure travelers. In this phase the customer is searching where he wants to travel	Browsing through travel service provider's website, traversing through OTA sites, clicking on ads on social media sites like Facebook, using marketing promotions by travel service providers, using travel search sites, online searching	Online travel agencies logs, social media sites like Facebook, travel service providers' analytical logs, travel search site logs, Google web logs
Planning: Before reaching this phase the traveler has narrowed down on the destination. Now he is planning various details of his travel, like, mode of transport to the destination, what kind of accommodation will he take, what mode of transportation will he use at the destination, places he would like to see, restaurants he would like to eat at etc.	Calling up the call centers, browsing OTA sites, surfing websites of travel service providers, reading other travelers' experiences on social media sites and blogs, surfing through travel review sites such as Tripadvisor, see pictures and videos	Call center logs, OTA web analytics logs, travel review sites database, social media sites and blog sites analytical databases, Google internet search database
Booking: After the traveler has planned his trip the next step would be to make all the necessary bookings like flight, hotel, transportation, tourist attraction sites etc	Travel service provider's website/call center/social media page/on property, travel agency, OTA	Travel service provider's web database, call center logs, social media database, OTA database, travel agency database
Experiencing: In this stage the traveler is using the travel services i.e. he is flying through the airline he booked, staying in the hotel, driving the car he rented, having dinner at the restaurant he booked etc	Traveler's on property feedback, complaints registered via call centers, his movements, time spent on the service	Feedback logs, feedback with employees, location/movement database
Sharing: After the traveler has completed his travel, he goes on and shares his experience with his own and outside network	Word of mouth, writing blogs, sharing experience on social media sites, travel review sites	Social media database, user's web profile database, travel review sites' databases

for airlines should achieve the integration of multi-channel information, and support the analysis of consumer preferences and personalized recommendation services. Table 12.1 describes how and where the customer leaves footprints during a typical travel life cycle.

Using big data techniques can help the airline companies to develop precision marketing strategies, and further increase the conversion rate of the whole network airlines [4]. For example, the likes of Delta, Emirates, British Airways, Iberia, KLM and Alaska have already armed their cabin crew with tablets and other handheld devices to ensure they are informed of passenger preferences and well equipped to push ancillary sales. In 2013, Delta Airlines equipped 19,000 flight attendants with Windows Phone 8 handheld devices, which make it easier for passengers to buy ancillary items onboard [3]. In November 2010, the international airline KLM surprised its customers: As passengers arrived at security checkpoints and gates, flight attendants were there to greet them by name and give them a personalized gift—something that the passenger could use on his or her trip, or enjoy when they returned home. In November 2010, the KLM Twitter feed was viewed more than 1 million times. What made this particular campaign stand apart from other run-of-the-mill marketing campaigns is personalization, which enabled the airline to offer customers something that held real, tangible value [5].

12.3 Passenger Data Mining Application

In order to illustrate how the massive passenger data can be utilized for business decision making, this chapter presents a real-world case of China southern Airlines. Using various data mining methods, including Weibo customer value modeling, social network analysis, website click-stream analysis, customer activity analysis, cluster analysis, Recency-Frequency-Monetary (RFM) analysis, and principle component analysis, this chapter presents how to apply big data techniques to explore passengers' travel pattern and social network, and predict how many times the passengers will travel in the future. The findings will provide airline companies the ability to become more effective in customer relationship management.

12.3.1 Weibo Customer Value Modeling

Along with the popularity of social media, the airline industry has gradually utilized this platform to further improve passenger services and enhance its own competitiveness. For example, according to a report by *Washington Post*, more and more American airlines including Southwest Airlines, United Airlines and Delta Air Lines have started to utilize social media to solve passenger complaints. KLM is the first airline that integrates social networking websites into the flight reservation process, which released the service of "meeting & sitting in the same flight", so that the passengers can link the data of Facebook or LinkedIn into the flight reservation process, and it is convenient for them to know who sits in the same flight as theirs [5]. The amount of information of social media is larger and larger, and if the airlines can utilize their resources reasonably, they can provide better services to the passengers, retain old customers and develop new customers, thus bringing better development for the airlines [6].

Currently, there are three primary models for evaluating the social media customer value: Klout scoring, Kred scoring and Weibo data mining.

12.3.1.1   Klout User Scoring Model

Klout scores website users based on a set of data mining algorithms and according to the indexes such as if a user has social media accounts or not, his/her number of fans, his/her update frequency, if his/her content is praised by others, his/her number of comments, and his/her number of forwarding, and so on. Klout score social media users with 100 as the standard. Its specific scoring mode is: if the customer has an account of Twitter or another social media website, and your messages can be seen by others, you already get certain scores. Based on this, Klout will score you according to the indexes such as your number of fans, frequency of your information update, Klout scores of your friends and fans, number of people who like your things, number of replies, number of forwarding, and so on.   .

The Klout Scoring Model has three main factors: true reach, amplification and network impact. True reach refers to the number of people that a user has influenced, amplification mainly refers to the number of people who forwarded your posts and frequency impact, and network impact refers to the network impact of a user.

12.3.1.2   Kred Scoring Model

The main data source of Kred is Twitter, and it established a Scoring Model based on surrounding followers, likes or shares with others. The final score of Kred consists of two parts: influence score and external connection score. The influence score reflects the breadth of a user's influence, and the external connection score reflects the influence depth. The influence score measures the ability of a user to motivate others, from 1 to 1000, which depends on the number of the user's Twitter messages forwarded, the number of new followers and the number of replies of the user. The influence depth level refers to the influence score of a certain topic posted by a user. The influence depth level does not consider the number of followers or other statistical data, but is based on what a user has already shared, said and done in a specific circle. In different circles, a user has different influence scores and influence depth scores. It is clever to be in accordance with the right methods.

The main difference between Kred and Klout is that the transparency of Kred is comparatively high, which will display how a user gets the final score, even the value score of a specific forwarding. The value of a common forwarding might be 10, but the value of a forwarding of a user with high Kred score might be 50. The score of being mentioned by others is higher than the score for being followed by others, and so forth. The score of each person is calculated in real time. In addition, Kred attempts to link virtuality with reality, which brings the achievements such as honors, medals and certificates, etc. that a user has in the realistic world into the Kred scoring calculation.

12.3.1.3 Weibo Data Mining Algorithm

The user scoring of micro data mainly inspects factors in three aspects: a user's activity, spreading capacity and reach, and its specific scoring algorithm is as below:

$$\text{Influence} = \text{activity} + \text{spreading capacity} + \text{reach} \qquad (12.1)$$

In this algorithm (12.1), spreading capacity refers to the number of valid posts and number of valid people forwarding and commenting posts. Reach refers to the number of active fans. Activity refers to the number of valid posts of posting, forwarding and commenting Weibos.

12.3.1.4 Airline Passenger Weibo Value Algorithm

In the context of the airline industry, we applied the third model of Weibo data mining, and evaluated the value of airline passengers on *Sina Weibo* in terms of three aspects: influence, activity and relevance with the airline company's Weibo. The influence factor includes number of Weibos posted, number of Weibos forwarded and number of fans, and so on. Activity factor includes number of Weibos posted by the user, number of Weibos forwarded by the user and number of check-ins of the user, and so on. Relevance factor includes the Weibo interactions between a passenger and the airline company, and the influence of the user's Weibo.

We model the airline passengers' value of Weibo in the algorithm as below:

$$SNvalue = \omega_1 * IF + \omega_2 * ATC + \omega_3 * Corr \qquad (12.2)$$

In this algorithm (12.2), SNvalue is the airline passenger's value on Weibo. IF is influence. ATC is activity. Corr is relevance, and $\omega_1, \omega_2, \omega_3$ are the weights of the factors.

Influence Factor (IF) IF refers to the potential spreading influence of a user. IF index is mainly related to the number of fans and quality of the fans of a user. The bigger the number of fans of the passenger, the bigger the number of people who might see the passenger's activities (posting and forwarding Weibos, etc.), and the bigger the number of people who are influenced. The higher the quality of the fans, the bigger the number of people who spread outwards and influence. Based on the idea of PageRank, we can define a PassengerRank for the passenger in the social networking websites. As to the passenger in the social networking websites, the bigger the number of "important people" in his/her friends is, the higher the rank that the passenger corresponds to is. Three indexes used for measuring PassengerRank:

- Number of fans
- If the fans have comparatively high PassengerRank values
- The number of people that the fans pay attention to

Activity Factor (ATC) At present, *Sina Weibo* uses number of fans as the basis to rank the users. User ATC index is related to number of fans, number of Weibo posted by the user and number of Weibo forwarded by the user, and so on. If we adopt the weighted approach, we can get the algorithm as below:

$$ATC = \omega_1 * \text{wb\_num} + \omega_2 * \text{trans\_num} + \omega_3 * fans\_num \qquad (12.3)$$

In this algorithm (12.3), wb_num is the number of Weibo posted. Trans_num is the number of Weibo forwarded. Fans_num is the number of fans. ω is weight factor of Weibo forwarding.

Relevance (Corr) Corr refers to the relevance degree between a passenger and the airline industry. In *Sina Weibo*, Corr is mainly related to the Weibo user properties and Weibo content. User properties mainly refer to the properties such as industry category of a user, which can directly reflect the potential possibility of the interaction of a user with the airline industry. Weibo content refers to the relevance degree of the Weibo posted by a user and the Weibo forwarded by a user with the field of airline industry. Taking one step further, we can analyze the role of a user in the public opinions related to airlines from the Weibo content, which is an important index in the relevance measurement. At present, through the analysis on the emotion of a user's Weibo towards the airline industry, we get the relevance factor as below:

$$Corr = \sigma * (\omega * SF) \qquad (12.4)$$

σ refers to the relevance degree between the Weibo content and China Southern Airlines, and the value range is between 0 and 1. ω refers to the degree of impact on the result of Weibo emotion analysis. SF refers to public opinion factor, mainly considering the relevance degree of the Weibo content of a user with the public opinions on the airline industry.

12.3.2 PNR Social Network Analysis

In the airline industry, there are three important types of travel data: passenger name record (PNR), share of wallet (SOW) and webtrends. These three data types can be joined by the user's identity with the addition of user name and the order number, then be imported into a big data platform. The PNR, SOW, and webtrends data were retrieved from the passenger database of China Southern Airlines.

PNR archives the airline travel itinerary for individual passenger and a group of passengers traveling together. Usually, passengers and their accompaniers are close to each other, such as families, friends, lovers, colleagues and so on. Therefore, the social network between passengers and their accompaniers can be constructed through exploring the PNR history data. The PNR data analysis will help the airline company to identify who are influential passengers in their social circles. The following steps can be applied to develop PNR social network:

1. Take every passenger as a node, if two passengers have travelled together, then there is a connection.
2. Add two directed connections to every pair (assume passenger A and passenger B who travelled together before are a pair), every connection strength is determined by the following factor: the proportion of "go together" times to single travel times. For example: Passenger A (a corporate executive) travelled 100 times in total. There are five times that he went with B (executive's mother), so the connection strength directed from A to B is 0.05. However, B only took five trips in all her life, then the connection strength from B to A is 1.
3. Count and show the detail information of passengers; such as gender, age and travel times.
4. Once the network is developed, the featured relationship and value of passengers can be determined. Figure 12.1 illustrates an example of PNR social network.

SOW is a marketing term representing traveler's value and contribution to a company, which refers to the amount of the customer's total spending that a business captures in the products and services that it offers. The technical measurement of SOW is a ratio of tickets purchase amount from an airline company to passenger's total travel times. With SOW data analysis, the airline identifies who are potential high-value travelers, and suggest corresponding marketing segmentation and promotion strategies based on different SOW level.

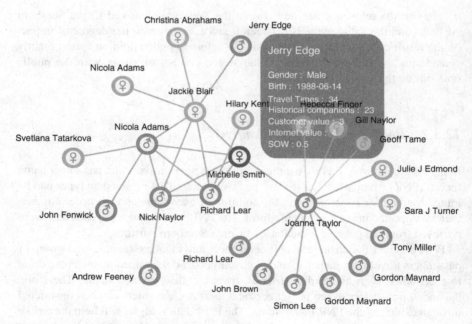

Fig. 12.1 An example of PNR social network

12.3.3 WebTrends Analysis

Airlines also can analyze webtrends data to explore passenger behavior of websites and mobile usage. Passenger's webtrends information includes mobile number, membership number, identity number, and other web browsing records. Connecting these webtrends data with other information sources provides an overview and insights on individual passenger's website and mobile usage. The following session demonstrates how the accessing event flow on WebTrends can be configured and incorporated into the sequence analysis of passenger events.

12.3.3.1 Customer Relevance

Associate the login account information (mobile number, member No., ID number, etc.) with a single view of customer (SVC) information to obtain detailed information of individual passengers. This part only targets those passengers with log data.

In addition to WebTrends, other event data of this user can be found after the users association, such as phone booking history. All these events will show in the sequence diagram of passenger events illustrated in Fig. 12.2.

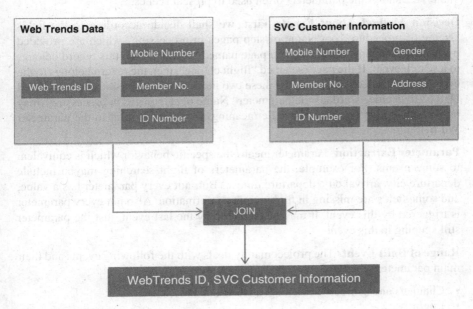

Fig. 12.2 Customer relevance

Table 12.2 Parameters in WebTrends analysis

Parameters	Description of WebTrends	Description of airline company
WT.si_n	Name of the scenario analysis	Name of procedure
WT.si_p	Identifies the step by name	Name of step pages in processing
WT.si_x	Identifies the step by position	
WT.si_cs	Identifies the step in which conversion occurs for Visitor Data Mart profiles.	

12.3.3.2 Scene Definition in WebTrends

The Parameters si_n and si_p are used in WebTrends event analysis. Because the data from the Chinese airline company are relatively rough and the scene categories defined by WebTrends are not subdivided very clearly, the Parameter ti (page title) is also used in practical applications.

Regarding the process of different events, the specific scene can be defined by client. For example, client sets up the related code on login page. Once login behavior occurred, the log will automatically classify it into the login scene. Table 12.2 shows the parameters often used to present scenes.

Decision Method About Events First, we shall decide according to the fields "Name of procedure" or "Name of step pages in processing" which are provided by Airline company. Such as a step page named "search", then this record belongs to a search event. If the page is named "flight choice", then the record belongs to the event of flight selection. Second, if these two fields show no specific events, we find "URL" to decide. Third, as the parameter "Name of step pages in processing" may not be subdivided into more specific meaning, we still will refer to the parameter WT.ti.

Parameter Extraction Parameter means the specific behavior which is equivalent to some events. For example, the parameters of flight searching maybe include departure city, arrival city, departure time ... But, not every parameter has a value, and some fields are missing in flight inquiry information. Also not every parameter is triggered by this event, it may be triggered by the last event, just the parameter still keeping in this event.

Range of Built Event The project mainly deals with the following events and their main parameter types:

- Channels and sources (Searching, advertisement ...)
- Login
- Users login events
- Flight searching (Extract flight information ...)
- Flight selection (Extract flight information ...)

- Passengers Information (Submitted information of passengers ...)
- Orders (Order information and the Information of the finalized flight ...)

12.3.3.3 Statistical Analysis

The following rules are made for every single passenger, and all the specifics will be decided according to practical application context.

1. How many times does the passenger login in before the ticket purchase on average (in a certain time)?
2. How many pages does the passenger browse before the purchase on average (take every page view as a unit)?
3. How many times did the passenger click advertisement before the ticket purchase?
4. How many advertisement hits after the ticket purchase?
5. Distribution of access sources (Baidu, Google, direct access etc.)
6. Distribution of passenger flight inquiries (in a certain time)

12.3.4 Display and Application of WebTrends Event Flow

The access event flow on WebTrends also is included in passengers' sequential analysis, so that all customers' event behaviors can be integrated and displayed. The event sequence diagram is based on different event types of each passenger, such as login, inquiry, order and its detail information.

The building methods are as follows:

1. Count the customer events, and show them and their frequency in time sequence.
2. After the clicks of "recent events" or "all events", the detail information in specific period can be seen, such as flight number, departure time, arrival city, and so on.

Figures 12.3 and 12.4 show examples of customer events.

12.3.5 Customer Activity Analysis Using Pareto/NBD Model

The Pareto/NBD model was originally proposed by Schmittlein et al. [7]. This model calculates customer activity level and predicts their future transactions based on their purchasing behavior. The model assumes that customers make purchases at any time with a steady rate for a period of time, and then they may drop out. The mathematical assumptions of this model are listed as below [7]:

1. While active, the repeat-buying rate λ of customer behavior follows Poisson distribution.
2. The transaction rate of different customers follows a gamma distribution $\Gamma(\gamma, \alpha)$. γ is the shape parameter and α denoted the scale parameter.

Customer Events Overview:

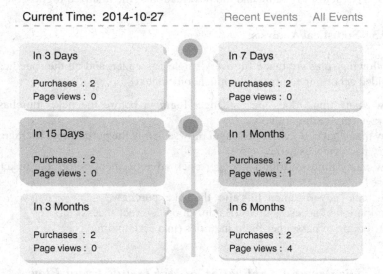

Fig. 12.3 Passenger event overview

Occurring Time	Event Details
2013-03-10 10:12:31	2013-03-10 10:12:31 We chat Check-in
2013-01-14 09:33:23	2013-01-14 09:33:23 Log in member card 692212812028 though B2C website
2013-01-11 09:33:17	2013-01-11 09:33:17 Transfer service
2013-01-11 09:33:44	2013-01-11 09:33:44 Buffet service
2013-01-08 09:33:41	2013-01-08 09:33:41 Self-help luggage service
2013-01-07 09:33:24	2013-01-07 09:33:24 Counter check-in service
2013-01-04 09:33:18	2013-01-04 09:33:18 Ipad service
2012-12-25 09:33:50	2012-12-25 09:33:50 Book flight 20130117 TV5510 ZSSS-ZGGG though B2C website
2012-12-25 09:33:36	2012-12-25 09:33:36 Check flight 20130117 TV5510 ZSSS-ZGGG though B2C website
2012-11-27 09:33:41	2012-11-27 09:33:41 Click flight 20130117 TV5510 ZSSS-ZGGG though B2C website

Fig. 12.4 Passenger event details

3. The dropout rate μ obeys exponential distribution.
4. Heterogeneity in dropout rates across customers follows a gamma distribution $\Gamma(s, \beta)$. s is the shape parameter and β denoted the scale parameter.
5. The transaction rate λ and the dropout rate μ are independent across customers.

The Pareto/NBD model requires only each customer's past purchasing history: "regency" (last transaction time) and "frequency" (how many transactions in a specified time period). The information can be described as $(X = x, t, T)$, where x is the number of transactions observed in the time period (0, T] and t is the time of the last transaction. With these two key summary statistics, the Pareto/NBD model can derive $P(active)$, the probability of observing x transactions in a time period of length t, and $E\left(Y(t)\middle| X = X, t, T\right)$, the expected number of transactions in the period (T, T + t] for an individual with observed $(X = x, t, T)$[8].

With passenger activity and other conditions, airlines could analyze the influence factors of activity degree which could be used to improve passenger activity. Three pieces of information were selected from the database where large passengers' records stored.

ORD_FAR.Far_Idnum:Customer id
ORD.Ord_Bok_Time:Booking time
ORD_CAS.CASH_TOTAL_TICKETPRICE:ticket price

In the database provided by China Southern Airlines, we put the passenger data from 2013-01-01 to 2013-06-30 into the Pareto/NBD model, and forecast the purchase number of each passenger in July and August, 2013. The Pareto/NBD model was implemented with R language.

Figure 12.5 shows a density distribution of the passengers' activity. We can find that the activity of most passengers is between {0.1, 0.2}. Table 12.3 lists the range of the passengers' activity. The total number of passengers is 202,370. Based on the passengers' activity the number of flying times predicted, airlines could make more effective marketing strategy for their customers.

This customer activity analysis has several important implications.

1. Customer segmentation could be done based on the passengers' activity degree. For example, customers could be divided into highly active, active and inactive. Then, airlines can carry out targeted management.
2. With the average spent by passengers and predicted flying numbers, airlines could calculate the revenue this passenger would bring to them and predict future returns.

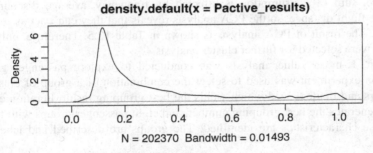

Fig. 12.5 Density distribution of the passengers' activity

Table 12.3 The scope of activity and corresponding number of passengers

The scope of activity P(Active)	Number of passengers	The scope of activity P(Active)	Number of passengers
[0,0.1]	8004	(0.5,0.6]	8337
(0.1,0.2]	96,269	(0.6,0.7]	5990
(0.2,0.3]	31,634	(0.7,0.8]	5722
(0.3,0.4]	19,538	(0.8,0.9]	6562
(0.4,0.5]	10,788	(0.9,1]	9526

3. Combining passenger active degree with life cycle length, airlines can calculate and estimate the customer lifetime value to allocate marketing resources and provide the basis for effective customer management.

12.3.6 Customer Segmentation by Clustering Analysis

Clustering analysis can be applied to segment airline passengers and explore their purchase behavior [9]. In this case of China Southern Airlines, the company website has around 6.2 million effective booking data, with passengers involved reaching the number of nearly 4 million in the past 2 years. A sample data set is retrieved from the company website, which includes 2.5 million booking data.

First, 12 variables of airline passenger behavior are selected for principal component analysis. Table 12.4 shows the 12 variables involved in principal component analysis (PCA).

Using PCA method, 12 analysis variables were integrated and transformed to nine principal component factors. The accumulative contribution of the nine extracted factors is over 0.98, indicating these factors carry more than 98 % of information which can be provided by the original 12 variables. Among the original variables, total mileage is affected by two indicators—frequency and average flight distance, average ticket price is affected by average discount and average flight distance, sum of consumption is affected by frequency, average discount and average flight distance, so the PCA analysis reveals that they can't act as separate factors. The result of PCA analysis is shown in Table 12.5. Therefore, only nine factors were selected for further cluster analysis.

Then, K-mean value analysis was conducted to explore passenger groups. Iteration experiment was used to select the combination of a group of clustering numbers and random seed which yields the best grouping result. Iteration experiment generates the best grouping number, and eight passenger groups with typical purchase characteristics are identified. The groups are described and labeled in Table 12.6.

Next, through comparing the mean values of group characteristics, we can identify the advantages and disadvantages of targeting different passenger groups. The following five findings would be useful for the airline company's business decision.

Table 12.4 Airline passenger lifetime value and purchase behavior

Characteristics	Indicators	Descriptions
Passenger lifetime value characteristics	Number of booking legs	Number of take-off and landing city pairs for client bookings
	Sum of consumption	Gross purchase sum
	Average ticket price paid	Quotient of purchase sum and number of flights
	Average discount	Price published for each city pair
	Number of days as of the last booking up to today	Difference between the last booking date and analysis date
	Total flight mileage	Sum of flight mileage of each city pair
	Average flight mileage	Quotient of Sum of flight mileage and number of flights
Behavior characteristics	Average number of days for booking upfront	Average of difference between purchase date and flight date
	Average booking time	Average of each purchase time point
	Rate of weekend flight	Quotient of number of weekend flight and total flights number
	Rate of holiday flight	Inclusive of certain days before and after the holiday
	Rate of flight for an international expo	Destination being Guangzhou in period of outward voyage, while departure from Guangzhou in the period of back trip

Table 12.5 The result of PCA analysis

Factors	Eigenvalue	Contribution	Accumulative contribution
F1: Frequency	2.89	0.241	0.241
F2: Average flight distance	1.89	0.157	0.398
F3: Average discount	1.46	0.122	0.520
F4: Advance booking	1.20	0.099	0.619
F5: Last flight trip	1.00	0.083	0.702
F6: Holiday flight trips	0.99	0.082	0.784
F7: Booking period	0.98	0.082	0.866
F8: Weekend flight trips	0.80	0.067	0.873
F9: Flight trips to an international expo	0.57	0.048	0.981
F10	0.10	0.008	0.989
F11	0.07	0.006	0.995
F12	0.03	0.005	1.000

1. Group 1, Group 5 and Group 7 have fewer numbers of bookings, with middle level of ticket price, supposed to be the ordinary mass groups, while the difference among the three groups is about the rate of flights on weekends, holiday and workdays.

Table 12.6 Passenger clusters

Clustering	Label	Advantage characteristics	Disadvantage characteristics
Group 1	Ordinary business client	None	Few number of booking, lower rate of flight trips on weekends
Group 2	Happy flight—not lost	Big number of days for advance booking	Few number of booking, the lowest discount
Group 3	Expo event	Higher rate of flight for an expo event	The smallest group
Group 4	Occasional high-end flight	High average ticket price, High average price	Few number of booking
Group 5	The masses—flight trips on weekends	Higher rate of flight on weekends	None
Group 6	Happy flight—already lost	None	Few number of booking, the lowest discount, the longest time interval since the last booking up to now
Group 7	The masses—flight trips on holiday	Higher rate of flight on holiday	None
Group 8	High-end, flight often	Big number of booking, high average price, big sum of consumption	None

2. Group 2 and 4 are groups purchasing discounted tickets, the difference is that Group 2 is still active, while Group 4 is basically lost already. Group 4 bears similar characteristics with A-type group supposedly.
3. Group 3 are travelers who flow in the same direction with those attending an expo, so we infer quite many of them are participants of the event.
4. Group 4 have a fewer number of booking, but with a higher price, while a small number of days for advance booking, suggesting this is a group with occasional travel needs, paying attention to prices seldom, so it could be a high-end group.
5. Group 8 have a big number of booking, with a high average price, and are a high-end group who fly often indeed. This high-end group are in pursuit of trends, and enjoy new technology while traveling. We can see this high-end group tend to handle special check-in, showing an obvious higher rate than other groups, at 40 %, especially online check-in and SMS check-in.

12.3.7   Recency-Frequency-Monetary (RFM) Analysis

Recency-Frequency-Monetary method is considered as one of the most powerful and useful models to implement consumer relationship management. Bult and Wansbeek [10] defined the variables as: (1) R (Recency): the period since the last purchase; a lower value corresponds to a higher probability of the customer's making a repeat purchase; (2) F (Frequency): number of purchases made within a certain period; higher frequency refers to greater loyalty; (3) M (Monetary): the money spent during a certain period; a higher value means that the company should focus more on that customer [9].

This case study adopted an extended RFM model to analyze the airline passenger behavior. The extended RFM model incorporated average discount factor as an additional variable, because average discount factor is an important indicator to measure the price level of passenger's airline purchase. The average discount factor defined here is ratio of purchase price to published price of the airplane seat. Therefore, the extended RFM model involves four variables: number of days from the last order date to modeling (R), number of flight trips (F), sum of consumption (M), and average discount factor (D). In this way, a traveler's ID generates the consolidated data.

Principal component analysis was used to score individual travelers based on the RFMD variables, and 16 consumer groups were identified. The findings could help marketers to recognize those most valuable consumers and establish profitable consumer relationships. The procedure of the RFM analysis is described below.

12.3.7.1 Exploratory Data Analysis

This step involves taking a closer look at the data available for investigation. Exploratory data analysis consists of data description and verifying the quality of data from the airline company's databases. Tables 12.7 and 12.8 provide a general understanding of the passenger data set.

Table 12.7 reveals that the difference between the maximum and the minimum of the two variables: number of flight trips and sum of consumption is huge. The data distribution plot also indicates that the original data is heavily right-skewed. Therefore, using the original data directly in our modeling will be a big problem. In order to fix this data problem, logarithmic transformation is used regarding number of flight trips, sum of consumption and average discount factor. We also take the opposite number regarding the difference of dates from the last order date to modeling date, and then standardize the data to remove dimension's influence.

Table 12.7 Descriptive data analysis of RFMD variables

Modeling variables	N	Mean	SD	Minimum	Maximum
R: Number of days from the last order date to modeling	1,624,293	188.34	175.07	1	730
F: Number of flight trips	1,624,293	2.25	2.11	1	128
M: Sum of consumption	1,624,293	1729	2062	18	173,190
D: Average discount factor	1,624,293	0.62	0.22	0.02	3.4

Table 12.8 Correlation matrix of RFMD variables

	R	F	M	D
R: Number of days from the last order date to modeling	1	−0.006	−0.06	−0.25
F: Number of flight trips		<0.0001	<0.0001	<0.0001
	−0.006	1	0.839	−0.075
M: Sum of consumption	<0.0001		<0.0001	<0.0001
	−0.063	0.839	1	0.197
D: Average discount	<0.0001	<0.0001		<0.0001
	−0.250	−0.075	0.197	1
	<0.0001	<0.0001	<0.0001	

Pearson correlation, N = 1,624,293; When H0: Rho = 0, Prob > |r|

Table 12.8 indicates that the number of flight trips positively correlates with income (sum of consumption). The more flight trips, the bigger sum of consumption, which corresponds with the flight reality.

12.3.7.2 Principal Component Analysis

Principal component analysis is used to determine the weight of each RFMD variables. Figure 12.6 shows the steps of principal component analysis of RFMD modeling.

Through the principal component analysis, the result shows that the three RFM modeling variables account for 95 % of the overall variance. The four RFMD variables and weights were determined to further depict the passenger's value model in Table 12.9. In particular, weight of number of days from the last order date to modeling is 1.23, weight of number of flight trips is 1.21, weight of sum of consumption is 1.43, and average discount factor is 0.54.

12.3.7.3 Clustering Analysis

K-mean value clustering method was applied to generate 16 passenger groups. The four RFMD indicators can be used to analyze specific target groups in more details [11]. The four RFMD indicators can help to rank the level of passenger lifetime values, and determine individual marketing strategy and realize precision marketing in respect of individual high-end travelers.

The concept of Customer lifetime value (CLV) is adopted to evaluate the profitability of each cluster. CLV is the present value of all future profit generated from a customer [12]. In this case study, the average CLV value of each cluster can be calculated with the equation:

$$CLV_{ci} = NR_{ci} \times WR_{ci} + NF_{ci} \times WF_{ci} + NM_{ci} \times WM_{ci} + ND_{ci} \times WD_{ci} \quad (12.5)$$

Fig. 12.6 Principal
component analysis steps

> Step 1: Data pre-processing. To take the data of modeling groups from the original database, and calculate corresponding derivative variable's value using basic variable's value. To analyze reasonableness of the variable value, and act accordingly.

↓

> Step 2: Standardize the data to remove dimension's influence on the result.

↓

> Step 3: Conduct relevant analysis over the data in step 2, check if the data are appropriate for principal component analysis; check the rules according to Pearson's correlation coefficient, and determine the data in step 2 are appropriate for principal component analysis.

↓

> Step 4: Conduct principal component analysis over the data after standardization, and select principal component for analysis based on demand due to the small number of variables considered currently.

↓

> Step 5: Calculate the comprehensive scores of the members, rank according to the scores, and present the score position of each member.

↓

> Step 6: Explain the scores of the members using principal component analysis result.

Table 12.9 Basic statistics of RFMD data

Modeling variables	Weight (all principal components)	Weight (the former three principal components)
R: Number of days from the last order date to modeling	1.23	1.23
F: Number of flight trips	1.32	1.21
M: Sum of consumption	1.32	1.43
D: Average discount	0.60	0.54

NR_{ci} refers to normal recency of cluster ci, WR_{ci} is weighted recency, NF_{ci} is normal frequency, WF_{ci} is weighted frequency, NM_{ci} is normal monetary, WM_{ci} is weighted monetary, ND_{ci} is normal duration of cluster ci, and WDci is weighted duration. The result of clustering analysis is shown in Table 12.10.

Based on the result of clustering analysis, some insights of customer segmentation and corresponding business strategies can be developed. For example, for those who don't take a flight for more than half a year, mark as low value directly, for example, group 16's score is 74.89, mainly because this group took flights a lot, but they fail to purchase on the website for more than 300 days, so they're treated as a lost group (lost herein refers to being lost to other channels or other companies).

Group 12 and 13 have higher average scores, value of variables is higher than average value, so they are company's important clients who are supposed to be developed and maintained; continuous client care is necessary, service measures and client experience need to be improved; these two groups aren't sensitive to prices, so market measures like promotion and fare reduction aren't suitable. Each client of each group has a score, and priority of resources can be given to these groups in light of scores and ranking.

Group 1 have lower value scores, because their average discount is low, but they made purchases in the last two months, indicating they're active relatively, so this group needs attention. Further study can be made, paying attention to age, purchase website source and other information of the group. It could be an individual traveler base that forms the long tail of website sales.

Figure 12.7 describes the characteristics of each cluster and corresponding business strategies.

12.4 The Construction of Passenger Intelligence Applications

In order to better utilize big data techniques, airline companies need to start to develop some big data applications. This chapter introduces a multi-channel intelligence customer marketing platform for airlines.

The platform is developed to build a scalable, high-efficient 360-degree view of customers. The platform collects passenger's multi-channel data through every trigger point of each client, analyzes the consumer behavior and shopping habits

Table 12.10 Result of clustering analysis

Group	Number of days from the last order date to modeling	Sum of consumption	Sum of consumption	Average discount	Customer lifetime value	Percentage	Label
1	64.86	2.121	876.8	0.394	47.77	7.78	Low value
2	94.95	1.004	1580	0.873 (↑)	62.25 (↑)	6.25	Customer to develop
3	601.5 (↑)	2.086	1100	0.386	7.303	6.36	Low value
4	76.42	3.637 (↑)	2254 (↑)	0.485	85.96 (↑)	5.58	Promising
5	301.1 (↑)	2.081	1476	0.564	45.94	7.55	Low value
6	322.9 (↑)	2.105	870.4	0.363	18.68	8.78	Low value
7	96.87	1.024	748.5	0.873 (↑)	36.98	8.08	Low value
8	88.22	1	1087	0.628 (↑)	40.79	8.29	Low value
9	85.95	1.004	532	0.599	17.08	8.9	Low value
10	494.2 (↑)	2.19	2122 (↑)	0.773 (↑)	44.76	4.96	Low value
11	121.1	2.291 (↑)	2450 (↑)	0.815 (↑)	82.94 (↑)	8.38	Customer to retain
12	100.2	5.476 (↑)	4808 (↑)	0.674 (↑)	96.22 (↑)	4.89	Customer to develop
13	75.09	14.31 (↑)	126,694 (↑)	0.705 (↑)	99.65 (↑)	1.38	Customer to retain
14	176.1	1.997	4016 (↑)	1.665 (↑)	88.33 (↑)	0.9	Customer to retain
15	79.64	2.07	1526	0.588	70.83 (↑)	8.27	Low value
16	333.9 (↑)	3.827 (↑)	2664 (↑)	0.508	74.89 (↑)	3.64	Low value
Mean	188.3	2.255	1729	0.619	50.5		

(↑) indicates the value for the cluster is higher than the mean

of travelers to recommend personalized travel products. This application gathers data from internal and external sources including website, ticketing robots, GDS, loyalty, check-in, flight, marketing, CRM, social media, and industry databases. It identifies records relating to the same individual to produce a single customer view, then further enhances the customer profile with external data, segment codes, and recommended treatments. The results are available to execution systems to use for

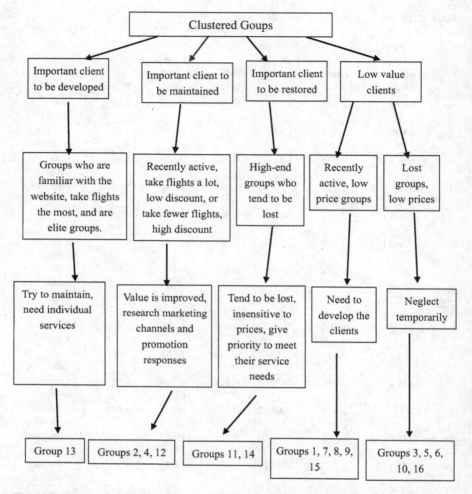

Fig. 12.7 The characteristics of each cluster and corresponding business strategies

personalization, offer and program selection, campaign execution, in-flight services and other purposes. The same data is also available for results reporting and other types of analysis.

This platform has two main benefits. First, it enables all systems to work from a complete, consistent customer view, enabling coordinated treatments across channels. Second, it saves each channel system from having to assemble its own detailed customer database. Traditional data warehouses require separate, expensive software to load and transform the data, to associate related records, and for modeling, analytics, and reporting. This all runs on expensive hardware and is operated by expensive IT staff and data scientists. These barriers have prevented all but the largest, most sophisticated B2B marketing organizations from building

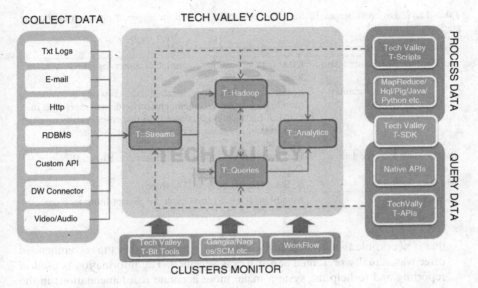

Fig. 12.8 Multi-channel intelligence customer marketing platform

a truly comprehensive central customer behavior and prediction database. In big data time, this is changing. Airlines and data solution providers cooperate with each other. Figure 12.8 presents an overview that shows how actionable insights can be derived out of big data. This platform has the following capabilities:

1. **Accept data from any source system.** This includes traditional, structured data such as purchase transactions right through to unstructured data such as web log files and contact center notes. The platform has an opt-in option to gather external data sources to enrich customer profiles.
2. **Allow access by external systems.** Upon request, the platform provides an Application Program Interface (API) that lets systems read its data during customer interactions.
3. **Associate different identifiers for the same individual.** The platform can chain together multiple identifiers: so if a Web system captures an email address and cookie ID, and the contact center captures email address and phone number, the system recognizes that the phone number, cookie ID, and email address all belong to the same person.
4. **Customer segmentation and customer behavior.** Behavioral segments can be created based on the aggregated customer data to combine transactional sights with shopping behaviors and social signals.
5. **Personalization and prediction.** The platform provides recommendations for customer treatment. The recommendations control which offers are considered and how they are prioritized and captures whether the recommended offer was actually presented and if it was accepted. This is controlled through an interface

Table 12.11 Different stages in the Big Data multi-channel intelligence customer marketing platform

Platform component		Source/products/technologies
Collect data	Structured data	CRM data, reservation system, call center logs, ERP, website logs,
	Unstructured data	Social media sites, blogs, location data, browsing behavior, mobile data, website content, enterprise data not recorded in CRM or ERP(e.g. marketing e-mail responses, survey results etc.), customer-employee interaction data, weather data, news, reviews etc.
Process data & query data (Technologies)		Hadoop (HDFS, Mapreduce), Cassandra, Hbase, Hive, Cognos, Hyperion
Big Data analytics		R, Sas, SiSense, Mahout, Datameer
Monitor		Mondrian, JGraphX, mxGraph, JavaScript Inforvis, Excel

that is accessible to non-technical users and captures whether the recommended offer was actually presented and if it was accepted. The information is used in reporting and to help the system make more accurate recommendations in the future.

Table 12.11 gives a few examples of the sources of structured and unstructured data, technologies and products that can be used for the different stages in the platform.

12.5 Conclusion and Implication

Using the data mining techniques discussed in this chapter, airline companies can learn important marketing implications of big data analytics. This chapter introduced Weibo customer value modeling, social network analysis, website click-stream analysis, customer activity analysis, clustering analysis, Recency-Frequency-Monetary (RFM) analysis, and principle component analysis, and the data mining results reveal passenger travel patterns, preference, travel social networks and other aspects of purchase behavior.

To help with formulating better business strategies, the airline companies may consider adoption of the following implications.

1. To set up an easier-to-use system: flight inquiry with high-level customization; ticket price calculation support with high-level customization, customized function design and product design, relevant product support, especially support for hotel products, and one-stop service should be provided to the greatest extent.
2. To track travel value chain closed loop further: from the whole process, such as inquiring products, reservation, payment, ticket issue, check-in, security check, waiting, cabin service, luggage claim, mileage accumulation, notice and start of next trip, record traveler's behavior details through contact of travelers with

the airlines, and provide prioritized individual services to important clients, for example, onboard seat preference or meal habit, etc.

3. Timely and effective client care, including SMS wishes, posted gifts, and so on. Weibo emotion analysis can be applied to judge if the attitude of a Weibo is positive, neutral or negative. It would be useful to extract information from the Weibo information and the social networking relationships (e.g., authentication information, number of fans and number of comments, etc.) of a passenger.

4. Individual online experiences. Priority can be given to important clients to be developed and maintained under the circumstance of limited resources, analyzing traveler's trip habit (behavior and preferences) to conduct cross-selling, identifying attractions to them based on user's preferences, filtering unnecessary information to present individual recommendations, and offering the most valuable product portfolio for clients during a specified time period. For instance, system analysis finds out that some clients purchase air tickets within a certain price range only. In this case, precision marketing can be applied to these clients, with SMS, mail, SNS and other means to keep them posted of product information.

References

1. Harteveldt HH (2012) The future of airline distribution: a look ahead to 2017. s.l.: special report commissioned by IATA
2. Davenport TH (2013) At the Big Data crossroads: turning towards a smarter travel experience. Available via AMADEUS. http://www.bigdata.amadeus.com/assets/pdf/Amadeus_Big_Data.pdf. Accessed 1 May 2014
3. Ghee R (2014) Top 5 in-flight trends to look out for in 2014. Available via http://www.futuretravelexperience.com/2014/01/top-5-flight-trends-look-2014/. Accessed 7 May 2014
4. Nicas J (2013) How airlines mine personal data in-flight. Available via http://www.wsj.com/articles/SB10001424052702304384104579139923818792360. Accessed 8 November 2013
5. Peveto A (2011) KLM surprise: How a little research earned 1,000,000 impressions on Twitter. Available via http://www.digett.com/2011/01/11/klm-surprise-how-little-research-earned-1000000-impressions-twitter. Accessed 11 January 2013
6. Chen J, Xiao YB, Liu XL, Chen YH (2006) Airline seat inventory control based on passenger choice behavior. Syst Eng Theory Pract 1:65–75
7. Schmittlein DC, Morrison DG, Colombo R (1987) Counting your customers: who are they and what will they do next? Manag Sci 33:1–24
8. Fader PS, Hardie BGS, Lee KL (2005) "Counting your customers" the easy way: an alternative to the Pareto/NBD model. Market Sci 24:275–284
9. Tan PN, Steinbach M, Kumar V (2005) Introduction to data mining. Addison Wesley, Upper Saddle River
10. Bult JR, Wansbeek T (1995) Optimal selection for direct mail. Market Sci 14:378–395
11. Khajvand M, Zolfaghar K, Ashoori S, Alizadeh S (2011) Estimating customer lifetime value based on RFM analysis of customer purchase behavior: case study. Procedia Comput Sci 3:57–63
12. Gupta S, Lehman DR (2003) Customers as assets. J Interact Mark 17(1):9–24

Printed in the United States
By Bookmasters